Gilded Mansions

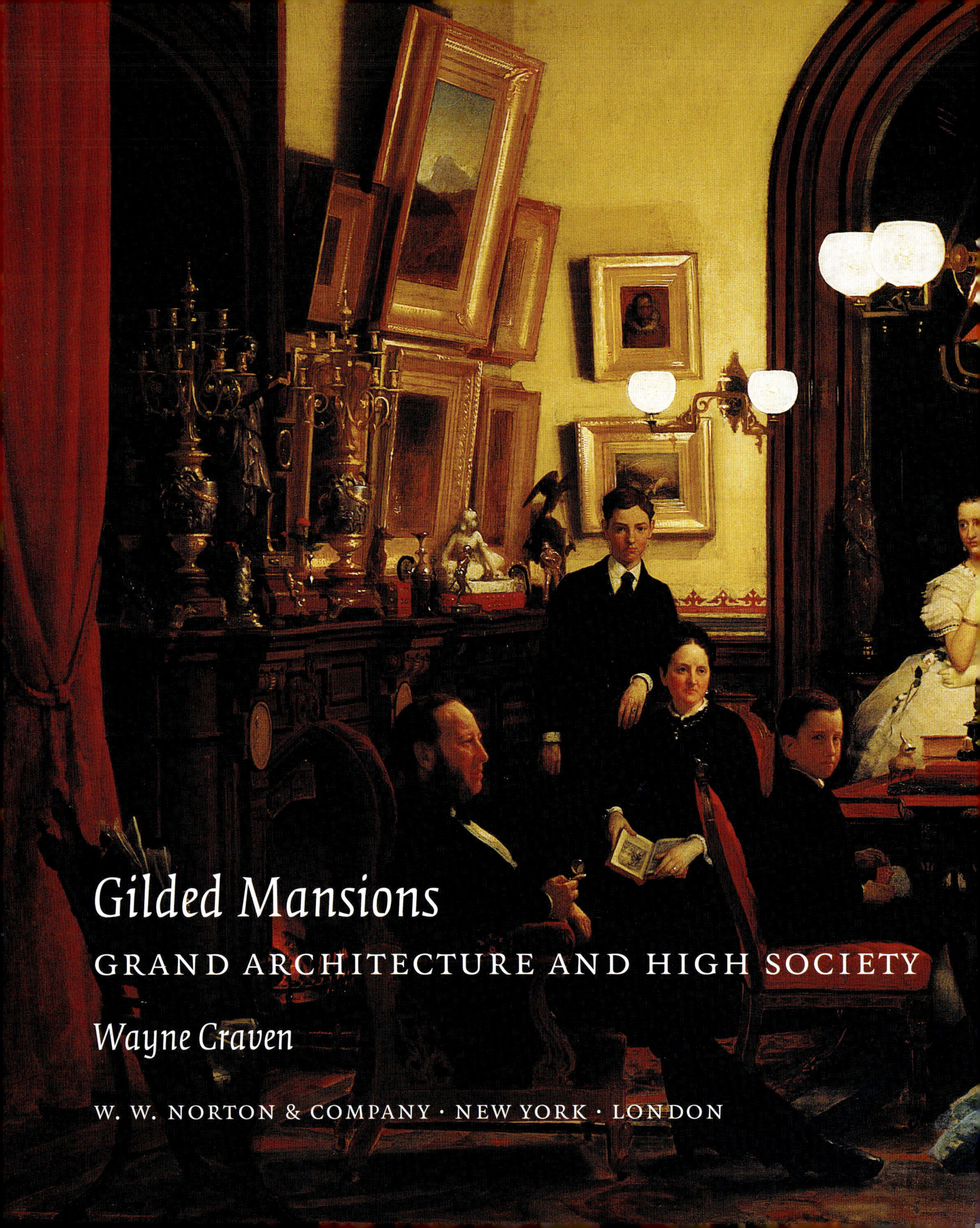

Gilded Mansions

GRAND ARCHITECTURE AND HIGH SOCIETY

Wayne Craven

W. W. NORTON & COMPANY · NEW YORK · LONDON

Gilded Mansions: Grand Architecture and High Society
Wayne Craven

Printed in Italy
First Edition

Publication of this book was partially underwritten by a grant from Furthermore, a program of the J. M. Kaplan fund.

Manufacturing by Mondadori Printing, Verona
Composed in Quadraat
Book design by Robert L. Wiser, Silver Spring, MD

Library Of Congress Cataloging-in-Publication Data
Craven, Wayne.
Gilded mansions : grand architecture and high society / Wayne Craven. — 1st ed.
p. cm.
Includes bibliographical references and index.
ISBN 978-0-393-06754-5 (hardcover)
1. Mansions—New York (State)—New York. 2. Millionaires—Homes and haunts—New York (State)—New York. 3. Architecture—New York (State)—New York—19th century. 4. Architecture—New York (State)—New York—20th century. 5. Architecture and society—New York (State)—New York—History—19th century. 6. Architecture and society—New York (State)—New York—History—20th century. I. Title.
NA7511.4.N4C73 2008
728.80973'09034—dc22 2008012309

W. W. Norton & Company
500 Fifth Avenue, New York, NY 10110
www.wwnorton.com

W. W. Norton & Company Ltd.
Castle House, 75/76 Wells Street, London, WIT 3QT

1 2 3 4 5 6 7 8 9 0

Frontispiece. Seymour Joseph Guy, *The William H. Vanderbilt Family*, 1873. Biltmore Estate, Asheville, N.C. (See caption on p. 86 for figure 48.)

This book is dedicated to Lorna.

Contents

Extravagance is the besetting sin of New York society. Money is thrown away. Fortunes are spent every year in dress, and in all sorts of follies. Houses are furnished and fitted up in the most sumptuous style, the building and its contents often being worth over a million dollars. . . . Each person strives to outdo his or her acquaintances. The rage for fine houses and fine clothes is carried to an amazing extent.

Junius Henri Browne, *Secrets of the Great City* (1869)

An Introduction to the Gilded Age

THE GILDED AGE it was called—the era from approximately 1865 to 1918 when American society hardened into a brazen gaudiness and American cities became blackened by the belated arrival of the Industrial Revolution. The years reached from the close of the Civil War, an internal conflict indicative of the nation's self-absorption, to the beginning of World War I, by which time the United States had transformed itself into a mighty industrial, economic, military, and political international power.

The term "Gilded Age" was first coined by Mark Twain in his novel of that name, published in 1873. From the beginning it was a derogative, for "gilded" refers to a bright, shiny veneer that but thinly veils a baser substructure, and the term applies equally well to a piece of furniture of that era, a massive picture frame, or to a portion of society itself. It was a gilded age, then, as opposed to a golden age.

The gilt of the Gilded Age pertained to that part of American civilization created by this country's first millionaire society—a unique and discrete sector, readily discernible from other contemporary American social and economic strata. As a distinct stratum within the broader cross-section of the population, the leaders of this restless, brassy, chest-thumping, sometimes vulgarly rich society called into existence icons and images of their new America by demanding them of artists, architects, and artisans as symbols of their own dynamic bravado. It was an America in which they reveled, joyously rejecting any lingering Puritan restraint that had for centuries held middle-class mercantile acquisitiveness and hedonism in check.

Then, as now, there was no one single, homogenous American society but instead many sociologically and economically identifiable groups—the poor and the immigrants, the tradesmen and the professionals, the urbanites and the agrarians, the middle class and the very rich, and so on. At the extreme poles were found the new groups—the wretchedly poor and the fabulously wealthy, polarized by the Industrial Revolution.

Within the arts, a broad diversity replaced the general unity of style and form that had prevailed prior to the Civil War. That complexity encompassed the Aesthetic Movement, the Eastlake Renaissance Revival, the Arts and Crafts Movement, the Beaux-Arts style in architecture and interiors as opposed to the form-follows-function theory of Louis Sullivan; in painting, it included Tonalism, Symbolism, Japonisme, Impressionism, a realism such as is seen in the paintings of Thomas Eakins and Winslow Homer and an urban realism of the sort found in The Eight—in the art of John Sloan and Robert Henri, for example. There were the early manifestations of Modernism, which attacked the very foundations of both Beaux-Arts academic idealization and the harshly frank images of realism. The unity of antebellum American art (i.e., the Hudson River School of landscape

painting and the genre pieces by, say, William Sidney Mount) would seem to be disintegrating into anarchy in the era that followed, but sociologically the nation was defining itself in clearly demarcated strata, and each of the numerous artistic movements identified above served some constituency, expressed some aspect of the multipartite soul of the new America.

The term "Gilded Age" cannot be applied to the whole spectrum of American civilization, from the poorest of the poor to the richest of the rich, between 1865 and 1918. To be precise, the title applies only to the socioeconomic faction made up of America's first millionaire society and perhaps the highest echelon of the upper middle class. It refers mainly to the world of the Astors, the Vanderbilts, the Whitneys, Morgans, Goulds, Fricks, Carnegies, Rockefellers, Huntingtons, and so on. It applies to a sector of their own making and their own defining, and although they frequently had only recently arisen from a lower social and economic status, once they arrived in the golden circle, they seldom had intercourse with those sectors whence they came.

That the resulting cultural distinctness had ramifications for the arts is easily demonstrated. Winslow Homer and Thomas Eakins are currently recognized as two of the greatest American masters of the period between the Civil War and World War I, and their art is seen as reflective of America in their day. However, their worlds did not intersect with the lives of the new millionaires. Homer and Eakins had nothing to offer them, and the latter in no way interested those two American painters either. The Gilded Age would find other artists—John Singer Sargent, for example—who would paint images reflective of its goals, values, and ambitions. In the 1870s and 1880s French academic paintings by Bouguereau, Gérome, Bonheur, and Meissonier were amassed upon the walls of grand ballrooms or private art galleries, but seldom indeed was any American artist represented among them. Later, if the plutocrats wanted paintings to adorn their mansions, they chose works by the European Old Masters—Van Dyke, Rembrandt, Titian, Reynolds, Gainsborough, and so on—rather than the somber images by Eakins or the commonplace subjects of Homer, or the squalor of the urban scenes by The Eight, for some of the newly minted had only recently escaped such scenes.

Figure 1. Charles Dana Gibson, *Mrs. Steele Poole's Housewarming*. From *Life* (2 January 1902), pp. 10–11. Like the novelist Edith Wharton, Gibson was a member of the very society from which he drew inspiration for his whimsical sketches. Knowing the Society of the nouveaux riches from inside its charmed circle, he could portray, with wit and satire, its mannerisms and foibles, its way of dress and its grand architectural interiors—the very same grand interiors discussed in this book. Here, the pudgy parvenu hostess, wearing a splendid gown from Paris, dozes in a glaringly empty salon as she awaits the guests who will never appear.

Consciously, by their enormous wealth, energy, imagination, and lifestyles, the new millionaires rapturously created a unique society within America itself, and they demanded a new range of art and architecture as the backdrop to their social order—an art and architecture that would separate them from the frumpy and still puritanical American middle class and align them with European aristocracy instead. The parvenus, as they were called, tried in various ways to emulate and even become connected with European aristocracy—for example, through the arrangement of marriages of their daughters to the sons of impoverished Old World noble families. Many a Gilded Age daughter was led unhappily to the sacrificial altar, by parental force when necessary, her bountiful dowry achieving two purposes: restoration of some measure of grandeur to a decaying but noble European house, and linkage of America's newly rich families with the aristocratic families of England, France, Germany, Italy, Hungary, Poland, or elsewhere.

Society and Architecture

One of the main themes I will explore within this distinct sector of the United States is the relationship between High Society and the architecture and art that it called into existence. Significant questions arise: What kinds of houses did this social group build for itself? What were the architectural modes and iconic images it deemed expressive of itself? What new rooms now appear as integral parts of grand houses? Ballrooms, for example, and art galleries—rooms that had not existed in the floor plans of antebellum American houses. Why were the ubiquitous brownstones of New York City suddenly unacceptable to this layer of society, while Italian palazzos and French châteaux were deemed expressive of the lifestyle of, say, an American coal merchant, meat-packer, or streetcar tycoon? What new professions were summoned into existence in service to architects and patrons? The interior decorator, for instance, and the professional art dealer and consulting connoisseur. Joe Duveen and Bernard Berenson, respectively, come to mind; they had no counterparts in antebellum America. And if an American socialite saw herself as a member of an international cosmopolitan set—in a way that few American women did prior to the Civil War—is it surprising that the architectural decor of two or three rooms in her new mansion should be created in Paris or London and then shipped to New York for installation?

The area of concentration in this study is New York City, because it became the capital of High Society in the United States. Of special interest is the development of Fifth Avenue in its evolution from farmland to shantytown to millionaires' row. But New York Society also leads us elsewhere—to one of its favorite watering places, Newport, Rhode Island, and to some of its distant retreats, such as Biltmore in the mountains of western North Carolina. All of this established a wellspring that nourished the Gilded Age in other centers, such as Boston, Philadelphia, Chicago, Washington, D.C., Cleveland, St. Louis, San Francisco, and Cincinnati—each of which deserves a Gilded Age study of its own.[1]

Merchant Millionaires in Europe

The rise of the powerful millionaire segment in American society—what would become an industrial-financial aristocracy such as this country had never known—should be seen against similar socioeconomic patterns that occurred in Europe. In England, the Industrial Revolution reached a full head of steam much earlier than it did in the United States, for there—beginning in the mid-eighteenth century—it made rich men of clever blacksmiths, tinkerers, and woolen merchants, through patents, commerce, or manufacturing; their enormous wealth soon brought these former laborers and shopkeepers great power and, in many cases, even elevation to the peerage. By the nineteenth century many of the parvenus had bought the elegant townhouses and noble country residences that England's true aristocracy could no longer afford to maintain, and their daughters were used as pawns to connect by marriage and offspring some formerly undistinguished name with the family lines of the British nobility.

In France a similar scenario unfolded, for there, too, in the reigns of the "citizen king," Louis-Philippe (1830–48), and Emperor Napoleon III (1852–70), the wealthy upper-middle class provided the political support and stability that allowed a king and an emperor to remain in power. In France as in England and other countries, the legitimate old aristocrats tended to despise the nouveaux riches upstarts even as the former saw their prerogatives and property pass into the latter's work-worn hands. During the Second Empire—the reign of Napoleon III—the rich *haute bourgeoisie* became the patrons of architects, painters, sculptors, interior designers, and craftspersons. The emperor commissioned Baron Haussmann to rebuild Paris in a manner that appealed to the tastes of the newly risen, and the results were edifices such as Charles Garnier's Opera House and Napoleon III's own newly built or remodeled palaces Compeigne, the New Louvre, the Tuileries. In and around Paris the great nouveaux riches families such as the Rothschilds erected townhouses and châteaux that rivaled the imperial residences.

European socioeconomic patterns such as these set the course for the emergence of America's own "aristocracy" in the decades following the Civil War. It was now relatively easy, for the Americans who had the money, to cross the Atlantic to see France's great Exposition Universelle of 1867, and while there, to observe the latest fashions preferred by the elegant crowd of the Second Empire, the flashy new architecture being erected everywhere that bespoke, above all else, the enormous wealth that came from *haute bourgeoisie* entrepreneurship. By the time Americans came flooding to Paris again for the colossal international trade exposition of 1889, they knew that they wanted those things that had previously been enjoyed only by Europe's true aristocracy. Inspired by the successful rise of the financiers and industrialists in France and England and determined to rival the splendor of Europe's aristocracy, they began to define their own society in its image and to create suitable architectural backdrops for its spectacular pageantry.

The New Wealth in the United States

The bloodiness and destructiveness of the Civil War had left the nation benumbed, feeling the loss of that romantic optimism and innocence that had characterized the antebellum years. The assassination of President Abraham Lincoln cast a pall over the land. The corruption of the administration of Ulysses S. Grant (1869–77) offered only a profound disillusionment, and the scandalous Boss Tweed ring carried political graft beyond anything previously known in America.

In 1869 Jay Gould and Jim Fisk tried, but failed, to corner the gold market, precipitating the panic of Black Friday. The failure of the financial house of Jay Cooke in 1873 inaugurated a deep economic recession that lasted for years. Capitalism raced on, impellent in its drive to riches, taking little note of the social abuses it left in its wake, but cocksure of its mission, of its vision of the new social, economic, and cultural patterns it was hell-bent to impose on America.

If the country lingered for a decade in the doldrums following the Civil War, its nascent Gilded Age refused to remain restrained or don the mournful black crepe for very long. The Philadelphia Centennial of 1876 brought joyousness and confidence to the land once more.[2] A national celebration, the Centennial looked both backward and ahead: It sparked a nostalgic sentiment for America's historied past, spawning a Colonial revival that had enormous ramifications for American architecture and decorative arts. It was also the kick-off party for industrialized America, the occasion to show off its wealth and manufactured wares, amid the riches and goods from around the world. Here was a great international emporium, with the dynamic Corliss steam engine as the symbol of a new industrial power. Also, the international exhibits made Americans aware of the rest of the world, and they now felt themselves to be a part of the global community in a way they never had before. They marveled, for example, at the art from Japan that they saw there, and they were fascinated by the exotic curiosities found in the Turkish bazaar. The experience of the Centennial was exciting and exhilarating, and it urged America to proceed with its new forms of Manifest Destiny, which were now economic, global, and imperialistic.

A New Form of Manifest Destiny

Having reached the Pacific Ocean in its westward expansion, the United States refused to relinquish the cherished philosophy it had inherited from the middle decades of the century—that of Manifest Destiny, the claim by the white race of its divine right to seize and occupy the broad lands of the western territories. Now, however, national energies went not into the acquisition of western lands but into an economic and imperialistic Manifest Destiny in which America became an industrial, financial aggressor, if not by divine right then by capitalistic and political might. American influence soon extended beyond the oceanic boundaries to distant places around the world as the United States acquired the Philippines, Guam, and a part of Panama; where actual military conquest was not involved, economic imperialism was used with comparable results.

The potential for fabulous wealth energized a people who had lived by a code of the Doctrine of Prosperity since the seventeenth century—a mercantile code that proclaimed that success in business was a sign of God's will and God's blessing. Wealth, the extraordinary wealth of the Industrial Revolution, became a major component of the social structuring of the United States. E. L. Godkin, in an article of 1896 titled "The Expenditure of Rich Men," addressed this very point and wrote that if previously there had been a foundation for American society it had been an "equality of conditions, that there should neither be an immoderate display of wealth, nor of poverty, that no man should be raised so far above the generality in outward seeming as to excite either envy, hatred, or malice. . . . The accumulation of great fortunes since the [Civil] War . . . has introduced among us the greatest of European curses—class hatred."[3]

The new socioeconomic condition engendered a debate in which sociologists and industrialists, respectively, attacked and defended the accumulation of great wealth. Foremost among the critics was Thorstein Veblen, who introduced the terms "conspicuous consumption" and "conspicuous waste" into the dialogue with the publication of his *Theory of the Leisure Class* in 1899. To counter Veblen's term "conspicuous consumption," W. A. Croffut coined the phrase "divine greed" as a term of high praise.

Andrew Carnegie presented the capitalists' side, in an article titled "Wealth," published three years after Godkin's. Carnegie declared,

> The problem of our age is the proper administration of wealth, so that the ties of brotherhood may still bind together the rich and the poor in harmonious relationship. The conditions of human life have not only been changed, but revolutionized. . . . The contrast between the palace of the millionaire and the cottage of the laborer with us today measures the change which has come with civilization.

This change, however, is not to be deplored, but welcomed as highly beneficial. It is well, nay essential for the progress of the race, that the houses of some should be homes for all that is highest and best in literature and the arts, and for all the refinements of civilization, rather than that none should be so.[4]

Even the clergy of the day—or at least some of them—defended the accumulation of wealth and its fashionable display, as when William Lawrence, Episcopal bishop of Massachusetts, declared that "material prosperity is helping to make the national character sweeter, more joyous, more unselfish, more Christ-like," or when Reverend Charles Nicholls wrote that "wealth, then, forms the principal ingredient entering into the composition of this big social trust whose subjective aim is pleasure, and whose objective one is to make a fine art of social life."[5] George F. Baer, president of the Philadelphia and Reading Coal and Iron Company, expressed divine sanction for the emerging socioeconomic order: "The rights and interests of the laboring man will be protected and cared for—not by the labor agitators but by the Christian men to whom God in His wisdom has given control of the property interests of this country."[6] Some thus saw the ascendancy of a few men to greater wealth and power over the multitude of their brethren as the rightful fulfillment of God's own plan. Others saw it as the playing out of the then popular theory of Social Darwinism—the survival, or emergence to dominance, of the fittest in the social and economic order of things.

American Fortunes

Previously, the extremes in American society had been between only the moderately poor and the moderately wealthy classes, as Godkin noted, and it had been considered to be in bad taste to flaunt such wealth as one possessed. But that changed as Gilded Age fortunes escalated to astronomical heights, relative to what "a fortune" had meant in antebellum days. When John Jacob Astor, the richest man in the United States, died in 1848, he bequeathed to his heirs a sum of $20 million. When William Henry Vanderbilt departed this life thirty-seven years later, in 1885, he left an estate of $200 million, ten times that of Astor's, providing an example of the meteoric quantum increase in American fortunes.

Godkin further observed, "It is only of late years that we have had among us a class capable of equalling or outdoing the European aristocracy in wealth. American fortunes are now said to be greater than any of those of Europe, and nearly, if not quite, as numerous."[7] If Europeans had previously looked upon America as a nation of moderately successful shopkeepers, that changed with the coming of the Gilded Age. To get a feeling for the disdain, even hostility that the Old World aristocracy felt for the newly rich of the United States, one need only read Henry James's *The American*, first published in 1877, or Edith Wharton's *The Custom of the Country* (1913). Both authors were fascinated with the uniqueness of America's gilded Society in relation to the high culture and social infrastructure of Europe's long-standing and authentic aristocracy.

Wealth came from many sources. Railroads created self-made millionaires out of men such as Cornelius Vanderbilt, Jay Gould, E. H. Harriman, Henry Villard, Leland Stanford, and Collis P. Huntington. Railroads needed steel, and steel and coke made Andrew Carnegie and Henry Clay Frick enormously wealthy. Railroads and industry needed capitalization, which made rich men of financiers such as J. Pierpont Morgan, while the Astors and the Goelets greatly increased their family fortunes through real estate investments. From the earth itself came the enormous wealth of John D. Rockefeller, who developed a monopoly in oil, and of James G. Fair, John W. Mackay, and Darius Ogden Mills, who owned gold and silver mines in the West. Philip D. Armour began packing meat in Chicago in 1868 and lived high on the hog ever after. In New York, A. T. Stewart and Benjamin Altman became department store tycoons, their great wealth enabling them to be among the earliest in America to collect art on a grand scale.

Industrialists by the hundreds joined the millionaires' club by manufacturing shoe strings, hair oil, corset stays, and detachable celluloid shirt collars and cuffs; steam locomotives and air brakes, telephones and typewriters; sewing machines, ready-made dresses, and spooled thread; printer's ink, patented medicines, electric light bulbs, and barbed wire. Riches from these and diverse other sources flowed into the pockets of the new millionaires, to pay for the expensive pleasures and symbols they demanded of architects, painters, sculptors, artisans, art and antique dealers, and interior decorators.

Figure 2. Charles Dana Gibson, *The Troubles of the Rich: At the Last Moment, Several who were Invited sent Their Regrets.* From *Life* (13 February 1902), pp. 130–31. Books that treat the interiors of bygone eras must, of necessity, deal with empty rooms, for the people who once dwelt within them are long since departed, and they seldom permitted the photographer to intrude on their family gatherings therein. But a book full of empty rooms can be a dull affair, and so I have sought to populate those rooms with the aid of Charles Dana Gibson's wonderful satires. He placed his characters within architectural settings that match those I describe in this book, and he captured both the grandeur that was aspired to and its anachronisms, at which we must smile, such as the servants who are liveried—that is, dressed in the costume of the French court of the eighteenth century.

Knickerbockracy vs. Parvenu Aristocracy

This dynamic explosion of energy and accomplishment was observed by the old "aristocracy" of New York, whose families traced their lineage back to early Dutch settlers or to colonial Englishmen: the Knickerbocker crowd. The walls of their brownstones were often lined with the silent images of generations of ancestors as subtle references to the antiquity of their pedigrees and therefore of their position in society, for their social pyramid was based on such things and not on money, of which they seldom had excessive amounts.[8] Conversely, in the drawing room of a Fifth Avenue mansion belonging to one of the newcomers would hang portraits by Reynolds, Romney, Gainsborough, Van Dyke, Titian, and the like, all obtained by the new-money people from old English country houses, French châteaux, or Italian palazzos—"borrowed" icons, as it were, falsely proclaiming ancient lineage.

One social commentator, writing in 1872, made the following unsympathetic assessment of society's Old Guard, "the pompous Knickerbockers":

> Those who claim precedence base their demand upon their descent from the original Dutch settlers, and style themselves "the old Knickerbockers." The majority of these . . . have inherited their fortunes from their ancestors. They are owners of valuable real estate, much of which is located in the very heart of the city. . . . They are frequently persons of cultivation, and were it not for their affectation of superiority, would, as a class, be decidedly clever people. . . . They make an effort to have their surroundings as clumsy and as old-fashioned as possible, as a mark of their Dutch descent. . . . They are extremely exclusive, and rarely associate with any but those who can "show as pure a pedigree." Their disdain of those whose families are not as "old" as their own is often times amusing.[9]

Society matron May Van Rensselaer, however, showed greater reverence for the descendants of the old Dutch families when she recalled that their names appeared infrequently in the Society pages and that they performed useful if unspectacular works. "Idleness and wasting time," she wrote, "are repugnant to people of Dutch blood. They live on quiet side streets, a little aloof from the turbid flow of current Society. . . . Society once connoted, first of all, family; its primary meaning at present is fortune."[10] She then added that "in the comfortable brownstone houses of Fourteenth Street and its neighboring thoroughfares there was no spectacular flaunting of wealth."[11] Mrs. Van Rensselaer published a book titled *New Yorkers of the XIX Century* (1897) in which she identified a number of the families who constituted the old Knickerbocker aristocracy, including the pedigree of each, thus defining that group as distinct from the new millionaires.

The restraint practiced by the Old Guard of New York Society is apparent in a book titled *The Last Days of Knickerbocker Life in New York* (1880) in which the author—well aware that his way of life was passing—reminisced about the principles that had guided his existence, and their erosion: "Knickerbocker life was too stable, too uniform, to countenance stag dinner-parties, when the consequent orgies would run far into the night. . . . Society under Knickerbocker rule was based on a strict observance of moderation in everything. . . . It looked with abhorrence upon the spendthrift; it condemned the idler. . . . Its pride was an honored home." The same author then continued: "Suddenly accumulated wealth has swept away its commemorative monuments. Boulevards and avenues have swallowed its winding streets. . . . Imposing structures of marble and granite have . . . displaced modest piles of homely brick, and costly luxuries have driven simple necessities to the wall."[12]

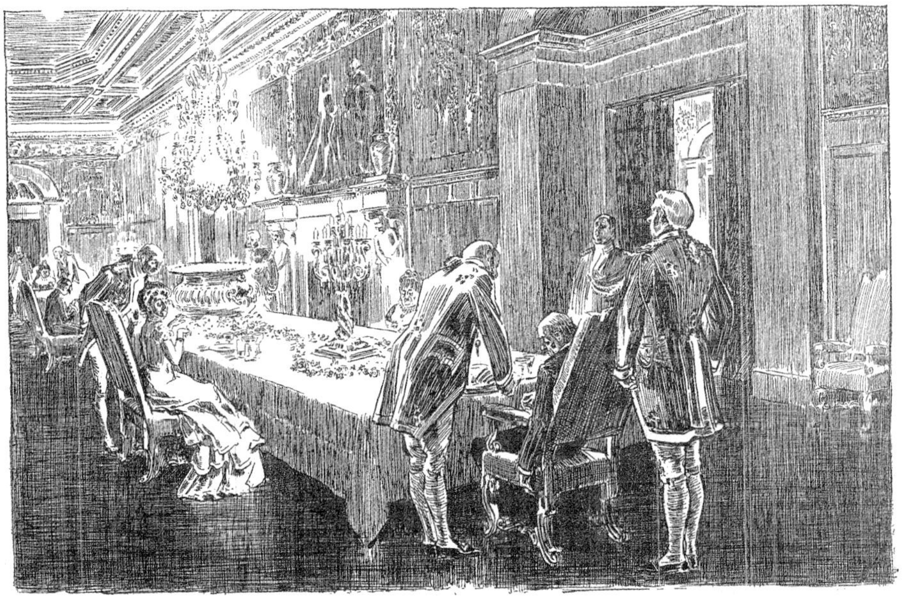

The New Rich

At the opposite end of Society from the old Knickerbockracy were those whom James McCabe caustically termed, in 1872, the "New Rich," or as they are sometimes termed, the "Shoddyites." They constitute the majority of the fashionables. . . . Every year makes fresh accessions to their ranks, and their follies and extravagances multiply in proportion. They occupy the majority of the mansions in the fashionable streets . . . and flaunt their wealth so coarsely and offensively in the faces of their neighbors, that many good people have come to believe that riches and vulgarity are inseparable. They make themselves the most conspicuous, and are at once accepted by strangers as the "best society" of the metropolis. They are almost without exception persons who have risen from the ranks. . . . They are ashamed of their origin, and you cannot offend one of them more than to hint that you knew him a few years ago as a mechanic or a shopkeeper.[13]

From her historical vantage point, May Van Rensselaer recalled that a great change in Society was noticeable already in the decade immediately following the Civil War, observing that until then Society—that is, Old Knickerbocker Society—remained static and "unthreatened by invasion":

All at once it was assailed from every side by persons who sought to climb boldly over the walls of social exclusiveness. . . . But [all] attempts to keep birth and lineage as the primary requisite for social distinction were destined to fail. New York was entering its period of amazing, mushroom growth. It was becoming too large, too cosmopolitan for a comparatively small group of the patrician native-born to retain preeminence in Society. . . . In that period of great economic expansion, people were rushing to New York to make their fortunes. They and their children formed in the city a wealthy, extravagant, spectacular group of no orderly social growth. . . . Social prominence, as the city understood the term, was to be expressed henceforth in terms of millions rather than of lineage.[14]

Another social critic declared that "the leaders of gayety flutter in the admiring gaze of the stupid and ignorant masses, but they are not worthy to be named in the same category with those who can boast better claims to distinction than merely the possession of money." The same author then said, "It is not worth our while to treasure the names of ladies of this order, who have made themselves conspicuous entirely by the extravagance of their entertainments, the excessive costliness of their dress, or their disregard of feminine discretion."[15]

Contemporary social critics could easily identify the new segment then arising within Society, as James D. McCabe did when he characterized the group at its worst, saying the detested newcomers were instantly recognizable, for they dress "magnificently, making up in display what they lack in taste. They cover themselves with jewels, and their diamonds, worn on ordinary occasions, might in some instances rival the state gems of European sovereigns." McCabe voiced his concern over their origins as well when he wrote that "their rough, hard hands, coarse faces, loud voices, bad English, and vulgar manners contrast strikingly with the splendors with which they surround themselves. . . . They are utterly lacking in personal dignity, and substitute for that quality a supercilious hauteur."[16] But McCabe was drawing a caustic caricature of the American nouveaux riches, and if they did possess some of the traits he ascribed to them, their accomplishments were nevertheless greater than his description suggests.

To Mrs. Van Rensselaer, the intermarriage of old families and new money was particularly odious: "Men of no social distinction," she wrote, "have frequently become prominent in Society by marrying women of breeding. The Vanderbilts, the Astors, the Belmonts and other present leaders have attained their station largely through the infusion of aristocratic blood into their line through marriage with the old families. Their wives made them."[17]

McCabe also addressed this point, insofar as the daughters of social climbers were concerned, noting that it was not uncommon for a man of recent fortune to make the marriage of his daughter "the means of getting his family into society. He will go to some young man within the pale of good society, and offer him the hand of his daughter and a fortune." The obligation of the aforesaid young man was, of course, "to get the family of the bride within the charmed circle."[18]

The Robber Baron: The Aptness of the Term?

The Gilded Age has been called the era of the "robber barons." But whence came this term, and does it still possess sociocultural validity or historiographical aptness? Historians of the Middle Ages originally coined the term to describe predaceous lords who would swoop down from their castles in lawless times to plunder any luckless wayfarer or caravan that passed beneath their ramparts. Its application to late-nineteenth-century American financiers and industrialists—

who reportedly preyed on each other as well as on unfortunate middle-class investors, the laboring classes, and the poor—occurred soon after the rise of this new breed of capitalists. Charles Francis Adams used the expression in 1878 in his famous study of the railroads.[19] An early advocate of some sort of control on the rampageous tycoons was the statesman and journalist Carl Schurz, who wrote in 1882 that he expected soon to see a movement set in motion that would "put an end to the operations of the modern robber barons, who, by corporate rascality, supplemented with tricks of the stock exchange, manage to plunder at will not only their fellow gamblers, but the innocent bona fide investors in corporate enterprises."[20] It must be noted, however, that Schurz's attack was only on those who abused the privileges of the capitalistic system—a minority among essentially honest businessmen.

Still, by 1901 President Theodore Roosevelt perceived a great danger in so much wealth and power being localized in the hands of so few men, to whom he referred, not as robber barons, but as "malefactors of great wealth":

> In no other country in the world had such enormous fortunes been gained. In no other country . . . was such power held by the men who had gained these fortunes. . . . The power of the mighty industrial overlords of the country had increased with giant strides, while the methods of controlling them . . . through the government remained practically impotent. . . . Of all forms of tyranny the least attractive and the most vulgar is the tyranny of mere wealth, the tyranny of a plutocracy.[21]

With Roosevelt's administration (1901–9) began a period of federal prosecution, using the Sherman Anti-Trust Act of 1890, of gigantic corporations such as Standard Oil, United States Steel, J. P. Morgan's financial combine, and the railroads—that is, the very heart of the corporate, capitalist American enterprise that had grown titanic, largely through monopolies or near monopolies. The alarm bell that aroused the democratic instincts of the nation had been sounded in 1894 with the publication of Henry Demarest Lloyd's *Wealth against Commonwealth*, which was an attack on the excessive power of corporate capitalism and on the theory of Social Darwinism. Here was a call to arms for the great democracy to take a stand against the "malefactors of great wealth" and, through socialism, create the great society. But the so-called robber barons and the ideology of free enterprise stood in the way.

Matthew Josephson codified the concept of the robber baron in modern terms in his classic study, *The Robber Barons*, which was published in 1934—at a time, it should be noted, when the nation was in the depths of the worst economic depression it had ever experienced. The ordinary American saw the banks closed and the factories shut down, and under the influence of socialist political ideologues, economic theorists, and union organizers, it was easy to find—in America's wealthy class—a scapegoat for the grave woes that beset the nation. And so the leaders of American finance and industry were pilloried and vilified—as a group, extending back to the 1870s—as infamous robber barons, tarring all who attained great wealth with the same biased brush. By the mid-1930s, wealth had come to be associated with frivolity, excess, and something that was somehow un-American and undemocratic.

Robber Barons Who Earned the Name

To be sure, there were men who deserved the title of robber baron—Jay Gould, Jim Fisk, and Daniel Drew come to mind. All three men came from rural areas to make their millions in New York City following the Civil War, and all three were seemingly born to financial knavery. By the age of twenty-one, in 1857, Jay Gould (1836–92) had enjoyed his first fleecing, leaving his partner in the tanning and leather goods business, Charles W. Leupp, of a fine old Knickerbocker family, so ruined and shamed that he committed suicide. Daniel Drew (1797–1879), a sanctimonious Methodist and a drover, would load up his cattle with salt when taking them to market, which would cause them to drink vast amounts of water just before they were weighed—and Drew thus began, literally, "watering his stock" well before he moved to Wall Street. He made his first million with steamboats on the Hudson River and additional millions as a stockbroker. Swaggering Jim Fisk (1834–72) began as a ticket-seller for a circus but in 1866, with Drew's backing, established a brokerage house in Wall Street.

The confluence of their stories came in 1868 when they joined forces to battle Cornelius Vanderbilt in the Erie Railroad Wars.[22] Vanderbilt wanted the Erie, which ran from

Buffalo to Chicago, to hook up with his New York Central, which ran from New York to Albany to Buffalo; Gould, Fisk, and Drew wanted the Erie, which they controlled, because they had not yet finished plundering it by watering its stock. What followed was truly a battle of Titans, although at times it resembled a Mack Sennett comedic farce.

In the debacle, Gould, Fisk and Drew made great use of a printing press, with which they shamelessly ran off unlimited numbers of stock certificates that either ended up in their pockets or were used as collateral in nefarious business deals. One ploy was to buy a decrepit railroad, issue stock in its name, exchange those shares for Erie stock, which were highly valued, and reap an enormous profit. Or they would print convertible bonds, and whenever they ran short on shares, they simply converted their bonds into shares of Erie stocks. This practice enormously increased the number of shares outstanding, thereby reducing their value, and the poor souls—the "widows and orphans" and small investors—who did not sell out in time could only watch their life's savings disappear as the value of the watered stock plunged.

On another occasion, Gould, carrying a satchel that contained $500,000, slipped off to Albany, where he bribed a judge and some legislators to get his bogus Erie bonds declared legal. It worked, and the Gould gang managed to skin Cornelius Vanderbilt of over a million dollars. At this point Drew retired to other devious acts, but the Gould-Fisk partnership replaced him by bringing that pillar of civic corruption, William M. "Boss" Tweed, onto their board of directors. This trio continued its duping, looting, stock-watering ways until they hit upon a scheme to corner gold and drive up the price; in that misadventure, thousands of small investors were defrauded, while the Gould gang sold short and came away with several millions in profits.

Jay Gould went on to control vast railroad interests. For example, in 1879, having acquired control of the unimportant Kansas Pacific line, he threatened to extend it to make contact with the Central Pacific, thus making a second transcontinental railway to compete with the Union Pacific. At the thought of this and the rate wars that would inevitably ensue, the board of the Union Pacific panicked, and to preserve its near monopoly it agreed to consolidate with Gould's Kansas Pacific; according to Henry Villard, with no more effort than making a threat, Gould walked away with over $10 million in his pocket. With those profits he was able, the next year, to buy Lyndhurst, the great castle-like estate near Tarrytown, New York (see figure 30, p. 66).

Gould was a loner, content to make millions, with little interest in establishing a place for himself in the high social circles of his day. As he puttered with his orchids, his favorite leisure pastime at Lyndhurst, he knew he was an intensely hated man and an outcast of Society. But despite the many threats on his life, Jay Gould died of natural causes in 1892. Meanwhile, in 1872, that jovial, obese bounder Jim Fisk had come to his sorry end in a dispute over the affections of Josie Mansfield, one of his several mistresses, when the equally dissolute Edward Stokes fatally shot him in the Grand Central Hotel. Daniel Drew did leave some good behind, for his endowment of several hundred thousand dollars established a theological seminary in Madison, New Jersey, which exists today as Drew University. But in general, the vast majority of American capitalists of the Gilded Age did not indulge in the predatory manipulations of the unholy Gould-Fisk-Drew trio, and it would be unfair to apply the censorial term "robber baron" to all successful financiers and industrialists because of the antics of a few rogues. Indeed, fairness—as well as historical accuracy—demands that the benefactions of Gilded Age Society be examined, as well as the malefactions.

The Benefactions of Capitalist Wealth

One of the main theses of this book proposes that such a harshly judgmental term as "robber baron" addresses only the negative aspect of the Gilded Age and fails to recognize that some of the men and women of that era accomplished many spectacular things for the benefit of the ordinary people of their own time and ours.[23] In 1908 Henry Clews put forward the following argument regarding the beneficial effect that American industry offered:

> The Vanderbilt [railroad] system employs 200,000 people at better wages than they can obtain elsewhere, any place in the world. . . . The State is paid $1 for every $2.70 received by the stockholders. Nor can I think it possible that the paternal system of Government proposed by the Socialists . . . could accomplish as much in a century for

the well-being and advantage of the people of this State and of the whole country as the Vanderbilt system of railroads has done in half that time. Until the . . . Socialists demonstrate that their untried systems will confer greater happiness on humanity than honest enterprise . . . under our present social system, with all its defects . . . I shall be tardy in subscribing to the new order of things.[24]

Moreover, it was the new millionaires' initiatives and their money that brought into existence an impressive list of social and cultural institutions. Their wealth, for example, established medical schools, enlarged and updated hospitals, founded mental asylums, and supported colleges and universities. Even so harsh a critic of America as Anthony Trollope conceded as much when he wrote, in 1862,

In no city has more been achieved for humanity by the munificence of its richest citizens than in New York. Its hospitals, asylums, and institutions for the relief of ailments to which flesh is heir, are very numerous, and beyond praise in the excellence of their arrangements. And this has been achieved in a great degree by private liberality. . . . The millionaire when making his will very generally gives back a considerable portion of the wealth which he has made to the city in which he made it. The rich citizen is always anxious that the poor citizen shall be relieved. It is a point of honor with him to raise the character of his municipality, and to provide that the deaf and dumb, the blind, the mad, the idiots, the old, and the incurable shall have such alleviation in their misfortune as skill and kindness can afford.[25]

Several decades later, Andrew Carnegie articulated the philosophy of "giving back." Rich men, Carnegie wrote in his article titled "Wealth," "have it in their power . . . to busy themselves in organizing benefactions from which the masses . . . will derive lasting advantage." And, he continued,

this, then, is held to be the duty of the man of Wealth . . . : to consider all surplus revenues which come to him simply as trust funds, which he is called upon to administer. . . . [For] the best means of benefiting the community is to place within its reach the ladders upon which the aspiring can rise—parks, and means of recreation, by which men are helped in body and mind; works of art, certain to give pleasure and improve public taste; and public institutions of various kinds, which will improve the general condition of the people;—in this manner returning their surplus wealth to the mass of their fellows in the forms best calculated to do them lasting good.[26]

There were many who subscribed to Carnegie's "Gospel." Johns Hopkins, a financier and director of the Baltimore and Ohio Railroad, gave $7 million to establish a free hospital in Baltimore and to found a university, which would bear his name, dedicated to medical research. The University of Chicago opened in 1892 thanks to an infusion of funds from John D. Rockefeller Sr., who also, in 1901, established Rockefeller University in New York City, an institution devoted mainly to medical and social research; twelve years later he set up the Rockefeller Foundation, which his son, John D. Jr., ably administered, and over the next fourteen years endowed it with $183 million, designated primarily for work in medicine and public health.

From the so-called robber barons of the Gilded Age came an impressive list of institutions that even today are open to or intended to serve the general public. Carnegie's gifts alone totaled $350 million and included Carnegie Hall in New York City (1892), the Carnegie Institute in Washington, D.C., and over twenty-eight hundred libraries in towns, large and small, all across the United States. In the fine arts, the J. Pierpont Morgan Library, the Frick Collection, the Walters Gallery, and the Corcoran Gallery bear the names of their founders, but there are many other institutions in which such men were active as organizers—for example, the Metropolitan Museum of Art, the Museum of Fine Arts, Boston, the National Gallery of Art in Washington (which was founded a bit later but with Andrew Mellon's steel and banking money), the Chicago Art Institute, and the Saint Louis Art Museum, to name but a few of the more prominent. Libraries such as the Boston Public Library and the New York Public Library belong to the list of their benefactions, as do the American Museum of Natural History in New York and the Field Museum of Natural History in Chicago, plus the Chicago, Pittsburgh, New York Philharmonic, Boston, Philadelphia, and Cleveland symphonies and the Metropolitan Opera Company, among world renowned institutions of music.

And so the Gilded Age was like most societies at most times—a mixture of good and bad. As raucous and self-serving as the era could be, its leaders nevertheless possessed a sense of civic pride and a commitment both to the less fortunate of their own time and to the cultural heritage of future generations. As much of the architecture considered in the pages that follow consisted of monuments to themselves, much of it has also been bequeathed to the American people, who now visit and enjoy it by the millions annually.

America is the land of the self-made man—the empire of the parvenu. Here it is felt that the accident of birth is of trifling consequence; here there is no 'blood' to be coveted save the red blood which every masterful man distills in his own arteries; and here the name of parvenu is the only and all-sufficient title of nobility.

William A. Croffut,
The Vanderbilts and the Story of their Fortune (1885), p. v.

Chapter One

Society, Europe, and Aristocracy

The Empire of the Parvenu

Society Defines Itself

"To be married in or buried from Grace or Saint Thomas's Church, is the desire of every fashionable heart," wrote James McCabe in 1872.[1] Episcopalianism, the favored faith of fashionable Society, offered "magnificent processions . . . and the merest nibble . . . of the Roman Catholicism which upper-class Americans had wistfully viewed in the gorgeous ceremonies of St. Peter's, Rome, and Notre Dame, Paris. . . . It was also the faith of dukes and viscounts and marquesses."[2] Other Protestant denominations had denied the parvenus the pomp and show that was a part of their new existence while Episcopalianism condoned their wealth and their lifestyles, and so they flocked to Saint Thomas Church at 53rd and Fifth Avenue or to Grace Church at 10th and Broadway. At the latter, Society found assistance in an unexpected source.

Gilded Age Society called upon a series of functionaries to assist it in its effort to define itself. The earliest was "arrogant old Isaac Brown" (figure 3), the sexton of Grace Church who "transmitted invitations for the elect," as Mrs. Burton Harrison described him.[3] In the years following the Civil War, only the most foolhardy hostess would attempt a gala or a dinner party without first conferring with Brown. Elizabeth Ellet, writing in 1867, said of Brown that "every aristocratic fete, every occasion for a fashionable assemblage in New York, has been for some years under the management of . . . the portly sexton of Grace Church." She then described him as "happy, fat, and sleek," and further noted that "with easy mien he salutes the belles as they alight, amiably conscious that—'Where Brown is found, To Fashion's eye is hallowed ground.' "[4]

Another contemporary remembered that it was Brown who "passed on worthiness in life or death" and arranged every social event from christenings to bridal parties to fancy dress balls to funerals; "a fashionable lady," that author declared, "about to have a fashionable gathering at her house, orders her meats from the butcher, her supplies from the grocer, her cakes and ices from the confectioner; but her invitations she puts in the hands of Brown. He knows whom to invite and whom to omit." The same commentator then continued, noting that Brown could supply any number of handsome young men in white tie and tails who "in consideration of a fine supper and a dance, will allow themselves to be passed off as the sons of distinguished New Yorkers." The city has, the anonymous writer observed, "any quantity of ragged noblemen, seedy lords from Germany, Hungarian barons out at the elbows, members of the European aristocracy who left their country for their country's good who can be served up in proper proportions at a fashionable party. . . . No man knows their haunts better than Brown."[5]

Ward McAllister remembered his predecessor as Society's chargé d'affaires, writing that he knew everything about everybody, was a good-natured fellow who enjoyed making jokes, and had a good word for all who passed before him as they entered the ballroom: "You could hear him *sotto voce* remarking upon men as they passed: 'Old family, good old stock,' or 'He's a new man; he had better mind his p's and q's, or I will trip him up. Ah, here's a good fellow who intends

Figure 3. Isaac H. Brown, sexton of Grace Church, New York City, from a photograph by W. Kurtz, ca. 1890. New York Public Library. The "portly sexton of Grace Church," the first of Society's major duomos in the early years of the Gilded Age, controlled the social events of his wealthy parishioners like a ringmaster at a circus. As a contemporary noted, "At weddings and at parties, Brown makes out the list of persons to be invited. He allows no interference. He knows his invitations will be accepted. . . . He directs everything, and carries his arrangements out with the decision and authority of an autocrat." (Browne, *Secrets of the Great City*, p. 85) No one, but no one, entered the gilded gates without obtaining his approval, and good churchman that he was, no one excelled him in groveling before the rich or in snobbishness before lowly climbers.

to dance his way into Society. Here comes a handsome boy, the women are crazy about him.' "[6] Elderly Peter Marie immortalized Brown in verse:

> O glorious Brown! thou medley strange,
> Of church-yard, ball-room, saint and sinner,
> Flying in morn through fashion's range,
> And burying mortals after dinner,
> Walking one day with invitations,
> Passing the next with consecrations.[7]

Brown had been making himself indispensable as sexton and social major domo for longer than anyone in the parish could remember. Indeed, it was said that the congregation would miss him more than the rector, should one of them be called away. In fact, one rector once tried to dismiss old Brown, only to be informed by his congregation that he, the minister, should attend to religious matters and leave social matters up to his assistant.

Brown's usefulness is not difficult to understand: The *arrivistes* who had forged this new society were always deeply concerned that they not commit some social *faux pas*, and they needed someone with the savvy to prevent them from doing so. There will, in fact, arise a whole string of such persons who will act as a sort of sergeant-at-arms, guarding the recently arrived against unwanted intruders and social miscues.

Isaac Brown had begun his career as a carpenter in upstate New York, made his way to the great city, and ended up at Grace Church, which he once described as the most fashionable court outside of Heaven. From his central position at Grace Church he could observe who visited with whom on the steps as parishioners exited after the Sunday services—he could sort out those who had arrived and those who were "old family" and those who had not been admitted to the fashionable set. In the 1860s and 1870s he could make or break any social aspirant simply by including or withholding his or her name on the list of invitations to fancy balls or weddings or whatever.

Ward McAllister

But Brown was not himself a member of Society. He was rough, even gruff; he was impudent and servile—he was once described as the connecting link between Society and the curbstone, a reference to his hailing cabs for the elite as they exited Grace Church. What Society needed was someone of their own set who would serve as the arbiter of all aspects of social ritual. They found that person in Ward McAllister (figure 4) who, in the 1880s, became Brown's successor, with the advantage that he was one of Society's own.

The Gilded Age codified Society, even to a precise number—the "Four Hundred" they were called. Ward McAllister was in charge of all important Society affairs, for, following the tenure of Old Brown, it was he who made up and kept the list of names of the chosen ones. He took himself very seriously in this matter, and some wag mockingly referred to him as "Make-a-lister." The number four hundred itself was reportedly adopted because no more than that could fit comfortably into Mrs. William B. (Caroline) Astor's ballroom in her brownstone house at 34th Street and Fifth Avenue, the epicenter of American Society in the last quarter of the nineteenth century. Actually, the inner circle of Society was considerably smaller than four hundred while for certain social events one thousand to twelve hundred invitations might be extended. But when queried about the limiting number, McAllister replied, "Why, there are only about four-hundred people in fashionable New York society. If you go outside that number you strike people who are either not at ease in a ballroom or make others not at ease."[8]

McAllister (1827–95) was born in Savannah, Georgia, where his father was famous for his hospitality and entertaining. When Ward was about twenty he spent some time in New York and was introduced to Society's inner circle by a relative living there. Returning to Georgia, he passed the bar before moving to California with his brother and father, with whom he set up a law firm. By the mid-1850s he was wealthy enough to retire.[9] He traveled about in Europe for several years, observing the fine points of court life and the lifestyle of the aristocracy. Returning to the United States, he bought a townhouse in New York and a place called Bayside Farm near Newport, Rhode Island.

McAllister was well placed insofar as family connections were concerned. His full name was Samuel Ward McAllister, being named after his cousin, Sam Ward, who had married the sister of William Astor; another cousin was Julia Ward

Howe. He married well, taking Sarah Gibbons, daughter of a Georgia millionaire, as his bride. Being a man of leisure, he was able to devote himself to his growing passion for organizing Society. Socialite Elizabeth Drexel Lehr described him and his work:

> He devoted his whole life to compiling his famous set of rules for the guidance of social New York. He read books on heraldry and precedence, studied the customs of every court in Europe. . . . [As] McAllister [made] his round of the opera-boxes on Monday evenings [he] would listen to plans for forthcoming parties with the utmost gravity, offer his advice as to whom should be invited, restrict the number of guests. . . . And all the while his watchful eyes would be observing the neighboring boxes, noting the newcomers, whom they were talking to. . . . "You can never be absolutely certain whether people are in society or not until you see them at four or five of the best houses. Then you can make advances to them without the danger of making a mistake," was his favorite dictum.[10]

Mrs. Winthrop Chanler—also of the Astor clan—admitted that Society was a closed circle of privileged persons, to which one either belonged or did not belong, and acknowledged McAllister as the Cerberus who guarded its formidable gates. She noted that he even published a series of articles in a Sunday newspaper identifying Society's elect: "He mentioned them all by name and made a sort of diagram of the hierarchy, not unlike Dante's description of Paradise, with the greater and lesser saints circling in their appointed places about the Mystic Rose. He was laughed at [and] called a snob . . . but the expression 'the four hundred' passed into current usage and has not been forgotten."[11]

New York Society: A Stratum of Its Own

In our unstructured and informal social relationships today, we may smile at McAllister and the cause to which he devoted his life. But the quotations just cited reveal the earnest attempts of a new layer of American society to define itself from within and defend itself from without. This new sector knew it was no longer middle class by virtue of its fabulous wealth, the enormous power that it wielded, and the lifestyle it chose to pursue. But if not middle class, neither was it aristocracy in the Old World sense—that is, not the aristocracy comprising ten or more generations of blue-blooded nobility. Its estates were as new as its money, and even the Astors represented only second- and third-generation wealth and social standing. Many of these new American millionaires still had the scent of the brewery or the dust of the coal bins about them, or the manners of the roaring mining camps that were lingering reminders of their recent rise to wealth. Anthony Trollope took note of the special new breed of "aristocrat" that America was fostering, observing that New York City had a right to be proud of its wealth: "But . . . I know of no great man, no celebrated statesman, no philanthropist of peculiar note who has lived in Fifth Avenue. That gentleman on the right made a million of dollars by inventing a shirt-collar; this one on the left electrified the world by a lotion; as to the gentleman at the corner there,—there are rumors about him and the Cuban slave-trade. . . . Such are the aristocracy of Fifth Avenue."[12]

So this new segment of American society established itself somewhere between the comfortable but only moderately well-to-do middle class that was beneath it in the social pyramid, and the true aristocracy of the Old World above it. But it was the latter that became the model for its dress, social ceremonies such as galas and balls, its fascination with equipage and yachts, its architecture, and its passion for collecting art. While it may have remained mid-

Figure 4. *Snobbish Society's Schoolmaster*: Ward McAllister, "Uncle Sam, you must—aw—imitate this, or you will never be a gentleman." From *Judge* (8 November 1890), cover. Library of Congress, Washington, D.C. Isaac Brown's successor as social organizer of the new millionaires was Ward McAllister, the man who first defined Society's "Four Hundred." O. Henry, like many others, took exception to this elitism, and wrote his book *The Four Million* (1906) as a rejoinder, declaring the social value of every New Yorker. In the *Judge* cartoon, a sign

dle class itself in some ways, this new stratum usually chose to emulate European aristocracy in its rush to establish the level at which it wished to function. As noted earlier, even the old Knickerbocker aristocracy did not offer a satisfactory model, for it was too staid, too puritanical in its restraints, too inhibited in its vision of what enormous wealth could allow one to enjoy.

That America's new millionaires chose to pattern their lives after European aristocracy had enormous ramifications for their social life and for the art, architecture, and decorative arts that they commissioned. Frederick Martin, himself a member of the gilded set, assessed the situation perfectly:

> The advent of the American woman in English Society was almost unheard of before the [American] Civil War, and this was due to the fact that up to that time American Society was a negligible quantity. But a few years later a change set in, and New York was obliged to face the fact that it must adopt a more metropolitan tone. From the shores of the Pacific, from the banks of the Monongahela, and from the great plains of the west and middle east came millionaires with their wives and children who were determined to change the old order into something entirely new. The lines of hide-bound convention were speedily broken down, new blood was infused into feeble stock, and as a result Venus Victrix, dowered with loveliness and dollars, set forth to conquer England.[13]

This passage asserts that there was a new layer in American Society, it proclaims New York to be the magnet to which the socially ambitious were drawn from around the nation, and it addresses the matter of how American Society began to integrate itself with European Society.

Martin also infers something that has been generally overlooked by those who have studied this period—the tremendous influence the California contingent had on Society once it settled in New York City. Since the days of the Gold Rush and the enormous wealth of the forty-niners who struck it rich, California society had been unhampered by the restraint of the dowdy social establishment that had long been entrenched in Boston, Philadelphia, Baltimore, and especially New York where the old Knickerbockers reigned, quietly and sedately. The Californians, however, were bold and brash; they wanted to enjoy their newly gained riches to the fullest, and they did not mind spending money lavishly—something the Knickerbocker families found difficult even when they had it. When this roaring herd came storming into New York City bedecked in gold and pockets overflowing with dollars, it contributed to a new *joie de vivre* that was beyond the ken of old brownstone society. The same could be said of those who hit the "Big Bonanza" in the roaring mining regions of Nevada, as we will see.

The Reverend Nicholls, an Episcopalian, recognized this very point when he wrote in 1904 that "an annually increasing quota of candidates for metropolitan honors . . . is made up of rich—suddenly rich—western people," and in another passage he gave fuller consideration to the matter:

> [Mrs. Hermann Oelrichs] and Mrs. William K. Vanderbilt, Jr., have evidently inherited the artistic trend of their mother, the wife of the late U.S. Senator Fair, of San Francisco, whose dinners and balls were given on a scale of Oriental magnificence. The California '49ers, the Fairs, Floods, Hearsts, Crockers, D. Ogden Millses, Mackays and their peers . . . made up their minds that no matter how short some of their pedigrees were, they themselves would live well and long. Accordingly they set themselves to work to invent the art of dining. And Mr. Ward McAllister, during his stay in San Francisco as a young man, acquired the whole gastronomic art of war of the '49ers and came back and imparted what he knew to benighted New York, then in the throes of the mincing and pinched-up Knickerbocker regime.[14]

The Short List of the Ultra-fashionable

While Gilded Age Society at first numbered approximately four hundred persons, the number of the "ultra-fashionable" was much smaller, and a short list of names of the leaders quickly emerged. Throughout most of the era, Caroline Schermerhorn Astor—Mrs. William Astor, THE Mrs. Astor—was the reigning if sometimes challenged queen of Society. The grandsons and granddaughters of Cornelius Vanderbilt became glittering stars in the galaxy of the Gilded Age. August Belmont, who for decades represented the Rothschild interests in New York, introduced a European flavor to social life, and his wife, Caroline, was one of New York's foremost hostesses before Caroline Astor came upon the scene. The Whitney dynasty rose at this time in the person of William Collins Whitney, and the Morgan fortunes culminated in J. Pierpont Morgan. There were railroad tycoons such as Henry Villard, for whom McKim, Mead and White designed a palazzo on Madison Avenue (now the Palace Hotel), and Louisine Havemeyer and her husband,

declares that "No Gentleman is without a Coat of Arts. Take your choice," while the box on which the effete Englishman stands is inscribed "The Real Thing. An English Snob of the 19th Century." A manly Uncle Sam laughs uncontrollably at McAllister for suggesting that he, as the embodiment of the bold and vigorous American male, must try to be like the wasted nobleman who slouches before them. McAllister once told a reporter that now, "with the rapid growth of riches, millionaires are too common to receive much deference; a fortune of a million is only respectable poverty. So we have to draw social boundaries on another basis; old connections, gentle breeding, perfection in all the requisite accomplishments of a gentleman, elegant leisure and an unstained private reputation count for more than newly gotten riches. You would be surprised at the number of apparently eligible men this list of requirements strikes out of consideration. The truth is we are not a nation of Chesterfields and Bayards, Sidneys and Raleighs." (*New York Daily Tribune*, 25 March 1888, p. 11)

Henry, who converted a sugar trust into a great art collection. The formidable Mamie, Mrs. Stuyvesant Fish, appears regularly on the Gilded stage, and at Newport one of the indomitable social forces was Tessie Oelrichs, wife of the scion of a German transatlantic shipping line, for whom Stanford White designed Rosecliff, one of the great masterpieces among the cottages there. Also at Newport one encounters the Ogden Goelets and Edward Berwind, a coal baron for whom Horace Trumbauer created a beautiful white palace. From the steel mills and coke furnaces of Pittsburgh came Andrew Carnegie and Henry Clay Frick, both of whom erected elegant mansions on Fifth Avenue. The fascinating Arabella Huntington used the California fortune of her husband, Union Pacific Railroad magnate Collis P. Huntington, in an unsuccessful assault on Society, but ended up selling her house (which stood where the sculpture garden of the Museum of Modern Art is now located) to oil giant John D. Rockefeller; rejected, she departed for California with her late husband's nephew Henry to establish there what would become the world-renowned Huntington Library, Art Collections, and Botanical Gardens. These are a few of the central characters who dominated Society in the Gilded Age, whose art and architecture were symbols of their ambitions and their roles in American, indeed international Society.

Henry James, Edith Wharton and Cosmopolitanism

Many artists have chronicled the Gilded Age as they observed it, often from within, sometimes from the sidelines, where they could analyze with detachment the society that concerns us. Among them are two extraordinary literary masters: Henry James (1843–1916) and Edith Wharton (1862–1937), who transcribed the very soul of the era. One need only read James's *The American* (1877), *Washington Square* (1881), *The Portrait of a Lady* (1881), *The Spoils of Poynton* (1897), *The Wings of the Dove* (1902), or *The Golden Bowl* (1904), or Wharton's *House of Mirth* (1905), *The Custom of the Country* (1913), or *The Age of Innocence* (published in 1920 but set in the 1870s) to gain a keen perception of their Society, of its desire to define itself, and its use of art, architecture, and domestic furnishings to symbolize its aspirations.

Both James and Wharton were devoted to their native country—but they could not bear to live in it. Once they had tasted the culture of the Old World, they found America endurable only for brief visits. And yet in their novels, set in England, Venice, Rome, Paris, or wherever, Americans are almost always the main characters, Americans who had gone to Europe to find that culture, that cosmopolitanism, that worldliness, that romance of life that did not exist in the United States. These two authors, in fact, lived the expatriate life they wrote about.

Somehow the crumbling dampness of a Venetian palazzo—filled with the shadows of centuries of secrets, emblazoned by the brush of Tintoretto or Veronese, the setting of grand drama and noble ceremonies—held an allure that row upon uniform row of dull-mauve brownstones back in New York could never offer, and it was so very different from the parochial smugness of Boston or Concord. The "Queen of the Adriatic" became a favorite destination of peripatetic Americans in ways not understood by the occasional visitor of earlier generations. Poor old Ralph Waldo Emerson missed the whole point of Venice when he recorded in his journal in June of 1833 that Venice was "a great oddity—a city for beavers, but to my thought a most disagreeable residence. You feel always in prison, and solitary. . . . There is always a slight smell of bilge water about the thing. . . . I soon had enough of it."[15] But then Ralph Waldo Emerson never took a moonlight ride in a gondola, nor discussed aesthetics with James Abbott McNeill Whistler, nor sat in the salon of the Palazzo Barbaro with Henry James and talked of psychological romances and hidden, forbidden thoughts, nor attended Kate Bronson's regular salons to mingle with counts and dowagers and Oscar Wilde, or chanced upon Bernard Berenson and Isabella Stewart Gardner whispering secretly about the existence of a long-lost Titian with which some ancient family was now forced to part for the sake of American dollars. No, the Gilded Age was different in so many ways from the antebellum decades of Ralph Waldo Emerson.

The novelist William Dean Howells, American consul in Venice in the 1860s, caught more of the spirit when he reminisced that he always enjoyed an afternoon respite "at the Caffe Florian in the Piazza of Saint Mark, where we drank a cup of black coffee and ate an ice, while all the world promenaded by and the Austrian bands made heavenly music."[16] Howells's response to Venice was very different from Emerson's, as when he took note of the palaces, which "rose in the most delicate and fantastic beauty, and mirrored in the brine a dream of sea-deep strangeness and richness. You see much of the beauty yet, but the pride and the opulence which [Venice] called into being are gone forever."[17] In *The Aspen Papers*, Henry James spoke of "the gloomy grandeur" of the interior of one of the decaying Venetian palazzos, and in another passage wrote, "The gondola stopped, the old palace was there; it was a house of the class which in Venice carries even in extreme dilapidation the dignified name [of palazzo]. . . . It was not particularly old, only two or three centuries, and it had an air not so much of decay as of quiet discouragement, as if it had rather missed its career."[18]

If Henry James gives us splendid word-pictures of expatriate life among the palazzos of the Grand Canal, John Singer Sargent has left us an equally brilliant visual record (figure 5). In his *Interior in Venice* the viewer is invited into the story of the Daniel Curtises, and the scenario opens in the magnificent salon of the Palazzo Barbaro on the Grand Canal. Daniel Curtis had been a judge in Boston, leading a quiet, staid Brahmin life until he punched another judge in the nose, for which he was jailed. In his resentment of such a reprisal by his fellow townspeople, he quit Boston and settled permanently in Venice. There he and his wife—they are seen seated in the lower right corner of Sargent's painting—hosted a continuous salon, set amid the early-eighteenth-century grandeur of the architecture of Antonio Gaspari (c. 1658–1738) and the wall and ceiling paintings by Sebastiano Ricci (1659–1734) and Giovanni Battista Piazzetta (1683–1754). In that beautiful chamber Robert Browning was a regular visitor until his death in 1889. In the same room, Henry James sat and wrote. In fact, the Palazzo Barbaro was the inspiration for the palazzo that Millie Theale rents, in which to spend the last months of her life, in *The Wings of the Dove*.[19]

John Singer Sargent visited the palazzo regularly, for Ralph Curtis, the young man at the left, was a cousin of the painter. On 26 February 1911, Bernard Berenson wrote to Isabella Stewart Gardner telling her of his happy visit with Ralph Curtis and his wife, Lizette, also pictured here, at their villa on the Riviera, describing the charm of the garden, reporting that he stayed in the same room that she had occupied there as a guest, and exulting in having some free time to read: "I've actually read *The House of Mirth* at last," Berenson declared, "and a mighty fine thing it is, by the way."[20] Isabella Stewart Gardner, the godmother of the Ralph Curtises' daughter Sylvia, fell in love with the Palazzo Barbaro; beginning around 1890 she began renting it from the Curtises for the summer months, and its influence on her conception of Fenway Court, which she eventually built in Boston, is evident in the Venetian Gothic style she chose.

European Aristocracy and American Parvenus

Old World nobility often kept touring American millionaires at a safe social distance, considering them, as a group, to be crass and uncultured, a vulgar new-monied set with more brass in their manner than gold in their pockets. Edith Wharton expressed the rage that was sometimes felt when, in *The Custom of the Country*, she had Undine Spragg, the spoiled daughter of an American businessman, bear the brunt of a tirade hurled at her by her husband, a member of France's rural minor nobility:

> "And you're all alike," he exclaimed, "every one of you. You come among us from a country we don't know, and can't imagine, a country you care for so little that before you've been a day in ours you've forgotten the very house you were born in—if it wasn't torn down before you knew it! You come among us speaking our language and not knowing what we mean; wanting the things we want, and not knowing why we want them; aping our weaknesses, exaggerating our follies, ignoring or ridiculing all we care about—you come from hotels as big as towns, and from towns as flimsy as paper, where the streets haven't had time to be named, and the buildings are demolished before they're dry, and the people are as proud of changing as we are of holding to what we have—and we're fools enough to imagine that because you copy our ways and pick up our slang you understand anything about the things that make life decent and honorable for us!"[21]

But in spite of such hostility, the American nouveaux riches could not be dissuaded in their desire to associate with European aristocracy—indeed, to form familial alliances with it.[22]

Figure 5. John Singer Sargent, *An Interior in Venice*, 1898. Oil on canvas, 25 × 31 in. (63.5 × 78.7 cm). Royal Academy of Arts, London. Set in the interior of the ancient palace that became the model for Isabella Stewart Gardner's Fenway Court in Boston, this scene portrays American expatriate life in Venice with Judge Curtis and his wife, formerly from Boston, living luxuriously amid moldering Baroque magnificence, as their son Ralph and his wife look on. It was in this room that Henry James wrote portions of *Wings of the Dove*, the architectural settings of which were inspired by the Palazzo Barbaro.

One way to assure an association with the great family lines of Europe was the time-honored manner of forming what were now social and economic ties, but what in earlier times, as practiced by the heads of European states, had been political alliances. This was the custom, alluded to earlier, of marrying off the handsomely endowried daughters of American millionaires to impoverished sons of Europe's noblest and most ancient houses. Writing in 1872, James McCabe noted that a certain Mr. Briggs, who had risen from poverty to great wealth as a pork merchant during the Civil War, had married a woman named Van Duysen because she represented Knickerbocker aristocracy; Miss Van Duysen "married Briggs's money in order to spend it." Of their daughter Flora, McCabe further wrote, "So soon as Mr. Briggs can dispose of his business, Miss Flora is to be taken to Paris. Within two years afterwards she will be led to the altar by a French duke, marquis, or count, who will fall in love with her father's bank book."[23]

Henry James often explored this theme, most notably in his novel *The Golden Bowl*, in which wealthy American tycoon Adam Verver arranges for his daughter to marry an impoverished Italian prince. Anthony Trollope had taken up the subject even earlier, in his serialized *The Way We Live Now*, which appeared in 1874, at about the same time as Mark Twain's *Gilded Age*. In it two of Trollope's main characters discuss this very issue:

> "I wonder whether that will come to anything?" said Paul Montague to Miss Carbury. They had come back into the drawing room, and had been watching the approaches to love-making which the baronet was opening.
>
> "You mean [Baronet] Felix and Miss Melmotte. I hate to think of such things, Mr. Montague," [replied Henrietta Carbury]. "It would be a magnificent chance for him."
>
> "To marry a girl, the daughter of vulgar people, just because she will have a great deal of money? He can't care for her really. . . ."
>
> "But he wants money so dreadfully! It seems to me that there is no other condition of things under which Felix can face the world, but by being the husband of an heiress."[24]

In Trollope's story, the social-climbing Melmotte, it should be noted, was a Frenchman, not an American, but the aristocracy's disdain was almost as virulent, as when Trollope has Roger Carbury say to Lady Carbury, "No one pretends to think that [Melmotte] is a gentleman. . . . He is one whom we would not admit into our kitchens, much less to our tables, on the score of his own merits. Because he has learned the art of making money, we not only put up with him, but settle upon his carcass as so many birds of prey."[25]

Scores of American girls were taken abroad with dowry in tow for the express purpose of uniting an upstart industrial family in the United States with some wasted English, French, Italian, or Hungarian noble line. Edith Bronson, daughter of Kate Bronson, who was Henry James's friend in Venice, married the Florentine Count Cosimo Rucellai (of Rucellai Palace lineage) in 1895. Julia Grant, daughter of an American president and heiress to the royalties of her father's immensely successful *Memoirs*, married Prince Michael Cantacuzene of Russia. Gladys, daughter of Cornelius Vanderbilt II, who built The Breakers at Newport, was wed to the Hungarian Count Széchenyi and thereby became a countess. A long list of such cases could easily be composed.

These arranged marriages were sometimes less than blissful, a hapless condition explored by Henry James in *The Europeans*. Similarly, in Edith Wharton's *Age of Innocence*, the young American woman, Ellen, the Countess Olenska, returned to the United States somewhat in disgrace because she had left her noble husband. In a real-life example, Anna Gould, daughter of Jay Gould, divorced her first husband, the Count Boni de Castellane, who, before the separation, had managed to go through $5.5 million of Jay Gould's gaudy money that had comprised the nuptial dowry, much of it spent on the furnishing of the Palais Rose, a pink marble palace in Paris.[26] Never mind, if Jay Gould's father had been but a poor dirt farmer, his daughter was now a duchess, as the Parisian art dealer René Gimpel once noted in his diary after a chance meeting with Anna on the street: "She is accompanied by her new husband, the Duke de Talleyrand-Perigord, Boni's cousin. After her divorce, which plunged him [Boni] back into financial straights . . . , Boni's only moan was: 'I was deceived, Anna Gould wasn't rich enough for me.' "[27] Poor Boni, who was once again faced with selling off the family treasures, had just negotiated, through the dealer Gimpel, the sale of Largillière's grand eighteenth-century portrait of Madame de Parabere for one hundred thousand francs. In 1909 we find the charming Count Boni at it again, this time as an unsuccessful suitor for the hand of Anne Morgan, daughter of J. Pierpont Morgan.

In yet another example, Cornelia, daughter of the Bradley Martins and niece of Frederick Martin, married the penniless Earl of Craven in 1893, and thereby set his financial house in order again. Miss Goelet by marriage became the Duchess of Roxburghe, and the Marchioness of Anglesey, née Minna King of Georgia, went to live in the château called L'Ermitage at Versailles, once the residence of Madame de Pompadour. After being widowed, Mrs. John Jacob Astor became Lady Ribblesdale, while Mary Leitner became the bride of Lord Curzon, the viceroy of India, making this daughter of one of the founders of Marshall Field's department store in Chicago the vicereine of India.

The Gilded Age reveled in poking fun at this practice, so brilliantly satirized in Charles Dana Gibson's "The Hopewell-Bonds Abroad: Chucking the Ring," which appeared in *Life* magazine in 1894 (figure 6). In the illustration, the grumpy millionaire father and the puggy, socially ambitious mother (far right) have taken their three daughters to Europe for the purpose of finding them husbands. The three fashionably coutured beauties are seen laughing gaily as they toss large rings at Kewpie dolls that represent less-than-handsome European noblemen bearing shields of ancient coats of arms. The young women frolic merrily in their anticipation of which duke, count, baron, prince, or marquis they are to win on this excursion.

The extent to which these marriages of social and economic convenience were commonplace is demonstrated in an article in *The New York Times*, 23 February 1890, titled "HEIRESSES IN THE MARKET," which quotes a notice in the London *Globe*; although obviously written tongue in cheek, its story was based in actual practice:

> It is characteristic of the present day . . . that a German paper should contain an advertisement offering to supply rich American women to needy Germans of position. . . . The advertiser appeals to Germans having titles . . . to write to him in order to be put into communication with American heiresses with fortunes up to four millions. . . . The untitled heiress has been so much on the hunt for nobles that the transactions have, as it were, passed into the market, and the fortunes of rich young ladies are quoted on the Matrimonial Exchange. . . . The proceeding has lately identified itself particularly with American women of fortune. . . . It has been an openly avowed barter of money for title.

One of the best examples of this sort of thing involved the dukes of Marlborough, the masters of Blenheim Palace, perhaps the greatest of the great houses of England. The eighth Duke of Marlborough had wed an American purely to save Blenheim. Consuelo Vanderbilt noted in her biography that after his first wife divorced him, the duke married a woman by the name of Lily Hammersley, "an American widow, whose wealth had been freely spent installing central heating and electric lights at Blenheim."[28] In addition, the dissolute duke began going through his wife's $6 million by refurbishing his London townhouse.

Consuelo also remembered that Lady Paget, one of her mother's dearest friends, "was born Minnie Stevens of New York and with my godmother Consuelo Duchess of Manchester, Lady Randolph Churchill [née Jennie Jerome] and Mrs. Cavendish-Bentink, represented the American element of the smart coterie known as 'the Prince of Wales' set."[29] Similarly, Frederick Martin noted in his memoirs that "Lady Paget represents the best Anglo-American type. I remember her well when, as Minnie Stevens, she was the Belle of Newport. . . . Following Newport came a season in New York, and afterwards Mrs. [Paran] Stevens carried Minnie off to London. The late King [Edward VII], who was then Prince of Wales, wished to arrange a match between her and Arthur Paget."[30] Minnie Stevens was the daughter of Paran Stevens, owner of the Fifth Avenue Hotel in New York City, and is known to us today through John Singer Sargent's extraordinary portrait of her, with its inviting, come-hither stare that is nearly as enigmatic and intriguing as that of the Mona Lisa.

Leonard Jerome of New York had introduced Lily Hammersley to the eighth Duke of Marlborough at Mrs. Paran Stevens's house in Newport in 1887. Jerome's own daughter, Jennie, had married the duke's brother, Randolph Churchill, with whom she had a son named Winston. But the marriage of Lily Hammersley to the eighth duke came just in time, for him at least, for the family treasures were going fast. Sometime around 1885 London's National Gallery had bought from the collection at Blenheim the *Ansidei Madonna*, a great masterpiece by Raphael, for seventy thousand pounds. The

Figure 6. Charles Dana Gibson, *The Hopewell-Bonds Abroad: Chucking the Ring*. From *Life* (13 September 1894), pp. 168–69. Daughters of American millionaires were regularly taken abroad in the hope of securing for them a husband from among the European nobility. Here, Mr. Pipp's three beautiful "Gibson Girl–like" daughters are trying their luck in a ring toss at Kewpie dolls who represent dukes, counts, barons, princes, and the like, in an atmosphere that resembles a carnival side-show game of chance.

New York Times noted that a Van Dyck had also been included in the sale, as well as seven paintings by Rubens, among them *Portrait of His Wife and Son* and *Portrait of His Wife*.[31] Six more large canvases by Rubens were yet to be sold, several more by Van Dyck, and a number of smaller Dutch pictures. In need of funds, the duke had been forced to sell off his patrimony, bit by bit, until Lily Hammersley's dowry bailed him out. His son and successor, the ninth Duke of Marlborough, observed how his father's marriage to an American heiress could relieve such inconveniences.

Consuelo Vanderbilt: Duchess of Marlborough, Mistress of Blenheim

As a young girl Consuelo Vanderbilt, daughter of Alva and William Kissam Vanderbilt and great-granddaughter of "the Commodore" Cornelius Vanderbilt, had a handsome young man come into her life, whom she loved most dearly. He was of a good family and wealthy, but he was not good enough for Consuelo's mother, who became enraged when she heard of the innocent affair and locked her daughter in her room. Alva screamed that she would have a heart attack and die if Consuelo ever saw William Rutherford again, and to ensure that that did not happen she packed her daughter off to Europe for a protracted stay.

Once more back in Newport, at Richard Morris Hunt's recently completed Marble House (see figure 106, p. 162), Alva contrived Consuelo's coming-out party to coincide with a visit from the ninth Duke of Marlborough, on whom Alva had locked her sights. The duke, who was staying at Marble House, proposed to Consuelo in the Gothic room (figure 110, p. 167) on 28 August 1895, and they were married the following November in New York City. But on their honeymoon the duke informed his bride that he, too, had someone whom he loved very much and that she, Consuelo, could never hope to replace that woman, that he had merely sacrificed himself by marrying Consuelo so that Blenheim Palace might shine brightly with all its treasures intact.

The ninth Duke commissioned John Singer Sargent to paint a grand family portrait, to hang at Blenheim opposite Sir Joshua Reynolds's celebrated *Fourth Duke of Marlborough and His Family*. Sargent went to Blenheim to make studies of the hall and the Blenheim standard (top of the painting), but the portraits were painted in his Tite Street studio in London. The artist cleverly had the duke, being shorter than his wife, stand on a step or two lower than she, and thus his shortness is not noticeable.

Consuelo, at the very young age of eighteen, thus became mistress of one of the greatest palaces of Europe and assumed the duties of one of the most important social offices, as duchess, in England. She was a gracious and successful hostess at Blenheim, being accepted not only by English aristocracy but also by Prince Edward himself as one of his favorites; indeed, Consuelo was one of the four duchesses who bore the canopy of Queen Alexandra at the coronation of Edward VII in 1901. But eventually Consuelo could endure her unhappy marriage no longer, and she divorced Marlborough. She found joy at last in a second marriage to Claude Balsan, a dashing French aviator and hero of the First World War.

Meanwhile, the ninth Duke of Marlborough was again broke. René Gimpel recalled going to see him on 26 December 1919: "He wanted to sell me some pictures, as the palace has become a big expense since his divorce from Mrs. Vanderbilt, although she provides him with an [annual] income. . . . The fine furnishings were bought by the present duke in the first years of his marriage. . . . Marlborough has sold everything he is legally allowed to dispose of."[32]

The Ramifications of Cosmopolitanism

There are two primary reasons for recounting the lives of Americans who expatriated themselves and the innumerable examples of American young women of fortune being wed to impecunious European noblemen: First, we observe how this nouveaux millionaire crowd was determined to associate its new sector of American society with the cultural patterns and the family lines of the Old World rather than with the middle class of the United States. Second, those connections gave America's wealthy set a direct acquaintance with the ways of European aristocracy and with its art and architecture. Conduits were thereby established by which American millionaires of the Gilded Age became intimately familiar with the cultural forms of the Old World, which they took as their models. Those connections explain the types of mansions they built for themselves—Madison Avenue palazzos and Fifth Avenue châteaux—as well as the civic and cultural institutions—libraries and art museums, train stations and department stores, gentlemen's clubs and halls of justice—they erected.

The inspiration for such magnificent edifices had virtually no precedent in America; it came instead from Old World sources, which Americans, for all of their dependence on European styles, had not theretofore drawn upon—palatial sources such as the New Louvre, the Tuileries, Versailles, Blenheim Palace, and the Palazzo Barbaro. Rejecting the native architecture of old Knickerbocker New Yorkers who dwelt snugly in dreary brownstones, these new American millionaires demanded of their architects buildings that would proclaim their allegiance to a high style, in living as well as in architecture. Just as the enormity of their wealth established the wide gulf between them and their middle-class countrymen, their art and architecture, like their dress, their manners, their games—indeed almost everything—tended to become symbols of their alliance with European aristocracy.

To play on the words of an old song, how you gonna keep 'em in some old brownstone after they've seen Paris? After these socially ambitious Americans strolled the boulevards of Napoleon III's Second Empire city, climbed the magnificent stairs at Garnier's Opera House, or walked through the sumptuous halls of the Luxembourg Palace, recently renovated by imperial command; or visited Visconti and Lefuel's Ministry of Finance (1852–57) and entered the newly completed Hôtel de Ville (1873–83); after they visited the elegant Hôtel de Pavia and observed the splendid interiors of the Gare de Lyon, what impressions would they carry back to New York and elsewhere? A passage from Ward McAllister's autobiography demonstrates the remembrance of such experiences that Americans carried home, for he recalled a brilliant gala held at the Fifth Avenue mansion of William Henry Vanderbilt: "As I went up the beautiful stairs and passed along the gallery, looking down on a hall such as few palaces contain . . . it put me in mind of a scene I well remembered at the Hôtel de Ville, in Paris, at a ball given by Emperor Napoleon III to the King of Sardinia. It looked royal, and was most impressive."[33]

An American Challenge to the Grandeur That Was Rome

The impressions carried back to the United States served as models for a sector of American society that saw itself on the one hand as the new aristocracy and on the other as capable of challenging the grandeur that was Rome. In the noble edifices of the Old World the new aristocrats found suitably grandiose symbols to match their visions of their own place in the social, political, and economic order at the turn of the century—not only in their domestic architecture but also in civic structures. Their public buildings would be built of marble, while the new institutions they established would be filled with great Renaissance and Baroque masterpieces or with the rarest of rare manuscripts and early printed books. Their railway stations would resemble the Baths of Caracalla and their temple-fronted, domed banks would be reminiscent of the Pantheon; they would erect arches of triumph in Washington Square and Prospect Park, and they would build commercial buildings on Fifth Avenue in the manner of Venetian palaces. Even the scale of Richard Morris Hunt's and McKim, Mead and White's Metropolitan Museum of Art was a challenge to the glory that was Rome. And yet, for all the unabashed aping of Old World culture and styles, what emerged was truly expressive of this new breed of the American industrial or financial millionaire, who was partly a pillager of the past and partly a dynamic creator of the future.

Figure 7. Consuelo, Duchess of Marlborough, ca. 1898. Photograph. Lafayette Collection, Victoria and Albert Museum, London, England. When the Duke of Marlborough married young Consuelo Vanderbilt—a marriage arranged by her mother, Alva—her dowry allowed for the renovation of Blenheim Palace and it meant the duke no longer had to sell off the great artistic treasures of the place in order to meet expenses.

New York ranks fourth in size among the cities of the earth. Architecturally it ranks nowhere. . . . This is owing to its private residences being built wholesale by contractors, who dispensed with architects. . . . Fifth Avenue, like other streets, consists for the most part of innumerable brown stone platitudes, all depressingly alike. The incredible monotony is the only character the great street can boast.

Life (20 December 1892)

Chapter Two

The Early Mansions

Part One

NEW YORK, in the decades following the Civil War, asserted itself as the financial, commercial, cultural, and social capital of the nation, surpassing its East Coast rivals, Philadelphia and Boston. A major transformation in the urban architectural scene began to occur in the late 1850s and 1860s as a result of New York's emergence as a center of enormous wealth. Both Society and architecture had become increasingly cosmopolitan.

But earlier, in the 1830s and 1840s Gotham was, architecturally speaking, a monotonous grid of virtually identical brownstone row houses. Society had developed its main enclave around Washington Square at the foot of Fifth Avenue, ringing its four sides with comfortable but repetitious brownstone dwellings of moderate size. No great mansion of unique design dominated, but there was an equalizing uniformity of color, scale, and form. As one scholar noted, "Some of the owners were very rich indeed and socially well-connected, but you would not know it from the outside of their houses."[1] And this is the precise difference between the brownstone generations and those that followed, for the latter employed architecture to flaunt their wealth in extravagant ways, to a degree that was previously unknown in American society.

THE BERATED BROWNSTONE

Brownstone, applied in thin slabs over brick construction, had come into American architecture in the 1830s, and it received its official imprimatur, as it were, with its use in Richard Upjohn's Trinity Church (1846) in lower Manhattan. To the eyes of the parvenus, the very sameness of brownstone houses all in a row reflected the petrified social order that prevailed (figure 8).

Numerous commentators have left records of their disdain for brownstone, which after 1865 became increasingly old-fashioned, more expressive of staid old Knickerbockers than the *joie de vivre* of the burgeoning new millionaires who would demand a fundamental change of architectural style as a symbolic manifestation of their presence and ambitions. One critic noted, in 1872, that the general appearance of any given street was "somber, owing to the dark color of the [brown]stone. Nearly all the houses are built on the same design, which gives to it an air of sameness and tameness that is not pleasing. . . . The great defect of [Fifth] avenue is the poverty of resource in the designs of the buildings."[2] Mariana Griswold Van Rensselaer observed in 1886, "We once admired our brownstone very heartily . . . , but it is nevertheless one of the most unfortunate substances that ever went by the

honorable name of stone—cold and unattractive in color, and too poor in substance to receive carving well."[3] Franz Winkler, in an article of 1901, asked the question, "What can be drearier than a walk through any typical and unchanged brownstone district?" He then criticized "brownstone fronts that look primeval" and referred to the buildings generally as having "dingy, dull old fronts, which are quite innocent of art."[4]

Henry Adams, in his novel *Democracy* of 1908, went even further, seeing a correlation between the dullness of the brownstones and the people who erected them, for he has his heroine, Mrs. Lightfoot Lee, observe that New York Society was a "wilderness of men and women as monotonous as the brownstone houses they lived in," revealing the symbolic potential of architecture.[5] And Edith Wharton, in *The Age of Innocence*, has young Newland Archer speculate about the house his future father-in-law is about to present to him and his bride: "the house was built in a ghastly greenish-yellow stone that the younger architects were beginning to employ as a protest against the brownstone of which the uniform hue coated New York like a cold chocolate sauce."[6]

Griffith Thomas (1820–79), who came to New York from England in 1838 to join his father, Thomas Thomas, in the architectural firm of Thomas and Sons, made a specialty of erecting the sober dwellings the critics came to berate. But it was to him that Caroline Astor turned when she decided her clan needed a new architectural showplace that was indicative of their position in Society; her reasons for doing so require analysis.

By the mid-1850s Society had begun to desert Washington Square to move farther northward—although remaining faithful to Fifth Avenue—to the region around 33rd and 34th streets. In the early nineteenth century, Mary and John Murray had owned a farm which ran from what is now Madison Avenue to Lexington Avenue, between 34th and 38th streets, an area then on the outskirts of the city but already known as Murray Hill. An adjoining tract, reaching from Madison to Sixth Avenue, between 32nd and 36th streets, was the property of John Thompson, and in 1826 John Jacob Astor bought both properties, which, after Astor's death in 1848, were inherited by his sons, John Jacob II and William Backhouse Astor.

In 1856 Caroline Schermerhorn Astor, wife of William Backhouse Astor Jr., ambitious to become The Mrs. Astor, persuaded her husband to erect a mansion on the southwest corner of 34th and Fifth Avenue, a pioneering move that anchored a new region of Society's domiciles (figure 9). Shortly thereafter, in 1859, her brother-in-law, John Jacob Astor III, built a large house—sheathed in brownstone, of course—in the same block, on the northwest corner of 33rd and Fifth, and others of Society soon migrated to the area.

The house that Griffith Thomas erected for Caroline Astor was four bays wide, being, upon its completion, the finest "mansion" in New York. But it was still a brownstone in its architectural form, and in this, it looked backward rather than forward. Caroline—a member of one of the oldest of Knickerbocker families and now married to an Astor, assured of both wealth and social position—could have erected any type of dwelling she wished, but she made a

Figure 8. Row of brownstone facades, West 46th Street, New York City, ca. 1870. Andreas Ferninger, Photograph, Museum of the City of New York. In the brown decades of the middle of the nineteenth century, New York architecture had a unity and continuity that bordered on monotony, as seen in this row of brownstone houses that are typical of almost the entire grid of Manhattan's grand avenues and side streets. It is against this sameness that the rebellion arises in the form of French châteaux and Italian palazzos.

Figure 9. Griffith Thomas, Caroline (Mrs. William B.) Astor residence, 1856, southwest corner of Fifth Avenue and 34th Street, New York City, with the A. T. Stewart residence at right. Museum of the City of New York.

to a new element that had begun to encroach upon old Knickerbocker society, for by 1875 she was well aware of the existence of a separate chamber in the house of Caroline and August Belmont—a grand room that was designed expressly as the venue for galas, parties, cotillions, and fancy-dress balls. By 1875, the Belmonts had already been entertaining New York Society for nearly twenty years, and Caroline Belmont was the ruling *grande dame*; if Mrs. Astor were to succeed Mrs. Belmont as queen of New York's high society, a ballroom was imperative.

The Mansion Concept

The "mansion" concept itself is of interest here, for in reality Mrs. Astor's house was nothing more than a brownstone of the sort that lined the city's grid as far as the eye could see. Perhaps it was executed with more refinement and with more lavish interiors, but fundamentally it remained a brownstone. To Knickerbocker society the mansion concept was as foreign as it was pretentious. While it was permissible to make one's house a little larger than one's neighbors', one did not, through architecture, emphasize the gap between those of modest income and those blessed with greater fortune. But that separation, that ever-widening gulf, is exactly what the social lions and lionesses of the Gilded Age's new millionaire society were soon to insist upon: Their homes were to demonstrate the enormity of their wealth and to assert the difference between their social stratum and that of the upper-middle class and the antiquarian Knickerbocker relics. Architecture—in the form of the mansion—thus became a powerful symbol of a new layer of American society.

The history of the American mansion as a large and stylish residence filled with rare furnishings and great works of art is one of evolution rather than revolution, and it is somewhat surprising that it took as long as it did to catch on—but such was the strength of the entrenched architectural

conscious choice to remain with what was essentially the brownstone tradition, a tradition that in itself connoted the social order of Old New York.

So Caroline's house at 34th and Fifth was old-fashioned even before it was finished. It probably seemed so to Caroline herself, for by the mid-1870s, as she emerged as the "queen" around which New York Society organized itself, she realized the house lacked one component that had become indispensable to La Belle Époque: the ballroom. In 1875 she commissioned Griffith Thomas to add a large room to the existing house, a room that would serve a double purpose: as the space in which the annual Astor ball could be held and as the art gallery in which the Astor collection of nineteenth-century French academic narrative paintings could be displayed. Its size—a relatively modest thirty-five feet square—established the four-hundred-figure-limit that, according to Ward McAllister, defined New York Society. With the addition of that room Caroline made a concession

Figure 10. Detlef Lienau, Hart M. Shiff residence, ca. 1850, southwest corner of Fifth Avenue and 10th Street, New York City. Lienau Collection, Avery Architectural and Fine Arts Library, Columbia University.

traditions that it faced. Its story began in antebellum days, virtually stopped during the Civil War, then slowly changed in the years following the War. Even though many great fortunes had been made by the 1870s and there were many Americans who were wealthy enough to build enormous mansions, the concept was unfamiliar, and the first generation of millionaires took to mansion building with some reluctance. Herbert Croly, a contemporary social and architectural critic, observed this when he wrote, "Neither the first Vanderbilts, the first of the Goulds, the first of the Astors, or the first of the Rockefellers evinced any interest in domestic or any other kind of architecture." Croly then explained that "they were or are content with respectable, comfortable, and ugly houses, which might or might not be on Fifth Avenue."[7] During the era from about 1855 to 1880, the architectural—and social—question being pondered was, "What is the appropriate domestic backdrop for this new, fabulously wealthy level of Society?" The answer emerged only hesitatingly.

While American architecture, from the very beginning, had been derivative of one European style or another—Georgian, Adamesque, Greco-Roman, Gothic, Italianate, and Romanesque, to mention the more prominent—new models were now chosen, particularly those that carried aristocratic encodings—the Italian palazzo, the French Renaissance château or the Baroque and Rococo residences erected or occupied by Louis XIV, Louis XV, and Louis XVI, or the grand English townhouse or country house. Also influential was the nearly contemporary Second Empire Parisian hôtel de ville (i.e., townhouse mansion) with its omnipresent mansard-roofed exterior and luxuriously decorated interiors designed by architects who had been trained at (or strongly influenced by) the École des Beaux-Arts in Paris.

Detlef Lienau and the Hart Schiff House

Of the architects who studied at the École, Richard Morris Hunt was the first American and the best known. But he was not the first to bring the architectural style of the Second Empire to the United States. Detlef Lienau, who arrived in the United States in 1848, introduced the voguish new Parisian style of townhouse mansion in the early 1850s, several years before Hunt returned from France, in 1855.

German-born Lienau (1818–87) had studied architecture in Munich before going to Paris in 1842, where he was employed by Henri Labrouste during the years that architect was working on his famed Bibliothèque Sainte-Geneviève.[8] However, Labrouste's innovative technology made less impression on young Lienau than did contemporary Parisian urban domestic buildings and the École des Beaux-Arts concept of architectural design. These were among the baggage he brought with him when he fled the social upheaval of Europe in 1848 to settle in New York City. By 1850, he was a practicing architect in partnership with the young French émigré Léon Marcotte, who was then also an architect, and their first commission was for the Hart M. Schiff residence.[9]

Schiff was a French banker who had settled in New York. His house rose on the southwest corner of Fifth Avenue and 10th Street, a fashionable area in 1850, but was soon left behind as Society moved continually northward on the avenue (figure 10). Its design presented a fashionable new alternative to the omnipresent brownstone, for it introduced the mansard roof, with dormers, to the American cityscape. Moreover, it was the first to present the concept of the French townhouse as suitable for an urban setting in the United States.[10] Indeed, here was a Second Empire design executed in America two years before the political entity known as the Second Empire came into existence in France, in 1852.

Figure 11. Alfred R. Waud, *Mansard Roof—Fifth Avenue* (1877). Picture Collection, Branch Libraries, New York Public Library.

To many eyes the new design was shocking in its discontinuity with the architecture that surrounded it, and the Hart Shiff house was assailed by some as a disruptive intrusion amid the Greek Revival brownstones, which had become the signature architectural features of New York City. Nevertheless, the time for change had come.

The impact of the Second Empire style as set forth in the Shiff house was immediate, no doubt fostered by many New Yorkers being at that time especially receptive to almost anything French, from cuisine to parlor decorations. When Anthony Trollope visited the United States in 1861 he observed the infatuation with all things French: "In his tastes the American imitates the Frenchman. . . . I do not merely allude to actual household furniture—to chairs, tables, and detestable gilt clocks. The taste of America is becoming French in its conversation, French in its comforts and French in its discomforts, French in its eating, and French in its dress, French in its manners, and will become French in its art."[11]

Figure 12. Calvert Vaux, John A. C. Gray residence, 1856–57, Fifth Avenue between 10th and 11th streets, New York City. Morris Library, University of Delaware.

There was, of course, a specific reason to account for the French appearance of the Hart Shiff house, aside from the fact that the architect himself was fresh from his Parisian training. A critic writing in *Putnam's Magazine* observed that "this is the residence of a French gentleman; which may account for the owner's adoption of a style of building which would remind him of the courtly formality, and solid gentility of the olden time in his native country."[12] But whether praised or ridiculed, the mansion immediately became one of the attractions of the city, and it was recognized—in its size, stylishness, and feeling of grandeur—as exuding the very qualities associated with the mansion form, something the old brownstone had failed to achieve.

A Choice: New York Brownstone or Parisian Boulevard Architecture

On a plot just a short distance from the Shiff mansion, John A. C. Gray erected a Second Empire–style house, designed by Calvert Vaux, on the west side of Fifth Avenue between 10th and 11th streets (figure 12). Here, too, the feature that signaled its French origin was the mansard roof with dormers. The mansion dates from 1856–57, and, like the Shiff house, is indebted to Parisian urban or boulevard architecture. The Gray house, which is virtually contemporary with Caroline Schermerhorn Astor's new brownstone, also presented New Yorkers with an option to the brownstone insofar as the mansion concept was concerned. Indeed, several large houses erected in the city show the tug of war that was then being waged between the indigenous brownstone design and the Second Empire Parisian townhouse or hôtel de ville. The difference in the two styles is evident in an old photograph that shows the Astor brownstone juxtaposed to the A. T. Stewart mansion just beyond it, across 34th Street (figure 13).

Not all members of Knickerbocker society were hostile to the new gaiety that was being ushered in by the parvenus—the William Colford Schermerhorns, for example, who were among the bluest of New York's blue-blooded families.

Figure 13. Fifth Avenue looking southwest from 36th Street, ca. 1879. The A. T. Stewart residence (center) looks across 34th Street to the William B. (Caroline) Astor house, beyond which is the brownstone of Mrs. Astor's nephew (and rival) John Jacob Astor III and his wife. The Astors' houses are located on the site later occupied by the Empire State Building. The transformation from the ubiquitous brownstone to the French-inspired boulevard design is observed in a comparison of the Astors' houses with the Stewart mansion and its voguish new mansard roof.

William—who was descended from Jacob Schermerhorn, a Dutchman who had come to New Amsterdam in the 1630s—was a cousin of Caroline Schermerhorn Astor. A lawyer by profession, he was also an ardent public servant, clubman, and a man-about-town; later, he became a trustee of the Metropolitan Museum of Art, a warden at Grace Episcopal Church, and a trustee of Columbia University.[13] William's wife, formerly Miss Ann E. Cottenet, "was remarkable for beauty and grace, and for the elegance of her reunions."[14] May Van Rensselaer reminisced that "a forerunner of the epidemic of fancy balls that attacked fashionable New York . . . was the affair given by Mrs. Schermerhorn in her dwelling at Great Jones Street and Lafayette Place," and then added, "Society had become a contest among leaders of its organization to do the newest and most elaborate thing."[15]

George Templeton Strong's diary is laced with references to the Schermerhorns and to the gaieties and intrigues of a social order that was just beginning to be set by a parvenu element, as when Strong recorded on 13 April 1860,

> Walter Cutting called to inform me that I had been unanimously elected . . . [to] a committee of twenty, which is hereafter to take charge of polite society, regulate its interests, keep it pure, and decide who shall be admitted hereafter to "Bachelors' Balls" and other annual entertainments. . . . It is to pass on the social grade of everybody, by ballot—one blackball excluding. Outsiders have no voice and nothing to do but be thankful for the privilege of paying an initiation fee and annual subscription, if we concede them that privilege. . . . My colleagues are . . . Hamilton Fish, Anson Livingston, John Astor, William Schermerhorn, and others of the same sort.[16]

A month later Strong mentions going to Schermerhorn's house on Great Jones Street for "private theatricals, Sandeau's *Mlle. de la Seigliere*, translated by William Schermerhorn."[17] Many years later one of Strong's diary entries tells of going to the home of Edmund Schermerhorn, William's brother, one afternoon: ". . . very agreeable on the whole. Rubinstein's Trio, opus 53 is turgid, labored and obscure. The Chopin 'Polonaise' (piano and 'cello) is brilliant. Haydn's Quartette, op. 77, is full of sunshine and truth. To Philharmonic tonight . . . in our box were the imperial Mrs. Camilla Hoyt, William Schermerhorn, and others."[18]

Strong's diary reveals that the Schermerhorns were a part of the inner circle of Knickerbocker New York and that they enjoyed entertaining. But by the mid-1850s they realized that their old residence on Great Jones Street was inadequate and its location way downtown was inconvenient. Moreover, merely moving from one brownstone to another was not going to be satisfactory. At that point Detlef Lienau was called in.

In the spring of 1859 the William Colford Schermerhorns moved into their new house (figure 14). Lienau's design—of which, of course, his patrons approved—was again a rejection of the brownstone type and an essay in the new Parisian style. Its quoining at the corners was repeated at the central-axis bay; a large, arched opening at the front door welcomed guests graciously, and it had a mansard roof with dormers. Also, the amount of architectural decoration surpassed that normally associated with the New York brownstone, and that too came from Parisian, Beaux-Arts inspiration. The Schermerhorns clearly wanted a "modern" house that would serve as an appropriately impressive backdrop for their celebrated salons and soirees. The elaborateness of the facade suggested that within there dwelt a socially active couple who were determined to lead Society in its emergence from its doldrums.

Inside, the rooms were elegantly furnished and reflected the new pastimes of Society—there was an art gallery, for example, which contained several nude images, and a music room used for the Schermerhorns' renowned musicales. Mrs. Van Rensselaer made an interesting observation when she wrote, "This was one of the first houses in the city to be equipped by a professional decorator. All its furnishings were in the style of Louis XV."[19] That decorator was probably Léon Marcotte, Detlef Lienau's partner.

Mrs. Schermerhorn gave a grand ball in the winter of 1860–61. That, too, was a break with tradition, for when Henry Brevoort had given one fourteen years earlier, a scandal resulted from an elopement, and Society had thereafter dropped costume balls. But at the Schermerhorns' gala, all six hundred guests were instructed to come in the attire of the court of Louis XV, to blend with the hostess's decor. Even the servants were liveried in costumes and wigs a la Versailles, and the two-hour "German cotillion," made popular by the Empress Eugénie at the Tuileries in Paris, was introduced in America on that occasion.

But evolutions within Society sometimes presented perplexing problems. While for the ladies an excitement over the forthcoming Schermerhorn gala mounted with each passing hour spent at their couturiers, for the gentlemen a serious matter arose in the issue of facial hair. Throughout the ages the latter has often been a mark of masculinity and stylishness, and young and old, the men of 1860 took enormous pride in the sporting of mustaches, sideburns, and assorted beards. As if being asked to wear satin pantaloons

Figure 14. Detlef Lienau, William Schermerhorn residence, 1858–59, 51 West 23rd Street, New York City. Lienau Collection, Avery Architectural and Fine Arts Library, Columbia University. The Schermerhorns' old brownstone down at Lafayette Place had seemed "grim" once the new era of entertaining beset New York Society. The new house that Lienau designed for them, conversely, reflected the importance of entertaining in the home, for it had rooms that had been largely unknown in domestic architecture in America—a music room, for example, and an art gallery.

and silk stockings were not enough, it was soon pointed out to them that at the court of Versailles in the time of Louis XV, facial hair was forbidden! Mrs. Schermerhorn was unyielding when a delegation called upon her to accept muttonchops and the like as compatible with the elegant Louis Quinze attire—she insisted that all facial hair must go! A compromise was reached only after one of the gentlemen discovered that the musketeer guards at Versailles had been permitted mustaches and beards, and so a full battalion of mustachioed musketeers showed up for the great gala on 23rd Street. Furthermore, one should note, the emperor himself, Napoleon III, had made the neatly trimmed mustache and Van Dyck beard fashionable.

The Schermerhorns' ball was a great success and opened many eyes to the possibilities of new designs in architecture and interiors. It must be noted, however, that the Schermerhorns were unusual among the Knickerbockracy in their avant-garde attitudes, for most of their set were smugly comfortable to remain in their ancient and undistinguished brownstones.

The Advent of the Grand Gala

It was, in fact, unusual to host a grand ball in one's home in the 1850s and 1860s. Such things were usually held in a public place such as Delmonico's or the Academy of Music. The gala given on the occasion of the visit of the Prince of Wales, in October 1860, for example, took place at the Academy. Great indeed were the excitement and the anticipation of the royal visitation, sending New Yorkers into a flurry of activity at the dressmakers' shops, the booteries, the glovemakers, the lace and fabric boutiques and the perfumeries. In fact, the occasion was so special that for the first time two gowns appearing at an American ball had been obtained in Paris from the house of Charles Frederick Worth, who was just then becoming all the rage as the preeminent fashion designer for ladies. Those gowns, worn by Mrs. Abram Stevens Hewitt and Mrs. David Gardiner, survive and are preserved at the New-York Historical Society and the Museum of the City of New York, respectively.

As ballroom experiences were fairly new, a spate of manuals appeared that informed the gala-goers of proper conduct and acceptable attire.[20] Men were to wear a black suit and tie, white kid gloves, and black patent leather shoes. Women should take care not to overdress and should emphasize simplicity even if the raiment were luxurious and expensive, but they should also be cautious not to underdress, lest they expose more than they should. They too should wear white kid gloves (never silk ones, which were "cheap") and should carry a perfumed handkerchief. The latter was probably a good idea, as dances of that era were usually robust affairs—ranging in activity between waltzes, the mazurka, and the polka and lasting up to two hours, as in the case of the German cotillion.

Balls of the type held in honor of the Prince of Wales were so popular that they became a regular part of the social season. Accordingly, pressure mounted for holding such events in one's own home, where greater control of the invitation list could be maintained. Just as art galleries, billiard rooms, smoking rooms, and other new spaces began to force their presence into the floor plans of mansions, so too did the ballroom.

The John Taylor Johnston House

In New York City, once the homogeneity of the ubiquitous brownstone had been challenged in the 1850s, several possible new avenues of architectural design were tested. One means of breaking with the tradition was, quite simply, to cease using brownstone and use another type of stone, of another color. For centuries, marble has traditionally carried connotations of grandeur, refinement, costliness, and monumentality. And so began the displacement of the coarse, mauve stone of yesteryear with glistening white, smooth marble—from which temples and palaces of great ages past had been constructed.

In 1856, the same year that Caroline Astor moved into her large new brownstone, John Taylor Johnston erected his house at the corner of Fifth Avenue and 8th Street, just north of Washington Square (figure 15). Johnston's father had immigrated from Scotland in 1804; working in the countinghouse of James Lenox's father, he prospered and built a brownstone house on Washington Square. He sent his son, John Taylor, to college at New York University, also located on Washington Square, and then off to Yale to study law. But after returning to New York and being admitted to the bar, the younger Johnston became involved with railroads, eventually controlling the Central New Jersey line, of which, at the age of twenty-eight in 1848, he became president. When he acquired the Lehigh and Susquehanna shortly thereafter, he gained access to the anthracite coal fields of Pennsylvania, and his railroads made him wealthy.

When Johnston decided to build himself a house, he became the first in New York to turn to the use of marble instead of brownstone, sensing the disfavor of the latter and the iconographic symbolism attached to it. Marble had long been used for details in New York architecture, even in brownstones—for entrance steps and door framing, for example. Moreover, it had been used earlier as the facing for a number of commercial buildings; A. T. Stewart's grand department store—called the Marble Palace because its exterior was veneered in marble—was erected in 1846 at Broadway and Chambers Street. But before 1856, marble had seldom been used as a primary building material—for something more than decorative trim—for domestic architecture.

The house was three bays wide and four stories high, with a modest cornice and handsome but not elaborate window enframements. It was by no means a design that could be considered lavish or revolutionary. In size, design, and general concept the house was virtually identical to the other houses with which it shared the block. It was, in truth, merely another brownstone except its brick substructure was faced with marble.

Johnston's Collection and the Art Gallery

In the 1850s Johnston began collecting paintings, a hobby that eventually claimed nearly all available wall space within the house. The continual growth of the collection necessitated the addition of an art gallery, at the rear of the house; it was not, therefore, an integral part of the original house. The time would soon arrive, however, when an art gallery would become a part of the architectural design of a millionaire's mansion. Art galleries in private homes in New York go back to those in Luman Reed's house of about 1834 and in Samuel Ward's house in the mid-1840s, but the concept never caught on generally. That occurred in mansion design only after the Civil War, as in the A. T. Stewart house of 1864–69 (figure 37, p. 72). For John Taylor Johnston's house, the gallery was an appendage, added above the stables around 1860–65. Stewart undoubtedly knew of Johnston's new addition and decided he would have his gallery included as a part of the original design.

Johnston's collection, one of the foremost in the city, indeed, in the United States, was formed mainly in the 1850s, 1860s, and early '70s. Both large and varied, it contained a Corot landscape; a genre scene set in ancient Greece depicting a woman about to bathe a baby, by Charles Gleyre; a landscape by Jules Dupres; a cavalry charge by Horace Vernet; Léon Gérôme's *Death of Caesar* (figure 16); Gustave Brion's *Brittany Peasants at Prayer*; two paintings by Jean-Louis-Ernest Meissonier; a cattle piece by Constant Troyon; a Venetian scene by Felix Ziem; and many more by artists of the French and German academic schools of the mid-nineteenth century. The American school was represented by Thomas Cole's four-picture series *The Voyage of Life*, Frederic Church's *Niagara Falls* and *Twilight in the Wilderness*, Allston's *Sappho* and *Spalatro's Vision of the Bloody Hand*, as well as works by Eastman Johnson, Emanuel Leutze, John F. Kensett, Sanford R. Gifford, Daniel Huntington, and several others. The Johnston collection was of the new spirit in that a sizable portion of it was composed of tremendously popular European Salon pieces. But it was also traditional, by mid-nineteenth-century American collecting practices, in that it included many pictures by American artists. Later collections, at least those formed by members of the Gilded Age's millionaires' crowd, are virtually purged of American artists and instead concentrate almost totally on German and French academic Salon pictures. While money made in American industry and commerce might pay for the collections, taste shifted decidedly to Europe in matters of cultural preference.

Johnston opened his gallery to the public on a specified day of each week, declaring to his fellow collectors that art should not be hoarded for the exclusive enjoyment of the wealthy. In a democratic society, a *noblesse oblige* required that something as morally and socially uplifting as great art should be made available to the general public. This attitude eventually led to the founding of the Metropolitan Museum of Art only a few years later, in 1870, with John Taylor Johnston serving as its first president.

Figure 15. John Taylor Johnston residence, 1856, southwest corner of Fifth Avenue and 8th Street, New York City. Photograph, Bernice Abbott. Museum of the City of New York.

The Sale of the Johnston Collection

After the financial collapse of 1873, brought on by the failure of the banking house of Jay Cooke, a deep depression beset the American economy. John Taylor Johnston was one of its victims. To satisfy creditors, Johnston was forced to sell his collection in December 1876, and many observers took note of the fact, for the first time, that art can be an investment as well as a luxury, an investment that can be cashed in when funds are needed, sometimes even at a profit. This unquestionably scored points with bottom-line–oriented American businessmen who previously may have been reluctant to pay hard cash for something as frivolous as art.

The Johnston sale, conducted by Samuel P. Avery at Chickering Hall, was a landmark in the history of art dealings in the United States because of the items included and the prices they brought. Among the 200 oil paintings and 125 watercolors was J. M. W. Turner's *Slave Ship*, which Johnston had acquired four years earlier; it was sold to Alfred Pell of Boston for $10,000. Someone paid $9,700 for a landscape by Troyon while Meissonier's *Marshal Saxe and Troops* brought $8,000, and the same price was paid for Gérôme's *Death of*

Figure 16. Jean Léon Gérôme, *Death of Caesar*, 1867. Oil on canvas, 34 × 57 in. (0.855 × 1.455 m). The Walters Art Museum, Baltimore. Ex coll., Gérôme's *Death of Caesar* has an interesting provenance: After being shown at the great Exposition Universelle in Paris in 1867, the year it was painted, it was acquired by Jules Allard, the French decorator whose name appears frequently in connection with work he did for American architects such as Richard Morris Hunt (figure 192, p. 287) and Stanford White. The painting next passed into an American collection, that of John Taylor Johnston of New York, the first president of the newly founded Metropolitan Museum of Art. After a financial collapse that necessitated the sale of his collection, Johnston sold the *Death of Caesar* at a celebrated auction to John Jacob Astor III. After Paris Salon pictures such as this fell from aesthetic favor, it eventually appeared at the New York branch of the Parisian dealer Boussod, Valadon and Company, and was finally purchased, in 1937, by Henry Walters to add to the collection of the Walters Art Gallery in Baltimore.

Caesar. Avery himself bought William Bouguereau's *On the Way to the Bath* for $6,000; in fact, Avery—then the leading art dealer in New York City—was one of the biggest buyers, along with James Gordon Bennett, publisher of the *New York Herald*, William T. Walters of Baltimore, and W. W. Corcoran of Washington.

It was at that sale that Corcoran acquired Church's *Niagara Falls*, for $12,500, the highest price fetched at the sale. Other works by American painters did not do as well, however. For example, Thomas Cole's *Voyage of Life* commanded only $3,100 and Winslow Homer's *Prisoners from the Front* went for a mere $1,800. Altogether, the three-day sale brought in $327,792, a new record for an art auction in the United States. Many who had been hesitant to collect art were astounded at the figure, and when good times returned to the economy, the number of collectors in America increased greatly.

Eventually good times returned for John Taylor Johnston as well, and he began forming a second collection, more modest than the first, to be sure. In 1899, he retired from the presidency of the Met, leaving a well-established institution with a growing collection and a philosophy of providing great art for the enjoyment of the public. At the time, Johnston was in ill health, and he died four years later.

Caroline and August Belmont: A Gay New Element in Society

Similar to the John Taylor Johnston house, which did not signal any radical departure in architecture or its symbolism, the August Belmont house was transitional in that its exterior remained traditional. Its interiors, however, possessed a new spirit that represented a confluence of European flair, cosmopolitan tastes in furnishings, a joy in lavish entertainment facilities, and an unapologetic display of wealth.

August Belmont (1816–90) was born in a small town in the Rhineland, Germany, to a prosperous Jewish landowner, and so his youth was spent in moderate comfort and advantage (figure 17). At the age of fourteen he entered an apprenticeship with the house of Rothschild, by 1830 one of the foremost financial houses of the Continent. While serving in the Rothschild office in Naples, during negotiations with the Papal Court, he frequented the extraordinary collections there and began a lifelong passion to own art.

The Rothschilds next sent him to Havana, Cuba, but while he was there, the Panic of 1837 hit the United States. Sensing the opportunities that the financial collapse in America offered, he tendered his resignation to the Rothschilds and sailed for New York, where he opened his own banking firm, August Belmont and Company, on Wall Street. Recognizing his rare abilities, the house of Rothschild made Belmont its agent in the United States, which assured the success of his banking interests and gave him enormous financial clout. In the decades that followed, Belmont was often involved in arranging the financing of major enterprises as the Industrial Revolution arrived and virtually exploded in the United States. In the 1880s, for example, he served on the board of the Northern Pacific Railroad, a transcontinental line, the chairman of which was Henry Villard—of the Villard Houses on Madison Avenue.

One contemporary described him thusly: "August Belmont radiated power. . . . Living in a palace and maintaining almost royal state, he was vital, autocratic [and] . . . long of purse."[21] New York was powerless to resist Belmont's suave charm, cosmopolitan *savoir faire*, and astute command of business affairs. He further endeared himself by marrying, in 1849, into a distinguished American family when he took as his wife Caroline Slidell Perry, daughter of Commodore Matthew C. Perry—the man who would, in 1853–54, open Japan to trade with the Western world; Caroline's uncle, Oliver Hazard Perry, had been the hero of the Battle of Lake Erie in the War of 1812. Their wedding was held at the fashionable Episcopal Grace Church, where Isaac Brown was sexton.

Caroline responded appropriately to the cosmopolitan air that her husband exuded, and she was very beautiful (figure 18). As a young girl, one woman recalled, "I watched Mrs. Belmont at the opera, ermine and sables slipping from her shoulders, her slender throat wearing a string of pearls, the largest known in this Republic, and every opera-glass in the house turned upon her."[22] Another contemporary remembered Caroline as "a woman of charm and distinction, to whom fortune had allotted means and opportunity to take the lead in entertainments of the grandiose foreign order, in a great house, with an illuminated picture-gallery and everything on a corresponding scale."[23]

Caroline Perry Belmont was indeed queen of New York Society in the late 1850s and 1860s, and she established the pattern of lifestyle that would be followed by her successor, Mrs. William (Caroline Schermerhorn) Astor. She blossomed as a social hostess, and the Belmonts' dinner parties quickly became legendary, thanks in no small measure to the French chef August had imported. Ward McAllister once recalled that "Mr. Belmont . . . kept a chef at $60 or $70 a month, which was [then] thought exorbitant."[24]

Frederick Martin, of a later generation, recalled that in those early days the Belmonts were the most prominent leaders of Society, and "Mrs. Belmont's receptions were distinguished by the presence of every one who was really worth knowing. She surrounded herself with cultivated people, and the first thing that anybody of note took care of when they visited New York was to obtain letters of introduction to Mrs. Belmont. . . . [Her] entertainments were on a gorgeous scale."[25] But some in older New York Society did not agree with such assessments, as when Elizabeth Ellet took a snide shot at Caroline and others who were becoming infatuated with the new *joie de vivre*: "Mrs. August Belmont has obtained a celebrity for magnificent parties, attended by fashionables noted for gayety; and the same may be said of many ladies who have as yet no history."[26]

Nevertheless, Society was impressed by the Continental manner, the promise of exquisite cuisine and fine wines that awaited them at the Belmonts'. New Yorkers had not entertained extensively in their homes theretofore. Previously, if Knickerbocker hostesses wished to give a dinner for a few friends, they were apt to do so at a restaurant such as the one operated by Swiss-born Lorenzo Delmonico in New York. But the Belmonts were among the first to escalate the scale of such things. Whereas earlier generations of Knickerbockers might have entertained something like a dozen dinner guests, the Belmonts, once established in their new home, presided at a table that reportedly seated up to two hundred, each place setting laid with gold service, with guests attended by footmen wearing the colors of the Belmont livery, maroon and scarlet. The social change that was occurring in such activities began to dictate changes in architectural design and the scale of spaces as well, as the salon and dining room grew in size, and the ballroom became a new feature of any house that was to be considered a mansion.

Figure 17. August Belmont, ca. 1855. Daguerreotype. Library of Congress, Washington, D.C. Belmont is shown here about the time he was serving as American minister at The Hague. In addition to his being European by birth, his experience in the Netherlands and elsewhere on the Continent prepared Belmont and his young wife for entertaining on a scale unknown to New Yorkers previously—and that necessitated innovations in architecture and interior decoration.

Figure 18. George P. A. Healy, *Portrait of Caroline Perry Belmont*, ca. 1860. Oil on canvas, 65 × 52 in. (165.1 × 132.1 cm). Museum of the City of New York, gift of August Belmont IV, grandson of Mrs. Belmont (51.317). Caroline Slidell Perry came from a notable family that included men who had distinguished themselves as naval heroes. Her father was Commodore Matthew C. Perry and her uncle, Oliver Hazard Perry. In the middle decades of the nineteenth century Mrs. Belmont was the reigning queen of New York Society, giving way to Caroline Schermerhorn Astor—THE Mrs. Astor.

August Belmont's Jewishness waned with his increasing Americanization. When his back was turned, there were whispers about his origins, among some of his Episcopalian, Methodist, Presbyterian, and Catholic acquaintances, but he overcame all that and was thoroughly accepted by Society—a Society that could be anti-Semitic at times. Edith Wharton, for example, used August Belmont as the model for the character of Julius Beaufort in *The Age of Innocence*, in which Beaufort is portrayed unsympathetically as a man of murky reputation and of Jewish ancestry. One historian of the Jewish community in New York commented on Belmont's Jewishness: "Before his marriage, his contacts with the Jewish community had been few; now his fellow-Jews refused to consider him a Jew at all. On the other hand, members of society now courted Belmont. Philip Hone, who never invited a Jew to his home, invited Belmont to dinner in 1850 and, in turn, dined at Belmont's home."[27] For the most part, Belmont was as accepted at any gentleman's club as he was at the increasing number of dinner parties and balls, as he was at gatherings at horse shows and racetracks, where the charming *bon vivant* became especially popular.

One of Belmont's greatest interests, when he was away from Wall Street, was horses. He had world-class racing stables and one of the first and finest strings of polo ponies in America. In later years his son, August Jr., developed Belmont Park Race Track (opened 1905) and named it after his father. Even today, one of racedom's most coveted prizes is the Belmont Stakes trophy, also named after August Belmont.

The Belmonts in Europe

Belmont had been involved in politics virtually since the day he arrived in the United States, and for his good efforts on behalf of the Democratic Party, President Franklin Pierce appointed him chargé d'affaires to The Hague in 1853. For the next four years the Belmonts lived in the Netherlands. Their furniture was stored in New York City until a fire swept through the warehouse, destroying all of their belongings there. While this was at first considered a disaster, it offered an extraordinary opportunity, which they seized, to start from scratch in the furnishing of the new home they were planning, *in absentia*, in New York.

In the Netherlands and at other places across the Continent, August and Caroline began to acquire furnishings, the likes of which had rarely been seen in the United States. As early as 1855, nearly two years before he would return to America, Belmont began shipping the first of 250 crates of goods back home. A partial list of items reveals the splendor in which the Belmonts intended to live, once their house was remodeled and furnished:

> . . . an antique carved wooden mantelpiece, a "mother-of-pearl dish held by two gilt bears," . . . a bronze barometer, a carriage, . . . jardinieres and etageres, bureaus, armoires, dressing cases, . . . penholders, inkstands, lampstands, . . . candlesticks, candelabra, chandeliers, . . . snuffboxes, card boxes, music boxes, . . . sugar bowls, salt cellars, gravy boats, breadbaskets, fish dishes, toothpick stands, napkin rings, . . . teapots, coffeepots, milk pots, mustard pots, chocolate urns, . . . champagne coolers, . . . 18 tablecloths, 24 towels, 30 pillowcases, 60 sheets, 72 napkins, . . . 90 forks, 109 knives, 150 spoons, Florentine china, Dresden china, French china, Berlin china, 183 cups and as many saucers, breakfast plates, soup plates, salad plates, dinner plates . . . made of Majolica, silver, gold, and china (422 plates in all, and 79 dishes), claret glasses, champagne glasses, water glasses, Madeira glasses, liqueur glasses . . . (213 glasses in all), punch bowls, decanters, pitchers, . . . 110 paintings, 179 books, and dozens of carved figures and pieces of sculpture, glass falcons, Delft cows, . . . a bronze bird, a bronze bear, a bronze bull, a bronze Puss-in-Boots. . . .[28]

In the decades that followed, as importations of this magnitude became multiplied a thousand times or more among households of the Gilded set, as the rooms in American mansions became filled with new or ancient Continental furnishings, a shift in aesthetic taste took place: the American interior became Europeanized. Charles Tiffany's New York emporium profited greatly by the importation of *objets d'art* from around the world.

The Belmont Mansion

The Belmont house in New York City raises poignant social and architectural issues. In his early years in the United States, August Belmont had acquired a place on 14th Street, but this eventually proved to be not sufficiently grand for the lifestyle he pursued. His father-in-law, Commodore Perry, urged him to build near the proposed Central Park

(begun 1857, opened 1859), an area that was then, however, a repository for rubble and a squalid assortment of squatters' shacks. In one of his rare instances of a lack of vision, Belmont decided against that location and selected a safer spot in a well-established part of the city, buying a house that was already standing, at the corner of 18th Street and Fifth Avenue.

As remodeled, the house had double porches on the avenue and a bay window on 18th Street (figure 19). In elevation it was not unlike the ever-present row houses of the city, except larger, being five bays wide; but the exterior had a veneer of brownstone applied to its surfaces, thus associating it with traditional New York architecture of the middle decades. The choice of the 18th Street location and the brownstone veneer perhaps indicates the desire of an outsider—a European and a Jew—to associate himself with established local traditions.

The Belmont mansion was noted for several special features, one of which was its beautiful and spacious ballroom, one of the first in New York to be built into a house when it was remodeled (as opposed to being added onto a house). In many of the homes erected by the wealthy of the Gilded Age, the art gallery or large drawing room doubled as a ballroom, for a ballroom would probably be used as such only one or two nights out of the entire year. At Mrs. Astor's house at 34th and Fifth, for example, her art gallery became her ballroom on occasion.

But for those who wanted to flaunt their wealth, a separate room was wrought into the design of the house, and according to Edith Wharton and Ogden Codman, writing much later, it was a mistake to try to make one room serve two purposes—as a salon in which the family gathered each evening and a ballroom that was used as such infrequently. They ridiculed rich Americans who failed to recognize the separateness of the two spaces, saying that "living and gala rooms have been confounded in an agglomeration of apartments, where the family, for lack of a smaller suite, sit under gilded ceilings and cut-glass chandeliers, in about as much comfort and privacy as are afforded by the public 'parlors' of one of our new twenty-story hotels." The authors further noted,

> Gala rooms are meant for general entertainments, never for any assemblage small or informal enough to be conveniently accommodated in the ordinary living-rooms of the house; therefore to fulfil their purpose they must be large, very high-studded, and not overcrowded with furniture, while the walls and ceiling—the only parts of a crowded room that can be seen—must be decorated with greater elaboration than would be pleasing or appropriate in other rooms. . . . Nothing can be more cheerless than the state of a handful of people sitting after dinner in an immense ball-room with gilded ceiling, bare floors, and a few pieces of monumental furniture ranged round the walls. . . . A gala room is never meant to be seen except when crowded; the crowd takes the place of furniture.[29]

If Society were now to engage in elaborate entertainments to amuse itself, certain architectural requirements must be respected, a fact recognized by Caroline and August Belmont. Moreover, even as early as the mid-1850s, it was understood that, as the purpose of the ballroom was to serve for festive occasions, its decoration was to be lavish, even extravagant.

Figure 19. Caroline and August Belmont residence, as remodeled ca. 1857, Fifth Avenue and 18th Street, New York City. Museum of the City of New York.

The Belmont Art Gallery
At the rear of the house, Belmont erected a spacious addition that served as an art gallery. The latter was required for the 110 paintings and several sculptures he had shipped back from Europe. Here was yet another instance of a new type of room being added to the mansion plan, at about the same time that Caroline Astor was doing so in her new mansion and that John Taylor Johnston was building his art gallery at the back of his house, above his stables.

Belmont's gallery signaled the new direction that collecting was to take in the Gilded Age, for it consisted almost totally of works by European painters—another instance of the Europeanization of taste, aesthetics, and furnishings. It made a statement that American art was provincial and somehow inferior, suitable only for middle-class tastes. To Belmont, an art collection was in itself symbolic of a high level of civilization and culture; he had seen English country houses, French châteaux, and Italian palazzos—the homes of the European aristocracy and even of nouveaux riches such as the Rothschilds—with their grand collections of paintings.

This new room in the American mansion presented design problems, such as proper lighting, for which large skylights became a popular solution. Another was to maximize wall surfaces on which to display the paintings; windows reduced that space, were a distraction from the pictures, and by night were useless for lighting anyway.

While views of Belmont's own gallery are not available, it was probably similar to William Aspinwall's gallery, which contained approximately the same number of paintings, most of which were by or attributed to European artists. An illustration from *Harper's Weekly* depicts one of Aspinwall's two galleries (figure 20). An accompanying notice reported that his galleries too were added onto his house, and that the architect was James Renwick, who at that very time was at work on Saint Patrick's Cathedral on Fifth Avenue. The same account observed that the collection was well lit by skylights. In the custom of that day, the walls were virtually covered, from floor to ceiling or from cabinet tops to ceiling, with paintings that nearly abutted one another.

Guests were awed by the size of Belmont's gallery and its airiness and light. Descriptions tell us that its ceiling was a huge rectangular glass dome that was supported, visually, by four sets of allegorical figures, one pair representing painting, a second music, another sculpture, and the fourth architecture. Belmont's was the first domestic art gallery in New York to be lit by a skylight, and by night the collection was illuminated by gaslight, as was William Aspinwall's gallery.

The Belmont collection existed as an entity from the moment in 1857 when, soon after August and Caroline returned from The Hague, the paintings were uncrated. All of New York soon knew of it. Nearly every major artist of the academic schools of the Continent was represented—Vibert, Meissonier, Munkácsy, Madrazo, Bouguereau, to name but a few. The pictures were mainly of genre scenes, domestic animals in farmyards, military events, and an occasional exotic subject set in Morocco or Istanbul. The collection set the pattern for others who were soon to follow Belmont's lead—A. T. Stewart and William Henry Vanderbilt, for example, or Caroline Astor, John Taylor Johnston, and William Aspinwall.[30]

Like many collectors Belmont had the urge to share his treasures with others. Not long after his return from The Hague he agreed to loan his paintings to the National Academy of Design for an exhibition to benefit several charities in New York. A reporter reviewing the show called it a "superb collection," and further noted, "Mr. Belmont has displayed rare taste in their selection and has very wisely preferred the finest works of modern artists to the mediocre productions of the old masters."[31] The writer then praised the "exquisite finish" of the small-sized French and Belgian pictures that had seldom been seen in New York prior to that time. He also identified a number of the artists and paintings in the collection, including Rosa Bonheur's *Gathering for the Hunt*, which he claimed to be the equal of her celebrated *Horse Fair*; four landscapes by Andreas Achenbach; and Paul Delaroche, Horace Vernet, and Gabriel Alexandre Decamps.[32] The reviewer then concluded with the observation that

> there has never been exhibited here a collection of pictures which contained so large a number of works of unquestionable excellence. . . . It is to be hoped that the liberality of Mr. Belmont, in affording the public an opportunity to examine his collection, may

Figure 20. Art gallery, William Aspinwall residence. From "Mr. Aspinwall's Gallery," *Harper's Weekly* (26 February 1859), p. 133.

induce the owners of other fine collections to follow his example. It is a positive injury to art to take its finest works and shut them up in the rooms of a private house, where they can be seen only by a limited number of its inmates.[33]

The last comment poses an interesting issue: the democratization of art collections by making them available to the masses. Several collectors of the Gilded Age tried to solve this problem by opening their galleries to the public one day a week, but this was only a stopgap solution. In the end, the matter led to the founding of the Metropolitan Museum of Art (1870), the Museum of Fine Arts (1870) in Boston, the Art Institute of Chicago (1879), the Cincinnati Art Museum (1881), the Saint Louis Art Museum (1879), and many more across the country—institutions that were born during the Gilded Age with the ideas, energies, wealth, and collections of its millionaire society.

The New York Times for 8 February 1858 observed that the Belmont benefit exhibition raised $2,800 for several local charities, among them the Association for Improving the Condition of the Poor, the New York School of Design for Women, the "Colored Home," and the Home for Penitent Magdalenes, which was under the care of the Nuns of the Good Shepherd.[34]

The Celebrated Belmont Wine Cellar

Nothing suggests the swing toward an upscale mode of life more than the wine cellar that August Belmont kept. He brought back from his European travels 48 bottles of champagne, 81 bottles of sherry, 139 bottles of French wine, and 169 bottles of German wine, and he regularly imported more by the case. The story, undoubtedly apocryphal, is told that Belmont's neighbor, the somewhat parsimonious James Lenox, died of a heart attack when he heard that August's wine bill for one month was $20,000.

The extensive and expensive wine cellar was but a manifestation of a new glorification of the good life in which Belmont and his friends reveled. Belmont deserves much credit for introducing a *bon vivant* way of life to New Yorkers, who had theretofore, by comparison, been a rather stodgy group. The good life that August and Caroline Belmont enjoyed was indicated in a statement made by one of August's closest friends (and a rival in horsemanship), Leonard Jerome, who announced that he was about to challenge the Belmont stud line: "After all, I'm fond of the fellow," Jerome declared, "but one can't let him have the pick of everything—he's got the best pictures, the best porcelain, and the best chef in New York as it is."[35] And, Jerome might have added, the finest wine cellar too.

In the joyous lifestyle proffered by August and Caroline Belmont and in their employment of architecture, decorative arts, and fine arts to create the proper backdrop of that lifestyle, a new mode of living emerged that provided wealthy New Yorkers with a model that they took to at once. In its lavishness it challenged the staid old ways of the Knickerbocker crowd, and it pointed the way for others to follow as the Gilded Age gained a full head of steam. All of this was established in the years immediately before the outbreak of the Civil War. The latter, of course, caused a cessation of the impellent march toward bigger and more sumptuously furnished architecture, but with the Belmonts' exquisite house, the die was cast. A gay new way of life would place new requirements on American architects, and a new kind of architecture would eventually be born in the creations of Richard Morris Hunt, Stanford White, George B. Post, Horace Trumbauer, and a host of others.

To secure wealth is an honorable ambition, and is one great test of a person's usefulness to others. Money is power. Every good man and woman ought to strive for power, to do good with it when obtained. Tens of thousands of men and women get rich honestly. But they are often accused by an envious, lazy crowd of unsuccessful persons of being dishonest and oppressive. I say, Get rich, get rich! But get money honestly, or it will be a withering curse.

Russell Conwell, *Acres of Diamonds . . . the Safe and Sure Way to Amass a Fortune, Be a Benefactor, and Achieve Greatness* (1890)

Chapter Three

The Early Mansions

Part Two

THE YEARS 1859 AND 1860 saw only a few important mansions rise, giving a faint indication of what loomed on the social and architectural horizons in New York. Then came the Civil War (1861–65), which completely distracted the nation and temporarily halted most domestic construction. The war had barely ended, however, when a boom in building began, and it continued until the financial panic of 1873, which ushered in a severe depression that gripped the nation for half a decade. As the economic situation began to improve in the late 1870s, the great era of mansion building resumed. One by one, the residences of the wealthy arose, more grand and sumptuous than ever, breaking totally with the old brownstone tradition and becoming increasingly French in inspiration.

THE LEONARD JEROMES

One of the few important mansions built in 1859–60 was the "palace" Leonard Jerome gave to his wife. Leonard Jerome was a Wall Street financier who not only made enormous sums of money but also lost a couple of fortunes. He was occasionally a partner in railroad affairs with Cornelius Vanderbilt. In the spring of 1864, Vanderbilt's rival Daniel Drew, by bribing state legislators, thwarted the Commodore's plans for extending his Harlem Railroad line down into the center of New York City; Drew convinced the assemblymen that the price of the Harlem would plunge if they passed a bill denying such access, and the greedy politicians went for it, some of them even mortgaging their homes in order to sell Harlem short. Passing the bill, they watched as the price began to dive from about $140 to $110. They were sure it would sink to $50 and they would all become rich. But then Vanderbilt stepped in, joined by Leonard Jerome, and began buying. Up and up went the price, until it soared past $200 a share, and all who had sold it short were facing ruin. Knowing he had his enemies where it hurt the most, the Commodore roared, "Send it to a thousand! Send it to a thousand!" But Jerome cautioned the railroad magnate that if he pursued that course he would ruin half the brokerage houses in Wall Street and throw the entire country into a panic and depression. So on Jerome's sage advice the Commodore backed off, and Leonard made a fortune in the process.

On another occasion, later in 1864, Jerome and John Tobin—Cornelius Vanderbilt's longtime friend and sometime business partner—decided to purchase controlling stock interest in the Erie Railroad, and to do so foolishly borrowed money from Daniel Drew. Part of the arrangement was that Drew would not sell shares he owned. Jerome and Tobin had hardly acquired a sizable block when Drew began dumping his holdings on the market. When the price of Erie collapsed, falling well below what Jerome and Tobin had paid for it, Drew called in his loan, and this time Jerome the speculator was wiped out, totally ruined financially. Such was the way business was done—by some, at least. But Jerome was irrepressible and was soon to rise again.

Julius Henri Browne knew Jerome more by reputation than personal acquaintance, and his description of the man seems to be more a censorial caricature than an objective portrait, but there was probably some truth to it nevertheless:

> He belongs to the present-day school of bold, often reckless operators; represents the fast financiers of the street. [He] has for years been a prominent operator in stocks. He is shrewd, resolute, full of expedients and resources; makes and loses fortunes every twelve months, but manages to float conspicuous on the financial tide. He is . . . a man of the world and fond of pleasure; dresses showily; drives fast horses; has fast friends; enjoys display; gives expensive entertainments; is extravagant and careless; is called good-looking; lives with a free hand and a liberal heart in the sunshine of the passing hour.[1]

Earlier, when Leonard Jerome was a practicing lawyer in Rochester, New York, he supported Millard Fillmore's 1849 presidential campaign and was rewarded by being appointed American consul in Trieste, Italy. He, his wife, Clarissa, and their daughters lived there in the early 1850s and became familiar with the European cosmopolitan lifestyle. After returning to New York briefly, the Jeromes again traveled to Europe, in 1858 and 1860, this time living in Paris mainly, when the Second Empire was at its most dazzling heights. Daughter Jennie recalled the scenes of splendor and the degree to which some Americans were involved in the social events of the day:

> Although I was not old enough to go into society . . . the echoes of the Tuileries fetes and of the gay social life of Paris were heard in our house. . . . The Emperor Napoleon III was credited with a great liking for Americans, and he certainly showed his partiality by having many invited to the official festivities. Among them was my eldest sister, who made her debut at one of the Tuileries balls. . . . When the

company was assembled, the doors were flung open, and "*Sa Majeste l'Empereur*" was announced. Then after a pause, "*Sa Majeste l'Imperatrice!*" who that evening appeared a resplendent figure in green velvet, with a crown of emeralds and diamonds, spiked with pearls. . . . The Emperor and Empress walked round the circle of curtsying and bowing guests, addressing a few words here and there, and then proceeded to the ball room.[2]

In 1859 Leonard and Clarissa Jerome were, in fact, among the Americans who were presented to the Emperor and Empress.[3] Clarissa reveled in the gay social swirl in the Paris of Napoleon III and the beautiful Empress Eugénie, of the Prince Imperial and of Princess Mathilde, of ambassadors and ministers at court, of fancy-dress balls and dinner parties held at splendid palaces, grand Parisian mansions, or noble châteaux in the French countryside (figure 21). It was all so different from the more sedate entertaining she had known back in New York. Indeed, the lifestyle the Jeromes came to know in Paris was bound to affect their way of life once they returned to the United States—and, consequently, the architecture and the interiors with which they surrounded themselves.

The Jerome Mansion

Leonard Jerome promised his wife, "I'll build you a palace yet!" Soon after he and Clarissa returned to the United States he purchased the large corner lot at Madison Avenue and 26th Street, overlooking Madison Square which, in 1859, was a fashionable area. A brownstone stood on the adjoining lot, the house of a Mrs. Schermerhorn, who had earlier snubbed the Jeromes as parvenus. Clarissa, determined that her new house should be a mansion that would outshine Mrs. Schermerhorn's, insisted that it be wrought in the spectacular new French style of the Second Empire. Leonard too had his reasons for wanting an elegant mansion, for he was already engaged in a friendly competition with August Belmont over who should be New York's dandiest *bon vivant*; as noted earlier, Leonard and August competed in numerous areas, including over fine wines, the best French chefs, the attention of young ladies, and, especially, horses, the latter being an interest the two men shared with their friend Cornelius Vanderbilt.

Thomas R. Jackson was retained as architect, with instructions to make the house grand and to make it very French. The result was the most lavish statement of the Parisian Second Empire style as applied to domestic architecture in New York before the Civil War. Its design broke with the uniformity of the Knickerbocker brownstones, for the Jerome mansion possessed the signature mansard roof with dormers and a richness of decorated architectural surfaces, especially around doors, windows, and dormers (figure 22). For example, the central window of the mansard roof area was a joyous celebration of architectural and sculptural ornamentation. Moreover, the house was constructed of red brick with a profusion of white marble trim, its colorful surfaces further differentiating it from the monotone of the brownstones.

Horses, Music, and Architecture

Leonard Jerome drove as fine a set of four-in-hand as anyone in America, and he was the founder of the Jockey Club at Coney Island. At his private racetrack—Jerome Park, up in the Bronx—he erected bleachers that could accommodate eight thousand spectators. It was there that the Belmont Stakes was first run, before being transferred to the later Belmont Park; August Belmont had helped Leonard finance the building of Jerome Park. There, New Yorkers, in their insatiable quest for amusement and thrills, could cheer on the flying colors of their own stables or those of friends. In fact, Leonard's love of horseflesh had architectural ramifications.

The mansion at Madison Square was built in a somewhat curious sequence. Before he had the house itself built, Leonard first had the stables erected at the back of the lot, but in a manner almost as fine as any Parisian palace; costing nearly $80,000, the structure was three stories high with the stables occupying the lower floor. The interiors were paneled with black walnut while the floors were covered with crimson carpeting. The stables became the talk of the town, as were the exquisite thoroughbreds they housed.

Leonard Jerome had a fondness, too, for music and for young ladies with beautiful voices, and so on the floor above the stables he had a ballroom built. This may also have been in competition with August and Caroline Belmont, for the balls given at the Belmonts' mansion were, by 1859, already acknowledged to be the highest achievement of New York's social world. There, in the Jeromes' chamber, which was

Figure 21 (overleaf). Henri Baron, *Dinner at the Tuileries*, 1867. Watercolor on paper. Château de Compiegne, Oise, France. The Bridgeman Art Library. Emperor Napoleon III sought to restore to France the grandeur of the great Bourbon monarchs of the eighteenth century and to assist in establishing the legitimacy of his own reign, so he instituted a Rococo revival, especially noticeable in architectural interiors and the decorative arts. He seems to have particularly enjoyed the company of wealthy Americans who were visiting France, as they were regularly invited to the posh dinners and entertainments held at the Tuileries—and of course, they carried home visions such as one finds in Baron's watercolor.

H. BARON

> Furniture arrived in crates from the leading cabinetmakers of New York. Pieces of walnut, ebony, tulip wood, and rosewood ornately carved or inlaid with pearl crowded the large darkened rooms. Chandeliers threw rainbows of crystal from the center of her ceilings; glass decanters and goblets were bought from the new Brooklyn industries. . . . Bronze statues supported gas jets, while cast-iron mirrors, fountains, and balconies were inserted into unused corners. . . . Sevres, Dresden, and Worcester porcelain stood in niches.[4]

probably larger than any room in any house in America, theatricals were presented for friends, and private concerts were performed by attractive young female protégées. The auditorium was fully equipped with a stage and proscenium curtains, and it could comfortably seat about six hundred guests. The first to perform there was Mrs. Pierre Lorillard Rolands, the belle of the season, who gave a delightful concert before an assemblage of New York's choicest society.

Clarissa saw to it that the new house was lavishly furnished, as recorded by Leonard's biographer:

The Opening Ball

The house was officially opened with a spectacular ball to which members of New York's highest society were invited. The centerpieces of the ballroom were two fountains, one spouting eau de cologne, the other bubbling with champagne. It was evident that the Jeromes had joined with the Belmonts to make New York a city of gaiety and high fashion, and the design and furnishings of their house were devoted to that purpose. The strong French connection was maintained in the years that followed the Civil War, when the Jeromes again took up residence in Paris, in 1868, until the Second Empire was overthrown, in 1870, during the Franco-Prussian War.

Haute couture gowns worn by the women attending the grand balls at the Jerome mansion came increasingly from France, too; an example of the period 1867–70 survives, a creation by Worth and Bobergh of Paris (figure 23). The vision of a hundred or more such gowns swirling about the ballroom floor conjures a delightful and colorful visage of the early years of the Gilded Age.

Epilogue for the Jerome Mansion

Clarissa and her daughters remained in Paris, even when Leonard's business affairs required that he return hurriedly to the United States. Disaster struck again, in 1869, at the Jerome financial empire, and Leonard lost yet another fortune in the stock market. But he said nothing of this most recent calamity

Figure 22. Thomas R. Jackson, Clarissa and Leonard Jerome residence, 1859, northeast corner of Madison Avenue and 26th Street, New York City. Brown Brothers..

Figure 23 (opposite). Ball gown by Worth and Bobergh of Paris, 1867–70. Silk satin, lace, and tulle. Philadelphia Museum of Art, gift of Charlotte Hope Binney Tyler Montgomery, 1966 (1996-19-5).

to his wife, who was more content in Paris and then in London than she was in New York. He quietly closed the grand mansion he had built, and then leased it to the Union League Club before leaving to rejoin his family in Europe. In 1873 he packed his art collection and a few other belongings and shipped them off to France, where Clarissa had taken up permanent residence; unfortunately, the ship by which they were being transported, the *Ville de Harve*, went down at sea, taking with it many lives, as well as all the Jerome consignments.

The Jerome mansion-cum-Union League Club was, for many years, continually seen by, and served as a model for, the richest men of New York, even as they contemplated building their own mansions, which they would do when better economic times returned. The Jerome family never again lived in the house overlooking Madison Square, although the irrepressible Leonard did regain still another fortune on Wall Street. In time, their mansion became the University Club and then the Manhattan Club, but it was demolished in 1966.

LeGrand Lockwood and Elm Park

Detlef Lienau reappears in the story of mansion design in America with the house he created for LeGrand Lockwood and his wife, Ann Louisa, in Norwalk, Connecticut, in 1864–68. Lockwood (1820–72), a native of Norwalk, had made his fortune in New York City as a shrewd but honest financier in Wall Street, and he served for a time as treasurer of the New York Stock Exchange. His firm, Lockwood and Company, was one of the largest of the great brokerage houses. He was, for example, Jay Gould's broker, and he frequently assisted Cornelius Vanderbilt in the financing of railroad acquisitions. Indeed, Lockwood sat on the boards of several of the emerging railroad systems; by the mid-1860s he was in virtual control of the Lake Shore line, which skirted the southern edge of Lake Erie and—like the much fought-over Erie system—was a vital connector between the Michigan Southern and Indiana Northern railroad in the West and Vanderbilt's New York Central in the East, the link that allowed through passage and freight between Chicago and New York.

Elm Park, as the Norwalk estate was called, was the Lockwoods' country house (figure 24). It was not an urban mansion, for it was located on a plot of thirty acres rather than abutted to other houses in a row along a city street, and therefore more a villa or château. Among its sixty-two rooms were some of the new types that were just beginning to appear in the designs of houses—a music room, for instance, and two billiard rooms, as well as a smoking room, a bowling alley in the basement, an art gallery, large salons for entertaining, a private theater, and thirteen bathrooms.

In the mid-1860s there was no single established style for mansion architecture, although some French mode, in one form or another, was favored. Lockwood and his wife had been to Europe in the 1850s and early 1860s and were

Figure 24. Detlef Lienau, Elm Park, the LeGrand Lockwood residence, Norwalk, Conn., ca. 1868. The Lockwood-Mathews Mansion Museum.

therefore familiar with the historic and modern styles of Paris and the French countryside before they began Elm Park. Furthermore, their selection of Detlef Lienau assured a house in the French manner, and the result was a rambling château of the type found in the rural areas of France.

French Renaissance became one of the favored styles of America's new High Society. That is, while the influence remained French, its design was not based on Second Empire "moderne," but rather on châteaux of the sort the Lockwoods had seen in the Loire Valley. Thus, two French prototypes became available to American millionaires: the one urban and Second Empire in style—that is, Parisian boulevard architecture—and the other a French rural château type.

In plan Elm Park was organized asymmetrically around an octagonal court, which rose more than three stories to a dome than flooded the central core of the mansion with light. It was constructed of granite and marble. Stonemasons and woodcarvers were brought over from Italy and lived in tents on the site while construction progressed; they earned one dollar and fifty cents a day, respectively, and most of them returned to their homeland when the project was completed.

The New York Times for 5 August 1867 announced that the mansion cost $2 million, a new benchmark for the lavish spending of newly made fortunes on great houses in America. The *Times* article declared that when finished, the house "will stand with scarcely a rival in the United States," for here, the reporter opined, was an estate that would challenge the great châteaux and country houses of the European aristocracy.

The Interiors

For the fabulously wealthy American nouveaux riches there now arose a marked increase in the lavishness of domestic interiors and their furnishings. To that purpose LeGrand called in the firm of Herter Brothers as well as Lienau's former partner, Léon Marcotte, and George Platt, one of America's earliest professional interior decorators; Platt was probably known to LeGrand earlier as the designer of "palace cars" for the financier's Norwalk-Danbury Railroad. One of the leading decorative painters of the day, Pierre-Victor Galland of Paris, was commissioned to do ceiling and wall-panel paintings, which Herter Brothers installed (figure 25). Prior to the commission for Elm Park, Galland had become famous for his decorative work in the imperial palaces of the Tuileries and Saint-Cloud, and his talent was in demand in royal and aristocratic residences throughout Europe.

Marcotte and the Herter Brothers at Elm Park

Marcotte knew Detlef Lienau and Pierre-Victor Galland in Paris when all three worked in the atelier of Henri Labrouste in the 1840s. He maintained close ties with Paris even after he settled in New York, for he not only imported Parisian-made furniture but also traveled frequently to the French capital. Ann Lockwood once wrote to her daughter-in-law from Paris—in 1869, just when the interiors at Elm Park were being executed—that "yesterday morning Mr. Marcotte called,

Figure 25. Pierre-Victor Galland, painted wall panel in card room, Lockwood-Mathews Mansion Museum, Norwalk, Conn., ca. 1896. Galland had a very distinguished career as a decorative painter. As a youth he had attended the École des Beaux-Arts in Paris, where he later became professor of decorative painting. He also served as director of Art Works at Gobelins Manufactory, there creating designs for a series of tapestries for the Palais de l'Élysée. Examples of his ornamental painting are found in some of the most important Parisian buildings of La Belle Époque, including the Pantheon and the Hôtel de Ville.

having just arrived from America bringing with him a plan of our library [and] saying that he had received instructions to go on with the furnishings of that room. . . . I am going with [him] to select some bronzes."[5] Marcotte maintained a branch of his decorating company in Paris, thereby assuring easy access to the latest fashions in Second Empire furnishings.

The Herter brothers came from Stuttgart, Gustave arriving first, in 1848, and Christian immigrating in 1860 after studying at the École des Beaux-Arts in Paris. Gustave earned a reputation as a designer and maker of exquisite furniture in New York, and when Christian joined him, they established the firm of Herter Brothers. It too maintained close ties with Paris as the fountainhead of the latest in interior decorations, and in fact from 1867 to 1869, or just as the Elm Park interiors were being completed, Christian lived in Paris as head of the firm's branch there while Gustave ran the operations in New York.

Herter Brothers decorated several of the rooms at Elm Park, including the enormous drawing room, music room,

Figure 26. Herter Brothers, center table, ca. 1870. Rosewood, tulipwood, sycamore, black walnut, white oak, and gilding. Toledo Museum of Art, gift of Dr. and Mrs. Edward A. Kern (1986.65). This table is similar to one that Herter Brothers made for the drawing room of Elm Park, Norwalk, Conn. The veneer top of the table is an example of the floral and foliate designs wrought in marquetry, which is the art of creating decorative images in a manner similar to that of mosaic, using intricately cut-out pieces of different-colored woods that are fitted together as in a jigsaw puzzle; other materials, such as mother-of-pearl, bone, and brass, are sometimes used. The technique flourished in Holland in the early-seventeenth century and from there spread to other European centers of furniture making, especially to France in the era of Louis XIV; the great master of that period was André-Charles Boulle and marquetry is sometimes referred to by his name. In 1743 Louis XV established the Marqueters Guild to ensure the finest craftsmanship in the elegant furniture being produced for the royal palaces of Versailles and elsewhere. With the Rococo revival during the reign of Napoleon III (1853–70) marquetry once more flourished. In the United States, the workshops of decorators such as Herter Brothers employed numerous craftsmen from Germany and France who specialized in it. For the related work of intarsia, see figures 189 and 190 on pp. 284–85.

rotunda, card room, and staircase. Walls were paneled with rich and exotic woods—walnut, rosewood, or satinwood, for example, splendidly inlaid with ebony, boxwood, or cedar. Some of the furniture for the rooms was done in the Eastlake-inspired Renaissance Revival style that was then favored. For example, the Lockwoods owned an ornate center table made by Herter Brothers that was similar to one now in the collection of the Toledo Museum of Art (figure 26). In addition to the richly carved ornamentations, the table was enhanced by an elaborate marquetry floral design on its top surface. Fine craftsmanship such as this was typical of Herter pieces and suggests a collaborative effort involving several different artisans. Similar carving is seen in the elaborate newel post of the staircase, which was also the work of Herter Brothers (figure 27). But the Herters and their employees were more than craftsmen, for in the firm's work for Elm Park a transition was occurring, from furniture maker/artisans to interior decorators, as the profession of the latter was then developing.

The drawing room was large, measuring thirty by thirty-two feet with fifteen-foot-high ceilings; it was made to appear even larger by extensive use of huge mirrors, the frames of which resembled those surrounding the windows, doors, and niches (figure 28). The white marble fireplace was ornately carved, and several pieces of marble sculpture adorned the room.

Many of the furnishings at Elm Park were influenced, in their design, by objects displayed at the great Exposition Universelle held in Paris in 1867, or just prior to work at Elm Park; Christian Herter, then residing in Paris, attended the famous industrial and commercial fair, and Ann Lockwood indicated, in a letter home, that she went several times too.

Almost all were made or purchased in France or were created in New York by craftsmen trained in Europe or working from French designs. The long-standing tradition of American decorative arts being made by American craftsmen in their little shops in New York, Boston, or wherever was replaced, at least for the mansions of the new millionaire society, by the international trade in high-style goods, usually a Second Empire version of the French Renaissance or Rococo mode.

Among the few truly American objects in the mansion was Albert Bierstadt's enormous painting *Domes of the Yosemite*, which was displayed in the central court (figure 29). His western landscapes, painted from his on-site sketches after he returned to his studio overlooking the Hudson River, were enormously popular in the 1860s. In 1867, Lockwood paid the artist the then enormous price of $25,000 to paint a picture of The Domes for him. Installed at Elm Park in 1868, the *Domes* worked well with the other paintings in the collection at Elm Park which was dominated by mid-nineteenth-century German—especially Dusseldorf—landscapes.

Figure 27. Newel post, Elm Park, ca. 1869. Lockwood-Mathews Mansion Museum, Norwalk, Conn.

Epilogue for Elm Park

In the late 1860s, consolidation of the major railroads had not yet occurred, and the East Coast and Midwest were crisscrossed by numerous independent lines. As the controlling officer of the Lake Shore Railroad, LeGrand Lockwood began to play Cornelius Vanderbilt against Jay Gould, for each coveted his connecting line. Lockwood borrowed heavily to purchase more and more shares of Lake Shore, using Elm Park as collateral. At that same time Gould and Jim Fisk were attempting to corner the gold market, a reckless gamble that caused a panic on Wall Street. Amid such wild speculation in stocks and commodities, a crash was inevitable, and it came—Black Friday—on 24 September 1869. Gould and Fisk bailed out just before the bubble burst, but many investors,

Figure 28. Drawing room, Elm Park, ca. 1869. Lockwood-Mathews Mansion Museum, Norwalk, Conn.

big and small, lost everything, and Lockwood was among them. As the Lake Shore shares plummeted, Cornelius Vanderbilt bought them up voraciously at bargain-basement prices, thus gaining control of the vital link between Chicago and New York City. When the $10 million Lockwood received from disposing of his Lake Shore stock and other holdings proved insufficient to cover his indebtedness, Vanderbilt ended up holding the mortgage on Elm Park.

LeGrand died only a few years later, in 1872. Two years after that, Vanderbilt foreclosed on the mortgage, and the house was sold in 1876 to Charles D. Mathews, an importer in New York City. Under Mathews's ownership, Elm Park continued to be recognized as an example of a new kind of architecture, its lavishness exuding a new level of wealth, its stylishness pointing to European aristocratic models.[6] The mansion is now a historic house, open to the public.

Figure 29. Albert Bierstadt, *Domes of Yosemite*, 1867. Oil on canvas, 10 × 15 in. (294.6 × 457.2 cm). St. Johnsbury Athenaeum, St. Johnsbury, Vt.

Lyndhurst

The mansion of Lyndhurst was originally a small Gothic Revival cottage retreat, built in 1838 on a site near Tarrytown, New York, overlooking the Hudson River and adjacent to Washington Irving's estate, Sunnyside. It was designed by A. J. Davis for William Paulding, who named it the "Knoll." In 1865, close to when Elm Park was begun, its new owner, New York merchant George Merritt, had the residence enlarged according to plans drawn up by the same architect. That is when it took the form that is seen today (figure 30). Merritt also renamed it.

Under Merritt's ownership, the structure became a pastiche of Gothic features with tourelles, towers, crenelations, and steeply slanted roofs, all asymmetrically adjoined in a wonderful re-interpretation of a medieval fairy-tale castle. It was wrought in white marble, obtained from the nearby quarries at Sing Sing. Merritt added the high tower and a large dining room, which was ornamented with a richly carved wooden ceiling that recalled the flamboyant phase of Gothic ribbed vaults, and stained-glass windows with ornate tracery. What had been Paulding's dining room was transformed into Merritt's library, and a billiard room was added, another instance of a new type of room being incorporated into domestic design. Davis was in charge of the architectural interiors and even designed the Gothic Revival furniture that went into them, as he had done earlier for Paulding; this in itself was unusual, for normally architects, upon completing a house, departed the scene, leaving rooms in a vacuous state, devoid of furniture and furnishings.

Meanwhile, in New York City, Jay Gould (figure 31) and his family lived in an unimposing brownstone at 579 Fifth Avenue. But after Merritt died, Gould began renting Lyndhurst in 1877 as a summer retreat where he could relax and enjoy his children. When he bought the estate in 1880 its construction was essentially complete. It became his favorite escape from the hassles of Wall Street (which were usually of his own making) and the hostility of people he had ruined (who at times became an angry, fist-shaking, threatening

Figure 30. Alexander Jackson Davis, Lyndhurst, near Tarrytown, New York, 1865. National Trust for Historic Preservation.

mob that surrounded his house in the city). Also, suffering from tuberculosis, he found the fresh air of the countryside beneficial, and he enjoyed puttering with his famous orchid collection.

In the parlor, Gould installed furniture of French Beaux-Arts design, which became popular about 1880, and examples of Herter Brothers' furniture survive there. The Gothic Revival furniture designed by Davis all became Gould's with the purchase of the mansion (figure 32). A large hall on the second floor was converted into an art gallery, which displayed Gould's substantial collection of French salon paintings by prominent artists such as Meissonier; his numerous Barbizon pictures by Diaz, Daubigny, Corot, and Rousseau, among others, suggest that his aesthetic tastes were running about one generation behind contemporary painting in France—but that made it possible to be certain of what was acceptable and what was not. Upon Gould's commission, Louis Comfort Tiffany created several large stained-glass windows for Lyndhurst.

Gould died at Lyndhurst, in 1892, and the estate passed to one of his daughters, Helen (Mrs. Finley Shepard), who lived there until her death in 1938. Her sister, Anna, purchased Lyndhurst from Helen's estate; her husband, the Duc de Talleyrand-Perigord, had died the year before, and Anna returned each year from France to spend summers at the beautiful Tarrytown castle. Just before World War II she returned for good to live in the United States, and it was she who left Lyndhurst to the National Trust for Historic Preservation. The property was opened to the public in 1965.

A. T. Stewart

Alexander Turney Stewart (1803–76) was born in County Antrim, Ireland, into a Scotch-Irish Protestant home of moderate comfort (figure 33).[7] After attending an academy briefly in Belfast, this quiet, studious young man decided to visit America, arriving in New York in 1820. He returned to Ireland to collect a small inheritance with which he bought $3,000 worth of Irish lace with which to open a store in New York in the summer of 1823, and from that first small shop he continually expanded his dry-goods business. With his remarkable talent for marketing and an uncanny eye for

Figure 31. Portrait Sketch of Jay Gould, 1883, from The Review of Reviews (January 1893), p. 622.

Figure 32. Dining room, Lyndhurst, ca. 1865. National Trust for Historic Preservation.

current fashions, he pioneered the phenomenon known as "one-stop shopping" in 1846, when he opened the world's first department store.

The concept of the department store expanded rapidly, especially in Paris: Au Bon Marché was founded as a drapery shop in 1852; Les Grands Magasins du Louvre, in 1855; Au Printemps, a decade later; La Samaritaine, from 1869; and Les Galeries Lafayette, in 1893. But the original idea was Stewart's, and he kept control of every aspect of his business, and a Scotsman's eye on every penny of expenditure and profit.

In 1862 Stewart moved his business into an eight-story, steel and stone palatial emporium, designed by John Kellum, a building that occupied a full block between 9th and 10th streets and Broadway and Fourth Avenue. Each floor of the new building provided two and a half acres of space, and opened to a large, elegant rotunda in the center, with a skylight that admitted light to all levels. For this, then the biggest retail store in the world, Stewart became America's largest single importer of international goods—a full fourteen years before such things were so proudly displayed at the Philadelphia Centennial.

In order to stock his opulent department store, he acquired mills and factories throughout New England, New Jersey, and New York, and he opened offices in several European countries to manage the flow of imported goods. According to *Harper's Weekly*, Stewart had "a warehouse in Manchester [England], where all English goods were collected, examined and packed; another in Belfast, for linens; one in Glasgow, for Scotch goods; warehouses in Paris and Lyons, for silks; and one in Berlin, for woolens. In addition . . . there are a number of American and European manufactories which worked exclusively for the firm of A. T. Stewart & Co." And he also had stores in Boston, Philadelphia, and Saratoga Springs.[8]

Stewart made a huge fortune by catering to the rising, prospering middle class and making available to it, in a pleasant, even social setting, the abundant harvest of manufactured objects produced by the Industrial Revolution. He filled his shelves and counters with a world-wide variety of goods that were theretofore unknown to American consumers; his stock became the middle-class counterpart of the more expensive and exotic objects carried by Tiffany's or Gorham.

The department store not only offered to the women of that day a place to acquire the necessities of life for their families, but also was one of the first places where they could congregate for social enjoyment outside the home; previously, their world had been confined largely to the house itself, Sunday church services often being the extent of their weekly outings. The story of their joyous, often frenetic but always exciting excursions into consumer-land is well told in Emile Zola's tale of the department store, *Au Bonheur des Dames (The Ladies' Paradise)*, published in 1883 and based on the rise of the Parisian store Au Bon Marché.[9]

Stewart was a pioneer in the creative advertising and marketing of merchandise, and the money came pouring in. By 1860 he was already the third richest man in the United States and, next to William Astor, the largest landowner in New York City. But Stewart was one of the first of America's millionaires to declare, by example, that rich men had an obligation to give back a portion of the wealth they had been

Figure 33. Late Alexander T. Stewart, engraving. From *Harper's Weekly* (26 April 1876, cover).

fortunate enough to amass. When Ireland was "suffering from famine, he sent over at his own charge a ship-load of provisions . . . [and] to the sufferers by the Franco-German war he sent [many] thousand barrels of flour, and for the relief of the victims of the Chicago fire his check for fifty thousand dollars."[10] He also commissioned a "Women's Hotel," which was erected at Fourth Avenue and 32nd Street, for he was concerned that the young women—who came pouring into the city from small towns and rural areas, attracted by employment opportunities, new to women, such as his department store offered—should have clean, safe and morally supervised housing; it accommodated fifteen hundred women and provided them with dining and laundry services as well as a library of twenty-five hundred volumes. Some years after Stewart's death the Women's Hotel became the Park Avenue Hotel.

Another of his ambitious philanthropic projects was the garden community he began developing on Long Island. Altogether he acquired ten thousand acres in what was then called Hempstead Plains and asked his architect, Kellum, to lay out a green city, designed for and affordable to working people, so they would have a fresh-air option to the wretched conditions of most tenement buildings. He even arranged for transportation connections between his tract and Manhattan, and included schools, churches, and stores into the design. Stewart died before seeing his dream completed, but the area eventually became Garden City, Long Island.

Stewart never entered the political arena directly, although he was often called on to serve his country in other ways. He was, for example, chairman of the American commission sent to the great international exposition in Paris in 1867, and he had many high-placed friends around the Continent, among them Otto von Bismarck and several members of the Rothschild family. He was an admirer of Ulysses S. Grant and worked toward his election in the presidential campaign of 1868.

The A. T. Stewart Mansion

Even after attending to civic duties and philanthropies that interested him personally, A. T. Stewart had ample money left over. With it, he built himself a sumptuous marble palace in which to live, and he formed a very large art collection.

Under the date of 21 March 1864, George Templeton Strong, a dedicated member of the old Knickerbocker crowd who often expressed resentment at the doings of the parvenus, noted in his diary that the "great, hideous one-hundred-thousand-dollar" Townsend-Sarsaparilla house "has just been bought by A. T. Stewart, who has razed it to the ground and tells William Astor he is going to lay out one million on a new white marble palazzo. I suppose it will be just ten times as ugly and barbaric as its predecessor, if that be conceivable."[11]

The remarkable Stewart mansion, completed in 1869, was located on an oversized lot measuring 150 by 112 feet on the northwest corner of 34th Street and Fifth Avenue (figure 34).[12] It was set back on the lot, the perimeter of which was marked by a handsome stone balustrade. The brownstone house of William and Caroline Astor was directly across 34th Street, but in contrast, Stewart's mansion was built of marble, and its Beaux-Arts design was derived from the Parisian Second Empire style. No American model for such a house existed—the inspiration was thoroughly European and aristocratic.

Figure 34. John Kellum, A. T. Stewart residence, 1869, northwest corner of Fifth Avenue and 34th Street, New York City. New-York Historical Society.

Stewart was well acquainted with European architecture, for he traveled frequently to England, Scotland, France, and elsewhere on the Continent. Among his friends in England was the Baron Ferdinand de Rothschild, whose lavish country house outside of London—the celebrated Waddesdon Manor (figures 128 and 129, pp. 191–92)—he had visited; the splendor of the furnishings and the art collections at Waddesdon were undoubtedly on his mind when he began to envision his own grand mansion in New York City.

The Stewart mansion was capped, not with the modest cornice of the brownstones, but with a richly ornamented mansard roof. Each face had a central pavilion, also characteristic of the Second Empire style, with emphasis provided by double columns supporting projecting cornices. Further architectural ornamentation was applied in the form of pilasters on the main floor and quoining at the second and third stories, while each window enframement was carved in Italy from Carrara marble. It was the marble—most of it was Tuckahoe marble obtained from a quarry in Westchester County—that made Stewart's residence most remarkable.[13] The mansion was, in fact, referred to as A. T. Stewart's Marble Palace.

From the beginning, Stewart was determined to create a domicile that was different from, and implied greater wealth than, the Astor brownstone across the street, with which it invited constant comparison. There were few ways in which the upstart new millionaires could outdo the Astors, but they quickly learned that one means was through architecture—by building something of higher fashion, more costly, connoting European sophistication and aristocracy more than Knickerbocker sedateness. In that sense, Stewart succeeded.

As noted, the architect of Stewart's Marble Palace was John Kellum (1809–71). In the 1850s and 1860s his firm had produced many commercial buildings with cast-iron fronts.

Before he designed the Marble Palace, his best-known work was the County Courthouse in lower Manhattan, that monument to the greed, fraud, and graft wherein dwelt the Boss Tweed gang. Starting out as a mechanic, Kellum had neither formal training as an architect nor first-hand experience with the great architectural traditions of Europe, but he became one of New York's most successful designers of public and commercial buildings.[14] Despite his achievement, he was never admitted to the inner circle of American architects of the mid-nineteenth century. He died while working on Stewart's planned community out on Long Island.

The Interiors

A broad flight of marble steps, on the 34th Street facade, led up to the rosewood doors at the entrance of the Marble Palace. The foyer was a clarion declaration of the richness that was to be found throughout the mansion—"magnificence, splendor, luxury," one critic had exclaimed (figure 35).[15] The walls were lined with glistening white marble, and large mirrors reflected the light from gas torches. Lavishness saturated the eye, in the richness of the Corinthian capitals, in the ornateness of the large, globed lamps, in the details of the architectural decoration of the cornice and ceiling.

The most distinctive features of the entrance hall were the marble statues, which were approximately life-size. To the left was Antonio Tantardini's *Water Nymph*, beyond which stood *Demosthenes* by Thomas Crawford. At the right was Scipione Tadolini's *Fisher Girl*, then came Harriet Hosmer's heroic enchained queen, *Zenobia*, and at the end wall were placed Randolph Rogers's *Nydia, the Blind Girl of Pompeii* and Crawford's floating marble maiden, *Flora*. These statues, which represent only a portion of the sculpture in Stewart's collection, suggest the presence of a system for the brokerage of art—that is, the services of art dealers, a relatively new profession then arising in America.

From the entrance hall, one entered, to the right, a reception room, or, passing straight ahead between the two statues, one traversed a short hallway which led to an enormous drawing room that ran the full length of the Fifth Avenue side. Further on in the entrance hall a door led into a music room. At the far end of the foyer was the doorway to the art gallery. To the left as one entered the entrance hall was a door to the dining room and beyond that came the door to a breakfast room.

The drawing room had three large windows facing Fifth Avenue, between which were two enormous mirrors, themselves icons of wealth (figure 36). Before the middle window stood R. H. Park's marble monument to sentimentality, FIRST LOVE, flanked by two tall Sevres vases, which reportedly cost $10,000. The wall decorations were painted by an Italian artist named Brigaldi "who came from Europe to execute them."[16] Brigaldi (1806–ca. 1875) was a well-known decorative designer and painter in his day. Born in Milan, Italy, he came to the United States in 1832, working mainly in New York. About 1848 he was called to Rio de Janeiro to

Figure 35. Entrance hall, A. T. Stewart residence, New York City. From George W. Sheldon, *Artistic Houses* (New York: D. Appleton, 1883–84), plate 5. Morris Library, University of Delaware. In the entrance hall of Stewart's mansion stood a remarkable collection of marble sculptures, assembled in the early 1870s. Although galleries of paintings were not unusual during this period, collections of sculptures were rare. Stewart was probably inspired by the assemblages of marble figures that he saw in English and European grand houses. Both American and European sculptors are represented here.

Figure 36. Drawing room, A. T. Stewart residence, New York City. From Sheldon, *Artistic Houses* (plate 9). Morris Library, University of Delaware.

of architectural gilding, in American domestic interiors, for the purpose of suggesting great affluence. The salon furniture was of the fashionable new Second Empire mode.

The art gallery, which extended most of the width of the house, at the rear of the first floor, measured thirty feet wide by seventy-five feet long and was fifty feet high, with a skylight for illumination (figure 37). One end wall was dominated by Rosa Bonheur's *Horse Fair* (1851–53), one of the most celebrated pictures of the nineteenth century (figure 38); the wall at the other end displayed *Landscape with Cattle*, a huge painting by Rosa's brother, Auguste Bonheur. Hiram Powers's *Greek Slave* and *Eve Disconsolate* are among the sculptures on display in Stewart's gallery.[17]

Academic Salon Paintings

Nearly all the paintings were by French, Belgian, or German artists. In forming his collection, Stewart followed the pattern set by August Belmont after his return from Europe in 1857. The paintings reveal a shift in taste and collecting from mid-century, when New York merchants took pride in the productions of American artists. Moreover, most of the paintings date from the third quarter of the nineteenth century and belong to the contemporary "salon school," as opposed to being works by the Old Masters, which would be preferred by the great American collectors of the next generation, such as J. Pierpont Morgan, Henry Clay Frick, and Benjamin Altman.

On the walls of Stewart's picture gallery one found Meissonier's eight-foot canvas *Friedland, 1807*, for which the great dry-goods merchant paid the artist the unheard-of sum of $60,000 (figure 39). There too was Bouguereau's *Return from the Hunt*. Fortuny was represented by his *Snake Charmers* and Gérôme by *The Charioteers*, a pictorial re-creation of Romans

design a new palace for Emperor Dom Pedro. After completing that task he moved next to Spain and then to London, where he was involved with the designing of theaters as well as townhouses for the wealthy. He then returned to New York and spent most of the remainder of his life executing the ornate decorative painting in several of the major rooms of Stewart's mansion, including the reception room and the breakfast room, devoting about a year to them altogether. Brigaldi's story of peregrinations on three continents demonstrates how the arts of interior decoration were by then becoming thoroughly internationalized.

Stewart commissioned a large Aubusson carpet to match the patterning of Brigaldi's ceiling decorations in the grand salon. The pilasters, their capitals, and the ceiling cornice—all of which were gilded—contributed to the splendor of the drawing room. That was one of the earliest uses

Figure 37. Art gallery, A. T. Stewart residence, New York City. From Sheldon, *Artistic Houses* (plate 11). Morris Library, University of Delaware. Prevailing on the back wall is Rosa Bonheur's *The Horse Fair* (figure 38). In the fashion of the day, paintings—of the French Salon type—were hung, floor to ceiling, with their frames abutting, and the surplus were leaned against the bases of the sculptures or against the walls. Stewart was personally acquainted with the art scene in Paris; he was, for example, one of the commissioners of fine arts for the great Exposition Universelle of 1867 held in the French capital. Among the membership of that committee were fellow collectors John Taylor Johnston and Robert L. Stuart and art dealer Samuel P. Avery.

Figure 38 (opposite, top). Rosa Bonheur, *The Horse Fair*, 1851–53. Oil on canvas, 96 × 199 in. (244.5 × 506.7 cm). Metropolitan Museum of Art, gift of Cornelius Vanderbilt II, 1887 (87.25).

Figure 39 (opposite, bottom). Jean-Louis Ernest Meissonier, *Friedland, 1807*, ca. 1875. Oil on canvas, 53 × 95 in. (135.9 × 242.6 cm). Metropolitan Museum of Art, gift of Henry Hilton, 1887 (87.20.1).

racing chariots in a vast amphitheater, and also by his *Pollice Verso*, or *Gladiators contending before Caesar* (figure 40). Alfred Stevens's *Après le Bal* and Munkacsy's *Visit to the Baby* are saccharine genre subjects of the type that were then so popular. Stewart delighted in knowing the artists who produced his paintings, and on several occasions he visited them in their studios in Paris. He and Meissonier, for example, once had an easy discussion about art, and a warm relationship is suggested by the letters that survive.

Altogether 150 pictures were shown in the gallery, but when Earl Shinn catalogued the Stewart collection he listed a total of 179 paintings and 19 sculptures.[18] That inventory listed several works by Old Masters, but, because attributions were rather casually applied then, it is not certain whether a piece was genuine, or done by a student of the Master or by a nineteenth-century copyist. The list included paintings by or attributed to Hobbema, Titian, Murillo, Rembrandt, and Horace Vernet. Among the few American artists represented in the collection were Eastman Johnson, Albert Bierstadt, Frederic Church, and Daniel Huntington.

While Stewart may have had the advice of several art dealers in the United States and Europe, the collection was composed of works he personally selected and found enjoyable. This refutes the accusation that Gilded Age collectors merely bought wholesale lots of paintings or had their collections formed for them by obliging art dealers; that may have happened occasionally, but usually it was not the case. Several years after Stewart's death a critic known as "Cicerone" observed, "It is evident that the collector knew what he liked, and did not mean to be mystified. On the whole, believing it to be fully a representation of the owner's choice and taste, we uphold it as a noble example of the aesthetic discernment of a merchant-prince."[19]

It is noteworthy that Cicerone referred to Stewart as "a merchant-prince," suggesting that Gilded Age industrialists, railroad tycoons, financiers, and department store entrepreneurs were viewed as the present-day counterparts to the likes of the Medici princes of the Italian Renaissance.

One writer made an interesting comment in an article in *Harper's Weekly* just as the Stewart mansion was being finished, in 1869—a year before the Metropolitan Museum of Art was founded, and a time when New York City had no art museum other than the New-York Historical Society, which had accumulated an assortment of portraits and random bequests. The author observed that the mansion, "with scarcely an alteration in the arrangement of the rooms, could be transformed into a magnificent art-gallery."[20] One can only speculate if A. T. Stewart had something like that in mind, for discussions of the conversion of private collections into public art museums were then "in the air." But if he did, he did not provide for it in his will, and Judge Henry Hilton, his executor, had other plans for both the building and the collection.

Figure 40. Jean Léon Gérôme, *Pollice Verso*, 1872. Oil on canvas, 38 × 58¾ in. (96.5 × 149.2 cm). Phoenix Art Museum, Phoenix, Ariz. Bridgeman Art Library.

Epilogue for the A. T. Stewart Mansion

Alexander T. Stewart died on 10 April 1876. His body had hardly been laid to rest when it was kidnapped from its grave in St. Mark's burial grounds in the Bowery and held for a ransom of $200,000. A dark comedy followed, of secret and continual removal of the body from one hiding place to another while his executor, Judge Henry Hilton, refused to pay, forcing the kidnappers to continually lower their demands. Finally the judge produced a body—*some* body, that is—for which he said he had paid $25,000 in ransom.[21] But the suspicion was that he had obtained some unclaimed cadaver which he called A. T. Stewart's mortal remains and left the kidnappers in possession of a body that nobody wanted. The farce, which was widely covered in the newspapers, subsequently led to numerous commissions for architects to design individual or family mausoleums, often monumental in scale, erected by rich men who wanted to feel secure that their remains would not undergo similar humiliation.

Since Stewart's three children had predeceased him, his estate went to his wife, Cornelia. Society had not welcomed the Stewarts into its fold, but then there is little indication that they desired to become a part of High Society. Stewart's wealth would have qualified him for membership in the millionaires' club, and among business colleagues he was well respected. When his name appeared in the newspapers, however, it was in the business section or in a notice of philanthropy, almost never in the society columns. The widowed Cornelia seldom left the draped interiors of her mansion, and she took no interest in the art collection. Her greatest concerns were with her wigs and her wrinkle-resistance skin creams. Her husband had probably suspected as much, for he left the estate in the hands of Judge Hilton.

The estate was estimated at around $40 million, but under Judge Hilton's supervision, within a decade it had been reduced to a fraction of that amount. Meanwhile, Mrs. Stewart sat at her 34th Street window, increasingly reclusive, absorbed with the dream of restored youth, watching the comings and goings at Mrs. Astor's house across the street. After Cornelia's death in 1885 Judge Hilton decreed that a great sale of the Stewart collection should be held, in 1887. The sale established a landmark in the brokerage of art in the United States, for a substantial, illustrated book—which catalogued and described the individual pictures and sculptures—was published in association with the auction, setting a pattern for such events in the future.[22] At the sale, Judge Hilton bought Meissonier's *Friedland, 1807* for $66,000 and magnanimously presented it to the Metropolitan Museum of Art. Cornelius Vanderbilt II, through his agent Samuel Avery, purchased Rosa Bonheur's *Horse Fair*, for $53,000, and likewise gave it to the fledgling Met.

As for the Marble Palace itself, it stood empty for a while, but in 1890 it became the home of the Manhattan Club (figure 41). In 1899, however, the latter found a new clubhouse in the

Figure 41. Childe Hassam, *The Manhattan Club (The Stewart Mansion)*, ca. 1891. Oil on canvas, 18¼ × 22 in. (46.4 × 56.2 cm). Santa Barbara Museum of Art, Santa Barbara, Calif., gift of Sterling Morton for the Preston Morton Collection.

old Leonard Jerome mansion down on Madison Square. Two years later Stewart's grand house was torn down, its brief life-span being only thirty-two years. The Knickerbocker Trust Company acquired the site and erected a temple-like bank building designed by Stanford White, which opened in 1904. By that date the area around Fifth Avenue and 34th Street had changed from residential to commercial, for where the great brownstones of John Jacob Astor III and Mrs. William (Caroline) Astor had stood now rose the towering Waldorf-Astoria Hotel (figure 42). By then, Society had once again moved farther north on Fifth Avenue.

Mary Mason Jones and Marble Row

Between 57th and 58th Streets on Fifth Avenue rose the building called Marble Row (figure 43), designed by Robert Mook for Mrs. Isaac (Mary Mason) Jones, whose husband had owned Chemical Bank. As the Gilded Age dawned, the long-widowed Mrs. Jones, one of the *grandes dames* of mid-century New York Society, was already approaching her seventieth birthday, making her move way uptown seem all the more daring. She and her sister, Rebecca (Mrs. Colford Jones), had been living on Broadway near Washington Square, in adjoining houses, where they enjoyed reputations as gracious hostesses among old Knickerbocker society.

Upon the death of their father, John Mason, the sisters had each inherited a tract of land on Fifth Avenue in the vicinity of 57th Street. With the opening of Central Park (which was then far from central within the city) in 1859, land values in that area began to rise, and consequently so did the taxes levied on them; in 1855 Rebecca's parcel was assessed at a little over $30,000, but by 1866 its evaluation had reached nearly $300,000. The sisters' properties were thus too valuable to leave undeveloped, and the solution was to erect multiple-unit structures on the two sites. Rebecca turned to Detlef Lienau to design and build for her a row of eight houses on the block between 55th and 56th streets, facing Fifth Avenue

(figure 44). The design was, of course, in the French mode of boulevard architecture, with a mansard roof and a continuous cornice uniting the several units in a single block.[23] The houses were built of Ohio limestone and had four slightly projecting pavilions.

In 1869, when Mary Mason Jones's Marble Row was completed, 57th Street was still "way uptown." Henry James tells about this northward migration of Society in his novel *Washington Square*, published in 1881. In it, one of the characters, Arthur Townsend—the cousin of Morris Townsend, the suitor of the heroine Catherine Sloper—speaks about his own impending marriage and the house he would acquire, and his expectation to "move every three or four years" because then "you've always got the last [most fashionable] thing," and "that's the way to live in New York." Townsend explained:

> "It's because the city's growing so quick—you've got to keep up with it. It's going straight up town—that's where New York's going. If I wasn't afraid [my fiancee] Marian would be lonely, I'd go up there—right up to the top—and wait for it. Only have to wait ten years—they'll come up after you. But Marian says she wants some neighbours—she doesn't want to be a pioneer. She says that if she's got to be the first settler she had better go out to Minnesota. I guess we'll move up little by little."[24]

Edith Wharton, Mary Mason Jones's niece, also wrote about the movement way uptown. Wharton (née Jones) used her aunt and her peripheral mansion as the models for Mrs. Manson Mingott and her house in *The Age of Innocence*, which, although written in 1920, is set in the 1870s—that is, in the years just following the completion of Marble Row. "A visit to Mrs. Manson Mingott," Wharton wrote,

> . . . was always an amusing episode to the young man [Newland Archer]. The house itself was already an historic document, though not . . . as venerable as certain other old family houses in . . . lower Fifth Avenue. . . . Old Mrs. Mingott, who had built her house later, had bodily cast out the massive [Greek Revival] furniture of her prime, and mingled with the Mingott heirlooms the frivolous upholstery of the Second Empire. It was her habit to sit in a window of her sitting-room on the ground floor, as if watching calmly for life and fashion to flow northward to her solitary doors.[25]

Within a decade, others did indeed follow Mary Mason Jones's northward migration, beginning with the Vanderbilts, who moved into the area around Fifth and 52nd. In the early 1880s, Cornelius Vanderbilt II built his mansion-to-top-all-mansions (figures 85–98, pp. 132–49) across the street from Marble Row. For the decade of the 1870s, however, Marble Row was one of the residential showplaces in New York City, standing alone, in virtual isolation from the fashionable sections of Fifth Avenue far to the south.

Earlier in her life, Mrs. Jones had closed up her house on Broadway and gone to Paris to live for a protracted period. While there she observed the architecture of the Second Empire—the hôtels des villes and the manor houses of the châteaux country. She saw, too, the glittering interiors of aristocratic and imperial residences such as the Tuileries, the Louvre, and Compiègne. When she returned to New York she chose to build in a similar fashion, for by then the old brownstone type of house would have seemed, to her, stodgy and provincial.

Indeed, at times Edith Wharton herself sounded very much like her aunt, stating in her autobiography the anguish she felt upon returning to New York after she had lived for a while in Europe. New York was, she wrote, "a cramped horizontal gridiron of a town without towers, porticoes, fountains or perspectives, hidebound in its deadly uniformity of mean ugliness. . . . How could I understand that people who had seen Rome and Seville, Paris and London, could come back to live contentedly between Washington Square and Central Park?"[26] Only a rather blurred line separated Wharton's own real-life experiences, those of her aunt Mary Mason Jones, and those of her delightful character, Mrs. Manson Mingott:

> [Mrs. Mingott] put the crowning touch to her audacities by building a large house of pale cream-colored stone (when brown sandstone seemed as much the only wear as a frock-coat in the afternoon) in an inaccessible wilderness near Central Park. . . . The . . . house (supposed to be modeled on the private hotels [des villes] of the Parisian aristocracy) was there as a visible proof of her moral courage, and she throned in it, among . . . souvenirs of the Tuileries of Louis Napoleon (where she had shone in her middle age), as placidly as if there were nothing peculiar in living above Thirty-fourth Street, or in having French windows that opened like doors instead of sashes that pushed up.[27]

That New Yorkers were ready for some change in their cityscape is evident, by 1869, in a passage from Junius Henri

Figure 42. Fifth Avenue from 35th Street, ca. 1898, showing (left to right) the Waldorf-Astoria Hotel, the Stewart residence/Manhattan Club, the Fifth Avenue Art Galleries, and the New York Club, ca. 1900. Library of Congress, Prints and Photographs Division. The northward advance of commercial usage is seen here, already by the turn of the century, for the great hulking form of the Waldorf-Astoria has replaced the brownstone houses of Caroline Astor and her nephew, John Jacob Astor III. The home of A. T. Stewart has become a gentlemen's club, as has the ivy-covered building in the foreground, and businesses—such as the art gallery (center)—have replaced domestic residences. To see the changes that have occurred, compare this view with that seen in figure 13 on p. 39.

Marble Row

Marble Row was a Fifth Avenue house designed in the mode of a French château, by definition a large house erected in the country and therefore surrounded by broad, open spaces. As an architectural form, it was transplanted, in America's Gilded Age, from a rural to an urban setting. It was a harbinger of things to come. Remembering fondly such nonurban palaces as Fontainebleau, Mrs. Jones herself produced the basic design for her house before turning it over to Robert Mook, who, although a successful architect, was not an innovator capable of something so original.

Like the nearly contemporary palazzo of A. T. Stewart, Marble Row broke with the entrenched architectural tradition of New York in its building material, for as its name implies, it was faced with a glistening cream-colored marble that set it apart from almost all other houses of the wealthy in the years following the Civil War. In Parisian fashion, the entire block between 57th and 58th streets was treated as a single

Browne's *Great Metropolis*, which suggests that the monotony of the architecture was a reflection of those who lived within it:

> Block after block, mile upon mile, of the same lofty brown-stone, high-stoop, broad-staired fronts wearies the eye. . . . One longs in the Avenue for more marble, more brick, more iron, more wood even—some change in the style and aspects of the somber-seeming houses, whose occupants, one fancies from the exterior, look, think, dress and act alike. One might go, it appears, into any drawing-room between the Park and the old Parade-ground, and he would be greeted with the same forms; see the same gestures; hear the same speeches. . . . The slavish spirit of imitation, with poverty of invention, has spoiled the broad thoroughfare. . . . It is a grievous pity that where there is so much money there is so little taste.[28]

Mary Mason Jones was determined to change all that.

unit, although there were actually five houses within the block. Mrs. Jones took the one at the corner of 57th and Fifth for herself and rented the other four to wealthy socialites.

Mary Mason Jones saw herself and her Knickerbocker crowd as New York's true aristocracy, and she resented the efforts of the new-money people to assert themselves as social equals. The confrontation of the two groups was nowhere more apparent than in the clash between Mrs. Jones and Mrs. Paran Stevens, the wife of the parvenu owner of the Fifth Avenue Hotel. Mary Mason Jones's animosity toward the "climber" Mrs. Stevens was so intense that she declared openly that the latter would never set foot in Marble Row by invitation, and she did not. But Mrs. Stevens did have her triumph in the end, for after Mrs. Jones's death, her husband,

Figure 43. Robert Mook, Marble Row, Mary Mason Jones residence, Fifth Avenue and 58th Street, New York City, 1867–69. Museum of the City of New York. One can well imagine Edith Wharton's *grande dame* of New York Society, Mrs. Manson Mingott, sitting at her window in Marble Row, watching and patiently waiting for Society to move "way uptown," from their enclaves around Washington Square and 34th Street, to the region of Central Park. Wharton was a keen observer of architecture and interiors and frequently employed them in her novels and short stories, encoding them with social and psychological significance.

Figure 44. Detlef Lienau, Rebecca Colford Jones Block, Fifth Avenue between 55th and 56th streets, New York City, 1869. Lienau Collection, Avery Library, Columbia University.

Paran Stevens, bought the property, and in 1893 Mrs. Stevens moved into one of the units of Marble Row, where she became ensconced as one of New York's presiding social queens.

But mansions came and went with amazing rapidity during this era, and Marble Row was eventually displaced by the Hermann Oelrichs's mansion, which in turn gave way to the splendid European-style Savoy-Plaza Hotel, which was replaced in time by the nondescript General Motors Building that occupies the site today.

A Scattered Assortment of Mansions, But French

By 1870 New York City possessed a number of mansions scattered about that broke with the old brownstone tradition: the Hart Schiff house at 10th and Fifth Avenue and the John Gray house just north of it, the Leonard Jerome mansion on 26th Street at Madison Square, the Marble Palace of A. T. Stewart at 34th and Fifth, and the two blocks of row houses belonging to Mary Mason Jones and her sister Rebecca, at or near 57th and Fifth Avenue. The new inspiration was decidedly French, either of the urban, Parisian hôtel de ville type or of the rural château sort. These homes set the course of architecture in New York in a new direction.

Scattered as they were, amid the endless grid of brownstone row houses, the mansions struck a discordant note in their respective neighborhoods. The next phase of their impellent assertiveness, as the new mode for the millionaires' pseudo-aristocratic pretensions, was to have the new style achieve hegemony and homogeneity by being clustered together in a specific sector of the city. That began to happen along Fifth Avenue when the Vanderbilts moved in, around 1880.

The great feature to be noticed in America is that all its citizens have full permission to run the race in which Mr. Vanderbilt has gained such immense prizes. In other countries, on the contrary, they are trammeled by a thousand restrictions. . . . Those who ought to be the Vanderbilts in England would shrink from employing their wealth in the magnificent manner adopted by their American friend. They would dread the effect of making any unusual display, which would surely subject them to the reproach of being millionaires and parvenus. Here is the difference between our two countries. In England a man is apt to be ashamed of having made his own fortune, unless he has done so in one of the few roads which the aristocracy condescend to travel by. . . . It is time that the millionaire [in England] should cease to be ashamed of having made his own fortune. . . . Let them take example from America.

"A Word about Mr. [Cornelius] Vanderbilt's Yacht," *Daily News* [London], 4 June 1853

Chapter Four

The Commodore and Beetlehead

The William Henry Vanderbilt Mansion

The Progenitor

Among the greatest American families of builders of grand mansions, the Vanderbilts must rank at or near the top. They also rank foremost among the new wealth of the Gilded Age. The Vanderbilts descended from a Dutch family that had come to America in 1650 from Bilt (hence the name), a small town in Holland. Though the family line was an old one, it was lowly and not a part of Knickerbocker society. Its appearance on the world stage arose only about the time of the Civil War when a rough and gruff old curmudgeon known as the Commodore made his debut (figure 45).

Cornelius Vanderbilt (1794–1877) was born on the family's scruffy Staten Island farm to a ne'er-do-well father, who, as the mood struck him, shuttled a ferry between the island and Manhattan.[1] As a boy, Cornelius detested formal education; throughout his life he boasted of his illiteracy while secretly lamenting it. During his youth he was harsh, abrupt, intimidating, dour, sarcastic, bad tempered, and famous for his profanity; he scorched the New York waterfront with his fists and his foul language.

But he was a strong lad and hard working, and he had an extraordinary genius for recognizing the potential for a profit. In 1810, at age sixteen, he borrowed a hundred dollars from his mother and bought his own small shallow-draft boat for ferry service. That was the beginning of the Vanderbilt fortune—the beginning that would eventually make him one of the richest men in the world. He sailed his little skiff alone, running both freight and passengers across the waters of New York harbor. Following the War of 1812 he built schooners that not only serviced New York bay but also ran up and down the East and North rivers. Then, modernizing with the times, he sold his entire fleet of sailing ships to enter the steamboat business, which also prospered mightily.

His large fleet plied the waters between Albany and New York and along Long Island Sound to New Haven, where his main competition came from Daniel Drew—thus began a rivalry that reached fever pitch during the railroad wars later in the century. Reveling in any kind of business warfare, he beat out Drew in the early steamboat competition by continually lowering his fares, forcing Drew to do likewise, until a person could go from lower Manhattan to Peekskill on the Hudson for less than thirteen cents. Drew gave in and sold out to Vanderbilt, whose policy, even in his early days, was to eliminate competition so he could obtain a monopoly that would allow him to charge any rate he wished. Once Drew was out of the picture, the price of a ticket shot up like a meteor.

Recognizing that New York City was the national center of commerce and finance, Cornelius moved there in 1829. Ten years earlier he had married his cousin, Sophia Johnson. When Sophia announced that she was content to remain in the modest comfort of Staten Island and refused to move to Manhattan, Cornelius promptly had her locked up in an insane asylum, as such institutions were then called, until she bent to his will and joined him in the city.

Sophia and Cornelius had thirteen children. Of their four sons, one died early in life. George, his father's favorite and heir apparent, attended West Point and became an officer in the Civil War, but he died young, of malaria. A second son, Cornelius Jeremiah, a cadaverous epileptic spendthrift who frequented every fleshpot and gambling house in sight, was an embarrassment to his father, who regretted that he had named him Cornelius. To stem his son's profligacy, Vanderbilt packed him off to an insane asylum—after all, that had been effective with Sophia. With son George dead and Cornelius Jeremiah a dissolute failure, that left, begrudgingly, the third son, William Henry, as Cornelius's primary heir, for the misogynist Vanderbilt felt only disdain for his wife and nine daughters.

In 1846 Cornelius built a house at 10 Washington Place, near Washington Square, a part of New York City that was still fashionable. But the house was not grand; it was, in fact, a typical brick-front row house of no particular distinction. The interior, too, was anything but magnificent. This reluctance to build grandly raises an interesting point: Cornelius Vanderbilt had little interest in stylish architecture and the building of fine mansions—as little, in fact, as he had in Society. For the Vanderbilt clan, these pursuits came in the next generation and especially in the generation of his grandchildren.[2]

Vanderbilt made about $20 million in the California Gold Rush, not by laboriously panning for the precious metal but by providing transportation—at a high price—to the gold fields for those who went to seek such elusive fortunes. His ships carried them to Central America, which they crossed by train to the west coast, where his Pacific coastline ships picked them up to take them to San Francisco. Those same ships were heavily laden with the supplies the forty-niners would need, available at scalpers' prices. By 1850, his steamboats had made him one of the wealthiest men in the nation. When the Civil War erupted he volunteered his services and his ships, being a staunch supporter of the Union cause. But war was war and business was business, and he turned a sizable profit by leasing to the government a number of his steamships.

Changing Careers at Seventy: From the Paddlewheel to the Iron Horse

Suddenly, in 1862, when he was almost seventy years old, Vanderbilt again decided to change with the times. He rid himself of his steamships to purchase rail lines, for he recognized the enormous potential of the railroad. He eventually put together a number of small, independent lines to create the great New York Central Railroad.

Daniel Drew now reappeared. Destruction of his old enemy became an obsession with Drew, who in 1866 formed an alliance with the Central. It ran from Buffalo to Albany, and Drew made an agreement with its board to route freight and passengers at Albany onto his Hudson River steamboats for the trip to New York City instead of connecting with Vanderbilt's New York and Harlem line. At first Drew's maneuver was ruinous to his raging adversary. But when the river froze that winter, making steamboat traffic impossible, the Commodore halted his trains well short of Albany and refused to take on any consignments from the Central. Both passengers and freight, arriving from the West, began piling up at the Central's Albany terminal, and the stock price of the Central plunged. Vanderbilt bought it by the tons at bargain prices, acquiring control by 1867. The Vanderbilt line now offered through traffic from New York City to Albany to Buffalo.

Then came the battle for the Erie Railroad, one of the rare occasions when the Commodore was outmaneuvered—by those scalawags Jay Gould, Daniel Drew, and Jim Fisk—in his effort to control a through line between New York and Chicago. But when Black Friday hit in late September of 1869, and the price of the stock of LeGrand Lockwood's Lake Shore and Michigan Southern Railway, which skirted the southern edge of Lake Erie, plummeted, Vanderbilt bought it up, thereby gaining controlling interest in it and assuring his line of a connection to Chicago, which was then emerging as the financial, transportation, and commodities capital of the Midwest.[3] By the time of his death Vanderbilt controlled a vast empire of rolling stock and some twenty-one thousand miles of track.

Fine Yachts and Fast Horses: A Rich Man's Toys

If Cornelius Vanderbilt had any passionate interests aside from making enormous amounts of money and demolishing competitors, they were driving horses and sailing yachts. He loved fast trotters and rejoiced in a competition with anyone on the road when he took his bays out for an exhilarating

Figure 45. *Cornelius Vanderbilt (the Commodore)*. Photograph by Howell, ca. 1870. Photography Collection, New York Public Library.

drive at breakneck speed, bullying those foolish enough to take up his challenge. So well known was this practice that Currier and Ives issued a color lithograph depicting Cornelius racing in Harlem Lane with Robert Bonner, the owner of several newspapers and a fellow equine enthusiast (figure 46).

While in the steamboat business Vanderbilt established new standards of luxury in the accommodations his floating palaces afforded their passengers. He also began building sumptuously appointed private yachts for his own enjoyment, which, in size, beauty, speed, and comfort, far surpassed anything known before. In 1847 the Commodore personally designed and supervised the construction of a grand yacht—modestly named *The Cornelius Vanderbilt*—marking the beginning of the rage for luxuriously outfitted, large-scale, oceangoing private boats, status-symbol toys of America's new millionaires. That craft was followed in 1851 by an even more lavish one, the 260-foot *North Star*, aboard which the Reverend John Overton Choules was a frequent guest. Throughout his life Vanderbilt had reveled in irreverence, but he liked the good Baptist minister from Newport, and Choules greatly admired his capitalist host; Choules recalled that on one long voyage he and the Commodore divided certain responsibilities—he being in charge of praying and Vanderbilt in charge of profanity. Choules left a description of the *North Star*:

> The state rooms . . . are fitted up in the first style of the upholsterer's [decorator's] art. The furniture throughout blends in one harmonious whole. . . . [The] saloon is of beautiful satin-wood, with just

Figure 46. Currier and Ives, *Fast Trotters on Harlem Lane, N.Y.*, ca. 1870. Lithograph. Metropolitan Museum of Art, New York City.

sufficient rosewood to relieve it, the work of which was executed by Mr. Charles Simonson [the builder of the yacht]. The cabinet furniture and the upholstery were furnished from the extensive establishment of Messrs. J. & W. Weeks. The furniture of the main saloon is of rosewood, carved in the splendid style of Louis XV.

According to Choules, the walls of the dining salon were sheathed in various tints of marble while the ceiling panels were painted white, with purple, gold, and light-green scrollwork creating medallions that contained portraits of Columbus, Daniel Webster, Henry Clay, John C. Calhoun, George Washington, Benjamin Franklin, and other distinguished persons from American history. Clay and Webster were friends whom Vanderbilt admired and supported politically; he named one of his steamships *The Daniel Webster*, and when in Washington lobbying the government for something or other, he often engaged in a game of cards with Henry Clay.

The luxury of the *North Star* and the willingness to spend lavish amounts on oneself for pure pleasure had hardly been known in America previously. They signal a change in cultural patterns, already in the 1850s, that would become one of the primary characteristics of the Gilded Age.

In 1853 Vanderbilt took his first vacation. Loading thirty-three members of his family, the Reverend Choules, and a few friends aboard the *North Star*, he sailed for Europe. Choules declared in the introduction to his chronicle of the voyage, "I felt glad that such a man, self-made as he is, should be seen by the accidental sons of nobility and fortune in the Old World," revealing the hero worship (perhaps mixed with a fearful admiration) that had begun to build around this rough-and-tumble American millionaire.

But if Cornelius Vanderbilt had great wealth, he had little interest in art, the sole exception being in portraiture of himself. While in Italy in 1853 he visited Florence, where he made the acquaintance of the famous sculptor Hiram Powers, whom he liked, according to Choules, who recorded their conversations.[4] In Powers's studio Vanderbilt posed for the modeling of his bust, while the likeness of his wife was being taken in the nearby studio of Joel Tanner Hart, another of the American expatriate sculptors living in Florence. Although modeled in 1853, the marble bust of Cornelius was not delivered until 1856, at which time the Commodore wrote to Powers the following letter, replete with the author's usual misspellings and errors of grammar: "Dear Sir The busts has arrived & paid for to your Eagent Mr. De hone and aire here named to be the best Ever Sean. I did not think you could make so goodlooking an article out of marble particularly after the man you had befour you when you packed up the Mud or Clay and beyond doubt you have dun justise to the Party."[5]

If Cornelius Vanderbilt did not concern himself with the arts or grand architecture, he was even less interested in philanthropy. A rare act of generosity occurred late in his life when he made a gift of $1 million to a small college in Nashville, Tennessee—Central University—which thereafter became known as Vanderbilt University. But philanthropy on a large scale was only then arising, in the 1870s, and in time, social theorists and public pressure would cause the new millionaires to reflect on how they could share the good fortune that had come their way, as advocated by Andrew Carnegie in his article, "Wealth," which appeared in June of 1889. The practice of philanthropy increased greatly when the generation of Cornelius's grandchildren came into prominence—and into their inheritances.

The Commodore died on 4 January 1877 at his comfortable but unspectacular house at 10 Washington Place. His remains were laid to rest in a mausoleum on Staten Island, especially constructed to prevent the disgracing of the corpse that poor A. T. Stewart's body had endured. Vanderbilt left an estate estimated at $100 million. The manner in which he disposed of his millions is in itself revealing, for he intended for the family name and fortune to be a commanding force in succeeding generations. Accordingly, he left almost everything to his son, William Henry Vanderbilt.

Beetlehead's Success

As noted, William Henry Vanderbilt (1821–85) was one of four sons born to Cornelius Vanderbilt (figure 47). Two sons had died and a third was a drunken gambler, and the nine daughters mattered little to their father. For many years the Commodore also felt nothing but disdain for William Henry, who as a youth was sickly and frail, unlike his father, the young muscular brawler who enjoyed intimidating other men physically. Even after William Henry became a man, his father thought him slow-witted and incapable of making

important decisions, much less managing the fortune the Commodore had amassed. The old man referred to his son as "good for nothing" and "Beetlehead."

When he was only nineteen William Henry further offended his father by marrying Maria Louisa Kissam, showing, in his father's eyes, poor judgment in taking as his wife the daughter of a penniless Brooklyn minister. To put his son out of the way, the Commodore bought a seventy-acre farm at New Dorp on Staten Island and sent him and his new wife into exile to manage it. There, William Henry and Louisa's eight children were born, nearly all of whom, along with their parents, would one day live in gilded mansions on Fifth Avenue.

Cornelius Vanderbilt did not often misjudge men, but he did his son. William Henry may have been slow and plodding—his contemporaries in later life made fun of him as such—but he was a thinker, and he was methodical, even imaginative in the affairs of business. His little farm at New Dorp grew from 70 to 350 acres and its profits increased annually.

When the depression of 1857 hit, William Henry—then thirty-six—noticed a little Staten Island railroad, only thirteen miles long but with considerable potential; he got himself appointed its receiver, thus becoming a railroad executive several years before his father did. This, too, he improved and made profitable.

Cornelius Vanderbilt took notice at last, and when he abandoned the steamboat business to acquire control of the New York and Harlem Railroad, he brought William Henry and his family back to Manhattan, in 1864, and made his son a vice president. After the Commodore obtained the Hudson River Railroad, his son became a vice president of that line as well. During the next several years William Henry learned much from his father, but he too contributed to the success of the family business. It was he, for example, who suggested that Cornelius gain control of the Michigan Central Railroad and LeGrand Lockwood's Lake Shore and Michigan Southern Railway, the last link in the chain that connected New York City and Chicago by rail.

Cornelius Vanderbilt did not want to see his enormous fortune dissipated by fragmentation into many little fortunes through an equal distribution to his two sons and nine daughters. To Cornelius Jeremiah he left only $300,000, and to each of his daughters he bequeathed about $200,000. To William Henry, the old Commodore left everything else, which amounted to nearly $100 million. Enraged by that arrangement, Cornelius Jeremiah and his sisters promptly sued. William Henry's skillful handling of this potentially disastrous situation was indicative of the adeptness that was so deceptively hidden behind his dull eyes and oversized, slow-moving bulk. By contributing another $500,000 to each

Figure 47 (above). Jared B. Flagg, *William Henry Vanderbilt*, 1877. Oil on canvas, 69 × 44 in. (175.3 × 111.7 cm). The Preservation Society of Newport County.

Figure 48 (opposite). Seymour Joseph Guy, *The William H. Vanderbilt Family*, 1873. Oil on canvas, 42 × 54 in. (152.4 × 182.9 cm). Biltmore Estate, Asheville, N.C. The family is shown in the parlor of the Vanderbilt residence at Fifth Avenue and 40th Street. William Henry is seated at the left. Beyond him stands Frederick, behind his mother, Maria Louisa; then young George (the future builder of Biltmore), and next are Florence and William Kissam (builder of Marble House at Newport), then fourteen-year-old Lila, seated at the table. Margaret is standing with her back to the viewer while Elliott Fitch Shepard (Margaret's husband) has his coat removed by a servant. Emily is wearing a white gown and standing before her husband, William Douglas Sloane (of the carpet and furniture family), who is seated next to Alice, who is married to the man standing at the far right, Cornelius Vanderbilt II, the head of the family in the next generation and the builder of The Breakers at Newport.

of his sisters from his own share of the inheritance, he pacified them, and he worked out a similar deal with his besotted brother. He thus emerged as head of both the Vanderbilt clan and the vast railroad empire that his father had built.

William Henry—diffident and soft-spoken—gained control of more and more lines, reaching farther into the continent, connecting Vanderbilt lines with great midwestern centers such as St. Louis and Indianapolis. He was a builder, an improver of whatever he acquired, and he made good judgments in the people he chose to assist him in his ventures. For example, when the agitation of an antimonopoly group made it wise for William Henry to divest himself of a quarter-million shares of railroad stock, he selected a young man who was just then beginning to rise in financial circles—J. Pierpont Morgan—to handle the sale of the shares without glutting the market and causing the price to collapse. Morgan went abroad, accomplished the sale while keeping the price high, brought much foreign capital into American business, and turned a very handsome profit for William Henry.

When William Henry died, only eight years after his father, he left an estate that had doubled what he had inherited from Cornelius—an astounding $200 million. In 1884 a Wall Streeter tried to put William Henry's wealth into comprehendible terms: "On interest and dividends alone Vanderbilt earns $28,000 a day, $1200 an hour, and $19.75 a minute."[6] Those figures were astronomical in the buying power of the 1880s.

William Henry enjoyed his last years surrounded by his many sons and daughters and their spouses (figure 48), as depicted in Seymour Guy's family portrait. It is interesting that The Commodore was still alive when Guy painted this family portrait, but William Henry chose not to include him,

having himself shown as the monarch of the clan. The painting portrays the family in their old house at the southeast corner of Fifth Avenue and 40th Street, diagonally across from the Croton Reservoir (and the spot where the New York Public Library now stands). William Henry had bought the lot in 1866, when it contained only a derelict, burned-out shell of a house, a victim of the Draft Riots of 1863. He erected a fine but not distinguished house at 450 Fifth Avenue, and there he and his family lived until 1881.

William Henry and the Great Fifth Avenue Land Rush

Within two years of the Commodore's death, William Henry, now possessing the necessary wherewithal, began planning a great new house—a mansion, or more specifically, a palazzo—that was grander and larger than anything New York Society had yet seen. It was not in William Henry's nature or personality to go seeking after Society; he enjoyed his home and his family, but he sensed that if the Vanderbilts were to be established as the preeminent family of the country, their patriarch must be headquartered in a palace that bespoke their primal position. While the interior depicted in Seymour Guy's painting seems comfortable enough, the architecture and decor do not proclaim great affluence; the new house that William Henry envisioned would have to express, above all else, the grandeur of the new aristocracy. So he followed Society in its impellent march up Fifth Avenue, where he acquired the entire block on the west side of Fifth between 51st and 52nd streets. On that plot Isaiah Keyser had long lived in a small house surrounded by his vegetable gardens, from which he sold produce to the neighborhood households, while his cows grazed pastorally about the property. Across the avenue stood Saint Patrick's Cathedral (begun in 1858), in majestic isolation. Neither Saks Fifth Avenue nor Rockefeller Center would arise in the immediate neighborhood for many years to come.

With the purchase of this large lot William Henry anchored the Vanderbilts firmly within what came to be known as Millionaires' Mile. But it was a pioneering move, for in addition to the property being less expensive in those northern reaches of Fifth Avenue, the family was establishing its independence from the old Knickerbockers of lower Fifth and the Astors at 33rd and 34th streets. The center of power once again shifted northward, for when William Henry Vanderbilt built there, soon to be followed by sons William Kissam and Cornelius II, the rest of Society raced to acquire nearby properties on which to erect their own mansions. It was as if someone had fired a gun and the land rush was on. Mary Mason Jones (model for Edith Wharton's Mrs. Manson Mingott) must have smiled to herself as she saw them from her window in Marble Row rushing northward up the avenue.

William Henry Vanderbilt's mansion was in reality a triple house (figure 49). The southern half, at the corner of 51st and Fifth, was for William Henry, Louisa, and seventeen-year-old George; William Henry's half of the building measured 80 feet wide and 115 feet deep. The northern half was divided into two parts, to be occupied by two of the Vanderbilt daughters and their husbands: Emily, who had married William Douglas Sloane, and Margaret, wife of Elliott Fitch Shepard. Even as the new mansion rose, another daughter, Lila, married William Seward Webb, and within a year the Webbs moved into a fine house "in the Gothic style" at 680 Fifth Avenue, near 53rd Street, next to Saint Thomas Church. Next door, at 684 Fifth, Lila's sister, Florence Adele Vanderbilt Twombly, and her husband, Hamilton, built their mansion in the Italian Renaissance mode. At the corner of Fifth Avenue and 52nd Street stood the handsome new French château that Richard Morris Hunt designed for one of the Vanderbilt sons, William Kissam, and his spirited young wife, Alva. Finally, six blocks north of his father's house, at 57th and Fifth, within a block's distance of Marble Row, Cornelius II—William Henry's eldest son—and his wife, Alice Gwynne erected their mansion. The Vanderbilts also bought up many of the neighboring properties along Fifth Avenue—a polyglot of vacant lots, garden plots, small undistinguished houses and derelict shanties—so they could control that stretch of the avenue, which was soon dubbed Vanderbilt Row.

William Henry's Palazzo

The architect usually credited with the design and plan for William Henry's mansion is John B. Snook, who had designed Vanderbilt's house at 40th and Fifth; when plans for the great palazzo were filed with the New York Building Department, Snook's name was on the application. However, there is

some evidence that Charles B. Atwood, who was then employed by Herter Brothers, was the architect. Christian Herter became prickly whenever Atwood and Snook were credited with the design, and on 11 April 1886 he or some official of Herter Brothers wrote a letter to the editors of a leading architectural journal, explaining, "It is a matter of record . . . that Herter Brothers were the architects of [Mr. Vanderbilt's house] . . . and are the only persons responsible for the designs, both of the exterior and the interior. . . . We might add that of the two gentlemen named by you, Mr. Atwood was employed by our firm at that time as a draughtsman and Mr. Snook by Mr. Vanderbilt as general superintendent."[7] The design of the mansion was probably a collaborative effort of Snook and Atwood, with Christian Herter in charge of the interiors. In any case, its construction began in 1879, and William Henry and his family moved into it in January of 1881.

In elevation, the house bears a vague resemblance to an Italian Renaissance palace. But a comparison with the Villard Houses (figure 164, p. 242)—erected only a few blocks away on Madison Avenue and only a few years later (completed in 1885) by the firm of McKim, Mead and White—shows the Villard mansions to be the more sophisticated and scholarly interpretation of a Roman palazzo. The Fifth Avenue facades of William Henry's grand mansion were set back from the street a short distance, the property line being defined by a low cast-iron ornamental fence that ran along the sidewalk.

There were two symmetrical, prismatic blocks to the house, with a central courtyard that one entered from Fifth Avenue. The roofline, perfectly flat and of a uniform level,

Figure 49. John Snook, Charles Atwood, and Herter Brothers, the Louisa and William Henry Vanderbilt residence, 1879–81, 640 Fifth Avenue, between 51st and 52nd streets, New York City (with William Kissam Vanderbilt's Petit Château seen just beyond 52nd Street). Brown Brothers. Herter Brothers was arguably the premier decorating firm of the post–Civil War era. Among its projects were the White House in Washington during President Grant's tenure; the Darius Ogden Mills mansion, on the spot now occupied by the *Atlas* at Rockefeller Center; the Jay Gould residence on Fifth Avenue; the Ruggles S. Morse house in Portland, Maine; the Philip D. Armour mansion in Chicago, and the interiors for J. P. Morgan and Benjamin Altman. The company also did major work at the St. Regis and the Bellevue Stratford hotels, at Delmonico's restaurant, and at the Minnesota state capitol.

was edged by a cornice, in good palazzo form as opposed to the French mansard termination employed in earlier New York City mansions. Bold stringcourses identified the three main floors, although there were actually five stories. The exterior was enriched by an exceptional amount of decorative carving, in the capitals of the broad pilasters and in panels on the third floor.

The house was originally to have been faced with white marble, which would have given it an entirely different appearance. However, William Henry, in advancing years and increasingly aware of his own mortality, was anxious to get into his magnificent new mansion, and realizing it would take considerably longer to get marble quarried and shipped to the site, at the last moment he instructed his contractor to switch to brownstone which could be obtained from nearby quarries in Connecticut and New Jersey.[8] Also, William Henry was undoubtedly aware that his enormous palazzo was going to be very different from anything else in New York City, and use of brownstone instead of marble would have given it some connection with both architectural and sociocultural traditions.

Over six hundred men worked day and night to complete the mansion in a year and a half. Reportedly, sixty sculptors and other artisans were brought over from Europe to create the architectural decorations, both exterior and interior. Although the family moved into the house in January of 1881, it took two additional years to complete all the details of ornamentation and acquire all of the luxurious furnishings. A house-warming reception was given in early March of 1882, with two thousand persons invited, to allow friends and reporters to inspect the splendid new mansion.[9]

The Interiors

One entered the house through an opulent vestibule, which served as a common foyer for both William Henry's portion and the sections provided for the two daughters. The walls were decorated with mosaics and the ceiling had a large skylight of stained glass. The first object encountered was a colossal, nine-foot-high vase made of brilliant green malachite with applied, gilded allegorical figures representing Fame (figure 50). It had been bought at auction by one of William Henry's agents at the sale of the effects of Prince Paul Demidoff, held at San Donato Palace in Florence, Italy, in 1880.[10] Earl Shinn, in his book on the Vanderbilt mansion, reported that the vase "was one of a pair made in 1819, and the other stands in the palace of the Czar in Russia."[11] The magnificent urns were made in Paris by Pierre-Philippe Thomire, and Czar Nicholas of Russia gave one to Count Demidoff.

To the left of the colossal malachite vase was the entrance to William Henry and Louisa's part of the house. The valves of the great doorway were reduced copies of Lorenzo Ghiberti's *Gates of Paradise* at the Florentine Baptistry. The collector

and art historian James Jackson Jarves commented on them soon after they were acquired, noting that they were about half the size of the originals and were made by the Barbedienne foundry in Paris: "They were exhibited at the London Universal Exhibition of 1851, where they were purchased for one hundred francs, and placed by Prince Demidoff in his palace of San Donato, near Florence, forming the entrance to his chapel. . . . At the great sale of his collection last year they were purchased on an American account, and sent to New York."[12]

William Henry, who paid $25,000 for them, thought he was buying solid bronze doors, but as it turned out they were made of "thin metal screwed to a common wooden frame."[13] The critic Clarence Cook declared that they had "a mean appearance," called them "an absurdity," and referred to their installation as a "most tasteless precedent."[14] But then, Cook was usually sharply critical of anything any Vanderbilt built.

Herter Brothers and the Aesthetic Movement

The interiors were such as had never before been seen in America, owing to the extraordinary artistry of Herter Brothers, which meant mainly Christian Herter, for by then Gustave, the older brother, had long since retired. As noted earlier, Gustave Herter (1830–98) and his half brother Christian (1840–83), sons of a skilled German cabinetmaker, were born in Stuttgart. Gustave gained valuable woodworking experience at the royal palace at Berg, but in 1848 he emigrated to the United States. He worked briefly for Tiffany, Young and Ellis, the forerunner of Tiffany and Company, but by 1851 he was on his own as a high-style cabinetmaker; several of his elaborate pieces, in the Gothic and Renaissance Revival styles, were singled out for special mention when they were shown at the Crystal Palace Exhibition in New York in 1853–54.

In 1860 Christian also emigrated, but he came to America after he had studied art at Stuttgart and at the École des Beaux-Arts in Paris; he returned to Paris for two years, 1867–69, to represent his brother's firm there and to study with Pierre-Victor Galland, a decorative painter whose work we have seen at LeGrand Lockwood's Elm Park in Norwalk, Connecticut (figure 25, p. 61). When he returned to the United States he bought out his brother, for Gustave wished to return to Germany. Christian then became the managing and artistic director of the firm of Herter Brothers, a position he held until his death.

Several matters greatly affected the aesthetic directions taken by Christian Herter: First was his knowledge of Japanese art gained from his several years in Paris, where the art of that country was immensely popular in the 1860s; that interest was reinforced by the Japanese exhibition seen at the Philadelphia Centennial. Second, there was the art-furniture theory of Sir Charles Eastlake, whose book *Hints on Household Taste in Furniture, Upholstery, and Other Details* was first published in London in 1868, with the first American edition appearing in 1872.[15] Also, Herter Brothers came along just as the Aesthetic Movement began to assert itself, with its emphasis on finely crafted, individually made objects of beautiful, rare, and exotic materials.

An example of the Eastlake Renaissance Revival style as interpreted by Herter Brothers' designers and craftsmen is the elaborate cabinet, made about 1873 (figure 51). The piece only loosely qualifies as being in the Renaissance mode, although it possesses classical components such as Ionic pilasters. In its richness of carving and variety of types and colors of woods, its exquisite marquetry and use of painted tiles, and its touches of gilding and its brasses, it is typical of Herter's work of the mid- and late-1870s. The plaques were probably imported from France or Germany, and the brasses are most likely French, but one of the firm's artisans carved the boldly three-dimensional beast heads on the end compartments and the classical bust in the center, while another specialist executed the intricate marquetry.

The total commitment to refined quality is evident in another cabinet produced by Herter Brothers around 1880, or about the time the decorators were working on William Henry's interiors (figure 52). The Japanese influence is seen in the simplification of the form and the litheness of the case piece itself, in the decorative panels of marquetry, and in the round, lacquer-work plaques that are painted with flowers and butterflies on a gilded background. The piece was, moreover, designed as a display vehicle, for its three top surfaces and the two lateral niches were meant to hold exotic bibelots such as fine Japanese porcelain, Persian ornaments,

Figure 50. Pierre-Philippe Thomire, malachite vase, 1819, from entrance foyer, William Henry Vanderbilt residence, New York City. Malachite with ormolu ornament, height (vase alone) 67½ in. (171.5 cm). Metropolitan Museum of Art, purchase, Admiral F. R. Harris gift, 1944 (44.152a,b). Ex coll., Count Demidoff, Florence, Italy, and William Henry Vanderbilt, New York City. Vanderbilt acquired this extraordinary piece from the great sale of the Demidoff collection, which was held in Paris in 1880. The Demidoffs, like the Vanderbilts, were wealthy industrialists who set out to vie with aristocracy. Anatole Demidoff lived in princely splendor at his estate, San Donato, outside of Florence. The *Times* of London, on 26 March 1880, reported, "The great fortunes of the family were chiefly due to the energy of Prince Anatole's father, in working his malachite and other mines in Siberia, and the money derived from this source he (the father) invested in works of art, of which he was passionately fond. . . . [Anatole] is said to have given the Pope $200,000 for his title of Prince of San Donato."

decorated folding fans, Moroccan water bottles, and the like—all of which would have been a perfect demonstration of the Aesthetic Movement assemblage, a kind of shrine to pure aesthetic sensibilities.

Herter Brothers excelled in the creation of the Aesthetic Movement room—one filled with *objets d'art*, often gathered from around the world, representing many different periods and cultures (a Moorish piece next to a European Rococo one, Japanese alongside contemporary American Arts and Crafts, and so on). Exquisite, beautifully crafted objects with lustrous surfaces and exotic patterns filled every space in such a room and bedazzled the eyes with color and texture. No piece was admitted unless it was of the highest aesthetic appeal, but the more there were, and the more variety in terms of style, culture, or period, the better for the total impact. A critic writing for *Harper's Monthly* in 1882 described the mix and clutter of an Aesthetic Movement room:

> The result was chaos. Witty callers declared that upon entering a fashionable house they found a bric-a-brac shop; they stumbled on a Smyrna rug, and broke their necks over the Dying Gladiator. It was not a parlor, but a china shop, in which the "curled and perfumed Assyrian bull" of modern fashion overturned the table and smashed the Dresden darlings. . . . A calico cow from Liverpool elbowed early

Figure 51. Herter Brothers, cabinet, ca. 1872–73. Rosewood, maple, satinwood, brass, stone, gilding, and paint. Los Angeles County Museum of Art, purchased with funds from the Michael J. Connell Foundation (M.85.27).

American, and Hispano-mooresque stood cheek by jowl with Capo di Monte. It was a jumble.[16]

The Aesthetic Movement room was an eclectic hodgepodge, in contrast to the so-called period room or culture room which was dominated by the style of one single era or culture, such as Louis XV, Queen Anne, American Federal, Japanese, or Moorish.

Herter Brothers enjoyed a clientele that reached from coast to coast. In New York they provided the interior decor and furnishings for the Collis P. Huntington and Pierre Lorillard residences; in Chicago, they received the commissions for the decoration of the Potter Palmer mansion and for H. H. Richardson's Glessner house. In California, two examples of their work were the Mark Hopkins mansion in San Francisco and the Darius Ogden Mills residence in Millbrae. Sometimes they were called on to "modernize" the interiors of existing houses, which they did for J. Pierpont Morgan's house on Madison Avenue in New York City.

Christian Herter acted as general contractor of aesthetics for the William Henry Vanderbilt mansion. In that capacity he procured choice pieces from around the world and arranged for American or Parisian decorators and craftsmen to create whole rooms or a chandelier or a stained-glass window or an exquisite bathtub, a doorknob, or whatever.

Figure 52. Herter Brothers, cabinet, 1878–80. Rosewood, ebonized cherry, maple, walnut, satinwood, brass, gilding, and paint. The Art Institute of Chicago, gift of the Antiquarian Society through the Capital Campaign (1986.26).

The Drawing Room

The drawing room overlooked Fifth Avenue and measured thirty-one by twenty-five feet. Its coved ceiling had a mural painted by Pierre-Victor Galland, the French decorative artist who had been Christian Herter's teacher in Paris; Herter had arranged the commission (figure 53). The scene in the Vanderbilt drawing room represented a festive procession of knights, ladies, and their peasant entourage bringing in the first grapes of the harvest. Some years later Edith Wharton and Ogden Codman, in their book *The Decoration of Houses* (1897), included a passage which reveals that Herter and Vanderbilt were re-creating in the drawing room of a Fifth Avenue mansion what they had seen in ancient Old World palaces; the authors noted that in

> many old Italian prints and pictures there are representations of these saloons, with groups of gaily dressed people looking down from the gallery. . . . In Italy the architectural decoration of large rooms was often entirely painted, the plaster walls being covered with a fanciful piling-up of statues, porticoes and balustrades, while figures in Oriental costume, or in the masks and parti-colored dress of the *Comedie Italienne*, leaned from simulated loggias or wandered through marble columns.[17]

The walls of the room were of red velvet with applied mother-of-pearl butterflies, which glistened in the gaslights of the chandelier. One awestruck visitor reported that "when the lights are burning, its splendor is akin to the gorgeous dreams of oriental fancy; and yet with all this dazzling opulence there is no hint of tawdriness . . . , and the profuse decorations are harmonized with consummate taste."[18] The author of *Artistic Houses* was similarly overwhelmed, writing that "everything sparkles and flashes with gold and color—mother-of-pearl, with marbles, with jewel-effects in glass . . . , every surface . . . weighted, with ornament: The walls with carnation-red velvet . . . [and] gilt applique work . . . [of] trees whose flowers are made of jewels, and from whose branches hang festoons of gold-thread."[19]

As beautiful as all of this was considered to be, it exemplified, of course, the very archetypal superabundance of ornamentation against which later generations of modernists and minimalists rebelled. But William Henry was so proud of the house he had built and the rooms he had furnished that he paid for the publication of four large volumes on the mansion with the text written by Earl Shinn (using the pseudonym Edward Strahan) and numerous large illustrations, plus several colored plates, which document the brilliant coloration of the rooms.[20]

For William Henry's interiors Herter Brothers' shops in New York City produced numerous pieces of exquisite furniture. A side chair that is now in the High Museum of Art in Atlanta is known to have been made for the grand house (figure 54). Its maple frame is gilded throughout, with inlaid mother-of-pearl and with gilded entwined serpents in the cross-splat; originally, the chair possessed a red fabric bearing Oriental motifs. It bears out the aesthetic philosophy of the decoration of the mansion, that every piece must be a work of art in itself, and the total ensemble should flood the eyes with exquisite surfaces, rich coloration, varied textures, beautiful craftsmanship, and elegant design. No one piece was to be "spotlighted" in this orgy of aestheticism.

Figure 53. Herter Brothers, corner of the drawing room, William Henry Vanderbilt residence, New York City, ca. 1883. Color plate from Edward Strahan's [Earl Shinn's] *Mr. Vanderbilt's House and Collection* (Boston: G. Barrie, 1883–84, vol. 1). Hirsch Library, The Museum of Fine Arts, Houston, Texas, gift of Sue Rowan Pittman.

Figure 54. Herter Brothers, side chair, made for drawing room of the William Henry Vanderbilt residence, New York City, 1881–82. Gilded maple, mother-of-pearl, and fabric, height 34 in. (87.6 cm). High Museum of Art, Atlanta, Ga., Virginia Carroll Crawford Collection (1982.316).

The Library and Dining Room

In the library too—located just north of the drawing room—every item contributed to the richness of decor, whether built-in bookcases, furniture such as the library table, walls that were hung with blue-green plush on a gold ground, or the innumerable bibelots (figure 55). Mother-of-pearl ornamentation was skillfully worked into the surfaces of the cornice, pilasters, and bookcases; such inlay was one of the hallmarks of truly fine furniture and architectural decoration of that era, being symbolic of both the wealth of the owner and the skill of the craftsman. George Sheldon, writing about William Henry's mansion, exclaimed, "Especially affluent and striking is the use of mother-of-pearl; very rarely, if ever, in the history of house decoration has this material been used so generously."[21] The pattern of the wallpaper in the library was repeated in the fabric of two of the upholstered, tasseled chairs.

The library table was designed by Charles Goutzwiller (1810–1900) and created in 1881 by artisans employed by Herter Brothers (figure 56). Into the polished rosewood surfaces of its end supports have been worked, in mother-of-pearl inlay, global designs showing North and South America on one end and Europe, Africa, Asia, and Australia on the other. The excellent craftsmanship was the result of a collaborative effort of several artisans, including a very skilled carver.

The various *objets d'art* seen throughout the room were chosen by William Henry and Louisa themselves, for this was not a case of wealthy patrons instructing their agents to surround them with cultural objects. William Henry and his wife exercised the power of veto over all objects before they were admitted to the house permanently. These objects often had interesting histories, as with the folding fan (seen on the bookcase at the left in figure 55) reportedly owned by Marie Antoinette, signaling a fascination with items that had once belonged to royalty. The fan leans against one of William Henry's most famous paintings, Jean Léon Gérôme's *Reception of the Duc de Conde at Versailles* (1878), the subject of which also alludes to the delight the Gilded Age took in the pomp and grandeur of the great Bourbon courts. Gérôme, one of the most celebrated French salon painters of his day, was famous for his visions of historical spectacles, whether set in the days of Julius Caesar or in one of the palaces of King Louis XIV.

Figure 55. Herter Brothers, library, William Henry Vanderbilt residence, New York City, ca. 1882. From Sheldon, *Artistic Houses* (plate 16). Morris Library, University of Delaware. This room is an archetypal example of the Aesthetic Movement room, the theory behind which is that if a single object is of high aesthetic merit, then a whole room full of such things would provide an even richer experience. From the exotic fabrics of the portieres at the doorways to the mother-of-pearl inlay of the library table (figure 56) to the richly patterned wallpaper to a painting by Gérôme, of the Duc de Condé being received by Louis XIV, above the Oriental fan and the Turkish water bottle—every object must be exquisite and a thing of beauty: in brief, the room is saturated with beauty.

The dining room, which was about forty-five feet long by thirty feet wide, overlooked 51st Street (figure 57). The ceiling was spectacular, for it was ribbed and between the ribs were "panels in low-relief representing flowers and fruits . . . glazed in transparent colors over a gold ground."[22] Sheldon, the author of *Artistic Houses*, reported that the ceiling painting—executed in Paris by E. V. Luminais, the central canvas measuring about twenty feet long—displayed a hunting scene set "in the olden days of France—a knight on horseback accompanying a lady, whose milk-white steed is led by a page, while a falconer near by has just let loose his bird—the whole briskly executed. . . . Two other hunting-scenes, by the same artist, fill the spaces formed at either end of the room by the arching of the ceiling." The same source reported that the walls were covered with wood panels, "generously carved with delicate Renaissance ornament—figures of little children, garlands of flowers and fruit, and horns of plenty." The dark-stained, carved English oak chairs were covered with stamped red leather, "relieved with gold in Cordova fashion" (figure 58). The built-in buffet, seen at the right in figure 57, was a collaborative creation of Herter's craftsmen.

Herter Brothers undertook the creation of almost any type of household furnishing for an impressive array of prominent,

Figure 56. Herter Brothers, library table, 1881–82, made for the William Henry Vanderbilt residence, New York City. Metropolitan Museum of Art Purchase, Mrs. Russell Sage Gift, 1972 (1972.47). While the ends of this table have mother-of-pearl designs representing two hemispheres of the world, the top has a celestial display, with the stars arrayed as they were on 8 May 1821—the date of William Henry Vanderbilt's birth. The carving includes lion's paws and palmettes and echoes the carving found in the paneling of the room.

wealthy clients. For example, a fire screen of about 1880 has a central panel of beautifully embroidered silk surrounded by an ornate gilded wood frame; it is believed to have been made for the Mark Hopkins mansion in San Francisco (figure 59). Specialists—usually women—did embroidery of this type, which truly reflects the Aesthetic Movement rather than the simple homey skills of sewing, for the piece here represents not only an extraordinary artistry but also a knowledge of that new element in Western aesthetics, Japonisme. A similar influence is found in a small cabinet, with its gracefully curved legs reminiscent of the hilts of Japanese samurai swords (figure 60). The central panel, one of the high points of furniture making in the period around 1880, displays a wonderful design of butterflies, cranes, and snakes. Without copying anything Japanese specifically, and working with furniture forms unknown to Japanese art, the Herter artisans demonstrated their comprehension of the aesthetics of patterning, design, and color in Japanese art.

Figure 57. Herter Brothers, dining room, William Henry Vanderbilt residence, New York City. From Sheldon, *Artistic Houses* (plate 15). Morris Library, University of Delaware. It should be noted that in the publication *Artistic Houses*—which is such a rich source of visual images of the interiors of the early Gilded Age—a number of illustrations were printed backward. It was simply an error, but one that accounts for the discrepancies found in pictures such as this one and other photographic views of the same room. The dining room chairs seen here may be studied in detail in figure 58.

Figure 58. Herter Brothers, side chair, made for the William Henry Vanderbilt residence, New York City, 1881–82. Oak, brass, and leather. Metropolitan Museum of Art Purchase, Margery Masinter, Shiela Wood Schwartz, Gloria Wells Sidnam, Julie Graham, Diana Landreth and Steven M. Kossak Gifts and Friends of the American Wing, 1994 (1994.80).

The Japanese Room

South of the drawing room was a Japanese room, which proclaimed to visitors that William Henry was *au courant* in his knowledge of and taste for the art of Japan, the country whose culture had burst on the European and American scenes only recently, following the expedition there of Commodore Matthew Perry in 1854 (figure 61). Herter Brothers "farmed out" this room to John La Farge, who had, in 1880, formed the La Farge Decorative Art Company, and this was one of his first commissions. Although La Farge himself had not yet been to the Orient—he did not make his journey to Japan until 1886—he was well aware of that new influence on Western art. A few traveling Americans had discovered Japanese art at the expositions in London in 1862 and especially in Paris in 1867, but for most, acquaintance with it dated from the Philadelphia Centennial of 1876, only three

Figure 59 (top left). Herter Brothers, fire screen, 1878–80. Height 53 in. (134.6 cm). Gilded cherry and embroidered silk. Cleveland Museum of Art.

Figure 60 (top right). Herter Brothers, cabinet, ca. 1880. Marquetry and gilding, ebonized cherry, maple, and satinwood. High Art Museum, Atlanta, Ga.

Figure 61 (opposite). Herter Brothers, Japanese room, William Henry Vanderbilt residence, New York City, 1879–81. From Sheldon, *Artistic Houses* (plate 19). Morris Library, University of Delaware. In 1880 the art and culture of Japan was still relatively new to Americans but very much in vogue. Commodore Matthew Perry's "opening up" of Japan to trade and cultural exchange in 1854 had piqued the Western world's interest. Christian Herter was among the earliest of decorators to take inspiration from the arts of Japan, probably because of his exposure to it in Paris in 1867. Few rooms decorated in the Japanese mode could approach the one that Herter Brothers helped William Henry Vanderbilt assemble in his new house on Fifth Avenue.

years before William Henry began his mansion. By 1876, as Marilynn Johnson has noted, artists were "already aware of the reforming influence of English design, the ordered simplicity of Japanese art, and the exotic drama of Moorish decorative objects, [but] for most Americans the displays at the Philadelphia Centennial were a first glimpse of foreign cultures."[23] William Henry's Japanese parlor must have been striking with its red lacquer beams set against a simulated bamboo frieze and ceiling, its walls hung with gold brocade, and the many lacquered cabinets, which displayed rare and beautiful Japanese objects.

The Stairway and the Bedrooms

The grand stairway to the upper floors made its way around an atrium that was open from the first floor to the top of the fourth, a light well that illuminated the inner parts of the house. Sheldon estimated this atrium to be about sixty feet long by forty feet wide, its central section "surrounded by galleries on each story, which are supported by superb colonnades of red Numidian marble, with bronze caps and bases." He then noted that the stairway contained a "superb newel [with] a life-size bronze figure of a girl, whose left arm encircles a massive urn . . . , her bracelets, belt, and head-dress being of *cloisonne* enamel sparkling with jewels, while out of the urn grows a lantern of intricate bronze work."[24]

At the main landings of the stairway were stained-glass windows designed by La Farge. On the first landing they depicted the fruits of commerce, an allegory showing ships and railroads upon which the Vanderbilt fortune had been founded. At the second-floor landing the windows represented hospitality and prosperity (figure 62).

In the custom of the times, the master and mistress of the house had separate bedrooms. The singular most important feature about Mrs. Vanderbilt's bedroom was that its architectural components had been fabricated entirely in Paris, by the internationally known decorating firm of Jules Allard et Fils, of which more will be said in subsequent chapters. For the ceiling of Louisa's room her husband had bought a large painting by Jules Lefebvre, representing the nude figure of Aurora "seated in a chariot, drawn through the air by two young women of pleasing mien and manner."[25]

The Art Gallery

On the first floor, one entered the huge art gallery (thirty-two by forty-eight feet) through broad archways (figures 63 and 64). The space was divided into a larger room and a smaller one, and the walls were covered with a dull red fabric and had mahogany architectural trim. Above, the skylight was composed of opalescent and tinted glass. By night, 169 gas jets blazed away for illumination.[26]

going into business here [Paris]!—it does seem as if our people are willing to do extravagant things at any one's bidding here while at home [in the United States] you cannot persuade the same person to do a reasonable thing."[29]

Besides Avery, Vanderbilt sometimes got advice from James Jackson Jarves, Earl Shinn, and an American dealer in Paris, George Lucas, but regarding acquisitions he always made the final decision; although he never considered himself a connoisseur, he knew what he liked and there was cohesion to the collection he formed. His preferences ran to anecdotal genre subjects, military scenes, and exotic (often Near Eastern or North African) themes—that is, his taste for French academic Salon art was exactly that of the French upper-middle class of the 1860s and early 1870s.

Jean-Louis-Ernest Meissonier (1815–91), who painted William Henry's portrait in Paris, was Vanderbilt's favorite painter. Henry James once reviewed Meissonier's *Friedland, 1807* (figure 39, p. 73), and his words offer insight into the appeal that the artist's work held for William Henry. "M. Meissonier is the great archaeologist of the Napoleonic era," James wrote, ". . . he understands to a buttonhole the uniform of the Grand Army." James further noted that Meissonier's pictures did not work as a totality, but were admirable in their detail: "The best thing [in the *Friedland*] is a certain cuirassier, and in the cuirassier the best thing is his clothes, and in his clothes the best thing is his leather straps, and in his leather straps the best thing is the buckles."[30] William Henry owned seven paintings by Meissonier.

At the earlier Manhattan house, at 40th and Fifth, paintings were hung about several rooms and among the other furnishings, as seen in Seymour Guy's painting of the family (figure 48, p. 87). That is, no room was designated specifically as an art gallery. The Vanderbilts' collecting habits started out modestly enough; Louisa Kissam recalled the circumstances of the first picture they bought: "We paid ninety dollars for it, and we were afraid to let our friends know how extravagant we had been. I have the picture yet, and there is more pleasure to me in looking at it than all the Meissoniers and other great pictures in the house."[27]

The early collection was small and mostly of paintings by American artists. According to the art dealer Samuel P. Avery, after the Commodore's death William Henry ceased to acquire American paintings and, with his new fortune and Avery's council, began "to buy the best and most costly in the world. He decided, at the outset, to procure nothing that was not important."[28] As early as 1872 Avery had written to John Taylor Johnston about the outrageous prices Vanderbilt was paying for paintings in Paris: "I have serious thoughts of

Among the treasures of the art gallery were three Salon pictures by Jean Léon Gérôme: *Louis XIV and the Grand Conde*, *The Sword Dance*, and *A Bashi-Bazouk*. Lawrence Alma-Tadema was represented by four oil paintings and two watercolors, typically depicting re-creations of the great days of the Roman Empire. Jules Breton, Thomas Couture and William Bouguer eau had two pictures each on the gallery walls, hanging near Leon Bonnat's *An Arab Plucking a Thorn from his Foot* and

Figure 62. John La Farge, *Hospitalitas* and *Prosperitas*, 1881. Stained-glass windows made for stairway of William Henry Vanderbilt residence, New York City. Now at Biltmore Estate, Asheville, N.C.

Figure 63 (opposite, left). Art gallery, William Henry Vanderbilt residence, ca. 1881. From Sheldon, *Artistic Houses* (plate 17). Morris Library, University of Delaware. William Henry's collection of paintings was archetypal of the 1870s and early 1880s, consisting mainly of Salon pieces depicting quaint genre scenes, military events, Arabs on horseback, or farmyard animals.

Figure 64 (opposite, right). Art gallery, William Henry Vanderbilt residence, ca. 1881. From Sheldon, *Artistic Houses* (plate 18). Morris Library, University of Delaware. Although William Henry was very much involved in the creation of his collection, he was assisted by men who were pioneers—

Eugene Fromentin's *Arabs Watering Horses*. The fascination with colorful North African subjects was also found in Alexandre-Gabriel Decamps's *A Bashi-Bazouk* and Mariano Fortuny's *Arab Fantasia at Tangiers*.

The Belgian artist Alfred Stevens was represented by his *Ready for the Fancy Dress Ball*, while the German painter Ludwig Knaus had four pictures there, including one titled *A German Village Fete*; the genre theme was similarly found in Jules Lefebvre's *Attending the Bride* and Edouard Frere's *The Young Washerwoman*. There were four oils by Rosa Bonheur, among them *Ready for the Hunt* and *A Flock of Sheep*, while Charles Jacque's *Sheep Stable* and Sir Edward Landseer's large *After the Chase* were indicative of the collector's love of animal pieces.

Among the pictures from the Barbizon school were six works by Jean-François Millet, four landscapes by Constant Troyon and two by Jean-Baptiste-Camille Corot, six pictures by Narcisse Diaz, and seven landscapes and genre scenes by Théodore Rousseau. Gustave Doré and Eugène Delacroix each had one painting in the collection. J. M. W. Turner's large oil *The Fountain of Indolence* was joined by three of his watercolors. Among the many other artists whose works were found on the gallery walls were Boldini, Cabanel, Ziem, Merle, Zamacois, Detaille, Isabey, Madrazo, Schreyer, and Vibert.

William Henry made frequent trips to Europe, where he enjoyed an acquaintance with the leading painters of the day. He was often accompanied by Avery, who had entree into even the most exclusive studios of the most arrogant of painters. Towner, in his book *The Elegant Auctioneers*, gives a nice word-picture of these visits:

> Many of Vanderbilt's pictures were custom painted. . . . On his estate at Bougival, Jean Léon Gérôme would receive suppliant millionaires from America with a graciousness that ebbed and flowed according to his foreknowledge of their bank accounts. . . . After he had . . . shown the bronze and silver trophies of his valorous painting campaigns, he would outline a picture at so many francs per personage, so much for the entourage, so much for each plume in the king's resplendent hat. . . . Meissonier was even more demanding, for by choice he would have painted no one but Napoleon. . . . [But] when William H. Vanderbilt . . . laid $40,000 on the table, Meissonier graciously contracted to reproduce a dazzling throng of society folk from the court of Louis XIII. . . . Cabanal was perhaps the most imperious of them all. . . . When Vanderbilt called on him in his sumptuous studio . . . the ultra-stylish artist received the applicant with a cold smile and a courtly manner, as if he himself might have been the ambassador

for the American market, at least—in the then-emerging profession of art dealer. Foremost among them were George Lucas, an American residing in France, and Samuel P. Avery. The latter's diaries are filled with notations about when he and William Henry were touring the galleries of London and Paris together, as in May of 1878, or about the time the great house on Fifth Avenue was being finished; "With Vanderbilt," Avery wrote, "to Agnews, Wallis, Tooths, McLeans, Marsden, Pilgeram. . . . bought for V. of Pilgeram 1 [painting by] Tadema [and a] Frere for 1500 £. From Wallis [a] Madrazo 600 £." Another time Avery wrote, "Went with V . . . to see new Rosa Bonheur at Pilgeram's" and on another occasion they visited artists' studios: "With Vanderbilt to Meissonier, Cabanel . . . Detaille, gave order to Detaille on [the account of] Mr. V." On May 14 Avery recorded "to Exposition with Mr. V. . . . & Lucas. visited picture galleries of Germany, France, Belgium, Spain, U. States, etc. met Madrazo, Rico, Gérôme, Knight." In late July Avery wrote, "To see Rosa Bonheur's picture for Mr. Vanderbilt. . . . to Detaille, saw Mr. Vanderbilt's picture commenced. . . . bought Millet of Petit for Vanderbilt for 15,000 *f*." A final example dates from the spring of 1880: "to Cabanel and Meissonier who agreed to paint Mr. Vanderbilt's portrait for about 20,000 [*f*]." Quotations from Beaufort et al., *Diaries 1871–1882 of Samuel P. Avery, Art Dealer* (pp. 456–58, 493, and 561).

from the monied world. . . . At the moment he was engaged . . . , but he would enter Vanderbilt's name on the waiting list.[31]

William Henry found pleasure in sharing the collection with others. He enjoyed strolling with friends among the 207 oils and watercolors, going from painting to painting, musing over their anecdotal content, admiring their details and their craftsmanship. For a while, with cards of invitation, the public was admitted to the gallery through a special door on 51st Street, between 11:00 A.M. and 4:00 P.M. on Thursdays, but because the public behaved so badly, this practice was stopped after a couple of years.

On 20 December 1883 William Henry invited three thousand people, mostly from the world of business but a few from art circles, to a reception to tour his gallery. Such events took on increasing social importance. As one contemporary noted, Society ladies vied to outshine one another; at the reception, for example, Alva, one of William Henry's daughters-in-law, appeared loaded with jewels, but she was outdone by Mrs. Chauncey Depew, "who wore a petticoat of red satin caught up with real birds of red and black plumage."[32]

Opening one's private art gallery to the public was not new, for other collectors in New York had already done so by then—for example, John Taylor Johnston, as noted earlier, but his collection was disbursed at auction in 1876. There was A. T. Stewart's extensive gallery, but he died in 1876, and the collection became unavailable to visitors until it was placed on the auction block in 1887. August Belmont also had a large collection, as did William Aspinwall and William Blodgett, and those gentlemen, in the spirit of civic duty, occasionally opened their doors to the public.

An interesting comment is found in William Croffut's account of the Vanderbilt family, published in 1886, the year after William Henry's death. It reads,

> Mr. Vanderbilt wished and meant to associate his name with some great gift to the City of New York . . . and this generous ambition at last, two or three years before his death, took the form of a public Museum, like the British Museum, to be . . . of incalculable value as an educator of youth. He decided to build such a museum of magnificent dimensions on the block opposite to his house on Fifth Avenue, and to endow it with $5,000,000. This would be a far greater endowment than that possessed by any other museum in the world, and it might be expected in a few years to excel all others in the extent and value of its collections. The delay in realizing this superb vision, and finally its failure through [his] death, resulted from the impossibility of obtaining the land.[33]

This suggests that William Henry was thinking of doing something similar to what William W. Corcoran had done in Washington, D.C., and what W. W. Walters was doing in Baltimore. Although his vision was not realized, William Henry did leave $100,000 to the Metropolitan Museum of Art, which in 1885 was still struggling to establish itself.

Gustavus Myers, the critic of great wealth, sneeringly opined in 1911 that in William Henry's case "neither knowledge nor appreciation [of art] were required; with the expenditure of a few hundred thousand dollars he instantly transformed himself from a heavy witted, uncultured money hoarder into a . . . surpassing 'judge and patron of art.' "[34] Indeed, as the authors of *The Opulent Interiors of the Gilded Age* have noted, "Art historians and critics have been hard on Vanderbilt, depicting him as an aesthetic dunderhead who, with little knowledge and even less feeling, sent Samuel P. Avery to Europe with a fistful of dollars to assemble a collection simply because owning art had become fashionable. Avery denied this in print."[35] Avery's denial was emphatic: "In the account of Mr. Vanderbilt's collection of pictures in this morning's *Times* the writer gives me credit for what I am not entitled to, viz: that I 'selected' them for him. Mr. Vanderbilt's collection is not a rapid accumulation. He has been a picture buyer for over 20 years and does not need the services of any person to 'select' for him, willing as he may be to be advised by friends."[36]

A Critical Assessment of the Mansion

The Vanderbilts had hardly settled into their new mansion before the critics began to denounce it. In May of 1881, one wrote that the house "is the result of entrusting architectural design to decorators, [and] it is to be hoped that the experiment may not be repeated."[37] The next year Clarence Cook derisively referred to the mansion as "a gigantic kneehole table," while Mariana Van Rensselaer, in 1886, described the houses as "brown-stone packing boxes."[38] A decade after it was finished, Montgomery Schuyler penned the following assessment, in which gold leaf appears to be the aesthetic cure-all of the Gilded Age:

> These houses have another misfortune in their lugubrious color. A vivid piece of painted decoration in the recessed balcony of the nearer

[house] is a grateful oasis in the gloomy waste of rubbed sandstone, and some relief to its monotony is also afforded by the gilded railings of the windows at each side of this balcony. But it is to be hoped that courage may be found to let loose a discreet decorator with unlimited gold-leaf upon the whole sad front.[39]

Writing from a more distant historical perspective, Herbert Croly noted in 1903 that the mansion's design, scale, and cost "testify to the growing desire for ostentatious magnificence. . . . The design of the exterior, indeed, is very far from being either coherent or interesting; and the material selected, the old smooth brownstone, indicates a blind ignorance of the drift of American architectural advance."[40]

If critics treated the exterior harshly, they were overwhelmed by the interior, one writing that it was too much for the senses to cope with, that the eyes became wearied in the presence of so much luxury: "The gustatory sense is sometimes cloyed by overstating. One longs to find out if there is not one single room where there might be found some repose."[41] Barbara Weinberg gave a late-twentieth-century analysis in her study of John La Farge: "If the nation were developing 'a taste of its own,' and if that taste were demonstrated in the home of William H. Vanderbilt, it was a taste dependent for expression on extreme wealth. The possessors of that wealth seemed more intent upon identifying themselves with their historical counterparts in other nations than in expressing the spirit of the nation from which their wealth derived."[42]

If the exterior was not as refined as one might wish, it must be conceded that the mansion was an important, bold step in the evolution of mansion design during the Gilded Age. Moreover, the idea of abandoning oneself to pure delight in the enjoyment of one's fabulous wealth signals a new spirit in America and American architecture, and men such as A. T. Stewart and William Henry Vanderbilt were surely role models, in that respect, for many who came after them.

Epilogue for the William Henry Vanderbilt Mansion

William Henry Vanderbilt died on 8 December 1885, not quite five years after moving into his new mansion. Reportedly he was the richest man in America. His will stated that the house was to be Louisa's for her lifetime and then pass to their youngest son, George, who had a special interest in beautiful objects and books and who at that time had no other home in New York. In the fullness of time it did go to George, who by then had no use for it, being happier at his baronial estate, Biltmore, in North Carolina. But George was forbidden by the terms of the will to sell it, so for several years he rented it to a man from Pittsburgh named Henry Clay Frick while Frick's own mansion at 70th and Fifth Avenue was being built and readied for him.

George had little use for the art collection his father had assembled. In 1902 he placed it on extended loan at the Metropolitan Museum of Art, where it was popular with visitors, but in 1920 it was withdrawn and returned to the great brownstone palazzo on Fifth Avenue. The collection was finally sold at auction at Parke-Bernet's in New York City.[43] By then, few were interested in Gérôme's re-creations of Roman times or Meissonier's detailed representations of Napoleon's legions, for by the 1940s the modern art movement dominated the art scene, and modernists detested nothing with greater ardor than mid-nineteenth-century academic Salon paintings.

When George died in 1914 the mansion passed to a male heir in a parallel line of the family, to Cornelius III, son of George's oldest brother, Cornelius II, and grandson of William Henry. Cornelius III had scandalized the family and Society by marrying Grace Wilson. Grace undertook a large-scale renovation with the aid of architect Horace Trumbauer, transforming the interiors into "period rooms" of the time of Louis XV, which by then had become all the rage. But by 1927, as commercial establishments increasingly moved into Fifth Avenue, as taxes rose in conjunction with the commercial value of the property, the northern half of the mansion—the part originally inhabited by two of William Henry's daughters and their families—was torn down to make way for a department store. Just before his death in 1942, Cornelius III sold the remaining portion of the property—the southern half, William Henry and Louisa's side—to William Waldorf Astor, who wanted to develop the site. It was demolished in 1947. Two years earlier a great sale was held at the house, at which the gutting of the palazzo was begun. Paramount Pictures, the movie studio, purchased several of the rooms and had them transported to California, where they were reassembled as sets for scenes to be shot in libraries, hotel lobbies, boardrooms, and ballrooms.

There should be no other standard of social test than that of merit; not judging individuals by what they were, but by what they are today; not judging by the ridiculous test of ancestry . . . but by the real worth of the living man or woman. . . . The young Vanderbilts . . . rank high in society, and are splendid specimens of nature's noblemen. . . . In the United States nature's nobility is at the front, as against the parchment nobility of England and the Continent. The personnel of the English nobility makes a sorry showing beside that of young George Gould, the young Vanderbilts, and others of our wealthy Americans.

Henry Clews, *Twenty-eight Years in Wall Street* (1888)

Chapter Five

Alva and William Kissam Vanderbilt

A Petit Château on Fifth Avenue

The Vanderbilt Fortune in the Third Generation

William Henry Vanderbilt's four sons—Cornelius II, William Kissam, Frederick, and George Washington—and four daughters—Margaret (Mrs. Elliott Fitch Shepard), Emily (Mrs. William Douglas Sloane), Florence (Mrs. Hamilton Twombly), and Lila (Mrs. William Seward Webb)—were all active as builders of great houses. In addition to ones they commissioned for themselves along Fifth Avenue, they added homes outside the city. Florence and her husband created a Georgian mansion in Madison, New Jersey, which they called Florham (combining the first syllable from each of their names); the building is now a part of Fairleigh Dickinson University. Emily and William Sloane built Elm Court in Lenox, Massachusetts, a summer retreat area favored by the wealthy. Margaret Shepard built Woodlea in Scarborough, New York, as an escape from the city, while Lila and William Seward Webb went off to the green hills of Vermont to establish Shelburne Farms, which would eventually house the extraordinary collection of folk art and Americana formed by their son, James Watson Webb, and his wife, Electra, daughter of the sugar-refining king and art collector Henry O. Havemeyer.[1]

Cornelius II, owner of one of the greatest mansions on Fifth Avenue, built the foremost showplace in Newport—The Breakers. William Kissam built Marble House in Newport as a gift for his wife. Frederick and his wife, Louisa, chose a site on the Hudson River for their country residence, while George developed the great North Carolina estate known as Biltmore. But the Vanderbilt clan erected many mansions; a list of an additional twenty-five could easily be drawn up. Alva alone would, in time, account for seven; indeed, she instigated so many buildings in her lifetime that she was offered membership in the American Institute of Architects, an invitation she declined.

To build so many houses on such a grand scale took enormous wealth. Although William Henry bequeathed to his heirs approximately $200 million, he recalled only too well the hard feelings—the jealousy, the recriminations, the threat of lawsuits—that beset the family when his siblings had been virtually excluded from the largess of the Commodore's estate. So he provided a more equitable distribution while keeping a large enough chunk of the fortune in the hands of two of his sons to retain the prestige of the Vanderbilt fortune. In addition to the Fifth Avenue mansion, his wife, Maria Louisa, received $200,000 annually and a gift of $500,000. Cornelius II and William Kissam each received $50 million. The two daughters who lived in the northern half of William Henry's mansion were given the houses they lived in. Then the sum of $40 million was divided equally among the eight children, each thereby receiving an additional $5 million, and another $40 million was set aside in trust from which all eight sons and daughters would receive an income for the rest of their lives. When it was all settled, Cornelius II, having also received anything left in the estate, came away with close to $60 million and William Kissam with about $55 million, plus the annuity to each.

William Henry, by his will, established the relative "pecking order" of the family by naming Cornelius II as its leader and William Kissam as vice chairman, so to speak. It is important to note that William Henry died relatively young, at age sixty-four, and his children were also relatively young at that time—Cornelius II, the eldest, was only forty-two and George, the youngest, was a mere twenty-three. That meant that all of the children had many years left in their lives to build houses, as well as the energy with which to do it, and in several cases, the social motivation to do it grandly.

Alva and William Kissam

Of the third generation, Alva was the first to employ architecture to thrust her immediate family in particular and the Vanderbilts generally into the mainstream of New York Society. For Alva, the term "socially ambitious" does her an injustice; perhaps "socially ferocious" would be more accurate. It was Alva, after all, who struck the first breach in the high, protective wall erected by Mrs. Caroline Astor and her major domo, Ward McAllister, to keep all upstarts at bay.

Prior to 1880 the Vanderbilts were not a part of Society. William Henry and Louisa found contentment and enjoyment in their own rather sizable family group, and they never pursued admittance into the charmed circle. Their offspring were held at a distance socially by Mrs. Astor, who saw them as social-climbing *arrivistes*. However, the Astor crowd was no match for Alva, not the lot of them. But

to give her her due, if Alva was at times willful and wrathful, she also had endearing qualities; Elizabeth Drexel Lehr, who knew her well, described her as "warm-hearted, impulsive, aggressive."[2]

Alva Erskine Smith was born in 1853, the daughter of a well-to-do cotton planter who had two plantations near Mobile, Alabama. After the family was ruined by the Civil War, her father tried to recover his fortune in Paris; there, Alva's eldest sister made her debut at one of the last grand balls given at the Tuileries by Emperor Napoleon III and Empress Eugénie. Her father being unsuccessful in Paris, the family moved to New York, where they opened a boardinghouse. Young Alva, however, began to wedge her way into Society through her friend Consuelo Yznaga, a Cuban heiress who was married to Lord Mandeville, heir of the Duke of Manchester.

Louis Auchincloss, in his book on the Vanderbilts, wrote of William Kissam's attraction to Alva, declaring: "There is something fascinating to world-weary second-generation heirs in a woman with the energy of their forebears, who knows just what she wants and just how to get it."[3] No doubt having lost wealth and social position as a result of the Civil War—Alva would have been twelve years old in 1865—she was determined to have it all once more and never again to lose it. She locked her sights on the handsomest of the Commodore's grandsons, William Kissam, and in 1875 they were married.

William Kissam Vanderbilt (1849–1920) was born on the farm at New Dorp, Staten Island, and was educated by a private tutor (figure 65). He was fifteen when his father was called to Manhattan by the Commodore to enter the management of his growing string of railroads. Shortly thereafter "Willy K.," as he was always known to the family, was sent off to Geneva, Switzerland, to attend private school; this period abroad established an enduring cosmopolitanism in his personality and an intimate acquaintance with European ways and culture. Upon his return to the United States he was assigned to a post at the Hudson River Railroad, where he proved to be a hard worker and skillful in the management of railroad affairs. By 1882, or about the time his Petit Château on Fifth Avenue was finished, he had risen to the office of president of the New York, Chicago and St. Louis Railroad. Following William Henry's death three years later, the advancement of the Vanderbilt family fortunes fell mainly on the shoulders of Willy K. and Cornelius II. When the latter became incapacitated in 1896, the mantel of family leadership was thrust on William, insofar as the Vanderbilt railroad interests were concerned. That was about the time he completed Marble House in Newport.

Whereas Cornelius II was sober and serious and seemed to like nothing better than the responsibilities of the family business, Willy K. was more carefree. He much preferred sailing on his yacht, the *Alva*, to far-off Constantinople or

Figure 65. William Kissam Vanderbilt, ca. 1885. Photograph. Brown Brothers.

India, and he would rather spend the day at the races than in the office, for he was an avid horseman. By 1903 he had resigned all his railroad offices, although he remained on the board of directors of the New York Central.

William Kissam's daughter, Consuelo, adored her father, and in her autobiography wrote of him and his relationship with her mother. "Generous and unselfish," she called her father, and said that his greatest "pleasure was to see people happy." She then continued: "But my mother—for reasons I can but ascribe to a towering ambition—opposed these carefree views with all the force of her strong personality. A born dictator, she dominated events about her as thoroughly as she dominated her husband and children."[4] If there was a happy, carefree side to Willy K., there was also a touch of melancholy in his life, as he revealed in the following comment:

> My life was never destined to be quite happy. . . . It has left me with nothing to hope for, with nothing definite to seek or strive for. Inherited wealth is a real handicap to happiness. It is as certain [a] death to ambition as cocaine to morality. If a man makes money, no matter how much, he finds a certain happiness in its possession. . . . But the man who inherits it has none of that. The first satisfaction, and the greatest, that of building the foundation of a fortune, is denied him. He must labor, if he does labor, simply to add to an over-sufficiency.[5]

The Petit Château

By 1878, William Kissam had already acquired a lot on the northwest corner of 52nd Street and Fifth (figure 66). It measured 100 feet on the Avenue by 125 feet deep. Richard Morris Hunt was the logical choice to design the mansion to be built on that lot for Willy K. and Alva, for he had, in 1876, been the architect of Idle Hour, their Oakdale, Long Island, retreat (now occupied by Dowling College).[6] The Fifth Avenue house, from the beginning, had to be special, a symbol of social primacy, of wealth, of power—it was, after all, to be the ram with which Alva was to attack the ramparts of Caroline Astor's social citadel. She immediately took charge of the project, and her friend Elizabeth Drexel Lehr later recalled that Alva told the architect he could choose any style he liked, as long as it was medieval: "She got her wish. Fortunately for her peace of mind she had never been to Bourges, so she did not know that she had a copy of the famous house of Jacques Coeur, the greatest upstart of the Middle Ages, the richest man of the fifteenth century." Lehr also informs us that when Hunt presented her with his designs, Alva exclaimed, " 'Oh, how lovely. Just what I want. A real Venetian palace like the Doges had. . . .' [Hunt] was too ironically courteous to contradict her."[7]

The result of Alva's directive was something quite new to New York City, or to any American city, for Hunt produced a design in the mode of a fifteenth-century French château; it was her mansion, more than any of its predecessors, that broke the pattern of urban architecture and issued in a whole new variety of Beaux-Arts interpretations of historic styles in radical juxtaposition to the endless rows of brownstones (figure 67).

The Petit Château, as it was called, was even significantly different from the colossal palace Willy K.'s father was erecting just across 52nd Street—different not only in its material (limestone as opposed to the traditional brownstone) but also in the excellence of its historic style–based Beaux-Arts design. After nearly thirty years of trial and error in mansion design, the Petit Château represents a maturity of concept and aesthetics that launched a new phase in the domestic architecture of America's millionaire society.

But one criticism surfaced early. Ernest Flagg, an eminent contemporary architect, observed that here was a château that was displaced and disoriented by being plunked down in an urban setting; that is, as a type, a château, like an English country house, was supposed to be surrounded by open spaces and acre upon acre of gardens, orchards, pastures, and so on. In Paris, Flagg noted caustically, "Rich men do not build country châteaux against the street lines of cities."[8] In reality, as Elizabeth Lehr noted, the inspiration for the Petit Château was not a château at all, but a large house in the medieval town of Bourges. Louis Auchincloss saw the association with the house of Jacques Coeur as entirely reasonable, writing, "Critics then and since have insisted that [the

Figure 66 (opposite). W. A. Rogers, *Fifth Avenue in the Afternoon: New York's Idea of a Pleasure Street*. From *Life* 20 (1 December 1892), pp. 318–19. Engraving showing the William Henry Vanderbilt and the William Kissam Vanderbilt residences at the left. New York Public Library.

Figure 67 . Richard Morris Hunt, Alva and William Kissam Vanderbilt residence (Petit Château), 660 Fifth Avenue and 52nd Street, New York City, 1881. Museum of the City of New York.

William Kissam Vanderbilt] edifice was more for kings than burghers and that it should have been surrounded by a vast park, but Alva and Hunt knew what they were doing. Jacques Coeur was a fourteenth-century [*sic*] Vanderbilt; he had put up his big house in the very center of his hometown."[9]

Flagg and other critics overlooked the fact that the house of Jacques Coeur was not the only house erected in France in the late fifteenth century. Hunt—who had lived for many years in France—undoubtedly knew many that were of the late Gothic style and were in every way "châteaux" for they were surrounded by the broad lands of country estates. Moreover, they were erected by the French aristocracy rather than by a rich merchant. A good example is found at the Château de Martainville of about 1485, which shares many features with the Vanderbilts' Petit Château (figure 68).[10] Be that as it may, to most critics at the end of the nineteenth century the Vanderbilt house was of a château type that should more appropriately be placed in the rolling countryside rather than in a compact urban setting.

Figure 68. Château de Martainville, ca. 1485, Martainville, France. Engraving.

Richard Morris Hunt

Richard Morris Hunt (1827–95) commenced designing the mansion in 1878 and construction was begun the next year. With the exception of some interior work, it was essentially finished in 1882. Hunt and his older brother, William Morris Hunt, were of an old New England family from around Brattleboro, Vermont, where Richard was born.[11] In 1843 his recently widowed mother took the family to Europe so William could study painting. Richard, while attending school in Geneva, determined to become an architect. In Paris, he was admitted into the atelier of Hector Martin Lefuel in 1845 and the next year became the first American to enter the school of architecture at the École des Beaux-Arts. When Lefuel was appointed architect of the New Louvre, he asked Hunt to assist him, and the young American, did so, working on the design for the Pavillon de Bibliothèque, gaining firsthand knowledge of the Second Empire style, which would sweep Paris and emanate to many parts of Europe and, through men such as Hunt, eventually to the United States. All the while, Hunt was touring Europe, studying various historic styles of architecture—from Rome to the Loire Valley, from Germany to London.

In 1855 Richard Morris Hunt returned to America and established his office in New York City. His most important project of this early period was the Tenth Street Studio Building (1857–58), done in conjunction with John Taylor Johnston and designed to provide studios for artists. Hunt himself had a studio there, where he housed his huge architectural library. Always concerned with the professionalism of his field, he was one of the founding members, in 1857, of the American Institute of Architects, with Richard Upjohn as president and himself as secretary.

Hunt married Catharine Howland, daughter of a prosperous and socially prominent shipping family, in 1861. Soon thereafter they purchased his mother's house at 49 West 35th

Street and moved into it. At that time that area was becoming a fashionable section of the city, for Caroline Astor had built her fine, new mansion less than two blocks away.

Although Hunt's office had plenty of work to do, he did not begin to design the buildings that made him historically famous until around 1870. In that year he began work on the Lenox Library (completed in 1877) on the site now occupied by the Henry Clay Frick mansion at 70th Street and Fifth Avenue. An exercise in Beaux-Arts design, the building had a noble monumentality about it, although it lacked the grace and elegance characteristic of Hunt's later work. Built of one type of stone throughout—a gray limestone—it differed from New York's brownstone buildings and from the brick-and-stone coloration of the High Victorian architecture of that era.

Hunt's domestic projects of that period include the Martin Brimmer houses (1870, Boston), in which he seems to have lost control of the Beaux-Arts style; the William Osborne and Jonathan Sturges houses (1870, 32 and 34 Park Avenue, New York City), which reveal his knowledge of the then popular Eastlake style; and the Marshall Field mansion (1873, Chicago), a less than inspiring display of the Parisian Second Empire mode. This brief survey testifies that Hunt was, so to speak, all over the map in the 1870s, successful, with plenty of commissions, but not yet having arrived at the sophisticated style, based on specific historic precedents, that characterizes his mature period. The turning point came when he received the commission for the Alva and William Kissam Vanderbilt mansion in 1878.

The Design

To satisfy the wishes of his clients (which is to say, Alva), Hunt employed a late-Gothic style—that is, a specific, identifiable historic style, redefined for modern use in the best Beaux-Arts tradition. Although William Kissam was never entirely out of the picture, Alva took charge from the very beginning. Hunt enjoyed working with her and found her intelligent regarding architectural matters.

The French character of the design reflected Alva's love of France. Consuelo, her daughter, wrote of this, saying that the family was never happier than during the two months of each year—May and June—that they spent in Paris. Consuelo reminisced that her playmates in the gardens of the Tuileries were Waldorf Astor (later Viscount Astor), May Goelet (who later married Marlborough's cousin, the Duke of Roxburghe), and Katherine Duer (later Mrs. Clarence Mackay).[12] Meanwhile, her mother was busy acquiring furnishings for the houses at New York, Newport, and elsewhere; "ransacking the antique shops of Europe," Consuelo wrote, "she returned with pictures and furniture to adorn the mansions it became her passion to build. She thus set the passion for period houses, which at that date were little known in this country."[13] Alva, in her turn, remembered fondly those happy years in Paris following the Civil War, when she was a girl, and her love of France had a direct influence on the design that Richard Morris Hunt produced for the Petit Château.

The mansion, in keeping with William Kissam's decree that there should be some "breathing room" incorporated into the design, was set back modestly from the perimeter of the lot. The exterior was of gray Indiana limestone, which became the new building material of fashionable New York, was monotone throughout, in contrast to the colorfulness of the High Victorian buildings then being erected. The roof was of blue-gray slate with copper trim. Reportedly the masonry firm of Ellin and Kitson employed some forty artisans to execute the architectural carving for the exterior and interiors, for there was a great amount of it.

There is a story, perhaps apocryphal, about a time when Hunt failed to provide the necessary designs for the architectural ornament; the carvers, becoming restless, began working on something on their own within a curtained enclosure on the building site. Whenever Hunt came around, he was diverted from entering the enclosure. Finally he insisted on being admitted, only to find that the artisans had carved a nearly life-size portrait of him with mallet and chisel, to go high atop a pinnacle of the Petit Château, a signature of his authorship of the design of the house, as was sometimes done in the Middle Ages. Hunt saw the humor in it and liked the piece so much that it became the image he used on his bookplate.[14]

The roofline was irregular, and both the street and avenue facades were asymmetrical, in keeping with the medieval, nonclassical spirit of the building. A picturesque little

tourelle paralleled the axis of the Fifth Avenue entrance, and a wealth of Gothic-style ornament added greatly to the beauty of the design (figure 69). In good Beaux-Arts fashion, Hunt was fastidious in his rendering of those details. However, to describe the mansion as no more than a pastiche of decorative details applied to a surface is to miss the real beauty of Hunt's creation. That is, this was a Beaux-Arts exercise in the late-Gothic mode, not a simplistic pasting of Gothic details onto an American frame building a la carpenter Gothic of earlier decades.

Figure 69. Richard Morris Hunt, Alva and William Kissam Vanderbilt residence (Petit Château),660 Fifth Avenue, New York City, 1881. Brown Brothers.

Although the eye is drawn primarily to the ornamentation, the mass of the wall was allowed to assert itself. Hunt understood the fundamentals of architecture as external mass and interior space. The ornamental details were clustered around specific features, namely, doors, windows, and the turret, leaving large expanses of wall surface to express the structure of the building. In turn, the broad, unadorned surfaces emphasized the decoration. One contemporary critic noted this feature, writing that "the richness of the design is much enhanced by the careful distribution of the ornamentation and the occasional breadth of plain wall-surfaces."[15] Prominent critic Montgomery Schuyler also noticed the skill of the architect in handling such things, remarking on "the simple and massive treatment of the walls and . . . the minute delicacy of the decoration."[16] Schuyler further declared that the exterior sculptural decoration was "much the most interesting work in decorative sculpture which is to be seen out-of-doors in New York." He then pinpointed exactly the historic style Hunt (and Alva) had chosen when he observed, "The style . . . is an attempt to summarize in one building the history of a most active and fruitful century in the history of architecture, which included the late Gothic of the fifteenth century and the early Renaissance of the sixteenth."[17]

A few years later another critic opined that the late-Gothic style of the Petit Château was the best of all those emanating from France's distinguished architectural history, even "more so than Louis XIV and Louis XV styles. It is the eclectic style par excellence, and is particularly suited to our modern taste for bric-a-brac, for movable decoration, for a picturesque mingling of forms and motives belonging to many lands, to many epochs."[18] The impact of this radical new type of architecture—new for New York, that is—is apparent in the words of appreciation expressed by the architect Charles Follen McKim, who made a point of walking past the Petit Château each night on his evening stroll; McKim reportedly declared that he "slept better after enjoying the sight of Hunt's W. K. Vanderbilt house."[19]

The Interiors

Author John Van Pelt, referring to the Petit Château, stated that "the original drawings of the Main Hall and Staircase with the cupola above, those of the Parlor, Dining or Banqueting Hall, the Moorish [Billiard] Room and Library were all produced in detail in Hunt's office."[20] Hunt then placed the execution of the interiors into the hands of the Herter Brothers of New York and Jules Allard et Fils of Paris, although the Moorish billiard room was done by Léon Marcotte and Co. Also, there is an infrequent reference to a man named Gilbert Cuel, a Frenchman, whom Alva employed as an interior decorator but of whom little is known.

The entrance, off of Fifth Avenue, led into a vestibule that gave entry to a grand hall (sixty feet in length), from which all the main rooms on the first floor could be entered (figure 70). Photographs of the area show a magnificent profusion of decorative relief carving throughout almost every available surface. As in most of the interior, this room was veneered in imported Caen stone, its surfaces beautifully worked. At the center of the long hall, on the right, was the grand staircase, opposite which was a huge, ornately carved fireplace (figure 71).

Immediately to the right was the library (eighteen feet by fourteen feet), which was in the French Renaissance style of Francis I (reigned 1515–47), the walls being lined with boiseries (decoratively carved wood paneling) taken from a French

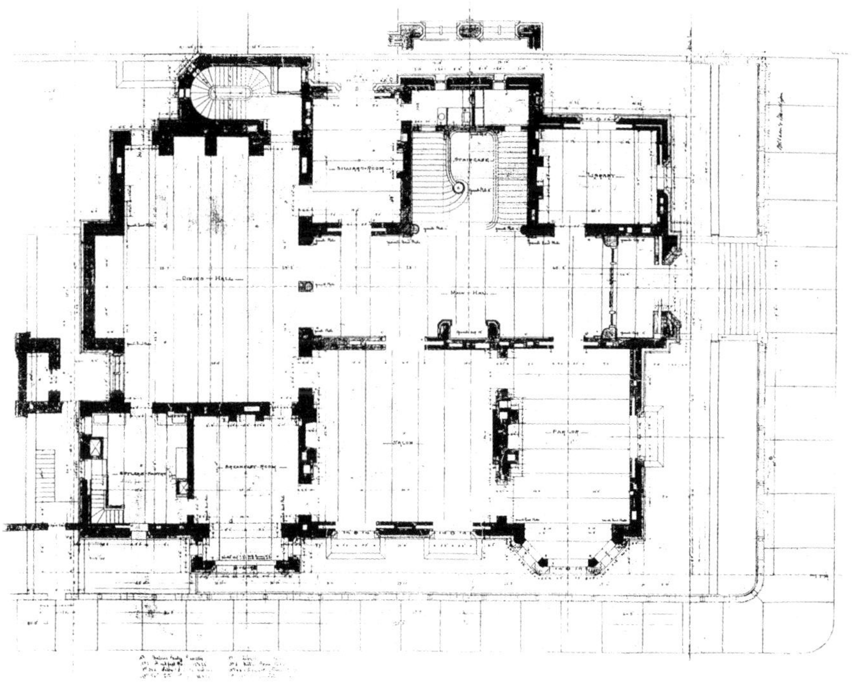

Figure 70. Richard Morris Hunt, floor plan, Petit Château, New York City, ca. 1882. From Van Pelt, *Monograph of the William K. Vanderbilt House* (plate 2). Morris Library, University of Delaware.

château of that period. This removal of wall paneling from ancient European grand houses for reuse in the mansions of American millionaires started and became a common practice in the Gilded Age, as will be seen in Chapter 12, which concerns Stanford White as decorator and dealer in antiquities.

Beyond the grand stairway was the billiard room, measuring twenty-four by eighteen feet (figure 72). For this interior, Léon Marcotte placed one of his most gifted assistants in charge, a young man named William Baumgarten, who later worked for Herter Brothers and eventually became head of that firm after Christian Herter died. Van Pelt mentioned the "stucco, tile, onyx column shafts and marble floor"[21] in describing the luxurious decoration of the room, which had Moorish arches and walls covered with colorful, richly patterned Moroccan tiles. A billiard room—one of several new rooms now being worked into mansion plans, creating new demands on architects and decorators—was typically treated as exotic and masculine, a space to which men could comfortably withdraw to have cigars, brandy, and a round of billiards while the ladies, after dinner, retired to elegant salons.

Returning to the hall, to the left was the parlor, the architectural decor of which was designed by Hunt himself and executed by Herter Brothers. The room was rather dark owing to the French walnut boiserie, and the center sections of

Figure 71. Richard Morris Hunt, main hall, Petit Château, New York City, ca. 1882. From Van Pelt, *Monograph of the William K. Vanderbilt House* (plate 35). Museum of the City of New York.

Figure 72 (opposite). Billiard room, Petit Château, 1882. From Van Pelt, *Monograph of the William K. Vanderbilt House* (plate 58). Morris Library, University of Delaware.

the paneling were filled with "a dull green damask" cloth. The parlor was referred to as the Grinling Gibbons Room because of its ornate woodcarving done in the manner of that seventeenth-century English master carver.

The Salon

Just west of the parlor was the large salon (thirty-eight by thirty-three feet), which was designed and executed in Paris by Jules Allard et Fils in imitation of the style of Louis XV. It was then shipped to New York, where it was reassembled by several of Allard's artisans, sent over expressly for that purpose. The salon had eight large white panels trimmed with gold and within each was hung a Gobelin tapestry taken from designs by François Boucher.[22]

The most important piece of furniture in the room was an ebony secretary with a black marble top and black and gold lacquer panels (figure 73). The cabinet was made by Jean-Henri Riesener (1735–1806), one of the most famous cabinetmakers of eighteenth-century France, and the exquisite ormolu mounts are the work of Pierre Gouthière (1732–1813), who was equally famous for gold and gilded adornments to Rococo furniture. This piece, given to the Metropolitan Museum of Art in 1920 by William Kissam Vanderbilt, was originally created for Marie-Antoinette for use at the palace at Saint-Cloud, and it represents yet another instance of American millionaires of the Gilded Age wishing to surround themselves with objects that had once belonged to royalty, as if by osmosis they would absorb aristocratic status.

THE PERIOD ROOM

An important development occurred insofar as room decoration of the Louis XV salon was concerned—the re-creation of a period room, which was something new to American domestic architecture. In a period room, the furniture and architectural setting were meant to re-create an ambience in the mode of a past historical style—in the case of the Petit Château's salon, that most extravagant era of one of the grandest of all the kings of France, Louis XV. Furnishings were either original antiques or reproductions that were so skillfully made it was virtually impossible to distinguish them from authentic pieces. Decorators such as Herter Brothers and Allard of Paris had in their employ master artisans who could reproduce antiques in the favored Louis XIV, XV, and XVI styles, and similarly replicate antique paneling, if actual old boiseries could not be bought out of some French chapel, château, nunnery, hôtel de ville, or wherever.

But the term "period room," as created in the Gilded mansions of the Vanderbilts, Astors, Whitneys, and so on, needs some qualification, for rarely did these parvenus set out to re-create archaeologically or academically correct period rooms; in the Gilded Age, the term must be loosely applied, for in a chamber called, say, the Louis XV room, furnishings from other eras, even from other cultures, were incongruously included. For example, in the Louis XV salon at the Petit Château, a tiger-skin rug is seen sprawled on the floor. Such an item would never have been found in an authentic re-creation of a mid-eighteenth-century French room from one of the royal palaces.

The period room is different from the Aesthetic Movement room such as the one in the mansion of William Henry Vanderbilt. An archetypal room of the Aesthetic Movement would be filled with a cluttered mix of exquisite pieces from diverse eras and cultures, whereas the period room would be dominated by a major object or architectural motif that identified it with a single era or style. Although the period room was attempted here and there some years earlier, it became popular in interior decor around 1880, thanks to Richard Morris Hunt, Stanford White, George B. Post, and other architects. It offered an alternative to the Aesthetic Movement mode of decoration, yet retained the potential for luxury and sumptuousness. "Culture" rooms—those done in the Moorish or Japanese mode, for instance—were a subtype of the period room. To maintain command of all this, architects and patrons called into existence the services of a new professional, the interior decorator.

The Salon Ceiling and the Painting Collection

The salon ceiling, a magnificent focal point of the room, was painted by Hunt's longtime Parisian friend Paul Baudry, who had done the ceiling paintings for Garnier's new Opera House in Paris; he had also executed twelve decorative panels for the Duc d'Aumale's splendid château, Chantilly—a château Alva and William Kissam had often visited as guests, so they were

Figure 73. Jean-Henri Riesener, desk (secretaire), 1783. Japanese black and gold lacquer and ebony, black marble top, and gilt bronze mounts by Pierre Gouthière. Metropolitan Museum of Art, bequest of William K. Vanderbilt, 1920 (20.155.11).

familiar with Baudry's work. A critic writing in *The Art Amateur* in 1887 reported to his American audience that Baudry's works generally have a certain "literary" side to them,

> based on an acquaintance with the classics and with history the likes of which few modern painters can boast. He was noted for his care in the representation of accessories and costume, and for the attention which he gave to the architectural scheme of which his paintings were to form a part. All this called for an amount and a kind of study which are seldom undertaken by modern decorative painters, who prefer, as a rule, to paint their ceilings and friezes without any regard to architecture.[23]

Baudry's ceiling for the Vanderbilt mansion no longer exists, but an article in *The New York Times* provided a general description soon after it was installed. A smaller rondelle depicted Phoebe, a goddess of the moon, while the larger one represented the wedding of Cupid and Psyche. In the latter, Cupid adores Psyche while Mars "toys amorously with charming Venus, and Proserpine fans her sleeping spouse [Pluto]."[24] Juno turned her back on Jupiter, who accepted a cup from Ganymede, and that group was balanced by the figure of Neptune.

Beyond the salon was a small breakfast room (twenty by twenty-seven feet) with an adjoining butler's pantry. The breakfast room was hung with Flemish tapestries, and the most notable painting there was Rembrandt's *Noble Slav* (figure 74). Although the paintings owned by William Kissam could hardly be called "a collection" such as Benjamin Altman and Henry Clay Frick would form, he did acquire a number of choice works. Among them, interspersed among the furnishings of rooms throughout the Petit Château, were François Boucher's *Toilette de Venus (Venus with a Dove*, figure 75) and Jean-Baptiste Greuze's *Broken Eggs*; Thomas Gainsborough's *Mrs. Grace Dalrymple Elliott* and Sir Joshua Reynolds's *Captain George K. H. Coussmaker*, both exquisite full length portraits, dominated the wall of the musicians' gallery in the banquet hall (figures 76 and 77). In 1907 Vanderbilt loaned to the Metropolitan Museum of Art, for special exhibition, a portrait of Lady Guildford of 1528 and a portrait of Queen Henrietta Maria by Anthony Van Dyck. All of the aforementioned paintings were given to the Met in 1920.

Figure 74. Rembrandt van Rijn, *The Noble Slav*, 1632. Oil on canvas, 60 × 43¾ in. (152 × 111 cm). Metropolitan Museum of Art, bequest of William K. Vanderbilt, 1920 (20.155.2).

Figure 75. François Boucher, *The Toilet of Venus*, 1751. Oil on canvas, 42 × 33 in. (108.3 × 85.1 cm). Metropolitan Museum of Art, bequest of William K. Vanderbilt, 1920 (20.155.9).

Figure 76. Thomas Gainsborough, *Grace Dalrymple, Mrs. John Elliott*, 1778. Oil on canvas, 91½ × 60 in. (235 × 154 cm). Metropolitan Museum of Art, bequest of William K. Vanderbilt, 1920 (20.155.1).

The Banquet Hall

The banquet hall—the largest room in the house, measuring fifty by thirty-five feet and two stories high—was done in a Gothic style and was placed at the western end of the grand hall (figure 78). This room, which doubled as a ballroom, was entrusted to Herter Brothers for decorating and outfitting, possibly with assistance from Léon Marcotte. Above the seven-foot-high oak wainscoting, the walls were of Caen stone, and on them were hung splendid tapestries. At one end was a huge double fireplace, richly carved with three pairs of marble caryatids supporting a great oak overmantel, the work of sculptor Karl Bitter. Above that was a gallery that displayed six sculptured figures in medieval costume. At the opposite end was the musicians' gallery, where music was performed when the Vanderbilts were hosting elegant balls such as the one illustrated by Charles Dana Gibson (figure 79). The room was illuminated by a large stained-glass window, created in France by Eugène Oudinot, who was then celebrated for such work; the window depicted Francis I and Henry VIII meeting on the Field of the Cloth of Gold, another example of a Gilded Age millionaire preferring a theme taken from the history of European royalty or aristocracy rather than one drawn from past events in America.[25]

Consuelo Vanderbilt recalled her childhood in the house and the gala evenings she and her brother observed from some hidden spot:

> How gay were the gala evenings when the house was ablaze with lights and Willie and I, crouching . . . behind a balustrade of the musicians' gallery, looked down on a festive scene below—the long table covered with a damask cloth, a gold service and red roses, the lovely crystal and china, the grownups in their fine clothes. The dining room was enormous and had at one end twin Renaissance mantelpieces and on the one side a huge stained-glass window, depicting the Field of the Cloth of Gold on which the Kings of England and France were surrounded with their knights, all not more magnificently arrayed than the ladies a-glitter with jewels seated in high-backed chairs behind which stood footmen in knee breeches.[26]

At a later date, around 1896–97, Edwin Howland Blashfield painted murals for the banquet hall, which Pauline King described as depicting scenes from the medieval period: "[In] the Sword Dance, young men dance, holding their swords over heads of maidens. Girls carry wine jars, and there is a queen of the dance. Stalwart gallants are dressed in armor and doublets and hose, while squires hold banners at the sides."[27]

Alva's Assault on Society: The Grand Ball at the Petit Château

Once the interiors of the Petit Château were completed, or nearly so, in 1882, Alva was barely restrainable. She was now ready for her final charge into New York Society, and the mansion was to be her field of battle. She planned a gala—a grand costume ball—which was set for 26 March 1883. Consuelo reported that one of her mother's greatest ambitions was "to become a leader in New York society. To this end she gave a fancy dress ball for the opening of her new house. . . . My godmother . . . Consuelo Yznaga, [who] had been my mother's bridesmaid, was our house guest and the ball was given in her honor. She was then Viscountess Mandeville and soon after . . . became Duchess of Manchester."[28] Alva was not one to allow an opportunity such as visiting aristocrats escape her, and the combination of the new mansion plus the presence of European nobility was formidable, so Alva put it to use.

All of New York Society began talking about the Vanderbilt grand ball. Devastated indeed were those parvenu hopefuls who did not receive an invitation. Reportedly, 140 dressmakers were kept busy for five weeks, day and night, creating the exotic costumes, and exotic and lavish they had to be, for Society sensed that this was to be an epoch-making event. Excitement built with each passing day.

Up to that point Society had not recognized the Vanderbilt clan, which had failed to gain the approbation of Mrs. Caroline Astor. Young Caroline, daughter of *the* Mrs. Astor, was as excited as the other girls her age about the prospect of dancing the quadrille and being attended by New York's handsomest young men. But she was crushed when she did not receive the eagerly awaited invitation. Questioned about the matter by a friend, Alva replied that she did not recall having met Mrs. Astor, and therefore could not invite to her house people she had not met. A few days later, Mrs. Astor paid a formal call on Mrs. Vanderbilt in her new mansion, and immediately thereafter an invitation was dispatched to the Astor residence—the old-fashioned brownstone-type mansion down at the corner of 34th and Fifth Avenue. Alva

Figure 77. Sir Joshua Reynolds, *Captain George Coussmaker*, 1782. Oil on canvas, 94 × 57 in. (238 × 146 cm). Metropolitan Museum of Art, bequest of William K. Vanderbilt, 1920 (20.155.3).

Figure 78. Richard Morris Hunt, banquet hall, Petit Château, New York City, ca. 1882. Avery Library, Coumbia University.

Figure 79 (opposite). Charles Dana Gibson, *The Social Push. Almost In.* From *Life* (1 January 1903), pp. 10–11.

had forced the ultimate showdown, and with this single stroke the Vanderbilts were everafter admitted into the inner circle of New York Society.

One thousand guests had been invited. They began to arrive at 11:00 p.m., the ladies rivaling each other in their dazzling, bejeweled costumes. Alva greeted them in her guise as a Venetian princess, wearing a gown inspired by a painting by Alexandre Cabanel, its cream-colored brocade richly adorned with jewels (figure 80). She wore a jeweled peacock in her hair and a long strand of pearls, which were extremely rare at that time and, of special importance, reportedly once belonged to Catherine the Great of Russia. At her side stood William Kissam, attired as Henri, 5th Duc de Guise, grand chamberlain at the court of Louis XIV; in his yellow satin costume he resembled a court dandy who had just stepped out of a seventeenth-century portrait by Anthony Van Dyck. His older brother, Cornelius II, came as Louis XVI while his wife, Alice Gwynne, was a sensation in her illuminated costume representing those wonderful new phenomena, electricity and the electric light (figures 81 and 82). Mr. and Mrs. Bradley Martin were dressed as Louis XV and Mary Queen of Scots, and Mrs. Paran Stevens seemed more regal than ever in her costume as Queen Elizabeth I.

Elizabeth Lehr remembered fancy-dress balls such as that one and the significance of the costumes connoting European royalty, writing of the "strange complex that made us who belonged to a society so new seek always inspiration for our amusements in the past! No one would have dreamt of anything so plebeian as modern fancy dress; we had all to be kings and queens and courtiers. Princes of trade could represent none lower than princes of the blood."[29] Richard Morris Hunt and his wife attended the grand ball, Catharine as a courtier from the time of King Francis I, and Richard in the costume of the early Renaissance painter Cimabue. Catharine described her impressions of the event:

> It was the first time the house was thrown open to the public, and a more beautiful setting for a costume ball could not well be imagined, Mrs. Vanderbilt's knowledge and taste combined with unlimited expenditure made it a memorable entertainment. The ball was said to have cost $50,000 and a series of quadrilles were danced in the dining room, at one end of which is a gallery from whence the music [came]. . . . Calcium lights filled the room with silvery splendor, which fell with extraordinary effect on Oudinot's [stained-glass] window.[30]

Ward McAllister reveled in such events and recorded the minutest details, noting that in the "Hobby-horse Quadrille" the men were all dressed in pink and the ladies in red hunting-coats with white satin skirts from the period of the Sun King, Louis XIV. For the "Dresden Quadrille," all of the ladies appeared in white satin, the men in white satin knee breeches, and all wore white powdered wigs.[31] The next morning the *New York Herald* carried the following headline: "Like an Oriental Dream . . . The Wealth and Grace of New

York in Varied and Brilliant Array," and the article reported that the scene had never been equaled "in Republican America and never outdone by the gayest court of Europe."

As hoped, the gala grand ball established Alva and the Vanderbilts at the epicenter of New York Society, while the mansion and Richard Morris Hunt set a new course for domestic architecture among America's millionaires of the Gilded Age of the 1880s and 1890s. The Petit Château was more than a picturesque bauble ornamenting Fifth Avenue—it was a statement of a new frame of mind as to how architecture should serve the ambitions of a new aristocracy, an American aristocracy of wealth that arose from railroads and steel, coal and coke, finance and commerce, pork and shoe polish. It was a dramatic culmination—a fulfillment, an architectural climax toward which mansion building had been evolving for several decades. A new course for such things was thereby charted.

Figure 80. Alva Vanderbilt, in the costume of a Venetian princess worn at the fancy-dress ball at the Petit Château, 26 March 1883. The Preservation Society of Newport County.

Epilogue for the Petit Château

Surprisingly, the Petit Château did not survive long, but it did last longer than Alva's marriage to William Kissam, which ended in divorce in 1895. Thereafter Alva had little interest in the house, and Willy K. died in 1920. In 1926, Herbert Croly, the most notable architectural critic of his day, wrote an epitaph for the Petit Château, declaring that "of all the Hunt buildings which are now about to be demolished, the one which we ourselves will most regret is the former home of Mr. W. K. Vanderbilt." He went on to say that it was the best of the great houses Hunt had designed, writing of the building's "ease, its grace and its urbanity." Croly then lamented that "the part of Fifth Avenue on which it was situated . . . has become completely transformed by a business invasion. . . . This part of Fifth Avenue has become altogether too busy, too noisy and too valuable to provide desirable sites for residences."[32]

There was an unsuccessful attempt to save the Petit Château as a museum, but Van Pelt, in 1925, saw the inevitable coming when he commented that it and its neighbor, the William Henry Vanderbilt house across the street, "now stand on ground that has become immensely valuable for commercial purposes, and it seems almost certain that their destruction must soon take place, and their beauty and past glory . . . swiftly dissolve and be lost in oblivion." He found ironic satisfaction in the fact that "he who tears it to pieces will have undertaken a Herculean task. The shades of the workmen of the past may thus have some measure of vengeance on the destroyers of the present."[33] As beautiful as the Petit Château was, it was not a house that Alva and William Kissam's children or grandchildren wanted to live in; its time had passed. In February and March of 1926 it was razed, and within a few years a portion of Rockefeller Center rose on its site.

Figure 81 (opposite, left). Costume of Louis XVI, worn by Cornelius Vanderbilt II to the fancy-dress ball at the Petit Château, 26 March 1883. Museum of the City of New York, gift of Countess Laszlo Széchenzi (51.284).

Figure 82 (opposite, right). "The Spirit of Electricity" costume, worn by Alice Gwynne (Mrs. Cornelius II) Vanderbilt at the fancy-dress ball at the Petit Château, 26 March 1883. Museum of the City of New York, gift of Countess Laszlo Széchenyi (51.284).

Life at its best is seen in this splendid mansion, where all is warmth, and color, and richness, and perfume. The gilded drawing-rooms are crowded with a confusion of silks, and velvets, and laces, and broadcloth, and flowers, and jewels; and from the seeming-happy crowd arises a pleasant hum of low-toned voices, as if passion would never lift them, or pain make them discordant, from the cradle to the grave.

Julius Henri Browne, *The Great Metropolis* (1869)

Chapter Six

The Cornelius Vanderbilt II Mansion

Alice and Cornelius Vanderbilt II

In 1879, soon after his father, William Henry Vanderbilt, and his brother, William Kissam, began their great houses at Fifth Avenue and 52nd Street, Cornelius Vanderbilt II (1843–99) commenced his grand mansion at the northwest corner of 57th and Fifth. As the eldest son of William Henry, he inherited the titular headship of the clan and assumed the mantle of leadership insofar as the Vanderbilt business interests were concerned.

Born at New Dorp, Staten Island, Cornelius II was a quiet, sober, straight-laced youth who grew up to be a quiet, sober, straight-laced man (figure 83). He attended private schools in New York City, but at age sixteen he went to work as a clerk in a bank. By 1863 he had entered the banking house of Kissam Brothers, where he earned fifty dollars a month—and lived within his income. Once, when his grandfather, the Commodore, invited him to join the rest of the family on his magnificent yacht, the *North Star*, to sail to Europe, young Cornelius asked the founder of the family fortunes if he would continue to pay him his salary while he was on the trip; when grandpapa said of course not, Cornelius II paused thoughtfully and then replied that he had better not go.

Figure 83. Benjamin C. Porter, *Cornelius Vanderbilt II*, 1899. Oil on canvas, 51 × 42 in. (129.5 × 107.7 cm). The Preservation Society of Newport County.

But his grandfather liked the diffident young man and in 1867 took him on as assistant treasurer; he soon became treasurer of the New York and Harlem Railroad, then vice president in 1880 under his father. After William Henry died in 1885 he assumed control of the Vanderbilt lines, by then largely consolidated into the New York Central Railroad. Maud Howe Elliott remembered Cornelius in her book, *My Newport*: "He was a serious man with a quiet, resolute manner. One who knew him intimately said, after his too early death: 'He killed himself with overwork. He was too conscientious and took over heavy responsibilities for the entire family. He worked harder than any of his clerks.'"[1]

Even after inheriting $60 million from his father, Cornelius continued to work long hours: he was not a yachtsman, he did not race horses or maintain a string of polo ponies, he did not philander or gamble—he worked. A biographer of J. Pierpont Morgan noted that Cornelius II was the only Vanderbilt that the great financier liked and that Morgan "worked easily with him . . . on New York Central affairs."[2] Over the years, Morgan and Cornelius collaborated on numerous civic projects, as when each contributed $25,000 to a fund to establish the New York Botanical Gardens in the Bronx in 1891; four years earlier Vanderbilt had given $100,000 to one of Morgan's cherished projects, the building of the Cathedral Church of St. John the Divine just north of Central Park.

In time, Cornelius found himself not only as head of the New York Central Railroad but also on the board of directors of forty-five corporations. In his prime he directed "the policy of about 16,000 miles of railroads, which furnish employment to nearly 120,000 men." The same source tells us that Mr. Vanderbilt "holds himself bound by the responsibilities of citizenship to a far greater extent than do most men of wealth and social position," and then followed with a long list of charitable and cultural organizations to which

Cornelius gave both time and money—for example, he was on the board of trustees of Columbia College and of the American Museum of Natural History; he was at one time or another a manager or director of St. John the Divine, of the YMCA, of the Seamen's Missionary Society, the Home for Incurables, the College of Physicians and Surgeons, the Vanderbilt Clinic and the Sloane Maternity Hospital, the Eye and Ear Infirmary, and on and on.

Although a quiet person, he was sociable. "With all his business cares," wrote a *New York Times* correspondent, "Mr. Vanderbilt is fond of society. He likes to meet intelligent and agreeable people, and, with his refined and gracious wife, he responds cordially to the social requirements imposed upon him in consequence of his conspicuous and influential station in life."[3]

On 4 February 1867, Cornelius married Alice Claypoole Gwynne, whom he had met when they taught Sunday School together at Saint Bartholomew's Episcopal Church (figure 84). They had four sons and two daughters: William Henry, who died young as a student at Yale and in whose memory Cornelius had Vanderbilt Dormitory erected on the campus; Cornelius III, or "Neilly," as the family called him; Alfred Gwynne, who was lost on the *Lusitania* in 1915; Reginald; Gertrude, who married Harry Payne Whitney, thus becoming Gertrude Vanderbilt Whitney, founder of the Whitney Museum of American Art in New York; and Gladys, who became a countess when she married Count Laszlo Széchenyi of Hungary.

At first Cornelius and Alice had a house at the corner of 32nd Street and Fifth, which around 1870 was still considered a fashionable part of town, being only two blocks south of Mrs. Astor's mansion. But as their family grew, they needed more room, and a rivalry within the Vanderbilt family had begun to foment even then—a rivalry that was to be waged, in part, on the architect's drafting table.

Cornelius and his brother William Kissam got along nicely and worked well together, Willy K. gladly deferring to his older sibling in business matters. And although Cornelius was never a great one for social flourish, still, he and especially his wife were conscious of the pecking order within the tribe—that is, Cornelius and Alice were to be recognized as its leaders, ahead of William Kissam and Alva—something

Figure 84. Raimundo de Madrazo y Garreta, *Mrs. Cornelius Vanderbilt II (Alice Claypoole Gwynne)*, 1880. Oil on canvas, 70 × 40 in. (178 × 102 cm). The Preservation Society of Newport County.

Figure 85. George B. Post, Alice Gwynne and Cornelius Vanderbilt II residence, northwest corner of Fifth Avenue and 57th Street, 1881–82. Museum of the City of New York.

to which Willy K. was more willing to accede than was Alva. The latter seemed determined to outdo Alice, and if Alva had the most magnificent mansion at Newport, Alice countered with the even more splendid Breakers; if Alva erected the luxurious Petit Château at 52nd and Fifth, Alice rejoined with an even larger palace farther up the avenue.

In 1879 Cornelius and Alice commissioned George B. Post to design their new house on the lot they had purchased on the corner of 57th and Fifth.[4] The first phase of the mansion, completed in 1882, occupied only half of the block between 57th and 58th streets, and its main entrance faced south on 57th Street (figure 85).

A decade later, as it became necessary to increase the stakes in the social poker game with Alva, Cornelius managed to purchase the other five houses on the block along Fifth Avenue, although acquisition of some of them proved difficult. "To make room for the addition," *The New York Times* reported, "the five houses on Fifth Avenue . . . will be taken down. The last two will not be touched at present. . . . The Seventh Regiment Veterans' Club has a lease of the corner house, which has five or six years yet to run."[5] But Cornelius was anxious that plans for his mansion not be impeded, and by January 1893 he had convinced the members of the Seventh Regiment Veterans' Association that they could meet elsewhere; the "Silk Stocking Regiment" rebuilt up at Park Avenue and 66th Street, and that is where Louis Comfort Tiffany created his famous Veterans' Room, an archetypal Aesthetic Movement interior. The last of the five brownstones on Fifth Avenue were demolished, and the mansion expansion proceeded northward to 58th Street.

The Great Mansion at 58th Street

The new mansion was to occupy a site 125 by 125 feet, and its style was determined by that of the earlier section, for the sake of continuity. George B. Post was the architect of the expansion as well, although he did consult with his former mentor, Richard Morris Hunt, who was then at work on Cornelius and Alice's Newport cottage, The Breakers.

In the expansion, which more than doubled the size of the house, the existing structure was gutted. By January of 1893 the western end of the old part had been "completely torn away and the north wall taken down. The great mansion is now almost an empty shell."[6] Sometimes as many as six hundred workmen were employed on the site, often laboring under floodlights at night as well as during the day. By November of that year the *Times* reported that the house was nearly complete and that the family should be able to move in before Christmas.

With this expansion, the main facade of the house now faced 58th Street and looked across a broad plaza to the southeast corner of Central Park (figure 86). Eventually the Pulitzer Fountain would be erected in this plaza just opposite the house, while farther across the way the Grand Army Plaza would be laid out, dominated by Augustus Saint-Gaudens's gilded equestrian statue of General William Tecumseh Sherman. To the immediate west stood the mansion of W. J. Hutchinson, also designed by George B. Post in the style of Francis I. On the western edge of the open square would soon rise the Plaza Hotel while to the east, on Fifth Avenue, stood Mary Mason Jones's Marble Row (figure 43, p. 78). At its prime, this was one of the handsomest urban landscapes in America.

George B. Post's rendering of the new main facade of the mansion shows the formal entrance marked by the arched porte cochere, or carriage porch. The house was set back, with a tall, iron perimetral fence enclosing the grounds. It was, like the earlier part of the house, constructed of red brick and limestone, adding a note of color that was absent in the monochromatic gray edifice built by William Kissam and Alva.

Post's design, in the French Renaissance mode, was a Beaux-Arts version of the great châteaux of the Loire Valley, and contemporary critics often cited the château at Blois as the model—again, a château type transplanted to an urban setting.[7] By 1885 an architectural alternative to this, in the form of an urban palazzo of Italian origins, had already arisen only a few blocks away, on Madison Avenue—McKim, Mead and White's Villard Houses (figure 164, p. 242).

The Critics

Architectural critic Montgomery Schuyler observed that the Vanderbilt mansion was inspired by "a French chateau of the period after the transition, when all detail had been thoroughly classicized, and only a romantic wilfulness and freedom of composition recalled the architecture of the Middle Ages."[8] Schuyler was basically correct, although details such as the little tourelles do indicate a lingering medievalism, and the design is totally asymmetrical, a violation of true classical principles; it took French architectural style a long time—much of the sixteenth century—to become completely classicized and purged of its great Gothic heritage. That transitional style became popular with American millionaires. If Alva's Petit Château followed the fifteenth-century model of the house of Jacques Coeur, Alice's mansion was sure to emulate the manner of the next historical phase, the early French Renaissance style of Francis I.

In the Cornelius Vanderbilt mansion the great amount of decoration causes one to yearn, architecturally, for the plain wall surfaces and solid masses found in Hunt's Petit Château (figure 67, p. 111). Schuyler, in the essay just quoted, observed that "in the matter of color, it is undeniable that the brickwork has in places a patchy look by reason of the comparatively small quantities in which it is used."[9] And another commentator similarly expressed his displeasure: "The huge house is by no means remarkable for beauty, grace or sympathy. It strikes the observer simply as a very, very large structure, and suggests rather a pretentious family hotel than a luxurious and elegant home."[10] Cornelius and Alice, in their jockeying for preeminence with the other members of the family, wanted a profusion of decorative detailing, employing expensive and abundant ornamentation of surface, to declare their greater wealth and social standing. But since most people would never gain admittance to view the luxury of the interiors of the Cornelius Vanderbilt house, the architectural declaration of wealth and primal social position had to be expressed through the splendidness (and costliness) of the exterior.

Edith Wharton, who noted in *The Decoration of Houses* that wealth and taste did not always go hand in hand, wrote to Ogden Codman in 1897, "I wish the Vanderbilts didn't retard culture so very thoroughly. They are entrenched in a sort of Thermopylae of bad taste, from which no force on earth can dislodge them."[11] In one of Wharton's fables, a man who had seen the Parthenon builds a temple to his god, but then he becomes despondent when his temple,

Figure 86. George B. Post, Cornelius Vanderbilt II residence, Fifth Avenue and 58th Street facades, New York City, 1895. Museum of the City of New York.

made of mud and straw, was not equal to the beautiful Athenian temple; the author has a passerby remark, "There are two worse plights than yours. One is to have no god; the other is to build a mud hut and mistake it for the Parthenon."[12] This was probably directed, at least in part, at the Vanderbilts, who had the money but, in Wharton's opinion, lacked taste in architecture. Wharton could hardly claim to be unbiased, however. She was, after all, a member of the old Knickerbocker crowd, and in her novels and stories about the Gilded Age she often dimly expressed a rather snide attitude as she defined the character of the parvenus. Although she moved freely in their society, she tended to be smugly critical of their behavior as well as their architecture. All that aside, the Alice and Cornelius Vanderbilt mansion was one of the showplaces of New York City, and for sheer grandeur, none was more impressive.

When guests arrived at the Vanderbilt house, their carriages would take them through the elaborate iron gate, onto a semicircular drive, and under the porte cochere.[13] The latter was ornamented with six sculptured reliefs executed by Karl Bitter, a sculptor favored by both Post and Hunt. These reliefs depicted musical groups of seven boys and seven girls singing, reminiscent of similar bas-reliefs by the Italian Renaissance sculptor Luca Della Robbia, such as those on the cantoria at the Cathedral in Florence (figure 87). When the house was demolished in 1927, two of the limestone reliefs were salvaged and installed in the entrance of the new Sherry-Netherland hotel that was then being erected at Fifth Avenue and 59th Street.

John La Farge and the Interiors at the 1882 House

The interiors of the mansion offer a complex problem for analysis because some parts were created for the 1882 portion of the house, some were then reused in different rooms as part of the 1894 expansion, some were discarded, and other parts were shipped to Newport to be used in The Breakers. But the story must start with John La Farge, who was put in charge of the decoration of several of the main rooms in the house of 1882.[14] Two years earlier, Cornelius's father had turned to Herter Brothers for coordination of his interiors, but Christian Herter had announced that William Henry's house was to be his last project before retirement, and so Cornelius and Post had to seek expertise elsewhere. La Farge had recently demonstrated his ability to coordinate a lavish, complex interior—consisting of murals, stained glass, and architectural decorations—as supervisor of the interior ornamentation at H. H. Richardson's Trinity Church in Boston, in 1876–77. At that time, he was better known as a "general contractor" decorator than his later rival, Louis Comfort Tiffany.

John La Farge (1835–1910) was a remarkable artist. The son of French parents, he was born in New York City and grew up not far from Washington Square. He seemed destined for a career in law, but in Paris in the mid-1850s his long-standing interests in literature and painting increased. He admired the art of Delacroix and even studied briefly with Thomas Couture, although he had not yet determined to become an artist. Back in New York and evermore disinterested in the practice of law, he became friends with Richard Morris Hunt, who suggested he go to Newport, Rhode Island, to study painting with his brother, William Morris Hunt. There he reveled in the discourses on literature and art with his new friend, Henry James.

In the years that followed, as he worked mainly on easel paintings of landscapes, La Farge's fascination with architectural decoration grew. His great opportunity came when Richardson asked him to take charge of the interior of Trinity Church in Boston, which he did, collaborating with a gifted young designer whom Richardson had recently hired, Stanford White. Mural painting in the mid-1870s was all but unknown in the United States, and with his work at Trinity, La Farge virtually single-handedly inaugurated the movement that became known as the American Renaissance (about 1885–1915). His best-known works in that genre are those he did for three New York City churches—Saint Thomas (1877–78, burned 1905), the chancel murals at the Church of the Incarnation (1885), and the choir wall at the Church of the Ascension (1887)—plus the lunette titled *Athens* (1893) for the interior of McKim, Mead and White's Walker Art Gallery at Bowdoin College and several civic-virtue murals at the Minnesota state capitol (1903). He became the foremost painter and aesthetician for the American Renaissance, he assaulted the barriers that separated the "decorative artist" of architecture from the "fine art

designer for fine furnishings. If his murals were influenced by Italian Renaissance classicism, his interest in the Middle Ages led him into experiments in stained glass, in which medium he became a master, his only rival—later—being Louis Comfort Tiffany. La Farge's work in achieving brilliant colors in glass and their interplay with light won him appointment to the French Legion of Honor when he displayed his work at the great international exposition at Paris in 1889. Moreover, La Farge was one of the earliest of artists to travel to the Far East, journeying to Japan in 1886 in the company of his friend Henry Adams, and to the South Pacific in 1890–91, arriving there to study the art of that non-Western culture a full year before Paul Gauguin did.

With regard to Cornelius and Alice's new residence at 1 West 57th Street, the intention from the beginning was to create Aesthetic Movement interiors in which every detail of the architectural decoration and furnishings was to be a superb work of art, all coordinated into a glorious artistic symphony. That is, the interiors were not to be executed as period rooms. This decision to go with a "modern" style contributed to the selection of La Farge as coordinator. Also, Cornelius Vanderbilt already knew La Farge because he was then engaged in making several stained-glass windows for the house of his father, William Henry Vanderbilt (figure 62, p. 102).

With a contract for $100,000 in hand, La Farge set out to design and execute some parts of the interiors himself or to provide the designs for other artists and craftsmen to follow,

artist" of easel painting, and he became a leading exponent of the Aesthetic Movement.

La Farge's restless fascination with various media and art's interplay with architecture and the decorative arts led him into collaborations with architects and sculptors and into a career as a professional interior decorator and a multimedia

and in general to orchestrate the whole artistic endeavor. The main rooms in the 1882 house for which La Farge was responsible were the entrance hall, the dining room, and the watercolor room, which was essentially a reception room in which a number of watercolors painted by Alice Gwynne Vanderbilt were displayed.

Figure 87. Karl Bitter, *Singing Youths*, 1893. Limestone, from carriage porch, 58th Street entrance to the Cornelius Vanderbilt II residence, New York City, now installed in entrance to The Sherry-Netherland hotel, New York City.

Figure 88. Entrance hall, Cornelius Vanderbilt II residence, Fifth Avenue and 57th Street, New York City, 1882. George B. Post Collection, New-York Historical Society.

ENTRANCE HALL

The entrance hall was dominated by a huge fireplace with life-size reddish brown marble caryatids by Augustus Saint-Gaudens, representing Pax and Amor (Peace and Love); the mosaic overmantel, by La Farge, depicts a classically robed maiden sitting on an excedra (figures 88 and 89). The fireplace bore a Latin inscription supplied by Cornelius Vanderbilt himself, which reads in translation, "The house at its threshold gives evidence of the master's good will. Welcome to the guest who arrives: Farewell and helpfulness to him who departs." This whole ensemble was transferred to the family sitting room on the second floor of the expansion section of 1892–94; before the mansion was demolished in 1927, it was given to the Metropolitan Museum of Art. Aesthetic Movement ensembles of this sort were popular in fashionable interiors, not only for fireplaces but also for fountains, as in the one executed around 1905–15 by Tiffany Studios (figure 90). There the border and the central scene are masterpieces of the mosaicist's art and, as with the use of stained-glass windows, add brilliant color to an interior.

Augustus Saint-Gaudens recalled his collaborative role in the decoration of the Vanderbilt mansion interiors:

> Mr. George B. Post gave me an order to make all the models for the great entrance-hall. . . . The undertaking required not only the two caryatids for the monumental mantelpiece . . . but as well the superintendence of the models for all the wood-carving in the hall, which was enormous, beside the creating of medallion family-portraits to be introduced in certain of the panels. For some reason these were not entirely completed. Those that I did do were

Figure 89. Augustus Saint-Gaudens with Louis Saint-Gaudens, Frederick MacMonnies, and Philip Martiny, from designs by John La Farge, mantel, from Cornelius Vanderbilt II residence, Fifth Avenue and 57th Street, New York City, 1882. Height 180 in. (457.6 cm). Metropolitan Museum of Art, gift of Mrs. Cornelius Vanderbilt II, 1925 (25.234).

Figure 90. Tiffany Studios, *Garden Landscape and Fountain*, 1905–15. Favrile glass mosaic, height 8 ft. 7½ in. (263 cm), fountain, 24 × 77 in. (61 × 195.6 cm). Metropolitan Museum of Art, gift of Lillian Nassau, 1976 (1976.105).

Figure 91. George B. Post, dining room and art gallery, Cornelius Vanderbilt II residence, Fifth Avenue and 57th Street, New York City, 1883. George B. Post Collection, New-York Historical Society.

the portraits of young Cornelius and George Vanderbilt, Gertrude Vanderbilt . . . , William H. Vanderbilt [II], and Cornelius Vanderbilt, the first of the family.[15]

Although Saint-Gaudens did not mention where the bronze portrait image of The Commodore was placed in the house, the portrait of little Gertrude and the double portrait of young Cornelius III and William Henry II were set within architectural enframements in the dining room of the 1882 section.

The Dining Room

In its richness, the dining room of the 1882 house, which served also as the art gallery, was one of the most remarkable rooms of the Gilded Age (figure 91). The critic Mary Gay Humphreys exclaimed that it was "the most ambitious decorative work which has yet been attempted [in America], and is only paralleled in magnificence and in the luxuriousness of its material, by the decorative work of the [Italian] fifteenth century."[16] In the ceiling, ornate coffers surrounded large skylights provided by La Farge, the glass being opalescent and decorated with jewel-colored pieces. At the time of the expansion, this glass was removed and installed as the skylight over the great staircase at The Breakers in Newport. The new dining room of the 1894 expansion, which again served as an art gallery, had a coved ceiling with an opalescent skylight; while a skylight of that type lacked the spectacular coloration of some of La Farge's stained glass, its main function was to illuminate the paintings, so although some aesthetic effect beyond mere plate glass was desired, it had to be essentially translucent.

The great oak beams enframing the coffers in the dining room of 1882 were inlaid with mother-of-pearl in a double Greek fret motif, and an iridescent hammered bronze leafage and egg-and-dart design edged the panels within the coffers. Saint-Gaudens collaborated with La Farge in the design of the coffer panels, and he was assisted by several young sculptors then working in his studio, among them Philip Martiny and Frederick MacMonnies. Four of the coffers contained handsome reliefs depicting mythological personages. One of these, *Ceres*, was carved from mahogany and holly wood with ivory, mother-of-pearl, marble and bronze inlay; the panel was about five feet in length (figure 92). The other three panels represented Pomona, Bacchus,

Figure 92. Augustus Saint-Gaudens, *Ceres*, 1882. Pear wood, mother-of- pearl, marble, and repousse copper, 62 × 25 in. (159 × 64 cm). Saint-Gaudens National Historic Site, Cornish, N.H., gift of the Trustees of the Saint-Gaudens Memorial.

and Actaeon, while additional reliefs in the ceiling depicted Apollo with cupids.[17] Still other panels, representing Dionysiac and Orphic rites, were designed by La Farge and inspired by the carvings of a late Roman, fifth-century A.D. ivory diptych; they were executed in Saint-Gaudens studio.[18]

Such superb artistry was not to be discarded, of course, when the mansion was expanded, and so the ceiling was dismantled and reassembled as part of the billiard room on the second floor of the new addition. Some of the decoration just discussed may be seen in a photograph of that new room of 1894, in which the relocated Saint-Gaudens fireplace is also visible (figure 93).

La Farge painted several murals for the watercolor room, which was removed in 1892–94 to a location just inside the new main entrance on 58th Street, where it served as a reception room. He also designed and his studio made several additional stained-glass windows, some of which are known from his preparatory sketches for them. Textiles were used throughout the 1882 house, particularly as portieres, draperies that were hung in doorways; after he created the designs, La Farge placed Mary E. Tillinghast in charge of the hand-embroidering of them. The *Aeneas* portiere is visible in the doorway of the 1882 dining room (figure 91).

To summarize an important point, most of the decoration of the early mansion was a celebration of the work of contemporary American artists and craftspersons. That is, the interiors were, thoroughly, examples of the American Aesthetic Movement, as opposed to rooms inspired by historic European styles, or period rooms. Between the earlier portion of the house and the building of the later, larger part, a shift in taste occurred that introduced the period room into the mansion's interiors.

The Interiors of the 1894 Expanded Mansion

John La Farge was not involved with the interiors of the new part of the house in 1892–94. Committed to artistry of the highest level he could produce, he had often been impractical in the amount of time he devoted to his creations, and the resulting delays were frustrating and irritating to his patrons; moreover, his cost overruns—for which, as general contractor, he was responsible—not only alienated Cornelius Vanderbilt but also brought financial ruin upon the whole enterprise La Farge had established in his many-faceted firm of interior decorators. By the time of the expansion, Cornelius Vanderbilt wanted nothing to do with La Farge, even though a number of the artist's creations of 1882–84 were reinstalled in the new addition or reused at Newport.

In the plan of the house as expanded, the main entrance was still off of 57th Street, with the grander 58th Street entrance reserved for special events, such as the arrival of guests for a gala ball. From 57th Street one entered a great hall that measured forty by fifty feet, executed entirely in Caen stone. To the immediate right was the library (twenty-five by thirty-five feet) at the corner of 57th and Fifth Avenue; next to it, facing onto the avenue, were two salons—the small salon (twenty by twenty-five feet), a period room in the style of Louis XVI, and the large salon (fifty by thirty-five feet), executed in the period style of Louis XV. Then, at the corner of 58th and Fifth was the transplanted watercolor room, now a reception room, which contained the grand staircase that was modeled on a prototype from the Loire Valley. Across the part of the building fronting 58th Street was the huge ballroom, while to the west of the grand hall were the dining room, Cornelius's office, and the Moorish smoking room.

The Moorish room combined—in a crescendo of design and detail—colorful tiling, Oriental carpeting, and a most extraordinary chandelier (figure 94). The Moorish element had come into American architecture in the mid-1870s. The landscape painter Frederic Church had employed Persian and Moorish motifs in the creation of his mansion, Olana, which was perched high above the Hudson River, and almost anything of Islamic design was called Moorish then. Americans generally were introduced to the native arts of the Moors through the Moroccan exhibition at the Philadelphia Centennial of 1876. The theme of a Moorish interior had been given artistic sanction when the renowned British painter and tastemaker Sir Frederick Leighton created a room called the Arab Hall in his London townhouse. In the 1880s and 1890s the architectural journals of the day carried numerous illustrated articles on buildings such as the Alhambra and the Alcázar; there is a high correlation between what is depicted in some of those plates and the appearance of Vanderbilt's billiard room. In fact, the Moorish room was said to be an exact replica of a room in the Alhambra in

Figure 93. George B. Post, billiard room, Cornelius Vanderbilt II residence, Fifth Avenue and 57th Street, New York City, after 1895 renovation, showing the Saint-Gaudens fireplace, which had been removed from the entrance hall of the 1882 house. George B. Post Collection, New-York Historical Society.

Granada. Although "exact" is perhaps too strong a characterization, Cornelius and his architect did send agents to Spain to make studies of the original tiling and mosaics, which were then duplicated for the mansion.

Lockwood de Forest, sometime-partner of Louis Comfort Tiffany and Aesthetic Movement craftsman par excellence, supervised the completion of the Moorish room in the Vanderbilt house. Such a room was not an anomaly, for Henry G. Marquand's New York City mansion had a Moorish smoking room, and there was a similar type of room in the house that Arabella Worsham (later Mrs. Collis Huntington) created in her remodeled townhouse on West 54th Street, which she later sold to John D. Rockefeller for his New York City residence. Before the Vanderbilt house was torn down, the smoking room tiles and mosaics were bought by movie mogul Marcus Loew, who had them installed in the Midland Theater in Kansas City.[19]

As if the Moorish room were not decorative and colorful enough with all its tiling, mosaics, and carpets, it also included one of La Farge's most brilliant stained-glass windows—a version of the famous *Peonies Blown in the Wind* (figure 95). While the version for the Vanderbilt mansion has not been located, three of the six versions have survived. The original *Peonies* window had been made about 1880 for the Newport "cottage" of Henry Marquand, and it is now in the Metropolitan Museum of Art; a variation was made for the John Hay house in Washington, D.C., and it is currently in the collection of the Smithsonian Museum of American Art, while another version, which was originally created for the studio of Sir Lawrence Alma-Tadema in London in 1886, is now in the Museum of Fine Arts, Boston.

The Ballroom and Grand Salon

The sumptuous, fancy-dress, costume ball was an annual event for any *grande dame* of the Gilded Age who had aspirations to social primacy, and for Alice Vanderbilt it was especially obligatory. Accounts survive of several she gave in the 1882 house, accounts that are interesting because that house had no ballroom. To the grand ball that Alice gave on the evening of 19 January 1891 came the cream of New York Society—Willy K. and Alva, Mrs. Astor, Mrs. Paran Stevens, Ward McAllister, Mr. and Mrs. Elbridge Gerry, and Mr. and Mrs.

Figure 95. John La Farge, *Peonies Blown in the Wind*, ca. 1879, from the Henry G. Marquand house, Newport, R.I. Glass and lead, 75 × 45 in. (190.5 × 114.3 cm). Metropolitan Museum of Art, gift of Susan Dwight Bliss, 1930 (30.50).

Figure 94 (opposite). George B. Post, Moorish smoking room, Cornelius Vanderbilt II residence, Fifth Avenue and 57th Street, New York City, 1882. George B. Post Collection, New-York Historical Society.

Ogden Mills being among the several hundred handsomely attired guests. The central hall and the library had been cleared of furniture for the pleasure of those who wished to dance. Dinner was served at midnight. The following year, on the night of February 5, the guests began to arrive about 10:00, led by Mrs. Astor, Mr. and Mrs. Ogden Goelet, Mr. and Mrs. John Jacob Astor, Mr. and Mrs. Chauncey Depew, and the ubiquitous Mr. McAllister, to name a few. Various members of the Vanderbilt clan were also among those who attended: brother George, another brother, Frederick, and his wife, Louise; sisters Margaret, Florence Adele, and Lila with their husbands.

That year, dancing was held in the white and gold parlors on the second floor, with the musicians concealed behind a screen of palms in a bay window overlooking the hall—hardly a satisfactory deployment of space.[20] By then, Alice could endure such makeshift arrangements no longer, for when Alva gave her annual galas at the Petit Château they were held in a spacious ballroom that was obviously designed for that very purpose. The new, much larger house must have a ballroom that was grander than the one at 52nd and Fifth. Less than one month after Alice's ball in February of 1892, construction started on the expansion of the mansion, and on March 5 Robert Maynicke, office manager of the George B. Post architectural firm, was quoted as saying that "the addition will include a ballroom of considerable size."[21]

Alice finally outdid Alva in the lavish new ballroom of her expanded mansion. It was perhaps the largest of any such room in the United States, measuring sixty-five by fifty feet and thirty-five feet in height. To span a space of that size it was necessary to employ large steel beams, as frequently noted by newspaper correspondents who covered the development of the great house; such technology was, of course, concealed behind the veneer of a historic style.

The ballroom was wrought in the mode of Louis XIV and therefore was a period room, copied from a chamber in the Hôtel de Valois in Paris. Its focal point was the decorated ceiling executed by Edouard Toudouze, a Parisian decorative artist famous for his murals at the Opéra-Comique and the Sorbonne.[22] Toudouze painted it in Paris and by April of 1893, had been working on it for nearly a year. Descriptions of the ceiling report that the composition evolved around a painted stone balcony with pale blue sky and whispy clouds in the center. On either side were "groups of beautiful women," one representing dance and the other music, appropriate themes for a ballroom. At the four corners were medallions that bore symbols of the four seasons, and in between were images of large vases filled with flowers. "Cupids frisk about, darting their love shots about rather carelessly," according to an art correspondent in Paris, who then concluded that "it is just the right thing for a ballroom [and] it is a comfort to find such artists [as Toudouze] working for our home decoration."[23] When finished, the canvas segments were shipped from Paris and installed in the Vanderbilt mansion.

The grand salon, done in the style of Louis XVI, was also created in Paris, the work of the decorator firm Jules Allard et Fils (figure 96). When this room is compared with one of the rooms done by La Farge, the difference between an Aesthetic Movement room and a room done in a fashionable historic style becomes apparent. The tardiness of its completion was the source of irritation to Cornelius, who chided Allard for not giving him enough time to review the designs before work started on their execution, indicating that Vanderbilt wanted to be involved in the aesthetic decisions. The grand salon reflects the intentions of an American industrialist millionaire to forge an association between his family and Old World aristocracy by means of a newly manufactured interior and its furnishings.

The Art Collection

Cornelius Vanderbilt II had a genuine interest in art, and on his frequent trips to Europe he enjoyed visiting the great museums and circulating among the finer galleries, where he purchased paintings and sculptures. "If Mr. Vanderbilt has a passion," a reporter once wrote, "it is love of art and love of the beautiful objects in nature and art. He has a fine collection of pictures and of books, and he is one of the most intelligent and appreciative of art critics."[24]

In the new dining room of 1894, as in the old one of 1882, were displayed the major paintings owned by Cornelius and Alice. As with the collection formed by William Henry Vanderbilt, their's was dominated by the work of contemporary European academic Salon painters. Regarding Cornelius's interest in art, an intriguing notice appeared in *The*

Figure 96. George B. Post and Jules Allard et Fils of Paris, grand salon, Cornelius Vanderbilt II residence, Fifth Avenue and 58th Street, New York City, ca. 1894. New-York Historical Society.

Art Amateur in 1886, less than a year after the death of William Henry; it read, in part,

It is to be regretted . . . that the late Mr. [William Henry] Vanderbilt was balked in his munificent intention to build and endow a public art gallery as a perpetual home for his splendid collection of pictures. It may not be rash, however, to predict that the family name will yet be identified with some such gift. The name of William H. Vanderbilt naturally was the more prominently connected with art, but it is known by many that, in knowledge and appreciation of pictures, Mr. Cornelius Vanderbilt greatly surpassed him. Indeed the present head of the family is a man of taste as well as of public spirit, and, while it may be impracticable for him to carry out the original intentions of his father as to the disposition of the Vanderbilt collection, it would not be surprising if, in his own way, he should, one of these days, do something hardly less munificent.[25]

Cornelius's collection was not as large as his father's, but it had its jewels. In 1890, for example, Cornelius bought from the Earl of Dudley one of Turner's greatest paintings, *Grand Canal, Venice*, which according to the terms of Vanderbilt's will went to the Metropolitan Museum of Art in 1899, at a time when that young institution was in need of world-class masterpieces (figure 97). He also gave to the same museum a collection of 650 Old Master drawings that he had acquired from James Jackson Jarves; although later scholarship has declared the attributions of many of these to be spurious, Vanderbilt's intention was laudable. The collection was, as in the house of 1882, displayed in the dining room (figure 98).

Cornelius took a genuine interest in the Met during its early years of development. In 1880 he was named a trustee, and by 1893 he was serving as chairman of the board's executive committee, all the while contributing both funds and works of art. *The Art Amateur* took note of this in 1887 and, after observing that the A. T. Stewart collection had been dispersed at auction, wrote that "its gem," Rosa Bonheur's *Horse Fair* (figure 38, p. 73), "has, through the generosity of Mr. Cornelius Vanderbilt, been acquired by the Metropolitan Museum. . . . Mr. Vanderbilt certainly set a splendid example.

There was at first much speculation as to the buyer, but the mystery only remained such until Mr. Vanderbilt could duly give the first notice of the presentation to the President of the Museum."[26] Cornelius's only instruction to the director of the Met was that Bonheur's great painting be placed where it could be seen by the general public, for he subscribed to the theory that exposure to art had a beneficial effect in elevating the working class, culturally, morally, and socially.

Epilogue for the Cornelius Vanderbilt II Mansion

Cornelius did not have long to enjoy the great house that he had built, for two years after it was finished, in 1896, he suffered a massive stroke from which he never fully recovered. He and Alice withdrew from Society's spotlight, and on 12 September 1899 Cornelius died of a cerebral hemorrhage. Alice lived in the mansion for a while before she moved to a smaller house; she had precious few opportunities to use her grand ballroom for joyful fancy-dress galas. The mansion became unused and boarded up, a white elephant amid the commercial establishments that began to encapsulate it. In 1926 she sold it to the Braisted Realty Corporation for nearly $7 million. One week before it was scheduled to suffer the fate of the wrecker's ball, in January 1927, she arranged to have the house opened to the public, charging fifty cents' admission to raise money for charity. The public flocked to see how the highest of High Society had lived during an era that was by then fading. Alice also arranged for the visitors, as they filed into the house, to sign the Vanderbilt guest book, which they enjoyed doing. Soon thereafter she had a few pieces removed from the mansion, and the remaining items became widely dispersed. In the spring of 1927, the great house came tumbling down to make way for a multistoried commercial building that was to house Bergdorf Goodman's elegant emporium of ladies' couture.

Figure 97 (opposite). J. M. W. Turner, *Grand Canal, Venice, from the Porch of the Madonna della Salute*, 1835. Oil on canvas, 36 × 48 in. (91.4 × 122.2 cm). Metropolitan Museum of Art, gift of Cornelius Vanderbilt II, 1899 (99.31).

Figure 98. George B. Post, dining room and art gallery, Cornelius Vanderbilt II residence, Fifth Avenue and 58th Street, New York City, 1894. George B. Post Collection, New-York Historical Society.

I have never even dreamt of such luxury as I have seen in Newport. . . . Is this really your America or have I landed on an enchanted island? Such an outpouring of riches! It is like walking on gold.

The Grand Duke Boris, brother of the Czarina of Russia, when he visited Newport; quoted from Lehr, *King Lehr and the Gilded Age* (1935)

Chapter Seven

Newport

Vernacular versus Grandeur

In the late 1880s and early 1890s Newport became Society's most fashionable resort. "Newport, not the White House, is the supreme court of social appeals in the United States," declared The Reverend Charles Nicholls, who continued, "Mrs. Astor, and not the wife of the President of the United States, is the first lady of the land, in the realm of fashion."[1] Newport outshone such places as Saratoga and Bar Harbor. The architecture at Saratoga was more modest and "the season" lasted only about a month—August—primarily for thoroughbred and racing enthusiasts. Long Island mansions, although numerous, were used more for weekend retreats once Society had returned to New York for the season there, which began in late September or early October.

Reverend Nicholls drew a remarkable comparison, especially for a clergyman, when he observed that "wealth and the highest fashion have become so much more centralized in Newport every year, that it has become as imperative for a social aspirant's claims to be passed upon by Newport, as it was for a potentate of the era of Charlemagne to go to St. Peter's, Rome, for coronation."[2] The "Holy of Holies," Elizabeth Drexel Lehr called it. "The playground of the great ones of the earth from which all intruders were ruthlessly excluded by a set of iron-clad rules."[3] Not every aspirant passed the test; Alexander Graham Bell, for example, spent many summers in Newport, only to be ignored by Society.[4] And Reverend Nicholls advised that if snubbed at Newport, the disappointed climber should "spread sail for Narragansett Pier or Bar Harbor."[5] Still, Society admitted a sufficient number into its inner circle to assure itself of a gay and amusing two months away from New York each summer.

Old Newport and Its Cultural Life

During the Colonial era, Newport, Rhode Island, was a prosperous seaport that also enjoyed great popularity as a summer resort. To it came not only New Englanders but also the wealthy from New York and the Carolinas, as well as well-to-do planters from the Caribbean Islands. It was nicknamed "Carolina Hospital" by the Carolinians who sought its cool breezes during the summer's heat and the malaria season. Following the American Revolution, however, Newport became rather seedy as its shipping interests diminished. Philip Hone—the celebrated diarist and former mayor of New York—recalled that when he began visiting Newport in 1834 only twelve families from Boston, New York, and Charleston owned houses there. In the 1840s the town began to experience something of a revival when several large hotels were erected to accommodate guests.

The grand thoroughfare of Newport was, and is, Bellevue Avenue, which beginning in 1852 was extended to Bailey's Beach as land speculators began to develop waterfront properties; prices rose from $7 per acre in 1845 to $450 an acre in 1865, just at the beginning of the Gilded Age.

In the years before the Civil War a sizable and active intellectual contingent, composed largely of people from Boston and Cambridge, took up residence at Newport during the season. Maud Howe Elliott, who has left a record of the cultural life at this favored watering place, and others of her set were concerned that summertime removal to Newport not become a boring hiatus from the energetic intellectualism they thrived on at home. They organized themselves informally into a little club, the activities of which revolved around essay readings, literary criticism, discussions of the newest scientific knowledge, theories of morality, mortality, and religion, and tea sandwiches. The membership was impressive, for it included Henry Wadsworth Longfellow, Charles Eliot Norton, Louis Agassiz and his son Alexander, Reverend Phillips Brooks, Henry James the elder, the historian George Bancroft and his wife, astronomy professor Maria Mitchell of Vassar College, Kate Hilliard, Helen Hunt and Kate Field, the writer Bret Harte, an assortment of professors from Harvard, and Albert, younger brother of Senator Charles Sumner. "A little band of us combined to improve the beautiful summer season," Mrs. Elliott related, "by picnics, sailing parties, and household soirees, in all of which these brilliant literary lights took part."[6]

Sometimes Maud read, for her own pleasure and in quiet seclusion—as in the summer of 1868 when one of her selections was Plato's *Phaedo* "in the original Greek." On occasion she was invited by Reverend Charles Brooks to read a program of her essays at his Unitarian Church on Sunday afternoons. A typical "club meeting" might consist of pleasurable intellectual high jinx, as when one afternoon Mrs. Elliott presided, with Colonel Higginson—fellow-Brahmin, founder of the Boston Symphony Orchestra, and successful businessman—as her aide:

Figure 99. Malcomb Strauss, *Bathing Hour at Narragansett*, 1905. From *The New York Times*, 5 July 1905.

> We once held a "commencement," the Latin programme of which was carefully prepared by Professor Lane of Harvard University. . . . [Colonel Higginson and I] marched up the aisle in Oxford caps and gowns, and took our places on the platform. I opened the proceedings by an address in Latin, Greek, and English; and when I turned to Colonel Higginson, and called him "Filie meum dilectissime," he wickedly replied with three bows of such comic gravity that I almost gave way to unbecoming laughter. . . . A class was called upon for recitations from Mother Goose in seven different languages. At the head of this Professor Goodwin, then and now of Harvard, honored us with a Greek version of "The Man in the Moon."[7]

In the late 1850s and early 1860s artistic life in Newport centered around William Morris Hunt, the older brother of Richard Morris Hunt. William returned to Newport in 1856 after studying in Europe for several years, bringing with him the Barbizon style, which he introduced to America as an alternative to the native-born Hudson River School. In the little harbor area at the head of Narragansett Bay, Hunt established an art school which soon attracted a number of students. Henry James recorded that his family left Paris, in a curious reversal of the usual transatlantic pattern, to go to America so that Will, his older brother, could study painting in the studio of William Morris Hunt. The Hunts and the Jameses became contributors to the easy social and intellectual life of the resort. Henry James would later detest what Society did to Newport, and what it built there.

The architecture inhabited by the pre-Gilded Age summer residents was generally of an unpretentious vernacular sort. May Van Rensselaer reported that "along Bellevue Avenue . . . small white farmhouses occupied the ground now taken up by the flamboyant 'cottages,' . . . [and] the summer residents . . . and natives mingled on terms of equality."[8] In those halcyon days, even when new residences were built, the local vernacular tradition was respected; there was nothing "palatial" about the simple frame houses surrounded by verandas, and they were more comfortable than grandiose. "Architecturally," Mrs. Van Rensselaer recalled, "they were generally influenced by what was left of the 'Queen Anne' movement; . . . a deliberate irregularity, breaking out into bay windows, and all kinds of projections, was the key-note of this type of design. . . . Appreciation is particularly due to some of the rambling unpretentious shingled houses designed by McKim, Mead and White . . . and the late Richard Morris Hunt."[9] The Isaac Bell house (figure 158, p. 234) of 1883, designed by McKim, Mead and White, comes to mind, or the Will Low house of about the same date. But Newport was about to change.

Society Invades Newport

May Van Rensselaer remembered that entertainments at Newport, at first, were simple (whist and picnics), and life was slow-paced and relaxed. But then came Ward McAllister, who bought Bayside Farm: "Life, for him to enjoy it, had to be gilt-edged and multi-colored."[10] Picnics were no longer simple country outings, but *fêtes champêtres* at which one nibbled at *pâte de foie gras* and sipped iced champagne. Or there were outings on the many yachts that had begun to anchor in the harbor. Furthermore, McAllister

> introduced the summer colony to the cotillion dinner. The meal was usually served in the garden of his estate by the light of delicately tinted lanterns and shaded candles. After dinner the guests strolled about the garden and went to the barn where Mr. McAllister had a hardwood dancing floor laid . . . , and there, to the music of a specially imported orchestra, [his guests] danced half the night away.[11]

Frederick Martin, younger brother of socialite Bradley Martin, remembered the Newport of his youth, which "was very different from the town which it now is. I remember it as a charming countrified watering-place to which people went on account of its natural attractions, and I must say I preferred its vanished rose-embowered houses and cottages to the marble palaces that have taken their place." He then continued, wistfully, that he often looked back on those quiet days at Newport with deep-felt regret: "Then it was a place one went to meet friends, not to make them; culture and charm were the passports into society, but now wealth seems to be the Golden Key which unlocks most doors in this place of rich men's houses." And Bellevue Avenue had become "artificial," Martin observed. "What a contrast to the dignified Avenue as I remember it! But it is an age of change, and Newport has shared the universal fate."[12]

Figure 100. William Kissam Vanderbilt Jr., Harold Vanderbilt, and Harry Lehr at Bailey's Beach, Newport, ca. 1890. Photograph. Newport Historical Society, Newport, R.I.

Maud Elliott too saw the passing of her beloved Newport summertime cultural life, for she observed that the friendly, old village had disappeared and was replaced by the "splendid festivities of fashion." She mourned that "under this influence it still abides. . . . Dances can be enjoyed only by those who can begin them at eleven o'clock at night, and end in the small hours of the morning. . . . [Newport's] exquisite social atmosphere, half rustic, half cosmopolitan, and wholly free, is found no longer."[13]

A great schism developed between the local townspeople and the boisterous, demanding, invading hordes of Society. The socialites referred to the regular residents as "Footstools," and the two no longer mixed well. The townies, for example, went to Easton's Beach to swim, while the rich swam at Bailey's Beach (figure 100). "Between 'The Footstools' and those who availed themselves of them there waged a continual guerilla warfare," Elizabeth Drexel Lehr recalled, for "the townspeople despised the 'cottagers,' the summer colony of millionaires." Then, becoming the advocate of the local folk, she queried, "What harm was there in charging the idle rich prohibitive prices for two months and then living in comfort for the rest of the year on the proceeds? The millionaires must have their luxuries? Well, let them have them, but make them pay ten times the proper value." Mrs. Lehr then shifted to the Socialites' position, which was to keep the

"Footstools" at arm's length and out of the sacred precincts of Bellevue Avenue and Ocean Drive, where their stately "cottages" rose.[14]

Fashionable Newport

It was along Bellevue Avenue and Ocean Drive that Society organized its grand architectural enclave of magnificent "cottages"—called such because summer residences at Newport had always been so designated. Bellevue was the connecting artery—the Fifth Avenue of Newport.[15] Before the advent of Society, it had been a quiet country lane, but in the 1880s and 1890s it became the thoroughfare of the coaching crowd.

The masters of the Gilded Age loved their horses, and each afternoon and early evening the avenue was filled with the two-way traffic of handsome landaus, victorias and barouches wheeling behind some of the finest horseflesh in the world. Competition was as keen in equine excellence as it was in the brokerage houses and boardrooms of the great corporations. Choking clouds of dust arose as young bucks sportingly raced each other up and down the unpaved road, while fashionable ladies spent the afternoon delivering their *cartes de visites*—which were taken, by footmen, to the doors of other fashionable ladies, who were not at home because they too were out delivering their calling cards.

This daily ritual stretched from the Casino to Bailey's Beach, with its participants dressed in pressed linen and pastel-gauzed dresses, perched in their carriages beneath parasols that coordinated with the attire of the hour, nodding or smiling or bowing to acquaintances as they passed, and liveried coachmen in stoic attendance to assist their mistresses in exiting and boarding. Stables and carriage houses became palaces in their own right, and a few of these—at Belcourt, for example—survive today to reveal the architectural and interior splendor devoted to such things in the era just before the arrival of the automobile. Even today, coaching remains one of the exciting, if anachronistic, devotions of the Newport season.

Among those things that so impressed the Grand Duke Boris when he visited Newport were the lovely, cantilever-bosomed ladies wearing Parisian gowns and trying to outweigh each other in applied diamonds, rubies, sapphires, emeralds, and overattenuated strands of pearls, even in daytime hours. But there were also the lavish entertainments held amid the splendor of the architectural settings designed by Richard Morris Hunt, McKim, Mead and White, and others who toiled in service to the new millionaire society.

Elizabeth Drexel Lehr, recalling Newport during the Gilded Age, reflected that America would never again witness entertaining on such an extravagant scale, for into those six or seven weeks of "the Season"

> were crowded balls, dinners, parties of every description, each striving to eclipse the other in magnificence. Colossal sums were spent in the prevailing spirit of rivalry. I remember Mrs. Pembroke-Jones telling me that she always set aside $300,000 at the beginning of every Newport season for entertaining. Some hostesses must have spent even more. A single ball could cost $100,000, even $200,000. No one considered money except for what it could buy.[16]

Mrs. Lehr further noted that the social scene at Newport was dominated by women while the men seemed content to follow their lead, and pay the bills. As the total purpose of the Newport season was social, at least among the glitzy millionaire set, little more was expected of men than that they be reasonably social at the entertainments their wives planned. Sometimes they failed to do even that, according to Mrs. Lehr, who confessed that the Newport millionaires were in general "dull companions at the dinner table." While they might be brilliant on Wall Street, they showed little or none of that brilliance on social occasions, for they either talked of business at dinner parties "or sat silent and apathetic through course after course, too nerve-racked by the strain of building a fortune to be able to relax. They were prepared to spend their last cent in gratifying the whims of their womenfolk, but they were incapable of amusing them themselves."[17]

And so, Society became queen at Newport, where the three most prominent hostesses were Alva Vanderbilt (later, Mrs. Oliver Hazard Perry Belmont), Tessie Oelrichs, and Mrs. Stuyvesant (Mamie) Fish. For them to entertain on a properly grand scale, lavish architecture was essential, even though the house might be in use only a few weeks of the year. Moreover, the building of a Newport cottage seemed to offer American millionaires and their wives a special outlet for their audacious taste.

Figure 101. Château-sur-Mer, Newport, 1852, remodeled by Richard Morris Hunt, 1873 and 1880s. The Preservation Society of Newport County, Newport, R.I. The Château-sur-Mer is the first, in point of time, of the great "cottages" of Newport.

Château-sur-Mer and the Great Era of the Cottages

Château-sur-Mer was built in 1852 for a wealthy China trade merchant, William Shepard Wetmore, on a large waterfront site on Bellevue Avenue (figure 101). Designed by a local builder, Seth Bradford, it was constructed of stone rather than the traditional wood, and for many years it was the grandest house in Newport. By its scale and splendor Château-sur-Mer looked to the future of Newport; moreover, it had the first large ballroom in the summer colony, where Wetmore entertained some twenty-five hundred guests at a gala in 1857. Change was in the air—but then came the lull in such things during the long years of the Civil War.

Wetmore died in 1862, and the mansion passed to his son, George Peabody Wetmore, who several years later, in 1871, asked Richard Morris Hunt to update the place. But it was no easy task to "modernize" this massive pile of granite blocks, which insistently retained its original form in spite of the architect's efforts. In the 1880s Hunt was again called in, and this time he replaced the old roof with one of mansard design, which had become popular in the style-setting Paris of the Second Empire.

Architectural historian Winslow Ames has observed that Hunt was more effective in interior renovations, noting that he "provided for elaborate interior paneling, carvings, and painted decorations and even suggested furniture for the principal rooms."[18] Between 1876 and 1878, on Hunt's recommendation, Luigi Frullini, a decorator and sculptor of Florence, Italy, executed the paneling and architectural decoration for the library and dining room in a Renaissance Revival style; the work was done in Frullini's workshop in Florence and shipped by boat to Newport, where one of his Italian artisans installed it (figure 102). Another updating of Château-sur-Mer occurred about 1903 when Wetmore, under pressure from his wife, agreed to have Ogden Codman redecorate the southwest salon in the style of Louis XV.

But Château-sur-Mer was a reworking of an older building and a sprucing up of its interiors, so Richard Morris Hunt was constrained in his creative efforts. Although by its size alone it stood out among other Newport houses, still it seemed old-fashioned when compared with what was about to arise along Bellevue Avenue and Ocean Drive. By 1870 there were some 250 summer cottages in Newport, most of which were of the shingle style, inspired partly by vernacular architecture and partly by the Queen Anne mode, which was then passing out of fashion. Not until the 1880s was the great era of the spectacular mansions inaugurated.

As early as 1882 the critic Clarence Cook complained of the extravagance that was beginning to dominate Newport architecture, declaring that this was "a time of universal self-indulgence and love of ostentatious display."[19] Cook pleaded for a simple cottage type that was inspired by Colonial

Figure 102. Fireplace, *Bacchus and Cherubs*, carved by Luigi Frullini of Florence, Italy. Château-sur-Mer, Newport, ca. 1880. The Preservation Society of Newport County, Newport, RI. Frullini (1839–97) specialized in carving wood paneling and figures in the Renaissance Revival style, and his work is now collected by such places as the Metropolitan Museum of Art, the Philadelphia Museum of Art, and the Victoria and Albert Museum in London. When George Peabody Wetmore and his wife went abroad for an extensive tour in the 1870s, leaving Hunt in charge of the remodeling of Château-sur-Mer, they may have seen examples of Frullini's work at the great expositions in Vienna in 1873 or in Paris five years later; Frullini himself came to the United States in 1876 on the occasion of the Philadelphia Centennial at which he displayed his artistry.

American architecture. But the big spenders of the Gilded Age had their own ideas about what their houses were to declare to the world, and it had nothing to do with either simplicity or American vernacular; it was more concerned with Old World aristocracies and palaces and châteaux. In most cases the architects' patrons made a conscious decision to reject the indigenous American mode in favor of the Continental palatial. By 1890 the change in the architectural character of Newport was obvious.

"Money is the universal requisite," wrote Mrs. Van Rensselaer in *The Social Ladder*, for unless one "has financial resources and the willingness to spend them lavishly, he can never hope to reach that eminence on which dwell the folk hailed by the society pages of the press as 'socially prominent.' Unless he is willing to keep on spending after he has attained that envied height, he cannot hope to remain there."[20] Much of the requisite money for a grand mansion on Bellevue Avenue came from Wall Street, and if there was one thing the Newport hostesses knew how to do, it was spend money lavishly—much of it on gowns or jewels or dinner parties or fancy-dress balls, to be sure, but a lot of it went into their great cottages as well. With each new cottage that rose, the next one had to outdo it, and the architects were instructed to do so. The race was on.

James Van Alen, handsome and debonair, married Emily, the daughter of William B. and Caroline Astor, and circulated in the privileged innermost sanctum of Gilded Age society. Wakehurst, the Van Alens' cottage on Ochre Point in Newport, was one of the earliest of the truly magnificent mansions (figure 103). Completed in 1887, its history is unusual in that it is an exact copy of a country house of Elizabethan vintage called Wakehurst Place (1570) in Sussex, England. Van Alen, a dedicated anglophile, commissioned the English architect Charles Eamer Kempe to replicate its design, and at Newport its construction was supervised by leading local architect Dudley Newton.

The steep pitch of the roof and its slate tiles are characteristic of late-sixteenth-century English architecture, as is the complex design of the roofline, which is constantly broken by dormers and gables. The windows were done in small diamond panes, as appropriate to the era being imitated. Once the limestone shell was completed and the historic details such as chimney pots and finials were in place, several of the interiors were decorated with rooms plucked from Old World grand houses—the appointments of the study being brought over from Lady Fitzherbert's London townhouse, while the dining room, in its earlier life, had adorned a house in Bourges, France, and the neoclassical drawing room had originally been the creation of Robert Adam, the celebrated eighteenth-century British architect-decorator.

Newton also oversaw the installation of the Jacobean paneling in the Long Hall as well as the Dutch Renaissance assemblage in the den, and the rooms were filled with old English furniture. Mrs.

Figure 103. Charles Eamer Kempe (plan) and Dudley Newton, Wakehurst Place, Newport, 1884–87. Replicates Wakehurst (1570) in Sussex, England. Built for James J. Van Alen, acquired by Salve Regina University, Newport, R.I., in 1972.

Lehr's recollection of how James Van Alen furnished his house provides an insight into the decoration of interiors of the Gilded Age mansions; on his visits to England, she noted, Van Alen rummaged through countless antique shops in Chelsea and Bloomsbury and toured the villages of Devon and Warwickshire "in search of 'period furniture' to add to his collection. His English tapestries were famous, his hall bristled with oak settles and dower chests, grandfather clocks and pewter tankards; every bedroom had its copper warming-pan, its Hogarth engravings."[21]

Wakehurst was inherited by the Van Alens' grandson, James Henry Van Alen, the noted tennis enthusiast who was instrumental in establishing the International Tennis Hall of Fame Museum at the Newport Casino. His wife, Candice, worked to save the Casino when it was under threat of destruction. In 1972 Wakehurst was purchased by Salve Regina University and currently serves as faculty office space and a student center.

The Goelets of Ochre Court

Emily and James Van Alen were neighbors of the Ogden Goelets, whose cottage was called Ochre Court, designed by Richard Morris Hunt in 1888, and completed four years later (figure 104). Its cost, an astronomical $4.5 million, was theretofore unheard-of for a summer place, but the Goelets of this generation were beginning to learn how to spend money in a carefree way, whereas their forebears had been exceedingly parsimonious. The family was of ancient lineage but lived miserly lives apart from Manhattan Society. Although by 1870 the family owned enormous tracts of land—from Union Square to 47th Street, their value estimated at $100 million—Peter Goelet, Ogden's uncle, still mended his own socks, milked his own cows, and performed any other farmyard chores that would save him a penny. The decorative painter Edward Simmons recalled the two Goelet sisters of the preceding generation:

> On the corner of Nineteenth Street and Broadway, in the midst of one of the busiest parts of town, was a quiet dwelling, occupying almost a whole block of land. Here were green trees and shrubbery with grass, and in the "back yard" they still kept chickens and a cow! This was the home of the Misses Goelet, who had lived here all their lives, and even the influx of business, theatres, etc., could not make them sell and give up the home they cared for.[22]

Peter Goelet III, who remained a bachelor, lived at the family's little urban farm with his two sisters. His brother Robert Goelet II was the father of Robert III and Ogden. Peter III and Robert II had inherited not only large tracts of Manhattan real estate but also controlling interest in Chemical Bank, which their ancestors had founded. They also had large holdings in the Illinois Central Railroad and in Western Union Telegraph Company. These brothers died within months of each other in 1879, leaving almost everything to the two sons of Robert II. In turn, Robert III and

Figure 104. Richard Morris Hunt, Ochre Court, the Ogden Goelet residence, Newport, 1888–92. Salve Regina University.

Ogden were astute managers of their fortunes and increased them. Stanford White designed a couple of business buildings for them, and for Robert, a dedicated yachtsman, he designed the Goelet Cup, schooner prize. White also designed the Goelet mausoleum at Woodlawn Cemetery.

The brothers married well. In fact, their wives became rivals—in the manner of the Astors and the Vanderbilts—over the issue of which branch of the Goelet family was to have predominance. That, of course, had ramifications for future architectural projects. Harriet Louise Warren Goelet, Mrs. Robert Goelet, was the sister of the architect Whitney Warren, and she was also an artist who took a studio on the eighth floor of the tower of White's Madison Square Garden. When her husband died—aboard his yacht in Naples—she commissioned a statue in his honor for the new campus that McKim, Mead and White were designing for Columbia University, which Robert had attended; McKim commissioned Daniel Chester French to do the bronze piece—*Alma Mater* that sits so majestically on the steps in front of Low Library.

Ogden Goelet married Mary Wilson, daughter of Richard T. Wilson, who had reportedly profiteered in the South by selling cotton blankets to the Confederate Army when he was supposed to be providing wool blankets. Mary's sister, Grace, married Cornelius III, son of Cornelius and Alice Gwynne Vanderbilt, and her brother Orme Wilson was wed to one of Caroline Astor's daughters. Mary Wilson Goelet was a prominent hostess at Newport, and her daughter May became a duchess when she married the Duke of Roxburghe, who promptly carried his bride and her $8 million dowry off to England.

By 1881, when the estates of Robert II and Uncle Peter III were settled, Ogden was a very wealthy young man with the wherewithal to build a grand cottage at Newport. The next year his brother Robert asked Stanford White to design a house for him and his wife at Newport. But Southside, as it was called, was of the old, picturesque, shingle-covered style cottage. For the Ogden Goelets, that just would not do, so they turned to Richard Morris Hunt, who created for them a grand château in the French Renaissance mode, which, at the time of its completion, was considered the finest French château in America. Ochre Court, as the mansion was dubbed, is located on Ochre Point, just off Bellevue Avenue, with lovely views of Narragansett Bay. Ochre Point is so named because of the ochre-colored lichen that gives a yellowish cast to the rocks along the coast.

If Alva and Willy K. Vanderbilt's Petit Château had been inspired by late French Gothic architecture, Ochre Court was based on sixteenth-century French sources, from the era of Francis I. One of the first buildings of the Gilded Age to take inspiration from that much-admired period, it anticipated what Hunt brought to full flower in George W. Vanderbilt's Biltmore a few years later. Excluding remodeled structures such as Kingscote and Château-sur-Mer, Ochre Court ranks among the earliest of the monumental cottages, built from scratch, as an expression of the new Society that now dominated Newport. In its prime, the rambling mansion required the services of twenty-seven house servants, a dozen gardeners, plus eight grooms and coachmen.

Upon entering the estate one passed through a beautiful iron gate that, from the avenue, enframed the house. The entrance pavilion, which was set to one side of the asymmetrical facade, had a porte cochere, above which was a huge stained-glass window. The design was characterized by irregularity, with parts projecting here and there, chimney stacks rising beyond the roofline, dormers jutting through cornices and into the roof. On the sea side the dominant motif was the grand loggia tucked between two pavilions of a facade that was also asymmetrical and irregular; above the loggia were three large stained-glass windows that looked down on a broad terrace. The fifty-room edifice was constructed of Indiana limestone and trimmed with copper, which oxidized to a beautiful soft green.

Here, indeed, was a monumental pile, designed in a favored French mode, that suggested more an association with European aristocracy than with anything indigenous to New England. It must have put ideas into the heads of many other members of Newport's gilded social set, for cottages that would rival or surpass Ochre Court were soon to rise on the shores of Narragansett Bay.

The interiors were supervised by Richard Morris Hunt himself, and they continue the lavish treatment that he began at the Petit Château.[23] The guiding spirit of the major rooms was sumptuousness, and many of the appointments were obtained from dealers in Europe who could supply everything from a carved stone fireplace to a magnificent stained-glass window. The great window above the porte cochere, for example, was purchased in Germany.

The three-story main hall has piers, on the first floor, of light-colored Caen stone, and arches and pilasters, all ornately decorated, which give way to gilded architectural ornamentation on the second level, with paintings enhancing the lunettes. The ceiling, which is supported visually by a dozen large caryatids, contains a large painting depicting a feast attended by mythological gods and goddesses, all of which call to mind the palace interiors or the grand-style buildings that had been recently restored in Paris (figure 105). The focal point of the hall was a large, hooded fireplace in the style of Francis I or Henri II. The decorative carving about the walls was executed by the firm of Ellin, Kitson and Company, architectural carvers of New York City. Here, as in many other of his buildings, Hunt turned to Karl Bitter for especially fine ornamental sculptures, such as those in the spandrels just below the vaulted ceiling.

Figure 105. Richard Morris Hunt, ceiling of the great hall, Ochre Court, the Ogden Goelet residence, Newport, Rhode Island, ca. 1892. Salve Regina University.

Equally rich in its heavy gilding and lavish carving is the dining room at Ochre Court, with its huge double fireplace, tapestries, pilasters and cornices, and painted ceiling. But the Louis XV ballroom is perhaps the most ornate of all, with its French doors and large arched, mirrored panels that reach to the full height of the room. The ceiling has a large ornamental painting set within a scalloped enframement. On an evening when a gala was being hosted, the room was lighted by three brilliant crystal chandeliers.

Ochre Court remained in the Goelet family until 1947, when Robert—Ogden's son, a successful railroader and real estate developer—presented it to the Roman Catholic diocese of Providence, Rhode Island. The property thereafter became a school, Salve Regina University, and the mansion house today serves as the administration building. The grand ballroom is now a chapel.

Marble House: Willy K.'s Gift to Alva

While the grandeur of Ochre Court may have established the pattern for the millionaires' cottages that began to spring up along Bellevue Avenue and Ocean Drive, the house that set the standard for lavishness in Newport was Marble House, which William Kissam Vanderbilt had Richard Morris Hunt design as a gift for his wife, Alva (figure 106). Vanderbilt acquired a waterfront lot located between the estates of William Waldorf Astor on one side and Caroline (Mrs. William) Astor on the other. Usually one tried to avoid being caught between the two social adversaries, but in this case it worked out, and it was just as well to have a buffer between them.

In 1888 Hunt was commissioned to design the finest house money could create. Alva knew of the project and was

in on every decision concerning it, and she knew it was going to be grand, but she wanted to keep it a secret, the bigger splash to make when she had the gala unveiling. So a high fence was built around it, keeping Newport neighbors in suspense about what Alva was up to with all that Vanderbilt money at her disposal.

Artisans, mostly imported from Italy and France, worked for four years to complete the building, which, including the interiors and furnishings, gobbled up $11 million, before it was finished. For Hunt it offered "an unparalleled opportunity to practice his Beaux-Arts skills, regardless of cost."[24] The grand opening bash that Alva gave was on the evening of 19 August 1892, and Richard Morris Hunt and his wife, Catharine, were among the guests.

The Design

Marble House is eighteenth-century French in style, a monochromatic off-white throughout, a cross between the Petit Trianon at Versailles and the White House in Washington, the symbolic intent of which is unmistakable. It is called Marble House because of the marble used throughout.

The facade has a portico of four colossal Corinthian columns with richly carved capitals, modeled on those of the Roman Temple of the Sun at Heliopolis in Egypt. The row of arched windows on the ground floor has an elegant cadence while the rectangular windows of the second floor possess a refined simplicity. Stringcourses mark the two-story design of the building within. The rhythm of the free-standing columns in the portico is continued across the face of the wall in handsome Corinthian pilasters, which define each bay and unite the first and second levels while visually supporting the heroic cornice. Consistent with its classical heritage, the roofline is perfectly horizontal, or appears so to the eye, the low pitch of the roof being concealed by the balustrade across the top, which repeats the pattern of the banisters enframing the driveway. Alva may have expressed to her architect a desire for something entirely different from the Petit Château, for the two take their inspiration from entirely different sources: at Marble House, there is no taint of the domicile of some upstart merchant burgher of Bourges; when gazing upon it, one thinks instead of the great Bourbon kings of Versailles.

Figure 106. Richard Morris Hunt, Marble House, Newport, 1895. Built for Alva and William Kissam Vanderbilt. The Preservation Society of Newport County. Photograph copyright, Richard Cheek.

Figure 107. Richard Morris Hunt and Jules Allard et Fils of Paris, gold ballroom, Marble House, Newport, 1895. The Preservation Society of Newport County. Photograph copyright, Richard Cheek.

The Interiors

Inside, the marble theme is evident in the entrance hall, from which one views the ten-ton bronze grill that spans the broad glazed section. Hunt designed this splendid grill, which at the time was considered the finest example of that type of work in the United States. Consuelo Vanderbilt recalled in her autobiography that "there were fine tapestries flanking the entrance depicting the Death of Coligny and the Massacre of Saint Bartholomew's Eve."[25]

The architectural interiors of the main rooms on the first floor are the work of Jules Allard et Fils, modern-day re-creations of rooms of the time of Louis XIV and Louis XV; they were produced in Allard's workshops in Paris. The gold ballroom is a restatement of the grandeur of the hall of mirrors at Louis XIV's palace at Versailles (figure 107). Never had so much gold—or rather, gilding—been seen in any American interior. The room was intended to be festive and celebratory, and it was meant to flaunt the wealth and power of the young Midases of the New World,

for here it does appear as if everything touchable has been turned to gold. Great chandeliers provide a joyous play of light, flickering and gleaming as they dance across the gilded room. The large painting on the ceiling recalls the manner of Tintoretto, and the huge fireplace has life-size bronze figures, modeled by Karl Bitter, which are heroic candelabra bearers. The arcade of mirrors and mirrored doors along the walls continues in enormous full-length arched windows along the outer wall.

The dining room at Marble House is almost as grand, and it too recalls the days of the Sun King of France (figure 108). Lest one miss the connection, a large full-length portrait of Louis himself looks down from one end wall. The walls are lined with pink Numidian marble extracted from a Roman quarry in Africa that had been closed since antiquity, but reopened, at Vanderbilt's expense, in order to obtain just the color of marble that was desired. "The beautiful dining room, built of red marble," Consuelo recalled, "glowed like fire."[26]

A detail of the upper corner of the dining room reveals the splendor of the architectural decoration (figure 109). The motif is of a gilt stag's head on the shaggy skin of a hoofed animal, with a branch of an oak tree seen between the antlers; the oak branches continue from the extended hoofs into the gilded decorative band of the cornice, all in conjunction with a large Baroque ormolu cartouche. Lovely little heads adorn the corbels of the cornice and are repeated in the gilded-bronze capitals.

The Louis Quatorze and Louis Quinze furniture for Marble House was made by Allard's firm and by Henri Dasson, also of Paris. In her recollections of life in the house in its early years, Consuelo remembered that the dining room chairs were so heavy (about seventy pounds each) that each required a footman to assist a guest to be seated at the table and to depart from it. William Kissam Vanderbilt was so pleased with the results in his house that he had relief medallion portraits of Jules Hardouin-Mansart, the celebrated seventeenth-century architect of Versailles, and of Richard Morris Hunt placed on either side of a marble bust of Louis XIV in the upper hall. The symbolic purpose here is inescapable: Marble House was no mere Beaux-Arts folly, but rather an association of the Vanderbilt line with the great Bourbon Sun King of France who had built the palace at Versailles.

Figure 108. Richard Morris Hunt and Jules Allard et Fils of Paris, dining room, Marble House, Newport, 1895. The Preservation Society of Newport County. Photograph copyright, Richard Cheek.

A Party for the Duke of Marlborough and Consuelo

Several impoverished sons of European nobility crossed the Atlantic to petition their claim to the fabled "Consuelo dowry," but Alva knew the value of her goods-in-trade and was not about to market her daughter for anything less than a duke. Three years after Marble House opened, the Duke of Marlborough was a house guest, and Alva gave a ball in his honor, arranging for it to coincide with Consuelo's coming-out party. Over five hundred people attended what was described as "the most beautiful fete ever seen in Newport," with the Vanderbilt livery highly visible in their Louis XIV costume; in the entrance chamber hummingbirds and butterflies hovered above floating lotus blossoms in a fountain. Three orchestras played for the dancing pleasure of the guests, while nine French chefs prepared gourmet dishes to delight their palates.

Figure 109. Richard Morris Hunt and Jules Allard et Fils of Paris, detail of upper corner of dining room, Marble House, Newport, 1895. The Preservation Society of Newport County. Photograph copyright, Richard Cheek.

Of the Gothic room (figure 110), which was used as the family's sitting room, Consuelo later wrote in her autobiography,

> On the ground floor . . . a Gothic room held a collection of majolica, cameos, and bronzes which a French connoisseur, Gervais [Gavet] by name, had brought together. . . . [Its] stained-glass windows from some famous church [in Europe] kept out the light, creating a melancholy atmosphere in which a della Robbia Madonna suggested the renunciation of a worldly life. It was here that Marlborough later proposed to me.[27]

The stained-glass windows—which completely shut out any view of the sea beyond—have long since been removed, although the handsome carved Gothic-style window enframements are still in place. The late-Gothic fireplace remains; it had been displaced from its original home in the Old World and given a new existence in this American millionaire's resort cottage. An elaborate ribbed ceiling carries out the Gothic motif. The furniture that was originally in this room was made by Henri Dasson of Paris. The collection of French medieval decorative arts, which Alva had bought in toto—specifically for her Gothic room—in Paris from the dealer Emile Gavet, was sold in the 1920s to the Circus King, John Ringling, and may now be seen in the John and Mable Ringling Museum of Art in Sarasota, Florida.

According to Consuelo, her second-floor bedroom, like everything else in the house, came under the dominance of Alva, who, for example, bought and arranged each object on the dressing table and forbid her daughter to change the arrangement or to add personal items. Consuelo remembered the room as "austere." Alva's own bedroom was done in an elegant Rococo Revival style, its furniture being made to order by Allard or Dasson. A silver grooming service by Tiffany and Company adorned the dressing table. William Kissam's bedroom was on the opposite side of the house, but it might as well have been on the other side of the moon.

The Scandal of Divorce

Willy K. had once arranged a long cruise to India on his grand yacht, the *Alva*, and had invited, among other friends, Oliver Hazard Perry Belmont to join him and Alva (figure 111). Oliver, the son of August Belmont (see Chapter 2), had no interest in his father's business and cared only for breeding horses. He had married once, but on the honeymoon he

Figure 110. Richard Morris Hunt, the Gothic room, Marble House, Newport, 1895. The Preservation Society of Newport County. Photograph copyright, Richard Cheek.

had deserted his wife and gone wandering off to Spain with a French dancer. Elizabeth Drexel Lehr recalled that he was a good-looking man, for she wrote,

> I used to think Oliver Belmont one of the handsomest men at the Coaching Parade [the Coaching Club's annual parade held in May in Central Park], with his dark eyes, clear-cut profile and slender, faun-like grace. Mrs. W. K. Vanderbilt [Alva] often sat at his side on the box behind the four famous bay [horses]. . . . The women glanced at her as she sat wide-eyed and innocent-looking, and whispered to one another.[28]

Most agreed that Oliver was, in the words of one biographer, "lost to frivolity." One such frivolity occurred aboard the *Alva* and was continued on a second cruise; by then it was obvious that Oliver Belmont and Alva Vanderbilt were attracted to each other.

Back then divorce was considered a scandal that just did not happen in the best families. But Alva was an iconoclast and ever ready to blaze new trails in defiance of any rules that displeased her. In January of 1895 she divorced William Kissam and virtually exiled him from his own houses; he was not permitted to attend the great bash at Marble House, for example, in honor of the Duke of Marlborough and the coming-out of his beloved daughter, Consuelo. The latter remembered that when they returned to New York at the end of that season, "we settled at 660 Fifth Avenue [the Petit Château], from which my father had . . . been banished. Society, not yet hardened to divorce, was inclined to take sides. . . . My mother resented my seeing anyone whose loyalties were not completely hers."[29]

Alva's socialite friend Elizabeth Drexel Lehr (figure 112), who was the daughter of John W. Drexel, J. Pierpont Morgan's partner, had discovered on her wedding night that her husband, Harry Lehr, loathed her and could not stand the thought of touching her, ever, although he wanted her to understand that they were to be cordial to each other in public, and he even said he would occasionally call her "darling." In time, Elizabeth met someone new who was kind and in love with her. But when she went up the Hudson River to her family's estate to inform her mother, she was greeted at the door with the news that her mother had a bad heart condition and anything shocking—such as her daughter's impending divorce—would surely be fatal.

Figure 111. The William Kissam Vanderbilts and friends on an excursion to the Near East, ca. 1890, showing, left to right, William Kissam Vanderbilt, Consuelo (seated), Winnie Rutherford (center), William Kissam Jr. (standing), Perry Belmont (seated, wearing white jacket), and Alva (reclining). Photograph. The Preservation Society of Newport County.

So Elizabeth returned to New York, determined to remain married to Lehr, but Alva Vanderbilt scolded her: "You ought to leave him [and] I'll help you. I don't believe in marriage anyway. . . . You are the old-fashioned woman, Bessie, I am the woman of the future." Alva "was immersed just then in the cause of the Women's Suffrage Movement. [Her friends] remembered that Alva had always been a fighter, that she had always championed her own sex, taken the woman's part in any discussion."[30] To Harry Lehr himself Alva said, "You know perfectly well I don't believe in marriage. I never shall until we have true equality of the sexes."[31] And Mrs. Lehr remembered Alva saying,

> "I always do everything first. . . . I blaze the trail for the rest to walk in. I was the first girl of my 'set' to marry a Vanderbilt. Then I was the first society woman to ask for a divorce, and within a year ever so many others had followed my example.

They had been wanting a divorce all the time, but they had not dared to do it until I showed them the way." She quickened to the sound of an argument as to a clarion call to arms.[32]

One year after her divorce Alva married Oliver Hazard Perry Belmont. She moved out of Marble House in 1896 and went to live at Belcourt, her new husband's estate at Newport, which was a grand house erected above stylish stables. Guides escorting groups of tourists around the prominent sights of the resort used to stop in front of Belcourt and announce, "Here you see before you the new home of a lady who is much in the public eye. . . . A society lady who has just been through the divorce courts. She used to dwell in marble halls with Mr. Vanderbilt. Now she lives over the stables with Mr. Belmont!"[33] Of course, those were no ordinary stables, for as Elizabeth Drexel Lehr observed, to Oliver Belmont, "coaching and racing devotee as he was, the stables were by far the most important part of [Belcourt]. Nothing was too good for them. They were steam-heated in winter and fitted for all the latest devices. The whole ground floor was given over to them and to the quarters of the eight smart grooms whom he had brought over from England."[34]

When Alva moved out of Marble House she closed it but not entirely, for she had her washing and ironing done there, the facilities for such things being better than at Belcourt. And after Oliver's death in 1908, when her suffragist activities were at their peak, she occasionally opened Marble House to use it as a base of operations.

Alva contributed $10 million to causes such as women's suffrage, the right to vote. She championed other women who were devoting their lives to equality, women such as Alice Paul and Christabel Pankhurst, whom she brought to the United States from England and sent on a speaking tour. She was among the leaders of the legions of women who marched down Fifth Avenue in 1912 demanding the right to vote. With Elsa Maxwell she wrote a suffragist operetta, titled "Melinda and Her Sisters," which was performed at the Waldorf-Astoria in 1916. Alva became president-for-life of the National Women's Party, and after women finally did get the right to vote, she refused to do so because there were no women candidates. It was Alva who reportedly coined the saying, "Just pray to God—she will help you."

Figure 112. Giovanni Boldini, *Elizabeth Drexel Lehr, Later Lady Decies*, ca. 1900. Oil on canvas, 86 × 46 in. (218.4 × 116.8 cm). The Elms, The Preservation Society of Newport County.

Alva spent several summers at Marble House after Oliver's death, and in 1913 added the Chinese teahouse on the lawn down by the ocean's edge. Two of Richard Morris Hunt's sons, Richard Howland and Joseph, who were architects, designed it for her. In connection with this commission the Hunt brothers traveled to China for proper inspiration for their design. Alva opened the little teahouse in 1914 with a conference of women activists.

Epilogue for Marble House

Marble House was closed for good about 1919, for after World War I Alva went to France, where she lived the rest of her life. She was, however, still a builder, as recalled by Consuelo, who was by then divorced from the Duke of Marlborough and happily married to a French aviation hero named Jacques Balsan:

> Her life was a lonely one and she decided to join me in France where I had determined to live. . . . I thought that her decision to live in France might be actuated by more than just the desire to be near me; always an inveterate builder, she welcomed . . . the opportunity to build a new home in the country, being really happy only when thus employed.[35]

Meanwhile, following his separation from Alva back in 1895, William Kissam had gotten on with his own life. His second marriage was a happy one, to a woman named Anne Harriman Sands Rutherford, who was just the opposite of all Alva had been. According to Consuelo, "Visits to my father were particularly pleasant, for I rejoiced in the happiness he had found in his second marriage. My stepmother had a gay and gentle nature."[36]

After his marriage in 1903 William Kissam moved to Paris, where he lived until his death. He became well known in both New York and Paris for the clinics he founded. His "small" house and racing stables at Poissy near Paris had their own racing track, and he ran his famous horses in the Grand Prix and the Prix du Jockey Club, content in the happiness that had eluded him during the stormy years of his life with Alva. He died in France in 1920.

Shortly before her death in 1933 Alva sold Marble House to Frederick H. Prince, president of the Armour Meat Company. It was bought from the Prince Trust in 1963 by the Preservation Society of Newport County. The Trust donated the furniture while the money for the purchase was a gift from William Kissam and Alva's youngest son, Harold Vanderbilt, the noted yachtsman. Marble House is now open to the public.

The Breakers

Marble House may have been built a few years earlier, but the grandest of all the grand houses in Newport was The Breakers, the cottage of Alice Gwynne and Cornelius Vanderbilt II, whose palatial mansion in New York City has already been discussed (figure 86). When Cornelius bought the waterfront property on Bellevue Avenue in 1885, a house already stood on the site. It had been designed in 1877 by Peabody and Stearns of Boston in the picturesque shingle style for tobacco tycoon Pierre Lorillard. Cornelius and Alice seemed to have been content with this behemoth and in fact added a north wing, greenhouses, and a children's playhouse. But in November of 1892 sparks escaping from a chimney ignited a conflagration that reduced the wood-framed house to ashes.

Alice was determined to rebuild their cottage but in a lordly fashion befitting her family's position as head of the house of Vanderbilt. Three months before the fire, Alva had held her dazzling house-warming, and Marble House immediately became the glory of the resort. Comparisons were inescapable, and in relation to Marble House, Alice's Breakers—the old Breakers—looked absolutely dowdy and frumpish. Indeed, for Alice, the burning of the old place prepared the way for her to beat Alva at her own game, which was to be undertaken only by the most courageous—and the most wealthy.

The Design

Richard Morris Hunt was sent for as if he were a physician being summoned on a life-or-death emergency. He prepared two watercolor studies to present to Cornelius and Alice, one proposal being in the style of the early French Renaissance of the time of Francis I (figure 113), the other being decidedly Italian and classical. The former is closely related to Hunt's design for Biltmore (figure 130, p. 197), then being erected outside Asheville, North Carolina. But Alice may have felt that the round towers and steeply pitched roof

were too similar in style to the Petit Château that the architect had created for Alva Vanderbilt in New York City (figure 67, p. 111), and the hint of imitation would have made it unacceptable. The classical design was chosen.

For the eleven-acre plot on Ochre Point, Hunt designed an Italian palazzo that was as much a break with American vernacular traditions as could be imagined, but no more so than Ochre Court and Marble House, which were also of his creation. The five-story palazzo design, of the type often seen in the area around Genoa, Italy, was as Italianate as Alva's Marble House was French, with classical cornices, arched openings, loggias, and a red-tiled roof (figure 114). The footprint of the mansion measured 250 feet across by 150 feet deep, and when finished it contained seventy rooms.

Cornelius was a cautious man, always thinking ahead to avoid disasters or emergencies; to that end, knowing that roofs often needed to be replaced, he had enough tile made to completely replace the roof three times. The original roof is still in place, and all those extra tiles still exist, stored away for when they may be needed.

At times there were over two hundred workmen on the site, setting stone, laying bricks, placing beams, doing carpentry, creating mosaic floors or ceilings for the loggias, carving architectural details, laying the tiles of the roof, and so on. Whereas Cornelius had paid only $375,000 for the original house and property, this new mansion cost him $7 million. But when it was finished, Alice had surely won the contest, for many would agree that no cottage in Newport—including Marble House—could match the splendor and grandeur of The Breakers.

The exterior was enlivened with a considerable amount of ornamentation. In addition to the architectural carving such as the quoining, the moldings, and the trophies in the metopes, there were figural sculptures—of mythological

Figure 113. Richard Morris Hunt, study for The Breakers in the style of Francis I, 1892. Watercolor and ink on paper, 20 × 28 in. (50.8 × 71.1 cm). The Octagon, Museum of the American Architectural Foundation, Washington, D.C.

Figure 114 (overleaf). Richard Morris Hunt, The Breakers, the Alice and Cornelius Vanderbilt II residence, Newport, 1892–95. The Preservation Society of Newport County. Photograph copyright, Richard Cheek.

personages—in the spandrels of many of the arched openings (figure 115). At Newport the outdoors was meant to be enjoyed in the sunshine and bay breezes of the summer months, and Hunt designed a wonderful loggia area on the second floor, facing the bay, that blended indoor and outdoor living. The ceiling of this area is covered with beautiful mosaics that add colorful decoration to the architecture (figure 116).

Construction was begun in 1893. The house was officially opened with a gala ball two years later, a ball given, on the evening of 14 August 1895, to celebrate the coming-out of one of Cornelius and Alice's daughters, Gertrude Vanderbilt, the young woman who would eventually marry Harry Payne Whitney. Indeed, the main purpose of the "cottages" at Newport was for entertaining, and architects were instructed to address this foremost requirement. In addition to dinner parties and grand galas and costume balls and coming-out parties there were pleasant afternoon fetes on the lawn, as seen in figure 117.

Figure 115. Karl Bitter, allegorical figures, side porch, waterfront, The Breakers, Newport, ca. 1894. Newport Restoration Foundation, Newport, R.I.

The Interiors

The interiors have been beautifully preserved, thanks to the good efforts, first of Vanderbilt descendants, then of the Preservation Society of Newport County, which now owns the property. Visitors enter into the great hall, which rises to a height of forty-five feet (figure 118). This hall is in the form of a Roman atrium, except it is enclosed. The ceiling is painted to imitate the open sky, and is framed by a great gilded cornice, the detailing of which, in both its sculptural decoration and its color scheme, is magnificent. Loggias of the upper story look out on this inner courtyard in the manner of Italian palazzos. The walls are of imported cream-colored Caen stone, inlaid with several different colors of marble; alternating marble and alabaster piers and columns define the bays of the gallery. Eight sets of matching doorways lead to other rooms and the grand stairway, which rises at the left to a landing and then divides. The carpet was one of several obtained from the William Morris manufactory in England. A fireplace—with carvings by Karl Bitter—warms the room. Along with the music room, this hall was of such a scale that it could be used for grand receptions and balls.

The music room is one of the two most splendid rooms in the house—indeed, in Newport—the other being the state dining room (figures 119 and 120). The ceiling of the music room is beautifully decorated with a central panel, painted in colorful but softly muted hues, recalling the designs of Roman murals at Pompeii. Intricately detailed coffers, with rosette centers, are rendered in off-white and gilt, as are the walls with their columns and pilasters. Russet and orange drapery swags hang at the doorways, a color scheme that is carried into the chairs, sofas, screens, and other pieces. The lavishness of the room is nearly overwhelming—the crystal chandeliers, the carving on the gilt furniture, the extraordinary pale blue marble of the fireplace and its surround as well as in the tabletop. Touches of Roman ornamentation are repeated in the pilasters with their gilded capitals and bases.

This masterpiece of a room was the work of Jules Allard et Fils of Paris, executed from designs drawn up by Richard

Figure 116. Loggia mosaics, waterfront porch, The Breakers, Newport, ca. 1895. The Preservation Society of Newport County. Photograph copyright, Richard Cheek.

Hermann Bouwens van der Boijen. Hunt sent to Allard the exact dimensions of the room, indicating the location of each doorway, window, recession, fireplace, or whatever. The room was then constructed in Paris, and when completed, it was disassembled and shipped over to the United States. Cornelius Vanderbilt paid to have the French artisans who created the room come over to attend to the installation.

Allard et Fils of Paris and New York

The decorating house of Allard et Fils is an interesting phenomenon in the creation of grand houses, both in Europe and in America. The firm's first commission in the United States was for the boudoir of Louisa Kissam Vanderbilt in the William Henry Vanderbilt mansion on Fifth Avenue, installed about 1880–81. This was perhaps arranged through Christian Herter, who was in charge of the Vanderbilt interiors and who had studied art in Paris. Thereafter, Allard's was frequently called on by American architects who were designing and decorating gilded mansions for their wealthy clients.

Allard had worked for Alice and Cornelius Vanderbilt before, executing the Louis XVI music room in their New York City mansion, and he had also done rooms in Alva and William Kissam Vanderbilt's Petit Château on Fifth Avenue. After Allard completed the latter commission in December of 1882, Richard Morris Hunt made him his primary source

Figure 117. Lawn fete at The Breakers, the residence of Mrs. Vanderbilt, ca. 1900. Photograph. Newport Historical Society.

Figure 118 (opposite). Richard Morris Hunt, great hall, The Breakers, 1895. The Preservation Society of Newport County. Photograph copyright, Richard Cheek.

for fabulous interiors, for the house of Allard could supply everything—its craftsmen could decorate the walls and the coffered ceilings, it could provide antique furniture or new pieces that simulated the antique, it had sources for obtaining ancient fabrics if upholstery were required, it could produce eighteenth-century chandeliers that were wired for that new invention, the electric light. Allard's workshops in Paris employed expert artisans in cabinetry, woodcarving, plaster work, painted and gilded decorations—whatever was needed to produce a *piece de résistance* such as the music room at The Breakers.

In anticipation of a lucrative market in the United States, Jules Allard established a branch in New York in 1885 in partnership with designer Eugene Prignot. Both Hunt and Stanford White turned to Allard's designers and craftsmen constantly for furnishings and architectural interiors in the styles of Francis I, Louis XIV, Louis XV, and Louis XVI. Their creations were knowledgeable interpretations of period rooms that were possessed with something of the effulgence and bombast of the Second Empire and *fin de siècle*.

Some years later, in 1905, the house of Allard in New York transformed into that of Alavoine. Lucien Alavoine had begun his career as an employee of Eugene Roudillon, whose fine furniture had long been known to Americans who went to Paris to shop for such things. Alavoine was assigned to execute the interiors of the Paris mansion of wealthy Edouard Mamelsdorf, and the latter was so impressed with his work that he offered to finance Alavoine in setting up his own business in 1890. In the following decade Alavoine collaborated with Allard on several Newport projects, including Marble House and The Breakers.

Alavoine bought out Roudillon in 1893, and, following the lead of Allard, opened a branch office in New York City. Twelve years later he bought out Allard in both Paris and New York. The New York branch frequently worked with the architect Horace Trumbauer, as at The Elms in Newport, or at the Edwardian Room in Henry J. Hardenberg's Plaza Hotel in New York City. In New York the business was run by Edouard Hitau, a decorator who was consultant to the Metropolitan Museum of Art in setting up its eighteenth-century period rooms. The firm of Alavoine was later managed by Martin Becker, who presided over it until it closed in 1965.

Figure 119. Richard Morris Hunt and Jules Allard et Fils of Paris, the music room, The Breakers, Newport, 1895. The Preservation Society of Newport County. Photograph copyright, Richard Cheek.

Figure 120 (opposite). Richard Morris Hunt and Jules Allard et Fils of Paris, state dining room, The Breakers, Newport, 1895. The Preservation Society of Newport County. Photograph copyright, Richard Cheek. One of the most magnificent rooms of La Belle Époque in America, the state dining room nearly overwhelms one upon entering it. Nearly every aspect of fine arts decoration known at that time was called into service here—painting, sculpture, extraordinary furniture making, carpet weaving, the artistry of crystal chandeliers, decorative stucco work, bronze casting, wrought iron, stone masonry, gilding, and more. All of this was coordinated in the Paris workshops of Jules Allard et Fils.

Figure 121 (above). Grand salon of Napoleon III, Richelieu Wing, Palais du Louvre, Paris, ca. 1860. Art Resource. Wealthy Americans who traveled to Paris were frequently invited to the imperial apartments, from which they carried home visions of their extraordinary grandeur. Although Hector Martin Lefuel was the architect in charge of Napoleon III's New Louvre, the interiors were created by Fould. For this magnificent chamber he commissioned Charles Raphael Marechal to paint the ceiling panel depicting *The Re-Uniting of the Louvre and the Tuileries by Napoleon III.* The scenes in the lunettes represent the many phases of construction of the two palaces during the reigns of Francois I, Catherine de Medicis, Henri IV, and Louis XIV, while the elaborate cornice decorations and stucco caryatids were executed by Louis Alphonse Tranchant. Gilding abounded, on the pilasters, door moldings, gigantic mirror frames, and on the furniture, often set off by rich, red walls or upholstery. Enormous chandeliers consisting of thousands of crystals each illuminated the room. Comparison of the state dining room at The Breakers and the grand salon at the Louvre is inevitable—it was in Paris, after all, that the Vanderbilt's great dining room was designed and created.

The State Dining Room and Other Rooms

Returning to the interiors at The Breakers, the state dining room—meaning the formal dining room as opposed to the smaller room in which the family normally had their meals—is one of the great rooms of the Western world (figure 120). Its beauty is in its totality as well as in its details, for it presents a flood of richness that delights the eye with its color, pattern, texture, and figural ornamentation. The scale of the room, two stories high and measuring forty-two by fifty-eight feet, is set by the twelve colossal columns of rose alabaster with gilded capitals. The walls are veneered in Cippolino marble, the ceiling is adorned with a painting of Aurora, goddess of dawn, and the cornice is a work of art in itself. The figurative and decorative work above the cornice adds to the grandeur of the room, as do the gilded arches with their keystone cartouches. The fireplace replicates one from the period of Louis XIII, while the enormous chandeliers are of baccarat crystal. This Beaux-Arts masterpiece by Allard et Fils rivals, in lavishness, the salons of seventeenth-century Venetian palaces, which was exactly what was intended, and it challenges the splendors of the grand-style interiors of Napoleon III's Second Empire in Paris (figure 121)—the grand foyer and stairway of the Paris Opera House come to mind, or the renovated royal apartments of the New Louvre.

The library, too, is a beautiful room, although not as grand as the state dining room or the music room (figure 122). Designed by Richard Morris Hunt himself, its walls are paneled with Circassian walnut and green Spanish hand-tooled leather. Here, the fireplace is ancient, having been bought from the sixteenth-century Château d'Arnay-le-Duc in France's Loire Valley; it bears an ironic inscription, which in translation reads, "Little do I care for riches, and do not miss them, since only cleverness prevails in the end."

The billiard room has walls of gray-green Cippolino marble and is handsomely ornamented with mosaics on both floor and ceiling (figure 123). In the billiard room Cornelius and his gentlemen friends found a haven, after dinner, where dinner jackets could be removed, business matters discussed, cigars smoked, and brandy savored—away from the fussy splendor of the more formal rooms and the obligation to make polite conversation with a dinner partner.

Figure 122. Richard Morris Hunt, library, The Breakers, Newport, 1895. The Preservation Society of Newport County. Photograph copyright, Richard Cheek.

Figure 123. Richard Morris Hunt, billiard room, The Breakers, Newport, 1895. The Preservation Society of Newport County. Photograph copyright, Richard Cheek.

The family bedrooms at The Breakers, located on the second floor, are handsomely done but are nowhere near as lavish as the main rooms on the first floor. Here, as in many mansions, the upper regions were seldom seen by anyone other than the immediate family. There is a marked difference in the amount of money spent on the public rooms below and the family's quarters above, and much less was expended on the servants' rooms on the upper floor. For the decoration of the family bedrooms at The Breakers, the commission went to a young architect from Boston who would soon exchange his architectural career for that of interior decorator—Ogden Codman, to whom we will return later.

Epilogue for The Breakers

Alas, not long after the palatial cottage was completed, Cornelius Vanderbilt suffered the severe stroke from which he never fully recovered. His last three years were spent mainly in his mansion in New York City, where, when he was first recovering, automobile traffic was diverted off of Fifth Avenue alongside his home and the streets were covered with tanbark and sawdust so the noise of horses' hooves and carriage wheels would not disturb him. Such was the power of the family.

Cornelius Vanderbilt II died in 1899. The funeral was held in Saint Bartholomew's church, then located at the corner of 44th Street and Madison Avenue, with Bishop Henry Codman Potter presiding. Soon thereafter, the family asked Stanford White to design, as a memorial to Cornelius, a three-portal entrance to the church. White followed, as his model, the facade of a Romanesque church he had seen in Arles, France, and among the sculptors who executed portions following White's design were Philip Martiny, Daniel Chester French, and Andrew O'Connor. The bronze doorways were cast by the Henry Bonnard foundry in New York City and were dedicated in 1904. When the church moved to its present location at 50th and Park Avenue in 1918, the architect, Bertram Goodhue, incorporated the Vanderbilt Memorial doors into the facade of his new building.

Alice Vanderbilt continued to use The Breakers as her summer retreat, and after her death it passed to one of her daughters, Gladys, who, having married a Hungarian nobleman, had become the Countess Széchenyi. She leased the estate to the Preservation Society of Newport County for one dollar and helped raise funds for its restoration. The Preservation Society acquired the property in 1972 and opened it to the public.

By 1895 Newport had several landmark residences that set a new standard and a new concept of the summer resort "cottage"—Ochre Court, Marble House, and The Breakers being foremost among them. These represented a conscious break with the American vernacular tradition of shingle-covered wood-frame houses that had prevailed in the region, for the "cottages" were clearly in the manner of the great houses, châteaux, and palazzos of European aristocracy. That was exactly what the architects' clients wanted, to display their enormous wealth and to ally with Old World nobility and separate from New World middle class.

Figure 124. Charles Dana Gibson, *Their Last Day of Summer*. From *Life* (1 October 1896), pp. 250–51. Summer romances blossomed among the young at the Newport cottages, and the end of the season often meant a sad parting, as captured here by Gibson.

Whether we think with some that [Biltmore] and the whole estate are un-American and out of accord with our nineteenth-century feeling and civilization, or whether we think with others that this marks the beginning of an era of great American . . . country houses, we must at least accept it as a great work of art. So able and cool a critic as [Charles Follen] McKim ranks it with the very best work of the century throughout the world, and considers Mr. Hunt to have bettered his instructors in the Early French Renaissance. At all events it stands as the best work ever done by the leading architect of the century.

Rick Olmsted to a Miss Clerque, 17 February 1895; quoted from Brendel-Pandich, "Biltmore in Asheville" (1980)

Chapter Eight

Richard Morris Hunt

Biltmore and The Rothschild Factor

For Richard Morris Hunt, the period between 1884 and 1895—the year of his death—was one of almost superhuman creativity in the area of grand domestic architecture. And that was in addition to the other enormous projects that came out of his office, such as the Administration Building at the World's Columbian Exposition (1893) in Chicago and the central section of the heroic new Metropolitan Museum of Art in New York City. A partial list of the houses he designed during that span of little more than a decade makes the point:

1881–84	Henry G. Marquand house, New York City
1885–87	Ochre Court, the Ogden Goelet house, Newport, R.I.
1885–87	Ogden Mills house, New York City
1888–92	Marble House, Newport, R.I.
1888–95	Biltmore, Asheville, N.C.
1891–95	Elbridge Gerry house, New York City
1891–94	Belcourt, Newport, R.I.
1892–95	The Breakers, Newport, R.I.
1891–95	John Jacob III/Caroline Astor houses, New York City
1893–95	Josephine Schmid house, New York City

Logistically, travel time alone, between his New York office and Chicago, Newport, Biltmore, or anywhere else when his presence on the building site was required, placed extraordinary demands on him. Moreover, each was a sizable commission for which each patron expected nothing less than his full attention.

Influence of French Architecture on Hunt

Richard Morris Hunt's lifelong penchant for French architecture of the fifteenth through the nineteenth centuries began in his youth when, in 1852, he and his mother traveled throughout the Loire Valley, visiting the châteaux of Chambord, Chenonceau, Blois, and Amboise, among others. His devotion to it was reinforced by his years of study at the École des Beaux-Arts and then by the almost annual visits he and his wife Catharine made to France once he became a successful architect. The admiration he felt for those noble edifices of the French aristocracy was shared by his patrons. It is therefore not surprising that the influence of numerous French châteaux appeared regularly in his own creations in the 1880s and early 1890s. Examples include his great houses built between 1885 and 1890: the William Borden mansion (Chicago, 1885–89), Ogden Goelet's Ochre Court at Newport, and ultimately the most grandiose of all, the Astor residence in New York City and Biltmore in western North Carolina.

Evidence for Hunt's passion for historic French architecture abounds, with Catharine's biography of her husband serving as an especially rich source. This typescript biography appears to have been written to provide the Hunts' grandchildren with a knowledge of their grandfather and his work. Among other things, it tells of the excitement of visits to one or another beautiful château, as, for instance, when the Hunts were traveling in Europe with George W. Vanderbilt while Biltmore was still in the planning stage; Catharine recalled the three of them being in England in the spring of 1889, but then Richard

> was called to Paris by the William K. Vanderbilts who were clamoring for his presence to arrive at certain decisions for the interiors for Marble House; I stayed behind in London with George W. Vanderbilt. . . . In Paris, the Vanderbilts insisted upon his going to the races at Chantilly on Sunday. . . . As the Vanderbilt's four-in-hand drove on the grounds, the old Duc [d'Aumale] exclaimed [from the royal pavilion,] "Tiens, c'est mon ami Hunt," and he sent his equerry to call him to his side. When RMH told him I was coming from London and that George W. Vanderbilt was with us, he said we must all come out to breakfast at Chantilly, so a few days afterward found us in the train in response to a formal invitation.[1]

Henri-Eugène-Philippe-Louis d'Orléans, the Duc d'Aumale—fourth son of King Louis-Philippe—had only recently restored the lovely old Château de Chantilly and presented it, along with its extraordinary furnishings and its collection of Renaissance and Baroque paintings (Musée Condé), to the Institut de France—that is, to the nation of France (figures 125 and 126). What the Hunts and George Vanderbilt saw there, in Henri Daumet's restoration, left them breathless, and surely enlarged young Vanderbilt's visions of the desired effect of Biltmore.

This wish to identify with Europe's ancient aristocracy through the medium of architecture was supported by the fact that the French nouveaux riches had behaved similarly, erecting fairyland castles and grand châteaux in imitation of the highest social class with whom they wanted to integrate their family lines. A spectacular example is Challain-la-Potherie, a wonderfully picturesque pastiche of late-Medieval

and early French Renaissance architectural motifs, which was, however, erected in 1854. Eugène-Emmanuel Viollet-le-Duc, the famous mid-nineteenth-century architect and restorer of architecture, observed the irony of a nation of people who had so recently dispatched its aristocracy, either at the guillotine or into exile, yet now raised a class of merchants and moneylenders who wanted to live like nobility in nouveaux châteaux of ancient appearance.

But even the imperial family of Napoleon III and Empress Eugénie engaged in such architectural patronage for the purpose of establishing their rightful place among the long line of rulers of France, for they commissioned Viollet-le-Duc to rebuild the old Pierrefonds (Oise, 1858–70), starting with no more than the ruined walls of the fourteenth-century structure and raising up a fabulous Second Empire château in the late-Gothic mode. In 1873, Richard Morris Hunt accompanied his friend Viollet-le-Duc out to Pierrefonds to inspect the place. It might also be noted that in 1856 Viollet-le-Duc had been asked to design the imperial train for Napoleon III and his empress; a specially designed private rail car was something that would not have gone unnoticed by visiting American railroad and industrial tycoons.

Figure 125. Château de Chantilly, Oise, France, originally constructed 1560, rebuilt by the Duc d'Aumale, 1876–83, and presented to the Institut de France in 1886. Bridgeman Art Library. Americans flocked to the Château de Chantilly to see the Duc d'Aumale's famous restorations, which were widely covered in American journals and newspapers. The estate dated back to Anne de Montmorency, High Constable of France, in the sixteenth century. It later passed to the Great Condé in the time of Louis XIV, when the grounds were laid out by the landscape architect Andre le Notre, who also did the grounds at Versailles. During the French Revolution the château was razed, but beginning in 1876 the Duc d'Aumale began its restoration—rebuilding, actually, from the ground up—completing that task, with the help of the architect Daumet, in 1883—that is, just as Americans were beginning to build châteaux of their own along Fifth Avenue and in the mountains of western North Carolina.

The Rothschilds as Role Models

There was no better example of a nouveau riche family utilizing architecture extensively to promote its social aspirations—just as the Vanderbilts and other American parvenus were to do—than the Rothschilds, whose fortunes were, like those of many Americans, founded on finance and railroads. Here was a family that delighted in building large, impressive homes, filled with the choicest examples of the decorative arts, paintings and sculptures, plus boiseries, fireplaces, doorways, and the likes plucked from ancient châteaux and palazzos across the Continent. But the Rothschilds did this a generation or two before the Americans did, and touring Vanderbilts could, in the 1880s, visit their great houses, even as they were beginning to plan similar edifices back home, on Fifth Avenue or in western North Carolina.

Figure 126. Bedroom of Monsieur le Prince, Château de Chantilly, Oise, France, as restored by the Duc d'Aumale, ca. 1883. Bridgeman Art Library. The interiors of Chantilly were magnificently done and contained a splendid library and art collection. The latter probably exerted considerable influence on Americans who, soon after Chantilly's completion, began to collect works by European Old Masters. A sense of the collection that the Duc d'Aumale assembled there is given in a contemporary account: "Quite lately the Duke acquired . . . the Earl of Dudley's famous Raphaels. Besides a historic portrait gallery of great interest, the great masters of Italy and the various schools of French art are here worthily represented. The Poussins, the Ingres, the Greuez, the Delacroix, the Decamps, form a collection worth making a pilgrimage to see. Then there are Raphaels, Da Vincis, Titians—in fine, the Duke has not only been one of the most assiduous, but one of the most fortunate collectors in this world. There are also magnificent Beauvais and Gobelins tapestry, faience, miniatures, marqueterie, engraved gems and jewelry [and] enamels." (*American Architect and Building News*, 17 July 1886, p. 35.)

The Rothschild saga began in Frankfurt, Germany, with the progenitor, Mayer Amschel Rothschild (1744–1812), the son of a shopkeeper who through diligence and business acumen rose to become financial adviser to the Elector of Hesse-Kassel. Mayer sent his five sons out to the leading centers of Europe to establish an interlocking financial network, one that has never been rivaled: While Mayer Amschel (1773–1885) remained in Frankfurt, Salomon (1774–1885) went to Vienna, where the Hapsburgs became his main clients, Nathan Mayer (1777–1836) arrived in London in 1798, Karl Mayer (1788–1855) was sent to Naples, and James (1792–1868) settled in Paris. This generation and especially the next built great townhouses and country houses and formed extraordinary collections of art and domestic furnishings.

Although almost all of the Rothschilds built prodigiously and lavishly, only a few instances can be surveyed here, and focus will be limited to one example—Waddesdon Manor. In London, Lionel (Nathan Mayer's son) built his fine townhouse adjoining the Duke of Wellington's Apsley House, while his brother, Mayer Amschel, erected Mentmore, which established a standard for nouveau riche grandeur. When James, of the Paris branch, saw Mentmore, he immediately found an architect whom he commanded to build a greater house, suggesting an architectural rivalry, similar to what occurred later among the Vanderbilts and other American families. For James, Joseph Paxton accordingly designed Château de Ferrières, erected just outside Paris between 1853 and 1860 (figure 127). Alphonse (1827–1905, James's son) built the beautiful Château de Pregny near Geneva, and Albert, of the Viennese line, commissioned a sumptuous townhouse, while Alfred, son of Lionel and a noted collector as well as playboy, built Halton House in Buckinghamshire. Many more examples include either refurbished residences of aristocracy or homes built anew in a grand manner. Most of this activity, all across Europe, was occurring between about 1850 and 1890—that is, in the decades just ahead of the American millionaires who followed the pattern exactly.

Sometimes the Rothschilds committed the parvenu error of mistaking lavishness for excellence in architecture and interiors, at least Lady Frances Balfour thought so, as noted in her diary after she visited Alfred's Halton House: "I have seldom seen anything more terribly vulgar. . . . Outside it is a combination of a French château and a gambling house. Inside it is . . . gaudily decorated. . . . Oh! but the hideousness of everything, the showiness! the sense of lavish wealth thrust up your nose!"[2] One is reminded of Edith Wharton's comment that she wished the Vanderbilts did not build houses that demeaned the art of architecture (see p. 134).

Figure 127. Joseph Paxton, the great hall, Ferrières, near Paris, France, ca. 1855. Art Resource. Ferrières, the residence of Baron James de Rothschild, is an example of the "architectural warfare" in which the great banking family engaged throughout Europe; members of the Vanderbilt family would, a few years later, follow a similar practice, using grand architecture to establish their position in society and their place in the pecking order within the family. From the outset, Ferrières was intended to rival, even surpass, Waddesdon (figures 128 and 129), the creation of Baron James's nephew. At Ferrières the noted historical and decorative painter Eugène Lami was commissioned to execute the interiors, which he did, somewhat in the manner of stage sets. Lami had earlier been commissioned by King Louis-Philippe to paint a series of military pictures for the palace at Versailles, and his work is known in America through his *Battle of New Orleans*, which is in the Cabildo in New Orleans.

A number of the Rothschilds established estates in Aylesbury, Buckinghamshire, about twenty miles northwest of London. Mentmore was created by Joseph Paxton in 1850. For Mayer Amschel, Paxton erected a Victorian version of a famous Elizabethan edifice—Wollaton Hall in Nottinghamshire—a direct borrowing from an ancient residence of aristocracy. By this time the heads of nearly all of the Rothschild branches had been ennobled to the rank of barony, and on the Continent the prefix "de" or "von" or "van" now appeared before the name. It was therefore obligatory to build like aristocracy.

If the English considered Halton House gaudy, they admired Mentmore greatly, especially the interiors. The entrance hall was grand, being two stories high with an arcaded gallery overlooking the splendors of antique and eighteenth-century marble sculptures, rare tapestries, a black-and-white marble fireplace from Peter Paul Rubens's own house in Antwerp and designed by the great artist himself, plus assorted carved, gilded, and tapestried furniture. The walls of the dining room at Mentmore were lined with white and gilded boiserie taken from the eighteenth-century Hôtel de Villars in Paris. The richly carved and gilded tables flanking the fireplace were extraordinary pieces, and Mayer Amschel loved to fill his rooms with such treasures as chandeliers from the Doge's Palace in Venice and a few trinkets from the Ducal barge as well.

Baron Ferdinand de Rothschild's Waddesdon Manor

Ferdinand de Rothschild (1839–98) was the son of Anselm, head of the Vienna branch of the family; his mother, Charlotte, was the daughter of Nathan Mayer of the London branch. Ferdinand settled in England in 1860 and five years later married Evelina, daughter of Lionel, who was by then head of the London line. But within a year Ferdinand was widowed, and he turned to collecting paintings and decorative arts as a distraction from his grief.[3] In 1874 he purchased, from the sixth Duke of Marlborough, a tract of thirty-two hundred acres in Buckinghamshire, only a few miles from Mentmore. On a hill amid the rolling countryside he erected an architectural masterpiece, a French château designed by a Parisian architect named Gabriel-Hippolyte Alexandre Destailleur (1822–93), renowned for his restorations of noble châteaux throughout France.[4]

Destailleur foreshadowed American architects such as Stanford White, among others, in that he collected ancient boiseries and all sorts of antique decorative items for later use in his restorations; he was there, on the spot, in Paris as Baron Haussmann razed innumerable ancient hôtels des villes and other structures to make room for his broad new boulevards. Destailleur raced ahead of the wrecker's ball to salvage the interiors of such places, to give them new life in the renovations he was executing for France's *haute bourgeoisie*. Destailleur's grandfather and father had been architects to the Duc d'Orléans and he himself had been trained at the École des Beaux-Arts, so he possessed every credential required by Baron Ferdinand.

Waddesdon was begun in 1874 and, although the Baron had moved into the château as early as 1880, it was finally completed in 1889 (figure 128) a few years before Richard Morris Hunt began designing Biltmore for George Vanderbilt. Indeed, in 1889, at about the time that work on Biltmore began, Vanderbilt and the Hunts toured England and the Continent to study châteaux and country houses that might inspire the designs of Biltmore; among the many places they visited was Waddesdon, and according to Catharine Hunt, her husband and Vanderbilt actually spent several days at Waddesdon, which she noted was "said to be the handsomest country place in England."[5] The scale, style, and lavishness of that splendid country estate had to make an impression on someone who was about to commence his own baronial retreat.

Destailleur produced the design of Waddesdon, in plan and elevation, and he assisted Baron Ferdinand in obtaining architectural interiors such as ancient boiseries, fine old carved fireplaces, richly coffered ceilings, and the like. But Rothschild was directly involved in every step of the project. As a young man he had toured the châteaux of Touraine in France and reportedly declared that if he were ever to build a great house, its design would be based on a French model of the type he saw on that trip. When the time came, in the mid-1870s, it was he who specified that a French château be erected on the English countryside, for while he preferred living in England, he wanted his house to be French. This was, to say the least, unusual in England, which had its own architectural traditions for country houses.

Figure 128. Gabriel-Hippolyte Alexandre Destailleur, Waddesdon Manor, Buckinghamshire, England, 1874–89, residence of Baron Ferdinand de Rothschild. National Trust, England. Bridgeman Art Library.

Destailleur's design called for a large rambling mansion that contained specific reminiscences from several examples of French Renaissance architecture: "the two towers of the Château de Maintenon; the dormer windows of Anet; the chimneys of Chambord; and two versions of the open staircase of Blois."[6] The style chosen, there as at Biltmore, was that transitional moment between Gothic and Renaissance classicism—Gothic in its asymmetry, coned towers, steep roof with irregular roofline interrupted by dormers, chimney stacks, and tourelles, but classical in the employment of pilasters, cornices, and strapwork decorative motifs.

Waddesdon was constructed of an ochre-colored Bath stone and was surrounded by vast formal gardens laid out by the Frenchman Elie Lainé, with fountains (from the palazzo of the Duke of Parma) strategically placed and marble statues (copies of ancient works) lining the garden paths and avenues. The main house was surrounded by auxiliary structures such as stables, a dairy building and various other farm buildings, an aviary, and so on; near the estate the baron developed a support village. Altogether, the manor comprised a grand baronial layout almost identical to that devised by George Vanderbilt at Biltmore only a few years later.[7]

The Interiors at Waddesdon

While Destailleur may have been of assistance in producing the eighteenth-century paneling that he rescued from renewal projects, the interiors at Waddesdon were the creations of Baron Ferdinand de Rothschild himself. The furnishings were almost totally French, of the reigns of Louis XV and Louis XVI with an occasional piece from the era of Louis XIV.[8] The baron shared with the American nouveaux riches a passion to possess objects that had been made for or owned by royalty and aristocracy. To fill his new mansion, for example, Rothschild bought heavily at the famous Hamilton Palace sale of 1882, a sale that has been called the greatest dispersement of high-style French furniture since the French Revolution. He also acquired things from the Prince Demidoff sale in Florence—where the agent of William Henry Vanderbilt had been one of his competitive bidders—and he regularly purchased *objets d'art* from the English nobility who were in need of money.

Numerous important pieces came into Waddesdon that had been made for Louis XVI or Marie-Antoinette for the palace at Versailles or at one of the Trianons, crafted by such masters as Jean-Henri Riesener and Charles Cressent—magnificent examples of the *ébéniste*'s artistry, with rich marquetry of rosewood, fruit woods, mother-of-pearl, and lapis lazuli; with gilded ormolu ornamentations; with delicately painted Sevres plaques worked into the designs. There were eleven Savonnerie carpets that had been commissioned by French royalty, and a sixfold woven screen by Savonnerie, from designs by François Desportes, that had previously been owned by Louisa, Marchioness of Waterford. From Sir Henry Hoare of Stourhead, Rothschild acquired a set of gilt bronze sconces and an elaborate Rococo desk, while from Lord Fitzwilliams's country house at Milton he bought a monumental black and gold secretary.

Of the many grand rooms, the most splendid is the Red Drawing Room, so-named because of the brilliant crimson eighteenth-century fabric with which the walls are lined (figure 129). The ceiling, by the Dutch painter Jacob de Wit (1695–1754), depicts "The Apotheosis of Hercules," with the hero's chariot driven by Mercury amid the assembled gods and goddesses of Mount Olympus; it dates from about 1725 and was probably taken from a palace in Amsterdam. The Savonnerie carpet had been commissioned by Louis XIV for the grand gallery at the Louvre, and the two elegant commodes had been crafted by Riesener, *ébéniste* to the French royal family. Above one door was placed a marble profile portrait of Louis XIV, inscribed with the date of 1699. Choice pieces of Sevres and Meissen served as focal points amid the lavish decor.

If Baron Ferdinand preferred French furnishings, his major paintings were English, for he possessed no fewer than nine works by Sir Joshua Reynolds and seven by Thomas Gainsborough, most of which were full-length portraits.[9] Many of these were acquired through Agnew, the noted art dealer of London, rather than bought directly from the families. In the Red Drawing Room were hung Gainsborough's *Prince of Wales (later George IV) with His Charger*, *Lady Sheffield*, and *Mrs. John Douglas*, plus Reynolds's *Colonel St. Leger*. But in other rooms were displayed the latter artist's *Mrs. Abington as the Comic Muse*, and *Lady Jane Halliday* as well as Gainsborough's *Duchess of Cumberland* and *Pink Boy*, showing a lad in Van Dyckian costume, the "pink" counterpart to the famous *Blue Boy* that is now in the Huntington Library in San Marino. One recent historian remarked that "the collection of these is so large and so choice that it goes a long way to make up for the masterpieces of English portraiture which left England for America in the dozen or so years after the 1914–18 War."[10]

Almost all of the Gainsboroughs and Reynoldses were images of ancestry, but from some family other than the baron's; that is, the walls of the manor were not lined with portraits of the Rothschilds, but rather with aristocratic icons appropriated for the grandeur and pedigree they could bestow, however tenuously, on their new owner. Like the furnishings, the paneling, and even the style of the exterior of Waddesdon, the portraits too were borrowed from the culture and traditions of aristocracy in the hope that the mantel of nobility would elevate the new owner's social position.

In fairness, Baron Ferdinand de Rothschild collected beautiful things out of a sincere admiration for their aesthetic merits, and the same could be said of George W. Vanderbilt. However, that did not conflict with the desire to acquire—by osmosis, as it were—the status of aristocracy. This precise pattern is repeated innumerable times among the American nouveaux riches as they built and furnished their own gilded mansions on Fifth Avenue, at Newport, in St. Louis, San Francisco, or in the remote western portion of North Carolina. That places such as Waddesdon had an influence on, and were often compared with, George Vanderbilt's Biltmore is observed in a comment by Henry James, who was a guest at both places several times. He described Biltmore as "a thing of high Rothschild manner, but of a size to contain two or three Mentmores and Waddesdons."[11]

George Washington Vanderbilt of Biltmore

The great estate of Biltmore, near Asheville, North Carolina, is arguably the grandest house in America (figure 130).[12] It was built by George W. Vanderbilt (1862–1914), the youngest of Louisa and William Henry's eight children (figure 131). George did not go into the family business the way his older brothers, Cornelius II and William Kissam,

Figure 129. Red drawing room, Waddesdon Manor, Buckinghamshire, England, ca. 1880, residence of Baron Ferdinand de Rothschild. National Trust, England. Sir Francis Watson has shown, in his 1959 article in *Gazette des Beaux-Arts*, that most of the "fitment" at Waddesdon—the walls, ceilings, windows, doors, and fireplaces—actually came from France, mostly from Paris, becoming available as a result of the large-scale reshaping of the city by Haussmann at the command of Napoleon III. The paneling in the green and gold room and in the breakfast room, for example, came from the Hotel de Richelieu, while that of the gray drawing room was obtained from the hôtel of the Duc Lauzun. The Savonnerie carpet (ca. 1680) in the red room was originally woven for the grand galerie of the Louvre, and the ceiling painting, the *Apotheosis of Hercules* by de Witt, came from a palace in Amsterdam. So, by 1880, here was a practice in place, of the wealthy Rothschilds buying up whole rooms and transporting them to be installed wherever they were building their great estates—and this was occurring just before American architects such as Richard Morris Hunt and Stanford White began the practice of doing the same thing on behalf of their clients in New York, Newport, and elsewhere. The association with aristocracy, even royalty, is found in the red room in the portrait of King George IV and the bas-relief by Antoine Coysevox of Louis XIV above the door.

did, nor did he sit on numerous boards of directors as did another brother, Frederick. Instead, he became the family's first scholar and intellect—a bibliophile, collector, connoisseur, horticulturist, and, above all, a builder of one magnificent mansion.

Educated by private tutors, George was the shy, studious Vanderbilt. He loved books more than the intrigues of New York Society, and the remote beauty of western North Carolina more than the frenzied summers of Newport's social swirl. While still in his teens he became interested in prints, and by the time he was twenty his collection contained 251 etchings by (or then attributed to) Rembrandt, 175 wood engravings by Albrecht Dürer, and 122 mezzotints after paintings by Sir Joshua Reynolds. He began to acquire books just as avidly, with the affection for a thing loved dearly, not just as trophies for display. His personal library would, in time,

Figure 130. Richard Morris Hunt, Biltmore, Asheville, N.C., 1892–95, residence of George ' Vanderbilt. Biltmore Estate, Asheville. The nouveaux castles and palaces built by George Vanderbilt and the Rothschilds were not the only fairyland monuments erected to the Romantic spirit and in imitation of the grand houses built by European aristocracy of past eras, for Old World royalty also indulged in the whim. For example, between 1869 and 1880 King Ludwig II—greatly under the influence of the operas by Richard Wagner—created, high atop a craggy mountain with panoramic views, the extraordinary Neuschwanstein was completed—seventeen-year-old George Vanderbilt visited Bavaria, and while his travel journal does not mention a trip to King Ludwig's castle, he did make a point of visiting other castles in the region. He undoubtedly knew of Neuschwanstein and probably did visit it. Eight years later, as he traveled through western North Carolina with his mother, he began to dream of erecting his own mountaintop palace with commanding views, and soon thereafter he began to acquire the 125,000 acres with which to fulfill that dream.

grow to twenty thousand volumes. He could read eight different languages; one of his favorite pastimes was translating modern prose into ancient Greek.

George Vanderbilt was twenty-three years old when his father died. He inherited $5 million plus an annual income from another $5 million placed in trust; William Henry's will also stipulated that after Louisa's death, the large brownstone palazzo and the huge collection of French academic paintings should go to his youngest son. George lived quietly with his mother at 640 Fifth Avenue (figure 49, p. 89) until her death in 1896, by which time that mansion had become a "white elephant." By investing his inheritance wisely he was able to increase it, but in the end his baronial estate in Carolina—which he began planning soon after his father's death—would consume almost all of his resources.

In 1898, three years after the completion of Biltmore, George Vanderbilt married Edith Stuyvesant Dresser, a Newport socialite and a descendant of Peter Stuyvesant (figure 132). One can only imagine her reaction on the day she first arrived at the château her husband had built and of which she was to become mistress, getting her first breathtaking view of the great mansion after their motor car had traversed the long private road and finally emerged into the clearing that presented the house as its centerpiece (figure 133).

Biltmore: The Prelude

Many years earlier, George and his mother had passed through western North Carolina, and he was struck by the natural beauty of the area—its remoteness and untouched, unspoiled character, and the loveliness of the tree-covered mountain range of the Appalachians. In 1888 he began to acquire parcels of land—quietly and anonymously, so as not to run up the price per acre—until he eventually owned an estate of 120,000 acres.

The place would be called Biltmore, he decided, combining "Bilt"—the name of the town in Holland whence came his ancestors—and "more," which in Old English meant a remote tract of high ground. Even before the first designs were drawn up, young George envisioned not only an enormous house but also a working farm with various livestock, a dairy, vegetable gardens, vineyards, and orchards to make the barony as self-sustaining as possible, all

Figure 131. James Abbott McNeill Whistler, *George Washington Vanderbilt*, 1903. Oil on canvas, 82 × 36 in. (208.6 × 91.1 cm). National Gallery of Art, Washington, D.C., gift of Edith Stuyvesant Gerry (1959.3.3). Whistler's portrait of George Vanderbilt is rather dark and moody and tells more about the painter than about his subject's personality. Vanderbilt was affable and quick-witted, of exceptional intelligence, a bibliophile, and devoted to the high culture of literature and art. From early youth he was the scholarly member of the Vanderbilt clan.

Figure 132. Giovanni Boldini, *Edith Stuyvesant Dresser Vanderbilt*, 1902. Oil on canvas, 80 × 36 in. (203.2 × 91.1 cm). Biltmore Estate, Asheville.

set amid carefully attended forests, an arboretum, and landscaping that took advantage of sweeping vistas of mountain ranges and picturesque valleys. To execute his vision he called in three specialists: Richard Morris Hunt as architect, Frederick Law Olmsted as landscape designer, and Gifford Pinchot as chief forester.

In the beginning there was only the forest. Gifford Pinchot (1865–1946), one of the first professional foresters in America, came from a wealthy family, for whom Hunt had designed Grey Towers, a mansion in Milford, Pennsylvania. Twenty-six-year-old Pinchot had graduated from Yale University and studied forestry in France by the time George Vanderbilt hired him in 1891. At Biltmore he found the forests in shambles, having been burned, slashed, and generally misused by the local folks. He began by thinning, planting, and harvesting, and by the end of the first year his operations even showed a small profit. It was he who set the plan for the forests of Biltmore, establishing the first comprehensive program in practical forest management in the United States. Reportedly, in the early 1890s he had a larger forestry staff than the U.S. government did.

But in 1895 Pinchot left Biltmore to become the head of the Division of Forestry (later the U.S. Forestry Service) in the Department of Agriculture, and, working closely with President Theodore Roosevelt, inaugurated a vast national conservation program; he later became a two-term governor of Pennsylvania. At Biltmore, Pinchot's place was taken by Carl Alvin Schenck from the University of Darmstadt in Germany. In 1898, Schenck set up the much-admired Biltmore Forest School. After George's death in 1914, over eighty thousand acres were deeded over to the federal government to become part of the Pisgah National Forest, and additional land from the estate became part of the Blue Ridge Parkway.

Frederick Law Olmsted was involved with the layout of the estate from the beginning. As early as 1888, Olmsted, assisted by his son, Frederick Law Olmsted Jr. (known as Rick), had drawn up a working plan for the estate. From the public road some miles away Olmsted laid out a drive through a long stretch of forest that permitted no sight of the mansion until, suddenly and dramatically, the visitor came to the open yard before it and a full view of the building. The effect was—and is—wonderful. In its siting, the

Figure 133. Richard Morris Hunt, Biltmore, central section of facade, 1895. Biltmore Estate, Asheville.

great house was approached from the east, and directly in front of the building Olmsted placed a large circular reflecting basin. The terrain beyond the western facade fell away to the French River before rising again in the Mount Pisgah range, which was especially spectacular at sunset.

At Olmsted's suggestion, stables and other auxillary buildings (greenhouses, barns, winery, etc.) were placed lower on the slope of the hill, out of sight, so they would not contend with the grandeur of the main structure. Hunt designed these buildings, along with the coachman's house and a gardener's cottage. As part of the master plan Olmsted designated areas for a chicken farm, a pig farm, kitchen gardens, nurseries, and several tenant houses, as well as large areas for vineyards.

To the south of the house Olmsted laid out the formal Italian gardens, which provided lovely avenues for evening strolls. Below this area he placed a four-acre walled garden that contained the rose beds and the greenhouses, for Biltmore was always adorned with large bouquets of beautiful cut flowers.

Richard Morris Hunt at Biltmore

George Vanderbilt's relationship with his architect was very close. Catharine Hunt noted in her unpublished biography that in December of 1894, when her husband's health had already begun to decline, Richard "always went to Biltmore full [of] anticipation of pleasure, for here George Vanderbilt watched over him with affectionate solicitude. . . . Even his professional work was made easy by the perfect harmony between himself and his client."[13] George sometimes traveled in the company of Catharine and Richard, as in the summer of 1889 when they were in Europe together, and when George went to Japan in 1892, Richard accompanied him as far as Chicago, where he had business connected with the World's Columbian Exposition.

Vanderbilt had employed Hunt on several projects previously—remodeling a house on West 53rd Street in New York; erecting some buildings on the New Dorp, Staten Island, farm that he had inherited; and designing a small library on West 13th Street, which George later gave to the city—but nothing big. With the Biltmore commission, he gave Hunt the grand opportunity that had eluded him in all his other projects for the Vanderbilt family: the chance to design a true château, on the scale of the châteaux of the Loire Valley, a grand house that was not crammed in among other buildings in a congested urban setting or confined to the relatively small size of oceanfront lots at a summer resort. When completed, the house spanned a breadth of about 380 feet across the main facade and contained 255 rooms, making it the largest private home in the world.

The style of the mansion was to be a regal one, such as that of Francis I, with connotations of the palace at Fontainebleau (begun 1528) or one of the grand châteaux of the Loire Valley, for both Hunt and Vanderbilt particularly admired the noble edifices of Blois, Chambord, and Chenonceau. But Biltmore is not a replica of any one French building; rather, it is a true creation springing from the Beaux-Arts imagination of a very talented architect and an enlightened patron.

While early-sixteenth-century French architecture still possessed details that survived from the Medieval period, it also evidenced the arrival of the new classical mode being imported from Italy. Hunt's design for Biltmore was asymmetrical, the entrance tower set slightly off center, with the exterior staircase to the left—inspired by the one at Blois (1515–24)—different in form from, but balanced by, the glazed conservatory to the right. The high pitch of the roof and the intrusion of dormers into the cornice are typical of the style of Francis I, as are the irregular profile of the roofline and chimneystacks, the gables and pointed arches, the turrets and pinnacles, and the traceried windows. To further associate the house of Vanderbilt with France and with royalty, Karl Bitter was commissioned to carve life-size figures of Joan of Arc and St. Louis, the saint-king of thirteenth-century France, to adorn the exterior staircase at the second level (figure 134).

Building Biltmore

Old photographs, taken in the early stages of construction, show the remoteness and isolation of the site. Roads in the area were little more than wide paths in the valleys and on mountainsides, so one of the first projects entailed building a railroad spur, three miles long, to the location so the necessary materials could be brought in. Nearly all of the stone, for example, was transported by train some six hundred miles from the limestone quarries in southern Indiana.

At the peak of activity around 1893, several hundred workmen were employed on the site, and a man named Francis M. Weeks was master contractor. Regarding Weeks the editors of *Architectural Record* observed that it was "fortunate that the man upon whose shoulders rests the responsibility of executing this glorious creation of the Master Architect's mind, the man to solidify into stone . . . the refined and carefully adjusted ideas of the designer should be Francis M. Weeks, of the long established firm of D.C. Weeks & Son."[14]

Biltmore was completed in time for George to host the Vanderbilt family and its entourage for Christmas of 1895. About one hundred of them (including assorted valets, nannies, maids, etc.) arrived by private railroad cars. Sadly, Richard Morris Hunt was not among the guests, for he had died by then.

Figure 134. Richard Morris Hunt, Biltmore, detail of exterior stairway showing statue of Joan of Arc by Karl Bitter, ca. 1894. Biltmore Estate, Asheville.

The Interiors

When the Vanderbilt clan arrived on that cold and wintery Christmas Eve, they must have been overwhelmed by the sheer size of the house, the 255 rooms and staff of fifty or so servants easily accommodating them, as well as the beauty of the setting and the interiors. After passing through the marble-paved entrance they could see to the right the conservatory or winter garden, with bowers full of flowers in brilliant bloom surrounding the central focal piece, a fountain topped with a bronze figure of a nude boy with two geese, the creation of Karl Bitter (figure 135). From the entrance hall they could also enter the great tapestry gallery (ninety feet long) to the left, with its series of sixteenth-century Brussels tapestries. The loggia of the west (rear) facade opened off of this long gallery, offering spectacular views of the surrounding mountain range, with Mount Pisgah looming above all other peaks, basking in the late-day sun.

George Vanderbilt had made a life's work of collecting bibelots and furnishings, large and small, for his grand château. His numerous trips to Europe were devoted to making the rounds of antique dealers in London, Paris, Brussels, or wherever, purchasing a small nineteenth-century bronze here, a magnificent set of sixteenth-century tapestries there, a set of forty chairs somewhere else, and so on. The zeal

Figure 135. Richard Morris Hunt, conservatory or winter garden, Biltmore, ca. 1895. Biltmore Estate, Asheville.

with which he gathered things and the scale on which he bought objects seemed to some observers to be frantic, but even before his house was built he was anxious to find treasures with which to fill it. For example, Catharine Hunt recalled their visit to London in 1889, noting that "one morning we spent at the great oriental carpet warehouse of Robinson, where G.W.V. selected three hundred rugs for the house yet to be built."[15]

The Great Hall (Gallery) and Breakfast Room

By the late 1880s and early 1890s George Vanderbilt had already become an avid collector of *objets d'art* other than books and prints, and it was evident that his house would have to be very large to accommodate the innumerable treasures he kept acquiring. For instance, he had purchased five large, splendid tapestries, and it was around them that the great hall was designed—thus were architectural decisions of scale determined, at least in part, by objects that Vanderbilt possessed and wished to display.

The great hall is of palatial dimensions, measuring forty-three by seventy-two feet and seventy feet in height (figure 136). The dining table, designed by Hunt, in the center of the room could seat sixty-four guests in eighteenth-century Italian chairs (or replicas thereof) covered in red damask. The five great sixteenth-century Flemish tapestries represented the story of Venus, Mars, and Vulcan; Vanderbilt had acquired them in Paris.

The room is so large that a single fireplace would have been both out of scale and inadequate to provide the entire space with the requisite warmth, so a tripartite design was devised, grouping three fireplaces together in the sixteenth-century French Renaissance mode. The carved overmantel, by Karl Bitter, is twenty-five feet long and represents "The Return from the Chase," an appropriate subject for a Francis I–type great hall where, in olden days, the post-hunt feasts were held. For the opposite end Bitter created five large relief panels depicting scenes from Wagner's opera, *Tannhauser*, carved in oak and decorating the organ gallery balustrade. The room is lighted by day by large windows high above the tapestries and by night by three huge circular chandeliers. In the manner of the style being imitated here, the arched ceiling is ribbed. Flags and banners add color to

Figure 136. Richard Morris Hunt, great hall, Biltmore, ca. 1895. Biltmore Estate, Asheville.

the space, while moose and stag heads remind one of the importance of the hunt in times gone by.

When George, Edith and their only child, Cornelia, dined alone, they did not eat in the great hall but rather in the much smaller breakfast room. On its walls were hung the family portraits, and from above the door the bust-length likeness of the Commodore looked down on his grandson and family. The chairs were covered with a red-rust Spanish leather, while the dinner service, in maroon and gold on white, was English Minton and Spode. Wedgewood-type jasperware reliefs, made from clay found in western North Carolina, were worked into the fireplace.

The Library

George Vanderbilt's favorite room was the library (figure 137). Located at the south end of the house, it had approximately ten thousand handsomely bound volumes on its shelves, mostly on art, history, architecture, landscape architecture, forestry and horticulture; another ten thousand books were shelved elsewhere throughout the house.

Among these collections were important items, such as a rare first edition (1667) of John Milton's *Paradise Lost* and a copy of Alexander Pope's *Essays on Man in the Four Epistles to a Friend* (1737), which contains numerous handwritten notations by Pope himself. There is similarly an 1817 copy of Samuel Taylor Coleridge's poetry, with the author's appended notes for a later edition. The range of the library's collections is indicated by the presence of a rare first edition of Charles Darwin's *On the Origin of Species*.

The paneling of the library was of Circassian walnut, and its focal point was the great black marble fireplace, above which were figures of Demeter (goddess of the earth) and Hestia (goddess of the hearth) carved from oak by Karl Bitter; they flank a seventeenth-century tapestry overmantel. Bitter also made the bronze andirons in the fireplace, ornamented with figures of Venus and Vulcan.

The ceiling painting in the library, *The Chariot of Aurora* by the Italian artist Giovanni Antonio Pellegrini (1675–1741), depicts the goddess bringing the new dawn as she crosses the sky. It once decorated the ceiling of a Venetian palace and was acquired by George on one of his trips abroad. The furniture is mostly English and Italian, although some of it is the work of the artisans of Biltmore Industries, workshops established by George Vanderbilt to train local North Carolina folk in various crafts.

Figure 137. Richard Morris Hunt, library, Biltmore, ca. 1895, with fireplace sculptures by Karl Bitter. Biltmore Estate, Asheville.

Biltmore Village

At the entrance to the grounds of the estate was Biltmore Village, for which Vanderbilt erected All Souls Episcopal Church, a school and a railroad station, a hospital and a post office, some stores, and a number of houses for people who worked on the estate. An editorial in the *Asheville News and Hotel Reporter* for 20 February 1897 reveals the attitude of the local folk toward the agricultural interests of the lord of the manor:

> It is Vanderbilt the farmer, not Vanderbilt of the Château, who has proven to be the great benefactor of Western North Carolina. He has shown the Carolinians the productive capacities of their virgin soil . . . by the scientific drainage, the improved machinery, the importation of fine stock, the judicious and lavish use of fertilizers, and the most up-to-date and scientific methods of farming.[16]

Each day, George Vanderbilt would make the rounds of his estate, preferring to do so on horseback even after the advent of the motor car. He would ride to a certain part of the forest where thinning was being done, or in the springtime he would ride out to see how the azalea garden—a whole hillside—was coming along under the direction of Chauncy Delos Beadle, who began work at the estate under Olmsted and remained for sixty years as superintendent.

Life at the Estate

Many distinguished guests made the journey to this far out-of-the-way baronial estate, just to see it because it had become one of the seven wonders of the modern world. Isabella Stewart Gardner visited there in 1903 and wrote to Bernard Berenson about it: "I am just back from Biltmore, where I spent a week with the George Vanderbilts. . . . Fancy owning 150,000 acres. It is quite wonderful."[17] John Singer Sargent (figure 138) went there in 1895 to paint the full-length portraits of Hunt and Olmsted "on location" (figures 139 and 140). So great was Vanderbilt's admiration for Hunt and Olmsted that he also commissioned two stained-glass windows depicting them, for All Souls Episcopal Church in Biltmore Village.

Henry James came to visit too, in February of 1905—perhaps not the best time of year to be in the Appalachians. Also, James was suffering from a cold and the loss of a front tooth when he arrived, and soon thereafter developed gout in his left foot, so his opinion may have been jaded by his infirmities. He found the house dreary, the estate pretentious, and he said so in a letter to Edith Wharton that is vintage James in style and poisonous eloquence:

I arrived here . . . five days ago, & was instantly taken with a most deplorable & untimely little attack of gout . . . , the result of which has been that I have not once left the house, & but scantly my room. But I am sufficiently better to intend to depart, at any cost, tomorrow afternoon. . . . The whole land here is bound in snow & ice; we are 2,500 feet in the air; the cold, the climate, is well nigh all the "company" in the strange, colossal heart-breaking house; & the desolation & discomfort of the whole thing—whole scene—are, in spite of the mitigating millions everywhere expressed, indescribable. There has been no one here but little pleasant squinting Miss [Kitty] Hunt, of Washington [the architect's daughter] & a pleasant . . . little old British soldier-man General Sir Thomas Fraser, who departed yesterday. I am now alone with the good G. V. & Huntiana; & it has all been verily a strange experience. . . . I mean one's sense of the extraordinary impenitent madness (of millions) which led to the erection in this vast niggery wilderness, of so gigantic & elaborate a monument to all that *isn't* socially possible there. It's . . . like a gorgeous practical joke—but at one's own expense, after all, if one has to live in solitude in these league-long marble halls, & sit in alternate Gothic & Palladian cathedrals, as it were. . . . Since writing the above, I have been down to luncheon & been able to see more of the house—& feel a bit shabby at failing to rise to my host's own conception of the results he has achieved. They *are*, in a way, magnificent. . . . Still, I repeat—for a tasteful Southern *home*, it merely makes me weep![18]

In a later assessment of Biltmore, Henry James made the inevitable comparison with the great houses erected by the Rothschilds: "Roll three or four Rothschild houses into one, surround them with a principality of mountain, lake and forest, 200,000 acres, surround that with vast states of desolation and make it impossible, through distance and time, to get anyone to stay with you, and you have the bloated Biltmore."[19] James's opinion of the estate was, however, atypical.

Edith Wharton and her husband, Teddy, had a very different reaction to Biltmore. They had known George and Edith Vanderbilt for a number of years before they journeyed to western North Carolina to spend Christmas of 1905 with them. On 26 December 1905, Edith Wharton wrote to her friend Sara Norton to describe her experience of Biltmore and a holiday event that occurred there:

The journey here was frightfully fatiguing, but this divine landscape, "under a roof of blue Ionian weather," makes up for all the hardship. . . . Yesterday we had a big Xmas fete for the 350 people on the estate—a tree 30 ft high, Punch & Judy, conjuror, presents & "refreshments." It would have interested you, it was done so well & sympathetically, each person's being thought of, from mother to last baby. In this matchless weather the walks thro' the park are a joy I should like to share with you—great sheets of fruited ivy pouring over terrace walls, yellow stars still shining on the bare branches of the nudiflora, jasmine, & masses of juniper, heath, honeysuckle, rhododendron & laurel making an evergreen covert so different from our denuded New England lanes. Alas, that it is so far from everything.[20]

As early as 1900 Biltmore had become known, to some, as "Vanderbilt's Folly," and others were asking how it happened that the poorest of the Vanderbilts had built the biggest of the houses, one that cost $3 million to erect and still more to furnish. Even so astute a modern critic as Richard Morris Hunt's biographer, Paul Baker, had trouble coping with Biltmore as a social entity, concluding his remarks about it with these words: "Ostentatious, indulgent, grandiose—the house was all of these, and it was irrelevant to much of American life."[21]

Figure 138. Charles Dana Gibson, *John S. Sargent*, 1903. From *Collier's Weekly* (28 March 1903), p. 30. Sargent, an American artist who lived in England, was at the height of his career as an internationally celebrated portraitist when he visited Biltmore to paint Richard Morris Hunt's likeness in 1895, the year of the architect's death.

Epilogue for Biltmore

By the time George Vanderbilt died in 1914, he had spent so much money building and furnishing Biltmore that the executors of his estate had insufficient funds to care for it properly. It was soon necessary to sell off large tracts of land or donate them to the federal government to be used as parklands. Edith Stuyvesant Dresser Vanderbilt continued to live there, but by the time of her death the estate had shrunk to a mere 12,500 acres. The property then passed to the Vanderbilts' only child, Cornelia, who had married a member of the English aristocracy, John Francis Amherst Cecil, and the Cecils lived at Biltmore.

In the 1930s the great house was opened to the public in an effort to help pay the estate's bills. By the early 1960s it had become the property of George Vanderbilt's grandson, William Cecil, who has turned it into a self-sustaining institution, in that it pays its own expenses—no small task for a historic house—and has become a major cultural attraction of the nation. Cecil hopes to be able to pass it on to his son and daughter—if estate and death taxes do not prevent it.

Figure 139. John Singer Sargent, *Richard Morris Hunt*, 1895. Oil on canvas, 92 × 60 in. (234.7 × 132.4 cm). Biltmore Estate, Asheville.

Figure 140. John Singer Sargent, *Frederick Law Olmsted*, 1895. Oil on canvas, 92 × 62 in. (234.7 × 157.5 cm). Biltmore Estate, Asheville.

I had not been aware that [Central] Park was such a very nasty place. In fact, the low grounds were steeped in the overflow of the pigsties, slaughter houses, and bone-boiling works, and the stench was sickening.

Frederick Law Olmsted (1857); quoted from Patterson, *Fifth Avenue: The Best Address* (1998)

Chapter Nine

The Astor Mansion

The Avenue, North of 59th Street

With elegant facades lining its eastern side and Central Park extending along its western side, it is difficult to imagine today's Fifth Avenue as a region of swamps, cesspools, and shanties, with goats and pigs roaming at will, an area of filth and foul air, of poverty and crime (figure 141). Such was the case, however, before its development began, the first stage of which was the opening of Central Park in the winter of 1859. But the grand residences did not begin to rise along its eastern perimeter until much later, in the late 1880s and early 1890s, and many contemporary commentaries survive to remind us what Fifth Avenue was like before the Astors, Carnegies, Gerrys, and others began to displace the squatters' shacks and rubble heaps. One source recalled,

> The squatters' settlements in the Park were surrounded by swamps, and overgrown with briers, vines, and thickets. The soil that covered the rocky surface was unfit for cultivation. Here and there were stone quarries and stagnant pools. In this wilderness lived the squatters, in little shanties and huts made of boards picked up along the river fronts and often pieced out with sheets of tin, obtained by flattening cans. . . . [There were] about two hundred shanties, barns, stables, piggeries, and bone-factories. . . . Some of the shanties were dug-outs, and most had dirt floors. In this manner lived, in a state of loose morality, Americans, Germans, Irish, Negroes, and Indians. Some were honest and some were not; many were roughs and crooks. . . . It is said that the Park area contained no less than one hundred thousand [mongrel dogs], which, with cows, pigs, cats, goats, geese, and chickens, roamed at will, and lived upon the refuse, which was everywhere.[1]

Such scenes lived on in fiction too, as in Edith Wharton's description of the area in *The Age of Innocence*. In her story Wharton went to great lengths to create a picture of the building of Mrs. Manson Mingott's mansion way up north, taking as her model, as we have seen, Marble Row, erected by Mary Mason Jones at 58th and Fifth (figure 43, p. 78). Old Mrs. Mingott, the *grande dame* of Wharton's story, had built her large house "in an inaccessible wilderness near Central Park," and there she awaited the migration of Society into that forsaken region: "She was sure that presently the hoardings [battered wooden fences], the quarries, the one-story saloons, the wooden green-houses in ragged gardens, and the rocks from which goats surveyed the scene, would vanish before the advance of residences as stately as her own."[2] And Mrs. Mingott was

right, for Fifth Avenue north of 59th Street eventually began to develop residentially, evolving rapidly, thanks particularly to the presence of Central Park and the lovely green prospects it offered once Frederick Law Olmsted's plan was executed.

The Great Wall of Châteaux

A brief notice in *The New York Times* captured the frenetic zeal to erect fine houses along Fifth Avenue in the early 1890s:

> WORK ON NEW MANSIONS. Ground is being broken at Sixty-fifth Street and Fifth Avenue for John Jacob Astor's new home. . . . Commodore Gerry's house, a few blocks below, has reached the third story, and through the network of scaffolds the outlines of an imposing mansion can be seen. From a point on Fifth Avenue, Cornelius Vanderbilt's house looks like a huge grist mill. . . . As fast as the stone wall grows, so fast grows the boarding in front, so that not a bit of the stone work can be seen.[3]

One of the mansions mentioned in that passage is the subject of this chapter—the great double house erected for Caroline Astor and her son, John Jacob Astor IV, and designed by Richard Morris Hunt.

In the design for Alva and William Kissam Vanderbilt's Petit Château (1879–82; figure 69, p. 114), Hunt had hit upon a style that America's new millionaires found both pleasing and expressive of their social ambitions and their great wealth. The style of the Astor mansion was inspired by a slightly later phase of French architectural history, but the encoded message was the same, for the late-Gothic, early French Renaissance style—called the style of Francis I—was evocative of the desired associations with European aristocracy and of pedigrees that exceeded a generation or two. The evolution of Hunt's work began with the Petit Château and culminated in the magnificent residences of Biltmore and the Astor mansion.

A Palace for the Astors—At Last

The William Kissam Vanderbilts opened their Petit Château with a gala costume ball on 29 March 1883, and everyone who attended realized that a new standard of opulence and something new in style had been created. But it was easier for Alva Vanderbilt to come charging into Society with something new than it was for Caroline Astor, who, being a Schermerhorn herself, was committed more to old Knickerbocker ways than to the energized brashness of the new-money people. So, even as she reigned as queen of New York Society, she ruled from her dowdy old brownstone down at 34th Street, an area of Fifth Avenue that, by 1890, fashion had left behind in its northward migration (figure 9, p. 35). She remained entrenched there—the antithesis of Wharton's Mrs. Manson Mingott—holding out against the rise of handsome, richly decorated mansions like the Petit Château, until the spitefulness of a nephew, the encroachments of commercial enterprises, and the architectural challenges of Society's newcomers forced her into action, which resulted in a new palace, erected on a large plot way uptown at 65th and Fifth.

To understand Caroline Astor's motivation to leave her nearly forty-year-old brownstone (see Chapter 2), the origins of the Astor fortune and its history must be retraced.[4] The founder of the family fortune was John Jacob Astor I, who was born in Waldorf, Germany, in 1763, the son of a butcher. He began his career in his older brother's musical instrument business in London, but in 1783, at age twenty, he came to America, with five pounds in his pocket. His crossing was steerage class, but on the voyage he met a dealer in furs who convinced him that once in New York he should sell the six flutes he had brought with him as his stock-in-trade, and use the money to purchase furs. He did so, and the foundation of the Astor fortune was laid.

After working for a furrier to learn the trade, Astor went off to Canada, where he made long treks, trading with the Indians for furs, curing the pelts himself, and doing all other aspects of the business. By 1800 he was wealthy, and while he remained in the fur trade, he began investing heavily in New York City real estate. When he died in 1848 his holdings in property were large, and his estate was valued at $20 million—at that time the largest fortune in America.

Astor had two sons, William Backhouse and John Jacob II. The latter was demented from birth and required care all his life, so the bulk of Astor's fortune went to William Backhouse Astor, who died in 1875, leaving two sons—John Jacob III and William Backhouse Jr. Thus were sewn the seeds of a blood feud. Upon their father's death, John Jacob III inherited two-thirds of the fortune, William only one-third, indicating which line of the family should assume dominance. George Templeton Strong, the noted diarist, knew the Astors

Figure 141. Ralph Blakelock, *Fifth Avenue at 89th Street in 1868*, 1868. Oil on canvas, 16 × 23½ in. (40.6 × 59.1 cm). Museum of the City of New York, gift of Archer M. Huntington (32.333).

well for he was the "old family lawyer" who handled many of their financial and real estate transactions; in the summer of 1873 he observed, "Strange how these millionaire families quarrel among themselves about money—brother alienated from brother, sister at daggers drawn with sister—and all about property, of which every one of them has more than enough."[5]

The obituary in *The New York Times* described the life of John Jacob Astor III as "a singularly calm, peaceful, steady, uneventful one." An editorial in the same issue observed that

> this tranquil, uneventful career presents a wonderful contrast to the bustling and at times almost turbulent lives of the two Vanderbilts [Cornelius II and William Kissam] and of Mr. Jay Gould. . . . These men have been examples of the trade of multiplying millions by speculation, while Mr. Astor practiced and illustrated the art of multiplying millions by wise investment and careful management. . . . If at times [these other men] added to their millions more rapidly than Mr. Astor added to his, the process was far less sure than his, and far less constant. . . . John Jacob Astor's business involved no invasion of the rights of others, no spoilation of innocent or misguided persons and no injury to society.[6]

The Astors were clearly held to be a cut above the upstart Vanderbilts and such reckless speculators as Jay Gould, and the means of accumulating the Astor fortunes was considered—by some, at least—more genteel, even more honorable. Moreover, both John Jacob III and William Backhouse had married into fine old established families, the former choosing a southern belle from Charleston society, a Miss Gibbes, and his brother selecting a young woman of the Schermerhorn line.

Caroline Webster Schermerhorn was the daughter of Abraham Schermerhorn and the great-great-great-granddaughter of William Beekman, founder of the Beekman family line in New York, and through her mother, née Helen White, she was a descendant of the Van Cortlandt family. When Caroline married William (she convinced him to drop the name Backhouse) at Grace Church on 20 September 1853, a union was thereby established between one of the oldest pedigrees of Knickerbocker New York and the greatness of the Astor fortunes.

But in point of fact the Astors of fortune were only one generation older than the Vanderbilts, Cornelius Vanderbilt I being born in 1794, thirty-one years after John Jacob Astor I. Nevertheless, by the 1880s, when the Vanderbilts and others began their assault on Society, there was a stratification that placed the Astors at the peak of the pyramid, well above any of the upstarts. The question was, which line of the Astors was to be the ruling line—that of John Jacob III or that of Caroline, Mrs. William Backhouse Jr.?

John Jacob III insisted that the honor of being queen of New York Society belonged to his wife, Charlotte Augusta Gibbes Astor, for as he was the dominant Astor, his wife should be THE Mrs. Astor. They lived comfortably in the brownstone house at the corner of Fifth Avenue and 33rd Street (figure 13, p. 39), never feeling the need to enlist ostentatious architecture in their ongoing skirmish to establish their position in Society, even though they were good friends with Richard Morris Hunt and his family.

Architects and Patrons: Social Relationships

To be sure, not all architects of this period established close personal relationships with the privileged glitterati of America's millionaire society, but a few did—among them Richard Morris Hunt, Charles Follen McKim, William Rutherford Mead, Stanford White, and Whitney Warren. Hunt and his wife, Catharine, in particular moved easily in the highest social circles. A passage from Catharine Howland Hunt's biography of her husband reveals the bond that developed between them and the family of John Jacob Astor III, especially with Charlotte Augusta:

> Our dear friend Mrs. John Astor was very ill at Beaulieu [their Newport house] all the latter part of the summer, and our hearts were very heavy as we knew her illness could only end fatally. [Our] dear friend, who for years blessed us with continual kindness and affection, and whose rare intelligence and exceptional qualities of mind and heart, made the very knowing of her a privilege, and how much more the intimate relations of a close friendship. . . . She was Kitty's [the Hunts' daughter's] godmother, and you all called her "Aunt Augusta." She was devoted to your father, and in every sickness and trouble, both she and her husband were ready with constant devotion. Their home . . . was famed for its intelligent hospitality, and there one met not only the best that the social side represented, but all that was interesting in Art, Literature, Science and Philanthropy. . . . [Richard Morris Hunt] was one of her pallbearers as well as one of her most deeply attached friends.[7]

As another indication of the closeness between the two families, a photograph survives of Catharine Hunt wearing the exotic costume she wore in a *tableau vivant* that was held at the Union League Club to publicize the forthcoming Philadelphia Centennial; in it, she posed as the personification of Asia, standing, with her right hand resting on the head of a stuffed striding tiger—and "loaded down with borrowed Astor jewels."[8]

As early as 29 December 1868, George Templeton Strong noted in his diary that the Hunts were a part of the elite New York social scene, writing that he, Strong, had "dined with Ellie at John Astor's. Convives, Mr. and Mrs. Dick Hunt, Denning Duers, Hayward Cuttings, G. G. Howlands . . . , and young Willy Astor, the son of the house."[9]

It helped that Hunt's wife was heiress to a shipping fortune of ancient vintage, the firm of Howland and Aspinwall; William Aspinwall was, in fact, her cousin as well as her guardian, and when the Hunts returned from their honeymoon at Niagara Falls, Aspinwall gave a ball and reception in their honor. Also, Catharine was a niece of Philip Hone, former mayor of New York and noted diarist.

On the international scene too, the Hunts fit comfortably into a variety of social situations. When they were in Paris in 1867 to see the great exposition staged by the Second Empire (Hunt was one of the U.S. commissioners), they were invited to an imperial ball given by Napoleon III and the Empress Eugénie in honor of the visiting Czar of Russia, Alexander II, to whom the Hunts were presented on that occasion. Back home, the Hunts entertained dignitaries, as when one night at Newport Catharine was hostess of a dinner party during which President Ulysses S. Grant sat on her right. One night in 1888 the Hunts were house guests at Ellerslie—that vaguely Elizabethan half-timber mansion near Rhinebeck on the Hudson River that Richard had designed for Levi P. Morton—the night that Morton, former U.S. minister to France, was elected vice president of the United States under Benjamin Harrison.

Richard Morris Hunt himself came from a family that was socially well positioned, if not wealthy. He was dapper and witty, a convivial conversationalist, as pleasant as a dinner partner for Society ladies as he was among his male friends enjoying cigars and brandy after dinner. He was casually cosmopolitan, and because he had spent most of his early life in France, he spoke with a slight but charming French accent, which contributed to an air of elegance. No doubt he understood his clientele well because he was himself a part of their set, and that helped him design the architectural symbols exactly as they desired.

THE *Mrs. Astor and William Waldorf Astor's Revenge*

Charlotte Augusta Gibbes Astor died in 1887, and when John Jacob III passed away three years later, he left almost his entire estate to his son, William Waldorf Astor, who contended that he then became titular head of the Astor clan. His Aunt Caroline quietly refused to recognize his claim, and the issue reached crisis proportions when Caroline had her calling cards printed simply "Mrs. Astor." To William Waldorf, that very act declared publicly that his wife was not acknowledged as THE Mrs. Astor, and the ill-feeling between the two intensified, which led directly to the architectural consequences that will soon unfold.

Caroline Astor did not interest her husband very much after their marriage in 1853, for William preferred to go off on his yacht for extended voyages rather than engage in his wife's social skirmishes. Rumors circulated about just who his companions on those bacchanalian sprees were, but William's drinking problem was known to all—in fact, an acquaintance of the family referred to him as a one-man temperance society who was determined to drink up all available spirits to save his fellow man from that fate. Elizabeth Drexel Lehr recalled the strange and strained relationship that existed between Caroline and her husband:

> No one ever knew what thoughts passed behind the calm repose of [Mrs. Astor's] face. She had so cultivated the art of never looking at the things she did not want to see, never listening to words she did not wish to hear, that it had become second nature with her. New York would ring with gossip concerning the latest doings of William Astor; stories would be circulated of wild parties on board his yacht. The rumors grew more and more exaggerated as they flew from mouth to mouth. . . . When someone would ask tentatively after her husband she would reply placidly: "Oh, he is having a delightful cruise. The sea air is so good for him. It is a great pity I am such a bad sailor, for I should so much enjoy accompanying him. As it is I have never even set foot on the yacht. . . ." Whatever the world might think of William Astor, his wife would never give vent to the faintest criticisms of anything he did.[10]

To Caroline, who was anxious to keep the Astor name and to keep it unblemished, divorce was unthinkable, for it was not until 1895 that Alva Vanderbilt would burst the bonds of that social taboo. Louis Auchincloss observed that Caroline Astor "probably would have been content to lead a quiet, unspectacular life had her husband wished to share one with her."[11] Thus shunned by her husband, she found her solace in Society, a Society she came to rule, and, as an Astor biographer put it, she was determined that if New York had no "king" of Society, it would at least have a "queen."

About 1870, through fancy-dress balls, the wearing of brilliant diamonds as she sat majestically in her private box at the opera, and the entertaining of such distinguished guests as President Benjamin Harrison and his wife, she began to assert her position as the centrum around which Society should organize itself. When Mrs. August Belmont retired from Society a few years later, Caroline stood alone at the peak of the social pyramid of the Gilded Age. Ward McAllister—the era's social arbiter, by self-appointment and by acclamation—dubbed her heir to the throne and on social occasions became her escort as surrogate for her perpetually absent husband. Moreover, Caroline had borne four daughters before presenting William with a male heir, and each daughter, of course, required a grand coming-out celebration. These occurred in the mid-1870s and were given with such lavishness that they contributed greatly to the establishment of Caroline Schermerhorn Astor's position of supremacy in the social swirl that New York had become.

And so she became "Queen Caroline." Elizabeth Drexel Lehr referred to her as "a *grande dame* in everything she said or did."[12] Mrs. Lehr also remembered that as "despotic and strong-willed as she was, she could on occasion be sentimental. . . . [She] was always dignified, always reserved, a little aloof. She gave friendship but never intimacy. She never confided."[13]

Caroline Astor's house at Fifth Avenue and 34th Street possessed most comforts of the day and many of the luxuries, such as an art gallery that doubled as a ballroom. Its interiors throughout were stylish. For many years she did not feel anymore compelled to use architecture to establish or maintain her social position than her brother-in-law did in his brownstone at 33rd and Fifth. But by 1890 even she had to see that her house was old-fashioned when compared with the splendid gilded mansions arising farther uptown. It was, however, a spiteful move by her nephew, William Waldorf Astor—who had inherited his father's house in the same block as Caroline's brownstone—that galvanized her into moving northward to join the main enclave of Society.

In a fit of pique engendered by the persistence of Caroline as THE Mrs. Astor, William Waldorf Astor moved out of the house at 33rd and Fifth, and on its site erected an enormous hotel—the Waldorf, named after himself and the town in Germany from which the original John Jacob Astor had come. When completed in 1893, the Waldorf towered many stories above his aunt's house. At last he had succeeded in placing her in his shadow, literally, and with a stroke had turned the quiet residential area into a bustling, noisy commercial district. Thus triumphant, William Waldorf packed up and moved to England, permanently, where he bought Cliveden, the palatial home of the dukes of Sunderland and Westminster. He became an Englishman, and with the help of his fortune, was dubbed the first Lord Astor. His son, William Waldorf II, married Nancy Witcher Langhorne, who became the first woman to sit in Parliament.

William Waldorf I thus abandoned the struggle for supremacy of the Astor line in America by becoming totally English, but he had his revenge through the Waldorf Hotel. The Waldorf hosted a gala opening night in 1893, a description of which is given in the book about the establishment, *Peacocks on Parade*.[14] The depth of the animosity between Caroline and her nephew was demonstrated a few years later when she spitefully refused to cancel a dinner party on the evening of the funeral in London of William Waldorf Astor's wife, Mary.

When Caroline Astor could no longer endure the commercial invasion of her world around 34th Street and Fifth Avenue, she vacated the old brownstone. Her son, John Jacob Astor IV, urged his by-then-widowed mother to follow Society uptown. In 1894 the old brownstone was torn down to make way for the building of the Astoria Hotel, which was designed to integrate with the Waldorf (figure 42, p. 76). The result was New York's most fashionable hotel at the turn of the century, the Waldorf-Astoria, with its famous lounge, Peacock Alley, and its celebrated host, Oscar of the Waldorf. Both sections of the hotel were designed by master hotel designer

Figure 142. Richard Morris Hunt, Caroline (Mrs. William B.) Astor and John Jacob Astor IV residence, northeast corner of Fifth Avenue and 65th Street, 1895. Museum of the City of New York, Wurts Collection. As with many of the great Fifth Avenue mansions, the Astor residence—as grand as it was—survived a remarkably short time; in 1926 it was torn down and replaced by the Temple Emanu-El.

Henry J. Hardenbergh, whose finest works include the Plaza Hotel in New York City, the Willard Hotel in Washington, D.C., and Boston's Copley Plaza Hotel.

The Astors' House at 65th Street

One day, at Newport, Caroline Astor offered her friend, Richard Morris Hunt, the commission to design for her a new house on property she owned at the northeast corner of Fifth Avenue and 65th Street (figure 142). The lot was unusually large, measuring one hundred by one hundred feet, but the structure was actually to be a double house with a single entrance on Fifth Avenue, John Jacob and his family occupying the corner portion while Caroline resided in the other half. As designed by Hunt it was grander, although less picturesque, than the William K. Vanderbilts' Petit Château, its period of inspiration being less late-fifteenth-century Gothic and more French Renaissance of the early sixteenth century. There were a few Gothic ornaments around the doors and windows and elsewhere, and the main medieval, nonclassical feature was the prominent and steeply pitched roof, the eave line of which was broken numerous times by dormers.

The influence remained French, for the roofline of a classical Italian palazzo would have emphasized the horizontal axis rather than the vertical reach, and the eave line would have been unbroken. But a classicizing process had purged tourelles, crockets, and pointed arches, and replaced them with pilasters, round-headed arches and other classical motifs. Also, there was a perfect symmetry in the Astor mansion, as opposed to the rambling additive asymmetry of the Petit Château. The design shunned the bombast of recent Second Empire neo-Baroque exuberance, and it possessed

instead a calm, classical grandeur in the Beaux-Arts manner, its inspiration coming from such models as the palace at Fontainebleau (1528–40) or the château of Villandry (Indre-et-Loire, 1532). The mansion, which also reflected the architect's visits to the château of Chantilly, was constructed of a monotone light gray limestone, with which the slate roof blended nicely.

The Purpose of the Mansion

To fully comprehend the importance to Society of lavish architectural backdrops such as this, one must take note of the character of the social season in New York. The following diary of events suggests at least as much an endurance test as a gay social swirl. A perusal of the society columns in newspapers of the day, covering a two-week period, around the time of the gala housewarming at Mrs. Astor's new château provides a sense of the continuing, sometimes overlapping juggernaut of Society, and gives us a feeling for the importance of a proper architectural setting for the events described. Although only a few individual names were mentioned, these were events for which much of Society turned out:

Monday, January 27, 1896: The Monday Evening Dancing Class was followed by the opera (Monday was the night Society attended). At midnight, guests attended a supper at Perry Belmont's house, Fifth Avenue and 67th Street.

Tuesday, January 28: Run of the Lakewood [NJ] Ocean County Hunt and Country Club, at which George J. Gould took a bad fall at the third jump. Charity Ball for the benefit of the Nursery and Children's Hospital, held at the Metropolitan Opera with Lander's one-hundred-piece orchestra performing.

Thursday, January 30: Cornelius Vanderbilt and William Watts Sherman are among the guests at dinner honoring The Rev. Dr. David Greer. Mr. and Mrs. Alfred Stevens host a theatre party for one hundred with dinner and dancing at the Waldorf.

Friday, January 31: Albert Morris Bagby hosted a musicale at the Waldorf in the morning with a program that included Saint-Saens, Haydn and Schumann. Later, Mr. and Mrs. John D. Rockefeller gave a reception with music at their home at 4 West 54th Street.

Saturday, February 1: The Badminton Club met in the afternoon with Mrs. John Jacob Astor, Mrs. Nicholas Fish and Mrs. William Rhinelander among those participating. Between 4:00 and 7:00 PM Mrs. Astor presided at a tea given at her new mansion at 840 Fifth Avenue, on the day she moved in. That night, Ogden Mills had a dinner party at his house at Fifth and 69th Street.

Monday, February 3: Mrs. Astor's ball in her new house, with guests arriving after the opera for supper and dancing.

Wednesday, February 5: The Cinderella Cotillion was held at Sherry's with Mrs. Anson Phelps Stokes, Mrs. Stanford White, Mrs. William Watts Sherman, and Mrs. Frederick de Peyster among the patronesses. That evening, Mr. and Mrs. Anson Phelps Stokes hosted a dinner and dance at their home, 239 Madison Avenue.

Thursday, February 6: A dinner party given by Chauncey Depew, at his residence at 43 West 44th Street, was attended by Mrs. Astor, Darius Ogden Mills, Mr. and Mrs. William D. Sloane, Mr. and Mrs. Cornelius Vanderbilt, Mr. and Mrs. William Rhinelander Stewart and Perry Belmont, among others.

Figure 143. Charles Dana Gibson illustration. From "The Seven Ages of the American Woman," *Scribner's Magazine* 26 (December 1899), p. 675.

Friday, February 7: A musicale—a piano concert—was hosted at the Hotel Majestic by Mrs. Henry Villard and Mrs. George J. Gould. That evening was the Bachelors' Ball at the Waldorf, with dinner served in the Empire Room.

Saturday, February 8: A musicale was held at the studio of artist Alexander Charles Robinson. That evening, the cotillion of Joseph T. Low's dancing class was held.

Monday, February 10: A tea and bazaar was held at the home of Eugene Kelly for the Association for Befriending Children and Young Girls. A cotillion occurred at Sherry's and the Met that evening performed *Die Meistersinger*, after which many of the patrons attended the ball given by Mr. and Mrs. John Jacob Astor IV at 840 Fifth Avenue.

Tuesday, February 11: Society turned out for "a musicale and dramatic entertainment" that raised funds for St. Andrew's Convalescent Hospital.

Wednesday, February 13: The Spinsters' Ball was held at Sherry's on St. Valentine's eve.

Thursday, February 14: The Assembly Ball took place at the Waldorf, among the subscribers to which were Mrs. Astor, Mr. and Mrs. John Jacob Astor, Mrs. August Belmont, Mrs. Isaac Bell, Mrs. Ogden Goelet, Mrs. J. Pierpont Morgan, Mrs. Watts Sherman, Mrs. William C. Schermerhorn, Mrs. Ward McAllister and Mrs. Stuyvesant Fish; supper was provided in the Winter Garden.

Saturday, February 16: St. Valentine's Kettledrum was presented at Sherry's to raise money for the Samaritan Home for the Aged; among the sponsors were Mrs. William Kissam Vanderbilt, Mrs. William Waldorf Astor, Levi P. Morton, and J. Pierpont Morgan.

Figure 144. Charles Dana Gibson, *The Weaker Sex. VIII.* He goes to the play, but finds it impossible to become interested in the piece. From *Collier's Weekly* (September 26, 1903), p. 15. Gibson was one of the highest-paid illustrators of his day, and in 1902 he wrote to P. F. Collier, "I hereby accept your offer of $100,000 for 100 double page cartoons, to be delivered to you during the next four years." The buying power of $100,000 was very high during the years 1902–6.

Society thus raced frenetically from one event to another, to and from venues that included both gala ballrooms and private dining rooms, glittering boxes at the opera and the elegant salons with bejeweled receptions (figures 143 and 144). For all of this, lavish architecture and interiors that displayed enormous wealth and the joy of spending it were expected, if one were to place one's self and one's family at the forefront of that impellent herd.

The Gala Opening

As we have seen, Caroline Astor moved into her new house on 1 February 1896, and that same afternoon she hosted a tea. Two days later, as part of the housewarming that was to introduce New York Society to her new palace, she held a grand ball. Excitement and anticipation prevailed as the nearly six hundred guests began to arrive for what *The New York Times* called the "largest and most elaborate private ball given this season, and . . . the first one that Mrs. Astor has given in many years."[15]

William Backhouse Astor had died in 1892, in Paris, whence he had gone to retrieve a wayward daughter (Charlotte Augusta Astor Drayton), who was reportedly having an affair with a married man named Hallett Borrowe, the son of a successful insurance mogul from New Jersey. There followed a year of both scandal and mourning, which precluded the annual Astor ball. The next year saw juicy details of Charlotte Augusta's divorce smeared across the newspapers, and then the death of another daughter, Helen Astor Roosevelt, and another year of mourning. Then Caroline's major domo, Ward McAllister, died in January of 1895, causing her further sorrow. The building and decorating of her new mansion helped occupy her during this trying period, and the grand ball of 1896 was to be her reentry into Society.

Standing in her salon, Mrs. Astor received her guests as they arrived—

Figure 145. Richard Morris Hunt, salon, Caroline Astor residence, Fifth Avenue and 65th Street, New York City, 1895, photograph ca. 1908. Brown Brothers. In the far corner is Carolus-Duran's full-length portrait of Caroline Astor, draped in black crepe in mourning for the *grande dame*'s death in 1908.

Figure 146 (opposite). Jules Allard et Fils of Paris (attributed to), armchairs, ca. 1895, made for the John Jacob Astor IV residence, Fifth Avenue and 65th Street, New York City; purchased in 1926 by John Ringling for his residence, Cà d'Zan, Sarasota, Fla. The John and Mable Ringling Museum of Art, the State Art Museum of Florida.

the Ogden Millses, Lispinard Stewart, the Philip Rhinelanders, the Henry Clewses, the August Belmonts, the Pierre Lorillards, and on and on (figure 145). They arrived late—some not until midnight—because many of them had come from their boxes at the opera house, where they had seen the Met's production of *Carmen*. Caroline herself had attended the performance that night, sitting like the social queen that she was, greatly bejeweled, in her private box, number 7.

A supper had been prepared for her friends as they arrived, and there was dancing in the brilliantly lit (with electric lights in the coved cornice) ballroom/art gallery. A week later John Jacob Astor IV and his wife held their grand ball to show off their part of the great mansion, to which nearly four hundred paid proper homage. There was dancing until midnight, then a supper from midnight to one o'clock, followed by a spirited cotillion that lasted into the wee hours amid interiors described by the press as "superbly decorated."[16]

The Interiors

Guests entered the double mansion through a large, central entrance hall (sixty-four by fifty-five feet) that served both halves of the house, with Caroline Astor's portion being to the left while her son and his family occupied the corner section. The walls of the entrance hall were veneered with a lovely Caen stone, and on them were hung handsome tapestries. In the center of the hall rose a grand staircase, which led to the second story of each half of the house where the private quarters were located—the bedrooms, sitting rooms, and so forth. At the upper level the walls were decorated with marble life-size waist-length herm-like female figures, the creations of Hunt's favorite sculptor, Karl Bitter. Between these were placed eighteenth-century portraits, mostly English. The hall was lighted by a rose-tinted glass skylight and a large and ornate chandelier.

The entrance hall gave access to several rooms used for entertaining—the acknowledged primary purpose of the first floor. These rooms could serve both Caroline and her son when the entire first floor was thrown open on the occasion of a grand ball or a large reception. Upon entering the hall, guests found a small Rococo reception room to the left and another to the right before coming to Caroline's large Louis XV–style salon at the left, with its walls done in white and gilt, and in the spirit of the times, the gilding was lavishly applied. Huge mirrors reflected light in this room, which had no windows. A great circular peacock-tail carpet covered the floor, and the furniture was copied from that at the Petit Trianon at Versailles; an example, from John Jacob's side of the house, is seen in figure 146.

In this room Caroline would receive her guests as they arrived, always standing alone in front of a full-length portrait of her. She was resplendent in her recently acquired Worth gown and so burdened by the Astor diamonds that some wag remarked that she resembled the great Italian chandelier of her ballroom. Colonel Mann, that impious jokester of Society's scandal sheet, *Town Topics*, once suggested that it might be easier on Mrs. Astor if, at her next ball, she put all of her jewels in a wheelbarrow and just

wheeled them in before her. As if in defiance of Colonel Mann, when she had her portrait painted, she had the artist depict her well bedecked in diamonds and pearls.

The portrait, now owned by the Metropolitan Museum of Art, had been painted in Paris in 1890 by Carolus-Duran, who was then still one of the premier portraitists of the day (figure 147). As with many of her crowd, Mrs. Astor spent much of each spring in Paris, where she maintained a residence, located in the fashionable Faubourg Saint-Germain; the annual Parisian sojourn was obligatory so that one could acquire a sufficient number of Worth gowns for the year-long round of festivities. But Caroline was by no means a "Gibson Girl," and Carolus-Duran represented her not so much beautiful as regal, in the way a dowager of the Renaissance Medici family might have been depicted; to be sure, Caroline was endowed by nature with neither great beauty nor sparkling wit, and by the year she had her portrait painted she had reached her sixtieth birthday. Caroline no doubt approved of the image's Van Dyck–like quality with its aristocratic encodings. Even the style of her dress was inspired by fashions seen in paintings of the seventeenth century.

Beyond this salon was Mrs. Astor's dining room, which had black oak paneled wainscoting, carved with ornate arabesques that were gilded. "The tapestries and hangings harmonized in their dark effect, and when the lights from the crystal chandelier and golden candelabra greeted the guests the scene was brilliant," according to a contemporary social reporter, who further observed, "The table service of gold and the gorgeous flowers, usually American Beauty roses in gold vases, added to its charm."[17] Here, as in several other houses, Hunt called on the firm of Allard et Fils to produce the paneling and the reproduction furniture.

If being among the privileged souls who were invited to one of Mrs. Astor's balls was the defining blessing of membership in New York High Society, an even greater achievement was being included among those invited to dinner. At the latter, guests were seated at eight o'clock and were expected to depart at eleven. They dined on gold service while gold epergnes and candelabras adorned the table, amid great sprays of bright red roses, and they drank vintage champagne from crystal glasses.

Figure 147. Carolus-Duran, *Caroline Schermerhorn Astor (Mrs. William B. Astor)*, 1890. Oil on canvas, 83 × 42 in. (212 × 107.3 cm). Metropolitan Museum of Art, gift of R. Thornton Wilson and Orme Wilson, 1949 (49.4). If Carolus-Duran's image of Caroline Astor reminds us of portraits from the seventeenth century, there are two reasons why. First, as a young man the artist traveled in Spain where he became infatuated with portraiture by Diego Velásquez, and second, the aristocratic style of the Spanish court—in dress as in art—appealed to the newly wealthy of America, who saw themselves as the new aristocracy of their era. The portrait was painted in Paris.

On her son's side of the house, a large reception room was the counterpart to Caroline's main salon. It too was done in an eighteenth-century French mode. To the east of it was John Jacob's dining room, with windows facing 65th Street.

The Astor Ballroom and Art Collection

Beyond the entrance hall and stairway lay the grand ballroom, extending across the entire width at the rear of the double house, again a space that served both Caroline and her son and daughter-in-law (figures 148–150). Here, indeed, was the holy of holies, the inner sanctum of American high society. Newspaper society columns referred to the mansion as "the White House of New York" and declared that the ballroom could easily accommodate twelve hundred people—so much had Society expanded since Ward McAllister's days when only four hundred would fit into Mrs. Astor's ballroom in the brownstone down at 34th Street. One means she had of controlling the membership of who was and who was not admitted to the charmed circle of Society was by selecting who was to be invited to her annual ball; no other guest list of the *fin de siècle* defined that gilded world so precisely and maintained the bastions against the vulgar "climbers" and pretenders. Not until she was nearing the end of her reign did she feel compelled to loosen up a bit to introduce some of the "Bohemian" crowd of writers and artsy folk into her privileged group.

Elizabeth Drexel Lehr recalled the brilliance of those special evenings in the Astor ballroom:

> Even after all these years I have only to close my eyes to conjure up a vision of the Astor ballroom in all its splendours. The massive candelabra that William Astor had brought back [years earlier] from Italy, the walls lined with pictures of the nineteenth-century French school, New York's last word in European culture . . . , the musicians' gallery with the band in the familiar Astor blue liveries. And on a raised platform at one end was an enormous divan—"The Throne." No one ever dreamt of calling it anything else. But alas, . . . it could only accommodate a limited number on those ample red silk cushions and there was acute disappointment every year [if one were not chosen to sit on the divan].[18]

Edith Wharton, whose father was Caroline's cousin, experienced similar evenings in the ballrooms of Gilded Age Society and often included such scenes in her novels and stories, as when she wrote of Mrs. Bry's ballroom in *The House of Mirth* of 1905:

> The company, in obedience to the decorative instinct which calls for fine clothes in fine surroundings, had dressed rather with an eye to Mrs. Bry's background [decor] than to herself. The seated throng, filling the immense room without undue crowding, presented a surface of rich tissues and jewelled shoulders in harmony with festooned and gilded walls, and the flushed splendours of the Venetian ceiling.[19]

Then Wharton has one of the characters, Gerty Farish, declare, "Someone told me the ceiling was by Veronese. . . . And this room is wonderfully becoming—everyone looks so well! Did you ever see such jewels? Do look at Mrs. George Dorset's pearls—I suppose the smallest of them would pay the rent of our Girls' Club for a year."[20] Photographers were never permitted to preserve on film such scenes in Caroline's ballroom, but a few artists seized upon the subject, often with great wit and satire, as in Charles Dana Gibson's "Matrimonial Misfits," dated only a few years after Mrs. Astor's first grand ball in the new mansion (figure 151). In illustrations such as this, Gibson showed himself to be Society's counterpart to the political cartoonist Thomas Nast in the biting satirization of his own class.

Caroline Astor's ballroom was meant to be a space that connoted wealth and power. It measured sixty feet in length and was two stories high, with most of the ceiling given to a large

Figure 148. Charles Frederick Worth, evening gown, ca. 1888. Velvet and satin. Photograph, Doyle Auctioneers and Appraisers, New York City. This lovely gown was designed and made in Paris for Esther Maria (Lily) Lewis Chapin, for the occasion of being presented at a European court. It languished in a trunk for years thereafter, but when it was sold at auction in 2001 it commanded a high bid of $101,500, at that time a world auction record for an evening dress.

stained-glass dome. Above the cornice was a highly ornamented coved area, with four pairs of Atlas-type muscular, nearly nude male figures supporting the great cornice of the skylight. These figures, along with the two Amazonian goddesses on the monumental fireplace in the eastern wall, are consciously reminiscent of the elaborate decorations at Fontainebleau, the great palace of King Francis I. Heroic, heavily ornate cartouches abound at this level, each having as its capstone the head of a famous artist.

The walls were covered with pictures in bold, gilt frames. The paintings were displayed in the old-fashioned way of stacking them one above the other, virtually from floor to ceiling; the more modern way would soon prevail: lining up choice examples at eye level, in a single row along a wall, each masterpiece being surrounded by ample space to give it individuality and emphasis, as Henry Clay Frick did a few years later in his New York mansion.

In its day the Astor collection was praised as one of high culture. Newspaper reports estimated the total value of the collection to be over half a million dollars, with some paintings worth as much as $40,000. But there were few masterpieces, by today's aesthetic criteria, and even by 1895 the collection was, in fact, noticeably outmoded. By 1926, when Caroline's grandson Vincent decided to sell the great house and its contents, the paintings brought only about $400 to $2,000 each at auction.

Formed in the 1870s when the French academic school was at its height among European and American nouveaux riches, the collection remained essentially unchanged from the one that had adorned the walls of the Astor ballroom down at 34th Street. Favored subjects included homey narrative or story-telling scenes, landscapes, an occasional battle or military scene, and a few still-lifes. A work by Corot, *Monte Pincio, Rome*, was the closest concession to the incipient modern movement in French painting.

Approximately one hundred paintings adorned the walls of the ballroom, and a sampling will convey the character of the collection. Jules Breton's *Le Repos*, a large picture, depicted a group of resting picnickers, while Émile van Marcke's *Dans les Landes*, an enormous canvas filled with plodding cattle (visible at the left in figure 150) dominated one wall, with Jules Lefebvre's nude *Odalisque* reclining above it. At the Astor sale in April 1926 van Marcke's great bovine piece was bought by John Ringling for the museum he was about to open in Sarasota, Florida; he also purchased Ferdinand Roybet's *The Connoisseurs* (figure 152) and Jean B. E. Detaille's *La Campagne en Russie*, paintings seen at the lower right and lower left of the fireplace in figure 150.[21] Ringling also acquired Constant Troyon's *Dog Herding Sheep*. In addition, Mrs. Astor's collection contained William Bouguereau's *Young Girl Winding Wool*, Jean Vibert's *L'Atelier*, and Etienne Berne-Bellecour's *Dans la Tranchee, Petit Paris*.

The End of a Reign

By the year 1900 Caroline Astor had reigned as queen of New York Society for a quarter of a century. Others with ambitions to sit on the throne—Alva Vanderbilt Belmont, Mamie Fish, Mrs. Clarence Mackay, and Mrs. Hermann Oelrichs, among them—circled the dais, waiting. Although Caroline was still recognized as Society's greatest of the great *grandes dames*, by then the younger women had begun to form satellite groups of their own. Even her court jester and major domo, Harry Lehr—who had replaced the late Ward McAllister—defected, going over to the court of Mamie, Mrs. Stuyvesant Fish, of whose antics, jokes, and viperous tongue Mrs. Astor disapproved as detrimental to a well-ordered and polite society.

Caroline Astor gave her last ball in the season of 1904; in 1907 she held her last dinner party. By then servants sometimes overheard her conversing with imaginary visitors and with dinner guests who were not there. Edith Wharton was inspired by accounts of Mrs. Astor hosting dinners at an empty table but carrying on conversations all evening, and of

Figure 149 (opposite). Charles Dana Gibson, *In Paris. He [Mr. Pipp] has the Opportunity of enlarging His Horizon and of Developing an Interest in the Real Purpose of the Trip.* From the "Mr. Pipp" series, *Life* (6 October 1898), pp. 270–71. Charles Frederick Worth, an Englishman who had established his *couturer* in Paris in 1858, dominated the *haute couture* world for the remainder of the century. He demanded that his American customers come to Paris for custom fittings, a scene that Gibson re-created in one of his illustrations from his "Mr. Pipp" series.

Figure 150. Richard Morris Hunt, ballroom and art gallery, Caroline Astor residence, Fifth Avenue and 65th Street, New York City, 1895. Museum of the City of New York, Wurts Collection. Whereas Mrs. Astor's ballroom in her house down at 34th Street could accommodate only four hundred guests—*the* "Four Hundred"—this grand room was spacious enough for over twelve hundred of Society's chosen ones to disport themselves and their finery. Its reminiscence of the great rooms at Fountainebleau, the early-sixteenth-century Renaissance palace of King Francis I, is again testimony to the desire of Americans to emulate European aristocracy.

a way that it could eventually be converted into a single dwelling.

In 1909 the architectural firm of Carrère and Hastings was called on to renovate most of the first floor.[23] Carrère and Hastings had come into prominence about 1890 as practitioners of the Beaux-Arts style that had been defined, in America, by Richard Morris Hunt and McKim, Mead and White; Hunt died in 1895, Stanford White was murdered in 1906, and thereafter both McKim (died 1909) and Mead increasingly lost interest in professional activities. By 1909 Carrère and Hastings therefore emerged as the leaders of the Beaux-Arts movement, which still had another decade of dominance before the watershed of World War I occurred. The firm had gained great acclaim as early as 1894 with the archetypal Beaux-Arts fluffery of the H. T. Sloane residence (figure 234, p. 343) on 68th Street, just off of Fifth Avenue, followed a few years later by the winning of the competition for the design of the colossal New York Public Library at 42nd and Fifth, a civic Beaux-Arts masterpiece that achieved equality with Hunt's and McKim, Mead and White's Metropolitan Museum of Art. The firm's main rival, George B. Post, was also aging, but he too remained devoted to the Beaux-Arts tradition. Contemporary critics saw the mantel of architectural excellence being passed from McKim, Mead and White to Carrère and Hastings, as noted in *Architectural Record* in 1910:

> It may be emphatically asserted . . . that American architects could not select any one Renaissance sub-style better adapted to their needs than that of eighteenth-century France. . . . Carrier & Hastings have been as successful in giving a modern American version of these good French architectural manners of the eighteenth century as McKim, Mead and White have been in sympathetically interpreting some of the earlier phases of Renaissance architecture.[24]

Because of the firm's prominence, it was natural for John Jacob Astor IV to turn to Carrère and Hastings for the

servants announcing the arrival of invisible guests, all of which appears in Wharton's short story "After Holbein."[22] Then one day Caroline fell on the stairs and became confined to a wheelchair, which made entertaining all but impossible. She was now largely alone in her great mansion, attended by her companion, a Miss Simrock, and her faithful butler, Hade, who had waited on her and overseen the running of the house since 1876. Friends called regularly, and her son and daughter-in-law were just across the hall, but among society folk, Caroline Webster Schermerhorn Astor was now more a memory than the queenly leader she had once been. Caroline died on 30 October 1908, and black crepe was draped about the large, life-size portrait of her that Carolus-Duran had painted in Paris.

The John Jacob Astor IV House

The half of the house at Fifth Avenue and 65th Street that had belonged to Caroline Astor passed, upon her death, to her son, John Jacob IV, who lived in the other half. Two years later he began the conversion of the double mansion into one enormous house, suitable to the lifestyle and entertaining that his family led. Richard Morris Hunt, no doubt in collaboration with the Astors, had designed the house in such

Figure 151. Charles Dana Gibson, *Matrimonial Misfits. 12:30 A.M. The Husband who wants to go Home and the Wife who doesn't.* From *Life* (22 February 1900), pp. 150–51.

remodeling of his magnificent Beaux-Arts mansion, designed by Hunt only twenty years earlier. Neither the patron nor the architects had any interest in the revolution that was then occurring, a revolution that was destined to displace the Beaux-Arts mode with a style based on steel I-beams, glass walls, reinforced concrete, and modern technologies. Both Astor and his architects remained faithfully committed to the Beaux-Arts manner of the preceding generation.

And so Carrère and Hastings set to work, their inspiration continuing to come from classical Renaissance, Baroque, and Rococo sources, given new life in the variations explored within the Beaux-Arts perimeters. In the entrance hall, the dividing partition wall was removed along with the double staircase, creating one huge chamber that measured about fifty by sixty feet, adding enormously to the entertaining capabilities within the mansion. It was rimmed by a

Figure 152. Ferdinand Roybet, *The Connoisseurs*, 1876. Oil on canvas, 48 × 59 in. (121.9 × 143.4 cm). The John and Mable Ringling Museum of Art, the State Art Museum of Florida. Ex Coll., Caroline Astor. Roybet's *Connoisseurs* is seen just to the right of the fireplace in Mrs. Astor's ballroom (figure 150). Roybet, a much decorated and very popular French Salon painter of the *fin de siècle*, specialized in genre scenes, historical costume pictures of knights, courtiers, and musketeers, and exotic scenes from the Turkish and North African harems. He first exhibited at the Salon in 1866, and his future was assured when his picture was purchased by Princess Mathilde, daughter of Jerome Bonaparte.

monumental arcade that screened flanking hallways from which one gained entrance to the adjoining rooms. An ornate domed bronze and glass skylight now covered the area and flooded it with light.

What had been Caroline's main salon (the northwest salon) was transformed into an enlarged dining room, the walls of which were covered with a set of seventeenth-century Brussels tapestries, titled *The Visit of Cyrus to the Defeated Croesus* and *The Tribute of the King to Cyrus*, both by Jacob van Zeunen, a *Caesar in Gaul* by Garaert van der Streecken, and a *Flight of Pompey* by Guillaume van Leedfael. The conversion of Caroline's salon into a dining room made it possible for John Jacob to turn what had been his dining room (the southeast room) into a library for himself, and it was there that he hung the portraits of his father and his mother (figure 154). The dark paneling of the former dining room was appropriate for a library, and a splendid large tapestry of mythological subject adorned much of one wall. The fact that no book is visible in the photograph of the library suggests that it was more a room to which John Jacob Astor IV could retire and find solitude, a drawing room, rather than the den of a confirmed bibliophile.

Perhaps because it was so grand (in spite of being rather old-fashioned by then), the ballroom remained as it was. Despite the fact that the Astor collection of French academic narrative, rural genre, and military pieces—dating from the 1870s and 1880s—was no longer the standard by which culture was measured in New York, John Jacob did not seize this

moment as an opportunity to do away with it and move instead into the competition for rare works by Old Masters—the Rembrandts, Raphaels, Van Dycks, and Fragonards that J. Pierpont Morgan, Bernard Altman, and Henry Clay Frick had been acquiring. The ballroom and its collection remained essentially unchanged until the great sale of 1926 and the subsequent demolition of the mansion.

But soon after Caroline's death in 1908, life in the house began to change. Her son and daughter-in-law divorced the next year, Ava Lowle Willing Astor moving to London, where she eventually remarried and became Lady Ribblesdale, wife of the noted sportsman. In 1911 John Jacob Astor too remarried, taking Miss Madeleine Talmage Force as his second wife.

On 3 March 1910, John Jacob Astor held a grand ball to which all members of Society's gala crowd came, to dance, to dine, and to marvel at the lavishness of the renovations.[25] The guests included the Stuyvesant Fishes, the Winthrop Chanlers, Lady Paget, Alva Vanderbilt (now Mrs. Oliver Belmont), young Vincent Astor, Anthony Drexel Jr., Egerton Winthrop, Worthington Whitehouse, Stephen Van Rensselaer, and about 150 others from Society's "short list." Franco's orchestra played, and supper was served between midnight and 1:00 A.M., after which the cotillion was led by Harry Lehr with Mrs. Orme Wilson (Caroline's daughter) as his partner.

But John Jacob Astor IV was not to enjoy his grand mansion for very long, for he was among the victims when the *Titanic* went down on 15 April 1912. The newspapers published eyewitness accounts of the heroism with which he conducted himself during the disaster—how he assisted others into lifeboats and the like. Reportedly, he saw his young pregnant wife safely into the next-to-last lifeboat, and bravely told her he would see her in the morning, in an effort to reassure her.

Epilogue for the Astor Houses

In 1916, the mansion passed to Vincent, the son of John Jacob and his first wife. But Vincent belonged to that later generation who saw such houses as "white elephants" because of their tax liability and their expensive maintenance; Vincent and his wife preferred their Long Island estate and something more modest as their city residence. Also, commercialism had continued its incessant march upward along Fifth Avenue, destroying the other great mansions one by one and replacing them with income-producing structures instead—apartment buildings and hotels, for example. The Astor mansion occupied an exceptionally large corner lot, making it a valuable piece of property. And so the house was sold in 1926 to make way—not for a commercial building but for a synagogue, the Temple Emanu-el, which still stands on the plot today.

At the auction held on April 21 and 22, John Ringling just before demolition of the Astor mansion, bought not only the paintings mentioned earlier and tapestries for his museum but also two of the rooms—the corner (southwest) salon and John Jacob Astor's library; these rooms may now be seen installed in the John and Mabel Ringling Museum of Art.

Figure 153. Eighteenth-century drawing room, John Jacob Astor IV residence, Fifth Avenue and 65th Street, New York City, 1895 and 1910. Museum of the City of New York. Astor and his decorators were hoping to recall the elegance and grandeur of the salons of the great Bourbon monarchs, Louis XV and Louis XVI, just as Napoleon III had sought them in the apartment of his son, Monsieur le Prince, fifty years earlier, as a comparison with figure 126 reveals. By 1910 the French period room was well established in the homes of the wealthy and had begun to appear in re-creations in art museums and historical societies.

Figure 154. Drawing room, John Jacob Astor IV residence, Fifth Avenue and 65th Street, New York City, after remodeling, ca. 1910. Museum of the City of New York. Mr. Astor, whose portrait hangs above the fireplace, was educated at St. Paul's School and at Harvard University before settling down to manage the family fortune. His life came to an early end, at the age of forty-seven, when he died in the *Titanic* disaster, after comporting himself nobly in seeing to it that women and children were safely escorted into lifeboats while he remained behind and went down with the ship.

Horse-shows, dog-shows, tennis tournaments, etc., take place in [the Casino's] enclosures, that are always well patronized. It is a dazzling sight when the lawns are covered with well-dressed women, whose jewels sparkle in the sunlight. . . . The graceful sweep of their gauzy dresses, the flutter of ribbons or scarfs, the fanciful head-gear, the effective parasols make a picture not easily forgotten.

Mrs. John King Van Rensselaer, *Newport: Our Social Capital* (1905)

Chapter Ten

McKim, Mead and White

Origins of the Firm and the Early Work at Newport

THE FIRM OF MCKIM, MEAD AND WHITE passed through three main phases: The early work was characterized by a trial-and-error search for a signature design that meandered from Romanesque massiveness to Queen Anne picturesqueness to Colonial American vernacular. In the second phase, beginning about 1885, the Roman Renaissance Revival style of the Villard Houses established their trademark style and their reputation, and it provided America with a form of architecture that could stand up to the great urban environment and give it both dignity and order. The final phase followed the death of Richard Morris Hunt in 1895, which left McKim, Mead and White as the unchallenged, preeminent architectural firm of America, that is, until Stanford White's death in 1906 and Charles Follen McKim's demise three years later.

CHARLES FOLLEN MCKIM

Charles Follen McKim (1847–1909) came from a good Philadelphia family, graduated from Harvard, and, like Richard Morris Hunt a few years earlier, trained in architecture at the École des Beaux-Arts in Paris.[1] His father, in a touch of irony, had written in 1867 to a man named Henry Villard—the same man whose house design would ultimately give new direction to the firm of McKim, Mead and White—to ask the railroadman's advice about his son's education and about allowing Charles to go to Paris to study. There was, in fact, a distant family connection, for Villard's wife was a daughter of William Lloyd Garrison, whose son had married Charles Follen McKim's sister.

Charles did go off to Paris to study, but one of his biographers has noted that while McKim "appreciated the great worth of the Paris system of training, he never [as a student there] liked modern French taste, and was always . . . nearer to Rome than to Paris."[2] The same author further observed that to the simplicity of solution in a design, "it was his nature to add a scholarly . . . appreciation of character in detail which grew with his advance in years and his almost annual visits to Italy."[3]

Margaret Terry Chanler—wife of Winthrop Chanler, of the Astor clan—remembered him as a "charming man of exquisitely fastidious taste and ardent classical convictions."[4] Thoughtful, prudent, reserved, always keeping the steady course, McKim was the anchor to the impetuous Stanny White. His two main contributions to the firm, once it was established, were his ability to organize enormous projects in a beautifully logical plan, and his celebration of the city as the very center of civilization.

STANFORD WHITE

In personality and temperament, McKim could hardly have been more different from his eventual partner, Stanford White.[5] Born in 1853 in New York City, in a house on West 10th Street, White was the son of Richard Grant White, a prolific critic and author of seventy books. The father lamented the absence of an aristocracy in America and was troubled by a democratic tendency to vulgarize, all of which undoubtedly had its influence on his son, who later designed palatial mansions for the new millionaire aristocracy. In time, White's great role within McKim, Mead and White would be to transform his clients' natural penchant for ostentation in their domestic architecture into magnificence, their extravagance into a tasteful beauty and dignity. "For an American plutocracy," wrote Paul Baker in his biography of White, "often unsure of itself and attempting to mold an image rooted in the past, Stanford White was eminently appropriate as a creator of images."[6]

While still in his teens, Stanford declared that he wanted to be a painter, so his father took him to the nearby Tenth Street Studio Building to discuss the matter with a friend, John La Farge. The latter recommended he become an architect instead, and another friend, Frederick Law Olmsted (of Central Park fame) suggested that young Stan enter the office of the architect Henry Hobson Richardson. Upon showing Richardson some drawings that La Farge had admired, young White was hired, in 1872. It was then that he met another new member of Richardson's firm, Charles Follen McKim, who had recently returned from Italy and from whom White was to learn much in the practice of architectural drawing.

This was a propitious moment in the history of Richardson's firm, for work was just commencing on Trinity Church, overlooking Copley Plaza in Boston.[7] White was put to work on the project at once, gaining wonderful exposure to artistic collaboration, involving La Farge, who was in charge of interior decoration, as well as Kenyon Cox, Frank

Millet, Francis Lathrop, and Augustus Saint-Gaudens, among others. In the evolution of this project, White's natural ability to devise beautiful architectural interiors and their details first manifested itself. Eventually Richardson made him coordinator of the project. This was an especially important event in his career, for at this early stage he learned to coordinate a multi-media of arts—including painting, sculpture, mosaics, stained glass, and interior furnishings—into a harmonious whole.

White continued to live in New York City, with his parents, not far from Saint-Gaudens's studio on 14th Street and La Farge's rooms in the Studio Building. White, Saint-Gaudens, and La Farge were all members of the Tile Club, the arts and crafts group that met regularly in Edwin Austin Abbey's studio at 58½ West 10th Street.[8] Other members included Elihu Vedder, J. Alden Weir, William Merritt Chase, Winslow Homer, the mosaicist David Maitland Armstrong, and Richard Watson Gilder, editor of *The Century Magazine*. The evening meetings of the Tile Club fostered a male bonding that was always important to Stanford White, his numerous extramarital affairs with young ladies notwithstanding.

In addition to Trinity Church, Richardson's office in the mid-1870s was designing the William Watts Sherman house in Newport, Rhode Island. Watts Sherman was a wealthy New York banker, and his picturesque, multitextured house in Newport represents a transition between the more modest wood-frame, shingle-covered vernacular houses of old Newport and the lavish "cottages" erected after 1890 such as Marble House, The Breakers, and Rosecliff.

By that time McKim had left Richardson's office to begin his own practice, but White remained and attended to many of the architectural details of the Sherman house, which was essentially of the Queen Anne style made popular in England by Robert Norman Shaw. White's role was that of artist-designer, serving not only as architect but also as interior decorator, a new profession then just arising. He was responsible for much of the color and charm of its interiors. The Watts Sherman house represents the early stages of Stanford's main contributions to McKim, Mead and White: his infallible taste, exquisite detailing, flair for the elegant, and knowledge of color, surface, texture, and ornament in architecture, especially interior design.

The Call of the Old World

White, anxious to see Europe and its treasures, sailed aboard the *Pierre* on 3 July 1878. At the last moment, McKim decided to join him; McKim had married the sister of his business partner, William Bigelow, and when the marriage ended with divorce, the business partnership ended. In Paris, White and McKim joined their friend Augustus Saint-Gaudens, who was then working on the main figure for the Farragut Memorial. Before White left for France the sculptor had written to him to complain about the difficulties of making a heroic figure wearing contemporary clothing. And, Saint-Gaudens added, "When you come over I want to talk with you about the pedestal. Perhaps something might be done about that."[9] As it turned out, during the years 1878–81, one of the projects that occupied and intrigued White was the designing of the base of the Farragut Memorial, the result of which was a totally new departure in the concept of bases for sculptures, just at a time when America was entering its golden age of memorial statuary. The project marked the beginning of a quarter-century-long collaboration between White and Saint-Gaudens in the making of commemorative monuments.

At one point McKim, White, and Saint-Gaudens left Paris to embark on a walking tour of the Romanesque country of southern France, for the Romanesque Revival style was then the hot ticket in architectural designing, thanks mainly to H. H. Richardson. Back in Paris, White shared quarters with Saint-Gaudens, cementing a friendship by endless drinking, joking, and wenching—all of which was beyond the patience of Charlie McKim, who departed for home. Slightly over a year later, in 1879, White returned to New York, but not before he visited Rome, Venice, and Verona. The powerful influence of the Old World would not show up immediately in White's interiors, but it was not long before it did.

Establishment of the Firm

Upon returning, White entered the architectural office that had recently been set up by McKim and William Rutherford Mead (1846–1928).[10] The soon-to-be famous firm was thus established, although White's name did not appear in the title at first (figure 155). A division of responsibility shortly emerged, serving the firm well throughout its existence:

McKim was a master at devising a workable overall plan, especially in large-scale projects such as the Boston Public Library, Pennsylvania Station, and the new multibuilding campus of Columbia University in New York City. White became the consummate designer of beautiful details, materials, and color schemes. And Mead emerged as a highly efficient office manager who kept all the plans moving along for the various projects the firm was executing simultaneously. Mead supervised what became a small army of draftsmen, and he kept an eye on accounting and other paperwork. All three partners always insisted that no matter how much one or another of them might be responsible for the design of a given building, that building was the result of the collaborative effort of all three of them, with the assistance of their very gifted staff.

Early in their partnership, McKim, Mead, and White went on a tour of New England to study the Colonial architecture of the seventeenth and eighteenth centuries and the various revival styles of the early nineteenth century. This is noteworthy in connection with the Colonial Revival that arose in architecture following the Philadelphia Centennial of 1876, which made Americans aware of their origins and their national heritage, especially in architecture and the decorative arts. The fruits of this study of Colonial and revival styles may be observed in some of the firm's earliest commissions, such as the remodeling of Kingscote and the design for the Casino at Newport.

Kingscote

The era of the great mansions at Newport arrived in the late 1880s and the 1890s. Of the several distinguished houses that preceded that era, many were subjected to extensive renovation to make them suitably palatial. The story began, as we have seen, with Richard Morris Hunt's remodeling of Château-sur-Mer, and it continued with the picturesque Kingscote, designed by Richard Upjohn in 1839 and finished, in his inevitable Gothic Revival style, in 1841 (figure 156). Constructed of wood, the traditional material of the early Newport cottages, and modest in scale and irregular in plan and profile, Kingscote was like the many shingle-style houses of Newport except in two respects—its applied Gothic ornamentation and its coloration, for it originally had a cream-colored exterior.

Kingscote was built for George Noble Jones and his family who were planters from near Savannah, Georgia, but the house was purchased by the King family in 1864, at which time it acquired its name, for "Kingscote" means "King's cottage." First owned by William King, a merchant in the China trade, it passed in 1876 to his nephew, David King, who was a major builder in New York City; it was he, in fact, who constructed the Cornelius Vanderbilt II mansion on Fifth Avenue at 58th Street. He was also the contractor for several McKim, Mead and

Figure 155. William Rutherford Mead, Charles Follen McKim, and Stanford White (left to right). Avery Architectural and Fine Arts Library, Columbia University.

Figure 156. Kingscote, Newport, R.I., originally built 1839, remodeled by Stanford White ca. 1881. The Preservation Society of Newport County. Photograph copyright, Richard Cheek.

White projects: the Bowery Savings Bank, for example, as well as the great arch in Washington Square. He and White shared a hideaway in the Holbein Building, which they affectionately referred to as "The Morgue."

In the late 1870s King undertook extensive renovations at Kingscote. He had George Champlin Mason and Son enlarge the service section, and purchased several major pieces of furniture for the south parlor and dining room from Léon Marcotte, one of New York's most fashionable decorators. But in 1881 the family needed more room, and the commission to remodel Kingscote went to Stanford White, who moved the service portion of the house back thirty feet and inserted the expansion part between the two older sections. During David King's ownership the exterior was painted the slate gray that is seen today.

The main feature of the renovation was the dining room (figure 157). While White was anxious to retain the character of the original house in his exterior design for the expansion, he departed from the Gothic mode in the new dining room, which is thoroughly of the Aesthetic Movement.

Stanford White and the Aesthetic Movement

The Aesthetic Movement,[11] discussed earlier in connection with some of the decorations for the William Henry Vanderbilt house, began in England and occurred in the United States from about 1875 to around 1910. It stressed that every portion of an architectural interior should be a work of art, that each article of the furnishings should be stunningly beautiful and contribute to the beauty of the whole ensemble. Exquisitely wrought hand-crafted *objets d'art* were preferred over the machine-made pieces that were so readily available in mass-produced quantities but often of very low aesthetic threshold. The movement was, in fact, a reaction against the gaudy banalities churned out by the Industrial Revolution. Stanford White would eventually reject the Aesthetic Movement in favor of aristocratic antiquities of European origins, but the concept of overloading the interior with beautiful objects and curios never left him.

While working on Kingscote, White renewed his friendship with Samuel Colman, a painter and designer who was the son of a wealthy New York publisher, and for whom White designed a modest shingle-covered cottage. In 1879 Colman had joined with Louis Comfort Tiffany, Candace Wheeler, and Lockwood de Forest in a loosely linked business arrangement called Associated Artists, and in their collaboration they represented a powerful force in the creation of the Aesthetic Movement. Stanford White's contact with Colman and the activities of the so-called Associated Artists group came together in the remodeling of the dining room at Kingscote, for which Louis Comfort Tiffany created the stained-glass windows. Upon White's commission, Tiffany also fashioned the green glass tiles that were applied to the chimney above the brass-faced fireplace, which was surrounded with opalescent tiles that line the walls on either side of the green and blue tiles. White sheathed the walls and ceiling with cork. Thus did the architect experiment with new materials for interiors, based on their alluring aesthetic effect.

Kingscote eventually passed to Maude Gwendolyn King, who married the Aesthetic Movement mosaicist David Maitland Armstrong;[12] their daughter, Gwendolyn, inherited it in 1968, and four years later, upon her death, she bequeathed it and its furnishings to the Preservation Society of Newport County. But as charming as Kingscote is, it remained, even after the expansion and renovations, of modest scale and more quaint than grand, at least when judged against the grandeur of the numerous great houses that were soon to rise on Bellevue Avenue.

Isaac Bell House: Shingle Style

Another Newport project for the young firm of McKim, Mead and White was a house for Isaac Bell Jr., a cotton broker who was married to the sister of James Gordon Bennett, publisher of the *New York Herald* and the prime mover in the building of Newport's Casino. Reportedly, Bennett had the house built for his sister and her husband, which would have brought him into contact with the firm. Completed in 1882, the Isaac Bell house stands as a landmark classic of the shingle style, as influenced by the picturesque element of the Queen Anne mode (figure 158).[13] But there are other influences at play, and the "mix and match" manner became ingrained in Stanford White's aesthetic. For example, although the form of the house is essentially Queen Anne, there are also Adamesque details such as the elliptical window in the gable

Figure 157. Stanford White, dining room, Kingscote, Newport, as remodeled ca. 1882, with glass bricks and tiles by Louis Comfort Tiffany. The Preservation Society of Newport County. Photograph copyright, Richard Cheek.

to the right and Adam-like triple windows of the central gable. White's penchant for decorative effects is further seen in the bamboo-like columns and in the variation in the design, shape, and patterns of the shingles.

The Newport Casino

Aside from the individual cottages, Society's communal gathering place at Newport was the Casino (figure 159). Maude Howe Elliott, daughter of Julia Ward Howe, observed many years later that it "was the first thing of its kind in the country, and its building marks an epoch in Newport life."[14] The architectural critic Mariana Griswold Van Rensselaer described it as "dignified, without being formal or pretentious, rural but not rustic, graceful, intimate, cheerful, with just a touch of fantasy—a Casino which is a mere summer-house for 'society's' amusement."[15] The Casino was, in fact, the first multirecreational complex in America, a precursor to a new socioarchitectural form that would arise in the era of the Gilded Age in response to Society's need for it—the country club. Here was yet another example of the expanded demands placed on architects by the new millionaire society.

The central character in the founding of the Casino was James Gordon Bennett Jr., who had inherited the *New York Herald* and $7 million from his father. Stanford White and Bennett were friends, and for Bennett, White would later create the interiors of his yacht, the *Namouna*, and design the building in New York City for Bennett's newspaper, the inspiration for which was a fifteenth-century palazzo in Verona.

Truly one of Society's bad boys, Bennett brawled one day at Delmonico's restaurant with Ned Stokes and departed with a broken nose for his efforts; Stokes was the jealous lover who shot and killed Jim Fisk over a flouncy floozie named Josie Mansfield. Bennett was to be engaged to a young woman, Caroline May, of a prominent New York family, but on the evening of 1 January 1877, at a small party held in his future father-in-law's parlor to announce the engagement, Bennett behaved badly. In the midst of the festivities, Bennett, having consumed a goodly amount of champagne, announced there was no bathroom within a reasonable distance and proceeded to relieve himself into the fireplace, although another version of the story says it was into the grand piano. His fiancée swooned, her mother screamed, the enraged brother-in-law-to-be lunged at Bennett with a poker from the fireplace, and Bennett was heaved out the front door, the engagement being renounced before it was announced. Shortly thereafter, the brother of his intended fiancée caught him alighting from a carriage in front of the Union Club and gave him a sound horsewhipping; a ceremonial duel followed, in which both parties fired harmlessly into the air.

Figure 158. McKim, Mead and White, Isaac Bell residence, Newport, 1883. The Preservation Society of Newport County. Photograph copyright, Richard Cheek. At this stage of the famous partnership the famed architects were still in their Queen Anne shingle-style mode, a result of their earlier tour of New England and a study of its vernacular, shingle-covered architecture.

Figure 159. McKim, Mead and White, Casino, Newport, 1879–80. Photograph courtesy of the Newport County Convention and Visitors Bureau.

Society never completely trusted Bennett after that, and with good reason. Mrs. John Van Rensselaer told of another escapade:

Polo [like lawn tennis] was also imported from England, and the game was played almost daily during the season at the field now occupied by the New York National League baseball club [the Polo Grounds]. In one game there in which . . . James Gordon Bennett was playing on the same team with William Douglas, the latter, for some reason, did not pass the ball to Bennett when it was coveted by the newspaper man. Bennett, furious, put his spurs to his pony, charged down upon Douglas and struck him across the head with his mallet. Douglas pitched off his horse, senseless, and never recovered his full health thereafter. The matter was hushed up, as so many scandals were in that day.[16]

Bennett, remembered today as the man who sent Henry Stanley into darkest Africa in 1871 in search of Dr. David Livingston, sent poor Douglas into a permanent state of wooziness.

Polo was reportedly first played in ancient Persia and revived in India in the nineteenth century. From there it was imported into England, in 1869, and then brought to Newport, in 1876, by James Gordon Bennett Jr. One day in 1878 a guest of Bennett's, a British army officer named Captain Candy, on a bet, rode his polo pony right up the steps of a most exclusive gentlemen's club, the staid old Newport Reading Room, and into the great hall where members dozed in great leather chairs or quietly read their papers. When "Sugar" Candy's privileges were revoked on that account, Bennett became furious and resigned from the club, vowing to organize his own new club—that is how the Newport Casino came into existence.[17]

But tennis, not polo, would be the focal sport of the Casino. Tennis seems to have originated in 1873 with a man named Walter C. Wingfield (and presumably a partner) in Wales, and the first championship match was held in 1877 at a place called Wimbledon, England. Although the U.S. Lawn Tennis Association would not be organized until 1881, the architects of the Casino anticipated the popularity of the game by designing the structure around the courts. From the day it opened to the public, 2 August 1880, the Newport Casino became the epicenter for tennis in the United States, and its invitational tournament, an international event, was the high point of the Newport season. Although the U.S. Open tennis tournament has long since (in 1915) moved to its new location outside of New York City, the Newport Casino remains the home of the International Tennis Hall of Fame.

The Design of the Casino

The Casino was one of McKim, Mead and White's first important nondomestic commissions from Gilded Age Society. Several stores and shops formed the street facade of the club, with a passageway in the center leading into the inner court, as can be seen in the plan (figure 160). Within, along one side and at the far end, were piazzas, while at the other side were a cafe and a restaurant, all overlooking the courtyard. A picturesque quality was achieved by making the facade asymmetrical, and a tourelle completed the fantasy.

The architects chose to use a wood-frame shingle style for the Casino, just as they did in 1882 for Southside, the somewhat Queen Anne–style cottage for New York socialite and real estate entrepreneur Robert Goelet, and in 1883 for the Isaac Bell house, which is located nearby. The Casino shows the influence of seventeenth-century Colonial American vernacular architecture that McKim, Mead and White had studied only a few years earlier.

Charles Follen McKim may have been responsible for the overall plan of the Casino, but Stanford White was the main operative in its design, and according to one biographer,

> his use of treillage [lattice or trellis], his Japanese touches, and his verandahs, conjure up something of the spirit of the British Raj. It is absolutely the right setting for late Victorian and Edwardian golden afternoons when Vanderbilts and Astors, clothed in thin voile and starched white linen, were served cool drinks by silent servants with the only sound that of a ball against a racket or a Gilbert and Sullivan medley played by a modulated band.[18]

Social Activities

Lest the gilded society become bored during the ten or so weeks it resided at the seaside resort each summer, the Casino offered a variety of amusements. Young ladies in shirt blouses, long skirts, and broad-brimmed hats could challenge each other at archery, while the menfolk could find a masculine haven in the billiard rooms or club rooms, where gaming at cards was constant. Bowling was available for those who were but mildly athletic. Tennis was then an entirely amateur game, played by handsome swains dressed in white shirts, white trousers, white shoes, and sometimes a little white cap. No one dared walk onto a court in anything but white. For spectators, warm afternoons could be spent in the cool shade of the verandas, chatting and gossiping while ostensibly watching the matches of either lawn or court tennis, through Stanford White's beautifully designed lattices with their circular "moon windows," which overlooked the Horseshoe Court or the lower lawn near the entrance (figures 161 and 162). The gentle quietude was only occasionally broken by the engaging laughter of jokester Harry Lehr. Amid the galleries and private boxes one might chance upon Tessie Oelrichs whispering some scandalous morsel to a wide-eyed but attentive King Lehr, or Alva Vanderbilt/Belmont indignantly accosting her friend Mamie Fish: "Mamie! Is it true that last night at Tessie's you said that I reminded you of a frog?!!!" "Oh, no, no, my pet . . . , not a frog—a toad, dear, a toad."

Among the arranged entertainments were concerts, horse shows (which were inevitably followed by a grand ball), dancing and theatrical productions. When the theater was not hosting an amateur or professional performance imported from New York—everything from musicales to vaudeville acts to ballet—its floor could be cleared of seating and used as a ballroom. Maud Howe Elliott recalled the entertainments at the Casino: "Every summer, leading actors are presented in the latest thing in drama. . . . Tuesday, the opening night, the boxes are crowded with men and women wearing clothes and jewels worthy of a gala performance at the Metropolitan [Opera]. . . . In the open court of the Casino, afternoon concerts are given by an admirable orchestra. Tea is served to the groups sitting under gay striped umbrellas."[19]

While the men and women in Winslow Homer's paintings, as a class—a middle class—were promenading at such middle-class resorts as Long Branch on the New Jersey coast, or playing croquet on a modest lawn, the Gilded Age set were at Newport's Casino. Elizabeth Drexel Lehr described the scene as she remembered it:

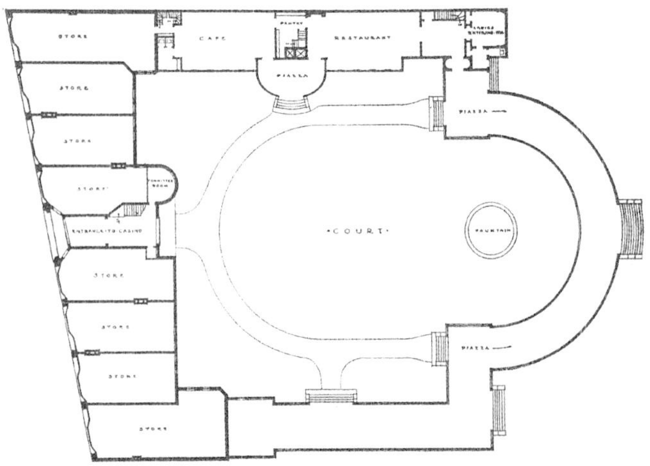

Figure 160. McKim, Mead and White, plan, Casino, Newport, 1879–80. From *A Monograph of the Work of McKim, Mead and White* (1915). Flanking an entrance tunnel, assorted shops face onto Bellevue Avenue. Once inside, a swarded lawn marked off into tennis courts is flanked by galleries and piazzas and a restaurant.

Such clothes! How they swished and rustled! Petticoats of satin, of lace, of taffeta; petticoats embellished with elaborate designs of plump cupids playing gilded lyres, true-love-knots interspersed with the doves embroidered in seed pearls. Parasols to match every dress, enormous flopping feather hats assorted to every costume. White gloves to the elbow, three or four new pairs every day, priceless lace ruffles at throat and wrists, yards of lace flouncing on underskirts, thousands of dollars' worth dragged over the Casino terrace. Different dresses for every occasion, eighty or ninety in a season, worn once or twice and put aside. On the Casino courts the "moderns" represented by Edith Wetmore and Mrs. John Jacob Astor played a strenuous but inefficient game of tennis in sports costumes considered the last word in daring—white tennis shoes and black stockings, white silk blouses, pleated skirts which fluttering in the breeze exposed . . . oh, horror, bloomers! Sailor hats to which were attached double veils protected their faces from the outrages of the sun.[20]

McKim, Mead and White at Newport: A Conclusion

For its several projects in and near Newport around 1880, McKim, Mead and White turned to the picturesque Queen Anne style and to the shingle-covered wood-frame vernacular architecture of colonial New England. But this was not the avenue that the firm would pursue to fame and fortune in the future. Their work of the late 1870s and early 1880s in and around the Narragansett Bay resort town stands as a discreet sector in the history of the partnership. Nowhere in it is found the kernel that will become their hallmark style, for neither the Queen Anne nor the Colonial Revival style would be employed to bring an urban dignity and order to the burgeoning American metropolis that was already suffering greatly from an unorderly urban sprawl. Something else arose that would serve McKim, Mead and White for that very purpose and make it the leading architectural firm at the turn of the century.

Figure 161 (above). Casino, courtyard and verandah, 1895–1900. Photographic Archives, Newport Restoration Foundation, Newport, R.I.

Figure 162 (right). Malcomb Strauss, *The Playtime of the Year, The Tennis Tournament at Newport*, *New York Times*, 9 July 1905. Broad-brimmed hats with matching parasols in pastel colors and the rustle of many layers of underskirts characterize the observers in Strauss's drawing of the gallery at Newport's Casino. Gentlemen wore white linen and straw hats.

[The wealthy American] was beginning then to import [European] pictures, tapestry and furniture by the great masters. His house must be worthy of them. Obviously the picturesque but coarse Romanesque of Richardson and his school was ill suited to house the finest objets d'art of the Renaissance. Something more elegant and restrained was required, and it was exactly this that McKim, Mead and White were equipped to give.

Charles H. Reilly, *McKim, Mead and White* (1924)

Chapter Eleven

McKim, Mead and White

The Villard Houses

By 1883 several mansions of one description or another had risen along Fifth Avenue, but collectively they represented something of a hodgepodge among the ubiquitous brownstones that still formed a uniform grid from Washington Square northward. Mary Mason Jones's French château–like Marble Row had opened up new territory in the vicinity of Central Park. The great houses of A. T. Stewart and William Henry Vanderbilt loomed big, different, and impressive, but no one seemed sure of their stylistic pedigree, or even if they should be liked, aesthetically. But then of greater sophistication and refinement came the Petit Château, which Richard Morris Hunt had designed for William Kissam and Alva Vanderbilt, and the first stage of the mansion George B. Post had designed for William's brother, Cornelius II, and his wife, Alice, in the style of Francis I.

Here and there one encountered a few other experiments, but those five were the really great houses standing by 1883. The two houses erected for the Vanderbilt brothers pointed the way for a new kind of millionaire's mansion in America, but, as we have seen, they were criticized because their styles were derived from architectural models that were basically of a château type—that is, of a rural type, and not of an urban form. Certain skillful architects could and did make this adaptation work, in the years that followed. One kind of urban architecture was admired—the boulevard architecture that was being imported from Paris—but though impressive, it did not lend itself well to palatial-scale mansions and it tended to connote more *haute bourgeoisie* than aristocracy. And so the question was raised, Was there not an urban model, from the great cities of Europe—expressive of the parvenus' aristocratic ambitions—to be found and employed in the service of America's Gilded Age? Was there not an architectural style from some past period that was truly at home in the burgeoning, bustling urban centers such as New York, Boston, Washington, Philadelphia, Chicago, and St. Louis?

The great contribution of McKim, Mead and White to the architectural history of the United States, and to the dignity of the American cityscape, was the discovery of a viable alternative to the French château style, in the form of the Roman palazzo. This first appeared in the complex of houses they designed for Henry Villard, erected on Madison Avenue between 50th and 51st streets in New York City. The commission for the Villard Houses established the reputation of the firm of McKim, Mead and White and sent it off in an entirely new direction in architectural design.

Henry Villard and the Villard Houses

Henry Villard (1835–1900) was born in Speyer, Bavaria, and educated at the universities of Munich and Wurzburg (figure 163). After emigrating to the United States in 1853 he made his way to Illinois, where his natural facility with languages led him into a career of journalism with newspapers published in German. As an ardent abolitionist he soon came to know a

Figure 163. Henry Villard. Photograph by Hoffert, Berlin. Baker Library, Harvard Business School.

young lawyer named Abraham Lincoln, and he became a correspondent for several English-language papers, covering first the Lincoln-Douglas debates, the election of Lincoln, whom he accompanied to Washington, and then the Civil War. In 1865 he married Fanny, the daughter of William Lloyd Garrison, and the young couple departed for Europe, where Henry wrote articles for the *Chicago Tribune* on such subjects as the great exposition in Paris in 1867.

Upon returning to the United States, Villard turned his interests to financial matters and to railroads. In Germany again in 1873, several businessmen asked him to look after their interests in the Oregon and California Railroad, which he agreed to do; appointed president of the line, he reorganized it and made it profitable. Shortly thereafter he became the receiver of the troubled Kansas Pacific Railroad, which brought him into conflict with Jay Gould who was trying to establish a competing line. Villard eventually won insofar as he got Gould to stop in exchange for a great quantity of the railroad's stock. But the wily Gould leaked the agreement to the press, and the price of the stock shot up meteorically, at which point Gould sold and made a profit of $10 million before the stock plunged as rapidly as it had risen. Meanwhile, Villard brought the Oregon Steamship Company under the wing of his transportation empire and then set his sights on the Northern Pacific line, of which he gained control and was made president in 1883. He was by then one of the most powerful men in the American Northwest, and he had become wealthy.

The money to build a fine mansion may have been made in the West, but Villard, and many others like him, recognized New York City as the social and financial capital of the nation. The Villards wanted a domicile in New York that would express their new high station in life and Henry's success within the capitalist aristocracy. In 1881 Villard bought the block-long plot on the east side of Madison Avenue between 50th and 51st streets, across the street from the back of Saint Patrick's Cathedral and, being familiar with Charles Follen McKim, turned to McKim, Mead and White to design a grand house.[1] Architecturally, this was a busy area: Saint Patrick's Cathedral had been finished only fifteen years earlier; William Henry Vanderbilt's brownstone palazzo had just recently been completed only a block away, over on Fifth Avenue; and William Kissam and Alva Vanderbilt's Petit Château was then nearly finished, at the corner of 52nd and Fifth.

The design called for six houses within the complex, Villard's portion being in the southern arm of the U-shaped plan, an arrangement similar to that of William Henry Vanderbilt's mansion in which William and his wife occupied the southern half while the rest of the structure was divided into two houses for his daughters. The Villards rented out the other five residences in their block; for example, the Edward Dean Adams and Artemas H. Holmes families lived in the two central houses, access to which was gained through what appeared in the overall design to be the main entrance, with its five-arched arcade looking out toward Madison Avenue (figures 164 and 165). The more modest entrance to the Villard section was in the center of the south arm, off the courtyard.

One entered through the Villards' foyer and proceeded to a large hall, which led, to the right, to the tripartite drawing room. At the opposite end of the hall was a large music room, and in between were doorways leading to a breakfast room and pantry while at the far corner was the dining room. Since most of the south arm was free standing and did not have long party walls abutting other structures, the plan permitted each room to have windows of its own. The plan thus avoided the dim, cavern effect often seen in brownstones, which, unless they were erected on corner lots, had windows only in two rooms, the front and the back, with inner rooms relying almost entirely on artificial lighting or small light wells.

Joseph Wells and the Elevation: The Classical Influence

The elevation of the unified block of residences, as at Marble Row and the Colford Block, offered a completely new alternative to brownstone row houses, and its design proved pivotal both for the firm and for the subsequent history of American architecture at the turn of the century. When McKim, Mead and White were given the commission for a large urban mansion for Charles Tiffany, built between 1882 and 1884—almost contemporaneously with the Villard Houses—the firm employed the style that had, in the previous decade, served Henry Hobson Richardson so well: the Romanesque. But the Romanesque was not the style of the future.

Figure 164. McKim, Mead and White, Villard Houses, Madison Avenue between 50th and 51st streets, New York City, 1882–85. Museum of the City of New York. The Villard Houses rose like a Roman palazzo on one of Manhattan's busiest thoroughfares, the dignity and nobility of its design serving well to counter the frenetic lifestyle of the emerging, bustling American megalopolis.

Figure 165 (opposite). McKim, Mead and White, plan, Villard Houses, Madison Avenue between 50th and 51st streets, New York City. From *A Monograph of the Work of McKim, Mead and White* (1915), plate 7. The Villard family occupied—unfortunately, very briefly—the southern (right) wing of the house, and rented out the rest of the structure, which was divided into five units.

The general scheme for the Villard Houses was McKim's. However, at an early stage the project was turned over to one of the firm's most talented draftsmen—Joseph Morrill Wells (1853–90)—who had been employed in the office even before White joined the partnership.[2] Wells, who had little formal education, was quiet and shy, yet he was a fanatic ready to destroy New York City in order to remake it. He lived alone in that famous bachelors' hotel, the Benedict, on Washington Square.

In 1889 McKim suggested to White that Wells be made a partner in recognition of his extraordinary contribution to the firm's success; to their surprise, Wells declined, saying wryly that he did not care to put his name "to so much damned bad work."[3] Wells probably did not want the responsibilities that a partnership would carry, for he cherished his freedom from such obligations. A month after the offer was made, Wells caught a cold, which worsened, and he died on 2 January 1890, at age thirty-seven.

Wells was a man who knew what he did and did not like. He once declared that he had no desire to see the great American West, for there was nothing there worth seeing; asked if he had ever been there, he replied he had never been farther west than Hoboken, and that was quite far enough. In 1880 he went to Europe for the first time, where he discovered he disliked English architecture, enjoyed some things about Paris, even more so the châteaux of the Loire Valley, but liked Italian architecture the best of all. For him, Bramante—the great Renaissance architect—became a god.

When the Villard commission came to the firm, McKim was in Oregon on other business for Villard and the Northern Pacific Railroad, and Stanford White was on a trip in the Southwest. The Villard project was, so to speak, dumped in Wells's lap, and he seized the opportunity. The design that he produced was modeled after the Chancelleria in Rome, which he had recently seen, and with this, the classical style of the Italian Renaissance became established as the appropriate model for grand urban architecture of the American Renaissance.

The Italian Renaissance palazzo style was not entirely new to mid-nineteenth-century revival architecture. In London, Charles Barry had used it for two clubs, the Travellers and the Reform. Its earliest appearance in America was probably John Notman's design for the Athenaeum (1847) in Philadelphia. Griffith Thomas employed it for his Union Club (1855) at Fifth Avenue and 21st Street in New York, and his design for the Fifth Avenue Hotel (1857) was generally of the palazzo mode. William Henry Vanderbilt's mansion was labeled "Renaissance" by the critics, but that was only vaguely true of its details and less so of the proportions and classical spirit of the total design. The Villard Houses offered a classical Roman design, based on specific Renaissance monuments, in which one finds a respect for historical tradition and an understanding of the aesthetics of the Roman urban models that inspired them.

Wells admired the Chancelleria and another influential building, the Palazzo Farnese, even before he actually saw them in Rome. Howard Walker, a friend of his, recalled an event early in their careers, in Boston, where Walker was working in the architectural office of John Sturgis, and Wells in that of Peabody and Stearns:

> He had a habit of dropping into my room of an evening. . . . One night . . . he appeared with two large rolls under his arm . . . and we tacked them on the wall. Two beautifully rendered large scale elevations of the Palazzo Chancelleria and the Palazzo Farnese. . . . I had never seen anything like them. I asked, "Did you make those, Joe?" [He replied] "Yes, that is architecture."[4]

Antonio da Sangallo's early-sixteenth-century Palazzo Farnese was the inspiration for some of the details of the elevation of the Villard Houses, while Baldassare Peruzzi's Villa Farnesina

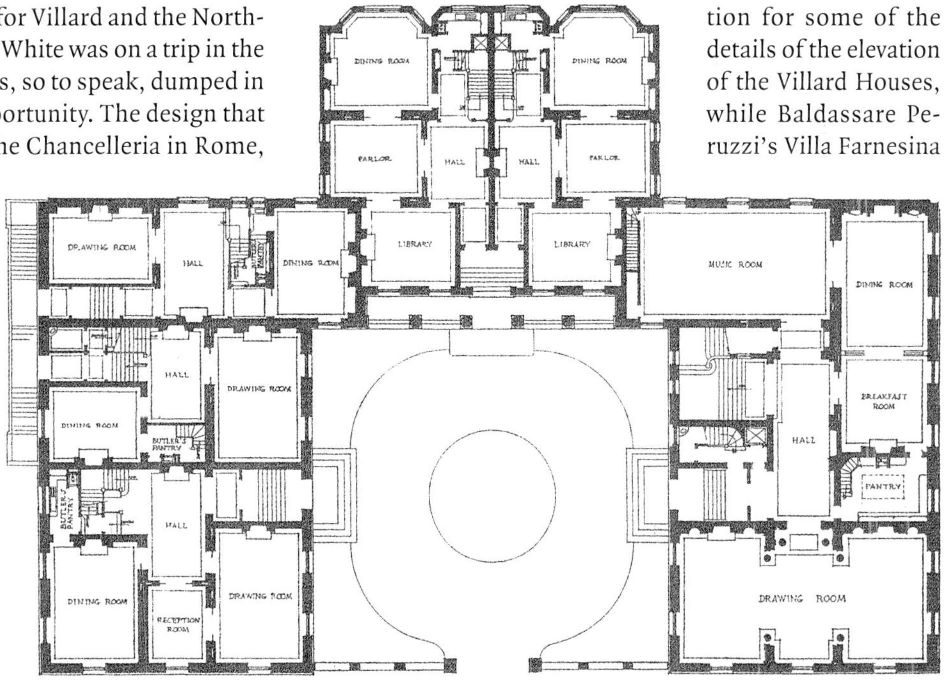

RAPHAEL · RIARIVS · SAVONENSIS SANCTI · GEORG CAMERARIVS · A · SIXTO · IIII · PONTIFICE · MAXIMO · H AVRENTIO · MARTYRI · DICATVM · ET · AEDIS · A · FVN

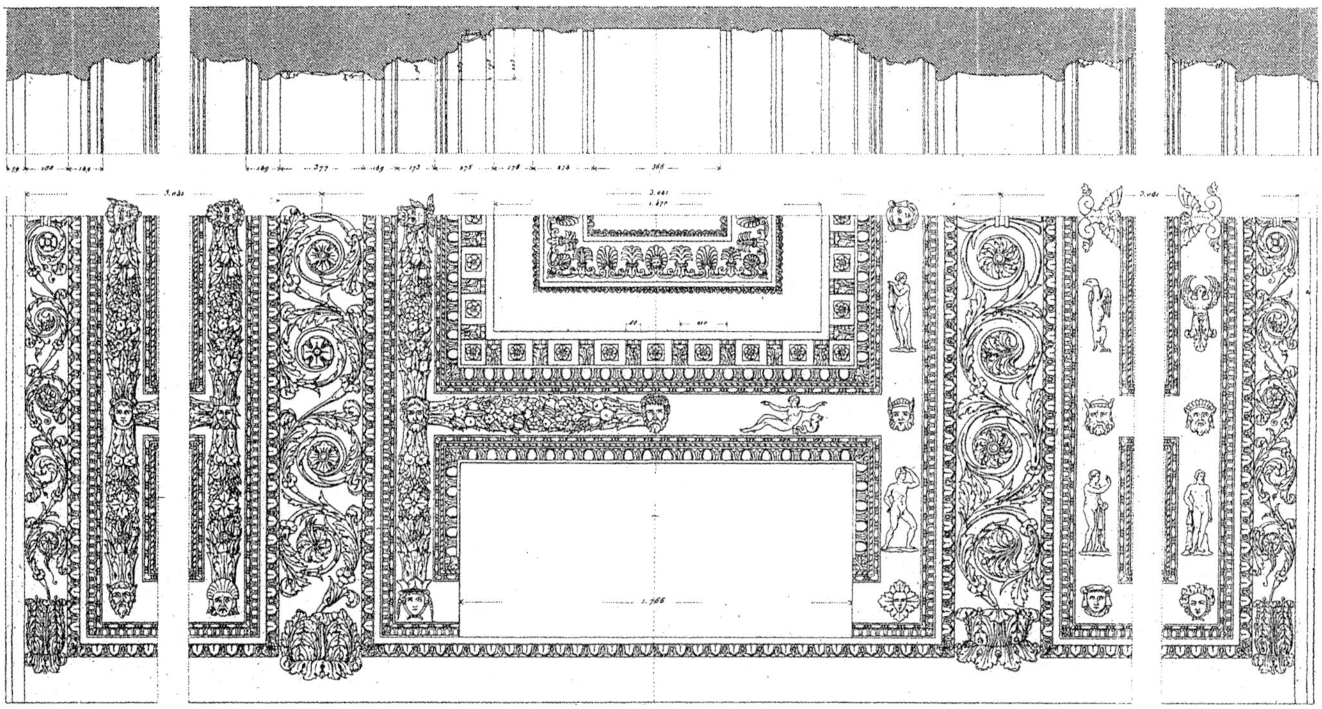

of 1510 may have been the model for the U-shaped plan with a central entrance of a five-bay arcade. For reference Wells would have found illustrations of such things in Paul-Marie Letarouilly's *Les édifices de Rome moderne*, three volumes of engraved plates published in Paris in 1840–57 (figures 166 and 167).

Since the eighteenth century, Americans have made great use of European architectural pattern books. Stanford White and Charles Follen McKim had extensive personal libraries of such things, and the firm of McKim, Mead and White had its own research library. Wells undoubtedly referred to his own favored publications as well. In Letarouilly's *Les édifices de Rome moderne* the architects had available to them a plate of the design of the facade of the Chancelleria as well as illustrations of ornamentation such as was eventually used in the interiors of the Villard Houses.

But there were also many publications with voluminous engraved plates depicting the ancient monuments and Renaissance palazzos, with meticulous details, as in Desgodets's *Les édifices antiques de Rome* of 1682 (figure 168). Dedicated classicists like Joseph Wells and Charles Follen McKim consulted these and other sources regularly, and the decorative details were a constant inspiration to Stanford White as he designed interiors for places such as the Villard Houses.[5]

The exterior of the Villard Houses is dominated by a severe restraint in the interpretation of classical design, with simplicity and monumentality being the guiding principles. Not counting the basement, the elevation consists of four stories, each clearly marked by a stringcourse and ultimately a bold cornice. The lower story, clearly rusticated, remains strong visually, and is not overly perforated, all of which is characteristic of classical Roman architecture. At the second level, the rustication has disappeared and decorative quoining appears at the corners, while the window design becomes rectilinear but aligned with those below and above, imposing a rational orderliness and symmetry not found in, say, the Petit Château; the central window at this level has a small balcony. In the third story the windows are both round-headed and rectilinear, and in the top floor the small, nearly square openings indicate the lesser portion of the houses devoted to the servants' quarters, storage rooms, and so on. The perfectly horizontal roofline is capped by a noble cornice and therefore differs from edifices of French

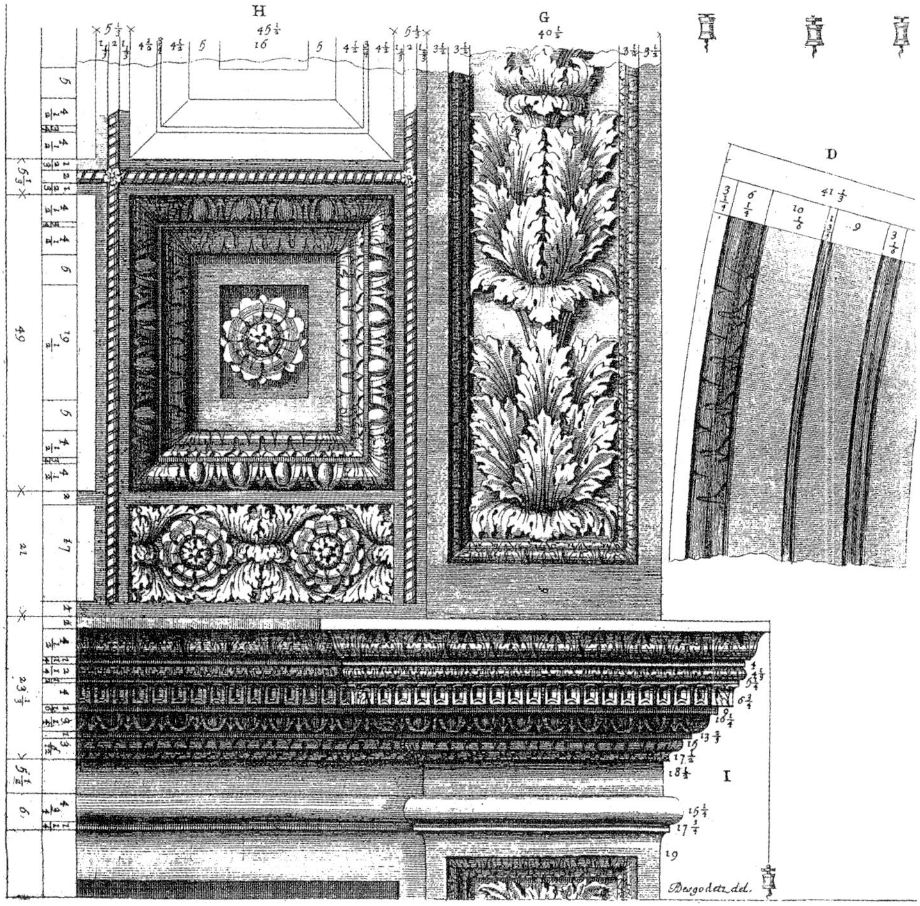

Figure 166 (opposite, top). The principal facade of the Chancellery in Rome. From Paul- Marie Letarouilly, *Les édifices de Rome moderne*, 3 vols. (Paris, 1840–48), vol. 1, plate 80. Morris Library, University of Delaware, Newark, Delaware. Letarouilly, a student in Paris of Charles Percier and Pierre F. L. Fontaine, traveled to Italy about 1820, where he became enamored of the grand architecture of Rome. He spent the next thirty years making beautifully detailed and accurate engravings of its buildings, which he published beginning in 1840. Thereafter, his volumes were required sourcebooks for any architect who was devoted to the classical style of antiquity or the Renaissance. *Les édifices de Rome moderne* alone contains 355 engraved plates of the type seen here.

Figure 167 (opposite, bottom). Vault decorations from the Palais Pietro Massimi. From Letarouilly, *Les édifices de Rome moderne*, vol. 1, plate 291. Morris Library, University of Delaware.

Figure 168 (above). Detail from the Arch of Titus, Rome, from Antoine Babuty Desgodets, *Les édifices antiques de Rome* (Paris, 1682). Morris Library, University of Delaware. As a young man Desgodets joined the Department of Buildings in Paris. To improve his knowledge of architecture he was sent to Italy to study, and while there he made hundreds of carefully measured and accurately studied drawings. The great minister Colbert arranged for them to be published, and they have served architects well ever since as sources for classical designs.

inspiration—that is, it is neither steeply pitched a la the medieval Gothic mode nor of the mansard type found in contemporary Parisian hôtels des villes.

The facade of the inner court has, as noted, an arcade of five bays but with double windows of the same design as those on the avenue fronts. Even the entrance doorways at the left and right of the courtyard are discreetly deemphasized in order to preserve the integrity of the wall. Clearly it is not a bombastic Baroque classicism that is being followed throughout the facades, nor is it a free-spirited École des Beaux-Arts interpretation. In its aesthetic essence, the design is permeated by a reserved, dignified, and simplified classicism that will become the hallmark of most of McKim, Mead and White architecture in the years that follow.

Stanford White had recommended that the Villard Houses be built of either limestone or granite, but Villard, like William Henry Vanderbilt before him, chose to use brownstone, thus linking the Villard Houses, in that respect, to *old* New York, in spite of the revolutionary new direction indicated by their design. But thereafter, McKim, Mead and White rejected brownstone as an exterior finish, just as Hunt had done when he built the William Kissam Vanderbilt house a couple of years earlier.

A Grand Style for Urban America

Following the completion of the Villard Houses, the Italian Renaissance style, along with classical Roman architecture of antiquity, became the trademark motif of McKim, Mead and White, although the firm did occasionally turn to other European styles from the seventeenth and eighteenth centuries.[6] The Romanesque and the picturesque Queen Anne shingle style of earlier years were purged in favor of this new mode, which seemed so appropriate for the needs of the times. The expressive aesthetic for the American Renaissance was thereby determined, for the Villard Houses were based on Italian Roman Renaissance *urban* architecture, and their style became the perfect solution for the urban palazzo in Gilded Age America. Moreover, that style proved adaptable to grand civic complexes as well, such as the Boston Public Library, Pennsylvania Station and the new campus of Columbia University; for commercial buildings such as Tiffany's and Gorham's new Fifth Avenue showrooms; and for gentlemen's clubs, the Harvard Club and the University Club being examples.

Here was a style the noble restraint of which served to impose a dignified order on sprawling American metropolises that seemed to be lurching out of control. Never mind that, in spite of extraordinary technological advances and social forces that promised a new world of "modernism," this style was historical and looked backward; it was what was needed at the moment, at least by an important, wealthy, and powerful sector of American society. Never mind, as well, that it was a style borrowed from another culture and another continent—Europe—rather than one that arose new and independent out of the land and culture of America itself. There were still many who saw the new iron age of America as blatantly crass and in dire need of refinement, and they were perfectly happy to appropriate what had served so well in European culture. An early scholar of the firm of McKim, Mead and White, Charles H. Reilly, even saw a similarity between the firm's architecture and the literature of Henry James, declaring that the firm did for American architecture what James "did for American literature. As he, so they too interpreted the old world to the new in such a way that the new was able to enter for the first time into its full inheritance."[7]

Thus there suddenly arose on the urban American scene an architectural option quite different from that offered by Richard Morris Hunt, for Hunt's domestic designs were firmly grounded in French architecture ranging from late Gothic to contemporary Beaux-Arts. The style that emerged from the offices of McKim, Mead and White was, as Paul Baker noted, symbolic of the great wealth of the American princes and the power they wielded, for "in times of considerable turmoil and disorder, the architecture of order, balance, and restraint, deeply rooted in the past, was increasingly appealing to many. More than any other architects, McKim, Mead and White would create the setting for America's turn-of-the-century Age of Elegance, inspired . . . by Italian Renaissance architectural ideas."[8] To be sure, a Fifth Avenue palazzo modeled after one belonging to the Medici or some other prominent family in Italy served well as an expression of an American client's place in society during an era that has been called the American Renaissance.

The Term "American Renaissance"

"American Renaissance" cannot be used as an umbrella term for the whole period of the late-nineteenth and early-twentieth centuries, for such things as Japanese parlors, Moorish smoking rooms, Colonial American and Georgian revivals, Aesthetic Movement library interiors, and Arts and Crafts/Craftsman/Mission–style design do not fit comfortably within it. As a phenomenon, the American Renaissance is discreet and separate from the other movements that coexisted within the varied spectrum of American civilization between the Civil War and World War I.

Also, its spiritual force was antithetical to that of a modern era yearning to assert and express itself; after all, the very years of the American Renaissance—about 1880 to around 1920—saw exciting new experiments in modern commercial architecture in Chicago and New York, the designs for which became increasingly ahistorical and expressive of structure, technology, and new materials. One is reminded of the much-quoted lament by Louis Sullivan that the triumph of the Beaux-Arts classicism of East Coast architects, in the designing of the main buildings at the World's Columbian Exposition in Chicago in 1893, retarded the march of modernism by at least a decade. Sullivan and those who subscribed to his architectural theories would, understandably, have taken offense should their work have been described as American Renaissance, for the term implies an association with the past.

The Villard Interiors

Stanford White's extraordinary talent for ornamentation was given a special opportunity in the interiors of the Villards' portion of the houses, for which he assumed responsibility. The interiors of Kingscote at Newport involved the remodeling of an existing building, which always has some limiting effect. But here, White could start from scratch, and he introduced into the interiors the inspiration from classical Italian sources that had dominated the exterior. A continuity was thus established between exterior and interior, unlike the relationship that existed at William Henry Vanderbilt's pseudo-Renaissance palazzo which had within a Japanese room, a Moorish room, and so on. White's interiors are all the more remarkable considering that no previous commission had offered him the chance to work in the classical Renaissance mode.

But the interiors were a collaborative effort, as they had been at Trinity Church and at the Cornelius Vanderbilt II house at 57th and Fifth. Although White was the guiding force in all interior schemes and the general supervisor in their execution, a whole host of artists and craftsmen contributed to produce the final results. Within the McKim, Mead and White offices, Francis Bacon (1856–1940) was probably the one who executed the architectural drawings. Bacon's work may be seen, in photographs, in the design of the woodwork or paneling of the major rooms. He was also a designer of furniture. At times he worked for Henry Hobson Richardson and Herter Brothers in that capacity, and in 1885 he joined the staff of the A. H. Davenport furniture-making firm of Boston.[9]

Others working on the project included Augustus Saint-Gaudens and his brother Louis, the mosaicist David Maitland Armstrong, and the decorative painter Francis Lathrop. John La Farge and Tiffany Studios were involved. That Joseph Cabus produced much of the wood paneling for the rooms is suggested by his bill for work at the Villard house, which totaled nearly $100,000; Cabus had earlier executed the woodwork for Villard's retreat at Dobbs Ferry, and his best-known effort is found in the paneling at the New York State Appellate Court in lower Manhattan. The well-known firm of Ellin and Kitson executed much of the elaborate stone carving, especially for the fireplaces in the major rooms.

Léon Marcotte was called on to provide some of the furniture while other furnishings were obtained from Sypher and Company of New York City, and still others came from A. H. Davenport of Boston. Candace Wheeler is believed to have provided some of the embroidered fabrics of the interiors.

The entrance vestibule, which contained a Tiffany stained-glass window, led into a large "living" hall—that is, a hall that was used as living space, not just a passageway connecting rooms. This hall, the walls of which were veneered with Mexican marble, had groined vaults adorned with colorful mosaics, designed by David Maitland Armstrong and executed by the firm of Pasquali and Aeschlimann, the same craftsmen who had done the mosaics in William Henry Vanderbilt's mansion; while no bill from Armstrong has been found among the McKim, Mead and White papers, there is a bill from Pasquali and Aeschlimann for $20,000. The focal point of the hall is the grand, ornately carved fireplace, above which is a lunette containing an allegorical female figure representing Peace—or Pax, as it is inscribed—with an infant on either side of her. This was the creation of Augustus Saint-Gaudens, who modeled it in clay before it was executed in stone by the master carvers of the Ellin and Kitson firm (figure 169). Although it lacks the grand caryatids, it is similar to the fireplace Saint-Gaudens designed for the entrance hall of the Cornelius Vanderbilt II house only a couple of years earlier. From the entrance hall one entered the ornate drawing room (figure 170), which led to the music room.

The music room was not completed when Villard moved in (and moved out), being finished only after the Whitelaw Reids acquired the house. This was a large room, rising to a height of two stories with a vaulted ceiling. Decorative, ornately carved panels lined the walls up to a height of about ten feet. Adorning the north and south end walls were casts of several groups of singing boys, taken from the originals of 1431–48 by Luca Della Robbia in the cantoria of the Cathedral of Florence; this may have been Saint-Gaudens's idea, for he brought back from Florence numerous casts of famous quattrocento sculptures which he displayed prominently about the walls of his studio in New York City. Judging by what can be seen in old photographs, taken about the time the Villards moved in, the furniture in this room may have been the work of Léon Marcotte and his craftsmen.

Figure 169. McKim, Mead and White, entrance hall fireplace, Henry Villard residence, Madison Avenue and 50th Street, New York City, ca. 1885. From *A Monograph of the Work of McKim, Mead and White* (1915), plate 9.

The grand staircase, which was twelve feet wide, was done in yellow marble and illuminated by two stained-glass windows by John La Farge. At the landing was the famous zodiac clock, designed by Stanford White and Augustus Saint-Gaudens.

The dining room was large, measuring twenty by sixty feet and rising to a height of about thirty feet (figure 171). It had a Roman-style fireplace of Nubian marble, above which were three allegorical figures, each placed on a corbel, designed by Saint-Gaudens and probably carved by Ellin and Kitson; they represented joy, hospitality, and moderation. The walls were covered with richly carved English black oak panels, and the ceiling was decorated with allegorical scenes and mythological busts painted by Francis Lathrop. The room contained two massive black oak tables and a sideboard, designed in the Tudor style by Francis Bacon and executed by the Boston furniture-making house of A. H. Davenport.

The largest space of all was the tripartite room, which extended the full width of the house that faced Madison Avenue. A reception room in the middle was flanked by drawing rooms on either end, creating an area that could be opened up, into one large room, for entertaining purposes. The reception room had red-stained cherry panels with delicate inlay on the walls, while the drawing room walls were hung with panels of embroidered silk, with that same material being used for the upholstery of the furniture. The ceiling had a decorative pattern wrought of plaster in low relief.

By comparison, the interiors of William Henry Vanderbilt's house presented a mixture of styles and cultures, from

Figure 170. McKim, Mead and White, drawing room, Henry Villard residence, Madison Avenue and 50th Street, New York City, 1885. From Sheldon, *Artistic Houses*, vol. 2, part 2, plate 34.

Figure 171. McKim, Mead and White, dining room, Henry Villard residence, Madison Avenue and 50th Street, New York City, 1885. From Sheldon, *Artistic Houses*, vol. 2, part 2, plate 33.

French Baroque to Moorish to Japanese motifs. Conversely, the rooms of the Villard house possessed a unity imposed by adherence to the principles of ancient Roman and Italian Renaissance art which were, to be sure, reinterpreted in late-nineteenth-century eclectic fashion but given continuity by the classicism that guided their creation. Stanford White never copied antiquity in a slavish manner or indulged in the dull banalities of academic-archaeological accuracy; instead, he used classical forms as points of departure from which his own creativity and good taste were allowed to soar, while respecting certain basic principles of classicism. That was, in fact, characteristic of both the age in which he lived and of the best productions of the Beaux-Arts tradition.

The critics approved of this new factor within the urban scene of New York City, the progeny of which proved its aptness. The author of *Artistic Houses*, writing just as the Villard Houses were finished, observed:

> With all its magnitude and costliness—its size is perhaps unequaled by that of any other similar edifice in the city, and its cost is believed to have been in the neighborhood of three quarters of a million dollars—it has preserved a chaste simplicity, both externally and internally. . . . No attempt at ostentation appears in any part of the architectural outline or the decorative scheme.[10]

There can be little quarrel with the description of the exterior as being chaste and restrained. But to understand how a contemporary critic could use a word such as "simplicity" to describe the interiors, the Villard rooms must be seen in opposition to such ostentatious chambers as those of the A. T. Stewart mansion and of the house of William Henry Vanderbilt (figures 36 and 53, respectively, on pp. 71 and 94).

Figure 172. McKim, Mead and White, dining room, end wall, Henry Villard residence, Madison Avenue and 50th Street, New York City, 1885. From *A Monograph of the Work of McKim, Mead and White* (1915), plate 11. Here, too, one finds the work of Augustus Saint-Gaudens who modeled the fish for the two wall-niche fountains. His brother, Louis Saint-Gaudens, sculpted the three allegorical busts placed on the wall above the fireplace. To White's good friends, John La Farge and Francis Lathrop, went the commissions for the murals in the house.

The Villards' Departure and The Reids' Arrival

Henry Villard and his family moved into their house in 1883, even before all rooms were finished, because they had nowhere else to go. Villard was ruined financially when the Northern Pacific went bankrupt, as were thousands of other stockholders, large and small. Furious mobs, inflamed by hostile newspaper accounts, gathered outside the mansion, angry because they thought that though they were broke, Villard was living in a luxurious palace. In early 1884, only three months after moving in, the Villards had to vacate the premises and move to their Dobbs Ferry house. Two years later their fine house was sold to Darius Ogden Mills, who presented it as a gift to his daughter when she married Whitelaw Reid.[11] Within a few years Villard did recoup his fortune, but by then he had lost his fine house.

Whitelaw Reid

Whitelaw Reid began his career as a young newspaperman in Ohio, and he became a war reporter during the Civil War. Horace Greeley, publisher of the *New York Tribune*, offered him a position after the war, causing him to relocate to New York City. Reid, who had long been interested in politics, managed Greeley's unsuccessful presidential campaign in 1872. In 1881 Whitelaw married Elizabeth Mills, and the couple embarked on an extended honeymoon throughout Europe, traveling to Paris, Amsterdam, Brussels, along the Rhine to Switzerland, to Italy and Rome, then to Venice for an extended visit, and to Vienna. In Paris they met Georges Clemenceau and in London they were introduced to William Gladstone, who, having ousted Disraeli, was beginning his second term as prime minister.

During the 1880s Reid was a friend of William C. Whitney, who masterminded Grover Cleveland's election to the presidency in 1884, and although they were on opposite sides in the political arena, they frequently consulted each other. In 1889 Whitelaw entered diplomatic life as President Benjamin Harrison's minister to France, arriving just as that nation was celebrating its centennial of the Revolution with a grand international exposition. He and his wife lived in Paris for about four years, taking careful note of all the exciting new Beaux-Arts edifices recently erected there during Napoleon III's Second Empire. While there they rented the mansion of the Comtesse de Grammont, which became a scene of constant entertainment. As testimony to Whitelaw's respected eye for architecture, the committee that was backing New York City as the locus for the World's Columbian Exposition of 1892 (1893) wrote to him in Paris for advice on the style of buildings they should propose.

Back in America, his political activities carried him onto the Republican national ticket as the vice presidential candidate in Benjamin Harrison's unsuccessful bid of 1892. Reid, through the *Tribune*, endorsed Teddy Roosevelt's gubernatorial run in 1898, and Teddy in turn backed Reid for the vice presidency two years later. During this period Elizabeth Reid and Edith (Mrs. Teddy) Roosevelt were especially close friends.

A few years later, Reid's friend President Theodore Roosevelt appointed him representative of the United States to the coronation of Edward VII, and in 1905 Reid became the American ambassador to the Court of Saint James. While in London, the Reids rented Dorchester House, further confirming their commitment to an aristocratic setting for America's leading figures of the Gilded Age.[12]

In 1881, the year that Reid married Elizabeth Mills, her father bought the *Tribune* and promptly made Whitelaw its editor. His advocacy for an expansionist policy for the United States—that is, of converting the doctrine of Manifest Destiny into one of global economic and military imperialism—was frequently voiced. For example, he wrote to President McKinley that "some day we will have Cuba as well as the Sandwich Islands [Hawaii]. To that extent I believe in Manifest Destiny."[13] And in a speech to his alma mater, the University of Miami in Ohio, he declared, in those chest-thumping days following the Spanish-American War, that "the old continental isolation is gone forever."[14]

Whitelaw Reid and the Arts

The *Tribune* not only flourished under Reid's leadership but also served as an outlet for his interests in architecture. For example, he instructed one of the paper's critics, Clarence Cook, to begin writing a series of articles pointing out the dullness of New York City architecture. "What I want," he wrote to Cook, "is first a crisp editorial on the prevailing lack of architectural taste in New York, the dreary miles of brown stone fronts, the worthlessness of brown stone as a material for building, the monstrosities given us by our wealthiest men."[15] His biographer, Royal Cortissoz, a noted art critic himself, observed that article after article followed, "discussing the question of architecture in our cities generally, but particularly in New York City. The 'frightful example' was to be fearlessly pilloried, and suggestions for a rational architectural reform were to be made."[16]

Reid, who became a trustee of the Metropolitan Museum of Art, was a friend, acquaintance, or sponsor of many artists and literary figures of his day. He spoke at the unveiling, in Paris, of the small version of Bartholdi's Statue of Liberty, and he negotiated with the famous sculptors Falguiere and Mercie to create the bronze equestrian statue of the Marquis de Lafayette for Washington, D.C. A frequent visitor to the studios of the leading Salon artists of that day—among them Bonnat, Gérôme, Cain, and Dubois—he was popular among them because of his political stance in favor of "free art" and his opposition to the U.S. policy of placing duties and tariffs on imported art. In London, at Dorchester House, the Reids entertained Rudyard Kipling and Sir Arthur Conan Doyle; in London, too, Whitelaw came to know John Singer Sargent and Edwin Austin Abbey, and he advised James McNeill Whistler in the difficult period of getting his *Gentle Art of Making Enemies* published.

In the United States, Reid had earlier helped Mark Twain and Charles Dudley Warner in the publication of *The Gilded*

Age (1873), and he assisted Lew Wallace, author of *Ben Hur* (1880), in getting his books published. He was acquainted with John La Farge, and his friend John Quincy Adams Ward received the commission to execute the bronze statue of Horace Greeley that was to be erected in the *Tribune* building. It was Reid who interceded with General Sheridan to smooth the way for Ward to make his western excursion among the Indian tribes, to study their culture, costumes, and customs. And it was Reid who finally persuaded William Tecumseh Sherman to pose for Augustus Saint-Gaudens; "I was concerned," Reid wrote,

> . . . in persuading General Sherman to give [Saint-Gaudens] the sittings which resulted in the magnificent statue at the entrance to Central Park, after the old veteran had profanely refused to be pestered any more with "d——d sculptors." Stanford White came to me in despair about it, and I tackled the old gentleman first through his daughter Rachel and afterwards in person. . . . He swore a little, but finally consented to give Saint-Gaudens the sittings.[17]

Ophir Hall

Elizabeth Mills Reid was ambitious and wanted to challenge Mrs. Caroline Astor as head of New York Society, and she was willing to spend the money to establish the architectural ambience that was needed if she were to make her run for the gold ring—or the gilded ring, in this case. The Reids had purchased, in 1887, Ophir Hall, an estate of one thousand acres near White Plains in Westchester County, but the next year a fire destroyed the Norman-castle manor house. Having become familiar with Stanford White when he designed a house for Elizabeth's brother, Ogden Mills, and his wife, Ruth Livingston Mills, on the banks of the Hudson River, they called in McKim, Mead and White to design, erect, and furnish a new Ophir Hall. Frederick Law Olmsted was placed in charge of landscaping the grounds. When finished, Ophir Hall evoked an ambience of ancient European aristocracy. White commissioned his friend Francis Lathrop to make leaded windows for the house, and H. Siddons Mowbray and George W. Maynard did several ceiling paintings while Frederick MacMonnies executed some of the sculptural ornamentation. The Reids moved into the new Ophir Hall in 1890. It presently serves as the administration building of Manhattanville College.

Remodeling of the Villard-Reid House

Soon after they acquired the Villards' house, the Reids asked Stanford White to remodel several of the rooms. Although some of the original decoration was lost in the process, other ornamental work was gained. In 1891, according to the Reids' wishes, White transformed the reception room and the two drawing rooms into one grand salon that ran the full length of the Madison Avenue frontage. The original paneling was removed and taken up to Ophir Hall where it was reinstalled. The "old" dark marquetry was replaced with lighter and brighter panels executed in the Rococo revival style by one of the leading decorative painters in Paris, Pierre-Victor Galland, who, as we have seen, had earlier created several ornate panels for Legrand Lockwood's early mansion in Norwalk, Connecticut (figure 25, p. 61). This commission was the direct result of the Reids' years in Paris (1889–91), when they became acquainted with the leading painters and decorative artists of that day.

By 1891 there was a new guiding spirit for interior decor—the re-creation of the eighteenth-century Louis XV or Louis XVI type of salon. This was the next stage of interior design, as American millionaires found in the French Rococo style the aristocratic elegance for which they yearned; the Rococo was very different from the more restrained classical mode of the original interiors of the Villard house. In Paris, Elizabeth went on a buying spree, acquiring furnishings and bibelots for the newly remodeled house that awaited her upon her return to New York City.

Other parts of the Villard house that were remodeled by the Reids included the music room (figure 174). For this grand chamber White designed a more elaborate ceiling, in the classical mode, than had been there before, and he had John La Farge paint lunettes for the end walls, depicting allegorical scenes of "Music" and "Dance," one of which reportedly represented Mrs. Reid herself languidly listening to a concert.[18] Five bas-reliefs, located just above the gallery, appropriately depicted singers and musicians in an Italian Renaissance style.

There were additional, periodical projects of remodeling, as in 1896 when the Reids asked Edwin Austin Abbey to paint a scene, depicting a dance, for the overmantel in the dining room. And in 1910, by which time both Stanford White and

Charles Follen McKim were dead, they commissioned the firm of McKim, Mead and White to remodel several of the second-floor rooms, transforming two guest rooms into an expanded library for Whitelaw.

Epilogue for the Villard-Reid Houses

Whitelaw Reid died in 1912. Elizabeth lived until 1931, although she spent much of her time at Ophir Hall. An auction was held in May of 1935 to sell off the grand furnishings of the house. For a while, Joseph P. Kennedy, father of the future president, owned the northern arm of the complex, opposite the Villard-Reid house, as an investment, until he sold it to the publishing firm of Random House. There Bennett Cerf held sway until 1969, committing only minor alterations to the respected interiors, even though the building had now become commercial properties. In 1948 the middle portion of the block was acquired by the archbishopric of New York, to be used for administrative offices, and for a while a portion of the structure was owned by Capital Cities Communications, parent of ABC, during whose occupancy serious and damaging renovation was done to turn the once-proud rooms into offices.

The worst, however, was yet to come. In 1974 Harry Helmsley, the real estate developer, leased the block and, despite the courageous efforts of preservationists and arts commissions, succeeded in gutting much of the total building and erecting a great towering glass-box skyscraper just behind the facade of the Villard Houses. Alas, a choice and rare masterpiece was essentially lost.

When the Villard Houses were new—in the mid-1880s—they presented to New York City a break with the brownstone architecture that Whitelaw detested so much. Even though they were sheathed in brownstone, their design seemed appropriate to the urban scene, for its ancient and Italian Renaissance style was derived from urban prototypes. Moreover, they imposed a classical restraint, an order and a dignity on the American metropolis that had until then seemed to sprawl at random. Finally, their classical style offered an alternative to the late-Gothic and French Renaissance styles then being used by Richard Morris Hunt and others for Fifth Avenue mansions—styles that were still partially Medieval, and styles that were derived not from urban, but from châteaux models. By 1886, American architects had two primary styles in which to design the palaces of the new millionaire society.

Figure 173 (opposite). Stanford White, library, remodeling of Villard residence for Mr. and Mrs. Whitelaw Reid, ca. 1886. Museum of the City of New York.

Figure 174 (above). Stanford White, music room, Villard residence, 1885. From Sheldon, *Artistic Houses*, vol. 2, part 2, plate 35. University of Delaware Library. While Augustus Saint-Gaudens was studying in Italy in the late 1860s he was drawn to sculptures by the great Renaissance masters—Ghiberti, Donatello, Mino de Fisole, Della Robbia, and the like; he purchased plaster casts of many of their works and brought them to America, where he had them installed on the walls of his studio. The relief groups of singing boys seen in this view may have been his suggestion, for they are replicas of the *Cantoria* series by Luca Della Robbia (ca. 1400–82), the originals of which, in the nineteenth century, were in the Cathedral in Florence. In spite of the decorative paneling, in this photograph the music room seems sparse and barnlike, for work was halted on it when Villard ran into financial troubles; it was completed—by Stanford White—only after the Whitelaw Reids purchased the house.

Restless as a whirlwind, [Stanford White] would flash into a roomful of people on his way from one show to another, shake hands here and there, tell us how lovely something was, or how much he hated something else, and rush out again into the white night of Broadway, leaving us all exhilarated and a little breathless. . . . Stanford White was a kind of gay pagan who enjoyed life to the utmost and did much to make others enjoy it; he hated convention, affectation, and pretense, and chose his friends in varied walks of life: artists, millionaires, and poor chorus girls shared his good will, and he was much beloved by all who knew him.

Margaret Terry Chanler, *Roman Spring* (1934)

Chapter Twelve

Stanford White

Collector, Dealer, and Interior Decorator

THE "GAY PAGAN WHO ENJOYED LIFE"

We have already been introduced to Stanford White's youth and his early career with McKim, Mead and White (see Chapter 10), as well as his work as an interior decorator for the Villard Houses (Chapter 11). But his personality and his remarkable activities as a collector and a dealer and in the founding of the profession of interior decorator must also be considered, for he played a major role in the decoration of the interiors of many of the great mansions.[1]

White was one of the fascinating personalities of the Gilded Age—no small accomplishment considering the rich tapestry of characters produced by La Belle Époque. Edith Wharton remembered him as one of only a few "men of exceptional intelligence . . . [whose] new ideas . . . stirred the stagnant air of old New York."[2] Margaret Terry Chanler recalled that White was "a big red-headed man with a warm pleasant voice; he seemed to tingle with potential energy; there was something meteoric about his exits and entrances."[3]

Elizabeth Drexel Lehr described how the whirlwind style of his life affected his social engagements, as one night at Sherry's restaurant: "Outrageously badly dressed, [his] untidy shock of red hair looking as though it had not had a comb passed through it for a week, he was not in the least embarrassed as he sat surrounded by some of the most elegant women in New York. A genius and an artist to his finger-tips, he was quite indifferent to his appearance." Mrs. Lehr then recalled an occasion when White arrived late for a dinner at Tessie Oelrichs's house, taking his seat at the table when the other guests were halfway through their meal: " 'It never takes me more than five minutes to dress,' he remarked. 'So I should imagine,' said Mrs. Oelrichs rather coldly. . . . 'But then just look at your idea of dressing!' He had merely flung

on a dinner jacket over his ordinary morning trousers, and had not even taken the trouble to change his shirt."[4]

White's motto seemed to be, Always live better than your clients. While this made for a delightful lifestyle, his living by the motto, together with his innate generosity and propensity to take risks in investments, contributed greatly to the severe financial problems that plagued the later years of his life. Until then, Stan, as he was called by his friends, lived the life of the *bon vivant* and was enthusiastically accepted into the lofty realm of Gilded Age millionaire society, whence came his clients in search of his special talents and his conviviality.

In 1887 he was elected a member of the exclusive Restigouche Club, a salmon-fishing club that leased vast acreage on the Gaspe Peninsula in the eastern part of Quebec Province in Canada. Although White did not build a lodge there, the wealthier members did—William Kissam Vanderbilt, for example, for whom White designed Kedgwick Lodge in 1897. Stan and Willy K. often went on fishing excursions together there. On 15 July 1888, Henry Adams wrote to Elizabeth Cameron to tell her "Stanford White has sent me a salmon from Restigouche."[5] Katherine Duer Mackay, too, gratefully acknowledged the gift of a fine salmon from her Harbor Hill architect, and in July of 1899 Frederick Vanderbilt, a younger brother of Willy K. and Cornelius II, sent White a note: "Please accept many thanks for the fine salmon you sent us."[6] Also, White served as sponsor for Robert Goelet, the New York City real estate millionaire, for his admission to the Restigouche Club.

Male Bonding and Clubman

Biographers have made much of White's friendships with a number of men, of his need for male bonding, and of his drinking and carousing with attractive young ladies—often showgirls—at secret hideaways. Among his closest friends was the sculptor Augustus Saint-Gaudens, but there were many others, as noted earlier in the discussion of the Tile Club. White and several of his artist friends were members of what they called the Sewer Club, and in 1888 he sent out a statement of dues owed, to Louis and Gus Saint-Gaudens, Thomas Dewing, Joseph Wells, and Francis Lathrop, among others. Socializing was constant and usually impromptu, as reflected in a note he sent to Edwin Austin Abbey, saying he had tried to get to Abbey's studio that morning but was detained by work at Madison Square Garden: "Fairchild is going to dine with me and go to see 'Kajanka' on Thursday," he wrote, adding that if "you are free won't you come too and dine with us . . . at my house. There will only be a few of the boys."[7] He sent the same letter to John Singer Sargent, who was then in New York painting portraits.

Artists' studios were frequently gathering places for Stanford White's Bohemian crowd, their meetings often arranged around musical entertainments. Once, in the fall of 1882, Joseph Wells, Francis Lathrop, and Augustus Saint-Gaudens discovered a musical group performing in a beer garden in Broadway. Gus—as Saint-Gaudens was known—arranged for the musicians to play in his studio for some of his artist and writer friends. The next year, Wells persuaded the Standard Quartet, a very accomplished group, to perform in Gus's studio on Sunday afternoons. Later, the Philharmonic Quartet was hired to play a program consisting of Beethoven, Mozart, and Schubert. This went on throughout "the season" in New York, from October through May in the 1880s. Among the regulars was Stanford White, sometimes with his father, Richard Grant White, a celebrity himself as literary and music critic; McKim occasionally joined them at these "smoking concerts" to which women were rarely invited, and the painter Thomas Dewing often appeared, as well as Richard Watson Gilder, the poet editor of *The Century Magazine*. Gus's brother Louis Saint-Gaudens frequently attended, as did the painter Edward Simmons, who recalled that while staying at the Players' Club, of which both he and White were members, he "got to know this very simple person [White], who was a child and an artist and never became an adult."[8] White regularly showed up at Society's balls and dinner parties (figure 175).

A jovial man-about-town, White was an inveterate clubman. He belonged to numerous groups; Paul Baker estimated that White was a member of about fifty clubs and organizations.[9] Indeed, because clubs were such an important part of his daily life, he was especially well qualified to design them. He was, for example, a member of the Century Association and the designer of its clubhouse at 7 West 43rd Street. After J. Pierpont Morgan and some others joined together to form

Figure 175. Stanford White and friends at the James Hazen Hyde Ball, photograph, 1905. Museum of the City of New York. White-tie occasions and fancy-dress balls were a routine part of life for the Gilded Society. In this photograph Stanford White, very much at home as a member of that Society, is seen standing, third from the right, and his friend, Mamie Fish, is seated. One of the most elaborate of Society's balls was given on 31 January 1905 by James Hazen Hyde, heir to the Equitable Life Assurance Association fortune; it was held in Sherry's ballroom, which had been designed by Stanford White, and was, for that evening, turned into the palace of Versailles at a cost of $200,000. Such extravagance brought down the censure of the press, a voice of concern from the board of directors of the Equitable over the misuse of corporate funds, and an investigation by the New York State attorney general, Charles Evans Hughes, which launched his political career.

men she had ever known, but she kept him at bay during a prolonged courtship. Their wedding took place three years later, on 7 February 1884, at the Episcopal Church at 46th Street and Fifth Avenue. Some of Stan's friends held a bachelor's party for him, at Martinelli's restaurant, and among those who attended were Gus Saint-Gaudens, J. Alden Weir, William Merritt Chase, Richard Watson Gilder, Charles Follen McKim, Richard Morris Hunt, Thomas Dewing, Frederick Law Olmsted, Joseph Wells, Loyall Farragut, and Francis Hopkinson Smith. The latter two ended the raucous festivities with an impromptu Spanish dance in which they became entangled with a vine that decorated the place.

Bessie and Stan departed for a six-month honeymoon in Europe, visiting Munich, Vienna, Rome, Naples, Paris, and Athens. All along the way White collected curios and antiquities in staggering amounts, a pastime to which we will soon return and one that required considerable wealth.

Bessie's great-aunt was Cornelia Clinch Stewart, whose husband, department store tycoon Alexander T. Stewart, died in 1876, and when the widow Stewart passed away in 1886, her will bequeathed $100,000 to Bessie Smith White; a sum of $250,000 was left to Bessie's mother, plus a quarter of the residue of the estate which *The New York Times* estimated to be $5 million. After Bessie's mother died in 1890, a portion of that amount went to her, bringing Bessie's inheritance to about $400,000—which she was smart enough to keep in her own name; she did, however, make "loans" to Stan on several occasions, and her money allowed the Whites to do things they could not have done otherwise. It was her money, for example, that allowed them in 1892 to buy and enlarge a country

the exclusive Metropolitan Club, they chose Stanford White to be the architect for their new clubhouse at Fifth Avenue and 60th Street, just off of Grand Army Plaza; both he and McKim were invited to become charter members, which they did.

Family Life

Bessie Smith, from one of New York's fine old families, being related to the Van Cortlandts, first met White about 1881 when McKim was designing a house for a prominent New York lawyer, Prescott Hall Butler, at St. James out on Long Island. Stanford White was one of the most handsome, exciting

Figure 176. Stanford and Bessie White, Mrs. Henry Clews, and Rawlins Cottulett. Photograph, ca. 1895. Costume balls were very popular throughout the Gilded Age. White, *bon vivant* and man-about-town that he was, was one of the organizers of the infamous "Pie Girl Dinner," held 20 May 1895 and attended by, among others, Augustus Saint-Gaudens, Charles Dana Gibson, Archie Chanler (of the Astor clan), and Henry Poor. Shapely young women poured wine—a brunette for red wine, a blonde for white, and scantily clad sixteen-year-old Susie Johnson, an artist's model, popped out of a great pie, to the raucous amusement of the thirty gentlemen in attendance. The events of the evening brought down the wrath of publisher Joseph Pulitzer, whose *New York World* declared in a crusade that such parties corrupted the morals of young girls.

place—Box Hill—out on Long Island, at St. James, overlooking the bay and the Sound. Stan had his salary from McKim, Mead and White, and the partners agreed that they could each withdraw up to $75,000 per year from the firm, but he never learned to live on his salary alone.

Stan and Bessie were happy together. They had a son, Lawrence, who graduated from Harvard in 1908 and then went to Paris to study at the École des Beaux-Arts. Larry married Laura, daughter of Margaret and Winthrop Chanler, a descendant of the Astor family. In 1914, by which time both his father and McKim were dead, Lawrence White joined William Rutherford Mead as a partner in the firm, from which Mead retired in 1920. Larry became a prominent figure in the art world, as a trustee of the Metropolitan Museum of Art and president of the National Academy of Design, while carrying on the architectural traditions of the firm of McKim, Mead and White.

The social and professional threads of Stanford White's life were frequently interwoven. He and Bessie entered into the social scene with full gusto, as when they attended a fancy-dress ball at the National Academy of Design in February of 1889; Stan went in a knight's full coat of mail, Bessie as a Byzantine princess. Their travels and social calendars often brought them into the company of the rich and powerful, as in 1903 when Stanford, Bessie, and Larry were invited to join J. Pierpont Morgan aboard his yacht, *The Corsair*, to watch the yacht races off Newport.

The Whites did the things that the favored members of the Gilded Society did, such as making annual visits to Europe. In 1893 they spent four months abroad, one of the high points of the trip being a visit to Egypt, where they climbed to the top of the great pyramid of Cheops. The literary figure Richard Harding Davis joined them as they rented a dahabeyah and took a trip up the Nile to Aswan. In London, the Whites and Davis visited the studios of artists John Singer Sargent and Edwin Austin Abbey, and in Paris Stan conferred with sculptor Frederick MacMonnies, who was working on the figures for the Washington Arch, which White had designed.

Back in New York, Stan was a hard man to keep up with, and Bessie sometimes excused herself or was purposefully out of town, as on the occasion of the Patriarchs' Ball at Delmonico's on 5 January 1891, which Stan attended alone. His evenings on the town—which meant most evenings—were spent with socialites such as William C. Whitney and James Deering, heir to the International Harvester fortune. Archie Chanler, Winthrop's brother, sometimes joined in, as did Robert Goelet, Charles T. Barney, and Henry Poor. For many of these men White either designed a fine mansion or remodeled an existing one.

Figure 177. Gertrude Kasebier, *Evelyn Nesbit*, ca. 1900. Photograph. Library of Congress, Washington, D.C. Seductive young Evelyn Nesbit became White's mistress while still in her teens, and many know of her today as "The Girl in the Red Velvet Swing," for reportedly White stashed her in one of his several hideaways where his nude love goddess performed for him by swinging in a swing suspended from the ceiling. Eventually White tired of her, although he continued to take good care of both her and her mother. In time, she married a deranged young millionaire from Pittsburgh, Harry Thaw, whom she could send into a rage by simply saying something like, "Well, Stanny would have gotten it for me!" As time passed, Thaw could stand it no longer. At the rooftop cabaret of Madison Square Garden, which White had designed, Thaw walked up to the table where the architect sat, pulled a pistol from his pocket, and shot White six times, killing him instantly, thus ridding the world of someone he considered a despoiler of young women. Thaw was acquitted on grounds of insanity, spent a brief period in an asylum, but then walked free; his domineering mother, meanwhile, had arranged his divorce from Evelyn, who rather disappeared thereafter.

THE WHITE HOUSE ON GRAMERCY PARK

In May of 1892 Stan, Bessie, and Larry moved into the townhouse White had renovated on the northwest corner of Lexington and 21st Street, on the north side of Gramercy Park. This was a suitably fashionable residence for the Whites as they rose in society. Gramercy Park was, as Elsie de Wolfe described it, "a spot hallowed by history, closed in from the outside world . . . where the oldest and most interesting American families had their houses."[10] Financier Henry Poor lived just across Lexington Avenue in a house remodeled for him by Stanford White. Samuel Tilden's residence was on the south side of the park, adjoining the Players' Club; the architect had designed a cottage at Newport, in the shingle style, for Tilden in 1881.

Margaret Chanler remembered that the Whites' house was full of beautiful and interesting things

> collected in many lands: pictures, statues, tapestries, old furniture, rich spoils of the past. There was much old Italian gilded carving on twisted columns, and elaborate picture frames. Stanford White was an initiator of the fashion for antique furniture that has since run its course. He started it with enthusiastic imagination: in the music room, a half-circle of eighteenth-century harps stood at the back of the stage; when there was music they seemed to listen and vibrate.[11]

Edward Simmons recalled the interior in his autobiography, writing that the decor of the music room was "more beautifully classic than anything I have seen in North America. A flight or two up was his room [the Green Room, figure 178]. Vercingetorix in his cave with all his spoils piled up around him! Everything he cared about . . . and a heterogeneous mass of priceless books, paintings, draperies, all in careless disorder, was happiness to him in his own den."[12]

In 1898 Stanford White purchased several ornate ceilings from Stefano Bardini, a contact in Florence who dealt in such things. From other dealers, such as Duveen Brothers of London, he frequently acquired ancient paneling that had been removed from French châteaux, Parisian hotels or townhouses, or from English country houses. The ceiling in the drawing room of his Gramercy Park house (figure 179), for example, was composed of richly carved and gilded moldings that enframed a large central panel depicting Angels bringing the news of Christ's birth, while in the outer portions were "four shields and four painted female heads" encased in a square red and gold frame, and beyond are "eight painted panels of Biblical subjects."[13]

The walls were resplendent in their covering of antique cardinal-red Genoese velvet, the seams of which were concealed by thin strips of dull gold galloon. The threadbare quality of the

Figure 178. Stanford White, the Green Room, Bessie and Stanford White residence, corner of Lexington Avenue and 23rd Street, New York City, 1898–1900. New-York Historical Society. The walls of White's study were lined with paintings, most of them by his friends and carousing buddies or by young artists whom he frequently helped financially by buying examples of their work.

Figure 179. Stanford White, drawing room, Bessie and Stanford White residence, corner of Lexington Avenue and 23rd Street, New York City, 1898–1900. New-York Historical Society. A more heterogeneous mixture of styles and cultures can hardly be imagined than one finds in this view of the Whites' drawing room. The elegant curves of a Rococo settee are juxtaposed to a great polar-bear-skin rug while a severe, rectilinear Cromwellian chair is matched against the ornate carving and gilding of a Louis XIV throne–like seat. Gilded pilasters, cornices, and ceiling moldings are set off by the scarlet red fabric that was applied to the walls.

velvet—all 114 yards of it—in no way diminished its appeal. An elaborate cornice decorated with swags was supported, visually, by pilasters with carved Corinthian capitals. The east wall contained a marble fireplace decorated with caryatids that White had picked up on his European travels, and above the mantel was a mirror with an ornamental gilded grill applied to it. This remarkable ensemble was enframed by a pair of twisted, richly carved columns upholding a broken cornice. Two large Baroque allegorical figures carrying cornucopia flanked the fireplace, while the original model of Saint-Gaudens's *Diana*, the full-scale version of which stood atop the tower of White's Madison Square Garden, graced the mantel, with a French bronze image of the goddess of the hunt at the right (figure 179).

The furniture of the room was a characteristic eclectic mix of styles, ranging from the curving elegance of the "Louis-something" settee to the severe, rectilinear oak-frame seventeenth-century–style armchair with gilded finials. Stanford White enjoyed a mix-and-match approach to decorating. Although this room may be termed a period room in that all of the furnishings are from one period or another, it is not a period room in the sense of one historic style being used consistently throughout—that is, it is not truly a period room because it is neither historically correct nor archaeologically accurate. The overall decorative effect was clearly of greatest importance in the aesthetic credo of Stanford White, who refused to be restrained by any academic commitment to correctness. Even a mixture of cultures was permitted in the name of decorative effulgence, as with the handsome Chinese rug placed before the fireplace and the huge polar bear skin thrown casually over the couch. Moreover, an artistic jumble effect was obviously desired, a kind of careless clutter of as many curios, bibelots, and *objets d'art* as could be packed into the space. The result was that the eye hardly knew on which object to focus. A similar situation existed in the dining room (figure 181). It too was a rich assemblage of diverse parts that White had picked up in antique shops in Paris, Rome, Naples, Berlin, and elsewhere. The ceiling was robustly ornate, and a "fantasy-classical" screen of carved columns, pilasters, and architrave provided an operatic entrance to the music room.

The several paintings in the parlor reflected White's eclecticism. For example, two small portraits were said to be by Holbein, the German-born artist who worked at the court of Henry VIII, but there was also a landscape titled *Durham* by White's friend Abbott Thayer; his prized painting of Lady Hamilton as Ariadne by the eighteenth-century Englishman George Romney hung near the likenesses of his parents painted by another friend, Daniel Huntington, and on the wall flanking the fireplace were hung life-size, full-length seventeenth-century images of Spanish noblewomen.

White's Art Collection

Paintings and sculptures were scattered throughout the house, but two rooms on the third floor contained the major part of the collection. The Green Room—the room Simmons described as White's den (figure 178)—fronted on Gramercy Park and contained pictures by American artists who were friends of or whose work was admired by White. There was a landscape by Homer Dodge Martin and three little pictures by Albert Pinkham Ryder, along with works by Arthur B. Davies, John Twachtman, Theodore Robinson, Dwight W. Tryon, John La Farge, J. Alden Weir, Kenyon Cox, and Willard Metcalf, as well as some early paintings by the photographer Edward Steichen. White owned four pictures by George Inness and three each by William Merritt Chase, Thomas Dewing, and Childe Hassam. Although not totally representative, his was a very personal and impressive collection of contemporary American art.

At the rear of the third floor was the art gallery, which contained the paintings White had gathered on numerous forays among European antique shops and art galleries (figure 182). If the Green Room housed his collection of contemporary American art, the art gallery was reserved for his European pictures, ranging from a thirteenth-century painting of the Madonna and Child said to be by Cimabue, to a marine painting by J. M. W. Turner of the nineteenth century.

Entrance to the art gallery was gained by passing through an elaborately carved and gilded Spanish Baroque doorway that White had acquired during his travels in Europe; it had the twisted columns that were prized, by White and his patrons, for their richly decorative effect, and to the inner frame of this structure he affixed an ornamental iron gate.

Upon entering, a visitor was confronted with the characteristic eclectic hodgepodge, for White's attitude here was

Figure 180. Italian ceiling, early eighteenth century, now installed in the Doge's Suite, Hearst Castle, San Simeon, Calif. Hearst Castle, California State Parks. The drawing-room ceiling was one of several purchased by White from the Florentine dealer Stefano Bardini. Paneling or ceilings such as this were carefully removed from the ancient palazzo that they originally adorned, each piece having been carefully numbered, then shipped to White's New York warehouse, where they remained until they were installed in one of the grand houses he was decorating for his ultra-wealthy clientele, or in this case, for himself. The original religious significance of the painted scenes was of little importance—it was the decorative quality of the ensemble that mattered to White and his clients. William Randolph Hearst bought the ceiling at one of the sales that followed White's death; once again it was removed, shipped to a new location, and given a new life in California.

"delighted in old Spanish carvings, altar-pieces, cloths, and reliquaries, and he favored Spanish painters like Coello, because of the strong decorative qualities of their stiffly clad and quaint figures."[15]

There were a few fine pictures within the assortment—Romney's *Lady Hamilton*, already mentioned, Thomas Gainsborough's *Lady Carr* and Sir Joshua Reynolds's *Miss Ridge* (once called *Kitty Fisher*), and additional portraits by Sir Thomas Lawrence and Sir William Beechey, as well as three genre scenes attributed to William Hogarth. Although the collection contained a number of religious paintings, portraits predominated, as noted by a reporter who wrote, "The picture gallery as it stands has too many portraits in it for the best effect; it suggests too much the wearisome rows of family portraits one finds at the country seats of old families in Europe."[16]

But of course, that was exactly the effect that White was hoping to create, for he and his clients eagerly donned the mantel of European aristocracy, hoping such collections of portraits would supply something they found lacking in a new country—the United States—and among a nouveau riche plutocracy. The whole idea of raiding Europe for everything from palazzo ceilings to ancient sarcophagi-cum-flower planters, from tapestries to "Louis-something" settees to ancestral portraits, was to endow this crass new generation of multimillionaires with the antiquity and gentility of Old World aristocracy, for these American Midases were acutely aware of their newness. Nor was Stanford White troubled by the ethical question of carrying off the treasures of ancient lands to give them new life in America on Fifth Avenue or on a Long Island estate, for he believed that the most powerful nations of the world had always looted the spoils of the less powerful or the conquered. Moreover, as John Taylor Russell pointed out in *The Art Dealers*,

the same as his attitude toward a period room—it was the overall decorative effect that was important, not a stylistic or historical grouping or a chronological presentation for the sake of academic edification such as one usually finds in an art museum today. The interspersing of great staghorns, hung between the open beams of the cathedral ceiling, with works of art mixed the exotic natural world with that of sophisticated artistry.

White's manner of collecting is immediately apparent as well. There were few masterpieces, for he bought something because he liked it, its decorative quality usually being the deciding factor, as a contemporary reporter observed: "It is generally understood that the architect purchased his paintings not for the names of artists that they represented, but because of their decorative effects and because they pleased him."[14] Another reporter commented that White

Figure 181. Stanford White, dining room, Bessie and Stanford White residence, corner of Lexington Avenue and 23rd Street, New York City, 1898–1900. New-York Historical Society.

"The art market was truly international because art was regarded as the prerogative of the rich individual rather than part of any one nation's patrimony."[17]

A Dealer in Antiquities and Opulence

Stanford White was not only a collector of rare antiquities and ancient architectural interiors. He was also in the business of dealing in such things, and occasionally items seen in photographs of his own home eventually turned up in the mansions of his clients. The large full-length portrait of a mother with a child, for example, which was in White's art gallery (far right, figure 182) reappeared at the weekend retreat he designed for William Collins Whitney in Wheatleigh Hills, out on Long Island. Furthermore, White frequently bought on speculation; that is, finding some choice piece—a fireplace, say, or a ceiling, a painting, or a tapestry—as he made the rounds of innumerable antique shops, he would buy it and have it shipped back to New York, where it might go into storage for two or three years before it eventually found a home in one of the residences he was designing for a client. In the fall of 1897, for example, he had bought a great many things from the Florentine dealer Stefano Bardini, and wrote to him to request a discount on the total price: "I ask you specially for this as many of the things I am buying at my own risk."[18] The following February, Bardini confirmed the shipment of forty-nine cases of goods purchased by White, including such items as six chairs covered with red damask, "2 tabernacles, 1 large and 1 small, carved wood, gilded," an oil portrait said to represent Ferdinand de Medici, "5 friezes on canvas, Venetian painting," one fifteenth-century marble mantel, and many more similar things.[19]

An Interior Decorator on Buying Sprees

White raced from dealer to dealer, all across Europe, having great fun spending his clients' money in prodigious amounts. When he and Bessie went to Paris in 1889 to see the great international exposition and the newly erected sensation, the Eiffel Tower, Stan was also on a mission of finding the treasures with which to fill the house of William C. Whitney at Fifth Avenue and 57th Street which the architect-decorator was then remodeling. Throughout the Continent, White had scouts or agents who alerted him to articles or collections of special interest. His man in Florence was Arthur Mario Acton, who had bought, restored, and furnished the Villa La Pietra, which eventually became a research center for the Institute of Fine Arts of New York University. Charles C. Coleman, the painter, lived on the Isle of Capri and informed White of many antiquities as they became available, while his agent in Rome was Waldo Story, the son of the sculptor William Wetmore Story. Even Augustus Saint-Gaudens, when he was working in France, would pass on word of objects he had seen in a French home that could be had inexpensively.

White's clients often left not only the architectural designing of their new mansions in his hands, but also the architectural interiors and the furnishing of the major rooms. Their confidence in him and his unerring eye for beauty and quality was expressed in a letter White received from a Parisian dealer in 1897: "Mr. and Mrs. Whitney have been a week ago at my place & they saw . . . several things they liked & wished me to draw your attention to. They said they left everything in your hands—therefore they took no decision."[20]

The usual arrangement was that the wealthy client would make a specified amount of funds available for White to draw on through a European bank. Frederick Vanderbilt—whose fine house overlooking the Hudson River had been designed by McKim, Mead and White and was nearing completion—placed $150,000 at White's disposal for his annual buying orgy in 1897, and the list of things he was to look for, made out in advance of the trip, fortunately survives; a staff assistant in White's office prepared a contract for Vanderbilt, so there would be no misunderstanding: "Dear Sir: We beg to acknowledge your [recent] favor in relation to the purchase of certain articles of furniture, for your account, by our Mr. White, during his approaching trip to Europe." Then followed the specifics in which the firm acknowledged the receipt of funds for the purchase of objects "as stated in your letter of Sept. 13th":

> It is understood that Mr. White is to exercise his own judgment in making the various purchases, which, however, are to conform, as far as possible, to the selection of such furniture, hangings, floor rugs, mantels and objects of a decorative character, in wood, metal, stone or marble, of Italian workmanship, as may, in his judgment, be appropriate for use in your house. While, necessarily, the nature of his purchases will be largely dependent upon the condition of the

market in such things, we have suggested to Mr. White your wish . . . to expend a considerable amount of the money upon objects possessing interest and character, but not necessarily representing intrinsic cost, the remainder to be applied to the purchase of certain more important pieces, on which the interior of your house will depend for its chief adornment.[21]

To guide Stanford White in his acquisitions for the rooms at Vanderbilt's Hyde Park house, Charles Follen McKim made out a list that same day:

Hall: . . . Large central table; long divan or sofa, opposite fireplace backing against table, with important chairs flanking the fireplace. Cabinet between lavatory door and lobby leading to dining room. . . . Fine chimney piece for this hall. . . . Staircase Hall: Trousseau just under stairs with chair on each side; also small table with mirror at foot of stairs; faience or marble pot under well in centre. . . . Reception Room: Look up old room in Paris, Style Louis XVI, and, if you find anything worth while, cable, but do not use any part of the money for this room. . . . [Dining Room:] The woodwork being mahogany, and consisting of a wainscot not higher than 4 ft., the rest of the trim being also of mahogany, very simple; walls to be covered with damask, or leather; ceiling of stucco. The columns indicated at the entrance of this room are also desirable. Two mantel pieces are needed, and one, two or three rugs; a table and twenty four chairs, or a type to be hereafter copied. . . . One or more sideboards, and at least two side tables. Walls to be covered with paneling in English oak, floor ditto; ceiling stucco; all to be executed under contract here. Chimney pieces and columns at entrance in stone or marble; arrangement of one, two or three rugs desired. . . . 2 pieces to be used as book-cases. . . . Type of a single and arm chairs, to be covered with silk; old Florentine or Roman mirrors. Miscellaneous: Any antique or finely wrought designs in metal work, such as fire-irons, candelabra, standing lamps, hanging lamps, etc. . . . Jardinieres [sarcophagi]. Stone or marble, for hall, as well as porticoes. Interesting screens of leather or silk. . . . Finally, you should use your own judgment about expending the whole, or, if you do not find satisfactory opportunity, only a part of purchase fund.[22]

The International Commerce in Antiques

Stanford White's activities lend insight into the fascinating world of antique dealing in the late-nineteenth and early-twentieth centuries. All things needed to furnish the interiors of newly risen American mansions were readily available in great variety—furniture, fabrics, ancient fireplaces, old stained-glass windows, coffered ceilings from palaces, walnut wainscoting from country houses, tapestries from French châteaux; indeed, even whole rooms were sometimes purchased, including the doors, windows, fireplaces, walls, ceilings, and possibly the furnishings.

Antiquities were constantly coming onto the market because many aristocratic families found themselves financially destitute but having to pay the bills for palatial maintenance and heavy taxes; of necessity, they began selling off family heirlooms that had been accrued over many centuries and generations. They had virtually nothing else to sell and no way of earning money. The American millionaires or their agents—such as Stanford White—had the money with which to buy those treasures, and in the middle of this burgeoning business were the brokers—the dealers, to whom the nobility came quietly, even secretly, to dispose of whatever was sellable to the American market.

The sheer number of professional dealers is surprising, for White had over fifty such men with whom he did business in almost every major city in Europe. And the dealers became increasingly aware of the financial backing that White brought with him when he made his annual pilgrimage. Two of the most important dealers White did business with were the house of Allard et Fils and that of Raoul Lowengard.

Allard et Fils of Paris and New York

White was always most welcome at Allard et Fils. When he was in France in October of 1897 Jules Allard, head of the great decorating house, wrote to him to say, "My son Georges . . . duly informed me that he has taken an appointment with you for tomorrow . . . morning at our showrooms. . . . I am very pleased to hear this as I have several new things of interest to show you and if you will kindly let me know at what time I may expect you I will arrange to be present."[23] The next day Georges Allard sent White a photograph of a painting by Jean-Baptiste Greuze that he had taken the American to see; Georges then suggested that "if Mrs. Whitney is looking for something really artistic it would be difficult to find anything more charming."[24] And then the day after that came a very interesting note from Jules Allard. It indicates that White did in fact go to see some of the extraordinary Parisian interiors that had been either created or renovated during Napoleon III's Second

Figure 182. Stanford White, art gallery, Bessie and Stanford White residence, corner of Lexington Avenue and 23rd Street, New York City, 1898–1900. New-York Historical Society. The paintings White acquired were chosen more for their decorative qualities than as great master works or for the presentation of a sequential history of European painting, whereas collectors such as J. Pierpont Morgan and Henry Clay Frick selected only the exquisite rare masterpiece by a given Old Master. This third-floor gallery was, in fact, a showroom or salesroom, for the paintings seen in this photograph are frequently encountered later in homes that White decorated.

Empire—that era of ebullient bombast and transmogrification in interior design.[25] Allard specifically mentions that he and White had an appointment to visit together the Senate and the Bank of France, the opulence of which could not but impress and influence an interior designer with a penchant for grandeur such as Stanford White.

Since 1885 the house of Allard et Fils had had a branch in New York City; Richard Morris Hunt was probably the first to make sufficient use of the company's talents to make it worthwhile to establish an office and factory/workshop in America, but McKim, Mead and White had also employed the firm's craftsmen in 1884 and 1885 for some of the interior work at the Villard Houses on Madison Avenue. Allard's letterhead told much about the international reputation it had earned and its high ranking among similar establishments, for it mentions the "Gold Medal, International Exhibition, 1878," and "Legion of Honor, 1878," and lists the firm's addresses as 52 rue Châteaudun and 437 Fifth Avenue; among their skills and wares were "Artistic Furniture, Interior Decorations, Old Tapestries, Antique Woodwork, Bronzes & Enamels."

White was notorious for not paying his bills in a timely fashion, as a pleading letter from Allard's indicates. It informs the architect that they had been "as poor as a churchmouse" all summer because of "your absence. We only have been able to collect from Mrs. Oelrichs one payment of $15,000 on a bill of $36,606.47. . . . Can't you favor us with a certificate for the balance of this account? We have had all of [Clarence] Mackay's work ready since three months and all this is money idle."[26] A few months later Allard's sent White another bill for some work done on his own house at Gramercy Park and for some executed for the ballroom of the William C. Whitney residence.

Additional letters and bills reveal the type of service Allard's could provide for an architect and decorator. In 1901, for example, White received a bill for two unspecified items for Mamie Fish's house with a note appended that "this bill is also three years due." Allard's craftsmen made a mock-up of what White was proposing to do for Whitney's house, and their bill of 18 March 1903, possibly for work being done at the Payne Whitney house, was for "putting up three panels of old ceiling at Glaenzer's warerooms."[27] In addition, Allard's skilled craftsmen could copy almost any piece of period furniture, and they were adept at repairing and restoring antiques; a bill of 1902 was for "repairing console tables in Dining Room [and] taking down partition and columns in Dining Room."[28]

E. Lowengard of Paris

At the turn of the century Stanford White bought heavily from the Parisian dealer Raoul Lowengard, who maintained an elegant establishment at 28 Champs-Elysées. Sometime in 1897 Lowengard sent a letter, now in the White Papers at the Avery Architectural and Fine Arts Library, informing the architect of an assortment of antiques he had recently acquired, including some Renaissance bronzes and a set of "very fine Louis Seize tapestry chairs & sofa which would go very well in a drawing & dancing room especially with some Boucher tapestry! And a set of embroidered Louis Seize chairs (silk) which are for a drawing room—they belonged to Prince Demidoff once of San Donato, Florence."

Lowengard wrote to White from Paris the following spring to tell him about an extraordinary set of tapestries he had just purchased:

> Among the things I bought is the finest set of 4 tapestries, Regency 1714, which were ever made. . . . These tapestries were only made once and never reproduced—like the Bouchers. . . . It is a series only made for & by order of the Regent de France for Madame

la Duchesse d'Orleans. It was once in the Palais Royal in Paris & sold by one of the members of the Orleans family. [They] were made according to the design conceived by the Regent himself. . . . They were never out of royal hands until they got sold 15 years ago. They represent as subjects the Pastoral history of Daphnis & Chloe. . . . I have sold the fine Boucher tapestry you would have liked for Mr. Whitney.[29]

Such letters revival the sort of exquisite artistry—the magnificent *objets d'art* that had once belonged to kings and queens, to dukes and duchesses—that America's millionaires could now purchase easily through dealers and bring home to ornament their Fifth Avenue palazzos and Long Island châteaux.

Duveen Brothers

The house of Duveen was operated in London by two brothers, Joel and "Uncle" Henry, who had transformed a satchel full of Delft ceramics into one of the great antiques enterprises of the era. By the 1890s they had established a branch in New York, which was eventually run by Joel's son, Joseph Duveen.[30] Much of Stanford White's dealings, however, remained with the London firm, which regularly notified him of special items it had acquired. But White bought not only furnishings on an object-by-object basis, but also whole rooms, which Duveen Brothers frequently offered him, as their correspondence reveals. If White wanted a Francis I room (French, early-sixteenth century), that could be had with a little searching, or if he preferred a Louis XIV chamber of excellent artistry, that too could be had, with Duveen Brothers as the intermediary; when the American architect told the brothers what he needed, their only question was, "Do you want it furnished or unfurnished?" In 1897 and 1898 White was working on a number of mansions, including the Ogden Mills residence at Staatsburg, New York, the Frederick Vanderbilt mansion at Hyde Park, the Thomas N. Page house in Washington, D.C., the Levi P. Morton residence and William C. Whitney's house in New York City, as well as his own place overlooking Gramercy Park, so it is difficult to identify the ultimate location of ceilings, wall paneling, or whole rooms that he purchased from Duveen Brothers. In a given summer—say, 1898—White might well be looking for European antique furnishings for five or six major rooms (drawing rooms, dining rooms, reception rooms, libraries, etc.) for four or five different mansions, meaning he had twenty to thirty large, important rooms to fill with sofas, chairs, tables, carpets, paintings and sculptures, lamps, bibelots, and lots of other objects. Whirlwind of energy that he was, he was equal to the challenge.

Of course, the room bought out of a French château or from a Venetian palazzo was inevitably of different dimensions from the room White had designed for an American client, so alterations were necessary. Duveen Brothers could provide that service, as could Allard's, or even Glaenzer's of New York. One can observe this in the following letter from Duveen Brothers: "In reference to the Louis XIV room, we intend starting alterations at once. . . . We conclude that you want the room altered according to the drawings [we have] sent to you; although we have a ground plan which you gave us, we do not feel satisfied with this; we want sizes of every wall and of every recess in the walls, in fact, we want a perfect architect's plan."[31]

On 28 May 1898, Duveen Brothers sent White photographs of "a pure old Venetian room," done entirely in carved and gilded wood, including doors, doorframes, windows, and cornices, calling it "the most wonderful Venetian room we have seen." It also contained antique chairs, sofas, and tables, and the dealers informed him, "We can sell you the furniture or the whole lot in bloc. If you like it, please wire us. . . . The whole thing is for sale in Italy."[32]

One gets an idea of the availability of such commodities in another letter from Duveen Brothers of later that same year:

In reference to the Italian carved Boiserie in Genoa, we beg to say that this is sold, but we are sending you by this mail, photographs of a room which is offered to us—It is belonging to an Italian nobleman near Turin and it consists of: 7 doors, with upper doors, beautifully painted; 7 door frames with the upper part painted; 5 fine Consoles with mirrors (marble tops); 2 fine Consoles without marble tops; 10 window frames; 4 mantel mirrors; about 190 feet of woodwork, 3 feet wide; 200 feet of molding; 8 room corners finely carved; 14 paintings above the door and door frames. All this is very richly richly carved and gilded and genuine of the period.

The letter closed with a note of urgency: "There is no time to be lost as [the palazzo] is soon to be pulled down if it is not sold and put up to auction."[33]

Vitall Benguiat and Antique Fabrics

Vitall Benguiat was another dealer with whom Stanford White did a considerable business at the turn of the century. Benguiat's letterhead lists him as an "Importer of Antique Embroideries, Brocades, Laces, Velvets, Fine Carpets, Jewelry, China, Works of Art, Etc. 11 Saville Row, Bond Street, London."[34] In anticipation of White's forthcoming trip to England in the fall of 1897, the jovial Benguiat wrote to invite him to visit his showrooms, adding, "I know of a very fine carpet that may suit you, and I also have some large pieces of velvet."[35] White did call to see the dealer's wares, for about three weeks later Benguiat informed him he was shipping to him in New York four crates containing two China vases, a pair of lamps, and some velvet; moreover, Benguiat had obtained the carpet he had mentioned from the famous London dealer Asher Wertheimer, adding that Wertheimer "is hurrying me for the money."[36] In London, Uncle Henry and the house of Duveen regularly served as Stanford White's agent and factor. For example, in April of 1898, White received a letter which read, "Received from Mr. Vitall Benguiat for Stanford White, Esq, of New York, 2 large Persian XVI century carpets, 2 large Blue and White China jars, 2 large lamps. [signed] Duveen Brothers, A. Chapman."[37]

Stanford White interiors consumed enormous amounts of fabrics—tapestries for the upholstering of furniture or for portieres hanging at doorways, antique velvets with which to cover the walls of whole rooms, brocades in great swags for draperies at the windows. When ancient fabrics could be obtained, they were preferred over modern materials, although there then arose, in response to the demand, a growing business in the weaving of reproductions of antique patterns. The American market for such things as Benguiat offered was increasing annually, and in early 1899 the London merchant wrote to White to tell him he was coming to New York with a very fine collection of goods; he hoped White would tell his friends and colleagues about the fine antique velvets, brocades, and carpets he would have to show them.

Duties and Taxes

Another letter from Benguiat in April of 1898 offered White an assortment of "Renaissance velvet, sets of cushions, and borders, also rich vestments."[38] White bought them, and they were shipped to him via Duveen Brothers. A letter written a few days later closes with a statement that reveals how dealers and importers got around the heavy duties then imposed on antiques that were brought into the United States from Europe: "I can value them much less," the wily old Vitall wrote, "and you will not have any difficulty in the Custom House."[39] This practice was widespread—placing a very low valuation on goods being imported so they would not be recognized as antiques and could pass without being held for payment of the duty tax. The Parisian dealer Lowengard once wrote to White on this same issue, saying he had seen the shipping agent who told him the duty on tapestries was forty percent, not sixty percent as White had thought: "He gave me to understand that he has means of passing things *very* much cheaper—and of course he took jolly good care not to indicate to me the means. He keeps his business to himself & I cannot blame him. I heard that even now goods (antiques) can be passed even free—if they are left for a certain time in a Paris dwelling."[40] In addition, customs officials were regularly bribed.

Godfrey Kopp: Source for Paintings and Antiques

Although many of the paintings that White bought were acquired mainly for their decorative attraction, he was occasionally offered some truly important masterpieces. A London dealer named George Donaldson, for instance, wrote to him excitedly in 1904:

> I have just had a big go—the biggest of my life, having bought two of the most famous pictures in England—one, the finest portrait in the world, by Titian—the "Ariosto"—and the other the great Vandyke of the two young brothers—Lords John and Bernard Stuart—one in white and blue with his foot on a step and his elbow coming out at you—life size of course. I tell you it's "some picture." From Lord Darnley, Cobham Hall. Very dear of course. The National Gallery wants them badly, but the war is not yet paid for and the treasury light. 50,000 pounds each is the price.[41]

White's contacts for the acquisition of paintings were many and varied. Godfrey Kopp, who worked out of Rome, was a valuable source, as the following letter indicates: "I have been entrusted with the sale of a old english Castle dating back from 1060 containing in over hundert Rooms most beautiful and unknown things, over 400 Paintings by

Italians, Van Dyck, Rembrandt, Romney, Gibson, Lawrence. Mostly portraits of the family. Early furniture, tapestry (14), China, panelings, etc."[42] Four years later Kopp offered White a painting of Danae which he himself owned and which he could document as having once been owned by the Duke of Modena: "I really think that your friend Mr. Whitney or Mr. Mackay or even Mr. Payne ought not to let such a rare opportunity escape and make acquisition of this most unique work of art."[43]

Kopp offered White the most extraordinary treasures, if they were indeed what they were said to be. For example, in April of 1898 he told the American architect that an Italian family had placed with him a large silver vase and its basin, claimed to be by Benvenuto Cellini. On another occasion the dealer asked White if he would like to buy six stained-glass windows from a viscountess who also had decided to part with a portrait by Philippe de Champagne and another, of Louis XV, by Hyacinthe Rigaud. Kopp also offered a portrait by Sir Joshua Reynolds from an English collection, the owner of which also had a large amount of beautiful furniture that he was anxious to sell.

Kopp offered White antique furniture as well as paintings. In October of 1897 he informed White of two ancient fireplaces, one in carved wood dating from the era of Louis XIII and another, in marble, from the Renaissance period. On another occasion the dealer told him of several items that he thought might be of interest—four Gobelin tapestries representing the four seasons, after designs by Pierre Mignard (1612–95), and "Grand Boiseries Louis XVI, with Clodion chimney, Falconnet garniture, ceilings, etc., Boucher tapestries, Nattier & Boucher Paintings."[44]

Mischief and fraud at times came to play in the international network of dealers, and at times Godfrey Kopp was, to be sure, a scoundrel. Henry Duveen warned Stanford White about him, saying that a certain party in Rome whose name is Kopp "is capable of almost anything and we warn you herewith to have nothing to do with him. . . . This man Kopff is a very dangerous person and you should be very careful to keep away from him."[45]

Kopp passed himself off as a Hungarian baron who had been forced to flee his native land because of a dalliance with a young woman of the royal family. In truth, he was the son of a Swiss pastry chef and began his career as a hotel errand boy. But he was impeccably dressed, charming, and suave, and he was for several years a correspondent of the connoisseur Bernard Berenson, whom he had met at St. Moritz. He became involved with a Parisian art dealer who sold forgeries produced by Gaston Duchamp (aka Jacques Villon), the elder brother of the Dada artist Marcel Duchamp.[46]

Kopp sold one such painting, a "Constable *Flatford Mill*," to John R. Thompson, a touring American who owned several restaurants in Chicago. Not one to miss an opportunity for a potentially enormous scam, Kopp offered to accompany Thompson on his tour of Italy. In Rome, Thompson became infatuated with the Arch of Constantine, which he ardently wished he could re-erect as the entrance to one of his restaurants back in Chicago. What good fortune, Kopp whispered to his gullible American mark, for the Italian government, then being in desperate need of funds, was willing to sell the sixteen-hundred-year-old arch. Such things had to be handled delicately and secretly, with Kopp as the go-between, but here was the deal: The government would sell the great Arch for a reasonable $500,000 if Thompson would give Kopp a $100,000 down payment, the balance being due when the celebrated monument arrived in Chicago. By the time Thompson realized he had been duped he was back in Illinois, and there was little he could do.

Kopp reportedly pulled the same ruse on Charles T. Yerkes, a traveling American millionaire who became enamored of the Column of Trajan, which Yerkes could have, Kopp declared, at the bargain price of $250,000. He later worked a similar deal on J. Pierpont Morgan, who thought he was buying the bronze doors from an ancient Italian church. Morgan and Yerkes asked the Duveens to look into this unscrupulous character, which they did by sending Edward Fowles, their senior associate, to make inquiries, and that is how Henry Duveen came to warn Stanford White to have nothing to do with the man.

Count Boni de Castellane assessed the matter precisely when he stated that American millionaires really believed that everything in Europe was for sale: "Americans imagine that American dollars can buy anything and anybody, and I shall never forget the laughable impudence of a *nouveau riche* who, upon seeing the Arc de Triomphe for the first time, thought that she would like to ship it to New York, and *actually imagined that it was for sale, provided the offer was high enough*."[47] In spite of Kopp's shenanigans, Stanford White bought a number of things from him, and even received the goods for which he had paid.

Bardini of Florence

As noted earlier, Stefano Bardini of Florence also supplied White with antiquities for his interiors. From him, White was able to obtain many ancient ornate Renaissance and Baroque ceilings and boiseries. Bardini dealt in ceilings as if they were commodities, notifying the American architect that he had shipped to him ceiling number 122 on the 23 July 1898, and number 1005 was sent off on September 8 of that year. And it was from Bardini that White secured the paneling from the chapel of the Bâtie, which was then placed in the entrance to the ballroom in the house that White was remodeling for William C. Whitney, as we shall see.

A letter from Bardini to White shows the reworking of an ancient ceiling, once the dealer had obtained it from its original owner. Bardini reminded White that when he bought number 122 it was "perfectly rectangular," but that in order to place it in his salon the dealer had to take it apart "in order to reduce it to the irregular shape to conform it to the lines of [my] salon," and continued,

> Now, I have had to make it true again, and to do this work according to your dimensions I have had to take it to pieces, even down to the smallest part. I have then put it together again with screws throughout, because if I had had it nailed together as it was originally the wood would have been split in every direction. . . . I have used the old cornice but I have suppressed the frieze and architrave. . . . It is all numbered [for reassembly] and I think it will go all right.[48]

Financial Problems

Stanford White had a steady stream of earthly delights laid before him by the multitudinous dealers who looked forward to his annual buying binges abroad. He had a passion to possess as many of their proffered treasures as he could, whether he could afford them or not. This, together with the high lifestyle he insisted on maintaining, his generosity to friends in need, and some very bad investments, brought him to the brink of financial disaster by 1904. He was hopelessly in debt, and even Bessie's money could not bail him out. A number of friends rallied to his aid—bankers, brokers, and financiers—but they took charge of his finances on the condition that he promise never again to engage in stock speculations.[49] Even so, he still remained in debt to the firm of McKim, Mead and White for over half a million dollars.

Deciding to have a grand sale of things that he owned but were not actually a part of his Gramercy Park house, White brought together his diverse collections of paintings, sculptures, decorative objects, and curios—from storage in warehouses or in friends' stables, from friends to whom he had loaned them or from clients who had them on approval, and from the excess in his own several residences, Gramercy Park, Box Hill, his bachelor's apartment in Madison Square Garden, and wherever else he lived.

By early February of 1905 they had been assembled in a warehouse in New York City, where they were tagged and catalogued in preparation for what would have been one of the most extraordinary auction events of the era. Shortly before the sale, however, disaster struck. The building had been modernized with that marvelous new phenomenon, electricity, but alas, some of the wiring was faulty, and the building caught fire on 13 February 1905. Everything in it was consumed in the conflagration, including White's collections. The next day *The New York Times* reported that White's objects were "priceless and . . . unique," and that the collection consisted of "tapestries, iron work, pottery, carved wood objects, and statuary. . . . The top floor of the building was under lease for storage purposes to Mr. White. . . . A personal friend said that . . . it was . . . one of the finest collections of its kind in the world. The majority of the antiques represented Spanish and Italian art of the fifteenth, sixteenth, and seventeenth centuries."[50]

Not only was White devastated by the loss of so many fine objects, but the financial loss was a severe blow as well, for he had neglected to take out insurance on the collections. The following year would bring an even greater disaster. But first there remain several important Gilded Mansions undertaken by him and his partners, and to their stories we now return.

[By 1893 Whitney] had finished with politics after having gratified every ambition, and swung the country almost at his will; he had thrown away the usual objects of political ambition like the ashes of smoked cigarettes; had turned to other amusements, satisfied every taste, gorged every appetite, won every object that New York afforded, and, not yet satisfied, had carried his field of activity abroad, until New York no longer knew what most to envy, his horses or his houses.

Henry Adams on William C. Whitney (1907),
quoted from Adams, *The Education of Henry Adams* (2007)

Chapter Thirteen

The William C. Whitney Houses

William C. Whitney

William Collins Whitney (1841–1904), founder of the family fortune that bears his name, was a successful lawyer, politician, financier and sportsman in an era renowned for its men and women of exceptional accomplishments (figure 183).[1] "At the age of fifty-seven years," *The New York Times* reported in 1898, he "is a highly favored man," being socially popular and financially powerful, and in matters of business, "his name is a synonym for success. He has never been identified with a business failure, and his successes have been great ones."[2] Whitney was described as being "of distinguished appearance," standing over six feet in height and "straight and vigorous as a West Point cadet"; he was social, gregarious, suave, possessed genteel manners and cultivated taste, a man whose companionship "is greatly enjoyed. . . . He is a staunch and generous friend, and a liberal-minded and public-spirited citizen."[3]

He was also one of the greatest builders of grand mansions in a period when architectural grandeur was a willful expression of a race of megalomaniacs. Ranking with the Vanderbilts in the number, size, and sumptuousness of the residences he built, his houses were filled with the choicest treasures that money could extract from the great private collections of Europe.

Born in Conway, Massachusetts, a descendant of the John Whitney who had come to the Bay Colony from England in 1635, William Whitney was the son of the Collector for the port of Boston. Following graduation from Yale College in 1863, he attended law school at Harvard before moving to New York City, where, in the year the Civil War ended, he was admitted to the bar—just as a period of spectacular fortune-making was about to be launched in the United States.

In 1869 Whitney married Flora Payne, daughter of Senator Henry Payne of Ohio and the sister of a Yale classmate, Oliver Hazard Payne, who was then making his way up the corporate ladder of John D. Rockefeller's Standard Oil Company in Cleveland. In time, Oliver Payne became treasurer of the mammoth oil monopoly, was second only to John D. himself in the number of shares of the company he held, and was one of the wealthiest men in the country. The Whitneys had four children—Pauline, Harry Payne, Payne, and Dorothy.

Whitney engaged in some of the great legal and political battles of his day, supporting Samuel J. Tilden in his run for the presidency, opposing Tammany Hall, and, as corporate council, successfully prosecuting the Tweed ring, including Boss Tweed himself, in the mid-1870s. He masterminded Grover Cleveland's presidential campaign in 1884, and the next year the Whitneys moved to Washington, D.C., where William served as Cleveland's Secretary of the Navy, a post in which he distinguished himself. Upon assuming his cabinet post, the U.S. Navy was afloat in decrepit ships and even the ones being built anew were being constructed from out-of-date plans and ordinance; Whitney disposed of many unseaworthy vessels and fought with shipbuilders to create a navy of steel-plated warships with modern weaponry. The

Figure 183. Unidentified photographer, *William Collins Whitney, Secretary of the Navy*. Brown Brothers.

age of American economic and military expansion—carrying the concept of Manifest Destiny beyond the borders of the continental United States—was about to dawn, and it was Whitney's fleet that possessed the naval power to impose American influence around the globe. That power first fully manifested itself in the Spanish-American War (1898), a few years after which President Theodore Roosevelt sent "The Great White Fleet" to the far quarters of the world to proclaim the might of the United States.

The Whitneys and Washington Society

Flora and William C. Whitney brought a new kind of high society and social entertainment to the national capital. Biographers have given reasons for this: First, other cabinet members did not possess the wealth that large-scale entertainments in the Gilded Age required, nor did they have the residential facilities—a ballroom, for example, or grand salons. Second, the social leaders of Washington society should have been Grover Cleveland and his wife, but shortly before being elected, Cleveland had had his wife committed to an asylum, leaving him essentially a bachelor in the White House, and it was consequently more difficult for him to entertain. The Whitneys, both of them sociable by nature, gladly stepped in to fill the breach and led the district to new levels of social gaiety.

This was a part of their plan even before they arrived in Washington. Their residence there having no ballroom, they arranged with Henri Watson, the New York decorator, to build and decorate "this cleverly devised extension of Mr. Whitney's house in seven weeks, it being imperative that it should be finished by a certain date." The Whitneys intended to commence entertaining immediately and needed the ballroom at once. The same article mentioned that the ballroom was "sumptuous" and that its walls were "a bright red relieved with yellow and gold."[4]

The Return to New York: The Business of Making a Fortune

At the end of Cleveland's first presidential term, William C. Whitney largely withdrew from politics to pursue his financial fortune. He and Flora moved back to New York City and took up residence in a house at Fifth Avenue and 57th Street. William C. Whitney knew that if he and Flora were to become the social leaders of New York, greater wealth than he then possessed would be required, and so he set out to make his fortune.

William had done well as legal council for the Standard Oil Company, a position obtained for him by his brother-in-law, although Whitney knew John D. Rockefeller personally and served on several committees with him. It was not in the law courts, however, that he made his millions, but rather in streetcars. In the 1880s public transportation in New York City involved eighteen different independent companies whose equipment had deteriorated and whose commitment to time schedules could best be described as indifferent. In a masterful stroke of financial and managerial entrepreneurship, Whitney and two other men consolidated the various slipshod entities into one well-run, efficient organization—the Metropolitan Street Railway Company. One of his partners was Thomas Fortune Ryan, who formed one of the foremost art collections of his day, and the other was Peter A. B. Widener, whose interests included the Pennsylvania Railroad, United States Steel, and the American Tobacco Company. Ryan was an astute businessman and Widener was experienced in public transit, for he had previously reorganized the Philadelphia system. As the citizens of New York increasingly climbed aboard the new electrified cars, which ran precisely on schedule, they dropped their coins into the fare boxes, collectively making millionaires of William C. Whitney and his partners, a nickel at a time.

2 West 57th Street

To assure that his sister and her husband had the proper house from which to launch their campaign to enter the gilded circle of New York's high society, Oliver Hazard Payne bought and gave to Flora a fine house standing at 2 West 57th Street. Its facade was of red brick with light gray stone trim, and it was formerly the residence of Mrs. Frederick Stevens, who, after being widowed, married a French nobleman, thereby becoming the Duchess of Talleyrand; she lived the rest of her life in France. Her fine house in New York City had been designed in 1875 by George Harney, who had gone to Europe to buy up such treasures as he could for the interiors. In this he actually preceded Stanford White; Harney may have been the earliest American architect to incorporate the spoils of European raids into the mansions of the wealthy along Fifth Avenue. "Much of the fine old wood-work used in the interior," one account stated, "was brought from Belgium by Mr. Harney himself, having been obtained by him from dismantled monasteries and nunneries."[5] Reportedly, the Flemish ballroom walls had originally graced the walls of a grand house in Ghent, Belgium, while the dining room walls were covered with "old Spanish leather, collected piece by piece laboriously in Spain, and put together here" in the Stevens house.[6] The house also contained ancient stone fireplaces, extracted from noble European dwellings, and Gobelin tapestries adorned many of the walls, while the antique furniture was upholstered in Beauvais tapestry. And, of special significance, the house had its own ballroom—not a room that doubled as a parlor or an art gallery, but a distinct ballroom that had been incorporated into the original design (figure 184).

In the late 1870s the Stevens house was—until surpassed by the newer mansions, such as William Henry Vanderbilt's and William Kissam Vanderbilt's—one of New York City's showplaces, and it probably had a considerable influence on Stanford White who was at that time in search of his own mode of interior decor for the Gilded Age. White remodeled the house in 1889–90, but Flora was not to enjoy it for very long.

The family had known for some time that Flora had a heart condition, and after a severe attack she died on 5 February 1893. Whitney went into a period of mourning, but he shocked Society—and especially his brother-in-law—when he married again three years later, the bride being Edith (May) Randolph. Oliver Payne became furious, believing Whitney had dishonored his beloved late sister by taking a second wife. He vowed to ruin Whitney, but when he was unsuccessful at that, he took his vengeance by luring away from their father two of the four children of William and Flora. Pauline and Payne sided with their uncle, who showered them with lavish gifts, but Harry Payne and Dorothy remained loyal to their father.

The ghost of Flora seemed to haunt 2 West 57th Street, and the second Mrs. Whitney had a right to have a house of her own. So her husband bought the house at 871 Fifth Avenue that had been built by sugar refinery king Robert L. Stuart. Whitney gave the house at 2 West 57th to his son, Harry Payne, who had recently married Gertrude Vanderbilt, daughter of Alice and Cornelius Vanderbilt II, whose mansion rose just across 57th Street. So before she was married, most of Gertrude's life had been spent on the northwest corner of 57th and Fifth, and after she was married it was to be spent on the southwest corner of that same intersection.

871 Fifth Avenue

The Stuart mansion had been completed in 1883, but Stuart had died the previous December so his widow oversaw the decorating and furnishing of the house, including the arrangement of the paintings in the famed art gallery. It was a large house on a plot fifty-five feet by two hundred feet, facing Central Park, and its four-story Italian Renaissance facade was constructed of brownstone, according to the designs of William Schickel. The original interiors are credited to William B. Bigelow—McKim's former partner—"the architect, who has general charge of the department of design of Messrs. Herter's establishment."[7] Mary Stuart died in 1891, and William C. Whitney purchased the mansion a few years later for Edith. Stanford White was again called in and given instructions to make it one of the grandest houses in New York City.

By 1896 the house, which was only thirteen years old, was already old-fashioned. The Stuart art gallery was an example of this outdatedness, for photographs of it show paintings stacked floor to ceiling and frame abutting frame, in the customary fashion of the 1870s and early 1880s, just as at William Henry Vanderbilt's gallery and that of A. T. Stewart. For Stanford White to achieve his grand visions, the house was gutted so he could start afresh. Whitney gave McKim, Mead and White *carte blanche*, and White, the partner in charge, spent lavishly over the next four years. It was estimated that the remodeling and the furnishings cost about $3.5 million.[8]

But tragedy struck once again when Edith died, in 1899, of head injuries suffered during a riding accident at the Whitney's estate in Aiken, South Carolina.[9] At that point William withdrew from society for an extended period of mourning, during which he turned his attention to the remodeling and furnishing of his house. In January of 1901 a reporter observed that it has been "Mr. Whitney's occupation in his leisure hours . . . to supervise [the alterations] and to secure, both abroad and in this country, the rarest and most remarkable furnishings, decorations, and paintings procurable. The purse of a Fortunatus, combined with rare good taste and judgment, have enabled him to transform the Stuart house into a palace filled with art treasures." The reporter then noted that here was an American millionaire who was attempting to re-create for himself an ambience that resembled more the abode of European aristocracy of old than anything that grew out of present-day America; the result was that "the owner has as near an approach to a Venetian or Florentine palace of the days of Leonardo da Vinci and Michael Angleo as it is possible to obtain." The reporter then continued: "There is hardly a piece of modern work to be found in the house. . . . The chimney pieces . . . are nearly all elaborate works in marble from old Italian palaces; the hangings are from similar sources, the ceilings of several rooms have been taken bodily from famous buildings in Europe, and the furniture and much of the woodwork are of the same unique character."[10] We have seen in the previous chapter that Stanford White had regular dealings with a vast network of dealers and decorators, not only in New York City but also in almost every major city of Europe. From them he bought richly coffered, gilded and painted ceilings, ancient fireplaces, and handsomely carved boiseries, as well as rare old fabrics, furniture, paintings, and assorted bibelots.

While he was working on the Whitney mansion, White received a letter from Duveen Brothers that is interesting because it concerns the professional secrets among dealers; Duveen's of London had sent to its New York warehouse "a rock crystal wall light intended for Mr. Whitney's Ball Room," with instructions for its men to set it up in White's office for approval; it was one of a pair: "I need hardly tell you that they are extremely fine and unique and the very thing for this room. They will, of course, be fitted for electric lights. . . . Kindly do not let any chandelier or wall-light manufacturers in New York get hold of this design."[11]

Another letter from Duveen Brothers informed Stanford White that "we have bought a most wonderful Louis Seize room, complete, carving by [Jean Charles] de la Fosse, and as fine in its way as the Louis Quatorze Room you bought for Mr. Whitney."[12] This was probably the Louis XIV room mentioned in the firm's letter of 22 December 1897 in which White was asked about his instructions for reworking its dimensions so it would fit one of the Whitney rooms.

William C. Whitney was a discriminating collector who knew what he liked and what he did or did not want to buy. In late 1897 Duveen Brothers, going through Stanford White,

Figure 184. George E. Harney, Flemish ballroom, Frederick W. Stevens residence, southwest corner of Fifth Avenue and 57th Street, 1875–76. From Sheldon, *Artistic Houses*, vol. 1, part 2, plate 9.

often came to the weekly salons she and her companion, Bessie Marbury, held: "One of the great feathers in our caps was the number of older men of distinction who liked to come to our 'at homes.' Among these was William C. Whitney, who seldom missed a Sunday when he was in town. He once made the remark 'You never know whom you are going to meet at Bessie's and Elsie's, but you can always be sure that whoever they are they will be interesting and that you will have a good time.' "[14] Among those Whitney might encounter at those salons were the actresses Sarah Bernhardt and Ellen Terry, Oscar Wilde, Count Robert de Montesquiou, Sara Hewitt, Mrs. Cooper Hewitt, Mrs. J. Pierpont Morgan, Charles Dana Gibson, Isabella Stewart Gardner, Henry Adams, Ogden Codman, and Stanford White.

As a "re-entrance into social life," as *The New York Times* put it, and as a housewarming intended to allow Society to see his splendid new residence, William C. Whitney gave a grand party—a debutante ball in honor of his niece, Helen Barney, daughter of his sister Lilly and her husband, Charles Tracy Barney, president of the Knickerbocker Trust Company and a close friend of Stanford White.[15] On the evening of 4 January 1901, as the first of the four hundred guests, many of whom had attended the opera first, arrived at William C. Whitney's new house, they passed through an entrance decorated with a wrought-iron and bronze grillwork that had been acquired from the Palazzo Doria in Genoa. That night, the vestibule—once part of an ancient Florentine house—welcomed Mrs. Caroline Astor, who wore black velvet which beautifully displayed all her superb diamonds. The vestibule was done in green onyx, with three grand chandeliers that made the ladies' jewelry sparkle with fire. Here, too, came Mr. and Mrs. John Jacob Astor, she wearing white tulle embroidered in gold, he, like all the

tried to sell Whitney a portrait of Diana, Lady Milner, by George Romney. The letter, describing the picture and the circumstances of its owner needing to sell it, is preserved, and on the verso is a note that reads, "Dear White, I do not care to consider this. [signed] W. C. Whitney."[13]

A Return to Social Life

Whitney was, by nature, a social creature, and he, Stanford White, and Charles T. Barney frequently spent an evening together "doing the town." Whitney was a consummate clubman, belonging to most of the same clubs that White did—the Century, the Metropolitan, the Knickerbocker, the New York Yacht Club, the Yale Club, and the Jockey Club. Once he returned to social life he was a welcome guest at any salon or dinner party. Elsie de Wolfe—an early interior decorator and a protégé of Stanford White—remembered that Whitney

Figure 185. Stanford White, stair hall, William C. Whitney residence, 871 Fifth Avenue, New York City, 1898–1900. Avery Architectural and Fine Arts Library, Columbia University, New York City.

other gentlemen, wearing formal black-and-white evening attire. Mr. and Mrs. Stanford White were in attendance, as was Charles Follen McKim, and they mixed easily among some of their past, present, and future clients—the Clarence Mackays, for instance, or Mr. and Mrs. Stuyvesant Fish, Mr. and Mrs. Whitelaw Reid, and Tessie and Hermann Oelrichs. There too were William Kissam Vanderbilt with Mr. and Mrs. William K. Vanderbilt Jr., for whom Stanford White had designed a little imitation of the Petit Château. Prince Troubetskoy and Prince Ruspoli added the attraction of Old World aristocracy to the glamour of the occasion, and many of the treasures they saw as they passed from one room to another they remembered seeing years earlier in Old World palazzos and châteaux.

Edith Wharton and her husband, Teddy, were present, the author no doubt observing the brilliant throng as well as the elegant ambience as potential material for some future novel, such as *The House of Mirth* (which was published only a few years later) or *The Age of Innocence*. In her book *The Decoration of Houses*—published in 1897, or about the time White began remodeling the Whitney house—Mrs. Wharton declared that eighteenth-century French interiors were suitable for copying in American homes, which is exactly what Stanford White did.

The Grand Hall, Dining Room, Library, and Salon

A grand staircase, the walls of which were adorned with beautiful tapestries (figures 185 and 186), led from the entrance hall to the main floor, admitting guests to the grand hall, which was two stories high and ran the full length of the house. From it, entrance was gained to the library, dining room, salon, and ballroom. White had bought the coffered, painted and gilded ceiling, an Italian Renaissance creation of the sixteenth century, from the Florentine dealer Stefano Bardini, and the great stone carved fireplace from the château of the Sieur Franc de Conseil at Aigues-Mortes, dated from about 1550. Most of the furniture was the work of either sixteenth- or seventeenth-century Italian or French craftsmen; much of it White had purchased from the Parisian dealer Émile Peyre when he was on one of his buying trips to Paris in 1898 or 1899.

In the grand hall guests encountered such treasures as the large equestrian portrait of King Charles I majestically astride a white horse, then attributed to Anthony Van Dyck—a prize recently taken by William C. Whitney; it was probably a later copy of the famous painting now in the National Gallery in London. The opposite wall was dominated by an impressive Italian altarpiece by Lorenzo Costa (1460–1535) representing a Madonna and Child seated between two standing saints. It was illuminated by a beautiful silver lamp of old Italian workmanship that was suspended from the ceiling. A huge black oak table from an Italian monastery and an ornately carved sarcophagus were also part of the furnishings of that area.

From the grand hall one entered, to the right, the dining room, the walls of which were decorated with sixteenth-century Italian murals, and the floor was covered with a "priceless" Persian carpet. The fireplace, which was of Italian Renaissance vintage, had above it three coats of arms carved in stone; White had purchased it from the dealer Simonetti of

Figure 186. Jean Cousin the Elder, *The Drowning of Britomartis*, 1547–59. Tapestry, probably made in Paris, wool and silk, 183 × 114 in. (465 × 290 cm). Metropolitan Museum of Art, gift of the children of Mrs. Harry Payne Whitney, 1942 (42.57.1). Ex Coll., William C. Whitney. Whitney was an avid collector of antique tapestries, and the *Britomartis* was one of his favorites. It had been designed by Jean Cousin the Elder for Diane de Poitiers, the mistress of King Henri II of France, and probably was hung, originally, at her famous Château d'Anet.

Rome. The ceiling of the dining room, which White also obtained from Bardini of Florence, was reportedly extracted from a palazzo in Genoa.

Next came the library, the stellar attraction of which was Sir Joshua Reynolds's *Portrait of Miss Jacobs*, purchased by Whitney at the famous Blakeslee-Fischoff sale (New York City, 1900). In this room too hung the *Portrait of a Venetian Nobleman* by Scipione Pulzone (called Gaetano), above the fireplace, which had been carved in marble in Italy in the fifteenth century and bought by White from Simonetti of Rome. On the library table stood a small panel painting said to be by Lucas Cranach the Elder, while a nearby Madonna and Child was attributed to Filippo Lippi.

The walls of the salon were covered with a figured crimson velvet; for this room alone Vitall Benguiat had supplied some two hundred yards of Renaissance fabric (figure 187). The ceiling—which once adorned a Roman palazzo before White obtained it from Bardini—was coffered in gold, green, and copper colors. The furniture, acquired in Paris, was mostly Henri II or Italian Renaissance.

Guests entering the salon were welcomed by Anthony Van Dyck's elegant full-length portrait of William de Villiers, Viscount Grandison, from the Buckingham collection in England; it had been recently obtained from a New York art dealer for a price said to exceed $60,000, reportedly the highest sum paid for a European painting in America, with the exception of Millet's *Angelus*.

In the salon the Van Dyck was joined by such masterpieces as a portrait of a man by Tintoretto, John Hoppner's *Mademoiselle Hillsburg, Dancing*, and a likeness of a woman by an artist of the eighteenth-century French school, possibly François Boucher. There was also "a large and fine portrait of a male member of the Medici family, by Justus Susterman."[16]

The Ballroom Passage and the Ballroom

Entrance to the ballroom was gained through a hallway, the walls of which were lined with richly carved boiserie and intarsia that dated from the middle of the sixteenth century, the era of Henri II (figures 189 and 190). This paneling, acquired by White through Émile Peyre, came originally from a chapel at the Château de la Bastie d'Urfe, St. Etienne, France, in the Loire Valley. The craftsmanship was not French, however, but Italian, for the work was signed "FRANCISCI ORLANDINI VERONENSIS OPUS 1547." The panels are inlaid with religious scenes such as "The Betrayal of Christ." This woodwork survives today as a gift of the children of Mrs. Gertrude

Vanderbilt Whitney, who presented it to the Metropolitan Museum of Art in New York just before the Whitney house was demolished in 1942. The hallway was lighted by a row of ancient stained-glass windows, also of Italian craftsmanship, as well as by iron and staghorn chandeliers. Through this hallway, on the evening of the grand housewarming, passed a continual stream of elegantly bejeweled ladies wearing beautiful gowns that had been acquired from Worth in Paris (figure 191).

The most brilliant room in the Whitney house was the ballroom, which was done in the style of Louis XIV (figure 192). If Whitney were to challenge Mrs. Astor and the Vanderbilts as a leader of New York Society, the ballroom—of all rooms—had to be truly grand. In size it measured sixty-three by forty-five feet, and the ceiling rose to a height of forty-five feet. To make room for such a large space in the remodeling project, White converted what had been Robert L. Stuart's art gallery into the ballroom. This was an interesting and revealing decision on the part of the architect and his patron, for it conceded that it was more important to have a splendid ballroom—which might be used only one or two nights a year—instead of an art gallery. Lavish entertaining took precedence over the cultural mantle of an art collection and art gallery such as A. T. Stewart and William Henry Vanderbilt had, and in the process the paintings and sculptures were distributed throughout the main rooms of the house, where they were treated more as ornamental decor than as an assembled collection to be viewed all together.

The ballroom walls were covered with carved and gilded oak panels from a seventeenth-century château near Bordeaux, that of Phoebus d'Albert, Baron of Pons and Foix and field marshal to the Sun King. This boiserie had been removed in the early-nineteenth century and taken to Paris to be installed in a grand house there, and it was in Paris that Stanford White bought it for installation at 871 Fifth Avenue.[17] The furniture was also French, mostly eighteenth century, for the stylish salons of King Louis XV were fast becoming the favored interiors to duplicate in American mansions of the Gilded Age.

The Whitney Tapestries and Paintings

As if the beautifully carved and gilded boiserie were not rich enough, the walls of the Whitney ballroom were further adorned by a number of splendid large tapestries taken from the designs of François Boucher and Jean-Baptiste Henri Deshays. These too survive, for at the 1942 sale of the furnishings of the Whitney house they were purchased by the Philadelphia Museum of Art. Tapestries were then out of favor in Europe and could easily be obtained by Americans who found in them symbols of antiquity and aristocracy, the very things they wished to have wrought into the decors of their new mansions, and so they were acquired in great numbers at the end of the nineteenth century.

William C. Whitney had an especially fine collection of them which included a set known as "The Wars of Flavius Titus," the largest of which measured about fourteen feet high by twenty-three feet long.[18] Other tapestries depicted such

Figure 187. Stanford White, drawing room, William C. Whitney residence, 871 Fifth Avenue, New York City, ca. 1902. Museum of the City of New York.

Figure 188. Charles Dana Gibson, *Advice to Snobs. If you wish to get on, devote Yourself to Those who Entertain.* From *Life* (18 December 1902), pp. 532–33. Gibson's satires provide a wonderful glimpse of life within the interiors of the Gilded Age. And although he was the creator of "the Gibson Girl," the idealized young American beauty in the prime of her womanhood, he also caricaturized the overweight, homely matron for whom even a Paris gown cannot work its miracles.

subjects as scenes from *The Iliad* and "The Battle of the Romans and the Sabines." Still another set represented "Les Beaux Pastorales," taken from cartoons by Boucher. Two tapestries from a set illustrating the myth of Diana are now in the collection of the Metropolitan Museum of Art (figure 186).

Stanford White had easy access to such treasures, once the European dealers learned that he was in the market for them. For example, at the very time he was working on the Whitney house he received a letter from Émile Gavet, which included photographs of three tapestries "of Raphaelesque design of which we spoke when you were last here. The tapestries have been made from designs attributed to Raphael, for the Palace of Duke Doria, at Genoa, the Duke's Arms being on the tapestries. . . . I ask 125,000 francs for them."[19]

Figure 189. Francisco Orlandini, intarsia paneling, 1547, originally in the chapel at the Château de la Bastie d'Urfé, St. Etienne, France; installed in the ballroom passage of the William C. Whitney residence, 871 Fifth Avenue, New York City, ca. 1902. Metropolitan Museum of Art, gift of the children of Mrs. Harry Payne Whitney, 1942 (42.57.4, 1–108). The craft of intarsia—or the intricate piecing together of different-colored woods to form a three-dimensional picture on a two-dimensional surface—first appeared in Italy in the thirteenth century, probably having been imported from Muslim countries. Its popularity reached a peak in the area around Florence in the late-fifteenth and early-sixteenth centuries, especially in the artistry of Fra Giovanni da Verona. Hundreds, even thousands of pieces of wood were precisely cut and fitted together for each panel; exotic woods from newly discovered parts of the world—from Africa, India, and South America—were used, and sometimes these were dyed to obtain just the right color.

Tapestries became so popular in America that the medium experienced a revival around the turn of the century. Candace Wheeler, for example, executed tapestry designs. Albert Herter, son of Christian Herter and otherwise known only as a painter, began a studio called Herter Looms in 1908, in which he attempted to re-create the spirit of late-Gothic tapestries. William Baumgarten, former manager of Herter Brothers who went into business for himself, also established a tapestry-weaving studio in New York City in 1893 as part of his decorating establishment; he started with four imported French weavers, and then soon increased the number of artisans to eighty, such was the demand for their creations: "A large number of important wall panels with figure compositions have been executed for the residences of wealthy men, and it is admitted by the best connoisseurs that these productions are not excelled by any made in France."[20]

There were few paintings by American artists in the Whitney collection, but one of note—actually a triptych—was by John La Farge. Many years earlier, in 1861, La Farge had painted a picture of St. Paul preaching for the Church of the Paulist Fathers in New York City, but it was not accepted by the religious order; two years later he added to it, on his own, accompanying wings, one devoted to the Madonna, the other to St. John, thus making a triptych. The piece languished in his studio until William C. Whitney acquired it in 1902. In that year Pauline King noted in her book on mural painting in America that when these were seen in the mansion, "word got about that Mr. La Farge had done some very remarkable things, of a kind it had been supposed would never be seen in this country, unless Italian churches and convent walls could be stripped of their frescoes."[21] That is, the type of art that La Farge was then producing fit in perfectly with the rest of the Italian Renaissance–French Baroque type of interior decoration of Whitney's rooms.

"The scene in the ballroom . . . "

After the open house, one society columnist singled out the grand hall and the ballroom for special adulation:

> The scene in the ballroom, when the cotillion was being danced, was reminiscent of some Court ball in a European palace. . . . The scene [in the grand hall] when the supper was at its height, with hundreds of beautifully gowned women, decked with flashing jewels and surrounded by Old World treasures of art, was more suggestive, save for the modern costumes, of a banquet in some old Venetian palace in the time of the Doges than one in the metropolis of the New World.[22]

That magical night at the Whitney open house there was dancing to the music of both Lander's and Franko's orchestras before supper, which was served at midnight. During the lavish meal, Louis Sherry's Hungarian Orchestra played. Dinner was followed by the cotillion, which was led by Worthington Whitehouse and Miss Barney, who wore a white mousseline de sole gown, embroidered in gold and trimmed with white flowers. One of the novelties of the evening was the entrance of

Figure 190. Fra Damiano da Bergamo, *The Last Supper*, ca. 1547. Intarsia panel originally in the chapel of the Château de la Bastie d'Urfe, St. Etienne, France; installed in the ballroom passage of the William C. Whitney residence, 871 Fifth Avenue, New York City, ca. 1902. Metropolitan Museum of Art, gift of the children of Mrs. Harry Payne Whitney, 1942 (42.57.4.108). At the Studiolo at Urbino, Italy, an entire room was created in the intarsia technique, in *trompe l'oeil* fashion in which cabinet doors seem to project from the two-dimensional wall surface, and shelves containing objects recede into the wall itself, the artisans experimenting with the recently discovered laws of perspective. *The Last Supper* panel is an example of the scenic type of decoration using the intarsia technique.

three stage horses representing three of William C. Whitney's prized thoroughbred racers, ridden by jockeys wearing the Whitney stable colors—pale blue and chocolate brown. To each guest the jockeys distributed riding crops as favors and mementoes of the evening.

Mr. Whitehouse also arranged a balloon figure for the cotillion in which the men stepped into paper balloons which concealed them down to their ankles; the women then selected balloons of their choice and, tearing them open, discovered who was to be their partner for the dancing of that figure. Although the older members of the assembly tended to leave after the first or second figure had been performed, the younger set danced on until three in the morning.

Other Whitney Properties

Altogether, William C. Whitney owned ten residences, totaling some 36,000 acres of estates in five states in addition to a "shooting box" in England. At Blue Grass Farms near Lexington, Kentucky, Whitney oversaw the breeding and training of a splendid stable of thoroughbreds; another—Stony Ford Farm, at Goshen, New York—was also a horse farm. There were two houses on Long Island, two in the Berkshire Mountains and two in the Adirondacks, and a lodge complete with golf course at Blue Mountain. In addition, he maintained a 2,000-acre estate with stables and racetrack in Aiken, South Carolina.

Whitney, an ardent conservationist, established several of his estates because he was anxious to accomplish privately what he could not get the federal government to do. At October Mountain, near Lenox, Massachusetts, he created an 11,000-acre game preserve, which he stocked with elk, black-tailed deer, buffalo, and moose as well as smaller game such as pheasant and quail. His love of the land included forests, and his 16,000-acre tract in the Adirondacks, which had over fifty lakes, became an early experiment in scientific forest management and dendrology. To see to it that logging on his Adirondack property was carried out properly and not rapaciously, he hired Gifford Pinchot, whom we met earlier as chief forester for George Vanderbilt at Biltmore.

Long Island estates became fashionable in the 1890s and thereafter, as easily reachable retreats when Society members were in New York City for "the season." William C. Whitney owned a 450-acre tract of land at Old Westbury, near Jamaica, where he maintained his famed racing stables, track, and bridal paths. There, McKim, Mead and White built a fine Tudor-style mansion in 1900–2, a rambling picturesque affair with many gables and high-pitched roofs, its surfaces covered with shingle and brick. At an early stage of the project Whitney instructed the architects regarding his conception of the house, saying, "I do not want a colonial nor a rectangular house. The nicest houses are those built a piece now and another later without much relation to each other but each room stuck out with windows in two or three directions. I have seen houses of this sort I liked, but, making no note of it do not now recall them."[23]

With Stanford White's assistance, the interiors at Westbury were filled with treasures found among the shops of the leading antiquities dealers of Europe.[24] The paneled walls were adorned with large portraits of European aristocracy, interspersed with great, many-pronged stag antlers in the manner of an ancient hunting lodge. Portraits played a specific role in the decor of a mansion of the Gilded Age, for they supplied, or at least gave the impression of, a family lineage of many generations, in the manner that portraits declared the ancient vintage of European aristocracy when they covered the walls of English country houses or Continental palaces. New York's old Knickerbocker aristocracy exhibited, in their parlors, portraits of five or six generations of the family—a legitimate ancestral portrait gallery, as it were.

Figure 191 (opposite). Charles Frederick Worth of Paris, evening gown, ca. 1900. Silk, satin, and velvet. Metropolitan Museum of Art, gift of Eva Drexel Dahlgren, 1976 (1976.258.1ab). This lovely evening gown was probably created for one of the younger set of the Gilded Age at the turn of the century, for its design incorporates the graceful curves of l'Art Nouveau—a design element found in the wrought-iron balconies and stair railings of the lavish new townhouses that were being built for the younger generations on the side streets, just off of Fifth Avenue. A gown such as this might well have been worn to the ball that William C. Whitney gave in 1905 in honor of his niece, and to show off his new house, the interiors of which were decorated by Stanford White.

Figure 192 (above) Stanford White, ballroom, William C. Whitney residence, 871 Fifth Avenue, New York City, 1902. New-York Historical Society.

But in the drawing room or library of the nouveaux riches would hang portraits by Reynolds, Gainsborough, Van Dyck, Romney, Lawrence, and the like, all raided by the new-money people from down-and-out European nobility with the aid of men such as Stanford White and Joseph Duveen, and bearing no familial relationship whatsoever to the new owners. Some years later a collector such as Henry Clay Frick at least treated such portraits as works of art rather than appropriated country house ancestral images.

For the Old Westbury house, as he did for Whitney's Fifth Avenue mansion, John La Farge created a set of stained-glass windows. They represented spring and dawn, and, while proving to be great challenges in their execution, were reportedly among the finest that he ever created (figure 193). He worked on them in the fall of 1901, suffering through such trials as a firing accident in the kiln that necessitated commencing the "Autumn" anew. "It has cost me," he wrote to Stanford White, "more than I shall get for it, but your instructions were to do the best I could and I was led away by the idea of doing something equal to anything Whitney could possibly have in his house unless he got a Titian or something of that kind."[25] John C. Van Dyke remembered seeing one of the windows in La Farge's studio and noted that it showed "a robed female figure scattering autumn leaves upon a pool. The brilliant autumn tints, the light from the reflecting water, would have been impossible to render fully with pigments, and the blending of light and air seems attainable only with La Farge's delicate opaline glass."[26] "Spring" stood before spring-blooming flowers—peonies and apple blossoms—while "Autumn" was surrounded by maple leaves and grapevines in their beautiful fall colors. To Henry Adams the artist expressed his belief that these windows represented "the high water mark of picture work in glass as far as skill and intelligence can go."[27]

William C. Whitney left the Old Westbury house to his son Harry Payne and his wife, Gertrude Vanderbilt Whitney. Gertrude built a sculpture studio on the property and spent many of her most enjoyable hours there, especially in her later life. Harry Payne and Gertrude left the estate to their son Cornelius Vanderbilt Whitney, who had the mansion demolished in 1942 in order to erect a new house on the site; that house is now the Old Westbury Golf and Country Club.

Epilogue of 871 Fifth Avenue House

William C. Whitney was not fated to enjoy the pleasure palaces he had created for very long, for he died in 1904 from complications of appendicitis. James Smith, a rather mousy little man who had recently inherited $40 million upon the death of an uncle, immediately purchased the Fifth Avenue house. Smith bought not only the property but all that the house contained, just as Whitney and Stanford White had decorated it. "He lived there alone," Elizabeth Drexel Lehr recalled, "the quarry of all the match-making mothers of New York."[28] But Smith soon blossomed, under his new riches, into a playboy who made off with another man's wife, sailing away with her to circumnavigate the earth. Alas, the poor man died when he was halfway around the globe, in Tokyo. Smith's estate was about to auction off 871 Fifth Avenue and all the treasures it contained when Whitney's eldest son, Harry Payne, and his wife, Gertrude, stepped in to buy the whole affair, lock, stock and gilded barrel—acquiring the house and its interiors virtually as they had been left when William C. Whitney died. Soon thereafter Gertrude and Harry moved from the home Whitney had given them earlier, at 2 West Fifth Avenue, to the house at 68th and Fifth.

On her deathbed, Flora Payne Whitney had asked her son, Harry Payne, to promise to marry Adele Sloane, Gertrude Vanderbilt's cousin, but Harry married Gertrude instead. He loved Gertrude at first, but then they began to drift apart. He drank heavily and gained so much weight that Gertrude once referred to him in her diary as "Fatty." As he began to see other women, she eventually turned to other men. Their interests were very different: his were horses, which he kept in the beautiful stables at Old Westbury; her interests were increasingly in art and artists. In New York City she involved herself in the careers of Robert Henri, John Sloan, and other members of the radical group known as "The Eight," being among the first and sometimes the only patron to purchase their paintings.

Harry Payne Whitney, noted socialite, horseman, polo player, and yachtsman, died in 1930. Gertrude continued to live at 871 until 1942, when she announced that its contents were to be auctioned off; within a few days she herself died. The auction began on April 30, and the next year the house was demolished.

Figure 193. John La Farge, *Spring*, 1900–2. Stained-glass window, 100 × 69 in. (254 × 175.3 cm). Philadelphia Museum of Art, gift of Charles S. Payson, 1977–33–1. This window was originally created for William C. Whitney's Long Island retreat at Old Westbury. In it La Farge employed opalescent glass and fired enamel glazes, for like his rival in this medium, Louis Comfort Tiffany, he was constantly experimenting to discover new effects that could be obtained.

Of the elaborate and eminently picturesque type of entertainment, Mrs. Cornelius Vanderbilt, Jr., Mrs. Hermann Oelrichs, Mrs. [Alva] Oliver H. P. Belmont, Mrs. Clarence Mackay, Mrs. George Gould [Jay Gould's daughter-in-law], and Mrs. Stuyvesant Fish may be cited as exponents. Mrs. Oelrichs's *bal blanc* at Rosecliff, her Newport villa, will go down into social history for a long time to come.

The Reverend Charles W. Nicholls, *The Ultra-Fashionable Peerage of America* (1904)

Chapter Fourteen

Newport Revisited

Rosecliff, Crossways, and The Elms

The Breakers and Marble House would appear to be beyond challenge in lavishness, that is until social aspirants such as Tessie Oelrichs and the Berwinds would achieve in their "cottages" at Newport an elegance that had hardly been attained since the age of Louis Quinze in eighteenth-century France.

Rosecliff and Tessie Oelrichs

The jewel of Stanford White's work at Newport is Rosecliff, which he created for Tessie Oelrichs. Before Tessie acquired the eleven-acre site, which ran from Bellevue Avenue to the water's edge, George Bancroft, the renowned historian and statesman, owned the property. Bancroft, an amateur horticulturist and the developer of the American Beauty Rose, had cultivated roses on its slopes overlooking Narragansett Bay, and hence the name of the site. The neighborhood was impressive, for next door was William Collins Whitney's place, and across the street lived—for the season, at least—the Henry O. Havemeyers, while just south of Rosecliff was the cottage of August Belmont.

After purchasing the parcel in 1891 Tessie dwelt for several summers in the old-style wooden house that the Bancrofts had built there. But in 1897 she asked White to design for her something in the upscale mode of Marble House and The Breakers, although of more moderate proportions. The result was what is arguably the most elegant of all the great Newport cottages, a masterpiece of the Rococo as reinterpreted by the Gilded Age (figure 195).

Tessie Oelrichs was one of the most engaging personalities of her era (figure 196). She was feisty, spirited, independent, of strong will, and outspoken. Her niece once wrote of her "racy and amusing monologues and up-to-the-minute profanity."[1] One day on the tennis courts of Newport's Casino she met a handsome and athletic young man named Hermann Oelrichs, and they married in 1890.

Hermann was the scion of the family that owned the North German Lloyd shipping company and transoceanic luxury liners, his family's wealth and position predating those of Tessie's family. Her father, James Graham Fair, was newly rich and "from the West," as an expression of that day categorized him and others like him. As a young Irish immigrant from Belfast, he had joined in the California Gold Rush of 1849. In the early 1870s he and his partner, John Williams Mackay,[2] struck it rich when they acquired the claims to what became known as "The Big Bonanza" in Nevada—the Comstock Lode, the largest silver deposit ever discovered and named after the prospector who originally laid claim to it, "Old Pancake" Comstock. Over the next twenty years their mines produced $500 million worth of silver and gold.

James Fair had two daughters—Theresa (always known as Tessie) and Virginia. The latter married the son of Alva and William Kissam Vanderbilt, and she and her husband—Willy K. Jr.—built the late Gothic-style townhouse, designed by Stanford White, adjoining the Petit Château on Fifth Avenue (figure 215, p. 318).

On the day that Tessie married Hermann Oelrichs, James Fair presented her with a gift of $1 million to give the young couple a proper start in Society. The Oelrichses set

Figure 194. Charles Dana Gibson, *A Northeaster. Some look well in It.* From *Life* (28 June 1900), pp. 550–51.

Figure 195. Stanford White, Rosecliff, Newport, 1899–1902, residence of Mrs. Tessie Oelrichs. The Preservation Society of Newport County, Newport. Copyright, Richard Cheek. Inspired by eighteenth-century European architecture such as the Trianon at Versailles, this *petit palais* on the shores of Narragansett Bay is one of the most exquisite of the summer cottages along Bellevue Avenue. Its gleaming white surface, although appearing to be stone, is actually glazed terra-cotta. The architect designed molds for details such as capitals, cornices, and swags, which made it possible to duplicate those parts quickly and relatively inexpensively when compared with the cost of carving each piece from stone.

up house in a splendid mansion on Fifth Avenue, at 57th Street. Their neighbors across the street were Alice and Cornelius Vanderbilt II. On the opposite corner was the great stone Romanesque pile erected by Arabella and Collis P. Huntington, and William C. Whitney's house (2 West 57th Street) sat on the other corner. But Hermann Oelrichs was more absorbed in his family's business than he was in Tessie's main passion, which was to be one of the queens of New York Society. Much of his time was spent in San Francisco or traveling to and from it. He died at sea in 1906.

By the turn of the century Caroline Astor was losing her grip—on Society and on reality. She sat alone in her great mansion, the one Richard Morris Hunt had designed for her at 65th and Fifth, and talked to herself or to imaginary guests at the dinner table. Her withdrawal left a void at the top of the social pyramid, and many then realized that the position, once so firmly held by *the* Mrs. Astor against all challenges, was up for grabs. As the new century opened, a triumvirate consisting of Alva (Mrs. Oliver Hazard Perry) Belmont (formerly Mrs. William K. Vanderbilt), Mrs. Stuyvesant Fish (the redoubtable Mamie), and Tessie Oelrichs dominated New York Society. To gain admittance to Society, one first had to get past this social Cerberus guarding the portal.

To occupy such an elevated position, Tessie Oelrichs had to create a properly impressive architectural backdrop against which to play out her grand lifestyle, not only in New York but in Newport as well. Thus Rosecliff came into being, as May Van Rensselaer noted: "Since Mrs. Oelrichs has built her beautiful white palace on the site of Mrs. Bancroft's house, the character of the place has been completely changed. Art has replaced nature, but it is an art that is perfect of its kind."[3] Construction of Rosecliff was begun in 1898.

Rosecliff: Plan and Exterior

At Rosecliff, Stanford White proved himself a genius as a planner as well as a designer of beautiful architectural details. The plan of the house looks like the letter H, with the marvelous ballroom forming the hyphen that connects the two wings (figure 197). Two courtyards were thereby created, one on either side of the ballroom. Each courtyard is accessible by any of the eleven large French doors that open onto it, and on evenings when Tessie was hosting a grand ball, all of the doors were thrown open, allowing easy access to and from any room on the first floor. The floor plan is a masterstroke of design.

The scheme of the elevation is dominated by the arcade of French doors, each door forming a bay that is separated from its neighbors by pilasters or beautiful Ionic columns. The attic story is reduced in scale and grandeur, allowing full focus to fall on the main floor; its bays align perfectly with those

Figure 196. Tessie Oelrichs, wearing the gown she wore at the Bal Blanc, 1904. Photograph. The Preservation Society of Newport County. Tessie Oelrichs was one of the great wits of the inner circle in Newport and New York Society. Like a number of others of her set, she often had to entertain alone, for her husband did not enjoy the social swirl that whirled around her, and he usually found it convenient to be away on business on the occasion of one of Tessie's big parties. To many, her Bal Blanc was the epitome of entertaining at Newport in the era of the Gilded Age.

Figure 197. Stanford White, plan, Rosecliff, Newport, ca. 1902. From *A Monograph of the Work of McKim, Mead and White* (1915), plate 173. From the ballroom (designated "Living Room" on the plan) one looked out across the terrace to lovely views of Narragansett Bay. The ballroom was the epicenter for the famous Bal Blanc, given by Tessie Oelrichs in 1904 when all of her lady guests were instructed to wear only white (including the powdering of their hair) and the gentlemen were requested to wear black. The design of Rosecliff was based on that of the Grand Trianon at Versailles.

below, but instead of arched doorways there are simple rectangular windows. The whole is capped by a graceful balustrade, which runs the entire perimeter of the building. The facades of the end portions, with their central arches and attic above, thus resemble the form of Roman triumphal arches, but with the lightness and delicacy of design of the eighteenth century.

White's genius is equally apparent in the details, which reflect the French spirit as manifested in both the seventeenth-century Grand Trianon and the eighteenth-century Petit Trianon at Versailles. As the years of the Gilded Age advanced, a strain of elegance and refinement, based on late Baroque or Rococo prototypes, emerged, thanks in no small measure to Stanford White. The heavy-handedness of A. T. Stewart's colossal pile of marble or of William Henry Vanderbilt's ponderous brownstone palazzo quickly became dated and old-fashioned. In monuments such as Rosecliff at Newport, and the Henry Clay Frick mansion of 1915 and the Duke Mansion on Fifth Avenue in New York City, the movement, many would claim, attained its zenith.

The exterior of Rosecliff appears to be stone, but it is not. White was then experimenting with a medium that assumes great importance in his architectural designing because of its potential for rich decoration at a relatively moderate cost. The walls are actually constructed of brick but then covered with a white-glazed terra-cotta tiling that resembles stone. The result is a surface that is itself as alluring as the architectural decoration. Being executed in terra-cotta, the details possess a crispness and a rich modeling of the figural and floral ornamentation, and once the molds were made, terra-cotta replicas could be produced much less expensively than if they had to be carved individually from stone.

The sensuously curving ironwork of the balconies and of the window grills reveals that White was well aware of the current mode for such things in Paris, for the curves reflect the contemporary Art Nouveau style.

The Interiors at Rosecliff

From the main entrance to Rosecliff, which is at the front of the right wing (figure 195), one steps into a grand white vestibule, beautifully detailed in the best Stanford White manner. The focal point of this area is a graceful stairway to the right, which, in its curves, creates a heart shape, repeating the lithe curves of L'Art Nouveau found in the exterior grillwork.

The main features of the salon or reception room are the handsome fireplace, carved from Caen stone in the French manner, and the elegant crystal chandeliers suspended from the decorative, coffered ceiling (figure 198). As on the outside, pilasters flank French doors, which flood this and other rooms at Rosecliff with light. The abundance of light reflecting off the near-white tint of the walls contributes to the joyousness that pervades the mansion.

The dining room, done in the style of Louis XVI, again has as its focal point the carved marble fireplace with its richly ornamented overmantel. In the evenings, matching crystal chandeliers and wall sconces illuminate the room.

The use of white or white with gilt interior marked the shift in taste from the colorful deeper tones of the era of Louis XIV to the lighter mode of Louis XV. The painter Edward Simmons noted in his autobiography that he believed "that Stanford [White] set the fashion here of building in our latitude. [He used] a decided lightening of the color scheme, so much so that a 'gag' was to call the firm 'McKim, White and Gold.' "[4]

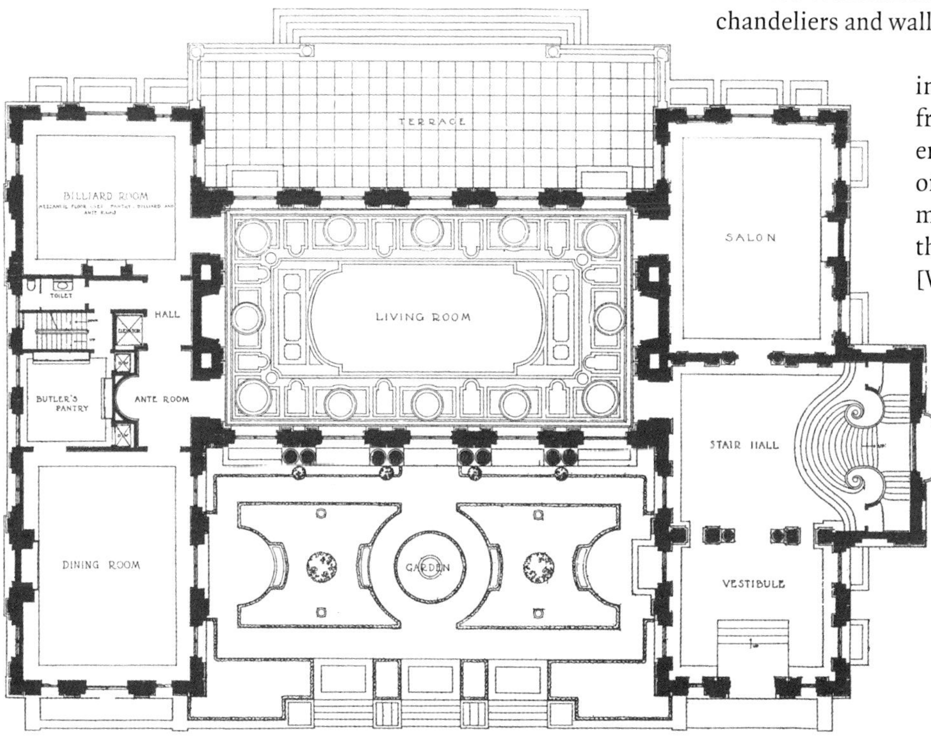

The Ballroom

The most important room in the house was the great ballroom. Measuring forty by eighty feet, it is the largest ballroom in Newport, and one of the most exquisite interiors by Stanford White ever designed (figure 199). Each of the two long walls of the ballroom has a row of five arched French doors. (Incidentally, this ballroom is where some of the most memorable scenes from the movie *The Great Gatsby*, starring Robert Redford and Mia Farrow, were filmed.)

The ballroom is in the mode of Louis XV, a style by then appreciated for its expression of quintessential aristocratic elegance. From its chandeliers and sconces to the painted *faux* sky on the ceiling, from the lavish plaster ornamentation of the ceiling to the exquisitely detailed pilasters and cornices, the decoration of the room makes this one of the most glorious chambers of La Belle Époque.

As noted, this room was the reason for the existence of the house, and its placement as the hyphen between the two wings declared it to be the central, primary section not only physically but also psychologically. This is all the more remarkable when it is recalled that thirty or so years earlier, the ballroom did not even exist in the plan and design of the large American house.

Of Balls and Ballrooms

Although ballrooms were known before 1870, they were seldom discreet rooms in private houses; that is, were a gala to be given, some other room in the house—such as a parlor or a large hall—would have the furniture removed to make space for dancing. Also, in earlier years, when large-scale entertaining was undertaken, which was not often, it commonly occurred at one of the numerous hotels or at a place such as Delmonico's or, later, Sherry's, for these establishments specialized in such things. But to give a ball in a home proved a challenge to most hosts and hostesses because even large brownstones had not been designed to accommodate that type of entertainment, as noted by Ward McAllister, who once gave a ball in his house on West 19th Street and discovered "what it was to turn a house inside out for a ball, and how contracted everything must necessarily be in a twenty-five foot [wide] house, to receive guests in it, give them a *salle de danse* and a supper room. . . . [I] then concluded that we

Figure 198. Stanford White, salon, Rosecliff, Newport, ca. 1902.
The Preservation Society of Newport County. Copyright, Richard Cheek.

Figure 199. Stanford White, ballroom, Rosecliff, Newport, ca. 1902. The Preservation Society of Newport County. Copyright, Richard Cheek. The ballroom—the connecting hyphen between the two wings at Rosecliff—was the major room of the entire house, indicating the importance of entertaining at Newport. Indeed, many considered entertainment to be the main reason for Newport's existence. Hostesses set aside hundreds of thousands of dollars each season for the giving of dinners and dances, and equal amounts were expended in Paris to acquire an assortment of evening gowns for those occasions. In her quest for an original theme for her evening's entertainment, for example, a hostess thought nothing of bringing the entire cast and orchestra of a Broadway musical to Newport for the evening, for the pleasure of her guests.

must go in most cases to a good-sized ball-room to give an enjoyable dance."[5]

One of the earliest of the great balls was, as noted earlier, the grand fete hosted by Annie Laight Cottenet (Mrs. William Colford) Schermerhorn, a costume ball given in late 1860 to which some six hundred guests came attired in the costumes of the court of Louis XV. They were greeted by servants wearing the livery of the royal palace of Versailles—a harbinger of things to come. The Schermerhorns had done their best to transform their dull and sedate house at Lafayette Place and Great Jones Street into the palace of Versailles for the occasion, but it did not work because the interiors simply were not transformable; the new mansions erected after the Civil War would be different in that they would have specific spaces for entertaining—specifically for fancy-dress balls—and, because of their scale, plan, and style, they could be transformed into a royal apartment at Versailles or at the Grand Trianon or whatever the theme of the evening required.

The idea of a very large separate room—one that could accommodate several hundred people for a festive occasion that included socializing, dancing, music, and dining—that might be used for only one night out of the year and otherwise left in deserted darkness, with shrouded windows and cloth furniture covers, was an invention of necessity during the Gilded Age. The ballroom, to some extent, set the very definition of Society for the term "The Four Hundred" derived from the capacity of Mrs. Astor's ballroom in the house at 34th Street and Fifth Avenue, which could accommodate only four hundred of Society's chosen ones, those whose names appeared on Ward McAllister's carefully selected list. "To be ultra-smart," Reverend Charles Nicholls declared, "one is ordinarily supposed to have received an invitation to an Astor ball."[6]

The ballroom also gave the new millionaires a way to display their enormous wealth—after all there was little point in having it if they could not flaunt it. It was not just the vast amount of money these parvenus possessed that separated them from the comfortable but dowdy middle class; it was their willingness to spend it lavishly on jewelry for the women, a string of polo ponies and club memberships for the men, fabulous ocean-crossing yachts that were floating palaces, magnificent art collections, great mansions, and, of course, entertainments, the zenith of which were the fancy-dress balls held amid the splendor of a grand ballroom.

In the time-proven and well-ordered society of Europe, a person knew if he or she were a member of the aristocracy by the bloodline that separated the privileged peerage from the middle and lower classes. But in America, where there was no true aristocracy, how was one's position at the peak of the social pyramid to be established and constantly reaffirmed? The primary means were by the possession of wealth and the vigorous display of it. The exhibition of a family's wealth therefore being essential, the new millionaires had to create occasions and environments where it could be shown: Monday nights at the opera, for example, an outing on one's yacht, a formal dinner party, or a fancy-dress ball.

Edith Wharton and Ogden Codman had much to say about ballrooms in their book, *The Decoration of Houses* (1897). The ballroom, they declared, was one of the two principal gala apartments, the music room being the other. Furthermore, a gala room was only meant to be seen when it was crowded with guests, "the crowd taking the place of furniture."[7] They took great care to define exactly what a ballroom was, and was not, noting that in Europe "gala rooms," as they were called, were used exclusively for entertaining and were, in the design of a great house, kept apart from the family's private apartments; they then noted that

> in many large houses lately built in America, with ball and music rooms and a hall simulating the two-storied Italian saloon, this distinction has been disregarded, and living and gala rooms have been confounded in an aggregation of apartments where the family, for lack of a smaller suite, sit under gilded ceilings and cut-glass chandeliers, in about as much comfort and privacy as are afforded by the public "parlors" of one of our new twenty-story hotels. This confusion of two essentially different types of room, designed for essentially different phases of life, has been caused by the fact that the architect, when called upon to build a grand house, has simply enlarged, instead of altering, the *maison bourgeoise* that has hitherto been the accepted model of the American gentleman's house.[8]

The authors of *The Decoration of Houses* said that the Italians had, over the centuries, excelled in the creation of ballrooms, in part because "the Italian decorator held any audacity permissible" in a room filled with people "whose mood and dress made them ready to accept the fairy-tales on the walls as a fitting background to their own masquerading."[9] They explained the Italians' recognition that house decoration is in reality interior architecture and should express its architectural affiliations: "To small dribbles of ornament [the Italians] preferred bold forcible moldings, coarse but clear-cut free-hand ornamentation in stucco, and either a classic severity of treatment or the turbulent bravura style of the saloon of the Villa Rotunda or of Tiepolo's Cleopatra frescoes in the Palazzo Labia at Venice."[10]

To Wharton and Codman, the archetypal ballroom must be large with a very high ceiling, and the walls and ceiling should be decorated more lavishly than would be appropriate for any other room. This made it unfit for any other use: "Nothing can be more cheerless than the state of a handful of people sitting after dinner in an immense ball-room with gilded ceiling, bare floors, and a few pieces of monumental furniture ranged round the walls; yet in any house which is simply an enlargement of the ordinary private dwelling the hostess is often compelled to use the ballroom or saloon as a drawing-room."

In addition, no ballroom was complete without its great chandeliers, and the room was always to be lit from above, never from the walls: "For a ball-room, where all should be light and brilliant, rock-crystal or cut-glass chandeliers are most suitable: reflected in a long line of mirrors, they are an invaluable factor in any scheme of gala decoration."[11] While the advice about the mirrored walls relates more to the ballroom at nearby Marble House than to Rosecliff, the glass of the French doors surrounding Tessie's gala room would have had a similar effect, by night, at least. Also, the Oelrichs's ballroom was decidedly more French than Italian, indebted more to the delicacy of the Louis Quinze Rococo style than to the bombastic "bravura" of its Italian eighteenth-century counterpart.

The Famous Bal Blanc at Rosecliff

As construction was nearing completion at Rosecliff, Mrs. Oelrichs went regularly to the site to give orders to the workmen. On one occasion she suffered a terrible accident when she was hit in the eye by a tack, which left her blind in that eye. But the indomitable Tessie continued supervising nevertheless, until the final touches were applied.

Although Rosecliff was not yet finished in August of 1900, it was far enough along that the impatient Tessie Oelrichs could host its official housewarming, a grand ball with 112 guests for dinner. It was held late in the season, on 19 August 1904, just prior to Mamie Fish's annual Harvest Festival ball at Crossways, her Colonial revival Newport cottage. However, Tessie had something even more grand in mind, and she began planning for it.

The scheme for the famous *Bal Blanc* was that white should dominate the evening. Tessie even asked President Teddy Roosevelt to get the U.S. Navy to anchor the Great White Fleet just off shore, as a backdrop for her soiree. When her request was denied, Tessie pouted only momentarily before swinging into action by ordering that a mock fleet be built—skeletal in construction and painted white—and floated into the waters off her property. The nautical theme seemed appropriate to Tessie because her gala was to be the climax to the day's activities, which included the famed yacht race in Narragansett Bay for the Astor Cup. The white theme was an extension of her villa, which was white externally and mostly internally as well.

On the enchanted evening of the Bal Blanc, bowers of white roses, orchids, lilies, hydrangeas and hollyhocks greeted Tessie's guests upon their arrival. The women had been instructed to dress in white; even their hair was to be powdered white in the manner of the eighteenth-century French court. The men were to wear black. Reverend Nicholls, who was invited to the event, observed that "dress not only heightens virtue, but actually creates beauty nowadays. This high aesthetic doctrine was seldom so vividly exemplified as by the fancy dress costumes worn at Mrs. Hermann Oelrichs's white ball, the crowning event of this Newport season."[12]

Epilogue for Tessie and for Rosecliff

Tessie spent every "Newport season" at Rosecliff until her death in 1926. Hermann, her husband, was usually not around for her summertime fetes, and in any case he had died only a few years after the white "cottage" was completed. The house passed to their son, Hermann Jr., who sold it in 1941 to Ray Alan Van Clief. Van Clief began restoring it the next year—by phone from New York City, where he was in the jewelry business.

When the restoration was complete in 1945, Van Clief gave instructions to set the table, prepare a feast on an appointed night, and send a limousine to pick him up at the Providence, Rhode Island, railway station. He looked forward with great anticipation to seeing his beautifully restored Rosecliff for the first time and to dining in its exquisite elegance. But fate decreed otherwise, for as his limousine was leaving Providence it was struck by a speeding fire engine, and Van Clief was killed instantly.

His widow sold the house the next year to Mr. and Mrs. J. Edgar Monroe, oil millionaires from New Orleans. They summered at Rosecliff until 1971, when they gave the entire estate—house, furniture, and grounds—to the Preservation Society of Newport County, along with an endowment in trust for maintenance and refurbishing. It is now open to the public.

Crossways and Mamie Fish

Maud Howe Elliott recalled that Mrs. Stuyvesant Fish—Mamie—was one of Newport's "brilliant social leaders" and that her cottage, Crossways, was "the scene of many original fetes. . . . She held high revels here—queen of a little court, with Harry Lehr wearing the cap and bells as court jester."[13] Elliott went on to say that Mamie "brightened the social heavens," conceding that her entertainments "bothered the more conservative but delighted the less conventional folk." But it was not only in Newport that this incomparable woman challenged Society's more quiescent souls, for she did as much wherever she was. Not especially attractive physically, her acerbic wit made up for her lack of beauty (figure 175, p. 258; Mamie is seated at the far right).

Alva's daughter Consuelo commented, in her memoirs, that Mamie was annoyed by any form of ostentation: "On one occasion [Mamie's] hostess, whose knowledge of history was as limited as her appreciation of art, announced, 'And this is my Louis Quinze salon!' Mrs. Fish, with a polite but studied insolence exclaimed, 'And what makes you think so?' "[14]

May Van Rensselaer also recalled Mamie's contributions to Society, writing that she "exercised a certain supremacy over the social life of Newport" and indeed saw her as one who rescued Society: "Through her endeavor Society was checked in its rapid slide down a gilded chute into crassness and vulgarity. She had great organizing ability, brains and taste. With the assistance of Harry Lehr, she contrived many original and charming entertainments in which wit and intellect occupied at least an equal place with extravagance."[15]

Mamie's wit and wrath at times terrorized Society, as when she and her jester, Harry Lehr, did not receive invitations to a musicale hosted by James Van Allen at Newport to honor J. Pierpont Morgan. Undaunted, Mamie searched out Van Allen and accosted him. He replied, "Very sorry, my dear . . . , but I can't have you and Harry Lehr at this party [because] you make too much noise." To this Mamie retorted, "Oh, so that's it! Well, let me tell you, sweet pet . . . that unless we are asked there won't be any party. Harry and I will tell everyone that your cook has developed smallpox, and we will give a rival musicale!"[16] Van Allen knuckled under; the "two disturbing elements" were permitted to attend the musicale, provided they remain on the terrace during the musical performance. On another occasion when a rival *grande dame*, Mrs. Ogden Goelet, planned a dinner party with the Archduke of Russia as the star attraction, Mamie scheduled one for the same evening at which Harry Lehr impersonated the Emperor of Russia; thus outranked, Mrs. Goelet saw Society parade to Crossways that evening instead of to the Goelets' Ochre Court.

Mamie's invitations were eagerly sought after because guests always knew they would have a good time and that usually something outrageous would occur. Her luncheons and dinners were presided over by her ultra-proper English butler, Morton, and her cook was by consensus among the world's best, while her wine cellar was unsurpassed.

Figure 200. Malcomb Strauss, *On Ocean Drive, Long Branch*. From *The New York Times*, 7 July 1905.

Mamie's husband, Stuyvesant Fish—son of Hamilton Fish—was of an old Knickerbocker family and was president of the Illinois Central Railroad; her role in life was that of an inveterate party giver. But the Fishes' fortune was not large in comparison to that of, say, the Vanderbilts, and at a dinner party in Newport one evening, as Mamie and Stuyvesant rose to leave, that outrageous clown Harry Lehr shouted to them, "Sit down, Fishes, you are not rich enough to be the first to leave!"[17] Still, Mamie and her husband lived well. Once when she was having a coughing fit, Stuyvesant inquired, "Is there anything I can get for you?" To which she replied, "Yes—that diamond and pearl necklace I saw today at Tiffany's."

In the 1880s Mamie decided to challenge Caroline, Mrs. William Astor, as the queen of Society, and architecture became one of the devices with which she set about her siege.

Stuyvesant and Mamie had been living in an old house on Gramercy Park, but in 1890 they asked Stanford White to design for them a mansion at the corner of Madison Avenue and 78th Street. Wrought in the style of a Venetian palazzo, it was often referred to as "the Palace of the Doges." Like many New York mansions of that day, its design was formed around the activities of large and lavish entertainments. At its core was a huge hall, done in white marble, that could accommodate large numbers of guests for a musicale or whatever, and its ballroom was one of the largest in New York City. The Fishes also had a lovely old estate, Glenclyffe, overlooking the Hudson River, near Garrison, New York.

At Newport their cottage, Crossways, was a Colonial Revival mansion on Ocean Drive. Mrs. Harry Lehr called the place a fine, solid house "which Stuyvesant Fish had designed himself, with its spacious dining-room, where two hundred guests could have supper at once, and its enormous hall which served as a ballroom."[18] Stuyvesant may have been the guiding spirit in the design of Crossways, but of course he needed the assistance of a professional architect to carry out his conceptions, and that architect was Dudley Newton, a local Newport architect of considerable prominence during the Gilded Age.

The Exterior at Crossways

Crossways, which is set well back from the road, is approached by a long driveway, which gives way to a landscaped circle in front of the cottage (figure 201). The facade of the house is symmetrical, with the central portion marked by a large portico supported by four two-story Corinthian columns. Three bays of windows flank the portico, aligned perfectly at the first and second floors, and there is a sunporch at either end, completing the symmetry. It is not a large house by comparison with The Breakers, but it is handsome, nicely thought out, and obviously inspired by the Colonial Revival then popular in the United States following the Centennial of 1876, which had awakened Americans' interest in their own historic past. Stuyvesant Fish's family reached back several generations to early Colonial times, and his house was a reflection of his pride in his venerable Knickerbocker ancestry.

The Interiors at Crossways

The interiors at Crossways continue the Colonial motif, with the Federal style showing up occasionally as well. In fact, the rooms there are unusual in that they are not attempts to recreate the grandeur of aristocratic European palazzos, châteaux, or country houses, but are forthrightly taken from America's own past. The broken-pediment, scroll mantel in the dining room was a reproduction of eighteenth-century American forms, and the furniture was of the Federal style as practiced by cabinetmakers such as Duncan Phyfe. In the library at Crossways the mantel was ornamented with delicate swag reliefs executed in the manner of the Salem woodcarver Samuel McIntire. The paneling in the central hall, while painted white, was a display of the cabinetmaker's and

carver's skills in the exquisite workmanship of the cornices, moldings, and pilasters, and the elliptical forms above the doorways and windows were reminiscent of fine American interiors of the Federal period.

The Elms and Edward Berwind

The Elms was designed for Herminie and Edward Julius Berwind on a site noted for its ancient elm trees, hence its name (those famous trees are now long gone, victims of the Dutch elm disease). Designed by Horace Trumbauer and completed in 1901, it was one of the last of the great mansions erected in Newport (figure 202).

Berwind was a coal king and a self-made man. The son of an immigrant German cabinetmaker who had settled in Philadelphia, Edward attended the United States Naval Academy, which had been temporarily relocated to Newport during the Civil War. After the war Berwind resigned his commission to enter the bituminous coal business with his brothers. The firm prospered, becoming the largest supplier of coal to the U.S. merchant marine. Berwind owned

Figure 201 (opposite). Dudley Newton, Crossways, Newport, 1900. Preservation Society of Newport County. Crossways, the Newport home of Stuyvesant and Mamie Fish, is a beautiful example of the Colonial American revival in architecture that occurred following the Philadelphia Centennial of 1876, a great fair that stressed the early history of our country. Stuyvesant Fish was a member of one of the oldest families of New York, his lineage dating back to the days of the Dutch settlement of New Amsterdam in the seventeenth century, which may well explain the choice of the Colonial style for his and Mamie's Newport residence. Nevertheless, Mamie often stood Society on its ear by her irreverent behavior—she was the first to have a jazz band perform for her guests, and she was the first to allow smoking at her dinner parties, other than when the gentlemen "retired" to have their cigars.

Figure 202 (above). Horace Trumbauer, The Elms, Newport, 1899–1901. The Preservation Society of Newport County. Photograph copyright, Richard Cheek. Trumbauer based his design for The Elms on a French model, the Château d'Asnières (ca. 1750) near Paris. The Parisian firm of Jules Allard et Fils provided much of the period furniture, the tapestries, and some of the paintings.

coal fields, railroads, steamships, and docks, and his millions made him eligible to move among the highest society of the Gilded Age. He had married well, which helped greatly as he wended his way through social escalation; Herminie Torrey was the daughter of the English consul to Italy.

At Newport, the Berwinds first lived in a modest Victorian house on Bellevue Avenue, until they acquired a parcel of fourteen acres for their new cottage. Ten of those acres are beautifully landscaped, to make up for the lack of an ocean view (figure 203).

Their new house was modeled after the Château d'Asnieres near Paris, which had been designed by Jules Hardouin-Mansart in the late seventeenth century. Also, Elizabeth Drexel Lehr remembered that "The Coal Baron" had been to England where he and his wife "admired Buckingham Palace, and [they] tried to reproduce some of its salient characteristics in the architecture of their own place."[19] The design of the exterior possesses a chasteness, a cleanness and crispness that is relieved by the gentle curves in the windows of the lower floor and in the central axis.

Figure 203. The Elms, Newport, 1901, view of the lawn from the terrace. The Preservation Society of Newport County. Photograph copyright, Richard Cheek.

The Interiors at The Elms

The walls in both the drawing room and the Louis Quinze–style ballroom are white. Handsome French furnishings adorn the drawing room, while the whiteness of the walls is enlivened by the exquisite ornamentation, and the ceiling has a large painting of mythological subject matter (figure 204). Appropriately, the decoration of the ballroom was the richest of any room in the house.

The Chinese breakfast room was the work of Alavoine and Company, the successor to the New York branch of Allard et Fils. There, Kang Hsi lacquered panels adorn the walls, and a painted chinoiserie border runs above the cornice. The dining room, one of the more lavish rooms of the house, was done in the Venetian mode, with two large paintings vying with the fireplace as the focal points (figure 205).

Berwind's interest in collecting art can be traced back to 1887 when he bought several items from the sale of the Henry Probasco estate. Probasco was an important collector in Cincinnati, and the sale was conducted by Thomas Kirby of the American Art Galleries in New York. Berwind purchased three French academic pieces at that time. Later, Mrs. Lehr remembered The Elms being "filled with the masterpieces of French and Italian art for which 'The Coal Baron' had ransacked Europe."[20]

René Gimpel gave an interesting recollection of Berwind in his autobiography, *The Diary of an Art Dealer*, under the date of 18 June 1918:

> He is a handsome old American with white hair and a stiff mustache who, despite his elegance, can't abide dandyism. He was the first American collector to appreciate our eighteenth-century paintings. . . . I have sold him a dozen pictures which rank among the finest in the world. The interior of his [New York] mansion is just brick-a-brac. Almost everything is fake. Because he believes he has taste, he has never asked anyone's advice, and he is too violent and authoritarian to stand the truth. He would possess nothing, if he had not had me, except two large superb Bouchers [tapestries], which are truly remarkable. The last painting he bought from me is the finest [Jacques Louis] David in the world, [a portrait of] Jeanne de Richemont.[21]

The *Self-Portrait with Two Pupils* by Adélaïde Labille-Guiard (1749–1803) is an example of Berwind's penchant for elegant eighteenth-century French paintings (figure 206).

In the spring of 1901 the Berwinds went to Europe, leaving instructions for the completion of the cottage on which they

Figure 204. Horace Trumbauer, drawing room, The Elms, Newport, 1901. The Preservation Society of Newport County. Photograph copyright, Richard Cheek.

had lavished several million dollars. They also left instructions for the housewarming that was to be held immediately upon their return. The party was arranged for 30 August 1901, when the Berwinds hosted over one hundred guests, with Herminie leading the cotillion.

Epilogue for The Elms

After Mrs. Berwind's death in 1922, Edward's sister, Julia, became the hostess of The Elms. Edward died in 1936, and Julia lived on there until her death in 1961. The Berwind heirs sold out to a developer, and the furnishings were disposed of at auction. At the last moment the Preservation Society of Newport County raised enough money to buy the property from the developer. The society was even able to buy back some of the furnishings. On 20 August 1962, The Elms was opened to the public.

Critiques of Newport during the Gilded Age

David Chase has written of the resort, "Unabashed splendor was not only accepted, it was celebrated. . . . These were the halcyon days of the leisured class. . . . [But] the Newport scene of popular imagination died with the Great Depression."[22] However, even before the great economic and social disaster struck in 1929, the idea of spending vast amounts of money on grand mansions was being called into question by social reformers and even by persons within the charmed circle itself.

Henry James, for example, as early as 1906, referred to Newport's sumptuous cottages as "white elephants." After remembering the quiet charm of Newport in earlier days, he wrote,

> . . . thanks to the "pilers-on" of gold . . . it now bristles with the villas and palaces into which the cottages have all turned. . . . The white elephants, as one may best call them . . . make now, for three or four miles, a barely interrupted chain, and I dare say I think of them . . . [and] the distressful, inevitable waste they represent. . . . They look queer and conscious and lumpish—some of them . . . really grotesque—while their averted owners, roused from a witless dream, wonder what in the world is to be done with them. The answer to which, I think, can only be that there is absolutely nothing to be done; nothing but to let them stand there always, vast and blank, for a reminder to those concerned of the prohibited degrees of witlessness, and of the peculiarly awkward vengeances of affronted proportion and discretion.[23]

Many of James's contemporaries—E. L. Godkin, for example, in "The Expenditure of Rich Men" of 1896—voiced similar criticisms.[24] But as Paul Baker concluded in his biography of Richard Morris Hunt, "The ambience was singularly appropriate for the display of costly furniture and art objects, expensive dresses and jewelry, and servants in livery."[25]

Figure 205 (*left*). Horace Trumbauer, dining room, The Elms, Newport, 1901. The Preservation Society of Newport County. Photograph copyright, Richard Cheek.

Figure 206 (*above*). Adélaïde Labille-Guiard, *Self-Portrait with Two Pupils*, 1785. Oil on canvas, 83 × 59½ in. (210.8 × 151.1 cm). Metropolitan Museum of Art, gift of Juila A. Berwind, 1953 (1953.225.5). Labille-Guiard, along with Vigée-Lebrun, was one of the few women in France eligible for election to the French Royal Academy. It is thought that this painting was a declaration that, in fact, more women should be considered.

The early W. K. Vanderbilt house has always been popular with New Yorkers. One frequently heard it asserted by people of some architectural discrimination that they preferred it to any residence in New York. . . . Not only was it the beginning of better things in American residential design, but the beginning it made was an extraordinarily good beginning. The twin houses built for Mr. W. H. Vanderbilt on the block to the south stand for the culmination of the old New York brownstone residence. The W. K. Vanderbilt house was one of the first signs of emancipation from a discredited convention, and its popularity was partly owing to this fact. It was liked, however, very much more because in itself it deserved to be liked. It possessed distinction, elegance, dignity and even repose.

"Notes and Comments: An Architectural Comparison," *Architectural Record*, May 1908

Chapter Fifteen

The Progeny of the Petit Château and the Villard Houses

Mansions Influenced by the Petit Château

In the design for Alva and William Kissam Vanderbilt's Petit Château, Richard Morris Hunt hit on a style that America's new millionaire society found both pleasing and expressive of their social ambitions as well as their economic attainments. The William Kissam Vanderbilts opened their Petit Château with a housewarming on 26 March 1883, and everyone who attended realized that a new standard of opulence and something new in style had been created. Soon thereafter, Hunt began to receive requests to design similar châteaux, as in the William Borden house on Chicago's Lake Shore Drive, begun in 1885 and completed in 1889 (figure 208). At Newport, as we have seen, Ogden Goelet's Ochre Court rose, on Ochre Point, between 1888 and 1892 (figures 104 and 105, pp. 159 and 161).

In the 1890s, as the Gilded Age reached full steam, millionaires such as Elbridge Gerry chose to dwell in their own versions of the Petit Château. Gerry built his on the southeast corner of 61st Street and Fifth Avenue, and he too turned to Richard Morris Hunt to design it for him in the early French Renaissance style in 1891–94. Even Caroline Schermerhorn, Mrs. William Astor—THE Mrs. Astor—recognized that her social position required a grand château in the new mode, and she commissioned Hunt to design something in the manner of the Petit Château, only grander (figure 142, p. 213).

What Hunt had devised around 1880 with the Petit Château also became a source of inspiration to other architects and their patrons. The architectural critic of 1908 quoted at the beginning of this chapter—writing some twenty-six years after the building was completed—expressed an affection for the Petit Château, and he identified the enduring characteristics that influenced so many grand houses following in its wake. Hunt's innovation—a total break with the old brownstone tradition of the city—was quickly picked up by a number of his fellow architects.

Tauranac, writing in *Elegant New York*, observed that "in 1890, there was hardly a fashionable house on Fifth Avenue north of 59th Street, but twenty years later Fifth Avenue was lined by millionaires' mansions with hardly a break from Elbridge Gerry's house on 61st Street to Andrew Carnegie's on 91st."[1] Several of those mansions rose as the progeny of the Petit Château, as did a number that were built on the side streets just off of the avenue. In this movement to create fairy-land castles, Richard Morris Hunt remained the central figure, and his work remained inspirational even after his death in 1895.

Figure 207 (opposite). Charles Dana Gibson, *A Castle in the Air: These Young Girls who marry Old Millionaires should stop Dreaming.* From *Collier's Weekly* 31 (30 May 1903), pp. 16–17. In *A Castle in the Air*, Gibson spoofs the practice, common in the Gilded Age, of young women marrying older men, rather blatantly for their money. Here, as her elderly husband dozes at one end of the long dinner table, the young woman at the other end daydreams of having children—and of having a husband who is young enough to romp with them.

Figure 208. Richard Morris Hunt, William Borden residence, Lake Shore Drive and Bellevue Place, Chicago, Ill., 1884.

The Josephine Schmid Mansion

One block north of Elbridge Gerry's mansion was that of Josephine Schmid, built of gray limestone on the southeast corner of 62nd and Fifth (figure 209). Designed by Richard Morris Hunt and completed in 1895, it imitated the late-Gothic style of the Petit Château, with decorative details in the Gothic mode enhancing the door and window surrounds, the balustrade above the third floor, and the peak of the roofline. The main feature, however, was the keep-like tower that occupied the corner of the house, with its high-pointed, conical roof. A series of four irregularly placed chimneys contributed to the picturesqueness of the structure.[2]

The Gertrude Rhinelander Waldo House

Farther north and one block over from Fifth Avenue, on the southeast corner of Madison and 72nd Street, was the Gertrude Rhinelander Waldo house (figure 210). In this urban château of 1894–99, the work of Richard Morris Hunt is again seen spreading through the efforts of other architectural firms, in this case that of Kimball and Thompson.[3] By the mid-1890s, even members of the old Knickerbocker families were building great mansions for themselves, for Gertrude Rhinelander was a descendant of Philip Jacob Rhinelander, who had first come to New Rochelle, New York, in 1696 and who became one of the major landowners in upper Manhattan.

When Gertrude married Francis Waldo, the newlyweds departed on a tour of Europe, where she discovered the lovely châteaux of the Loire Valley in France. When she and her husband returned home, nothing would do but for her to have her own château in New York City. The house was constructed of uniform limestone on a lot 40 feet wide by 102 feet long, and it rose to a height of five stories. Work was begun in 1894, just about the time Hunt's Biltmore and Astor mansions were nearing completion; the Waldo house owes much to the French Renaissance adaptations of those structures. The architectural decoration, which is extensive, is in the style of Francis I in which the design was influenced by classical forces. The facade on Madison Avenue, for example, is essentially symmetrical, while the facade of the Petit Château was picturesque and asymmetrical; similarly, the windows here are round-headed while at the earlier Vanderbilt mansion the arches were pointed, in the Gothic manner. But the complex, broken roofline, the high-rising chimney stacks, and the steeply pitched roof all testify that the main influence was a transitional phase when certain precepts of classicism had made their way north of the Alps, where they were blended with the indigenous Gothic style of France.

But the Waldos never moved into their fine château. Mr. Waldo died before it was completed, and Gertrude Rhinelander Waldo chose to live with her sister across the street. Upon Gertrude's death in 1914, her sister Laura inherited the property, but in time a bank foreclosed on it. For a while it became the home of a prominent antiques shop; after that

Figure 209. Richard Morris Hunt, Josephine Schmid residence, Fifth Avenue and 62nd Street, New York City, 1895. Museum of the City of New York.

Figure 210. Kimball and Thompson, Gertrude Rhinelander Waldo residence, Madison Avenue and 72nd Street, New York City, 1899. Brown Brothers.

it was leased by St. James' Episcopal Church. In 1986 it became the home of the Ralph Lauren and Polo lines of men's wear; its conversion to commercial usage probably saved it from destruction and replacement.

The Isaac D. Fletcher House

The Isaac D. Fletcher house stands at the northeast corner of Fifth Avenue and 79th Street, facing Central Park (figure 211). This time, the architect who picked up on what Richard Morris Hunt had begun with the Petit Château was Charles P. H. Gilbert (1860–1952). Fletcher asked Gilbert specifically to design for him a house that was like the William K. and Alva Vanderbilt house.

Isaac Dudley Fletcher, a native of Bangor, Maine, had come to New York City at the close of the Civil War and had prospered there as an industrialist, becoming president of the New York Coal Tar Company and then of the Barrett Manufacturing Company. Although he was a prominent clubman, he and his wife—the former Miss Marie Elizabeth Pickering—did not enter into the swirl of High Society. Their names are seldom found among those invited to costume balls or dazzling banquets at Delmonico's. Nevertheless, they too wanted a Fifth Avenue château of their own, as a symbol of their success. Fletcher bought the lot in 1897 and the mansion was completed two years later.

The 79th Street facade has three asymmetrical axes—one starting with the large opening for the doorway and proceeding up through four additional stories to a huge gable set within the roof. A second axis, to the east (or left) of it, is rather squeezed in between the first axis and the east end of the mansion. Set against the confusion of decorative features and numerous openings of the eastern half of the building is a single axis in the western portion, the fenestration of which is unlike either of the other two axes. The Fifth Avenue facade, with its slight bay, is different still from the three axes of the 79th Street facade. Ogive arches and decorative crockets and spires further suggest the late-medieval prototype that was being followed, as well as the absence of classical symmetry and simplicity; and yet there are some classical motifs—in the round-headed arches above some of the openings and in the rectilinear forms of some of the windows.

Figure 211. At the left, Charles P. H. Gilbert, Isaac D. Fletcher residence, Fifth Avenue and 79th Street, New York City, 1899. Museum of the City of New York. Born in New York City, Gilbert had studied architecture at Columbia University but began his practice in the roaring mining towns of Arizona and Colorado. Returning to New York in 1888 at the time of a great building boom, he designed townhouses in the fast-developing West Side and in Brooklyn. His versatility within the Beaux-Arts mode is seen by comparing his Fletcher, Kahn, and De Lamar residences (see figures 230 and 242 on pp. 335 and 355). The Fletcher mansion, along with the residence he designed for five-and-dime-store-magnate Frank W. Woolworth one block north, represents the apogee of Gilbert's work in the Gothic townhouse mode. The neighborhood was a good one; next door to the Fletcher house was the Payne Whitney residence, designed by Stanford White, and at the end of the block was the James (later, Doris) Duke mansion. But by 1939 *Forbes* magazine would declare that grand houses such as this were no longer symbols of power, "but of decay." The Ukrainian Institute of America bought it in 1955.

Both Fletcher and his wife became collectors, adorning the walls of their mansion with masterworks attributed to Rembrandt, Reynolds, Gainsborough, David, and other celebrated masters. In an admirable display of public spirit, they bequeathed their collection to the Metropolitan Museum of Art—then housed in the grand new monumental building at 84th Street and Fifth Avenue designed by Richard Morris Hunt. Altogether, the Met received from the Fletcher estate a total of 251 works of art plus a much needed gift of $3 million. Unfortunately, the paintings were not, in every case, what they had been believed to be, for, as Calvin Tomkins noted, the Fletcher bequest "included Rembrandt's *Head of Christ*, a good Rubens, and an embarrassing number of mediocre pictures."[4]

The Felix Warburg House

With each passing year, Society moved ever farther uptown. The Felix Warburg house of 1908, for example, stands on the northeast corner of 92nd Street and Fifth Avenue, one block north of the Andrew Carnegie mansion (figure 212). This was about the northernmost expansion of Society, for the great mansions of the Gilded Age tended to cluster south of the Warburg house.

Frieda Schiff was the daughter of Jacob H. Schiff, the senior partner of the great financial house of Kuhn, Loeb and Company; she is best known today as the little girl in Augustus Saint-Gaudens's low-relief portrait of her with her brother, which their father, a generous patron of the arts, presented to the Metropolitan Museum of Art when he was made a member of the board of trustees. Frieda married Felix Warburg in 1895 and her husband joined the firm of Kuhn, Loeb. Frieda's own interest in the arts is preserved today at the Brooklyn Museum in the form of the Frieda Schiff Warburg Memorial Sculpture Garden.

From Perry Belmont, son of August Belmont, the Warburgs bought a lot one hundred feet wide by seventy-four feet deep. Then, selecting Charles P. H. Gilbert as their architect, they did something unusual: They built a house that was only fifty feet wide, which allowed them a garden at the side that measured fifty feet in width.

The five-story house is monochromatic, being constructed of gray limestone. Although the style of reference is late

Gothic, the design left large areas of wall surface unadorned, just as Hunt had done in his design for the Petit Château. The first four floors possess only a modest amount of architectural decoration, limited to the ogive arches above the windows and to the balcony balustrades of the central axis of each facade. The upper part of the house, conversely, has a profusion of Gothic ornamentation. In style, the exterior recalls the Hôtel de Cluny in Paris, a well-known landmark of the period.

Two salons overlooked the avenue and the park, and they held Felix Warburg's major collection of early German and Italian woodcuts and Rembrandt etchings. The music room was on the second floor. Adjoining it was the red room, which housed the Warburgs' collection of Italian paintings, among them four panels painted by Pesellino that were once the base for the great altarpiece by Fra Filippo Lippi, which is now in the National Gallery, London. In a neighboring room hung a small painting, *Madonna and Child*, attributed to Botticelli. One of the most lavish rooms on the second floor was the dining room, which was used only on formal occasions. Its walls were hung with tapestries and it had an

Figure 212. Charles P. H. Gilbert, Felix Warburg residence, Fifth Avenue and 92nd Street, New York City, 1908. Now, the Jewish Museum. In this house lived Felix Warburg and his wife, Frieda, their five children, and thirteen servants. When the house was completed, Felix's father-in-law, Jacob Schiff, felt it was ostentatious and feared it would invite envy and anti-Semitism.

ornate fireplace. The house was described as "elaborately fitted out with fine marble work and woodwork which helped to form a fit setting for the extensive and costly decorations, tapestries, furniture and statuary gathered by the banker and his wife from all parts of the world."[5]

The Warburg collection of prints was one of the finest in the world, and when it was given to the Metropolitan Museum of Art in 1941 it was, according to the curator of prints Williams Ivins, "the most important gift . . . ever received for [the] Department of Prints."[6] The collection consisted of 228 pieces by fifteenth- and sixteenth-century graphic artists such as the Master E.S., Schongauer, Marcantonio, Lucas van Leyden, Albrecht Dürer, and Lucas Cranach. There were forty-four by Rembrandt, including three stages of the *Christ Presented to the People*, *The Three Crosses* (figure 213), a *Landscape with Cottages*, and a *Presentation of Christ in the Temple*. Warburg's commitment to making art available to all of the people was addressed in a statement made by his son, Edward, at the time of the gift: "In keeping with Mr. Warburg's interest in the history and appreciation of art, it is hoped that by making this collection accessible through the Metropolitan Museum to the student and the public at large, it will become a continuing source of interest and enjoyment."[7]

After Felix's death, Frieda continued to live in the house, but she was soon beset by the problem facing so many of the residents of Fifth Avenue's grand mansions—property taxes. The land itself continued to increase in value as more and more commercial establishments, hotels, and apartment buildings surrounded the great houses. By 1941, the taxes on the Warburg property were $665,000 a year, to which would be added maintenance and operational expenses. In short, such places became unaffordable even for the very wealthy, and their descendants often had little interest in inheriting or maintaining such places. In 1944 Frieda Warburg presented the house to the Jewish Theological Seminary and three years later it was opened as the Jewish Museum.

Figure 213. Rembrandt van Rijn, *The Three Crosses* (second state), 1653. Drypoint and burin on vellum, 15 × 17¼ in. (38.1 × 43.8 cm). Metropolitan Museum of Art, gift of Felix M. Warburg and his family, 1941 (41.1.31).

The William Kissam Vanderbilt Jr. House

It is appropriate to end this section on the progeny of the Petit Château with the house next door to it, which was built for William Kissam Vanderbilt Jr. He was the youngest of the three children born to Alva and William K. Vanderbilt, his siblings being Harold and Consuelo. Whereas Harold is best remembered as a yachtsman, William K. Jr.'s games were whist and bridge; he published two books on the latter, *Contract Bridge* (1929) and *New Contract Bridge* (1930). But he too was a yachtsman of note, building the *Enterprise*, which defeated Sir Thomas Lipton's *Shamrock V* in the America's Cup race of 1930. His interest in the sea was genuine; after serving in the U.S. Navy during World War I, he turned his attention to navigational studies and to ma-

Figure 214. Giovanni Boldini, *Virginia Graham Fair, Mrs. William Kissam Vanderbilt, Jr.*, ca. 1900. Oil on canvas, 80 × 45 in. (203.8 × 114.0 cm). Fine Arts Museums of San Francisco, Calif., gift of Mrs. Vanderbilt Adams (67.31.1). Next to John Singer Sargent, Boldini was the favorite portrait painter of the Gilded Age, especially for portraits of Society women such as Elizabeth Drexel Lehr (figure 112, p. 169), Consuelo Vanderbilt, Duchess of Marlborough, and Virginia Graham Fair Vanderbilt.

rine biology and engineering. His varied interests also found an outlet in the automobile when it first appeared, and in 1904 he founded the Vanderbilt Cup Automobile races that were held in Nassau County, Long Island.

But Vanderbilt was far more than a wealthy playboy with expensive diversions. After graduating from Harvard University he went to work for the company founded by his great-grandfather—the New York Central Railroad. By 1918 he was its president.

In 1899 William Kissam Jr. married Virginia Fair (figure 214). She was the sister of Tessie Oelrichs, for whom Stanford White had designed Rosecliff at Newport, and the daughter of James Graham Fair, who had struck it rich—big time rich—in mining ventures in the West.

For the newly married couple, Stanford White designed a house, in 1904, on Fifth Avenue between 52nd and 53rd, on a plot adjoining the elder Vanderbilts' Petit Château (figure 215). It was completed in 1907, by which date the house next door had become an architectural legend. Richard Morris Hunt's house of 1882 being the respected landmark that it was (figure 67, p. 111), White had the sensitivity to make the one he designed defer to it in its style. Stanford White did not often work in the French Late Gothic–Renaissance transitional style, and no doubt did so only out of respect for the distinguished neighbor of the one he was designing. The house for the younger Vanderbilts was considerably smaller than that for the elders, but White made certain features line up with its larger neighbor, thereby establishing some degree of continuity between them. In addition, White chose building materials to achieve a harmony between the two buildings, for he employed a limestone similar in color and texture to what Hunt had used some thirty years earlier.

There are differences in the exteriors, however. The older house was four stories high, the newer one was five stories, but White was careful to retain a similarity of scale nevertheless. He turned to a more classicized form of late Gothic, whereas the classical element is hardly present in Hunt's house. Also, White could not resist incorporating extraordinary areas of decorative detail, around the street-level doorway, for example, and in the main dormer on the Fifth Avenue facade. Moreover, Hunt's design was characterized by a delightful, fantasy-like picturesque quality with its little towers and such, while White's relied on a more sober, classicized arrangement.

The interior was sumptuously furnished, as one would expect considering that the patron was the son of Willy K. and Alva, who had furnished such places as Marble House as well as the mansion next door, places where young William had grown up. And although Stanford White was murdered in 1906, the year before the house was finished, he no doubt had designed interiors for it that were as opulent as the young Vanderbilts could afford. But the house was not destined to stand for long, for in less than two decades—in 1925—it was demolished to make way for a commercial property. Today the Tishman Building occupies the site of 666 Fifth Avenue.

Not all of the grand houses of the Gilded Age followed the pattern of the Petit Château, but a significant number did. In 1882 it represented a turning point both in the concept of domestic architecture for all that Society ruled, and in the career of one of America's most important architects, Richard Morris Hunt. One can but wonder if Hunt and Alva and William Kissam Vanderbilt fully realized at the time of its dedication—at that famous ball in March of 1883—what an impressive progeny it would have in the ensuing decades.

The Progeny of the Villard Houses

If the Petit Château was the wellspring for numerous millionaires' mansions in the late Gothic–early French Renaissance mode, so the Villard Houses were the fountainhead for a classical revival (figure 164). When Richard Morris Hunt referred to the Gilded Age's new tycoons of finance, commerce, and industry as the new Medici, he was comparing them, in terms of power and patronage within their society, with the greatest of Italian families of the fifteenth century who were not royalty, but merchants and moneylenders. Bernard Berenson noted in his first book the relationship between America and Italy during the Renaissance: "The spirit which animates us was anticipated by the spirit of the Renaissance. . . . That spirit seems like the small rough model after which ours is being fashioned."[8]

Even the term "American Renaissance" has become one employed by scholars and critics in their analyses of a certain sector of the socioeconomic and cultural life of the United States in the years from about 1885 to around 1915. In 1979–80 an exhibition presented at the Brooklyn Museum, a classical building designed by McKim, Mead and White, focused on an America which, in the Gilded Age, drew heavily from the art forms created by the Italian Renaissance of the fifteenth and sixteenth centuries, and from the original sources for that movement, the art of ancient Greece and Rome. One of the authors of the catalogue for the Brooklyn show wrote that the term "American Renaissance" concerned "the identification by many Americans—painters, sculptors, architects, craftsmen, scholars, collectors, politicians, financiers, and industrialists—with the period of the European Renaissance and the feeling that the Renaissance spirit had been captured again in the United States."[9]

If the times generally were being compared to those centuries of the Italian Renaissance, so was the firm of McKim, Mead and White in particular, for McKim was equated with

Figure 215. Stanford White, Virginia and William Kissam Vanderbilt Jr., residence, 666 Fifth Avenue, New York City, 1905. Museum of the City of New York. William Kissam Vanderbilt Sr. long lamented that he had not purchased the entire block, between 52nd and 53rd streets on Fifth Avenue, to protect his Petit Château from unwanted encroachment. But as it turned out his son, William K. Jr., and his wife, Virginia, became his next-door neighbors. Indeed, the house that Stanford White designed for them was an homage to the Petit Château, complementing it in style yet bowing to it in grandeur. The address, 666 Fifth Avenue, is well known to New Yorkers.

Bramante and White was seen as the reincarnation of Benvenuto Cellini. The spirit of the Italian Renaissance was in the air, and McKim, Mead and White seized on it to produce a solution for the reorganization of the great cities of the Gilded Age. The design of their buildings drew heavily from the architecture of ancient Rome and the Renaissance to express the ambitions, power, and self-image of America's new millionaire society. With a chest-thumping bravado that was worthy of the age they served, McKim, Mead and White set out to equal the Baths of Caracalla with their own Pennsylvania Station, with its iron and glass shed encapsulated within a classical shell. McKim imposed a grand classical order and logic on an urbanscape that was lurching out of control, and White adorned it with beautiful Roman or Renaissance details.

All of this began with the Villard Houses on Madison Avenue, and the firm's draftsman, Joseph Wells, deserves much credit for devising the architectural style that would, in its versatility, serve so well in the designing of gentlemen's clubs or train stations, art institutions or department stores, public libraries or private homes.

McKim, Mead and White and the Skyscraper

A brief digression regarding the skyscraper is necessary for these were the very years during which the tall building began to soar above the urban horizon. The tall office building was not the only type of skyscraper, for the high-rise apartment building was also a result of the technology centered around the elevator and the steel frame. But there was resistance to stacking millionaires one on top of the other, at first anyway, for the tall apartment building carried connotations of the tenements that occupied block upon block of the city's poorer neighborhoods and ghettos. The great moguls of finance, commerce, and industry almost unanimously rejected apartment dwelling in the Gilded Age, and so did their younger generation. While a few might take a resident apartment in one of the great new hotels—such as The Plaza—the ultra-wealthy chose to erect great mansions on Fifth Avenue or on Madison, and the young scions built sumptuous townhouses on the cross streets. Still, the question must be asked: What was the relationship of McKim, Mead and White insofar as the skyscraper was concerned?

McKim, Mead and White's neo-Roman-Renaissance mode has been criticized for never coming to grips with one of the major architectural forms of the day, the skyscraper. The firm did, in fact, on occasion, take up that challenge, but in truth, the skyscraper form was foreign to the humanistic scale within which the firm preferred to work. As designers they sensed intuitively that it would be unnatural to try to apply the forms and spirit of Roman and Renaissance architecture to the soaring thrust of the tall building and the new spirit of technology enframed within glass and steel. So they left it to others to evolve the structural and aesthetic solutions for the skyscraper, while they went about their business of creating an environment that laid a mantle of dignity over that impellent dynamo known as the Gilded Age.

That was precisely what McKim, Mead and White saw as its mission, indeed, its obligation. It would be for others to create an architectural environment that reflected an age of iron, steel, and glass, of powerful steam engines, screaming locomotives and roaring motor cars, of noisy, dirty factories and thousands of blackened, smoke-belching gigantic chimney stacks—in short, the crass, raging energy of the Industrial Revolution. Indeed, the firm's purpose was to devise an architectural vocabulary that would endow such raw, dynamic industry with a dignity, even a nobility, and a self-confident, assertive expression of accomplishment. For this, McKim, Mead and White should no more be criticized than should Brunelleschi, Alberti, Bramante, and Michelangelo for adapting the architecture of Roman antiquity to the vitalizing new forces of the Renaissance.

Therefore, let the complaint of what McKim, Mead and White failed to do in the age of the skyscraper be put aside. Furthermore, in humanistic terms, the skyscraper created nearly as many problems as it solved. Providing the solution to those very humanistic concerns within a virtually exploding megalopolis was the avowed intent of the firm. The problems inherent with the rise of skyscraper after skyscraper were openly declared during the Gilded Age, as when Elsie de Wolfe wrote that it took her and her companion a long time to make up their minds to desert their little house off Gramercy Park that had belonged to Washington Irving: "The skyscrapers put the finishing touch to our dilemma. Year after year they had encroached upon us, cutting off air, shutting out all the sunlight. Our chimneys, at the bottom of a well created by two towering giants, one on each side of us, refused to draw. The traffic made it impossible for us to sleep at night."[10] Ernest Flagg, one of the leading Beaux-Arts architects at the turn of the century, voiced the anti-skyscraper sentiment eloquently when he wrote that the invention of the elevator had given Americans the ability to build ever higher, no matter what the consequences to humanistic urbanistic values such as light, air, easy movement, and so on. The coming of the elevator, Flagg wrote, "opened a new field to American genius," and, he continued, ". . . our architects for some years have been trying to solve the impossible problem of building structures all out of proportion to the width of the streets and at the same time shall be successful as works of art." Then he touched on the very issue of humanism that concerned McKim, Mead and White:

> In a more civilized community where the arts are fostered, such greed on the part of the landowners to secure more than their legitimate share of light and space at the expense of their neighbors and the public in general, would have been promptly suppressed; not so here. With us it is allowed to go on without let or hinderance until some day we shall awake to the fact that to continue in this course means the conversion of our streets into dismal ravines and the congestion of traffic in thoroughfares already too contracted. Even now an irreparable evil has been committed and the city has been permanently disfigured by these monstrous overgrown structures which, ugly in themselves, dwarf into insignificance and injuriously affect the appearance and value of all neighboring buildings of more modest and reasonable proportions.[11]

Flagg then observed that in Paris a respect for humanistic scale had been maintained, and that Americans should learn from that example.

A strong sentiment for the continuation of European culture persisted in the United States at the turn of the century. Edith Wharton and Ogden Codman, for example, declared as much when they wrote that in our quest for originality we are constrained by a Western tradition that extends over two thousand years: "Does any but the most inexperienced architect really think that he can ever rid himself of such an inheritance? He may mutilate or misapply the component parts of his design, but he cannot originate a whole new architectural alphabet. . . . The styles especially suited to modern life . . . [are] those prevailing in Italy since 1500, in France from the time of Louis XIV, and in England since the introduction of the Italian manner by Inigo Jones."[12]

Another critic—writing in 1910, from a pro-Beaux-Arts, anti-Modernist bias—took up the same issue and declared that while the time may come when originality in American architecture may be appropriate,

> for the present, originality is necessarily revolutionary; and there is no meaning in a revolution without an established order from which to revolt. Carrère and Hastings joined McKim, Mead and White in an attempt to establish an order, and they looked in the same direction for the necessary material. They understood that a local American tradition must be founded upon an antecedent European tradition, because acceptable architectural forms must be served up with a garniture of splendid associations and of unimpeachable authority. The notion that Americans can . . . dispense with such associations and create a group of local realistic forms, based upon the peculiar function and structure of American buildings, can receive no countenance from a study of architectural history.[13]

Accumulatively, such statements declare a manifesto for the pro-humanistic, anti-skyscraper sector at the turn of the century, a sector that favored the continuum of Western tradition over the rise of iconoclastic, even anarchistic modernism. It is not intended, here, to denounce modernism or to belabor the dehumanizing factor of the ultimate expression of modernism in architecture—the eighty-five-story-high glass box. The point is that in the decades of the Gilded Age, many architects such as Ernest Flagg, Carrère and Hastings, Charles P. H. Gilbert, Richard Morris Hunt, and McKim, Mead and White had a positive, sound, legitimate foundation for their art that was based in humanism, Beaux-Arts theory, and eclectic historicism. That art should not be condemned as anti-progress, as attempting to forestall the inevitable march of modernism with tired old, worn-out academic architectural solutions. To be sure, that art had a purpose: To impose order on the urbanscape, to retain time-honored humanistic values of the Western tradition, and to encapsulate their own hyperdynamic age within a mantle of dignity and culture.

Although the Renaissance palazzo style commenced in domestic architecture, with the Villard Houses of 1885, it evolved, during the years that followed, in other types of buildings—in libraries, gentlemen's clubs, art museums, even commercial buildings. Its fullest statements are found in such commissions as the Boston Public Library (1887–98), the World's Columbian Exposition in Chicago (1893), and Columbia University in New York City (1893–1913), all of which are not domestic. The same is true of a number of clubs in New York City that the firm designed—the Century Club (1891), the Harvard Club (1893), the Metropolitan Club (1894), and the University Club (1899), for example. Of commercial buildings, the New York Herald Building (1893) for James Gordon Bennett could be mentioned, or the Gorham Building, or the Tiffany Building.

In the aforementioned structures the Roman Renaissance palazzo form became the trademark style for the firm of McKim, Mead and White. But following the completion of the Villard Houses in 1885, some time elapsed before an actual movement could be identified as the classical palazzo style in domestic architecture. That occurred mainly after 1900.

The Morton Plant House

The classical Renaissance style developed by McKim, Mead and White spread rapidly among other architects, just as the late Gothic–early French Renaissance mode of Richard Morris Hunt was quickly picked up by a number of his colleagues. They recognized in it a suitable style for domestic architecture and appreciated the fact that it was an urban form, having been employed in Renaissance cities such as Rome, Venice, Florence, and Genoa.

The Vanderbilts owned considerable property on Fifth Avenue north of 50th Street, not only as parcels upon which to erect their own mansions but also as protection against commercial encroachment. William Kissam Vanderbilt, for example, owned the southeast corner lot at 52nd Street, which he sold to Morton Plant in 1902 with the stipulation that the property remain residential for twenty-five years.

Morton Plant had inherited over $20 million from his father, Henry Bradley Plant, an officer of numerous corporations and chairman of the Southern Express Company of Memphis, Tennessee. As a young man Morton went to work at his father's firm, rising to vice president, an office he held until 1902, proving himself a capable administrator. He continued as a member of the board of directors of several companies and banks, among them the Chicago, Indianapolis and Louisville Railroad. Plant was a noted yachtsman and owner of the Philadelphia franchise of the National Baseball League, and he was a prominent clubman in New York City. Always maintaining close ties with Connecticut, where he was born, he was the founder of the Connecticut College for Women in New Haven.

After he bought the Vanderbilt lot, directly across from the William Henry Vanderbilt house and diagonally across the intersection from William Kissam Vanderbilt's Petit Château, Plant determined to build himself a fine mansion (figure 216). To design it he called on the architect Robert W. Gibson (1854–1927).

Figure 216. Robert W. Gibson, Morton Plant residence, Fifth Avenue and 52nd Street, New York City, 1905, now Cartier's. New York Public Library. Born in Essex, England, and trained at the Royal Academy in London, Gibson came to the United States when his design won the competition for the Episcopal Cathedral in Albany. In 1888 he moved to New York City, where he established a successful practice.

Gibson—who was born in Essex, England, and trained at the Royal Academy in London—settled in Albany, New York, about 1880 and began his practice; his most notable achievement there was All Saints' Cathedral, which attracted considerable attention to the young architect.[14] In 1888 he moved to New York City, where one of his first important commissions was for the Seawanhaka Corinthian Yacht Club, at Oyster Bay, New York, of which Morton Plant was commodore. The two men came to know each other at that time. Among Gibson's other major commissions were a building for the Bronx Botanical Gardens and a United States Clearing House, the latter a Baroque, Beaux-Arts extravaganza a la the World's Columbian Exposition in Chicago 1893.

Gibson created a classical block form with a horizontal roofline—that is, not a pitched roof of the Gothic mode or the Mansard roof of Parisian boulevard architecture. The building terminated in a balustrade and a large cornice, the rich decoration of which spreads down into the top row of windows. The rectangular windows have squared-off headers throughout, with the exception of the one arched header above the central entrance on 52nd Street; originally this portal was a carriage entrance. Gibson incorporated a temple front as part of the facade, rising above the corbelled balcony, with pilasters and a triangular pediment. The building is divided into three levels: the rusticated base, the central section of three stories with smooth wall surfaces but quoining at the corners, and the balustraded cornice. The whole is composed of a thoroughly classical vocabulary, but the parts are assembled with a Beaux-Arts originality and freedom while generally respecting basic classical tenets.

Gibson had created a beautiful building in the palazzo mode. But in time an all-too-familiar problem arose. By 1916 Plant could no longer endure the hustle and bustle of commercialism that had encroached on his fine mansion. He asked Vanderbilt to release him from their agreement. William Kissam did and even bought the house from Plant, who moved up to Fifth Avenue and 86th Street. The next year, Vanderbilt gave in to the inevitable and leased the building to Cartier's, the prestigious jewelry concern. And such it is today, the house having survived by becoming a commercial site instead of being replaced by one, as happened to so many of the great mansions on the Avenue.

The George Gould Mansion, New York City

Jay Gould, Commodore Vanderbilt's old adversary, was never accepted by Society, but his children were. As mentioned earlier, one daughter, Anna, married into European nobility—twice, in fact. Helen, another daughter, was also

admitted into the inner circle of fashionable New York, as was Jay Gould's son, George.

George Jay Gould (1864–1923) decided to forego college in order to enter his father's business. There, he was carefully trained, but he never became the astute tactician that his father was, always a step or two ahead of his opponents, or the diabolic schemer who pocketed millions of dollars at the expense of both friends and enemies. Although he showed promise, George possessed a very different personality from that of Jay Gould; Henry Clews, writing when George was twenty-three years old, spoke well of him: "He possesses good abilities, has an attractive presence, and is modest and retiring in his manners. He has, thus far, made an excellent record, and the Stock Exchange was glad to admit him to membership. . . . [He] is bright and agreeable, and a good husband. If Jay Gould has made enemies, that is no reason why his son should not be popular."[15] When Jay Gould died in 1892, George became his principle heir and, on behalf of the family, the manager of the vast empire of railroads and telegraph lines that his father had assembled; alas, he was not entirely successful as the head of the family's business enterprises.

In 1886 George married an attractive young actress named Edith M. Kingdon, who—equally surprisingly—was also accepted into a Society that normally rejected theater people. Few actresses of the Gilded Age actually landed their "stage-door Johnnies," but Edith Kingdon did, although George's parents strongly disapproved initially. However, she was vivacious, full of good humor, and a stunningly beautiful young woman, and she was eventually accepted by the Gould family. George had fallen madly in love with her, and he delighted in showering her with lavish gifts even after they married. Elizabeth Drexel Lehr remembered one of Mrs. Astor's balls where Edith appeared "in a dress of silver brocade shot with green and wearing her magnificent emeralds," creating a sensation: "Her husband . . . told Harry Lehr that he had just bought as a surprise for her some of the finest jewels in the world, the eight famous 'Peacocks' Feathers' of emeralds and diamonds which had once been the property of the Emperor of China."[16] A famous photograph of Edith shows her wearing a long rope of pearls, one of the great phenomena of her day, which Tiffany's had valued at $500,000—another gift from an adoring husband (figure 217).

The Goulds had a good family life, centered around their eight children. George built two splendid homes, one at the corner of 67th Street and Fifth Avenue, and a country place called Georgian Court in Lakewood, New Jersey. The latter, designed by Bruce Price in the late 1890s, was described as one of the most magnificent private residences in the United States.[17] Mrs. Lehr recalled with fondness her many visits there,

> for Edith was a delightful hostess, and the house and gardens were magnificent. I was always given the "Purple Guest Room" . . . and slept in the enormous marriage bed which George Gould had caused to be designed for his bride. It was a particularly hideous example of the artistic ideas of the 'eighties, and I believe [Léon] Marcotte had been paid a tremendous sum to embellish it with golden scrolls, lover's knots, entwined hearts and other appropriate devices. It reared an ungraceful head somewhere near the ceiling . . . the better to display its lavish coating of gold. Edith laughed as she drew my attention to the design of the painted frieze on its centerpiece [representing] eight cupids attending an altar of love. . . . "I shall never forget my feelings when I first saw it," she said. . . . "I just knew I should have eight children if I slept in that bed . . . and so I did!"[18]

In New York City, Edith and George had lived in a fairly modest house at the corner of Fifth Avenue and 47th Street, but when it proved inadequate for their social ambitions they moved farther uptown, to a pseudo-Gothic imitation—and a poor one at that—of the Petit Château, built on the northeast corner of Fifth and 67th Street. This, too, eventually was declared to be unsatisfactory, and by 1906 the Goulds were planning its demolition to make way for a new marble palazzo.

For their new home, the Goulds turned to fashionable architect Horace Trumbauer (1868–1938), who increasingly enjoyed the favor of Society's charmed circle. Trumbauer had started out as an office boy at one of Philadelphia's leading architectural firms, and, being a quick study, learned to be an architect in only a few years. After establishing his own office, he gained recognition with the mansion he designed for Peter A. B. Widener (1898) in Philadelphia. Soon thereafter he moved to New York, although he continued to design a variety of structures for the Quaker City—the Ritz-Carlton Hotel, for example, and the Edward Townsend Stotesbury house in nearby Chestnut Hill; the Philadelphia Free Library and the Philadelphia Museum of Art were also created from his designs. Trumbauer had scored a hit among

Figure 217. Edith Kingdon, Mrs. George J. Gould, and Kyrle Bellew, 1908. Edith Kingdon had been an actress before she caught the eye of George Jay Gould, son of Jay Gould. Their marriage infuriated George's mother, for stage women were then considered only slightly above prostitutes in the social scheme of things. But Jay Gould liked his daughter-in-law, and she eventually won over New York's High Society as well. Many years later she returned to the stage for a one-day performance in a play titled *Mrs. Van Vechten's Divorce Dance*, a benefit program that was covered in *The New York Times* in January 1908. It was held at the Hotel Plaza, and in this illustration Mrs. Gould is shown on stage with fellow-actor Kyrle Bellew. She wears a rope of pearls, of which she was very proud, for pearls were then rare and rivaled diamonds in value.

Society's golden circle as the designer of The Elms (1899–1901) in Newport for the "coal king," Ernest Berwind, and in 1912 he would create the James B. Duke mansion (later, the Doris Duke mansion-cum-Institute of Fine Arts) at 78th and Fifth Avenue. At The Elms a penchant for the delicacy of eighteenth-century French architecture is obvious, and this characteristic frequently shows up in Trumbauer's work, even in buildings otherwise judged to be of the Italian Renaissance palazzo type.

Figure 218. Horace Trumbauer, George J. Gould residence, Fifth Avenue and 67th Street, New York City, 1906. Museum of the City of New York.

Edith and George Gould moved into their new home in 1908 (figure 218). The simplified block-form house rose to five stories, although the top floor was hidden from street level by a classical balustrade that crowned the fourth story. The design was in the palazzo mode, but its classical severity was softened by delicate touches of decoration—as in the ornamental swags below the third-story windows and in the elaborate cornice. But the decoration notwithstanding, there was a classical respect for the plane of the wall and the cubic form of the block. Although the lower level was boldly rusticated, as were many Italian Renaissance palaces, the three levels above it were smooth. The several levels were united by the quoining that continued the rustication of the lower story. The entrance to the mansion, on 67th Street, was through a large archway that symmetrically anchored the central axis, with two bays of windows on either side.

The interiors were lavishly adorned, and like so many of his circle, George collected paintings to grace the more important rooms. For example, from Joe Duveen he acquired Thomas Gainsborough's large full-length portrait of Karl Frederick Abel, the celebrated musician and composer (figure 219). The portrait had once belonged to the subject's patroness, Queen Charlotte of England, and therefore held the appeal of having belonged to royalty.

Life was going quite nicely as the Goulds took up residence in their new Fifth Avenue palazzo. But then things began to fall apart. In business affairs, George Gould was not the mastermind that his father had been. In contests with Edward H. Harriman of the Union Pacific and with the Pennsylvania Railroad, Gould was badly outmaneuvered. Even his siblings turned on him for mismanaging the Gould estate, and he was stripped by the courts of his executor's role. One by one, he had lost the several railroads of the "Gould System" as well as the Western Union Telegraph Company. Edith died in 1921 and the following year George married Guinevere Jeanne Sinclair, a mistress he had kept in discrete but fashionable seclusion since 1913; he acknowledged the three children he had had with her. They withdrew from Society, of course, and rented an estate in Scotland. While traveling in France, George came down with pneumonia and died in May of 1923.

The mansion at 67th Street did not stand empty for very long, for it was soon rented by Alice, Mrs. Cornelius Vanderbilt II, whose great house overlooking the Plaza was demolished in 1926. The house was next occupied by Alice Vanderbilt's daughter, the Countess Laszlo Széchenyi, as her New York residence.

Figure 219. Thomas Gainsborough, *Karl Frederick Abel*, 1777. Oil on canvas, 88 × 58 in. (223.5 × 147.3 cm). Huntington Library and Art Gallery, San Marino, Calif. Ex coll., George J. Gould.

The Edward S. Harkness Mansion

In his day, Edward S. Harkness (1874–1940) was one of the most generous benefactors to the causes of education, medicine, and the arts (figure 220). He was the son of Stephen V. Harkness, who financed John D. Rockefeller at a time when the latter was about to go bankrupt, thereby turning a $70,000 investment into millions of dollars and becoming the wealthiest of Rockefeller's partners in Standard Oil. Born in Cleveland, Ohio, young Harkness attended St. Paul's School before going to Yale University, where his interest in art was awakened, along with interests in Shakespeare, French literature, and Egyptology.

Figure 220. *Edward S. Harkness*, ca. 1925. Charcoal drawing. Columbia University Health Sciences Library.

Harkness inherited a large fortune as his portion of his father's estate, which he increased through his own efforts in business and finance. In addition, in 1918 he was bequeathed $60 million upon the death of his brother, Charles, and another $93 million from the will of his mother. Altogether, it was estimated that he had given away well over $100 million to charities and cultural, educational, and medical institutions. Yale University, for example, received a gift of $12 million for the construction of Harkness Quadrangle and Tower. Harvard University was given an equal amount for dormitory buildings; one of his favorite projects was creating situations at colleges that brought students and faculty into closer contact, often by having them co-inhabit dormitories. It was also Harkness's money that brought about the merger of Columbia University Medical School with Presbyterian Hospital in New York City.

Insofar as the arts were concerned, he served on the board of trustees of the Metropolitan Museum of Art during J. Pierpont Morgan's tenure as president there, and was a generous sponsor of that institution as well (figure 221). For example, his interest in Egyptology continued and he visited the land of the Nile in the company of Howard Carter, the discoverer of King Tut's tomb; Lord Carnarvon had sponsored Carter's archaeological expeditions, and when Harkness heard that Carnarvon's own collection of Egyptian artifacts was going to come on the market, he bought the whole collection and presented it to the Metropolitan Museum of Art. Although he was an officer or director of several corporations—such as the Southern Pacific and the New York Central railroads—he always claimed that philanthropy was his real profession. He was shy and rather diffident, usually refusing to attend the ceremonies inaugurating new buildings or programs that his money had made possible.

Harkness built his mansion on the northeast corner of Fifth Avenue and 75th Street, with James Gamble Rogers (1867–1947) as the architect. Rogers was, at the time, just getting his career under way. After graduating from Yale University he had gone to Paris to study architecture at the École des Beaux-Arts. Back in the United States, he attracted attention with the mansion he designed for Peter G. Thomson in Hamilton, Ohio, in 1909, but he was still relatively unknown when Harkness tapped him to be the architect of his

Figure 221. *William*, hippopotamus, from the tomb of Senbi at Meir, Egyptian, XII Dynasty, ca. 1981–1885 B.C. Ceramic, blue-green faiance, height 4⅜ in. (11.2 cm). Metropolitan Museum of Art, gift of Edward S. Harkness, 1917 (17.9.1).

Fifth Avenue palazzo. Thus began a long working relationship between the two men. When Harkness gave Yale the money for the dormitory quadrangle, Rogers was selected as the architect, and he created a residential college (1916–19) based on those of Oxford and Cambridge universities in England. When Columbia University and Presbyterian Hospital in New York were united, it was Rogers who designed the new building (1923–28). Over the years Rogers became one of the leading architects of college buildings, specializing in the then popular collegiate Gothic style. Among his commissions were structures for Northwestern University in Evanston, Illinois, for New York University, and for H. Sophie Newcomb College in New Orleans, and it was he who designed Butler Library (1932–34), which terminated one end of the McKim, Mead and White campus of Columbia University in New York City. In the famous competition for the new Tribune Building in Chicago in 1922, Rogers's design received an Honorable Mention.

The grand house for Edward S. Harkness was erected on an oversized lot that measured thirty-five feet (instead of the usual twenty-five) on the avenue by one hundred feet on 75th Street (figure 222). The result was a very large and imposing structure that well deserved the title of "palazzo." Its design was, in its basic form, the requisite simplified block dominated by absolute symmetry. The entrance, on 75th Street, marked a central axis accented by a slightly protruding portico with Tuscan Order columns enframing a round-headed arch; atop the architrave was a window framed more decoratively than the others of the facade. Regularity and symmetry characterized the portions of the facade on either side of the central axis, with three bays to the left and three to the right. Typical, too, was the preservation of the wall plane, for even though there are many windows, the structural wall remains evident. Simply put, the design was an interpretation of the palazzo type found in Renaissance Rome.

The impressiveness of a mansion such as this lies not so much in its lavishness as in its monumentality and sensitivity to the true and basic principles of classical design. Although constructed of an expensive material, Tennessee marble, that is about the only concession to ostentation visible in the exterior. Domestic architecture in America prior to the Gilded Age was seldom monumental—large, perhaps, but seldom monumental. This changed with structures such as the Villard Houses and the Harkness mansion, which possessed a monumentality that is associated with, say, the Chancelleria in Rome and the Medici Palace in Florence.

If the exterior was reserved in its presentation of wealth, the interiors were lavish—again, a situation that paralleled the distinction between exterior and interior in many Italian Renaissance palaces.[19] From the entrance hall, which had figural paintings on the vaulted ceiling, one entered a reception room that extended the full length of the Fifth Avenue side, a chamber nearly thirty-five feet long, with windows overlooking Central Park. This room, done in the Louis XVI style (except for the tiger skin rug, of course), had an exquisite fireplace and overmantel, reaffirming that although the exterior was Italian Renaissance, interiors could be done in a wide variety of styles, changing from one room to another.

At the opposite end, on the first floor, was the dining room with its elaborately decorated beam ceiling. A large

tapestry, which extended nearly the length of one wall, was hung above an ornately carved sideboard, and the chairs were done in tapestry. A superb Oriental carpet covered the floor. The east wall had a window that would otherwise look out on the solid brick wall of the adjoining house (the Burden mansion), except for Kenyon Cox's window of opaque glass with its lovely design of a sea maiden wrought in a leaded pattern. The dining room had a handsomely carved fireplace with an eighteenth-century English portrait, said to be by George Romney, in the overmantel. Furnishings of a room such as this—in which most objects were of ancient European vintage—represented a fulfillment of what Stanford White had begun many years earlier in his decorating of the Villard interiors and the major rooms of the William C. Whitney house.

On the second floor, the library, above the reception room and like it, looked out on the park (figure 223). This room, too, was richly furnished in European antiques, with tapestries on the walls and Oriental carpets on the floor. The library also served as an art gallery, for in it were displayed a number of Harkness's French and English landscape and genre paintings, paintings of exceptionally high quality. There was, for example, Hans Holbein the Younger's *Portrait of a Member of the Wedigh Family* (ca. 1532), John Constable's *Salisbury Cathedral from the Bishop's Grounds* (ca. 1820), and Sir Thomas Lawrence's *Elizabeth Farren* (1790), all of which were bequeathed to the Metropolitan Museum of Art (figures 224–226).

At the eastern end of the second floor was the most sumptuously decorated room in the house, the music room, with its ornately coffered and gilded ceiling, which incorporated a number of allegorical paintings (figures 227 and 228). Several large paintings, often depicting musical themes, graced the decoratively patterned walls. In rooms such as this the eye was greeted everywhere with encoded symbols of sumptuousness and wealth that were intended to convey the idea of making life itself a work of art.

The author of a 1910 article about the Harkness mansion made an interesting

Figure 222. James Gamble Rogers, Edward S. Harkness residence, Fifth Avenue and 75th Street, New York City, ca. 1909. Photographs of the Harkness residence are taken from *Architectural Record* 27 (May 1910), pp. 382–99. Although trained as an architect at Yale University, Rogers was a midwesterner and began his practice in Chicago, where he was a friend of Frank Lloyd Wright, although Rogers preferred Beaux-Arts classicism to modernism. When he moved to New York City, he was still an unknown young architect, until he received the commission for the Harkness house. That work launched his career. The Harknesses wanted something in the reserved, Roman style—perhaps because they had seen the great Baroque extravaganza that Senator William A. Clark had built only two blocks away (see figure 244, p. 358).

Figure 223 (opposite). James Gamble Rogers, library, Edward S. Harkness residence, Fifth Avenue and 75th Street, New York City, ca. 1909. Courtesy of the Commonwealth Foundation.

Figure 224. Hans Holbein the Younger, *Portrait of a Member of the Wedigh Family*, 1532. Oil on wood panel, 16½ × 12¼ in. (42.2 × 32.4 cm). Metropolitan Museum of Art, gift of Edward S. Harkness, 1940 (50.135.4).

Figure 225. John Constable, *Salisbury Cathedral from the Bishop's Grounds*, ca. 1820. Oil on canvas, 34½ × 44 in. (88 × 111.8 cm). Metropolitan Museum of Art, bequest of Mary Stillman Harkness, 1950 (50.145.8).

Figure 226. Sir Thomas Lawrence, *Elizabeth Farren, Later Countess of Derby*, 1790. Oil on canvas, 94 × 57 in. (238.6 × 146.1 cm). Metropolitan Museum of Art, bequest of Edward S. Harkness, 1940 (40.135.5).

Figure 227 (top). James Gamble Rogers, music room, Edward S. Harkness residence, Fifth Avenue and 75th Street, New York City, ca. 1909. From *Architectural Record* 27 (May 1910), p. 390.

Figure 228 (bottom). Ceiling of the music room, Edward S. Harkness residence, Fifth Avenue and 75th Street, New York City, ca. 1909. From *Architectural Record* 27 (May 1910), p. 391.

comment: "It is imperative that a house of this type should not only be costly," he wrote, "but should look so," and he continued,

> It has become customary among Americans that their houses should be expressive of abundance and wealth. They usually desire also that this effect of opulence should be conveyed in an architecturally meritorious manner. . . . Such people are, as a rule, frankly proud of their wealth. It is the indication and proof of their success and their personal efficiency. They do not want necessarily to display it, but neither do they want to conceal it. . . . The majority of their associates have built houses which are frankly luxurious; and when they build a house of their own they naturally desire that it also should, in its appearance, constitute a celebration of their success.[20]

This, in its own way, was a forthright manifesto of the right of the wealthy to enjoy their wealth by surrounding themselves with domestic architecture and interiors that bespeak of their success and their indulgence in the finest that life has to offer. But, Edward S. Harkness would surely add, it is also imperative for the wealthy to give back to society through generous benefactions.

The Otto Kahn Mansion

Otto Hermann Kahn (1867–1934), the son of a prominent banker of Mannheim, Germany, grew up in a cultured home where he listened to his father's guests discuss art and literature, "heard young ladies sing Mendelssohn's 'Lieder ohne Worte' and long-haired pianists play Chopin and Beethoven and Schumann [in rooms containing] fine paintings and statuary. He heard his parents discuss . . . Heine and Schiller and Goethe. . . . The elder Kahn threw his home open to artists and literati."[21] Young Otto studied music—the violin and cello—as an avocation, and by age seventeen he had written two tragedies in blank verse.

Kahn began his career as an office boy in a bank in Karlsruhe. When he was twenty-one he joined a banking firm in London, working his way up to assistant manager before accepting an offer from Speyer and Company, then a leader in the financial world, to work in their New York office. Within three years after his arrival he joined the renowned banking firm of Kuhn, Loeb and Company, one of the major financial houses of that day. On behalf of Kuhn, Loeb, he became a valued adviser and financier for the Edward H. Harriman railroad enterprises, his shrewd mind proving essential in the reorganization of such vast holdings as the Union Pacific and the Baltimore and Ohio railroads. In 1896 Otto married Addie Wolff, daughter of one of the senior partners of Kuhn, Loeb, and the next year he became a partner of the firm. But when he was interviewed some years later, the reporter concluded that Mr. Kahn would much rather discuss art than dollars.

Interests outside the business world centered around his long-standing love of music. He became a stockholder of the Metropolitan Opera Company in 1903 and was elected chairman of the board eight years later; Kahn was named president of the company in 1918, a post he held until a few years before his death. Upon his advice, Arturo Toscanini was brought over from La Scala in Milan, Italy, to become the Met's conductor. Over the years Kahn remained the major financial benefactor of the Metropolitan Opera.

His democratic ideals led Kahn to believe that government should support the arts and that the arts should be available to all economic levels of the citizenry; when, in his opinion, government failed in its support, individuals should come forward to provide it. His philosophy on this subject, which was clearly stated as a credo of *noblesse oblige* for the successful financiers and industrialists of the Gilded Age, was similar to that espoused by Andrew Carnegie in his *Gospel of Wealth*, but addressing support for the arts specifically:

> No life is quite complete . . . which does not include a responsiveness to the call of beauty and art. Maecenases are needed for the dramatic stage, the operatic stage, the concert stage, for conservatories and art academies, for the encouragement and support of American writers, painters, sculptors, decorators—in fact, for all things which in Europe are done by princes, governments and communities. . . . To strive toward fostering the art life of the country, toward counteracting harsh materialism, toward relieving the monotony and strain of the people's everyday life by . . . creating opportunities to awaken in them the love and the understanding of that which is beautiful and inspiring, and aversion and contempt for that which is vulgar, cheap and degrading is, I think, a humanitarian effort eminently worth making.[22]

Kahn's generosity was directed in many directions, from a substantial gift in 1928 that allowed resumption of the restoration work on the Parthenon in Athens to the funding of prize money awarded to African-American artists in New York. Aside from his main interests in the Metropolitan Opera Company and the New York Philharmonic Orchestra, he served innumerable organizations; he was, for example, a trustee of the

Carnegie Institute of Technology and a member of the visiting committee of the Department of Art and Archaeology at Princeton University. He was, in brief, a modern-day Medici prince, for whom it was natural to wish to possess a palace.

Otto Kahn had prospered. Then, when his father-in-law died in 1916, Wolff's estate left $16 million to his two daughters; shortly after that, Addie's sister died, and Addie became the recipient of the entire amount. By 1916–18, therefore, the Otto Kahns were financially prepared to spend a sizable fortune to build a large palazzo on Fifth Avenue (figure 230). They were fortunate to find an oversized corner lot, measuring 145 feet along the avenue by 100 feet deep, just across 91st Street from Andrew Carnegie's great mansion, for Carnegie had bought up much of the surrounding property to protect his own site from unwanted commercial encroachment. Kahn knew the area well, from Felix Warburg, who was also a partner in Kuhn, Loeb and who had built his version of the Petit Château only one block north of the 91st Street lot; Warburg's architect was Charles P. H. Gilbert.

The Kahns selected J. Armstrong Stenhouse, an Englishman, as their architect, but Gilbert assisted him. Referring to the Kahn mansion, a contemporary critic wrote that "a rare perception of the ideals actuating the architect of the Renaissance stimulates the imagination of Mr. Stenhouse, without fettering it. His work is a virile reaction to sixteenth century [Italian] stylistic influences, venerated and thoroughly comprehended." The author then noted that Stenhouse had spent many years in Italy, studying specifically the architecture of the sixteenth century "with intense enthusiasm."[23] As with the Villard Houses, the design of the exterior was based on the Chancelleria, a sixteenth-century Roman palace. However, unlike McKim, Mead and White's palazzo prototype, which had a brownstone exterior, the Kahn mansion was faced with St. Quentin limestone, imported from France.

The design produced by Stenhouse and Gilbert resulted in what was arguably the quintessential Renaissance palazzo of the Gilded Age. If the Villard Houses stand at the beginning as the progenitor, the Kahn mansion exists at the end of the era as the culmination. It is truly a great house, its design imbued with a grandeur and nobility. Perhaps because of its enormous scale, it suggests an indebtedness to the several gentlemen's clubs designed in earlier years by McKim, Mead and White in the classical palazzo form.

The base is massive and boldly rusticated with relatively small arched windows. Above that is the grand floor—what the Italians call the *piano nobile*—which is evident in the exterior in the very tall windows that have alternating arched and pedimental headers. The rustication decreases at this level, and a delicate relief is given to the plane of the wall by the application of double pilasters between the windows and at the corners. A pronounced simplicity dominates the third and fourth stories, with a severe treatment of the rectangular fenestration. The entire massive block is capped by a handsome, though not large, cornice.

The 91st Street facade has two arched entrances that are cleanly cut into the massive wall; these allow a carriage to enter and exit a central courtyard. Many an Italian Renaissance palace encircled an open space within itself, designed in that fashion to protect the residents from the unruly life of the streets and even from the assault of enemies; in the Kahn mansion the courtyard allows light to enter interior rooms that

Figure 229. Otto Kahn. Photograph, ca. 1920. Library of Congress, Washington, D.C. Otto Kahn—always dapper, impeccably attired, his mustache neatly trimmed—was an international figure. Born in Mannheim, Germany, he began his career in banking there before moving to England, where he became a British citizen. But in 1893 he settled in New York City and three years later married Addie Wolff. In 1897 he became a member of the firm of Kuhn, Loeb and Company, where his colleagues were Paul and Felix Warburg and Jacob Schiff. Kahn became a leading figure in industrial financing and was heavily involved in the reorganization of several major railroads.

would otherwise be windowless. The design of the courtyard is dominated by classical components, with a beautiful arcade of round-headed Roman arches set on slender shafts, reminiscent of the work of the brilliant quattrocento Florentine architect, Brunelleschi.

The scale of the house itself is almost overwhelming. The major rooms were on the second story and were furnished with lovely antiques. The five rooms at this level—the library, the Italian room, the French salon, the dining room, and a music room—were palatial in scale, for the ceilings were twenty feet high. The two floors above the *piano nobile* contained fifteen bedrooms, each with its own bath, and there were forty servants' rooms, suggesting the extent of the staff needed for running a house that size. Kitchen and laundry facilities were located in the basement.

A newspaper reporter recalled that Otto Kahn's house, like that of his parents in Mannheim, was "thrown open to artists and art lovers," adding that Kahn "was a connoisseur of rare and fine paintings [and that he] owned one of the most splendid art collections in this country."[24] The walls of the major rooms on the second floor were hung with beautiful works by Old Masters, among which were a family group by Franz Hals and *Three Children of Captain Little* by George Romney. The art dealer René Gimpel remembered the "magnificent private mansion newly built, Italian Renaissance [with its] superb pictures and art objects." Gimpel also noted that Otto Kahn had commenced collecting by buying eighteenth-century French paintings, "starting with a fake Nattier, or rather an old copy, the original of which is in Stockholm. . . . He subsequently acquired two Paters and a Boucher tapestry, *La Halte de Chasse*; but his wife pushed her husband toward Dutch and then toward the Netherlandish primitives." Gimpel also recalled that Kahn had purchased, in 1906, "a wonderful Gerard David from me for $10,000."[25] Kahn also owned Carpaccio's *St. Eustace*, which he had acquired from Wentworth Castle in England; after his death it was sold to a Swiss collector, Baron Thyssen.

Otto Kahn died suddenly, of a heart attack, while attending a meeting at the offices of Kuhn, Loeb and Company, on 29 March 1934. He was survived by his widow and their two sons and two daughters. The decision to dispose of the great mansion was made almost immediately, and by May arrangements had been made to sell it to a Roman Catholic organization, the Academy of the Sacred Heart. At first several neighbors—among them Mrs. Andrew Carnegie, Mrs. Emily Vanderbilt Hammond, and Mrs. Florence Adele Burden—raised mild objectives, but the lawyers soon worked things out, satisfying one of the main concerns by promising never to erect additional floors atop the building.

The family took some of the furnishings—things that had sentimental value or would work into their own homes, and then a sale of the rest was held. Mrs. Kahn took an apartment at Sutton Place, and the Kahn mansion became a school for two hundred girls. It continues in that capacity today.

Figure 230. Charles P. H. Gilbert, Otto Kahn residence, northeast corner of Fifth Avenue and 91st Street, New York City, 1918. Museum of the City of New York, Wurts Collection. The Kahn mansion—the design of which was based on that of the Papal Chancelleria in Rome—was the largest private home in Manhattan. Its eighty rooms were cared for by a large staff of servants. An international music patron, Kahn sponsored not only the Metropolitan Opera but also the Russian Ballet and the Paris Conservatory Orchestra, and he contributed to the restoration of the Parthenon in Athens. In his Fifth Avenue palazzo he entertained such celebrities as Arturo Toscanini, George Gershwin, and Anna Pavlova in the music room, which had a small stage upon which musicians performed; Enrico Caruso, for example, sang there as part of Kahn's daughter's coming-out festivities.

The attractiveness of the French ideal in architecture is so great that it has imposed itself all over Europe, insomuch that the new quarters of nearly all European cities are becoming imitations of Paris.

Montgomery Schuyler, "Modern Architecture," *Architectural Record*, July 1894

[In the United States] no style today is quite so "taking" with the crowd as the modern French.

Anonymous critic, *Architectural Record*, April 1902

Chapter Sixteen

Facades in the Modern French Manner

THE PEOPLE for whom the houses discussed in this chapter were built were not the original creators of great fortunes, but rather heirs to those who were. They were the great-grandsons and the great-granddaughters, the grandnieces and grand-nephews of those who had first amassed the enormous wealth of the Gilded Age. This is the generation of cousins—of Gertrude Vanderbilt, daughter of Cornelius II and Alice Gwynne, who married the boy across the street, Harry Payne Whitney; of Gertrude's cousin Consuelo, daughter of Alva and William Kissam Vanderbilt, who wed the Duke of Marlborough; of Gertrude's and Consuelo's cousins Florence Adele and Emily, daughters of Emily Vanderbilt Sloane; of their cousins Louise and Edith Shepard; of Florence Adele Sloane and her cousin Florence Twombly, a granddaughter of William Henry Vanderbilt, who married the Burden brothers, James and William, sons of the ironmaster of Troy. And there were others.

For the first time, America had developed a true leisure class—a class of men and women who seldom did daily work but sought to make an art of living. Margaret Terry Chanler loved her husband, but in her autobiography she freely admitted that he was incapable of any kind of useful work, saying that his Etonian education had "unfitted him for American life, which was no place for charming idlers; yet he was essentially American and never wished to expatriate himself, only to move about the world in search of fun and adventure, and they generally came his way."[1] And Louis Auchincloss has often described his social class with the same precision as Edith Wharton, as when he wrote of Harry Payne Whitney:

> One sees in the pages of Gertrude's diary that her husband Harry Payne Whitney's life was stained with disappointment. He never cared for business, nor did he ever find other occupations in which to use his considerable talents. There were polo and horse racing, of course, in both of which he excelled, and in his investments . . . he was gifted with a Midas touch, vastly increasing the fortune that never brought him happiness. But in the eternal round of parties that bored him there was, as for so many of his set, the solace of the bar.[2]

If there is something delightfully frivolous about the architecture considered in this chapter, it is, perhaps, an appropriate reflection of the society for whom it was built.

Almost all of the third and fourth generations of America's wealthy built fine houses between about 1890 and 1910. They did not buy the large lots right on Fifth Avenue, overlooking Central Park, but instead erected more modest (but still sumptuous) townhouses just off of the avenue, on the cross streets between about 65th and 95th streets.

The architectural styles suitable for the large corner lots that faced the open greenery of Central Park were ill-suited for adaption to the rather cramped side-street lots, which usually measured only twenty-five feet across, with the house hemmed in between abutting neighbors on both sides. So other models were sought, and the number of styles multiplied; while the great mansions on the avenue were usually done in the Italian Renaissance palazzo or the French late-Gothic/early-Renaissance modes, the smaller structures ranged in designs from late Gothic to Colonial American.

One of the most popular was the decorative Modern French form as exemplified in innumerable Parisian townhouses, their design being transported to New York in the 1890s and reaching its full flowering in the first decade of the new century. Here was the latest thing in townhouse design, straight from the École des Beaux-Arts and the offices of the architects who had rebuilt Paris in the aftermath of Baron Haussmann's grand design for the city. But it had its critics, who referred to it condescendingly as "the cartouche style." That appellation has been retained, although it is no longer necessarily used disdainfully. The style is characterized by an exceptional amount of surface decoration, which, architectural purists claimed, overwhelmed the natural architectonic qualities of fine building.

Perhaps the reason for patron and architect resorting to increased ornamentation was that these buildings were smaller than the great palazzos and châteaux, and therefore relied on the application of extra ornament to convey the idea of the wealth and social importance of those who dwelt within. In scale, they were essentially the same as New York's omnipresent brownstones, which had long since become boring and reflective of the middle class, so in order to make their facades distinctive, a profusion of "schlag" was applied to the surface.

But the result was elegant. The elaborate style, which was decidedly French, was developed in Paris to serve the *haute*

bourgeoisie in the last half of the nineteenth century, and it was beautifully suited to the "Gay Paris" of the Second Empire (1853–70) and the early decades of the Third Republic (1871–1941). Contemporary critic Montgomery Schuyler noted the power of the Parisian architectural styles, throughout Europe as well as in the United States. He wrote of the increasing influence in America of "the Paris School of fine arts, of which the pupils . . . are every year returning in increasing numbers to take part in the building of the United States."[3]

The Modern Style in France

The Modern French style did have historical precedent, but it was derived from neither the austere palazzo manner nor the reserved early French Renaissance style. Instead, it drew heavily from more bombastic Baroque and decorative eighteenth-century prototypes. It was not so much a rebirth of those styles as it was a Beaux-Arts reinterpretation—a rather free use of, say, French Baroque or Rococo components, reassembled in an elegant and decorative manner. Elegance, luxuriousness and ornamentation were fundamental to the style. Moreover, it had a "modern" quality to it, which was attractive to the younger generation of wealth; as noted in *New York 1900*, "in the hands of skilled graduates of the École des Beaux-Arts it combined the authority of historical example with a sense of modernity."[4] As it turned out, it was an alternative to the contemporaneous Art Nouveau style, and it was an extension of aristocratic European architectural tradition instead of a denial of it, which turn-of-the-century "Modernism," as we have come to use the word, was eager to do.

To those who have become accustomed to using the term "Modern" to identify the totally new movements that burst

Figure 231. Charles Dana Gibson, *The Greatest Game in the World—His Move.* From *Collier's Weekly* (28 February 1903), pp. 20–21.

on the art scene in Paris and elsewhere around 1907 as a violent reaction against the traditions of the Renaissance, the use of "Modern" to mean a Beaux-Arts reinterpretation of Baroque and Rococo forms may seem strange indeed. But at the turn of the century, "modern" could also refer—for some, at least—to a townhouse designed in elegant form following a Parisian model that was of a quasi-Baroque style. To the scions of the Gilded Age, who were probably only remotely aware of the revolution in the arts known as "Modernism," as the term is now used, "modern" simply meant the latest thing from Paris, in architecture as well as in a new frock.

For an architect, it helped if he had lived in Paris for a few years and had studied architecture as defined and taught at the École des Beaux-Arts. But as throughout the history of American architecture, there were resources to which he could turn if he had never been to Paris—architectural design books with elaborately detailed plates that were sometimes richly colored. The Second Empire produced its share of such publications to assist the hundreds of architects who were rebuilding Paris and restoring favored palaces and châteaux throughout France, and who were active throughout much of Europe. The work of César Daly may be cited as an example; Daly was an art publisher in the 1860s and 1870s and two of his most important publications were *L'Architecture privée au XIXe siècle, sous Napoleon III. Nouvelles maisons de Paris et des environs*, originally published in 1864, and *Motifs historiques d'architecture et de sculpture d'ornament: Décorations exterieures empruntées à des édifices français du commencement de la Renaissance à la fin de Louis XVI . . .* , which first appeared in 1869, but there were numerous editions of both of these, in testimony to their use and popularity. In *L'Architecture privée* one could find exquisite plates of coffers, balustrades, moldings, capitals, pilasters, mosaic pavements, ceiling designs, wall paneling, mantles, and—of special importance for the current discussion—sculptured architectural cartouches. The latter were abundantly illustrated as well in *Motifs historiques d'architecture*, only for the exterior of houses, and one plate from the 1911 edition is reproduced here (figure 232).

American architects of the Gilded Age found a fountainhead of inspiration in the plates of such publications.

Figure 232. Style Louis XV. Maison rue de la Parchiminerie, a Paris, César Daly, *Motifs historiques d'architecture et de sculpture d'Ornament: Décorations exterieures empruntées à des edifices français du commencement de la renaissance à la fin de Louis XVI*, 2 vols., Paris, 1911 (originally published 1869), vol. 2, plate 16. Morris Library, University of Delaware. César Daly was perhaps the most influential French architectural critic of the second half of the nineteenth century. He was concerned with the theory of urban organization in the

Richard Morris Hunt not only knew them well but also knew the publisher, whom he visited at his country house in France; Hunt's biographer, in fact, tells of one of Daly's sons proposing marriage to the Hunts' young daughter, Kitty.[5]

American architects who had been to Paris and studied there, of course, found the city to be a grand repository of the new Second Empire style. They found its exciting creations almost everywhere they turned—in imperial palaces, in governmental buildings, banks, department stores, train stations, and the elegant hôtels des villes that increasingly lined the grand boulevards. At times it seemed that the exuberant architectural detail of the great buildings of the international expositions of 1867 and 1889 had been applied to the permanent architecture of the city. A splendid example—and one that exemplifies the "cartouche style"—is found in the decorative details of the Quai d'Orsay, the grand new Parisian train station (figure 233). Americans, returning from Paris in the Gay Nineties, were eager to create for themselves and their families townhouses that were of this stylish new "modern" mode.

The Sloane Family

In America, one of the earliest examples of this new type of building in the modern mode was the H. T. Sloane house on 72nd Street. Henry Thompson Sloane was one of six children born to William Sloane and his wife, Euphemia Douglas. William had been a penniless weaver in Scotland. He immigrated to New York in 1834 and there, with his brother, John, established a carpet store under the name of W. and J. Sloane. The firm prospered, expanding into the business of selling furniture as well as rugs and textiles and establishing branches in numerous American cities. After William died in 1879 the business was run by his sons, Thomas C., William Douglas, and Henry Thompson. The store was located, first, at Broadway and 18th Street, where auctions were held that had sales of well over a million dollars each—big money, for auctions in those days. But eager to move with Society, W. and J. Sloane's relocated uptown, on the southeast corner of Fifth Avenue and 47th Street. In spite of the firm's success, however, the stigmatism of being "shopkeepers" was attached to the Sloanes. Still, the Sloane boys married rather well—William Douglas, for example, married Emily Vanderbilt, a daughter of William Henry Vanderbilt, and they lived in a portion of the palace that William Henry had built at Fifth Avenue and 52nd Street (figure 49, p. 89).

Henry Thompson matriculated at Yale College in 1866 but withdrew soon thereafter for health reasons. Two years of travel followed before he entered the family business. In the early 1880s he married Jessie Robbins, daughter of Daniel Robbins, a founder of the Brooklyn-based pharmaceutical house of McKesson and Robbins. She was acclaimed one of the great beauties of her generation and was said to be the best-dressed woman in New York Society. Henry and Jessie established their residence on West 54th Street, where their two daughters—Jessie and Emily

modern city and was an interpreter of Haussmann's reorganization of Paris. As editor of *Le revue générale de l'architecture et des traveaux publics* (1839–1890), his criticism was read and respected on both sides of the Atlantic. He also published an important study of the domestic architecture of the era of Napoleon III, *L'Architecture privée au XIXe siècle*. The influence of his engraved designs is found in the facades of buildings on innumerable side streets, just off of Fifth Avenue.

Figure 233. Quai d'Orsay Station, Paris, decorative detail, ca. 1899. From *Architectural Record* 11 (October 1901), p. 575. The cartouche style had its first full architectural presentation at the great international fair held in Paris in 1889, and the style reached its apogee in 1900 with the Quai d'Orsay station (now a division of the Louvre devoted to modern art). While its richness seems appropriate for such edifices, it came under criticism from the Modern camp for its excessive application of ornamentation to architecture. In this detail from the Quai d'Orsay Station, notice the scale, established by the small figure of a man standing in the lower right corner.

Eleanor—were born. By the early 1890s, H. T. had prospered through the success of W. and J. Sloane's, of which he eventually became a director and treasurer. Conscious of the role of domestic architecture in asserting the place of one's family in Society, he and his wife decided to move uptown and to the east side.

The H. T. Sloane House

Not being one of the families of truly great wealth, the Sloanes did not purchase one of the favored corner lots on the avenue, but settled for a side-street location just off of Fifth—an extra-wide lot at 9 East 72nd Street (figure 234). A quick glance at its facade reveals that here is yet another radical departure from the ubiquitous brownstone of New York City.

In 1893, Carrère and Hastings, who were engaged to design the house, were among the earliest in the United States to experiment with the new type of Parisian townhouse facade. Both John Merven Carrère and Thomas Hastings were trained at the École des Beaux-Arts in Paris in the early 1880s; both returned to the United States in the mid-1880s to work for McKim, Mead and White just as the Villard Houses were being brought to completion. But they left that firm in 1887 to form their own partnership, and by the 1890s they were producing architectural designs in a bravura neo-Baroque style that would not have been tolerated at McKim, Mead and White, for such was beyond the conservative classicism of Charles Follen McKim and even more excessive than Stanford White could endure.

Insofar as the exterior was concerned, the facade was all that mattered, for the sides were snugly abutted to the walls of neighbors' houses and the rear of the building, being seldom seen, was of secondary importance. On a block-by-block basis in less affluent regions of the city, where generic and undistinguished brownstone townhouses were built row upon row, a certain architectural unity—which some would call sameness and dullness—resulted and carried connotations of general equality of social and economic standing (see figure 8, p. 34). But uptown, on the side streets between Fifth and Madison, strongly individualistic designs—such as that seen in the Sloane house—presented a problem insofar as unity within the block was concerned. Each facade might be lovely in its own right, but in a row of fifteen or so houses in which each was markedly different from its neighbors, unity was reduced to little more than a uniform height and a generally common spirit of design in the "modern" Parisian mode. In such areas, the monotonous old brownstone grid was therefore destroyed.

While the design of the Sloane house was a Beaux-Arts exercise in the historical style of the Renaissance-Baroque tradition, it was different from the palazzo type discussed in previous chapters—different from, say, the Villard Houses (figure 164, p. 242). There is an absence of broad planes of undecorated wall that were so admired in classical Roman and Renaissance architecture. Here, wall planes become obscured by the extraordinary amount of architectural ornamentation, which carried the facade into the Baroque phase of classical design. Also, the facade possesses a deep and rich three-dimensional quality, especially above the first floor, that similarly identifies it with a post-classical phase of Renaissance architecture. For example, instead of using flat pilasters to unite the two middle levels of the house, the architects employed columns, nearly in the round, and the plane of the windows is set beyond these; balustrades and cornices, too, help define a rich interplay of space and form, or three-dimensionality. The ornamental carvings of the capitals and above the windows of the second and third stories reveal a commitment to lavishness that narrowly escapes ostentation, but decorative carving in bold relief—and in abundance—became an integral component of the French Modern style on which such designs were based.

The middle level of the house is the real eye-catcher in which the architects made an aesthetic statement that prepared the visitor for the lavishness within. Five Ionic columns unite two stories and create four intercolumnar bays that are filled with ornamentation. Elegant French doors with glazed oculi above open onto narrow balustraded balconies and are capped with ornate keystones and flanked by sculptured brackets. The smaller windows of the third floor are similarly decorative, and the entablature is crowned by a balustrade, above which rises a Mansard roof with four dormers trimmed with scrolls at the sides and arched pediments on top.

Figure 234. Carrère and Hastings, Henry T. Sloane residence, 9 East 72nd Street, New York City, 1893–94.

The whole is a classicist's nightmare, a raging terror to the classical purist. One can imagine what Joseph Wells or Charles Follen McKim must have thought as they saw it rise and take form. But it was French, it was direct from Paris, it was elaborate and extravagant, and it proclaimed luxury without and promised sumptuousness within, all to the delight of Carrère and Hastings' nouveaux riches clients.

As a style, this cartouche mode had its following, not only in domestic architecture but in civic buildings as well. By the time the H. T. Sloane house was completed, many wealthy Americans had been not only to Paris to see the elaborate architecture of the great 1889 exposition there, but also to Chicago, where they saw America's own efforts at grandiose extravagance at the World's Columbian Exposition of 1893. Adele Sloane, niece of Jessica and Henry Sloane, recorded the impression the latter made on her and her family when they visited it:

> You do not get a very good view of the buildings until you are right in the grounds, and then they suddenly appear to you in all their beauty and grandeur. Everyone says it is impossible to describe the impression they first make on you. . . . It is a feeling one cannot tell of but which one never forgets. . . . It is truly what one should call "the Dream City"; it is too ideally beautiful to be real.[6]

The architectural creations at the Exposition Universal of 1889 in Paris and the World's Columbian Exposition in Chicago four years later form a backdrop for much of the architecture associated with the Gilded Age.

Life in the H. T. Sloane House

The doorway at the left of the facade opens into an arcaded great hall from which a stairway ascends to the main floor above and to the grand salon. The latter extended across the full fifty-foot width of the front of the house and was lighted by the four great French doors of the facade.

Immediately upon the completion of the house in 1894, Jessie Robbins Sloane began entertaining quite grandly. Perhaps her finest hour came on the evening of January 24, 1898, when she gave a ball attended by over 250 guests, among whom were New York's highest Society—"a much more exclusive affair than Mrs. Astor's recent ball," wrote the society columnist for *The New York Times*. Mrs. Sloane received the guests as they arrived in the gray room, which

Figure 235. Ernest Flagg with Walter B. Chambers, Oliver Gould Jennings residence, 7 East 72nd Street, New York City, 1899. From *Architectural Record* 10 (October 1900), p. 214.

opened onto the large ballroom, while behind a row of potted plants and bushes Berger's Gypsy Hungarian Orchestra played the entire evening. "Mrs. Astor wore a white satin gown and a dazzling display of precious stones," the *Times* reporter observed,[7] and she was accompanied by Mr. and Mrs. John Jacob Astor IV; the Stanford Whites were there, along with Mr. and Mrs. I. Townsend Burden and Mr. and Mrs. James A. Burden—Mrs. Burden being the former Adele Sloane, the hostess's niece. Mamie Fish was escorted by her husband, Stuyvesant, and Mr. and Mrs. Ogden Mills, Chauncey Depew, and William Kissam Vanderbilt also attended, along with several rising stars of the younger generation—including Mr. and Mrs. William Schieffelin, Miss Lila Vanderbilt Sloane, and Miss Emily Vanderbilt Sloane. Many of these names will reappear as we progress through this chapter.

Epilogue for the H. T. Sloane House

But merriment and happiness were not to reign for long at the fashionable new house at 9 East 72nd Street. Little more than a year had passed after the grand ball when, on April 28 at 3:30 in the afternoon, Henry Thompson Sloane was granted a divorce from Jessie, who at 8:00 p.m. that same evening married Perry Belmont, the youngest son of Caroline and August Belmont and brother of Oliver Hazard Belmont. The Perry Belmonts lived in Washington, D.C., for twenty years, where they were leaders of the social world from the administration of Theodore Roosevelt to that of Calvin Coolidge, and they summered at Newport, living at Belcourt which Perry had inherited from his brother. Jessie Robbins Sloane Belmont died in Paris in 1935, with Perry at her side, and she was buried in the Belmont mausoleum at Newport.

Meanwhile, H. T. Sloane did not wish to live in the fine house he had but recently built. He rented it briefly to Joseph Pulitzer and then sold it, in 1901, to James Stillman, president of the National City Bank of New York. H. T. remained active in business, but he never remarried. He died at his New York City home, at 18 East 68th Street, in the fall of 1937. After 1935 the house on 72nd Street—like its neighbor, the Jennings residence—was occupied by the Lycée Français de New York, a private school devoted to the study of French literature and culture, but both houses were sold recently.

Oliver Gould Jennings

The Sloane house was erected on the lot at number 9 East 72nd Street; adjoining it immediately to the west, at 7 East 72nd, is the grand townhouse of Oliver Gould Jennings (figure 235). A prominent businessman at the turn of the century, Jennings was a director of the National Fuel Gas Company and of Bethlehem Steel as well as the McKesson and Robbins Company, and thereby connected with the family of Jessie Robbins Sloane, who lived next door.

Jennings's father, Oliver Burr Jennings, began life as a dry-goods clerk, and when news of the discovery of gold in California reached New York City, he persuaded his employers to stake him to an inventory of supplies, which were then shipped around Cape Horn to San Francisco. By the time they arrived, Jennings was already there and had even obtained a small purse from mining for the golden nuggets. But he gave up prospecting to sell supplies to those who chased their dreams of instant riches. In little over a decade he had made enough money to sell out and retire, and he returned to New York about 1862. He married, and through his wife's sister—who was married to William Rockefeller—he was introduced to John D. Rockefeller just at a time when the Rockefeller brothers were reorganizing their oil business in Cleveland, in 1871–72. They needed capital, and Oliver Burr Jennings made a crucial but modest investment that was sufficient to get him appointed a trustee of Standard Oil Trust. Thereafter, the dividends rolled in, and Jennings became very wealthy, along with the Rockefellers, Oliver Payne, Henry Flagler, and others of the great trust.

His son, Oliver Gould Jennings, attended Phillips Academy and in 1887 graduated from Yale, where he was a member of the prestigious Skull and Bones Club, before attending law school at Columbia University. When his father died in 1893, young Jennings became wealthy in his own right and proved himself to be a very capable businessman. Jennings was an amiable man-about-town and clubman, being a member of the Metropolitan, Union, New York Yacht, and Yale clubs. His family connections placed him at the heart of New York Society; a sister, for example, married Hugh Auchincloss of Hammersmith Farms of Newport, Rhode Island. In 1896 Jennings married Mary Dows Brewster.

THE O. G. JENNINGS HOUSE

Three years later the young couple asked Ernest Flagg (1857–1947) to design for them a townhouse in the modern Parisian mode, to be erected on the lot at 7 East 72nd Street. William B. Chambers was Flagg's partner in the commission. Flagg was, at that time, one of the rising stars of the younger generation of architects, for he already had to his credit such important projects as St. Luke's Hospital (1896) in New York City, the Corcoran Gallery (1897) in Washington, and the buildings at the United States Naval Academy (begun 1896) in Annapolis. He had started his career as a land-and-development speculator in New York City in the 1870s and early 1880s, but in 1889 he went to Paris, where he entered the École des Beaux-Arts to study architecture.

The experience of the French capital itself and his training at the École made a lasting impression on Flagg; of especial importance were the teaching of Paul Blondel and the theories of Charles Blanc. By the time he returned to New York in 1891 to establish his practice, he was a committed Francophile, dedicated to discovering the proper relationship between the decorative and the structural in architecture. He addressed that issue in an article, "Influence of the French School on Architecture in the United States," which appeared in the *Architectural Record* of 1894. In the essay he declared that "if architecture in this country is to be elevated to a high plane, we must adopt the same honest methods and noble aims which are encouraged at the French school." Singling out Charles Garnier's Opera House in Paris for special admiration, Flagg declared that whatever one might think of the details, "all will agree that its author is a man of genius; his production will always rank as a work of art."[8] By the time he received the commission for the Jennings house, Flagg had already begun to apply his French-inspired principles to major architectural commissions.

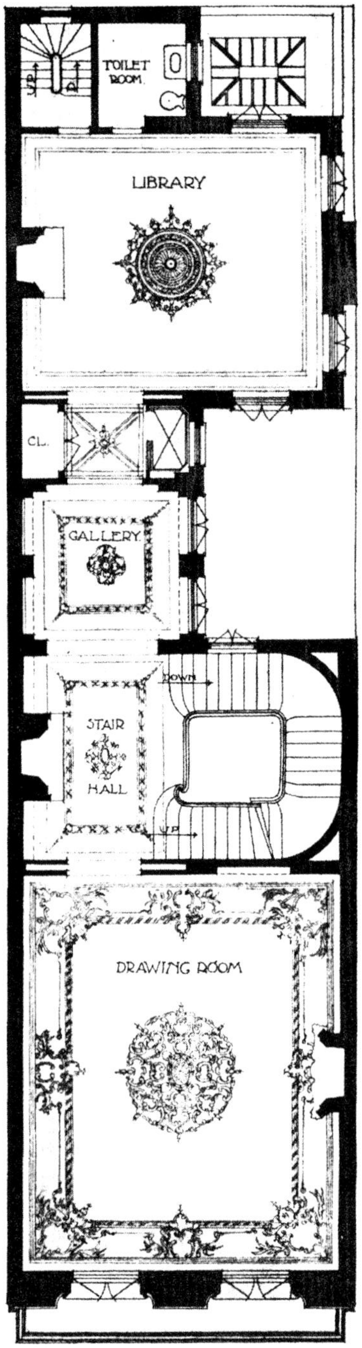

Figure 236. Ernest Flagg with Walter B. Chambers, plan: main floor, Oliver Gould Jennings residence, 7 East 72nd Street, New York City, 1899. From *Architectural Record* 11 (October 1901–2), p. 55.

The lot on which the Jennings house was erected—the first property east of the corner parcel on Fifth Avenue—measured twenty-eight feet wide, facing 72nd Street. The facade, built of Indiana limestone, reveals the influences of Parisian townhouses and the architect's training at the École des Beaux-Arts. Flagg had seen such houses along the boulevards of Paris, and the interest in them—as well as general knowledge of their appearance—is seen in a series of illustrations of such houses that appeared in the *Architectural Record* of 1898, just before Flagg began work on the Jennings house.[9] The rusticated walls—"pin-striped," as it were—of the first through the third floors establish a single plane that sets off the considerable amount of decoration found around the door and windows of the two bays. On the ground floor the openings—the one at the left being the doorway while its counterpart is a broad window—are arched and rather plain, giving a feeling of strength at that level. Above these features runs a balcony, almost the entire width of the building, supported by carved corbels and enclosed with ornamental wrought-iron decorative work.

At the second level, concave arched openings enclose French doors that open onto the balcony, while scallop-shell motifs decorate the area above the doors.

The windows on the third floor, which are smaller and rectangular, have small crescent balconies, supported by ornamental corbelling, and they have decorative wrought-iron balustrades. A boldly projecting cornice separates the third floor from the coved slate roof, which has a pair of dormer windows, the enframements of which are lavishly ornamented, as are the copper ribs of the roofline and the crowning decoration. The roof area is the most decidedly French feature of the facade and is related, in style and profusion, to the detail of the Quai d'Orsay seen in figure 233.

Flagg and Chambers took great care to make certain elements of the design correlate with that of the H. T. Sloane house next door—the balcony above the entrance of the Jennings house lines up perfectly with the cornice over the entrance to the Sloane residence. The openings of the first floor have round-headed arched openings in each house and the lower level in both facades is similarly rusticated; French doors are found in the windows of the second floor in each instance, and the main cornice, between the third floor and the roof area, of the one house lines up with that of the other. As a result, even though the facade designs are quite different, they do achieve a certain correlation.

Figure 237. Ernest Flagg with Walter B. Chambers, entrance hall, Oliver Gould Jennings residence, 7 East 72nd Street, New York City, 1899. From *Architectural Record* 10 (October 1900), p. 219.

The Interiors

As noted earlier, the lot was twenty-eight feet wide, and it ran the usual one-hundred feet in depth; in this it was like most side-street lots of the New York grid. There were no windows on the side walls but Flagg did design a sizable light well about two-thirds of the way back; this allowed light and air to enter the middle rooms and the stairway, whereas otherwise only the front and back rooms would have had natural lighting and a flow of air (figure 236).

Such matters were of great importance to Flagg during these years when solutions were being sought for the alleviation of dark, airless sections of the multitude of tenements then being erected to house the poor of the city. In 1894, in fact, Flagg published a tenement plan that contained a light court; it became the prototype for such buildings for several decades thereafter.[10] In the design of houses for rich and poor alike, the invention of the light well provided a great advantage over the plan of earlier brownstones, which had no openings in the entire length of the house, making interior rooms dim and filled with stagnant air.

One entered the house through richly carved wooden doors into an entrance hall, the walls of which were lined with Caen stone; the decoration of the exterior was continued here in the form of elaborately carved cartouches placed in the keystones above the flattened-arch doorways (figure 237). The lavish use of mirrors on the walls gave a feeling of increased spaciousness.

The rooms were arranged in Pullman fashion—that is, sequentially in a straight line from front to rear. About halfway back was the stairhall with the U-shaped staircase ascending to the right; a skylight illuminated the entire depth of the stairwell. At the front of the main floor was the large drawing room, measuring twenty-three by thirty-one feet, which was the center of entertaining in the house. It was an elaborate room with white paneled walls that had gilded cartouche designs in each panel. The richly ornamented coved ceiling had large cartouches at the corners. Just beyond the stair hall was the gallery that overlooked the light well. At the rear of the house was the library, which had lateral windows overlooking the garden behind the H. T. Sloane house; the library was twenty-five feet wide by thirty-one feet long. On the third floor were the family's private rooms—the bedrooms, baths, and sitting area—while the servants' quarters were on the fourth floor.

Thus, by 1899 there stood at numbers 7 and 9 of East 72nd Street a pair of houses that were as different in design as the old brownstones farther downtown were identical in appearance. But, aside from the formal similarities achieved by aligned cornices, the Jennings and Sloane houses were united by the common source of their design—the Parisian *haute bourgeoisie* boulevard townhouse. Soon whole blocks of cross streets, in the East 60s and 70s, would display proud facades in the voguish new French cartouche manner, each quite different from its neighbors but united with them in its origin in a common source.

Ernesto Fabbri

Ernesto Fabbri Sr. (1830–83) was born in Florence, Italy, where his father was a prosperous merchant. After being educated in England he came to the United States and became a partner of another merchant, John Randall, whose daughter he married. Fabbri returned briefly to Italy but was again in New York by 1865 where he joined the firm of Fabbri and Chauncey, which was headed by his older brother, Egisto. The latter retired from the firm in 1867, leaving Ernesto to run it. In 1875 Egisto became a senior officer of the successful banking house of Drexel, Morgan and Company, where he amassed a fortune estimated at $20 million. J. Pierpont Morgan soon learned to respect the council of Egisto in financial matters, and one of Egisto's shrewdest investments was when he backed a young genius of an inventor named Thomas Alva Edison when the latter incorporated his electric company in New York City—the company that became ConEdison.

One of Ernesto's children was a son, Ernesto Jr. (1874–1943), who was nine years old when his father died. His Uncle Egisto adopted him, who saw to it that he had a Princeton education, and introduced him into the inner circle of New York Society. Soon after graduation from college, young Ernesto married Edith, daughter of Margaret Vanderbilt (Mrs. Elliott) Shepard, granddaughter of William Henry Vanderbilt, and niece of Cornelius II, William Kissam, and George W. Vanderbilt. The wedding, which took place in Scarsdale, New York, was a very grand affair. Margaret Vanderbilt Shepard and Louisa (Mrs. William Henry) Vanderbilt were there, sitting next to Mrs. Cornelius Vanderbilt II; also in the Vanderbilt section at the front of the chapel were the bride's aunts and their husbands, Mr. and Mrs. William D. Sloane and Dr. and Mrs. Seward Webb. There, too, was her cousin with her husband, Mr. and Mrs. William J. Schieffelin. Across the aisle sat Mrs. Ernesto Fabbri Sr., near John D. Rockefeller. Edith's Uncle George, who served as one of the ushers, arranged for the newlyweds to go off to his estate, Biltmore, for a month as the beginning of their honeymoon.

Edith Shepard's parents, Elliott and Margaret, had long lived in a portion of the palazzo that William Henry Vanderbilt had erected on Fifth Avenue (figure 49, p. 89), but now widowed with her children grown and out on their own, Margaret retired to Scarsdale. Before doing so, however, she bought a plot at 11 and 13 East 62nd Street and on it erected a house for her daughter and her new husband.

The Fabbri House

The Fabbri house was designed by the architectural firm of Haydel and Shepard, the latter being Augustus Dennis Shepard, a nephew of the patron (figure 238). Haydel had studied architecture at the École des Beaux-Arts in Paris, which explains the French flavor in the design of the facade. In that design, as was often the case in cartouche-style houses, surface decoration dominated over basic architectural form.

The facade of the Fabbri house resembles an exercise in which the student was required to incorporate as many decorative features of the Beaux-Arts vocabulary as possible. More, in the way of adornment, would be difficult to work into the design. Yet that ornamentation is the very thing that gives the facade its character, and if that profusion of decorative detailing were meant to encode such signals as wealth, luxury, power, a touch of frivolity, and pseudo-aristocratic

Figure 238. Haydel and Shepard, Ernesto G. Fabbri residence, 11 East 62nd Street, New York City, 1900. Museum of the City of New York. Although not a large edifice by mansion standards, the Fabbri house possesses a grandeur nevertheless. It had its own ballroom, for example, and its mahogany paneled dining room measured twenty-five by forty-one feet.

social position, then it succeeded. A frank abandonment to sensual and materialistic pleasures was the avowed goal of both architect and patron, and we are reminded that America had never before reached such heights of hedonism in its architecture. No facade better illustrates the refusal to submit to any lingering vestiges of Puritanism by this youthful sector of American Society—here, indeed, is an American architectural *joie de vivre*.

The facade possesses an architectural gaiety that bespeaks more of its Parisian origins than those of a Knickerbocker heritage. A reminiscence of elegant eighteenth-century French architecture is found in the French doors of the second floor and the refined pilasters and richly carved capitals that define the three bays. The cartouche element is boldly presented as corbels supporting the wrought-iron balconies of the third floor, which are also gained by tall French windows. From pavement to roofline there is a pleasurable delight in carved sculptural and architectural ornamentation that is classical, Renaissance, Baroque, and Rococo in derivation, but reorganized and redesigned according to Beaux-Arts aesthetic theories.

Sculptural richness asserts its equality with architectural form, for this is a facade of multiple planes that are broken by lights and shadows: beginning with the plane of the windows one advances to the plane of the wall, beyond which is the plane of the pilasters, and finally the plane defined by the furthest extension of the corbelled cornice. Three-dimensionality prevails.

The ornate richness of the exterior was continued throughout the major rooms of the interior. But the Fabbris were not to enjoy their handsome house for very long. Ernesto, following in the footsteps of his Uncle Egisto, went to work for the firm of Drexel, Morgan, which in 1907 dispatched him to Europe, where he and Edith remained for several years. The house was rented to Edward Harriman, the railroad tycoon, while his own palazzo was being erected on the northeast corner of Fifth Avenue and 52nd Street. After Harriman moved out, the house was used for a while by James Smith. When Edith divorced Ernesto in Paris in 1923, the house remained in her name. Meanwhile, it seems Edith's affections had turned in the direction of Ernesto's brother, Alesandro. Edith died in 1954, but her beautiful townhouse was not, fortunately, a victim of the wrecker's ball and was given new life when put to new uses; for example, it was, for a while, the location of the Johnson-O'Connor Research Foundation.

Figure 239. Carrère and Hastings, E. K. Dunham residence, 35 East 68th Street, New York City, 1899–1900. Avery Architectural and Fine Arts Library, Columbia University.

E. K. Dunham and His Cartouche-Style House

Edward Kellogg Dunham (1860–1922) was born in Newburgh, New York, the son of Edward W. Dunham, president of the Corn Exchange Bank. After graduating from Columbia College in 1881 he attended medical school at Harvard, where he received his degree in 1888. In the years that followed he became a renowned physician, specializing in pathology and bacteriology; in 1898 he was appointed professor of pathology at the Bellevue Hospital Medical College and he served as a consultant to the New York City Health Department and the Health Commission. He early established his reputation through his diagnosis of cholera cultures.

In 1893, Dunham married Mary Dows, daughter of David Dows, a prominent financier and merchant of the city. He was an active clubman, being a member of the University, Century, Harvard, and Riding clubs. But he and his wife did not enter into the inner circles of New York Society, probably because he was busy with his ongoing medical researches and his professional career. Nevertheless, when it came time to acquire a house in an upscale neighborhood in the late 1890s, they chose a site just off of Fifth Avenue in the upper 60s, and they selected a design that was of the *au currant* "modern" French style.

To design their new house at 35 East 68th Street, on a lot that measured twenty-five by one hundred feet, the Dunhams selected Carrère and Hastings (figure 239). It was erected between 1899 and 1901, soon after that firm had completed the H. T. Sloane house. Unlike the reserved design of the grand palazzo type of mansion, frothy little baubles such as the Dunham house were popular among Society's younger set and soon became all the rage.

A critic, writing in the *Architectural Record*, described the Dunham house as "florid" with a "'pretentiousness' of architectural treatment." But then he admitted that

> the exuberance of ornament is handled with skill and discretion, and very clearly avoids defects of over-muchness inevitable in this sort of work when produced by designers of less experience. Indeed,

there are only a few architects in the United States who have acquired an idiomatic mastery of this style. . . . [The study of this facade] is recommended to the attention of the large tribe of bunglers who are busy disfiguring our streets with crude extravagances of the "French Style.' "[11]

The salient characteristic of this style is an unabashed delight in not only architectural decoration but also sculptured ornamental embellishment, often in the form of foliate carvings such as swags and festoons draped around cartouches. These are found above the doorway at 35 East 68th Street as well as above and below the window next to it. The elegantly arched windows of the second floor are capped by additional cartouches that support the balconies of the third floor, the rectangular windows of which are framed by rectilinear architectural decoration. On the fourth floor the rectangular windows are rather plain, and the circular lights of the mansard roof are enframed with a delicate ornamentation.

Wrought-Iron Work

In addition to all of the sculptured decoration, which virtually consumes the multiplaned facade, the wrought-iron railings of the third floor balconies add a delicate linear element to the design. Wrought iron was frequently used both on the facades and in the interiors of the gilded mansions. As early as 1892 the respected critic Montgomery Schuyler commented on the excellent design in "the railings which surround [the Vanderbilt houses], in which an original, characteristic, and successful treatment of metal has been attained, and which, as works of art, are really of more value than the houses they protect."[12] Wrought iron was popular at the turn of the century, often being used to express the new aesthetic of l'Art Nouveau, and it became a fine art medium in its own right. Many firms were able to produce such work as was incorporated into the facades of newly erected townhouses and mansions, not the least of which was the Gorham Company of Providence, Rhode Island. In New York City, the William H. Jackson Company excelled in decorative architectural metal work. Important artists and architects—from Louis Comfort Tiffany to Cass Gilbert—undertook commissions to design elaborate gates, fences, window guards, and stairway and balcony railings.

Matters of Construction and the Expediency of the Unaesthetic Steel Frame

The facades of houses such as those erected for the Sloane, Jennings, Fabbri, and Dunham families were constructed of limestone, often coming from the favored quarries around Bedford, Indiana. The rejection of brownstone, as much for social as aesthetic and structural reasons, has been noted. But the new houses had an additional advantage in that their framework was now of metal rather than wood, and therefore fire resistant if not fireproof. While the Beaux-Arts nature of the design of the facades does not prepare one for the cast-iron or steel skeletal frame within, that structural system was in fact employed. Numerous firms could provide the metal components for building fine houses, precisely according to an architect's specifications, just as was being done in the skeletal frames of the high-rising skyscrapers of that day.

One of the leading firms in New York City, and one of the oldest contract engineering firms in America, was Milliken Brothers, founded in 1857. By 1900 it employed about one hundred engineers and draftsmen in its main office. It was the firm that supplied the steel for Louis Sullivan's Wainwright Building in St. Louis, as well as a host of other buildings. An article in *Architectural Record* for 1902 reported that Milliken Brothers "can execute orders very rapidly, turning out the structural steel work for an entire building in five or six weeks. . . . The firm designs and constructs iron and steel work for armories, bridges, docks, office buildings, dwellings, and factories." The article also informs the reader that the firm will furnish fireproof and burglar-proof doors, balconies, balustrades, fountains, gates, and "all kinds of ornamental work, either from designs furnished in its office or by the architects."[13] It is known, for example, that Milliken Brothers executed the decorative metal-work, from designs drawn up by Ernest Flagg, for the Oliver Gould Jennings house. As we have seen, wrought iron was overtly used for decorative effects; but in obedience to the Beaux-Arts aesthetic code, where it was employed for structural purposes it was concealed behind a veneer of polished marble or Caen stone or some other such material, for its exposure was then considered coarse and aesthetically debasing. In that, of course, Louis Sullivan parted ways with the Beaux-Arts designers of his day.

The William Jay Schieffelins and Their House

Margaret Vanderbilt (1845–1924) was the eldest daughter of William Henry and Louisa Kissam Vanderbilt, the railroad tycoon and his wife. Margaret came between Cornelius II and William Kissam in the family genealogy. She married Elliott Fitch Shepard, with whom she had four daughters—Maria Louise, Edith, Alice, and Marguerite—all of whom grew up in the portion of William Henry's Fifth Avenue palazzo that he had designated for the Shepards. In 1891, Maria Louise married William Jay Schieffelin, and the wedding breakfast—for six hundred guests—was held in William Henry's grand picture gallery (figures 63 and 64, p. 103). Mrs. Shepard's wedding gift for the young couple was a house at 35 West 57th Street.

Louise's husband belonged to one of the grand old Knickerbocker families. His mother was a Jay, a descendant of the first Chief Justice, John Jay. William was no idler. After he was graduated from Columbia College he went to Munich, where he studied chemistry. Thereafter he entered the family business, a long-established wholesale drug firm that had been founded in 1793, of which he eventually became chairman of the board. In later years he was active with the Citizens' Union, an organization that promoted political reform—so effectively, in fact, that its efforts led to the downfall of the corrupt regime of Mayor Jimmy Walker. Schieffelin also worked to put an end to sweat-shop conditions in the garment industry, and he was a champion of improved educational opportunities for young black Americans, serving as a trustee for both the Hampton Institute in Virginia and the Tuskegee Institute in Alabama.

Figure 240. Hunt and Hunt, William Jay Schieffelin residence, 5 East 66th Street, New York City, 1900 (now, the Lotos Club). Courtest of the Lotos Club.

William and Louise lived in the West 57th Street house throughout the 1890s, until the hustle and bustle of that area made the residence undesirable. About 1898 Margaret Vanderbilt Shepard acquired the houses at numbers 5 and 7 on the north side of 66th Street, just east of Fifth Avenue. After having the houses demolished she commissioned Richard Howland Hunt, the son of Richard Morris Hunt, to design a house for her daughter and son-in-law, on the double-wide lot that measured forty-seven feet across. While his father had often turned to historical French architecture for inspiration, Richard Howland drew from a phase that Richard Morris had never used—the "modern" French or cartouche-style Parisian townhouse.

The lower level is rusticated and constructed of limestone, with three openings—a doorway to the left side with two windows in the center and at the right (figure 240). The house is set back a few feet, and the street perimeter and entranceway are enframed with a wrought-iron railing. A bold cornice with richly carved corbels separates that level from the second story which follows the three-bay arrangement but is built of limestone and red brick. The cornice serves as the floor of a full-width balcony with an attractive wrought-iron railing that matches the one on the street level. In the second story the windows, like the corners, are framed with stone quoining; they are slightly recessed from the plane of the facade, in shallow arched niches that allow for additional carved cartouche ornamentation above the windows.

architect's father for such places as Marble House and Biltmore. On the second floor a library extended across the width of the house, overlooking 66th Street.

William and Louise Schieffelin lived in the house at 5 East 66th Street until about 1925, when they moved into an apartment building—the latter type of dwelling by then having been granted approval for the residency of High Society. Sometime after that the house became a private club—The Lotos Club—and still functions in that capacity today. Paul Goldberger, recent architectural critic for *The New York Times*, while he rather liked the facade design, seemed uncertain if he should because of its frivolousness, expressing himself with uncharacteristic ambivalence when he wrote, "The detailing is lavish, and comes tantalizingly close to excess. The ability of Hunt . . . to push this design right to the edge and yet never lose control is impressive."[14]

The French doors of the second floor and the windows of the third floor are united by a continuation of the limestone quoining, and at the third story the window decoration is found just beneath the sills. An ornate cornice terminates the third floor, and recessed from it is the slate-covered mansard roof with three windows, each of which has a circular motif above it with a carved shell design; perhaps the most lavish carving of all is in the festoons and cartouches that are set between the windows and at the corners. At the fifth level the windows are oval with bold, three-dimensional frames. As with other cartouche-style houses, the exceptional amount of carved ornamentation and the polychromed effect of the red brick and light gray limestone were meant to connote the wealth and luxurious lifestyle of those who dwelt within.

One entered into a foyer that gave way to a reception room to the right, with a gracefully curving stairway beyond that with a wrought-iron railing. At the rear of the house was a ballroom, complete with an elaborately carved fireplace (figure 241), adorned by caryatids at either side, the work of Karl Bitter—the same sculptor employed so often by the

Figure 241. Hunt & Hunt, dining room, with fireplace by Karl Bitter, William Jay Schieffelin residence, 5 East 66th Street, New York City, 1900. Courtesy of the Lotos Club.

Mansions in the Cartouche Style

Occasionally, the motifs of the French facade were attempted on a grand scale, but the result was seldom successful for the very reason that bothered Goldberger: Architectural decoration on a small scale was manageable and acceptable to the eye, but when spread across the facades of a large mansion, it became effusive and excessive, obliterating those inherent architectural qualities that demand precedence. Only a couple of examples need be examined to prove the point—the mansions built by Joseph De Lamar and by Senator William A. Clark.

Joseph Raphael De Lamar

Joseph Raphael De Lamar was born in Amsterdam, where he spent his youth. He eventually became owner and captain of his own merchant ship and reportedly visited nearly every port in the world. When he came to the United States he settled in Vineyard Haven, on Martha's Vineyard, Massachusetts, where he operated a ships' salvage business. In 1878 he was lured westward by the discovery of gold in Colorado before returning east to Chicago, where he studied chemistry and metallurgy to inform himself about the mining business. Back in Colorado, his mining claims paid off handsomely, and he was soon a member of the millionaires' club. Like so many others who made their fortunes in the West, he was attracted by the financial opportunities in New York City. There he gained additional riches on Wall Street, where his quiet manner garnered him the title "Man of Mystery." De Lamar became an officer or director of numerous corporations, as diverse as the American Bank Note Company, the Delta Sugar Beet Company, and the Dome Mine Company of Canada. By the early 1890s, his was a brilliant American success story.

De Lamar married Nellie Sands, the daughter of a druggist of New York City, but although wealthy, the Lamars never became a part of the inner circle of Society. They had one daughter, Alice, and in the late 1890s they lived in Paris most of the time; wealthy Americans who were shunned by Society often tried their luck in European capitals. While there, they were exposed to the latest fashion in "Modern French" architecture. Also, while there they purchased paintings and furnishings, evidently for a grand house they intended to build when they returned to the United States.

But that marriage did not last, and after Nellie divorced him, Joseph and Alice returned to New York. In 1902, Joseph bought a choice piece of property at the northeast corner of Madison Avenue and 37th Street, for which he paid the then-astounding price of a quarter of a million dollars. It was another three years, however, before he selected his architect—Charles P. H. Gilbert—and gave him "a free hand so far as the dwelling itself [was] concerned," according to *The New York Times* for April 8, 1904. The selection of the location in itself reveals that De Lamar did not choose to break into the socially elite "millionaires row" of Fifth Avenue between 50th and 95th streets, but took a site in an area Society had long since abandoned. The neighborhood was still quite good, of course, for J. Pierpont Morgan lived nearby, and a block to the north stood the Havemeyer mansion—again, homes of people who lived the good life of the Gilded Age but lived largely aloof from the gilded Society.

The De Lamar House

Still, when it came to the house Joseph De Lamar was to build, it had to be something that would outdo every one of those splendid mansions on Fifth Avenue. To accomplish this he and his architect turned to the modern French style, relying on extraordinary amounts of architectural ornamentation to convey the message of enormous wealth and affiliations with European culture (figure 242). De Lamar was determined to have the finest mansion in New York City—at first, anyway, for midway through construction he seemed to have lost interest in such grandeur.[15] But the design he approved, as submitted by Gilbert, was a transmogrification of the grandest of the grand Beaux-Arts mode, a monument to extravagance and, to use economist and sociologist Thorstein Veblen's nearly contemporary phrase, to conspicuous consumption.

The entire exterior wall is rusticated, from pavement to the fourth floor, giving the granite surface a horizontal "pinstriped" appearance and bestowing on even the flat surfaces a continuous decorative effect. Pavilions at the corner and opposite end of the building contribute to the pronounced three-dimensionality of the facade, which culminates in a Louvre-like mansard roof that is punctuated with dormers. Embellishments were applied at every opportunity—in bold cornices, in ornamental trim around doors and windows, in pediments above dormers, in wrought-iron balconies, and elsewhere.

In its richness and in the type of ornamentation employed, the De Lamar mansion is related to something like the recently constructed Parisian train station, the Quai d'Orsay, or even to some of the buildings of the Exposition Universelle of 1900, also in Paris. However much it may have been appropriate for those latter two examples, the style of the house seems today—as it did in the days of its completion—overblown, effusive, and overdone, too much of a good thing. In the end, what worked well for the ornamentation of more modest side-street townhouses proved less than satisfactory for large mansions fronting on the avenues.

Figure 242. Charles P. H. Gilbert, Joseph Raphael De Lamar residence, Madison Avenue and 37th Street, New York City, 1906. Courtesy of the Consulate of Poland in New York City, photograph by Michael Wisniewski. The architect here showed his virtuosity and his ability to design in any one of several modes that were then popular, for his Fletcher mansion (figure 211, p. 314) is in the Gothic style while the residence he created for Otto Kahn (figure 230, p. 335) is in the manner of a Roman palazzo, and the De Lamar house is an exercise in Parisian Beaux-Arts style. After De Lamar's death the mansion served for fifty years as the home of the National Democratic Club, and in 1973 it became the Polish Consulate in New York City; the Consulate has undertaken extensive restoration programs.

Figure 243. Louis Shaettle, *Mythological Scene*, ceiling painting, Alice De Lamar's bedroom, fourth floor, Joseph Raphael De Lamar residence, northeast corner of Madison Avenue and 37th Street, New York City, ca. 1906. Courtesy of the Consulate of Poland in New York City, photograph by Michael Wisniewski.

Alice De Lamar, who never liked the house or living in it, recalled that the dining room, library, and billiard room were on the first floor, while the art gallery and ballroom were on the second level. In the art gallery, with its Pompeiian red walls, stood one of the seven marble replicas of Hiram Powers's *Greek Slave*. Near it hung Bouguereau's *Aurora*, which some claimed to be the artist's masterpiece. The music room was also on this entertainment floor, and it, like the other rooms of the first and second stories, was sumptuously decorated. Some rooms had large windows filled with Tiffany's stained glass, which were lighted electrically from behind; Alice reported that her father had taken her to the Tiffany Studios to observe them being made.

But the house was not a happy one. The little music room and the grand ballroom never once hosted a gala event or a fancy-dress ball. Joseph Raphael De Lamar died in 1918, leaving an estate of nearly $30 million. Of that he left large bequests to each of three medical schools, those at Harvard, Columbia, and Johns Hopkins. He also left $500,000 to the New York Association for Improving the Conditions of the Poor. The remainder of the estate—including the Madison Avenue mansion and the Long Island country house, Pembroke—went to his only child, Alice. She, wishing not to live in the mansion, immediately tried to sell it, although that proved difficult because of the residential restrictions of the area. For a while Alice thought she had sold it to the American Bible Association, but that fell through and the National Democratic Club eventually bought it. In 1973 the People's Republic of Poland purchased it to serve as its consulate in New York City.

Senator William A. Clark

William Andrews Clark (1839–1925) grew up on a Pennsylvania farm but made his way to Montana as a young man.[16] There he prospered by selling supplies to the miners, and with his profits he bought up claims around Butte and Helena. To learn more about the mining business, he spent a year at the School of Mines at Columbia University, following a pattern similar to that of Joseph De Lamar. As his gold and silver mines, and later his copper mines, prospered, he improved the smelting plants, acquired additional mines, sometimes as far away as Arizona, and began opening banks in Montana territory. He also controlled lead mines in Idaho and the Las Vegas and Tonopah Railroad. As his wealth begot more wealth, his business interests ventured into lumber, coal, coffee, sugar beets, and cattle.

Clark truly had the Midas touch. Copper had been discovered at Butte in 1875, and Clark and his adversary, Marcus Daly of the Anaconda mine, benefited from the demand for it caused by the rise of electrification of America and Europe at the turn of the century; during one period Clark's United Verde mine was earning about $400,000 a month for him. By 1900 his wealth was estimated to be approximately $50 million.

In the 1890s he began a colorful career in politics, his opponent, again, being Marcus Daly. Clark defeated Daly for the office of U.S. senator in a bitter, close, and scandal-riddled campaign in 1893, only to have the Senate declare the election void because of the numerous improprieties. But Clark was finally elected and seated as a U.S. Senator from Montana in 1901; however, he served but a single term in Washington. While in the national capitol, he became interested in the affairs of the Corcoran Gallery, which became a beneficiary of his generosity.

Even while in Washington, Clark realized that New York City had become the social, economic, and cultural capital of the nation, and he made plans to settle there. He had married Kate Stauffer in Montana in 1869, but she died in 1893; eight years later he married Anna La Chapelle of Butte. Anna was the daughter of a Canadian physician who had settled in Montana, and when her father died, she became the ward of William Clark. She was to exert an enormous influence on him, for she was interested in the fine arts and music. Clark made arrangements for her to go to Europe to study music, and in 1901, in Marseilles, she became his second wife. It is from about that time that the senator's activities as an art collector intensified, no doubt as a result of Anna's tutelage. The writer of his obituary noted that "without doubt, his second wife helped to bring out a side of Clark's character which had been latent . . . his love for the beautiful in art."[17]

In 1901 the "Copper King," as he was known, was in need of a grand house in New York City, and he had plenty of money to lavish on it. But Clark seems not to have intended

5th AVE

to use his wealth—as, say, Alva Vanderbilt did—as a ram with which to batter down the gates of New York Society and gain admission to its charmed circle. He had no taste for that society, and said so in an interview given while the house was under construction: "he cared little for formal society and said he was too busy to be fashionable."[18]

The Senator William A. Clark Mansion

As if one such French exposition-inspired mansion—the De Lamar house—were not enough to accost the eyes of New Yorkers and assail their architectural sensibilities, a second was rising at about the same time farther uptown, at the northeast corner of Fifth Avenue and 77th Street (figure 244). The Clark mansion, some said, would have been a fit dwelling for the great showman, P. T. Barnum, while one wag, Wallace Irwin, was moved to write poetry about it:

> Senator Copper of Tonopah Ditch
> Made a clean billion in minin' and sich,
> Hiked fer Noo York, where his money he blew
> Buildin' a palace on Fift' Avenoo.
> "How," sez the Senator, "can I look proudest?
> Build me a house that'll holler the loudest—"
> . . . Pillars Ionic,
> Eaves Babylonic,
> Doors cut in scallops, resemblin' a shell;
> Roof wuz Egyptian,
> Gables caniptian,
> Whole grand effect, when completed, wuz—hell.

The sentiment of the architectural community was expressed in the *Architectural Record*, in a series of articles devoted to bad examples of building design, for the Clark mansion was designated as "Architectural Aberration No. 21."[19]

Senator Clark was, to be sure, very wealthy, and he seems to have been committed to the idea that one of the best ways to show to the world that a person possessed great wealth was through the architectural design, scale, and lavishness of his house. He thereby commissioned the local firm of Hewlett and Hull to create for him a resplendent mansion. Perhaps with his encouragement the architects turned to the fashionable new French modern style, but it seems their design was not sufficiently lavish, so it was sent off to Paris to be reworked by the well-known architectural designer and professor at the École des Beaux Arts, Henri Deglane.

Figure 244. Hewlett and Hull, and Henri Deglane, William A. Clark residence, Fifth Avenue and 77th Street, 1902–7. Brown Brothers. Senator Clark's house was grand—in scale and in architectural adornment. It had a five hundred-seat theater with stage, its own astrological tower, and an eighteenth-century room imported from France, complete with crimson and gold draperies.

Only slightly earlier, Deglane had designed the elaborate exterior for the Quai d'Orsay railway station and the Grand Palais at the Exposition Universelle of 1900—both of which represent the cartouche style run rampant. But it worked there, where it seemed appropriate and was therefore both acceptable and enjoyable. The style was being employed elsewhere in Paris at that time, as in the apartment house at No. 7 rue Rembrandt (G. Rives, architect) and in the edifice that rose at No. 87 Boulevard de la Villette (M. Rabier, architect), both of about 1897–98 (figures 245 and 246).[20] At the time that Clark's mansion was being erected, the Ansonia Hotel, at 74th Street and Broadway, was rising in the same effusive style as these Parisian examples. And it should be recalled that the Pan-American Exposition opened in Buffalo in 1901, the very year that the Clark mansion was begun. Indeed, the bravado of the Clark facades would seem to have more in common with contemporary Parisian and American exposition architecture than with anything else, as a detail from the exterior of the Clark mansion demonstrates (figure 247). Although the firm of Hewlett and Hull is nominally accredited with the design, it was in fact the local overseer of the execution of Deglane's design.

Hardly a square meter of either facade was left to architectural elements alone and not covered with some form of ornamentation. Even the plane of the walls is broken by the rustication that spreads across the surfaces. The Baroque, in its wildest excesses, seldom reached the three-dimensionality of form that is seen here, and in places—especially in the upper level of dormers—architecture ceases to exist and is transformed into bloated sculptural bombast. The house proves the unfailing principle that whenever genius creates a good thing, it is only a matter of time until someone makes a mockery of it by pushing it into an excessive mutation.

The great house—built on a lot that measured seventy-seven feet on the avenue and two hundred feet on the street—reportedly cost $5 million to build. At one point Clark became impatient with its slow progress and with the mounting expenses. In a typical reaction, he bought a stone quarry and a bronze foundry so he could control the costs and the accessibility of the required materials. Many of the elaborate ornaments on the facades were cast in bronze, at the Henry-Bonnard foundry in New York City, and then painted to give the appearance of stone, thereby saving the time and expense of having them carved by sculptors from actual stone.

If the Clark mansion appeared to be hugely out of scale—as a house—from the outside, it was equally enormous within, for it had over 120 rooms, among which were the usual spaces—an art gallery, a ballroom, a salon, dining room, billiard room, and library, plus thirty-one bathrooms and twenty-seven servants' rooms. The Louis XIV salon was filled with authentic furnishings, including a Fragonard ceiling. From Vitall Benguiat, Clark purchased a number of fine Oriental carpets, and from Lowengard of Paris he bought a series of Boucher tapestries.

The collections and furnishings, taken as a whole, overwhelm the imagination, as one pieces together the entire ensemble of the several major rooms. One can gain some idea of the assemblage from the catalogues of items—nearly seven hundred pieces—that eventually ended up in the Corcoran Gallery in Washington; in addition, the accounts of the three-day sale of the pieces the Corcoran did not take were published in *The New York Times*.[21]

Figure 245. G. Rives, apartment house, 7 rue Rembrandt, Paris, ca. 1895. From *Architectural Record* 8 (July–September 1898), p. 77.

Figure 246. M. Rabier, 87 Boulevard de la Villette, Paris, 1895–1900. From *Architectural Record* 10 (April 1901), p. 438. Figure 245 and this one, depicting architecture from turn-of-the-century Paris, reveal how the "exposition type" of architecture of the great French fairs and of the Quai d'Orsay have spread to residential design as well. And from its use for domestic purposes in Paris, it soon spread to America—in examples such as the De Lamar and the Senator William Clark mansions.

The Clarks' collection was one of the marvels of the Gilded Age. Even before the great house on Fifth Avenue was completed, the senator had begun to acquire rare and beautiful furnishings on a grand scale. Under the influence of Anna, he began spending three months a year in Europe, where they made the rounds of the art museums and the dealers' galleries, always being welcomed warmly. Clark also bought things from American dealers—from the Knoedler art galleries, for example. He owned twenty-three paintings by Camille Corot, two Gainsboroughs, and his collection of works by Monticelli was said to be better than that of the Louvre; there were paintings by or attributed to Rembrandt, Van Dyck, Titian, Steen, Beechey, Lawrence, Romney, Constable, Delacroix, Boucher, Troyon, Theodore Rousseau, and Whistler—altogether, about 225 paintings throughout the main chambers of the house. There is some evidence that at one time, at least, Clark thought of creating a collection to leave to the public, housed within his own great mansion, similar to what Henry Clay Frick had done. But in the end, he left it first to the Metropolitan Museum of Art, which refused it because the bequest required that it be housed together in perpetuity. So the choicest paintings, sculptures, carpets, laces, and porcelains went instead to the Corcoran Gallery of Art in Washington, where they can be seen today.

Figure 247. Hewlett and Hull, and Henri Deglane, cartouche from exterior of the William A. Clark residence, Fifth Avenue and 77th Street, New York City, ca. 1907. Cast bronze. From *Architectural Record* 16 (July 1904), p. 147. The origins of decorative work such as this trace back to Paris, especially in the bombastic architectural designs for the great international exposition of 1889 and also to the Quai d'Orsay train station erected for the Parisian fair of 1900, as a comparison with figure 233 on p. 341 demonstrates.

By 1925, the year of Clark's death, the day of the grand Fifth Avenue mansion had passed. That same year saw the sale of Mrs. Astor's great house at Fifth and 65th Street, and its demolition the following year, to make way for Temple Emanu-El. Within a year or two of that, the wrecker's ball was assailing the colossal mansion that William Henry Vanderbilt had erected at 52nd and Fifth Avenue. Others met similar fates as they were replaced by commercial buildings, hotels, and apartment buildings for the wealthy. Neither Clark's widow nor his children wanted the great hulking white elephant, and so plans were made to tear it down—no easy task, by the way; even as early as 1906 a critic writing in the *Architectural Record* opined that the wreckers of future years would face a formidable task with the Clark mansion. But down it came, in 1927, barely twenty years old. In its place rose one of the earliest of the cooperative apartment buildings, known simply as 960 Fifth Avenue, designed by Rosario Candela and Warren and Wetmore, and opened in 1929.

* * * * *

The cartouche style—the French modern style, as it were—worked well enough for modest-scaled facades on the side streets, just off Fifth Avenue. But the same style lapses into architectural effulgence—as in the De Lamar and Clark mansions—when applied to the exterior walls in such abundance that architectonic forces are overwhelmed by it. On the relatively narrow facades of the side streets, the cartouche style is sprightly and gay, even a little frivolous, but joyfully so. When encrusted on the great mansions, it became ridiculous.

Endnotes

Introduction

1 An existing example is Gabriel P. Weisberg, DeCourcy E. McIntosh, and Alison McQueen, *Collecting in the Gilded Age: Art Patronage in Pittsburgh, 1890–1910* (Pittsburgh: Frick Art and Historical Center, 1997).

2 See James D. McCabe, *The Illustrated History of the Centennial Exhibition* (Philadelphia: National Publishing Co., 1876).

3 E. L. Godkin, "The Expenditure of Rich Men," *Scribner's Magazine* 20 (October 1896):500.

4 Andrew Carnegie, "Wealth," *The North American Review* 148 (June 1889):653.

5 Lawrence's quote is taken from Louis Auchincloss, *The Vanderbilt Era: Profiles of a Gilded Age* (New York: Scribner, 1989), p. 17, and that of Reverend Charles Nicholls is from his book, *The Ultra-Fashionable Peerage of America* (New York: G. Harjes, 1904), p. 25.

6 George F. Baer, open letter to the press in reference to the anthracite coal strike of 1902, August 1902; quoted in Louis Auchincloss, *Theodore Roosevelt* (New York: Henry Holt and Co., 2001), p. 46.

7 Godkin, "Expenditure of Rich Men," p. 497.

8 Contemporary social critic James D. McCabe mocked this practice, as when he wrote that every member of the Old Guard "can show a string of portraits of yellow-faced worthies, in leather breeches, and ruffles and wigs, which he points to with pride as his 'ancestors.'" McCabe, *Lights and Shadows of New York Life, or, The Sights and Sensations of the Great City* (Philadelphia: National Publishing Co., 1872), pp. 137–38. An illustration from *Harper's Weekly* for 4 January 1868, titled "New Year's Day among the Modern Knickerbockers," makes the point nicely, for it shows a number of such portraits about the room. But even more noticeable is the staid atmosphere, the quietness, the lack of any raucous *joie de vivre*. Although the illustration depicts New Year's Day, everyone seems engaged in whispered conversation, and one young woman sits alone, contentedly reading a book. That scene would never be confused with the celebrations of the new-money people.

9 McCabe, *Lights and Shadows of New York Life*, p. 136.

10 John King (May) Van Rensselaer, *Social Ladder* (New York: Arno Press, 1975; originally published 1924), p. 34.

11 Van Rensselaer, *Social Ladder*, p. 37.

12 Abram C. Dayton, *The Last Days of Knickerbocker Life in New York* (New York: G. P. Putnam's Sons, 1897; originally published 1880), pp. 213–14 and 368.

13 McCabe, *Lights and Shadows of New York Life*, p. 139.

14 Van Rensselaer, *Social Ladder*, pp. 53, 56, and 58. On this point Van Rensselaer and James D. McCabe were in agreement, for he wrote in 1872 that the parvenus were "rude, ignorant, uncouth in manner, but they have wealth, and that is all that is required." McCabe, *Lights and Shadows of New York Life*, p. 140.

15 Elizabeth Ellet, *The Queens of American Society* (Philadelphia: Porter and Coates, 1867), pp. 456–57.

16 McCabe, *Lights and Shadows of New York Life*, p. 140.

17 Van Rensselaer, *Social Ladder*, p. 16.

18 McCabe, *Lights and Shadows of New York Life*, p. 166.

19 Charles Francis Adams, *The Railroads: Their Origin and Problems* (New York: G. P. Putnam's Sons, 1878), p. 145.

20 Carl Schurz, *The Boston Herald*, Supplement, 1 June 1882, p. 30.

21 Theodore Roosevelt, *Theodore Roosevelt: An Autobiography* (New York: Charles Scribner's Sons, 1926), pp. 414–16. Roosevelt's opinion of the parvenu Society people in general was not high, as he expressed in a letter to Cecil Arthur Spring Rice: "As for society people—the Four Hundred, the men and women who at this moment find their most typical expression at Newport—they lead lives which vary from rotten frivolity to rotten vice." Elting Morrison, ed., *The Letters of Theodore Roosevelt*, 8 vols. (Cambridge, Mass.: Harvard University Press, 1951), 3:107.

22 See John Steele Gordon, *The Scarlet Woman of Wall Street: Jay Gould, Jim Fisk, Cornelius Vanderbilt, the Erie Railroad Wars, and the Birth of Wall Street* (New York: Weidenfelt and Nicholson, 1988).

23 On this subject, see Burton W. Folsom Jr., *The Myth of the Robber Barons: A New Look at the Rise of Big Business in America* (Herndon, Va.: Young America's Foundation, 1987), and Charles R. Morris, *The Tycoons: How Andrew Carnegie, John D. Rockefeller, Jay Gould, and J. P. Morgan Invented the American Supereconomy* (New York: Times Books/Henry Holt and Company, 2005).

24 Henry Clews, *Fifty Years in Wall Street* (New York: Irving Publishing Co., 1908), p. 394. Clews was a successful financier and political adviser on economic matters; he wrote numerous essays on social and economic issues.

25 Anthony Trollope, *North America*, Donald Smalley and Bradford Allen Booth, eds. (New York: Alfred A. Knopf, 1951; originally published 1862), p. 194. Trollope (1815–82), the son of Frances Trollope, was an English novelist of the mid-nineteenth century; he visited the United States in 1861–62.

26 Carnegie, "Wealth," pp. 661 and 663.

Chapter 1

Society, Europe, and Aristocracy

1 James D. McCabe, *Lights and Shadows of New York Life, or, The Sights and Sensations of the Great City* (Philadelphia: National Publishing Co., 1872), pp. 166–67. On Grace Church, see William Rhinelander Stewart, *Grace Church and Old New York* (New York: E. P. Dutton, 1924).

2 David Lowe, *Stanford White's New York* (New York: Doubleday, 1992), p. 16.

3 Mrs. Burton Harrison, *Recollections, Grave and Gay* (New York: Charles Scribner's Sons, 1912), p. 275.

4 Elizabeth Ellet, *The Queens of American Society* (Philadelphia: Porter and Coates, 1867), p. 453. Julius Henri Browne, writing two years later, assured his readers that any wedding over which the good sexton presided would be a success: "At weddings and at parties [Brown] makes out the list of persons to be invited. He allows no interference. He knows his invitations will be accepted, and as he knows who is in town, both stranger and resident, he can always make out a full list. He directs everything, and carries his arrangements out with the decision and authority of an autocrat." Browne, *The Secrets of the Great City* (New York: Jones, Brothers and Co., 1869), p. 85.

5 Quoted from Arthur Maurice, *Fifth Avenue* (New York: Arno Press, 1975; originally published 1918), p. 66.
6 Ward McAllister, *Society as I have found It* (New York: Cassell Publishing Co., 1890), p. 124.
7 Quoted from Maurice, *Fifth Avenue*, p. 67.
8 "Secrets of Ball-Giving, a Chat with Ward McAllister," *New York Daily Tribune*, 25 March 1888, p. 11.
9 On McAllister, see his autobiography, *Society as I have found It*.
10 Elizabeth Drexel Lehr, *King Lehr and the Gilded Age* (Philadelphia: Lippincott, 1935), pp. 23–24.
11 Margaret Terry (Mrs. Winthrop) Chanler, *Roman Spring: Memoirs* (Boston: Little, Brown, 1934), p. 234.
12 Anthony Trollope, *North America*, Donald Smaller and Bradford Allen Booth, eds. (New York: Alfred A. Knopf, 1951; originally published 1861), p. 214.
13 Frederick Martin, *Things I Remember* (New York: E. Nash, 1913), pp. 171–72. Edith Wharton took this same theme for the plot of her novel, *The Custom of the Country* (New York: Charles Scribner's Sons), also published in 1913.
14 Charles W. Nicholls, *The Ultra-Fashionable Peerage of America* (New York: G. Harjes, 1904), pp. 81 and 78.
15 Alfred R. Ferguson, ed., *The Journals and Miscellaneous Notebooks of Ralph Waldo Emerson*, 16 vols. (Cambridge: Harvard University Press, 1964), 4:186.
16 William Dean Howells, *Venetian Life*, 2 vols. (Boston: Houghton, Mifflin, 1892), 2:251. On Howells, see Susan Goodman and Carl Dawson, *William Dean Howells: A Writer's Life* (Berkeley: University of California Press, 2005).
17 Howells, *Venetian Life*, 2:228.
18 Henry James, *The Aspen Papers and Other Stories* (Oxford: Oxford University Press, 1983), p. 5.
19 See Henry James, *Letters from the Palazzo Barbaro* (London: Puskin Press, 1998).
20 Rollin van N. Hadley, ed., *The Letters of Bernard Berenson and Isabella Stewart Gardner, 1887–1924* (Boston: Northeastern University Press, 1987), pp. 484–85.
21 Wharton, *Custom of the Country*, p. 545.
22 The purchase of noble titles with American dollars or other barter was neither unusual nor difficult. Henry Clews was disdainful of the practice, and after asserting that "the modern nobility spring from success in business," he declared that English noble titles were regularly placed on the auction block and that American money now easily purchased aristocracy's treasures: "The antiquities, the bric-a-brac, the works of art, the rare furniture . . . are purchased by the new nobility raised up by success in finance and commerce. There is very little in Europe which is not obtainable at a price." See Henry Clews, *Fifty Years in Wall Street* (New York: Irving Publishing Co., 1908), p. 608.
23 McCabe, *Lights and Shadows of New York Life*, pp. 159 and 161. The matter was as practical as it was unsentimental. "The great invasion," Frederick Martin noted in his memoirs, "began a generation ago, when Miss [Jennie] Jerome of New York, married Lord Randolph Churchill, a wedding which may be said to have set the fashion for similar alliances." Martin, *Things I Remember*, p. 172.
24 Anthony Trollope, *The Way We Live Now* (London: The Trollope Society, 1992; first published in serial form in 1874 and as a book in 1875), p. 34.
25 Trollope, *Way We Live Now*, p. 125.
26 The loveable if fey little count continually tried to outmaneuver both his ex-wife and her financially astute family, as the following notice, quoted from the *Boston Transcript*, testifies: "The little Count Castellane has to work almost too hard for a count in trying to get money out of the Goulds. The awful rumor is about that work is stopped on the red marble Castellane Paris palace because the countess and her family found out that the count had an arrangement with the builders and architects by which he got forty per cent commission!" Quoted from *The American Architect and Building News* (29 October 1898), p. 38.
27 René Gimpel, *Diary of an Art Dealer* (New York: Farrar, Straus and Giroux, 1966), pp. 3–4.
28 Consuelo Vanderbilt Balsan, *The Glitter and the Gold* (New York: Harper, 1952), p. 42. See also James Brough, *Consuelo: Portrait of an American Heiress* (New York: Coward, McCann and Geohegan, 1979).
29 Balsan, *Glitter and the Gold*, p. 37.
30 Martin, *Things I Remember*, p. 176.
31 *The New York Times*, 24 March 1885, p. 4.
32 Gimpel, *Diary of an Art Dealer*, p. 123.
33 McAllister, *Society as I have found It*, pp. 369–70.

Chapter 2
THE EARLY MANSIONS
Part One

1 Jerry Patterson, *Fifth Avenue: The Best Address* (New York: Rizzoli, 1998), p. 72.
2 James D. McCabe, *Lights and Shadows of New York Life, or, The Sights and Sensations of the Great City* (Philadelphia: National Publishing Co., 1872), p. 207.
3 Mariana Griswold Van Rensselaer, "Recent Architecture in America: City Residences," *The Century Magazine* 31, no. 4 (February 1886):550. Another source referred to the brownstones as "the most vulgar type of dwelling ever erected by man." Harry W. Desmond and Herbert Croly, *Stately Homes in America* (New York: D. Appleton and Co., 1903), p. 531.
4 Franz Winkler, "Architecture in the Billionaire District of New York City," *Architectural Record* 11 (October 1901):684. Jersey freestone, as brownstone was sometimes called, was a mauve-brown sandstone that was quarried in Passaic, New Jersey, and in Connecticut. Exposure to the elements and pollutants turned it darker and browner. See Charles Lockwood, *Bricks and Brownstone: The New York Row House, 1783–1929* (New York: McGraw-Hill, 1972).
5 Henry Adams, *Democracy, an American Novel* (New York: Henry Holt and Co., 1908), p. 2.
6 Edith Wharton, *The Age of Innocence* (New York: D. Appleton and Co., 1920), p. 69.
7 Desmond and Croly, *Stately Homes in America*, p. 334.
8 See Ellen W. Kramer, "Detlef Lienau, an Architect of the Brown Decades," *Journal of the Society of Architectural Historians* 14 (March 1955):18–25.
9 The Schiff house offered Léon Marcotte his first important opportunity in interior design, leading to a distinguished career as one of the Gilded Age's earliest and foremost designers of interiors and exquisitely crafted furnishings.
10 A. J. Bloor declared that Lienau was the first to introduce the mansard roof into American architecture; see his "Report on Mansard Roofs," *Proceedings of the American Institute of Architects* (1874):45. However, notice should also be taken of another early example provided by Charles Lemoulnier, who arrived in the United States from France in the mid-1840s; he designed the Deacon mansion in Boston in 1847–48, and several of its rooms were paneled with boiserie brought over from the Hôtel de Montmorency in Paris.
11 Anthony Trollope, *North America*, Donald Smalley and Bradford Allen Booth, eds. (New York: Alfred A. Knopf, 1951; originally published 1861), p. 204.
12 "New York Daguerreotyped," *Putnam's Magazine* 3 (March 1854):238.
13 Much later, when the new campus for Columbia University at Morningside Heights was being designed by McKim, Mead and White, Schermerhorn was chairman of the board of trustees, and he gave the money for the building of Schermerhorn Hall.
14 Elizabeth Ellet, *The Queens of American Society* (Philadelphia: Porter and Coates, 1867), p. 452.
15 Mrs. John King (May), Van Rensselaer, *The Social Ladder* (New York: Arno Press, 1975; originally published 1924), p. 183. William Rhinelander Stewart recalled the social leadership of the Schermerhorns, noting that they "represented all that was best in the social life of New York in their time." Quoted from William Rhinelander Stewart, *Grace Church and Old New York* (New York: E. P. Dutton, 1924), p. 439.
16 Allan Nevins and Milton Halsey Thomas, eds., *The Diary of George Templeton Strong*, 4 vols. (New York: Macmillan Co., 1952), 3:20.
17 Nevins and Thomas, *Diary of George Templeton Strong*, p. 27, under date of 18 May 1860.
18 Nevins and Thomas, *Diary of George Templeton Strong*, 4:354, under date of 6 May 1871.
19 Van Rensselaer, *Social Ladder*, p. 183.
20 See Neville Thompson, "Terror in the Ballroom: What to Wear, How to Dance, What to Say," *Nineteenth Century* 23 (Spring 2003):35–36.
21 Quoted from David Black, *The King of Fifth Avenue: The Fortunes of August Belmont* (New York: The Dial Press, 1981), p. 173. Junius Henri Browne, who did not know Belmont from inside the charmed circle of Society, has left us a rather critical description of the man. After noting that his home on Fifth Avenue "is interiorly one of the most elegant and luxurious in town. His picture gallery alone is said to be worth $400,000 or $500,000," Browne described Belmont as "small, heavy set, with a short, thick nose, not inviting in appearance, nor conciliating in manner. Though a man of brain and character, he is not popular, nor does he wish to be—satisfied with his position and his unquestionable power. . . . He walks lame, having been wounded in a duel while living on the Continent; but in the peculiar understanding of Wall Street he is not likely to be crippled." Browne, *The Great Metropolis: A Mirror of New York: A Complete History of Metropolitan Life and Society, with Sketches of Prominent Places, Persons, and Things in the City, as they actually exist* (Hartford, Conn.: American Publishing Co., 1869), p. 616.
22 Quoted from Black, *King of Fifth Avenue*, p. 173.

23 Mrs. Burton Harrison, *Recollections, Grave and Gay* (New York: Charles Scribner's Sons, 1912), p. 279.
24 "A Chat with Ward McAllister," *New York Daily Tribune*, 25 March 1888, p. 11.
25 Frederick Martin, *Things I Remember* (New York: E. Nash, 1913), p. 218.
26 Ellet, *Queens of American Society*, p. 453.
27 Hyman B. Grinstein, *The Rise of the Jewish Community of New York* (Philadelphia: The Jewish Publication Society of America, 1945), p. 374.
28 Black, *King of Fifth Avenue*, p. 140.
29 Wharton, Edith, and Ogden Codman, *The Decoration of Houses* (New York: Charles Scribner and Sons, 1897), pp. 134–35.
30 At about the very same time that the Belmont collection was introduced to New Yorkers, another event occurred that further promoted contemporary European art: the exhibition of a large number of paintings of the Düsseldorf school and the establishment of the Düsseldorf Gallery which was quite popular in the last half of the 1850s. The Düsseldorf paintings, like those in Belmont's collection, represented a Europeanization of taste and a challenge to the native Hudson River School painters.
31 *The New York Times*, 19 December 1857, p. 4:5. For a more detailed account of the Belmont collection, see "Galleries of Belmont and Blodgett," *Putnam's Magazine* 5 (May 1870):534–40.
32 The only American artist mentioned by the reviewer in the Belmont collection was Eastman Johnson, who, after studying for two years (1849–51) at the academy in Düsseldorf, moved to the Netherlands, where he remained until his return to the United States in 1855. His tenure at The Hague, therefore, coincided with the Belmonts' residence there, and it may have been at that time that August acquired examples of his work.
33 *The New York Times*, 19 December 1857, p. 4:5.
34 The practice of holding art exhibitions to benefit one social program or another, inaugurated here, was followed during the years of the Civil War with the Sanitary Fairs, which were organized to help wounded soldiers and the families of those slain in the conflict. It is continued even today when special exhibitions or special opening events are held to raise money for charitable purposes.
35 Anita Leslie, *The Remarkable Mr. Jerome* (New York: Henry Holt and Co., 1954), p. 53.

Chapter 3
THE EARLY MANSIONS
Part Two

1 Junius Henri Browne, *The Great Metropolis: A Mirror of New York: A Complete History of Metropolitan Life and Society, with Sketches of Prominent Places, Persons, and Things in the City, as they actually exist* (Hartford, Conn.: American Publishing Co., 1869), p. 617.
2 Mrs. George Cornwallis-West, *The Reminiscences of Lady Randolph Churchill* (New York: The Century Co., 1909), pp. 9–10.
3 Anita Leslie, *Lady Randolph Churchill: The Story of Jennie Jerome* (New York: Charles Scribner's Sons, 1969), p. 11.
4 Anita Leslie, *The Remarkable Mr. Jerome* (New York: Henry Holt and Co., 1954), p. 65.
5 Letter, dated Paris, 19 July 1869, Archives of the Lockwood-Mathews Mansion Museum, Norwalk, Conn.
6 The Mathews family continued to live in the house until 1938; three years later it was sold to the City of Norwalk. It is now open to the public as the Lockwood-Mathews Mansion.
7 See Stephen N. Elias, *Alexander T. Stewart: Forgotten Merchant Prince* (Westport, Conn.: Praeger, 1992). See also Edward Crapsey, "A Monument to Trade," *The Galaxy* 9 (January 1870):94–101. Portraits of Stewart are rare, as noted by his contemporaries: "One of Stewart's peculiarities was his unwillingness to have portraits of any kind taken of himself, giving . . . as a reason, that he was such a commonplace-looking fellow." Quoted from "Alexander T. Stewart," *Harper's Weekly* (29 April 1876):345.
8 "Alexander T. Stewart," p. 346.
9 See also Michael Miller, *The Bon Marché: Bourgeois Culture and the Department Store, 1869–1920* (Princeton: Princeton University Press, 1981); W. Lancaster, *The Department Store: A Social History* (London: Pinter Publishers, 1992); and David Cheney, "The Department Store as a Cultural Form," *Theory, Culture and Society* 1 (1983):22–31.
10 "Alexander T. Stewart," p. 346.
11 Allan Nevins and Milton Halsey Thomas, eds., *The Diary of George Templeton Strong*, 4 vols. (New York: Macmillan Co., 1952), 3:416.
12 See Jay Cantor, "A Monument to Trade: A. T. Stewart and the Rise of the Millionaire's Mansion in New York," *Winterthur Portfolio* 10 (1975):165–97.
13 Stewart at one point became impatient with the tardy deliveries of marble from the Tuckahoe quarry and arranged a contract with its owner and operator, "fixing a heavy penalty, amounting . . . to the forfeiture of the quarry itself, for delay in delivery, beyond a specified time, of the marble." When the marble arrived late, Stewart foreclosed; reportedly, the distraught owner promptly died on the spot after pleading with the great merchant not to take his livelihood, and Stewart found himself master of a marble quarry. Thereafter, his marble arrived at the building site in a timely manner. See *American Architect and Building News* 58 (25 February 1899):1.
14 Kellum's obituary noted that "the most striking specimens of his work are the Mutual Life Insurance Company's building; the Stock Exchange; the Herald building; Mr. A. T. Stewart's store[s]; the extensive iron ferry-house of the Union Ferry Company at Fulton Street; the stores of Ball, Black and Co.; Tiffany and Co.," as well as the Women's Hotel mentioned earlier. Quotation from *Harper's Weekly* (12 August 1871):741.
15 George W. Sheldon, *Artistic Houses*, 2 vols. in 4 (New York: Doubleday and Co., 1883), 1:7.
16 Sheldon, *Artistic Houses*, 1:8.
17 The *Greek Slave* is the version now owned by the Newark Museum in Newark, N.J., and the *Eve Disconsolate* is now in the collection of the Hudson River Museum, Yonkers, N.Y.
18 Earl Shinn [Edward Strahan], *Art Treasures of America*, 3 vols. (Philadelphia: G. Barrie, 1879–82), 1:4–52.
19 *The Art Amateur* (July 1879):29–30.
20 "Mr. Stewart's New Residence," *Harper's Weekly* (14 August 1869):526.
21 For the satirical and irreverent coverage of the kidnapping of Stewart's body and the chastisement of Judge Hilton for his mishandling of the affair, see "A Voice from the Grave," *Puck* (13 November 1878):3, and "The Resurrection of the Body," *Puck* (27 November 1878):3.
22 See *Catalogue of the A. T. Stewart Collection of Paintings, Sculptures, and other Objects of Art, to be sold by auction . . . by order of Henry Hilton . . . and Charles Clinch . . . executors of the Estate of Mrs. Cornelia M. Stewart, deceased* March 23rd, 24th and 25th . . . continuing March 28th and following days, American Art Association, managers, Thomas E. Kirby, auctioneer (New York: Press of J. J. Little and Co., 1887).
23 On Lienau and the block of houses he designed for Rebecca Colford Jones, see Ellen W. Kramer, "Detlef Lienau, an American Architect of the Brown Decades," *Journal of the Society of Architectural Historians* 14 (March 1955):18–25.
24 Henry James, *Washington Square* (London: Macmillan, 1881), pp. 43–44.
25 Edith Wharton, *The Age of Innocence* (New York: D. Appleton and Company, 1920), p. 24.
26 Edith Wharton, *A Backward Glance* (New York: D. Appleton-Century, 1934), pp. 54–55.
27 Wharton, *Age of Innocence*, p. 10.
28 Browne, *Great Metropolis*, p. 222.

Chapter 4
THE COMMODORE AND BEETLEHEAD

1 Cornelius's childhood home was a small, wood-frame farmhouse, typical of Dutch regional architecture of the eighteenth century. It was destroyed by fire in the late-nineteenth century.
2 Even at work, after the Commodore had become a millionaire many times over, he did not build himself a large and grandiose office, but had only one small, stark room in Bowling Green, with a desk that had one drawer, in which he kept his box of cigars. Most of his business records were kept in his head, and his office staff consisted of one secretary.
3 Vanderbilt, who at last had access to the vast markets of the interior of the continent, then had $42 million in stock certificates for his New York Central printed up, which he sold, a stock-watering escapade of gigantic magnitude but a move that greatly increased the Vanderbilt fortune.
4 John Overton Choules, *The Cruise of the Steam Yacht North Star* (Boston: Gould and Lincoln, 1854), pp. 222–24.
5 Quoted from Richard Wunder, *Hiram Powers, Vermont Sculptor*, 2 vols. (Newark: University of Delaware Press, 1991), 1:300.
6 Arnold Lewis, James Turner, and Steven McQuillin, *The Opulent Interiors of the Gilded Age: All 203 Photographs from "Artistic Houses"* (New York: Dover Publications, 1987), p. 114.
7 Letters to the Editors, *American Architect and Building News*, 17 (2 May 1886):214.
8 Architectural critic Clarence Cook, commenting on the Vanderbilt mansion, observed that "it is carried out in its present material contrary to the earnest wish of the architect, who had intended a light-colored stone to be used. " Cook, "Architecture in America," *The North American Review* 135 (September 1882):249.

9 For an account of this reception. see *The New York Times*, 8 March 1882.

10 See the *Catalogue des Objets d'Art et d'Ameublement . . . a Florence, au Palais de San Donato, le 15 Mars 1880 et les jours suivants. . . .* (Paris, 1880), p. 7, no. 29.

11 Earl Shinn (Edward Strahan), *Mr. Vanderbilt's House and Collection*, 2 vols. (Boston: G. Barrie, 1883–84), 1:14. Rich, green malachite had been one of the sources of the early Demidoff fortunes, coming from mines in the interior of Russia that were owned and operated by the Demidoffs.

12 James Jackson Jarves, "The Gates of Paradise," *Harper's Monthly* 65 (June 1882):92.

13 *American Architect and Building News* (17 November 1894):66.

14 Cook, "Architecture in America," p. 249.

15 Eastlake's near-epoch-making book was rewritten, paraphrased, and popularized by American authors such as Clarence Cook and Harriet Prescott Spofford, each publishing his or her own book on interior decorating and furniture. See Clarence Cook, *The House Beautiful* (New York: Charles Scribner's Sons, 1877), and Harriet Prescott Spofford, *Art Decoration applied to Furniture* (New York: Harper, 1878).

16 Mary Elizabeth Wilson Sherwood, "Certain New York Houses," *Harper's Monthly* 65 (September 1882):681. On the Aesthetic Movement, see Doreen Bolger Burke, Jonathan Freedman, Alice Cooney Frelinghuysen, et al., *In Pursuit of Beauty: Americans and the Aesthetic Movement* (New York: Metropolitan Museum of Art, 1986).

17 Edith Wharton and Ogden Codman, *The Decoration of Houses* (New York: Charles Scribner's Sons, 1897), pp. 137 and 139.

18 Quoted from Jerry Patterson, *The Vanderbilts* (New York: H. N. Abrams, 1989), p. 86.

19 George W. Sheldon, *Artistic Houses*, 2 vols. in 4 (New York: Doubleday and Co., 1883), 1:113.

20 Shinn, *Mr. Vanderbilt's House and Collection*.

21 Sheldon, *Artistic Houses*, 1:114.

22 Sheldon, *Artistic Houses*, 1:116.

23.Burke, et al., *The Pursuit of Beauty*, p. 152.

24 Sheldon, *Artistic Houses*, 1:112.

25 Sheldon, *Artistic Houses*, 1:124.

26 Electric lights were installed in the Vanderbilt mansion in 1882, but some of the wiring proved faulty, causing a fire, Thomas Alva Edison had all of the wiring removed. Thereafter, illumination was by gaslight.

27 *The New York Times*, obituary for William Henry Vanderbilt, 9 December 1885.

28 *The New York Times*, obituary for William Henry Vanderbilt, 9 December 1885.

29 Samuel Avery to John Taylor Johnston, Paris, 31 July 1872, quoted in Madeleine F. Beaufort and Jeanne Welcher, "Some Views on Art Buying in New York in the 1870s and 1880s," *Oxford Art Journal* 5, no. 1 (1982):54.

30 Henry James, *Parisian Sketches: Letters to the New York Tribune*, Leon Edel and Isle Dusoir Lind, eds. (London: Rupert Hart-Davis, 1958), p. 38, letter dated 22 January 1876.

31 Wesley Towner, *The Elegant Auctioneers* (New York: Hill and Wang, 1970), pp. 30–31.

32 Towner, *Elegant Auctioneers*, p. 44.

33 William A. Croffut, *The Vanderbilts and the Story of their Fortune* (Chicago and New York: Belford, Clarke and Co., 1886), p. 246.

34 Gustavus Myers, *History of the Great American Fortunes*, 3 vols. (Chicago: Charles H. Kerr and Co., 1911), 2:213.

35 Lewis, Turner and McQuillin, *Opulent Interiors of the Gilded Age*, p. 119.

36 Samuel Avery in *The New York Times*, 10 March 1882, 2:6.

37 *American Architecture and Building News*, 21 May 1881, p. 243.

38 Cook, "Architecture in America," p. 249, and Mariana Griswold Van Rensselaer, "Recent Architecture in America: City Residences," *The Century Magazine*, 31, no. 4 (February 1886):554.

39 Montgomery Schuyler, *American Architecture Studies* (New York: Harper and Brothers, 1892), p. 66.

40 Harry W. Desmond and Herbert Croly, *Stately Homes in America* (New York: D. Appleton and Co., 1903), p. 255.

41 *The New York Times*, 25 August 1881, p. 2.

42 H. Barbara Weinberg, *The Decorative Work of John La Farge* (New York: Garland Publishing Co., 1977), p. 255.

43 See *The New York Times*, 5 April 1945, 38:1; 19 April 1945; 16:5; 20 April 1945, 16:6; and 20 May 1945, 29:2.

Chapter 5

ALVA AND WILLIAM KISSAM VANDERBILT

1 On the Vanderbilts as builders, see Montgomery Schuyler, "The Vanderbilt Houses," in *American Architecture Studies* (New York: Harper and Brothers, 1892), pp. 52–67, and Robert B. King, *The Vanderbilt Homes* (New York: Rizzoli, 1989).

2 Elizabeth Drexel Lehr, *King Lehr and the Gilded Age* (Philadelphia: Lippincott, 1935), p. 147.

3 Louis Auchincloss, *The Vanderbilt Era: Profiles of a Gilded Age* (New York: Scribner, 1989), p. 47.

4 Balsan, *Glitter and the Gold* (New York: Harper, 1952), p. 6.

5 Cornelius Vanderbilt Jr., *The Queen of the Golden Age: The Fabulous Story of Grace Wilson Vanderbilt* (New York: McGraw-Hill, 1956), p. 13.

6 Idle Hour, a rambling, shingle-covered Queen Anne–style house, was the first commission Hunt executed for the Vanderbilt family. It burned in 1899 and was rebuilt for Alva by one of Hunt's sons, Richard Howland Hunt.

7 Lehr, *King Lehr and the Gilded Age*, p. 177.

8 Ernest Flagg, "The École des Beaux-Arts," *Architectural Record* 4 (July–September 1894):40.

9 Auchincloss, *Vanderbilt Era*, p. 47.

10 The Château de Martainville now houses the Musée des Traditions et Arts Normand, and is located in Epreville, Seine-Maritime, France, east of Rouen.

11 Two excellent biographies of Hunt exist: Paul Baker, *Richard Morris Hunt* (Cambridge, Mass.: MIT Press, 1980), and Susan Stein, *The Architecture of Richard Morris Hunt* (Chicago: University of Chicago Press, 1986).

12 Balsan, *Glitter and the Gold*, p. 5.

13 Balsan, *Glitter and the Gold*, p. 7.

14 John V. Van Pelt, *Monograph of the William K. Vanderbilt House* (New York: J. V. Van Pelt, 1925), p. 15, says one "G. Bubert" modeled it, but that was probably an error of recording a name; he may have meant Caspar Buberl, who is known to have done carving at the house. For an illustration of the image of Hunt, see Baker, *Richard Morris Hunt*, p. 280, fig. 65.

15 Anonymous, *American Architect and Building News* 38 (29 April 1891):132.

16 Schuyler, "Vanderbilt Houses," p. 52.

17 Schuyler, "Vanderbilt Houses," p. 57. For a negative critique of the Petit Château, and of Richard Morris Hunt as an architect, see Clarence Cook, "Architecture in America," *The North American Review* 310 (September 1882):249–51.

18 Anonymous, *The Art Amateur* 19 (November 1888):137.

19 Charles Moore, *Daniel Burnham: Architect, Planner of Cities*, 2 vols. (New York: Houghton Mifflin, 1921), 1:116.

20 Van Pelt, *Monograph of the William K. Vanderbilt House*, p. 15.

21 Van Pelt, *Monograph of the William K. Vanderbilt House*, p. 21.

22 *The Art Amateur* 15 (November 1886):128.

23 Anonymous, *The Art Amateur* 16 (January 1887):29. This same critic observed that "the only works of Baudry's at all known in America are the ceilings which he executed, one for Mr. W. K. Vanderbilt . . . , and one for Mr. Cornelius Vanderbilt." Much later, Baudry's view of Olympus was painted to adorn the ceiling of the New Theater, designed by Carrère and Hastings in 1909, in New York City.

24 *The New York Times*, 11 June 1882.

25 Oudinot was the most famous artist working in stained glass in France between about 1860 and his death in 1890. As a youth he had studied, in Paris, with Eugène Delacroix, and, according to his obituary, "in 1862 he was appointed worker in stained-glass to the City of Paris. From that time his reputation rapidly increased, both at home and abroad, and, besides innumerable works for the City of Paris and the French Government, he executed many commissions for foreign countries, among them being . . . large windows for Trinity Church, Boston. His preference was for Renaissance design, which he understood perfectly." *American Architect and Building News*, 27 (8 February 1890):1.

26 Balsan, *Glitter and the Gold*, p. 10.

27 Pauline King, *American Mural Painting: A Study in the Important Decorations by Distinguished Artists in the United States* (Boston: Noyes, Platt and Co., 1902), p. 250.

28 Balsan, *Glitter and the Gold*, p. 6.

29 Elizabeth Drexel Lehr, *King Lehr and the Gilded Age*, p. 68.

30.Catharine Hunt, "Richard Morris Hunt," 3 vols., typescript biography (Washington, D.C.: American Institute of Architects), 3:280.

31.Ward McAllister, *Society as I have found It* (New York: Cassell Publishing Co., 1890), pp. 353–54.

32 Herbert Croly, "The Work of Richard Morris Hunt," *Architectural Record* 59 (January 1926):88.

33 Van Pelt, *William K. Vanderbilt House*, pp. 18 and 21.

Chapter 6

THE CORNELIUS VANDERBILT II MANSION

1 Maud Howe Elliott, *This Was My Newport* (New York: Arno Press, 1975; originally published 1944),

p. 161. A newspaper columnist put it even more succinctly: "Mr. Vanderbilt has no fads or hobbies." *New York Times*, 26 November 1893, 21:5.

2 Jean Strouse, *Morgan, American Financier* (New York: Random House, 1999), p. 249.
3 *The New York Times*, 26 November 1893, 21:5.
4 On Post, see Sarah Bradford Landau, *George B. Post, Architect: Picturesque Designer and Determined Realist* (New York: Monacelli Press, 1998).
5 *The New York Times*, 5 March 1892, 8:2.
6 *The New York Times*, 28 January 1893, 10:3.
7 "In its completed form the present mansion is an impressive reminder of the famous Blois Castle, the birthplace of Louis XII., and one of the historic landmarks of France." *The New York Times*, 26 November 1893, 21:5.
8 Montgomery Schuyler, "The Vanderbilt Houses," in *American Architecture Studies* (New York: Harper and Brothers, 1892), p. 62.
9 Schuyler, "Vanderbilt Houses," p. 61.
10 *The Illustrated American* (8 July 1893):22.
11 Letter from Edith Wharton to Ogden Codman, 2 May 1897, Society for the Preservation of New England Antiquities, Boston.
12. Edith Wharton, "The Valley of Childish Things, and Other Emblems," in *The Collected Short Stories of Edith Wharton*, R.W.B. Lewis, ed., 2 vols. (New York: Charles Scribner's Sons, 1968), 1:58–64.
13 In 1939 the magnificent gate was given to the City of New York by Gertrude Vanderbilt Whitney and installed at the entrance to Central Park at Fifth Avenue and 105th Street. It was designed by George B. Post.
14 The best coverage of this matter is Henry Adams, "John La Farge's Work in the Vanderbilt Houses," *American Art Journal* 16 (Autumn 1984):30–70, and James L. Yarnall, "Souvenirs of Splendor: John La Farge and the Patronage of Cornelius Vanderbilt II," *American Art Journal* 26, nos. 1 and 2 (1994): 67–105.
15 Homer Saint-Gaudens, ed., *Reminiscences of Augustus Saint-Gaudens*, 2 vols. (New York: Century, 1913), 1:349–50. The bas-relief profile portrait of Cornelius I, modeled in 1882 from photographs taken in 1873, is illustrated in Armin Brand Allen, *The Cornelius Vanderbilts of The Breakers* (Newport, R.I.: The Preservation Society of Newport County, 1995), p. 14, no. 17. A plaster replica of the double portrait of the two boys is preserved at The Saint-Gaudens National Historic Site, Cornish, N.H.
16 Mary Gay Humphreys, "The Cornelius Vanderbilt House: Decorations for the Dining-Room, Watercolor Room, and Smoking Room," *The Art Amateur* 8, no. 6 (May 1883):135.
17 A plaster replica of the *Actaeon* panel and a plaster version of *Apollo with Cupids*, taken from the original clay models executed by Augustus Saint-Gaudens, survive, respectively, at the J. B. Speed Art Museum, Louisville, Ky., and at the Saint-Gaudens National Historic Site, Cornish, N.H. The original of the *Apollo* panel is now in the Smithsonian American Art Museum, Washington, D.C.
18 Adams, "John La Farge's Work in the Vanderbilt Houses," pp. 49–50.
19 See *The New York Times*, 7 April 1927, p. 32:1.
20 For an account of the 1892 ball, see *The New York Times*, 6 April 1892, 5:5.
21 *The New York Times*, 5 March 1892, 8:2.
22 Edouard Toudouze (1848–1907) was the son of architect Gabriel Toudouze. As indications of his celebrity, he had won the Grand Prix de Rome in 1871 and a silver medal at the great Exposition Universelle in Paris in 1889, and that same year had been elected a Chevalier of the Legion of Honor.
23 *The New York Times*, 3 April 1893, 9:3.
24 *The New York Times*, 26 November 1893, 21:5.
25 *The Art Amateur* 14 (December, 1886):55.
26 *The Art Amateur* 16 (May 1887):122.

Chapter 7
NEWPORT

1 Charles W. Nicholls, *The Ultra-Fashionable Peerage of America* (New York: Arno Press, 1975; originally published 1905), p. 23.
2 Nicholls, *Ultra-Fashionable Peerage of America*, p. 35.
3 Elizabeth Drexel Lehr, *King Lehr and the Gilded Age* (Philadelphia: Lippincott, 1935), p. 112.
4 Mrs. John King (May) Van Rensselaer, *The Social Ladder* (New York: Arno Press, 1975; originally published 1924), p. 245.
5 Nicholls, *The Ultra-Fashionable Peerage of America*, p. 88.
6 Maud Howe Elliott, *Reminiscences, 1819–1899* (Boston: Houghton, Mifflin and Co., 1900), p. 402.
7 Elliott, *Reminiscences*, pp. 408–9.
8 Van Rensselaer, *Social Ladder*, pp. 223 and 227.
9 Harry W. Desmond and Herbert Croly, *Stately Homes in America* (New York: D. Appleton and Co., 1903), p. 376. On the architecture of Newport in general, see Antoinette F. Downing and Vincent J. Scully Jr., *The Architectural Heritage of Newport, Rhode Island, 1640–1915* (New York: C. N. Potter, 1967).
10 Van Rensselaer, *Social Ladder*, p. 228.
11 Van Rensselaer, *Social Ladder*, p. 229.
12 Frederick Martin, *Things I Remember* (New York: Arno Press, 1975; originally published 1913), pp. 63 and 70.
13 Maud Howe Elliott, *This Was My Newport* (New York: Arno Press, 1975; originally published 1944), pp. 408–9.
14 Lehr, *King Lehr and the Gilded Age*, p. 141.
15 See Eileen Warburton, *Bellevue Avenue: Newport's Legendary Stroll* (Newport, R.I.: Pondhouse, 1992).
16 Lehr, *King Lehr and the Gilded Age*, p. 138.
17 Lehr, *King Lehr and the Gilded Age*, p. 58.
18 Winslow Ames, "The Transformation of Château-sur-Mer," *Journal of the Society of Architectural Historians* 29 (December 1970):291–306.
19 Clarence Cook, "Architecture in America," *The North American Review* 135 (September 1882):246.
20 Van Rensselaer, *Social Ladder*, p. 162.
21 Lehr, *King Lehr and the Gilded Age*, p. 124.
22 Edward Simmons, *Seven to Seventy: Memories of a Painter and a Yankee* (New York: Harper, 1922), p. 204.
23 For illustrations of the interiors of Ochre Court, see *Architectural Record* 5 (October–December 1895):135 ff.
24 Thomas Gannon and David Chase, *Newport Mansions: The Gilded Age* (Little Compton, R.I.: Fort Church Publishers, 1982), p. 68.
25 Consuelo Vanderbilt Balsan, *The Glitter and the Gold* (New York: Harper, 1952), p. 25.
26 Balsan, *Glitter and the Gold*, p. 25.
27 Balsan, *Glitter and the Gold*, p. 25.
28 Lehr, *King Lehr and the Gilded Age*, p. 26.
29 Balsan, *Glitter and the Gold*, p. 40.
30 Lehr, *King Lehr and the Gilded Age*, p. 221.
31 Lehr, *King Lehr and the Gilded Age*, pp. 154–55.
32 Lehr, *King Lehr and the Gilded Age*, p. 121.
33 Lehr, *King Lehr and the Gilded Age*, p. 146.
34 Lehr, *King Lehr and the Gilded Age*, p. 145.
35 Balsan, *Glitter and the Gold*, p. 283.
36 Balsan, *Glitter and the Gold*, p. 184.

Chapter 8
RICHARD MORRIS HUNT
Biltmore and the Rothschild Factor

1 Catharine Hunt, "Richard Morris Hunt," typescript biography, American Institute of Architects, Washington, D.C., 3 vols., 3:338.
2 Lady Frances Balfour, *Ne Obliviscaris* (London: Hodder and Stoughton, 1930), 2 vols., 1:221 and 222. Quoted in Jill Franklin, *The Gentleman's Country House and Its Plan, 1835–1914* (London: Routledge and Kegan Paul, 1981), p. 246.
3 See Dorothy (Mrs. James de) Rothschild, *The Rothschilds at Waddesdon Manor* (New York: Viking Press, 1979).
4 See Sir Anthony Blunt, "Destailleur at Waddesdon," *Apollo* 105 (June 1977):409–15. This issue is devoted to Waddesdon Manor and its collections.
5 Hunt, "Richard Morris Hunt," 3:336.
6 Mark Girouard, "Waddesdon Manor, Buckinghamshire," *Country Life* 126 (20 August 1959):66.
7 Upon Ferdinand's death, Waddesdon passed to his sister, Alice. When she died in 1922 she bequeathed it to a cousin, James de Rothschild of the Paris line. In 1957, James left the manor, with a large endowment, to the National Trust of England.
8 See Forbes J. B. Watson, "French Eighteenth-Century Furniture at Waddesdon," *Gazette des Beaux-Arts* 54 (July–December 1959):17–36.
9 See Ellis K. Waterhouse, *Paintings: The James A. de Rothschild Collection at Waddesdon* (London: National Trust, 1967).
10 See Forbes J. B. Watson, "The James de Rothschild Collection at Waddesdon Manor," *Connoisseur* 143 (May 1959):206.
11 Quoted in Michael Hall, *Waddesdon Manor* (New York: H. N. Abrams, 2002):169.
12 See John M. Bryan, *Biltmore Estate: The Most Distinguished Private Place* (New York: Rizzoli, 1994).
13 Quoted in Susanne Brendel-Pandich, "Biltmore in Asheville, North Carolina, *The Magazine Antiques* 117 (April 1980):858.
14 *Architectural Record* 11 (April 1902):109–10. McKim, Mead and White also used Weeks as general contractor at the Levi P. Morton house, for example, at 681 Fifth Avenue. Weeks was also in charge of construction of Saint Thomas Church, designed by Charles C. Haight, at the corner of Fifth Avenue and 53rd Street, as well as at Rockefeller Hall on the campus of Vassar College in Poughkeepsie. He had earlier worked for William Kissam Vanderbilt in the building of Idle Hour, a Long Island estate.
15 Hunt, "Richard Morris Hunt," 3:334.
16 Brendel-Pandich, "Biltmore in Asheville, North Carolina," p. 856.
17 Rollin van N. Hadley, ed., *The Letters of Bernard*

Berenson and Isabella Stewart Gardner, 1887–1924 (Boston: Northeastern University Press, 1987), p. 315, letter dated 19 May 1903.

18 Quoted from Lyall H. Powers, ed., *Henry James and Edith Wharton: Letters* (New York: Scribner's, 1990), p. 47.

19 Louis Auchincloss, *The Vanderbilt Era: Profiles of a Gilded Age* (New York: Scribner, 1989), p. 60.

20 Edith Wharton to Sarah Norton, 26 December 1905, in R.W.B. Lewis and Nancy Lewis, eds., *The Letters of Edith Wharton* (New York: Charles Scribner's Sons, 1988), p. 100. Sarah, or Sally, Norton was one of six children of Charles Eliot Norton, and a spinster who took care of her father; she was a favorite correspondent of Edith Wharton's with whom Wharton could discuss intellectual and cultural matters.

21 Paul Baker, *Richard Morris Hunt* (Cambridge: MIT Press, 1980), p. 432.

Chapter 9
THE ASTOR MANSION

1 Quoted in Arthur Maurice, *Fifth Avenue* (New York: Arno Press, 1975; originally published 1918), pp. 298–99.

2 Edith Wharton, *The Age of Innocence* (New York: D. Appleton and Co., 1920), pp. 24–25.

3 *The New York Times*, 26 March 1893, p. 11.

4 On the Astors, see John D. Gates, *The Astor Family* (Garden City, N.Y.: Doubleday, 1981); Harvey O'Connor, *The Astors* (New York: Alfred Knopf, 1941); David Sinclair, *Dynasty: The Astors and Their Times* (London: J. M. Dent, 1983); and Derek Wilson, *The Astors, 1763–1992: Landscape with Millionaires* (London: Weidenfeld and Nicolson, 1993).

5 Allan Nevins and Milton Halsey Thomas, eds., *The Diary of George Templeton Strong*, 4 vols. (New York: Macmillan Co., 1952), 4:487, under date of July 2, 1873.

6 *The New York Times*, 23 February 1890.

7 Catharine Hunt, "Biography of Richard Morris Hunt," 3 vols., typescript, biography, American Institute of Architects, Washington, D.C., 3:316.

8 Paul Baker, *Richard Morris Hunt* (Cambridge: MIT Press, 1980), pp. 253–54 and fig. 56.

9 Nevins and Thomas, *Diary of George Templeton Strong*, 4:237, under date of 29 December 1868.

10 Elizabeth Drexel Lehr, *King Lehr and the Gilded Age* (Philadelphia: Lippincott, 1935), pp. 84–85.

11 Louis Auchincloss, *The Vanderbilt Era: Profiles of a Gilded Age* (New York: Scribner, 1989), p. 190.

12 Lehr, *King Lehr and the Gilded Age*, p. 85.

13 Lehr, *King Lehr and the Gilded Age*, p. 85.

14 Albert Stevens Crockett, *Peacocks on Parade: A Narrative of a Unique Period in American Social History* (New York: Sears Publishing Co., 1931).

15 *The New York Times*, 4 February 1896, p. 8:3.

16 See *The New York Times*, 9 February 1896, p. 20:1, and 11 February 1896, p. 8:2.

17 *The New York Times*, 6 December 1925, XI, 3:2.

18 Lehr, *King Lehr and the Gilded Age*, p. 88.

19 Edith Wharton, *House of Mirth* (New York: Macmillan Publishing Co., 1987), p. 175.

20 Wharton, *House of Mirth*, p. 176.

21 The paintings by Roybet and Detaille are illustrated in Mark Ormond, ed., *Legacy of the Circus King: John Ringling, Dreamer, Builder, Collector* (Sarasota, Fla.: The John and Mabel Ringling Museum of Art, 1997), plates 32 and 33.

22 Edith Wharton, "After Holbein," in *The Collected Short Stories of Edith Wharton*, R.W.B. Lewis, ed., 2 vols. (New York: Charles Scribner's Sons, 1968), 2:532–50.

23 See "The Residence of Col. John Jacob Astor," *Architectural Record* 27 (June 1910):470–82.

24 "The Work of Messrs. Carrère and Hastings," *Architectural Record* 27 (January 1910):44.

25 For an account of this party, see *The New York Times*, 4 March 1910, p. 3:1.

Chapter 10
MCKIM, MEAD AND WHITE
Origins of the Firm and the Early Work in Newport

1 On McKim, see Charles Moore, *The Life and Times of Charles Follen McKim* (New York: Da Capo Press, 1970; originally published 1929).

2 Charles H. Reilly, *McKim, Mead and White* (London: Ernest Benn, 1924), p. 10.

3 Reilly, *McKim, Mead and White*, p. 11.

4 Margaret Terry (Mrs. Winthrop) Chanler, *Roman Spring: Memoirs* (Boston: Little, Brown, 1931), p. 266.

5 On Stanford White, see Paul Baker, *Stanny: The Gilded Life of Stanford White* (New York: The Free Press/Macmillan, 1989); Lawrence Wodehouse, *White of McKim, Mead and White* (New York: Garland Publishing, 1988); David Lowe, *Stanford White's New York* (New York: Doubleday, 1992); and Charles Baldwin, *Stanford White* (New York: Da Capo Press, 1971; reprint of 1931 edition).

6 Baker, *Stanny*, p. 292.

7 On Henry Hobson Richardson, see Mrs. Schuyler Van Rensselaer, *Henry Hobson Richardson and his Works* (Boston: Houghton, Mifflin, 1888); Henry Russell Hitchcock, *The Architecture of H. H. Richardson* (Hamden, Conn.: Archon Books, 1961); Jeffrey Karl Ochsner, *H. H. Richardson: Complete Architectural Works* (Cambridge: MIT Press, 1982); James F. O'Gorman, *H. H. Richardson: Architectural Forms for an American Society* (Chicago: University of Chicago Press, 1987); and James F. O'Gorman, *Living Architecture: A Biography of H. H. Richardson* (New York: Simon and Schuster Editions, 1997).

8 See Ronald G. Pisano, *The Tile Club and the Aesthetic Movement in America* (New York: Harry N. Abrams, 1999). At the Tile Club members painted decorative designs, genre scenes, figural subjects or scenic views on eight-inch-square plaques; regrettably, most of the early tiles were destroyed in a fire 1881, although some specimens may be seen in the Guild Hall Museum in East Hampton, Long Island. The group disbanded in 1887.

9 Homer Saint-Gaudens, ed., *The Reminiscences of Augustus Saint-Gaudens*, 2 vols. (New York: The Century Co., 1913), 1:256.

10 On the firm, in addition to Reilly, *McKim, Mead and White*, see the following: Richard Guy Wilson, *McKim, Mead and White* (New York: Rizzoli, 1983); Leland Roth, *McKim, Mead and White, Architects* (New York: Harper and Row, 1983) and *The Architecture of McKim, Mead and White, 1870–1920: A Building List* (New York: Garland Publishing, 1978); and *A Monograph on the Works of McKim, Mead and White* (New York: Architectural Book Publishing Co., 1915, reprint with introduction by Leland Roth, 1973).

11 On the Aesthetic Movement, see Doreen Bolger, Burke, Jonathan Freedman, Alice Cooney, Frelinghuysen, et al., *In Pursuit of Beauty: Americans and the Aesthetic Movement* (New York: Metropolitan Museum of Art, 1986).

12 See Robert O. Jones, *Maitland Armstrong: American Stained Glass Master* (Tallahassee, Fla.: Sentry Press, 1999).

13 On the shingle style, see Leland Roth, *Shingle Styles: Innovation and Tradition in American Architecture, 1874–1982* (New York: Harry N. Abrams, 1999), and Vincent J. Scully, *The Shingle Style: Architectural Theory and Design from Richardson to the Origins of Wright* (New Haven: Yale University Press, 1955).

14 Maud Howe Elliott, *This Was My Newport* (New York: Arno Press, 1975; originally published in 1944), p. 154.

15 Mariana Griswold Van Rensselaer, "Recent Architecture in America: City Residences," *The Century Magazine*, 31, no. 4 (February 1886):548–58 and 677–87.

16 Mrs. John King (May) Van Rensselaer, *The Social Ladder* (New York: Arno Press, 1975; originally published 1924), pp. 176–77.

17 See Ward McAllister, *Society as I have found It* (New York: Cassell Publishing Co., 1890), pp. 355ff.

18 Lowe, *Stanford White's New York*, p. 79.

19 Elliott, *This Was My Newport*, p. 191.

20 Elizabeth Drexel Lehr, *King Lehr and the Gilded Age* (Philadelphia: Lippincott, 1935), p. 139.

Chapter 11
MCKIM, MEAD AND WHITE
The Villard Houses

1 See William C. Shopsin, Mosette Broderick, Sarah Landau, et al., *The Villard Houses: Life Story of a Landmark* (New York: The Viking Press, 1980).

2 On Wells, see C. Howard Walker, "Joseph Wells, Architect, 1853–1890," *Architectural Record* 66 (July 1929):15–18.

3 Quoted from Paul Baker, *Stanny: The Gilded Life of Stanford White* (New York: The Free Press, 1989), p. 152.

4 Walker, "Joseph Wells, Architect," pp. 15–16.

5 For a study that relates the architecture of McKim, Mead and White to the plates found in Letarouilly's *Les edifices de Rome moderne*, see John Barrington Bayley et al., *Letarouilly on Renaissance Rome, The Student's Edition of Paul Letarouilly's Edifices de Rome Moderne. . . .* (New York: Architectural Book Publishing Co., 1984).

6 See Royal Cortissoz, "Some Leaders of Our Architectural Renaissance," *Scribner's Magazine* 86 (July 1929):107.

7 Charles H. Reilly, *McKim, Mead and White* (London: Ernest Benn, 1924), p. 23.

8 Baker, *Stanny*, p. 105.

9 On Francis Bacon, see Doreen Bolger Burke, Jonathan Freedman, Alice Cooney Freylinghuysen, et al., *In Pursuit of Beauty: Americans and the Aesthetic Movement* (New York: Metropolitan Museum of Art, 1986), p. 418. Bacon, the brother of the architect Henry Bacon, earned a degree in architecture from Massachusetts Institute of Technology in 1877. After traveling about Europe and participating in

an archaeological excavation in Turkey he became a designer for Herter Brothers at a time when that firm was working on the William Henry Vanderbilt house, about 1880. In 1883 he joined the architectural firm of Henry Hobson Richardson, working on the interiors and furnishings of several of the architect's major commissions. But after two years he moved to Boston where he worked for A. H. Davenport and Company, translating the designs of handcrafted furniture into forms suitable for machine production. At Davenport's he often worked with McKim, Mead and White, as on the Mackay residence at Roslyn, Long Island.

10 George W. Sheldon, *Artistic Houses*, 2 vols. in 4 (New York: Doubleday and Co., 1883), 2:161.

11 See "Henry Villard's Estate," *The New York Times*, 12 January 1886, p. 8:3.

12 See E. Douglas Shields, "Dorchester House: The Home of the American Ambassador to the Court of Saint James," *Outlook* 81 (28 October 1905):467–73, and William Phillips, "An Ambassadress in the Golden Age," *Atlantic Monthly* 208 (November 1961):67–72.

13 Donald R. Contosta and Jessica R. Hawthorne, "Rise to World Power: Selected Letters of Whitelaw Reid, 1895–1912," *Transactions of the American Philosophical Society* n.s. 76, part 2 (1986):22.

14 Whitelaw Reid, *English and American Studies*, 2 vols. (Freeport, N.Y.: Books for Libraries Press, 1968; originally published 1913), 1:128.

15 Royal Cortissoz, *The Life of Whitelaw Reid*, 2 vols. (London: Thornton Butterworth, 1921), 1:231.

16 Cortissoz, *Life of Whitelaw Reid*, 1:231.

17 Cortissoz, *Life of Whitelaw Reid*, 2:379.

18 La Farge's murals of *Drama* and *Music* are illustrated in Pauline King, *American Mural Painting: A Study in the Important Decorations by Distinguished Artists in the United States* (Boston: Noyes, Platt and Co., 1902), pp. 24 and 25. See also *The New York Times* (1 February 1888), p. 4:17.

Chapter 12

STANFORD WHITE

1 See Channing Blake, "Stanford White's New York City Interiors," *The Magazine Antiques* 102 (December 1972):1060–67, and Stephen Garmey, "Stanford White: Designer for a Gilded Age," in *Gramercy Park, an Illustrated History of a New York Neighborhood* (New York: Balsam Press, 1984), pp. 115–31. See also Wayne Craven, *Stanford White: Decorator in Opulence and Dealer in Antiquities* (New York: Columbia University Press, 2005).

2 Edith Wharton, *A Backward Glance* (New York: D. Appleton-Century, 1934), p. 149.

3 Margaret Terry (Mrs. Winthrop) Chanler, *Roman Spring: Memoirs* (Boston: Little, Brown, 1934), p. 256.

4 Elizabeth Drexel Lehr, *King Lehr and the Gilded Age* (Philadelphia: Lippincott, 1935), p. 202.

5 Henry Adams to Elizabeth Cameron, 15 July 1888, in J. C. Levenson, Ernest Samuels, Charles Vandersee and Viola Hopkins Winner, eds., *The Letters of Henry Adams*, 6 vols. (Cambridge, Mass.: The Belknap Press of Harvard University Press, 1982), 3:126.

6 Frederick Vanderbilt to Sanford White (SW), 1 July 1899, Stanford White Papers, Avery Architectural and Fine Arts Library.

7 Copybook 3:50, 26 March 1890, SW Papers, Avery.

8 Edward Simmons, *From Seven to Seventy: Memories of a Painter and a Yankee* (New York: Harper, 1922), p. 237.

9 Paul R. Baker, *Stanny: The Gilded Life of Stanford White* (New York: The Free Press, 1989), p. 133.

10 Elsie de Wolfe, *After All* (New York: Arno Press, 1974; originally published 1913), p. 90. Miss de Wolfe and her companion, Bessie Marbury, lived only two blocks away in a small house once owned by Washington Irving.

11 Chanler, *Roman Spring*, p. 257.

12 Simmons, *From Seven to Seventy*, p. 241. Vercingetorix was the first-century B.C. leader of the Gauls whose revolt against Rome was put down by Julius Caesar.

13 *The New York Times*, 7 April 1907, part 2, p. 4:1. This ceiling is now installed at the William Randolph Hearst mansion, San Simeon, in California. For a color illustration of it, see Craven, *Stanford White*, plate 5.

14 *The New York Times*, 13 May 1907, p. 9:1.

15 *The New York Times*, 31 March 1907, part 2, p. 11:2.

16 *The New York Times*, 31 March 1907, part 2, p. 11:2.

17 John Taylor Russell, *The Art Dealers* (New York: Scribner, 1969), p. 75.

18 SW to Stefano Bardini, Paris, 27 October 1897, SW Papers, Avery.

19 Bardini to SW, Florence, 24 February 1898, SW Papers, Avery.

20 Émile Lowengard to SW, Paris, 29 October 1897, SW Papers, Avery.

21 McKim, Mead and White to Frederick Vanderbilt, 17 September 1897, SW Papers, Avery.

22 McKim to SW, 17 September 1897, SW Papers, Avery.

23 Jules Allard to SW, Paris, 28 October 1897, SW Papers, Avery.

24 George Allard to SW, Paris, 29 October 1897, SW Papers, Avery.

25 Jules Allard to SW, Paris, 28 October 1897, SW Papers, Avery.

26. Allard et Fils to SW, 25 September 1900, SW Papers, Avery.

27 18 March 1903, SW Papers, Avery. Eugene Glaenzer was a dealer and decorator in New York City who often acted as White's receiving agent. At times he was commissioned by McKim, Mead and White to decorate major rooms in the mansions they designed—as at the Frederick Vanderbilt house at Hyde Park, New York, for example.

28 31 December 1902, SW Papers, Avery.

29 Émile Lowengard to SW, Paris, 21 April 1899, SW Papers, Avery.

30 On Joseph Duveen, see Meryle Secrest, *Duveen: A Life in Art* (New York: Alfred A. Knopf, 2004). The Duveen papers are at the J. Paul Getty Museum in Los Angeles, California.

31 Duveen Brothers to SW, London, 22 December 1897, SW Papers, Avery.

32 Duveen Brothers to SW, London, 28 May 1898, SW Papers, Avery.

33 Duveen Brothers to SW, London, 17 September 1898, SW Papers, Avery.

34 On Benguiat, see Wesley Towner, *The Elegant Auctioneers* (New York: Hill and Wang, 1970), pp. 158–75.

35 Vitall Benguiat to SW, London, 1 November 1897, SW Papers, Avery.

36 Vitall Benguiat to SW, London, 19 January 1898, SW Papers, Avery.

37 Letter on Benguiat letterhead to SW, 15 April 1898, SW Papers, Avery.

38. Vitall Benguiat to SW, London, 16 April 1898, SW Papers, Avery.

39 Vitall Benguiat to SW, London, 20 April 1898, SW Papers, Avery.

40 E. Lowengard to SW, Paris, 7 October 1897, SW Papers, Avery.

41 George Donaldson to SW, London, 13 June 1904, SW Papers, Avery. Titian's *Ariosto* is now in the National Gallery, London, and the Van Dyck double portrait is in a private collection in England.

42 Godfrey Kopp to SW, London, 11 November 1897, SW Papers, Avery.

43 Godfrey Kopp to SW, Paris, 16 March 1901, SW Papers, Avery.

44 Godfrey Kopp to SW, Paris, 15 July 1900, SW Papers, Avery.

45 Henry Duveen to SW, London, 10 June 1898, SW Papers, Avery.

46 For the story of Kopp's escapades, see Colin Simpson, *Artful Partners: Bernard Berenson and Joseph Duveen* (New York: Macmillan, 1986), pp. 94–101.

47 Boni de Castellane, *How I Discovered America: Confessions of the Marquis Boni de Castellane* (New York: Alfred A. Knopf, 1924), p. 34.

48 Avery. Stefano Bardini to SW, Florence, 24 July 1898, SW Papers, Avery.

49 *The New York Times* reported on 29 March 1907, p.1:5, "In addition to Mr. White's indebtedness to his firm, it is understood that he lost a large amount of money in Wall Street speculations. . . . According to the story told by an intimate friend, Mr. White lost about $300,000 in stock speculations about a year ago. He appealed to his friends for assistance. They held a meeting and after an examination of his broker's accounts they agreed to take up the account and carry it until the losses were wiped out, provided that he would sign a promise never again to speculate. Mr. White agreed to this."

50 *The New York Times*, 14 February 1905, p. 10:1. The warehouse was at 114–120 West 13th Street in New York City.

Chapter 13

THE WILLIAM C. WHITNEY HOUSES

1 See the biography by Mark Hirsch, *William C. Whitney, Modern Warwick* (New York: Dodd, Mead, 1948), and W. A. Swanberg, *Whitney Father, Whitney Heiress* (New York: Scribner, 1980).

2 "William C. Whitney," *The New York Times*, 20 November 1898, Magazine Supplement, p. 2.

3 "William C. Whitney," Magazine Supplement, p. 2.

4 *The Art Amateur* 15 (June 1886):15.

5 *The Art Amateur* 17 (October 1887):107.

6 Mary Elizabeth Wilson Sherwood, "Certain New York Houses," *Harper's Monthly* (September 1882): 688. The dining room and two other rooms are illustrated in George W. Sheldon, *Artistic Houses*, 2 vols. in 4 (New York: D. Appleton and Co., 1883), 1:101.

7 Sheldon, *Artistic Houses*, 2:88. Bigelow was the former partner of Charles Follen McKim, who had

married Bigelow's sister. After McKim divorced Bigelow's sister the partnership ended and Bigelow went to work for Herter Brothers.

8 *The New York Times*, 18 February 1900, and the *New York Herald*, 22 May 1904.

9 On the estate in South Carolina, see "Mr. Whitney's Southern Home," *The New York Times Illustrated Magazine*, 16 January 1898, pp. 14–15.

10 *The New York Times*, 5 January 1901, p. 3:1.

11 Duveen Brothers to Stanford White (SW), Stanford White Papers, London, 22 June 1898, Avery Architectural and Fine Arts Library.

12 Duveen Brothers to SW, London, 20 April 1898, SW Papers, Avery.

13 Duveen Brothers to SW, London, December 1897, SW Papers, Avery.

14 Elsie de Wolfe, *After All* (New York: Arno Press, 1974; originally published 1913), p. 101.

15 White had remodeled the Barneys' house. Several years later Barney was ruined in the panic of 1907 and took his own life; the next year, Upton Sinclair published his novel *The Moneychangers*, in which he used the collapse of the Knickerbocker Trust and Barney's suicide as the plot.

16 *The New York Times*, 5 January 1901, p. 3:1.

17 This paneling is illustrated in Leo Lerman, *The Museum, One Hundred Years and the Metropolitan Museum of Art* (New York: Viking, 1969), p. 293.

18 This is probably the set of tapestries mentioned in a letter from a New York dealer, H. D. Gardiner, to McKim, Mead and White, dated 16 March 1901, in the SW Papers, Avery: "Kindly deliver to bearer the Renaissance #6876. Subject—'The Destruction of Jerusalem by the Armies of Titus' XVth century. Size 9′ × 8′. Price $1500."

19 Émile Gavet to SW, Paris, 28 October 1899, SW Papers, Avery.

20 "William Baumgarten," in *The National Cyclopaedia of American Biography* (New York: J. T. White, 1892), 11:466.

21 Pauline King, *American Mural Painting: A Study of the Important Decorations by Distinguished Artists in the United States* (Boston: Noyes, Platt and Co., 1902), p. 17.

22 *The New York Times*, 5 January 1901, p. 3:1.

23 Quoted from Hirsch, *William C. Whitney*, p. 582.

24 Several illustrations of the Westbury interiors are reproduced in *Architectural Record* 16 (October 1904), pp. 340–43.

25 John La Farge to Stanford White, 7 May 1902, The New-York Historical Society, McKim, Mead and White Papers, quoted from H. Barbara Weinberg, *The Decorative Work of John La Farge* (New York: Garland Publishing Co., 1977), p. 416.

26 Quoted from Weinberg, *The Decorative Work of John La Farge*, p. 418. John C. Van Dyke, *American Painting and Its Traditions* (New York: Charles Scribner's Sons, 1919), p. 138.

27 Weinberg, *Decorative Work of John La Farge*, p. 418.

28 Elizabeth Drexel Lehr, *King Lehr and the Gilded Age* (Philadelphia: Lippincott, 1935), p. 75.

Chapter 14
NEWPORT REVISITED
Rosecliff, Crossways, and The Elms

1 Quoted from David Lowe, *Stanford White's New York* (New York: Doubleday, 1992), p. 214.

2 John Williams Mackay was the father of Clarence Mackay, who married Katherine Duer and for whom Stanford White designed and furnished Harbor Hill on Long Island.

3 Mrs. John King (May) Van Rensselaer, *Newport: Our Social Capital* (New York: Arno Press, 1975; originally published 1905), p. 61.

4 Edward Simmons, *From Seven to Seventy: Memories of a Painter* (New York: Harper, 1922), p. 240.

5 Ward McAllister, *Society as I have found It* (New York: Cassell Publishing Co., 1890), p. 226.

6 Charles W. Nicholls, *The Ultra-Fashionable Peerage of America: An Official List of Those People who can Properly be Called Ultra-Fashionable in the United States* (New York: Arno Press, 1975; originally published 1904), p. 29.

7 Edith Wharton and Ogden Codman, *The Decoration of Houses* (New York: Charles Scribner's Sons, 1897), p. 138.

8 Wharton and Codman, *Decoration of Houses*, p. 134.

9 Wharton and Codman, *Decoration of Houses*, p. 139.

10 Wharton and Codman, *Decoration of Houses*, p. 136.

11 Wharton and Codman, *Decoration of Houses*, pp. 140–41.

12 Nicholls, *Ultra-Fashionable Peerage*, p. 52.

13 Maud Howe Elliott, *This Was My Newport* (New York: Arno Press, 1975; originally published 1944), p. 164.

14 Balsan, *Glitter and the Gold* (New York: Harper, 1952), p. 27.

15 Mrs. John King (May) Van Rensselaer, *The Social Ladder* (New York: Arno Press, 1975; originally published 1924), p. 242.

16 Elizabeth Drexel Lehr, *King Lehr and the Gilded Age* (Philadelphia: Lippincott, 1935), pp. 125–26.

17 Quoted from Lowe, *Stanford White's New York*, p. 250.

18 Lehr, *King Lehr and the Gilded Age*, p. 93.

19 Lehr, *King Lehr and the Gilded Age*, p. 117.

20 Lehr, *King Lehr and the Gilded Age*, p. 117.

21 René Gimpel, *Diary of an Art Dealer* (New York: Farrar, Straus and Giroux, 1966), p. 37.

22 Thomas Gannon and David Chase, *Newport Mansions: The Gilded Age* (Little Compton, R.I.: Fort Church Publishers, 1982), p. 7.

23 Henry James, "The Sense of Newport," *Harper's Monthly* 113 (August 1906):346 and 354.

24 E. L. Godkin, "The Expenditure of Rich Men," *Scribner's Magazine* 20 (October 1896):495–501.

25 Paul Baker, *Richard Morris Hunt* (Cambridge, Mass.: MIT Press, 1980), p. 370.

Chapter 15
THE PROGENY OF THE PETIT CHÂTEAU AND THE VILLARD HOUSES

1 John Tauranac, *Elegant New York: The Builders and the Buildings, 1885–1915* (New York: Abbeville Press, 1985), p. 162.

2 See Montgomery Schuyler, "The Work of N. Le Brun and Sons," *Architectural Record* 27 (June 1910): 364–81. The late Gothic style was so popular that it was sometimes used for nondomestic structures, as in Fire Engine House Number 31, which stands at the corner of Lafayette and White streets, near today's SoHo district in lower Manhattan. It was designed by Napoleon Le Brun (1821–1901), the quasi-official architect of the New York City Fire Department. Completed in 1896, it introduces the issue of civic pride assumed by America's millionaire society of the Gilded Age, for the parvenus wanted their civic buildings—and their palaces of culture for the people, such as libraries and art museums—to have the same dignity and grandeur that they were infusing into their homes.

3 Francis Hatch Kimball (1845–1919) and George Kramer Thompson (died 1935) are best known for their Manhattan Life Insurance Building, the first skyscraper in New York City to be erected entirely on a steel and iron skeletal frame, in 1895. They worked on theaters, churches, and commercial buildings more than on domestic projects. See Montgomery Schuyler, "The Works of Francis H. Kimball and Kimball and Thompson," *Architectural Record* 7 (April–June 1898):479–518.

4 Calvin Tomkins, *Merchants and Masterpieces: The Story of the Metropolitan Museum of Art* (New York: Henry Holt and Co., 1989), p. 189.

5 *The New York Times*, 24 May 1941, p. 29:4.

6 *The New York Times*, 14 January 1941, p. 17:2. See also "Warburg Gift," *Metropolitan Museum of Art Bulletin* 36 (February 1941):48–53.

7 *The New York Times*, 14 January 1941, p. 17:2.

8 Bernard Berenson, *Venetian Painters of the Renaissance* (New York: Meridian, 1957; originally published 1894), p. v.

9 Richard Guy Wilson, "The Great Civilization," in *The American Renaissance, 1876–1917* (New York: Brooklyn Museum, 1979), p. 11.

10 Elsie de Wolfe, *After All* (New York: Arno Press, 1974; originally published 1913), p. 122.

11 Ernest Flagg, "The Influence of the French School on Architecture in the United States," *Architectural Record* 4 (October–December 1894):215.

12 Edith Wharton and Ogden Codman, *The Decoration of Houses* (New York: Charles Scribner's Sons, 1897), p. 13.

13 "The Work of Messrs. Carrère and Hastings," *Architectural Record* 27 (January 1910), pp. 36–38.

14 Robert W. Gibson wrote two articles, titled "The Modern Cathedral," which were published in *Architectural Record* 1 (January–March 1892):286–94, and (April–June 1892):435–47.

15 Henry Clews, *Twenty-eight Years in Wall Street* (New York: Irving Publishing Co., 1888), pp. 606–7.

16 Elizabeth Drexel Lehr, *King Lehr and the Gilded Age* (Philadelphia: Lippincott, 1935), p. 105.

17 See M. Christina Geis, *Georgian Court: An Estate of the Gilded Age* (Philadelphia: Art Alliance Press, 1982). See also Katherine Hoffman, "George Gould's Home at Lakewood," *Munsey's Magazine* 23 (June 1900):301–9. For illustrations of the exterior and interior, see Harry W. Desmond and Herbert Croly, *Stately Homes in America* (New York: D. Appleton and Co., 1903):377–95.

18 Lehr, *King Lehr and the Gilded Age*, pp. 106–7.

19 The best collection of illustrations of the exterior and interiors of the Harkness mansion are found in "A Fifth Avenue Mansion," *Architectural Record* 27 (May 1910):382–99.

20 "A Fifth Avenue Mansion," p. 383.

21 *The New York Times*, 30 March 1934, p. 18:1.

22 *The New York Times*, 30 March 1934, p. 18:2.

23 Leon Solon, "The Residence of Otto H. Kahn, Esq., New York . . . ," *Architectural Record* 46 (August 1919):99.

24 *The New York Times*, 30 March 1934, p. 18:3.

25 René Gimpel, *Diary of an Art Dealer* (New York: Farrar, Straus and Giroux, 1966), pp. 91–92.

Chapter 16

FACADES IN THE MODERN FRENCH MANNER

1 Margaret Terry (Mrs. Winthrop) Chanler, *Roman Spring: Memoirs* (Boston: Little, Brown, 1934), p. 214.

2 Florence Adele Sloane, *Maverick in Mauve: Diary of a Romantic Age*, Louis Auchincloss, ed. (Garden City, N.Y.: Doubleday and Co., 1983), p. 189.

3 Montgomery Schuyler, "Modern Architecture," *Architectural Record* 4 (July–September 1894):4.

4 Robert Stern, Gregory Gilmartin and John M. Massengale, *New York 1900: Metropolitan Architecture and Urbanism, 1890–1915* (New York: Rizzoli, 1992), p. 316.

5 Paul Baker, *Richard Morris Hunt* (Cambridge: MIT Press, 1986), p. 325.

6 Sloane, *Maverick in Mauve*, p. 72.

7 *The New York Times*, 25 January 1898, p. 7:5.

8 Ernest Flagg, "The Influence of the French School on Architecture in the United States," *Architectural Record* 4 (October–December 1894): 210–28.

9 See "Examples of Recent French Architecture," *Architectural Record* 8 (July–September 1898), especially pp. 69 and 77, where such motifs as rusticated facades, projecting corbelled balconies with wrought-iron railings, French doors, cartouche carvings, and mansard roofs with dormers are shown.

10 See Ernest Flagg, "The New York Tenement-House Evil and its Cure," *Scribner's Magazine* 16 (July 1884):108–117.

11 *Architectural Record* 11 (October 1901):723.

12 Montgomery Schuyler, *American Architecture Studies* (New York: Harper and Brothers, 1892), p. 67.

13 For a list of buildings in which Milliken Brothers was involved, see *Architectural Record* 11 (September 1902):124.

14 Paul Goldberger, *The City Observed: New York* (New York: Random House, 1979), p. 232.

15 A notice in *The New York Times* (8 April 1904, p.5:2) reads, "according to a report . . . in real estate circles, [De Lamar] has practically decided to sell the mansion he is building. . . . Mr. De Lamar will finish the house, but it is said his desire to be the owner of one of the finest dwellings in the city and the costliest one on Murray Hill is not nearly so strong as it was three years ago, when he bought the site."

16 See Carl B. Glasscock, *The War of the Copper Kings: Builders of Butte and Wolves of Wall Street* (New York: Grosset and Dunlap, 1935), and William Daniel Mangam, *The Clarks of Montana* (Washington, D.C.: Service Printing Co., 1939).

17 *The New York Times*, 3 March 1925, p. 1:3.

18 *The New York Times*, 3 March 1925, p. 1:3.

19 "The House of Senator Clark, Architectural Aberration No. 21," *Architectural Record* 19 (January 1906):27–30.

20 For illustrations of these, see *Architectural Record* 8 (January–March 1899):76–77, and 10 (April 1901):438.

21 See *The New York Times*, 12 January 1926, p. 33:7; 13 January 1926, p. 47:1, and 14 January 1926, p. 8:4. See also *Illustrated Handbook of the W. A. Clark Collection* (Washington, D.C.: The Corcoran Gallery of Art, 1932), and *The William A. Clark Collection* (Washington, D.C.: The Corcoran Gallery of Art, 1978).

Bibliography

Unpublished Materials

Archives. The Preservation Society of Newport County, Newport, Rhode Island.

Hunt, Catharine. "Richard Morris Hunt," 3 vols., typescript biography. American Institute of Architects, Washington, D.C., ca. 1900.

McKim, Mead and White Archives. Museum of the City of New York.

McKim, Mead and White Papers. The New-York Historical Society, New York City.

Stanford White Papers. Avery Architectural and Fine Arts Library, Columbia University, New York City.

Stanford White Papers. The New-York Historical Society, New York City.

Published Materials

Adams, Charles Francis. *The Railroads: Their Origin and Problems*. New York: G. P. Putnam's Sons, 1878.

Adams, Henry. *Democracy, an American Novel*. New York: Henry Holt and Co., 1908.

———. *The Education of Henry Adams, A Centennial Version*, Edward Chalfant and Conrad Edick Wright, eds. Boston: Massachusetts Historical Society, 2007; originally published 1907.

Adams, Henry. "John La Farge's Work in the Vanderbilt Houses." *American Art Journal* 16 (Autumn 1984):30–70.

"Alexander T. Stewart." *Harper's Weekly* (29 April 1876):345–46.

Allen, Armin Brand. *The Cornelius Vanderbilts of The Breakers*. Newport, R.I.: The Preservation Society of Newport County, 1995.

Ames, Winslow. "The Transformation of Chateau-sur-Mer." *Journal of the Society of Architectural Historians* 29 (December 1970): 291–306.

Andrews, Wayne. *Architecture in New York: A Photographic History*. New York: New York Atheneum, 1969.

———. *The Vanderbilt Legend: The Story of the Vanderbilt Family, 1794–1940*. New York: Harcourt Brace, 1941.

Auchincloss, Louis. *Theodore Roosevelt*. New York: Henry Holt and Co., 2001.

———. *The Vanderbilt Era: Profiles of a Gilded Age*. New York: Scribner, 1989.

Baker, Paul. *Richard Morris Hunt*. Cambridge, Mass.: MIT Press, 1980.

———. *Stanny: The Gilded Life of Stanford White*. New York: The Free Press/Macmillan, 1989.

Baldwin, Charles. *Stanford White*. New York: Da Capo Press, 1971; first published 1931.

Balfour, Lady Frances. *Ne Obliviscaris*. London: Hodder and Stoughton, 1930.

Balsan, Consuelo Vanderbilt. *The Glitter and the Gold*. New York: Harper, 1952.

Beaufort, Madeleine F., and Jeanne Welcher. "Some Views on Art Buying in New York in the 1870s and 1880s." *Oxford Art Journal* 5, no. 1 (1982): 48–57.

Berenson, Bernard. *Venetian Painters of the Renaissance*. New York: Meridian, 1957; originally published 1894.

Black, David. *The King of Fifth Avenue: The Fortunes of August Belmont*. New York: The Dial Press, 1981.

Blake, Channing. "Stanford White's New York City Interiors." *The Magazine Antiques* 102 (December 1972):1060–67.

Bloor, A. J. "Report on Mansard Roofs." *Proceedings of the American Institute of Architects* (1874), p. 45.

Blunt, Sir Anthony. "Destailleur at Waddesdon." *Apollo* 105 (June 1977):409–15.

Bourget, Paul. *Outre-Mer: Impressions of America*. New York: Charles Scribner's Sons, 1895.

Brendel-Pandich, Susanne. "Biltmore in Asheville, North Carolina." *The Magazine Antiques* 117 (April 1980):855–67.

Brough, James. *Consuelo: Portrait of an American Heiress*. New York: Coward, McCann and Geoghegan, 1979.

Browne, Junius Henri. *The Great Metropolis: A Mirror of New York: A Complete History of Metropolitan Life and Society, with Sketches of Prominent Places, Persons, and Things in the City, as they actually exist*. Hartford, Conn.: American Publishing Co., 1869.

———. *The Secrets of the Great City*. New York: Jones, Brothers and Co., 1869.

Brownell, William C. "Newport." *Scribner's* 16 (August 1894):137–56.

Bryan, John M. *Biltmore Estate: The Most Distinguished Private Place*. New York: Rizzoli, 1994.

Burke, Doreen Bolger, Jonathan Freedman, Alice Cooney Frelinghuysen, et al. *In Pursuit of Beauty: Americans and the Aesthetic Movement*. New York: Metropolitan Museum of Art, 1986.

Cantor, Jay. "A Monument to Trade: A. T. Stewart and the Rise of the Millionaire's Mansion in New York." *Winterthur Portfolio* 10 (1975):165–97.

Carnegie, Andrew. "Wealth." *The North American Review* 148 (June 1889):653–64.

Castellane, Boni de. *How I discovered America: Confessions of the Marquis Boni de Castellane*. New York: Alfred A. Knopf, 1924.

Catalogue des Objets d'Art et d'Ameublement . . . a Florence, au Palais de San Donato, le 15 Mars 1880 et les jours suivants. Paris: 1880.

Catalogue of the A. T. Stewart Collection of Paintings, Sculptures, and other Objects of Art, to be sold by Auction . . . by Order of Henry Hilton . . . and Charles Clinch . . . Executors of the Estate of Mrs. Cornelia M. Stewart, deceased. New York: Press of J. J. Little and Co., 1887.

Chanler, Margaret Terry (Mrs. Winthrop). *Roman Spring: Memoirs*. Boston, Little, Brown, 1934.

"A Chat with Ward McAllister." *New York Daily Tribune*, 25 March 1888, p. 11.

Cheney, David. "The Department Store as a Cultural Form." *Theory, Culture and Society* 1 (1983): 22–31.

Choules, John Overton. *The Cruise of the Steam Yacht North Star*. Boston: Gould and Lincoln, 1854.

Clews, Henry. *Fifty Years in Wall Street*. New York: Irving Publishing Co., 1908.

———. *Twenty-eight Years in Wall Street*. New York: Irving Publishing Co., 1888.

Contosta, Donald R., and Jessica R. Hawthorne. "Rise to World Power: Selected Letters of Whitelaw Reid, 1895–1912." *Transactions of the American Philosophical Society* n.s. 76, part 2 (1986):13–27.

Cook, Clarence. "Architecture in America." *The North American Review* 135 (September 1882):243–52.

———. *The House Beautiful*. New York: Charles Scribner's Sons, 1877.

Cornwallis-West, Mrs. George. *The Reminiscences of Lady Randolph Churchill*. New York: The Century Co., 1909.

Cortissoz, Royal. *The Life of Whitelaw Reid*, 2 vols. London: Thornton Butterworth, 1921.

———. "Some Leaders of Our Architectural Renaissance." *Scribner's Magazine* 86 (July 1929): 100–8.

Crapsey, Edward. "A Monument to Trade." *The Galaxy* 9 (January 1870):94–101.

Craven, Wayne. *Stanford White: Decorator in Opulence and Dealer in Antiquities*. New York: Columbia University Press, 2005.

Crockett, Albert Stevens. *Peacocks on Parade: A Narrative of a Unique Period in American Social History*. New York: Sears Publishing Co., 1931.

Croffut, William A. *The Vanderbilts and the Story of their Fortune*. Chicago and New York: Belford, Clarke and Co., 1886.

Croly, Herbert. "The Work of Richard Morris Hunt." *Architectural Record* 59 (January 1926):88–89.

Dayton, Abram C. *The Last Days of Knickerbocker Life in New York*. New York: G. P. Putnam's Sons, 1897; originally published 1880.

Desmond, Harry W., and Herbert Croly. *Stately Homes in America*. New York: D. Appleton and Co., 1903.

Downing, Antoinette F., and Vincent J. Scully Jr. *The Architectural Heritage of Newport, Rhode Island, 1640–1915*. New York: C. N. Potter, 1967.

Elias, Stephen N. *Alexander T. Stewart: Forgotten Merchant Prince*. Westport, Conn.: Praeger, 1992.

Ellet, Elizabeth. *The Queens of American Society*. Philadelphia: Porter and Coates, 1867.

Elliott, Maud Howe. *Reminiscences, 1819–1899*. Boston: Houghton, Mifflin and Co., 1900.

———. *This Was My Newport*. New York: Arno Press, 1975; originally published 1944.

"Examples of Recent French Architecture." *Architectural Record* 8 (July–September 1898):67–81.

"A Fifth Avenue Mansion [Harkness]." *Architectural Record* 7 (May 1910):382–99.

Flagg, Ernest. "The Ecole des Beaux-Arts." *Architectural Record* 3 (January–March 1894):302–13; (April–June 1894):419–28; 4 (July–September 1894):38–43.

———. "The Influence of the French School on Architecture in the United States." *Architectural Record* 4 (October–December 1894):210–28.

———. "The New York Tenement-House Evil and its Cure." *Scribner's Magazine* 16 (July 1894): 108–17.

Folsom, Burton W., Jr. *The Myth of the Robber Barons: A New Look at the Rise of Big Business in America*. Herndon, Va.: Young America's Foundation, 1987.

Franklin, Jill. *The Gentleman's Country House and Its Plan, 1835–1914*. London: Routledge and Kegan Paul, 1981.

"Galleries of Belmont and Blodgett." *Putnam's Magazine* 5 (May 1870):534–40.

Gannon, Thomas, and David Chase. *Newport Mansions: The Gilded Age*. Little Compton, R.I.: Fort Church Publishers, 1982.

Garmey, Stephen. "Stanford White: Designer for a Gilded Age." In *Gramercy Park, an Illustrated History of a New York Neighborhood*. New York: Balsam Press, 1984.

Gates, John D. *The Astor Family*. Garden City, N.Y.: Doubleday, 1981.

Geis, M. Christina. *Georgian Court: An Estate of the Gilded Age*. Philadelphia: Art Alliance Press, 1982.

Gimpel, René. *Diary of an Art Dealer*. New York: Farrar, Straus and Giroux, 1966.

Girouard, Mark. "Waddesdon Manor, Buckinghamshire." *Country Life* 126 (20 August 1959): 65–69.

Glasscock, Carl B. *The War of the Copper Kings: Builders of Butte and Wolves of Wall Street*. New York: Grosset and Dunlap, 1935.

Godkin, E. L. "The Expenditure of Rich Men." *Scribner's Magazine* 20 (October 1896):495–501.

Goldberger, Paul. *The City Observed: New York*. New York: Random House, 1979.

Goodman, Susan, and Carl Dawson. *William Dean Howells: A Writer's Life*. Berkeley: University of California Press, 2005.

Gordon, John Steele. *The Scarlet Woman of Wall Street: Jay Gould, Jim Fisk, Cornelius Vanderbilt, the Erie Railroad Wars, and the Birth of Wall Street*. New York: Weidenfelt and Nicholson, 1988.

Grinstein, Hyman B. *The Rise of the Jewish Community in New York*. Philadelphia: The Jewish Publication Society of America, 1945.

Hadley, Rollin van N. ed. *The Letters of Bernard Berenson and Isabella Stewart Gardner, 1887–1924*. Boston: Northeastern University Press, 1987.

Hall, Michael. *Waddesdon Manor*. New York: H. N. Abrams, 2002.

Harrison, Mrs. Burton. *Recollections, Grave and Gay*. New York: Charles Scribner's Sons, 1912.

Hirsch, Mark. *William C. Whitney, Modern Warwick*. New York: Dodd, Mead, 1948.

Hitchcock, Henry Russell. *The Architecture of H. H. Richardson*. Hamden, Conn.: Archon Books, 1961.

Hoffman, Katherine. "George Gould's Home at Lakewood." *Munsey's Magazine* 23 (June 1900): 301–9.

Homberger, Eric. *Mrs. Astor's New York*. New Haven: Yale University Press, 2002.

"The House of Senator Clark, Architectural Abberation No. 21," *Architectural Record* 19 (January 1906):27–30.

Humphreys, Mary Gay. "The Cornelius Vanderbilt House: Decorations for the Dining-Room, Watercolor Room, and Smoking Room." *Art Amateur* 8, no. 6 (May 1883):135–36.

Illustrated Handbook of the W. A. Clark Collection. Washington, D.C.: The Corcoran Gallery of Art, 1932.

James, Henry. *The Aspen Papers and Other Stories*. Oxford: Oxford University Press, 1983.

———. *Letters from the Palazzo Barbaro*. London: Puskin Press, 1998.

———. *Parisian Sketches: Letters to the New York Tribune*, Leon Edel and Isle Dusoir Lind, eds. London: Rupert Hart-Davis, 1958.

———. "The Sense of Newport." *Harper's Monthly* 113 (August 1906):346–54.

———. *Washington Square*. London: Macmillan, 1881.

Jarves, James Jackson. "The Gates of Paradise." *Harper's Monthly* 65 (June 1882):92.

Jones, Robert O. *D. Maitland Armstrong: American Stained Glass Master*. Tallahassee, Fla.: Sentry Press, 1999.

King, Pauline. *American Mural Painting: A Study in the Important Decorations by Distinguished Artists in the United States*. Boston: Noyes, Platt and Co., 1902.

King, Robert B. *The Vanderbilt Homes*. New York: Rizzoli, 1989.

Kramer, Ellen W. "Detlef Lienau, an American Architect of the Brown Decades." *Journal of the Society of Architectural Historians* 14 (March 1955):18–25.

Lancaster, W. *The Department Store: A Social History*. London: Pinter Publishers, 1992.

Landau, Sarah Bradford. *George B. Post, Architect: Picturesque Designer and Determined Realist*. New York: Montacelli Press, 1998.

Lehr, Elizabeth Drexel. *King Lehr and the Gilded Age*. Philadelphia: Lippincott, 1935.

Leslie, Anita. *Lady Randolph Churchill: The Story of Jennie Jerome*. New York: Charles Scribner's Sons, 1969.

———. *The Remarkable Mr. Jerome*. New York: Henry Holt and Co., 1954.

Letarouilly, Paul-Marie. *Edifices de Rome Modern*, 3 vols. Paris: 1840–57.

Levenson, J. C. Ernest Samuels, Charles Vandersee and Viola Hopkins Winner, eds., *The Letters of Henry Adams*, 6 vols. Cambridge, Mass.: The Belknap Press of Harvard University Press, 1982.

Lewis, Arnold, James Turner, and Steven McQuillin. *The Opulent Interiors of the Gilded Age: All 203 Photographs from "Artistic Houses"*. New York: Dover Publications, 1987.

Lewis, R.W.B., and Nancy Lewis, eds. *The Letters of Edith Wharton*. New York: Charles Scribner's Sons, 1988.

Lockwood, Charles. *Bricks and Brownstone: The New York Row House, 1783–1929*. New York: McGraw-Hill, 1972.

Lowe, David. *Stanford White's New York*. New York: Arno Press, 1913.

Mangam, Daniel. *The Clarks of Montana*. Washington, D.C.: Service Printing Co., 1939.

Martin, Frederick. *Things I Remember*. New York: Arno Press, 1975; originally published 1913.

Maurice, Arthur. *Fifth Avenue*. New York: Arno Press, 1975; originally published 1918.

McAllister, Ward. *Society as I have found It*. New York: Cassell Publishing Co., 1890.

McCabe, James D. *The Illustrated History of the Centennial Exhibition*. Philadelphia: National Publishing Co., 1876.

———. *Lights and Shadows of New York Life, or, The Sights and Sensations of the Great City*. Philadelphia: National Publishing Co., 1872.

Miller, Michael. *The Bon Marché: Bourgeois Culture and the Department Store, 1869–1920*. Princeton: Princeton University Press, 1981.

A Monograph on the Works of McKim, Mead, and White. New York Architectural Book Publishing Co., 1915, reprint with introduction by Leland Roth, 1973.

Moore, Charles. *Daniel Burnham: Architect, Planner of Cities*, 2 vols. New York: Houghton Mifflin, 1921.

———. *The Life and Times of Charles Follen McKim*. New York: Da Capo Press, 1970; first published 1929.
Morris, Charles R. *The Tycoons: How Andrew Carnegie, John D. Rockefeller, Jay Gould, and J.P. Morgan Invented the American Supereconomy*. New York: Times Books/Henry Holt and Company, 2005.
Morrison, Elting, ed. *The Letters of Theodore Roosevelt*, 8 vols. Cambridge, Mass.: Harvard University Press, 1951.
"Mr. Stewart's New Residence." *Harper's Weekly* (14 August 1869):526.
Myers, Gustavus. *History of the Great American Fortunes*, 3 vols. Chicago: Charles H. Kerr and Co., 1911.
Nevins, Allan, and Milton Halsey Thomas, eds. *The Diary of George Templeton Strong*, 4 vols. New York: Macmillan Co., 1952.
"New York Daguerreotyped." *Putnam's Magazine* 3 (March 1854):238.
Nicholls, Reverend Charles W. *The Ultra-Fashionable Peerage of America*. New York: G. Harjes, 1904.
Ochsner, Jeffrey Karl. *H. H. Richardson: Complete Architectural Works*. Cambridge, Mass.: MIT Press, 1982.
O'Connor, Harvey. *The Astors*. New York: Alfred Knopf, 1941.
O'Gorman, James F. *H. H. Richardson: Architectural Forms for an American Society*. Chicago: University of Chicago Press, 1987.
———. *Living Architecture: A Biography of H. H. Richardson*. New York: Simon and Schuster Editions, 1997.
Ormond, Mark, ed. *Legacy of the Circus King: John Ringling, Dreamer, Builder, Collector*. Sarasota, Fla.: The John and Mabel Ringling Museum of Art, 1997.
Patterson, Jerry. *Fifth Avenue: The Best Address*. New York: Rizzoli, 1998.
———. *The First Four Hundred: Mrs. Astor's New York in the Gilded Age*. New York: Rizzoli, 2000.
———. *The Vanderbilts*. New York: H. N. Abrams, 1989.
Phillips, William. "An Ambassadress in the Golden Age." *Atlantic Monthly* 208 (November 1961): 67–72.
Pisano, Ronald G. *The Tile Club and the Aesthetic Movement in America*. New York: Harry N. Abrams, 1999.
Powers, Lyall H., ed. *Henry James and Edith Wharton: Letters*. New York: Scribner's, 1990.
"The Quai d'Orsay." *Architectural Record* 11 (October 1901):557–80.
Reid, Whitelaw. *English and American Studies*, 2 vols. Freeport, N.Y.: Books for Libraries Press, 1968; originally published 1913.
Reilly, Charles H. *McKim, Mead and White*. London: Ernest Benn, 1924.
Renehan, Edward J., Jr. *The Dark Genius of Wall Street: The Misunderstood Life of Jay Gould, King of the Robber Barons*. New York: Basic Books, 2005.
"The Residence of Col. John Jacob Astor." *Architectural Record* 27 (June 1910):470–82.
Roosevelt, Theodore. *Theodore Roosevelt: An Autobiography*. New York: Charles Scribner's Sons, 1926.
Roth, Leland. *The Architecture of McKim, Mead and White, 1870–1920: A Building List*. New York: Garland Publishing, 1978.
———. *McKim, Mead and White, Architects*. New York: Harper and Row, 1983.
Rothschild, Dorothy (Mrs. James de). *The Rothschilds at Waddesdon Manor*. New York: Viking Press, 1979.
Russell, John Taylor. *The Art Dealers*. New York: Scribner, 1969.
Saint-Gaudens, Homer, ed. *Reminiscences of Augustus Saint-Gaudens*, 2 vols. New York: The Century Co., 1913.
Schezen, Roberto, Jane Mulvaugh, and Mark A. Weber. *Newport Houses*. New York: Rizzoli, 1989.
Schuyler, Montgomery. *American Architecture Studies*. New York: Harper and Brothers, 1892.
———. "Modern Architecture." *Architectural Record* 4 (July–September 1894):1–13.
———. "The Vanderbilt Houses." *American Architecture Studies*. New York: Harper and Brothers, 1892, pp. 52–67.
———. "The Work of N. Le Brun and Sons." *Architectural Record* 27 (June 1910):364–81.
———. "The Works of Francis H. Kimball and Kimball and Thompson," *Architectural Record* 7 (April–June 1898):479–518.
Secrest, Meryle. *Duveen: A Life in Art*. New York: Alfred A. Knopf, 2004.
Sheldon, George W. *Artistic Houses*, 2 vols. in 4. New York: Doubleday and Co., 1883–84.
Sherwood, Mary Elizabeth Wilson. "Certain New York Houses." *Harper's Monthly* 65 (September 1882):680–90.
Shields, E. Douglas. "Dorchester House: The Home of the American Ambassador to the Court of Saint James." *Outlook* 81 (28 October 1905): 467–73.
Shinn, Earl. *Art Treasures of America*, 3 vols. Philadelphia: G. Barrie, 1879–82.
———. *Mr. Vanderbilt's House and Collection*, 2 vols. Boston: G. Barrie, 1883–84.
Shopsin, William C., Mosette Broderick, Sarah Landau, et al. *The Villard Houses: Life Story of a Landmark*. New York: The Viking Press, 1980.
Simmons, Edward. *From Seven to Seventy: Memories of a Painter and a Yankee*. New York: Harper, 1922.
Simpson, Colin. *Artful Partners: Bernard Berenson and Joseph Duveen*. New York: Macmillan, 1986.
Sinclair, David. *Dynasty: The Astors and Their Times*. London: J. M. Dent, 1983.
Sloane, Florence Adele. *Maverick in Mauve: Diary of a Romantic Age*, Louis Auchincloss, ed. Garden City, N.Y.: Doubleday and Co., 1983.
Solon, Leon. "The Residence of Otto H. Kahn, Esq., New York. . . ." *Architectural Record* 46 (August 1919):98–114.
Sparke, Penny. *Elsie de Wolfe: The Birth of Modern Interior Decoration*. New York: Acanthus Press, 2005.
Spofford, Harriet Prescott. *Art Decoration applied to Furniture*. New York: Harper, 1878.
Stein, Susan. *The Architecture of Richard Morris Hunt*. Chicago: University of Chicago Press, 1986.
Stern, Robert, Gregory Gilmartin, and John M. Massengale. *New York 1900: Metropolitan Architecture and Urbanism, 1890–1915*. New York: Rizzoli, 1992.
Stewart, William Rhinelander. *Grace Church and Old New York*. New York: E. P. Dutton, 1924.
Strahan, Edward. See Shinn, Earl.
Strouse, Jean. *Morgan, American Financier*. New York: Random House, 1999.
Swanberg, W. A. *Whitney Father, Whitney Heiress*. New York: Scribner, 1980.
Tahara, Keiichi, and Robert A. M. Stern. *Images of Fin-de-Siecle Architecture and Interior Decoration*. New York: Kodansha International/Harper and Row, 1988.
Tauranac, John. *Elegant New York: The Builders and the Buildings, 1885–1915*. New York: Abbeville Press, 1985.
Thompson, Neville. "Terror in the Ballroom: What to Wear, How to Dance, What to Say." *Nineteenth Century* 23 (Spring 2003):35–36.
Thorstein, Veblen. *The Theory of the Leisure Class: An Economic Study of Institutions*. New York: Macmillan, 1899.
Tomkins, Calvin. *Merchants and Masterpieces: The Story of the Metropolitan Museum of Art*. New York: Henry Holt and Co., 1989.
Towner, Wesley. *The Elegant Auctioneers*. New York: Hill and Wang, 1970.
Trachtenberg, Alan. *The Incorporation of America: Culture and Society in the Gilded Age*. New York: Hill and Yang, 1982.
Trollope, Anthony. *North America*, Donald Smalley and Bradford Allen Booth, eds. New York: Alfred A. Knopf, 1951; originally published 1862.
———. *The Way We Live Now*. London: The Trollope Society, 1992; originally published in serial form in 1874 and as a book in 1875.
"Two Miles of Millionaires." *Munsey's Magazine* 19 (June 1898):345–61.
Vanderbilt, Cornelius, Jr. *The Queen of the Golden Age: The Fabulous Story of Grace Wilson Vanderbilt*. New York: McGraw-Hill, 1956.
Van Pelt, John V. *Monograph of the William K. Vanderbilt House*. New York: J. V. Van Pelt, 1925.
Van Rensselaer, Mrs. John King (May). *Newport: Our Social Capital*. New York: Arno Press, 1975; originally published 1905.
———. *The Social Ladder*. New York: Arno Press, 1975; originally published 1924.
Van Rensselaer, Mariana Griswold. "Recent Architecture in America: City Residences." *The Century Magazine* 31, no. 4 (February 1886):548–58 and 677–87.
Van Rensselaer, Mrs. Schuyler. *Henry Hobson Richardson and his Works*. Boston: Houghton Mifflin, 1888.
Walker, C. Howard. "Joseph Wells, Architect, 1853–1890." *Architectural Record* 66 (July 1929):15–18.
Warburton, Eileen. *Bellevue Avenue: Newport's Legendary Stroll*. Newport, R.I.: Pondhouse, 1992.
Waterhouse, Ellis K. *Paintings: The James A. de Rothschild Collection at Waddesdon*. London: National Trust, 1967.
Watson, Forbes J. B. "French Eighteenth-Century Furniture at Waddesdon." *Gazette des Beaux-Arts* 54 (July–December 1959):17–36.
———. "The James de Rothschild Collection at Waddesdon Manor." *Connoisseur* 143 (May 1959):204–9.
Weinberg, H. Barbara. *The Decorative Work of John La Farge*. New York: Garland Publishing Co., 1977.

Weisberg, Gabriel P., DeCourcy E. McIntosh, and Alison McQueen. *Collecting in the Gilded Age: Art Patronage in Pittsburgh, 1890–1910*. Pittsburgh: Frick Art and Historical Center, 1997.

Wharton, Edith. "After Holbein." In *The Collected Short Stories of Edith Wharton*, R.W.B. Lewis, ed., 2 vols. New York: Charles Scribner's Sons, 1968, 2:532–50.

———. *The Age of Innocence*. New York: D. Appleton and Co., 1920.

———. *A Backward Glance*. New York: D. Appleton-Century, 1934.

———. *House of Mirth*. New York: Macmillan Publishing Co., 1987.

———. "The Valley of Childish Things, and Other Emblems." In *The Collected Short Stories of Edith Wharton*, R.W.B. Lewis, ed. 2 vols., New York: Charles Scribner's Sons, 1968, 1:58–64.

Wharton, Edith, and Ogden Codman. *The Decoration of Houses*. New York: Charles Scribner's Sons, 1897.

The William A. Clark Collection. Washington, D.C.: The Corcoran Gallery of Art, 1978.

"William Baumgarten," In *The National Cyclopaedia of American Biography*. New York: J. T. White, 1892, 11:466.

Wilson, Derek. *The Astors, 1763–1992: Landscape with Millionaires*. London: Weidenfeld and Nicolson, 1993.

Wilson, Richard Guy. "The Great Civilization." In *The American Renaissance, 1876–1917*. New York: Brooklyn Museum, 1979, pp. 10–73.

———. *McKim, Mead and White*. New York: Rizzoli, 1983.

Winkler, Franz. "Architecture in the Billionaire District of New York City." *Architectural Record* 11 (October 1901):681–99.

Wodehouse, Lawrence. *White of McKim, Mead and White*. New York: Garland Publishing, 1988.

Wolfe, Elsie de. *After All*. New York: Arno Press, 1974; originally published 1913.

"The Work of Messrs. Carrère and Hastings." *Architectural Record* 27 (January 1910):2–117.

"The Works of the Late Richard M. Hunt." *Architectural Record* 5 (October–December):97–180.

Wunder, Richard. *Hiram Powers, Vermont Sculptor*, 2 vols. Newark: University of Delaware Press, 1991.

Yarnall, James L. "Souvenirs of Splendor: John La Farge and the Patronage of Cornelius Vanderbilt II." *American Art Journal* 26, nos. 1 and 2 (1994):67–105.

Acknowledgments

I wish to thank a number of people at the University of Delaware for their encouragement and their support of my research and writing. First of all, this book welcomes our new president, Patrick Harker—I wish him every success during his tenure.

To Provost Daniel Rich and Associate Provost for Research Carolyn Thoroughgood I am especially grateful for the grant they arranged to help with the cost of the illustrations; although I have long since retired, they both recognize that intellectual curiosity does not end with retirement. I am grateful to my friend, J. A. Leo Lemay who, one evening over dinner, urged me to apply for a university research grant. I submitted an application the next day, and within twenty-four hours both Dan and Carolyn had approved it.

I want also to recognize the generous support of the Furthermore Foundation, which provided funding for the purchase of images and for the cost of the permissions to publish them. Such expenses, which increase each year, are now an impediment to scholarship, and without assistance from the Furthermore Foundation this book could not have been published in the form that it is.

Susan Brynteson, director of libraries at the University of Delaware, has made Morris Library an exceptional research center, and Timothy Murray has made Special Collections there a joy to work in. The entire staff of the new Media Center in the library have patiently guided me through the new technologies of publishing—which I thought I had escaped, but haven't.

In the Art History Department, I wish to express my gratitude to Ms. Eileen Larson and Ms. Tina Trimble, who have helped in more ways than I can enumerate.

At the Museum of the City of New York, Faye Haun was absolutely indispensable in ferreting out the very view of a building, or one of its rooms, that I needed. Her knowledge of the collections and her tireless efforts are hereby gratefully acknowledged.

Many people at museums, libraries, and historic houses around the country have been so helpful—among them are Andrea Carneiro at the Preservation Society of Newport County, and the society's talented photographer Richard Cheek. At Biltmore Estate, I should like to thank Erica Daves and Darren Poupore. At The New-York Historical Society, Itty Mathew, Sue Kriete, Jill Reichenbach, and Matthew Murphy were especially helpful, and at the Met, Eva Peters, Jeri Wagner, and Teressa Romito have earned my gratitude.

Special thanks go to my technology guru—the "Rocket Dude"—Kenneth Gerrish and his wife Barbara: Here's another one for your coffee table.

Regina Ryan, my literary agent, has been genuinely excited about this book from the beginning, for which I am especially indebted to her, as I am to my editor at W. W. Norton & Company, James Mairs, and his associate, Austin O'Driscoll. Their counsel has always been wise, professional, and welcome. I thank Robert Wiser for his beautiful designing of the book.

To Lorna, my dear wife of fifty-five years, again I say, "This one's for you."

Index